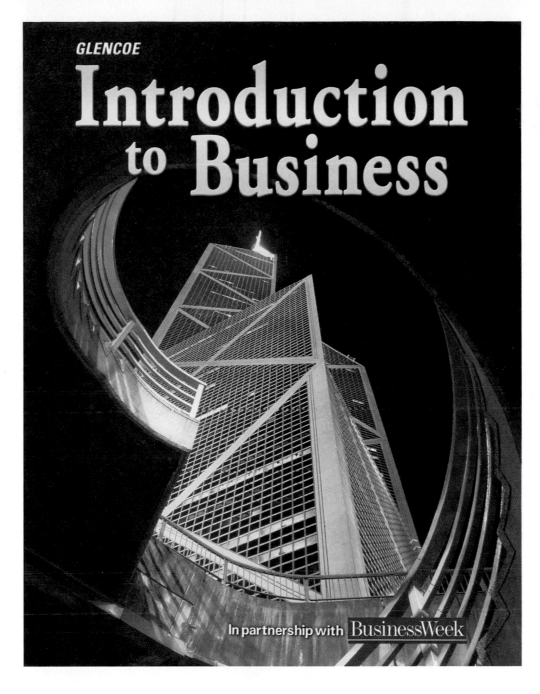

GLENCOE
Introduction to Business

In partnership with BusinessWeek

FIFTH EDITION

Betty J. Brown
Ball State University

John E. Clow
State University of New York, College at Oneonta
National Council of Economic Education, New York, NY

Glencoe
McGraw-Hill

New York, New York   Columbus, Ohio   Chicago, Illinois   Peoria, Illinois   Woodland Hills, California

ABOUT THE AUTHORS

Dr. Betty J. Brown is Professor of Business Education and Office Administration at Ball State University, Muncie, Ind. She was formerly Associate Professor of Technological and Adult Education, Business Education, and Office Systems Management, at the University of Tennessee, Knoxville. In addition to teaching at the secondary and postsecondary levels, Dr. Brown has written numerous articles, delivered speeches, and conducted workshops on the teaching of business.

Dr. John E. Clow is the Director of Leatherstocking Center for Economic Education at the State University of New York, College at Oneonta. He also serves as the National Program Consultant of the National Council on Economic Education in New York. Prior to that he was President of Berkeley College of Manhattan. Dr. Clow has taught at both secondary and postsecondary levels and has to his credit numerous speeches and publications in the areas of business and economic education.

Glencoe/McGraw-Hill

A Division of The **McGraw·Hill** *Companies*

Printed in the United States of America.

Send all inquiries to:
Glencoe/McGraw-Hill
21600 Oxnard Street, Suite 500
Woodland Hills, CA 91367

ISBN 0-07-825859-6

2 3 4 5 6 7 8 9   027   06 05 04 03 02

Table of Contents

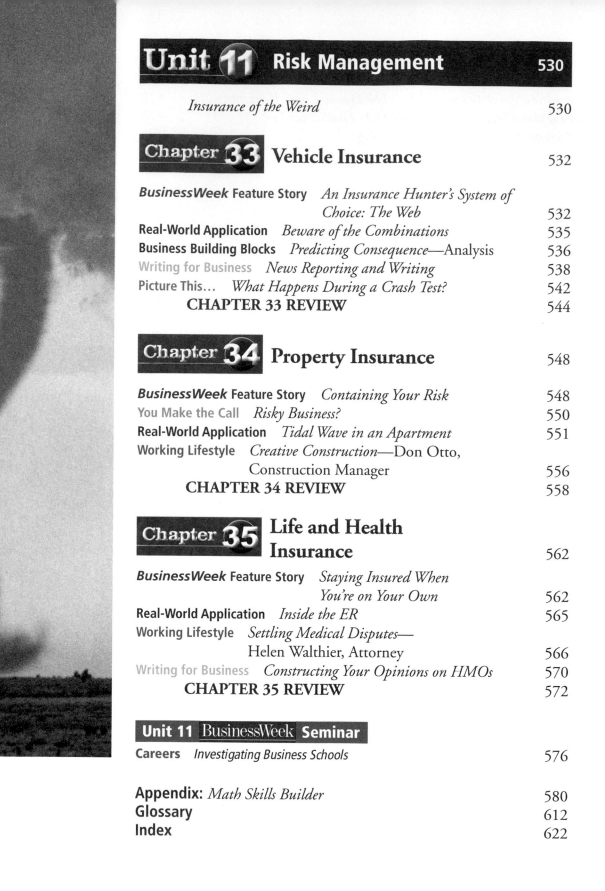

Understanding the Unit

Unit Structure

Introduction to Business is divided into 11 units, each beginning with a unit opener. The unit opener utilizes trivia to engage you in an introductory account of topics to come in the following chapters.

Introduction

The unit overview offers a real-world squib, with accompanying factoids about concepts covered in the unit. It introduces the concepts that will be explored, acting as a preview for what is to follow.

Unit 2

Owning and Operating a Business

Chapter 5
Entrepreneurship and
Small Business

Chapter 6
Business Ownership
and Operations

Chapter 7
Organizational
Structures

Chapter 8
Leadership in
Management

Chapter 9
Technology's Impact on
Business

Go Under the Hybrid's Hood

Disappointed that it's the twenty-first century and cars still can't fly? Well, don't be. There's a new car on the block, and it's called the hybrid model. This machine is a high-tech composite of old and new technology. Honda leads eco-cars on the roadways. Learn more about this car by reading the five important Ps.

- **Pounds**
  It takes about 1,000 pounds of batteries to store as much energy as one gallon of gasoline.

- **Power**
  The gasoline-electric hybrid car is a cross between a gasoline-powered car and a battery-operated car.

- **Pollutants**
  Hybrid cars have been traveling on Japan's roads since the late nineties.

- **Parity**
  The hybrid car was created to minimize tailpipe emissions and improve mileage.

- **Passage**
  An electric car can go between 50 and 100 miles between charges. A gas-powered car can go 300 miles before refueling. A hybrid car can go 720 miles before refueling!

BUSINESS Online
Idea Factory
To learn more about hybrid cars, visit the *Introduction to Business* Web site at www.introbus.glencoe.com, and click on Unit 2 Owning and Operating a Business.

Business Online

This section refers to the *Introduction to Business* Web site, which is created specifically for the book. At www.introbus.glencoe.com you will find more about the unit opener's topic as it refers to the concepts in the following chapters.

Understanding the Chapter
Chapter Structure

The chapter opener gives you a brief introduction to the new material that will be covered in the chapter. Each chapter begins with a list of the skills and knowledge you can expect to have mastered once you have completed the chapter. Photographs expand and reinforce the business and economic concepts presented in each chapter.

Learning Objectives

These direct your reading as you progress through the chapter. Use these as a tool for test review.

Chapter 5

Entrepreneurship and Small Business

BusinessWeek Feature Story
Paint by Numbers

Learning Objectives

After completing this chapter, you'll be able to:
1. **Describe** an entrepreneurship and a small business.
2. **List** the advantages and disadvantages of an entrepreneurship.
3. **Recognize** the advantages and disadvantages of a small business.
4. **Explain** why small businesses may fail.

Why It's Important

Entrepreneurships and small businesses bring vital energy and innovation to the economy. The risks involved energize entrepreneurs and small business owners to become successful.

Key Words

entrepreneurship
virtual business
or dot-com company
entrepreneur
risk taker
profit
small business

Gamblin Artists Colors Paints in Popular Hues. Martha and Robert Gamblin's work hangs in some of the world's top art museums. But don't bother looking for their names on gallery walls.

The Gamblins toil behind the scenes, manufacturing some of the world's finest oil paints. Each year, Gamblin Artists Colors in Portland, Oreg., ships more than 500,000 tubes and cans of paint in some 150 colors to artists and supply stores worldwide. Leading painters such as David Hockney and Chuck Close swear by them. "They make colors other companies just don't," says Wolf Kahn, a West Brattleboro (Vt.) landscape painter whose work is on display in museums nationwide.

Source: Excerpted with permission from "Paint by Numbers," *Frontier*, November 6, 2000.

An Extension Activity

Color is a science. Researchers have studied everything from how color affects brain activity to energy consumption. Study your classroom. Find out if the colors are "brain compatible."

BUSINESS Online
The Full Story
To learn more about Gamblin Artists Colors, visit the *Introduction to Business* Web site at **www.introbus.glencoe.com**, and click on *BusinessWeek* Feature Story, Chapter 5.

68

BusinessWeek Feature Story

Each chapter incorporates a different *BusinessWeek* story that applies to the chapter. The first part of the story is introduced in the chapter opener. The story in its entirety may be read on the *Introduction to Business* Web site at **www.introbus.glencoe.com**. It reappears again at the end of each chapter.

Extension Activity

After reading the *BusinessWeek* Feature Story, you're presented with a real-world situation. You'll be called on to apply common sense and business knowledge. Each activity is different.

Why It's Important

A brief paragraph explains why it is important for you to learn and understand these basic business concepts. It will help you to make a connection between the specific concepts being discussed and how they fit into the larger picture.

Key Words

This is a list of the key words that are introduced throughout the chapter. Key words are printed in boldface and highlighted the first time that they are introduced and defined within the text.

Understanding the Features

Introduction to Business Features

Each chapter contains a selection of the features you'll read about on the following pages. Each varies in length and focus. They help you understand the practical and real-world application of the concepts that you master throughout this book. While they vary in content, they all show a realistic and creative approach to business. Each feature ends with a question that asks you to expand on what you learned with critical and creative thinking.

Technology Toolkit

You'll find this in the margin in particular chapters. It informs you about a specific aspect of a technology gadget used in the business world. It expands the scope of technology to illustrate its impact on culture, language, ethnic heritage, political philosophy, social and economic systems, shared history, multinational economic unions, international trade, competition of resources, job specialization, and environmental factors. The Critical Thinking question in each feature asks you to analyze, interpret, and apply a concept in the feature.

Consider This...

You'll find this in the margin in particular chapters. Each highlights real-world companies or situations in the business world. Topics may encompass technology, community development, international business development, business's influence on the environment, contemporary business culture, sociological and environmental influences on business, economic development, and so on. The Analyze question at the end will allow you to tackle a business problem using your own unique critical- and creative-thinking skills.

Business Building Blocks

You'll find this feature in various chapters. This presents important skills that are necessary for success in school and on the job. Each feature focuses on communication, math, or analytical skills. First the topic is introduced and then you

Math

have an activity to practice the skill.

Usually the adjoining box includes tips or a how-to list. Often it is important to read the material in this box before completing the Practice.

Working Lifestyle

What are you doing at 10 A.M.?

This career profile appears in different chapters. Each chapter features a different person, one person representing an occupation from 1 of the 16 career clusters outlined by the U.S. Department of Education. The narrative is based upon what each person does on the job at 10 A.M. in the morning.

The "Salary" gives you the average income of an occupation profiled as well as the salary range. "Outlook for This Career" offers a few words about the particular position's future. The final question, "Connecting Careers Activity," focuses on recent developments in business and asks you to speculate how these might affect the career in an ever-changing world.

CAREER PATH — Health Science

You Make the Call

You'll find this in a variety of chapters in this book. This is a short feature, which poses an ethical quandary. You're asked a few follow-up questions about how to react to the situation. This takes into account many of the concepts you'll learn in the unit and its chapters. Often this is about weighing personal gain versus social responsibility.

Writing for Business

Portfolio Activity

You'll find this in a variety of chapters. This new, interdisciplinary skills feature asks you to plot and write your own original story. Creativity is highly encouraged in research and writing. The first paragraph introduces you to the subject and offers directions. It's important to carefully read this paragraph. Then you'll "Pick a Path."

This is your chance to select which story you want to pursue. Each is a little different, but only choose one. "The Setting" gives you the place of the story; "Rising Action"

offers specific events you'll need to take into account; and the two-step process is how to work your way to a climax, or conclusion (which you control).

Lastly, the "Conclusion" will ask you to evaluate your story by completing a specific language arts task in order to give your story structure and shape. This feature integrates and applies reading comprehension, written communication, application of business vocabulary, and the decision-making process.

Understanding the Features

Visual Narratives

Real-World Application

In every chapter you'll find a real-world photo essay on a company, a person, or contemporary issue. Each is a four-part photo essay, which falls at the top, right-hand corner of every page between the chapter opener and chapter review. This is a visual way of studying the concepts that are addressed in the chapter.

Real-World Application part 4

THE BIZ BEHIND BOZART
The Bozart Toys Web site shows consumers its products, but other online sites and toy stores sell the toys. What are some benefits of selling toys online?

Real-World Application part 3 o

THE BIZ BEHIND BOZART
Mangel manages all aspects of Bozart. He travels to China a few times a year to ensure quality control in the manufacturing of the...

Real-World Application part 2 of 4

THE BIZ BEHIND BOZART
...art Toys started wi... ...ess plan in '95. Or... ...ater Mangel acqu... ...oney and produc... ...st toy, Marco the ...ficent. ... you think Man... ...y became a suc...
...tinued on p. 75

Real-World Application part 1 of 4

THE BIZ BEHIND BOZART
In the early '90s, the art market slowed down. Larry Mangel, an art dealer, decided to change his career focus and open his own business, Bozart Toys. What makes Larry Mangel an entrepreneur?
continued on p. 73

Global Economy

Global Economy

Demand for Oil Americans demand oil for many purposes, but mostly as a fuel for their automobiles. About 101 million vehicles burn 122 billion gallons of gasoline a year. Domestic supplies meet about half of the demand for oil. The map below shows where we get the rest.

Canada supplies 13 percent

Europe supplies 7 percent (Leading Sources: Great Britain, Norway, Belgium)

Persian Gulf Region supplies 23 percent (Leading Sources: Saudi Arabia, Iraq, Kuwait)

Asia and Oceania supply 3 percent (Leading Sources: Australia, Indonesia, Brunei)

Caribbean Nations supply 4 percent (Leading Sources: Virgin Islands, Trinidad and Tobago, Netherlands Antilles)

Africa supplies 15 percent (Leading Sources: Nigeria, Angola, Algeria)

Mexico supplies 11 percent

South America supplies 24 per... (Leading Sources: Ve... Colombia, Argentin...

On average, a barrel holding 42 gallons of crude oil produces 21 gallons of gasoline

This narrative uses a map and squibs to expound on a concept presented in a chapter.

Picture This...

Picture This...
What Happens When You Type a URL?

There are seven of these visual narratives in the book. Each describes a particular technological process. People often take for granted how things work without really breaking down and understanding the construction. This gives you a deeper understanding of the world around you.

1. Type into a Web browser this Universal Resource Locator (URL): http://www.businessweek.com.

2. The Web browser communicates with a domain name server to find the www.businessweek.com Internet Point (IP) address.

3. The domain name server sends the BusinessWeek IP address to your Web browser.

4. Your Web browser then uses the IP address to connect to the BusinessWeek server and asks for the BusinessWeek home page.

5. The BusinessWeek server sends its home page file to your Web browser. That home page file is in HTML text.

6. Your Web browser changes (or formats) the HTML file to display the BusinessWeek home page on your screen.

Now You Take a Shot...

Research a Virtual Business. Remember you imagined inheriting $2,000 at the beginning of this chapter? You decide to open a savings account to hold your money. Visit a real-time online bank on the Internet. List the benefits of an online bank over a bricks-and-mortar bank.

To the Student   Features Contents

Understanding Assessment

Review Structure

Each major concept in each chapter ends with a section called Fast Review. The section assessment is a brief version of the Chapter Review found at the end of the chapter. This gives you an opportunity to review the major concepts just covered. Activities and questions help you review important business and economic terms and concepts.

Chapter 5 Review

Summary

1. An entrepreneur recognizes a business opportunity and organizes, manages, and assumes the risks of a business venture. Small businesses are vital to our economy. They employ more than half of all workers in the United States, and they're the main source of new jobs.

2. Entrepreneurs show expertise, may work from home, and gain the profit from their own work. On the other hand, entrepreneurs have to take total responsibility for the business, work long hours, and endure financial risks when they decide to start the business.

3. The advantages of running a small business include being your own boss, providing great personal service, and easy formation. A small business owner faces potential problems if he or she doesn't adapt to change and possibly lacks the managerial skills needed to successfully run the business.

4. Small businesses often fail because the owners start with little money, freely extend credit, have little business experience, and haven't mastered time don't plan for the ups and downs of business, and haven't mastered time management.

Using Business Key Words

Use these business terms correctly in the following sentences.
- entrepreneurship
- entrepreneur
- virtual business or dot-com company
- risk taker
- small business
- profit

1. A(n) _____ is a person who recognizes an opportunity and who organizes, manages, and assumes the risks of a business enterprise, with the intent of increasing the value of the business.
2. A person who likes to take chances is a(n) _____.
3. A(n) _____ is a business that operates on the Internet.
4. The money that is left over after a business has paid all the costs of producing its goods and services is called _____.
5. An independently owned business serving a limited geographic area is called a(n) _____.
6. A business started by someone who accepted the risk of starting and running a business is a(n) _____.

Summary

This reinforces the Learning Objectives that were introduced in the chapter opener. Each Learning Objective is summarized point by point in this small section. You may use this as a study tool to remind yourself of major concepts in the chapter. This is a list of the main ideas of the chapter for quick review and recall.

Using Business Key Words

This activity will call on your recollection of the vocabulary words introduced throughout the chapter. You'll be asked to complete the sentences or match the key word to its definition.

Review What You Learned

This exercise requires recall of information found in the text.

Critical Thinking

These questions offer you the chance to show your application and more in-depth understanding of the concepts in the chapter. You'll be asked to interpret, analyze, compare, or make judgments based on ideas from the chapter.

Understanding Business Concepts

This section asks you to apply the concepts and skills learned in the chapter.

Viewing and Representing

This section asks you to use your visual literacy skills to deconstruct an image, which relates to business and economics. The photograph may be metaphorical or straightforward. Use the concepts you have learned in a chapter to complete this activity.

Chapter 5 Review

Review What You Learned

7. What do all people who start a new business do?
8. What is an entrepreneurship?
9. What is a virtual business sometimes called?
10. How does the Small Business Association (SBA) define a small business?
11. What is profit?
12. Name the advantages and disadvantages of entrepreneurships.
13. Why may an entrepreneurship fail?
14. How do small businesses help the U.S. economy?
15. Why is it important for a small business owner to be aware of consumer trends?

Understanding Business Concepts

16. Why do you think it is important that entrepreneurs be take-charge, self-directed people?
17. Why are so many people starting home-based businesses?
18. Why might it be more satisfying to run your own company than work for someone else?
19. Why does the owner of a business usually put in more hours at work than an employee?
20. Why is the need for money considered to be the most serious problem an entrepreneur faces?
21. Why do you think small businesses are able to offer services that larger companies cannot?
22. Why is it so important for small business owners to be able to keep adequate financial records?

Critical Thinking

23. Why do you think some virtual businesses or dot-com companies fail?
24. What skills and attributes do you think a successful entrepreneur needs? Why?
25. Explain the difference between being self-disciplined and self-motivated.
26. A checklist is a good way to organize an entrepreneur's thinking when beginning to plan a business. What questions might be on the entrepreneur's checklist?

Viewing and Representing

Examining the Image. With a partner, examine this picture. What kinds of questions does this image seem to answer? Are the questions personal, creative, analytical, or informational? How effective is the image itself for drawing viewers or readers into the issue? Write a brief story based upon your perceptions of this image. Share your story with the class.

Chapter 5 Review

Building Academic Skills

HISTORY

Oral History

Brainstorm and write questions in order to conduct an interview with someone who is an entrepreneur or a small business owner. Prepare questions that will get the interviewee to tell how his or her life changed as the result of being an entrepreneur or small business owner. Present the interview to the class. Discuss how the interviewees' stories compare with the information in the text.

LANGUAGE ARTS

Journalism

Pick a partner to produce a newsletter that describes the successes and failures of the small businesses in your community. Some topics might include funding, laws, economic trends, consumer wants and needs, time management, risk management, help wanted ads, technology, and so on.

COMPUTER TECHNOLOGY

Charting Growth

The hottest market for small businesses isn't across a great ocean. It's right here in the United States. Currently, the combined buying power of U.S. minority groups totals $1.3 trillion, or some 20 percent of the country's purchasing power. The Commerce Department estimates that the spending power of non-whites will reach $4.3 trillion, or 32 percent by 2045. In a database program, create a chart or graph to show this likely purchasing power.

MATH

Calculating Closings

In the city of Orange, 187 new businesses opened in 2000. By 2001, 15 percent of businesses were no longer in operation. How many were open in 2001? One year later, another 12 percent were considered discontinued. How many businesses were still open in 2001?

Linking School to Home

Investigate Product Loyalties. Create an inventory of the products and services you and your family use that are produced by small businesses or entrepreneurs. Categorize them by family member. Then interview each family member, and find out why he or she purchases the products and services from the small business or entrepreneur. Compile your results and share them with the class.

Linking School to Work

Portfolio Project. Research the requirements for setting up a small business in your community. Investigate areas such as government regulations, financing, and the costs of leasing space and buying equipment. The local chamber of commerce might direct you in your research. Write a report with your findings.

Building Academic Skills

This section is an interdisciplinary approach to business and economics concepts. Language arts, computer technology, math, history, social science, and science are the subjects you might be asked to explore in this section in order to complete an activity.

Linking School to Work

These activities ask you to explore your work experiences, or the specific work experiences of community leaders or business owners. You may interview someone who is employed to gain his or her perspective. The principles in this activity relate to the business and economics concepts covered in the chapter.

E-Homework

This element consists of two activities which are designed to enhance your Internet and technology skills.

Linking School to Home

The activity is designed to relate business principles to your home environment. You may be asked to apply practical and analytical skills of business concepts to your home life.

Connecting Academics

This activity places you in a hypothetical situation where you have to make a decision. Math, computer technology, language arts, science, social science, and history are all subjects you might be asked to explore in conjunction with business concepts presented in the chapter.

Business Online

"The Full Story" heading contains a Web-based version of the *BusinessWeek* Feature Story. Read the entire article at www.introbus.glencoe.com.

Chapter 5 Review

E-Homework

Applying Technology

Electronic Survey. Use word processing software to create a survey that can be sent to local small business owners and entrepreneurs in your community. Through the survey, find out what type of skills they currently possess and what technology skills they think they'll need in the future. If possible, send out the surveys using e-mail. As a class, compile the results using a spreadsheet or database software.

High-Tech Callings. Research the technology classes that are available in high schools, technical centers, and colleges in your community. As a class, brainstorm a list of businesses that could be started by someone who has technology skills.

Connecting Academics

Math. Joaquin wants to start his own business for renting bikes at the park. He begins researching the age of his hometown's residents. He learns the following:

0–5 years of age	960 residents
6–11	1,840
12–18	4,500
19–35	8,225
36–60	2,960
Over 60	

Construct a bar graph to present this information. Use computer software if possible.

Language Arts. You want to strengthen your entrepreneurial qualities. Complete the following steps to learn more about other entrepreneurs and yourself:

- **Reading.** Go online or to the library to read articles and books about entrepreneurs and entrepreneurial activities.
- **Writing.** Write about individuals you know who are entrepreneurs. Did the person overcome obstacles to achieve success?

- **Watching.** Find films about athletes, businesspeople, or others who achieved success.
- **Practice.** Find case studies that involve goals, creativity, and risk taking.

BusinessWeek Analyzing the Feature Story

You read the first part of "Paint by Numbers" at the beginning of this chapter. Below are a few questions for you to answer about the Gamblins. You'll find the answers to these questions when you're reading the entire article. First, here are the questions:

27. What motivated the Gamblins to take the risk of starting a new business?
28. How does Gamblin Artists Colors use technology in its small business?
29. What's the purpose of the special line of paints the company recently introduced?

CREATIVE JOURNAL ACTIVITY

What are your hobbies or interests? List business ideas related to your hobbies. How can you reap the benefits of your talents?

BUSINESS Online

The Full Story

To learn more about Gamblin Artists Colors, visit the *Introduction to Business* Web site at www.introbus.glencoe.com, and click on *BusinessWeek* Feature Story, Chapter 5.

BusinessWeek Analyzing the Feature Story

The *BusinessWeek* Feature Story introduced at the beginning of the chapter closes the Chapter Review. This activity asks you read the entire feature article before answering the questions in this section.

Creative Journal Activity

This may be used as a portfolio activity, which offers you the opportunity to demonstrate the skills that you master after you have read the chapter. A portfolio or journal contains pieces of successful projects and samples of your outstanding work.

Understanding Unit Assessment
BusinessWeek Seminar

A four-page *BusinessWeek* Seminar asks you to explore career, small business, technology, or global business in-depth. Each seminar asks you to research a topic by using news magazines, newspapers, and the Internet. It requires research, exploration, interaction, critical thinking, analysis, and assessment.

Investigate the Images

These questions will focus on analyzing your observations when looking at photographs on the *BusinessWeek* Seminar opening page. Then you will think critically about the media and how it represents culture and newsworthy trends.

BusinessWeek Seminar

Unit 1
Global Business

保心安油

77

What Is Today's Chinese Business Trend?

In Chapter 3, you read about the Industrial Revolution. Many workers during this historical period worked in the factories and on the railroads. China, with its 1.2 billion people and abundance of natural resources, is facing its own economic revolution. This seminar asks you to investigate China's contemporary business trend.

62

BusinessWeek Seminar

Investigate the Images

Look at the photographic collage on the left page. What do you see? What do you think? What do you feel? The power of reading visuals is in analyzing and dissecting your observations. On a separate piece of paper, reconstruct the worksheet below in order to complete your investigation. The questions may help shape and focus your analysis.

Your Observations

1. How many photographs do you see?

2. Examine each photograph. How is each assembled in relation to the others?

3. What is the subject of each photograph?

4. Does color signify a message?

5. What issues do you take from these images?

Information

6. Summarize what you know about the photographs from your observations.

Exploring Culture

7. What do you know about China's culture— business, education, politics, and so on?

8. Where do you learn this information (for example, newspapers, TV, magazines, textbooks, films, etc.)?

Unit 1 *BusinessWeek* Seminar **63**

Factoids

Population. In 1200, Hangchow, China, was the fourth city in the world that had over a million people. (Nearly 700 years later, New York City's population reached a million people.)

Climate. The country has an extreme range of climates from its tropical south to its subarctic north.

Natural Hazards. Typhoons strike along the southern and eastern coasts about five times a year.

Geography. China is the world's fourth-largest country (after Russia, Canada, and the United States).

Downtown. China has half of the world's tallest buildings.

Greetings. A Chinese group applauds anyone introduced to the group. Applaud back.

Factoids

Here is your chance to learn more about the topic in little factoids. These are high-interest and may help direct your research or conclusion.

Introduction

This recaps concepts covered in the unit. Then it introduces the topic you will explore in the four-page seminar.

Understanding Unit Assessment
BusinessWeek Seminar

Preparation

This section offers a brief summary of the topic covered in the seminar and actual materials needed for completion. It introduces the concepts that will be explored in-depth, acting as a preview of what is to come.

Procedures

This step-by-step process informs you of how the seminar will be completed in an organized manner.

Chart It

A brief paragraph explains how to create a graphic organizer about your topic. The illustration is also an example of how your version might look. Often this is an individual and group discussion activity. It requires you to use your conceptual and analytical skills.

Analyze and Conclude

After analyzing, discussing, and studying "Chart It," this section presents you with critical thinking questions. These will ask you to examine all of your research and to give conclusive answers.

Becoming an Informed Consumer

This is the last section of the four-page *BusinessWeek* Seminar. Here is your chance to polish your business knowledge by applying it to your own life. Evaluate the concepts you explored in the unit and the seminar. Make decisions based on ideas from the unit.

BusinessWeek Online

This element consists of further research about the topic you explored in the seminar. The "Further Exploration" heading contains the Web site and specific topic for you to enhance your knowledge and Internet skills.

BusinessWeek Seminar

Taking Aim at Global Business

Preparation

Find out why Chinese workers are migrating from farming villages to industrial cities, and how their moves affect business trends in China.

Objective

In this *BusinessWeek* Seminar, you will:
- **Research** the media to find articles on Chinese workers' migration patterns.
- **Investigate** the topic by using a journalist's arsenal of key questions—who, what, where, when, why, and how.
- **Interview** a classmate who poses as a migrant worker.

Materials Needed
- ✓ Recent copies of *BusinessWeek*, the *Wall Street Journal*, or Internet access
- ✓ Paper
- ✓ Pencil
- ✓ Small tape recorder (if it's available)
- ✓ Poster board
- ✓ Markers

Procedures

1. Choose a research partner.
2. Find and read a recent article written about the migration of Chinese workers. If possible, use the Internet to access the Web site of a business publication. For example, access the *BusinessWeek* Web site at **www.businessweek.com**. Click on the tab labeled "Global Business" or use the internal search engine to locate the topic...

BONUS: THE NEW SOFTWARE STARS

BusinessWeek

THE GREAT MIGRATION

3. Consider the following issues:
- Why are people migrating to the cities?
- What problems do they encounter?
- Are the benefits worth the risks?
- How does this affect China's economy?

4. Create a role-play in which one partner plays a newspaper reporter interviewing a migrant worker, and the other plays the worker. In your role-play, you should describe why the worker left his or her village and what his or her feelings are about living and working in a big city. Make sure to discuss living conditions in the village versus working conditions in the city. The role-play...

64 Unit...

BusinessWeek Seminar

Chart It

With your partner make two lists: "Advantages of Migrating to the City" and "Disadvantages of Migrating to the City," and list what you think are the three most important of each. As a class, reproduce the table that is below and create a comprehensive list on the board.

Migrating to the City

Advantages	Disadvantages

Becoming an Informed Citizen

Congratulations, you finished the seminar. Now it's time to reflect on the decisions you made.

Critical Thinking. Why did you choose to report certain aspects of your research and not other parts of the information? Did an article's images play any part in your decision making? Or did you pick an article based on its title?

Analyzing Your Future. How will China's migration patterns affect you as a citizen of the world?

BUSINESS **Online**

Further Exploration

To find out more about workers' migration patterns in other countries, visit the Glencoe *Introduction to Business* Web site www.introbus.glencoe.com.

Analyze and Conclude

After studying the comprehensive list on the board, answer the questions below:
1. **Making Inference.** What is the most important reason a worker has for migrating to a city in China?
2. **Recognizing Cause and Effect.** What are the dangers of migrating?
3. **Interpreting the Facts.** How will the migration of workers influence the economy of China and, therefore, business in China?

Reviewers

Doug Ahlers
Sutter, Calif.

Gwen Alsburry
Oakdale, La.

Stephanie Andrejcak
Burnt Hills, N.Y.

Jane Babcock
Petoskey, Mich.

Michael Baker
Winnetka, Ill.

Paul Beskid
Doylestown, Ohio

Angela Black
Park Hills, Mo.

Sandy Blackman
Benton, Ill.

Marilyn Blum
Garden Grove, Calif.

Ron Bonhaus
North Bend, Ohio

Teresa Boulds
Eldorado, Ill.

Jeremy Brady
Coleman, Wis.

Jay Brown
Frankfort, Ill.

Jay S. Brown
Brodheadsville, Pa.

Ruby Bullen
South Holland, Ill.

Linda Burkett
Clinton, Ind.

Susan Case
South Beloit, Ill.

Becky Ceniceros
Forsan, Tex.

Genie Chaney
Edmond, Okla.

Janene B. Chisek
Freeland, Mich.

Todd Christman
Woodsfield, Ohio

Susan Cleavenger
Waynesburg, Pa.

Sharon Clem
Brodheadsville, Pa.

Margaret Colvin
Manahawkin, N.J.

Larry M. Condra
Abilene, Tex.

Richard Corbo
Bronx, N.Y.

Rosalynd Cravin
Houston, Tex.

Janice Curtis
Plymouth, Ind.

Nancy Dague
Remus, Mich.

Barry Danziger
Somerset, N.J.

Chandra Darr
Thomasville, N.C.

Elizabeth Deaton
Hamshire, Tex.

Jimmie Dedmon
Walters, Okla.

William Delaney
Cresson, Pa.

Cora DeMott
Thomasville, Ga.

Donnajean deSilva
Columbus, Ohio

Melissa S. Dornbusch
West Milton, Ohio

JoAnn Dotson
Hanford, Calif.

Brian Dudley
Selma, Ind.

Michael Duncan
Newburgh, Ind.

Lonney Evon
Quincy, Mich.

Wil Farrell
McHenry, Ill.

Gerald Finsen
Mt. Holly, N.J.

Kimberlee S. Fish
Davison, Mich.

Janet Fisher
Beavercreek, Ohio

Joyce Fleming
Alexandria, Ala.

Renee Flory
Mount Joy, Pa.

Jane Foreman
Valparaiso, Ind.

Holly Gast
Marblehead, Ohio

Charlotte Gibson
Madison, Ind.

Joyce Hagen
Newburg, Mo.

Kim Hancock
Blanchard, Okla.

Claudia Harris
Clarksburg, Calif.

Susan Harshbarger
Graceville, Fla.

Madeline Hatcher
Waskom, Tex.

Lisa Heid
Noblesville, Ind.

Ellen Heim
Wheeling, Ill.

Evelyn Holderieath
Mendon, Mo.

Lynda Johnson
Mooreland, Okla.

Thelma K. Jones
Baton Rouge, La.

Jane Keegan
Brookville, Ind.

Connie Kelley
Graham, Tex.

Tommy G. Kindig
Randlett, Okla.

Jayne Klingel
Marion, Ohio

Brenda Knight
Cedar Park, Tex.

Brad Knoche
South Milwauhu, Wis.

James Kramer
Marrlenny, Fla.

Wayne L. Kurlander
Statehill, N.Y.

Sharon Larson
Crystal Lake, Ill.

Sally Layman
Norwalk, Calif.

Arlene Lent
Clyde, N.Y.

Bob Lieber
Houston, Tex.

Donna Lyde
Petersburg, Tex.

Robert D. Madison, Ph.D.
Brooklyn, N.Y.

Alan Magee
Painted Post, N.Y.

Teresa Marcella
Bensalem, Pa.

Tamera McCarthy
Oconto, Wis.

Patricia McRobert
Kansas City, Mo.

Joan Miller
Darlington, Wis.

James Monroe
Snow Hill, N.C.

Cheryl A. Moore
Killeen, Tex.

Helen Morris
Westhampton, N.J.

William Morrison
Windber, Pa.

Joyce Muhlenkamp
St. Henry, Ohio

Edward J. Murphy
Hopewell Junction, N.Y.

Rachel Nichols
Arnold, Mo.

Angie Niebrugge
Charleston, Ill.

Susan Nunnally
Cumming, Ga.

Debby Odom
Gruver, Tex.

Azzie Olds
Vivian, La.

Beth Patzke
Baldwin, Wis.

Jan Payne
Beaver, Okla.

Elaine Peeters
Wolcott, N.Y.

John R. Pehle
Frankfort, Ill.

Bobbi Pulver
Three Lakes, Wis.

Olivia Ramirez
Tornillo, Tex.

Lynn Retz
Auburndale, Wis.

Paul Richmond
Elmia Heights, N.Y.

Marlene Roberts
Johnstown, Pa.

Tim Rohlinger
Kewaskum, Wis.

Teri Roscka
Monticello, Ind.

Sherry Rouner
Mt. Vernon, Mo.

Jason Russell
Frenchlick, Ind.

William Sanderson
Flossmoor, Ill.

Keith A. Schneider
Cambridge, Wis.

Sandra Schroeder
New Lisbon, Wis.

Bernice Scozzafave
Lansing, Mich.

Katie B. Shaw Clements
Havana, Fla.

Mary Shroyer
Middlebury, Ind.

Susan Siler
Huntley, Ill.

Gail Sobel
DeRuyter, N.Y.

Joan Sountis
Cliffside Park, N.J.

Kathy Speichinger
Belle, Mo.

Lois Stadtmiller
Curwensville, Pa.

Diane Stefanisko
Atglen, Pa.

Deborah Surnbrock
St. Leon, Ind.

Sandra Talley
Fullerton, Calif.

Karen Teach
Clear Springs, Md.

Vince Tesi
Colts Neck, N.J.

Brandi Thomas
Soledad, Calif.

Jim Tiedeman
Benton, Wis.

Scott Truelove
W. Unity, Ohio

Tresa Twenter
Green Ridge, Mo.

Joe Ward
Jackson, Mich.

Mary Warnke
Brillion, Wis.

Libbey Watkins
Sibley, La.

Tracy Weller
Albany, Mo.

Diana White
Mound City, Mo.

Lance White
Round Lake, Ill.

Ruth Ann White
Wabash, Ind.

Judy Williams
Bicknell, Ind.

Nancy Yankee
Holden, Mo.

Unit 1

The Economy and You

Confectionary Consumption

Valentine's Day. Halloween. You've all seen the bins and bins full of chocolate ready for sale and consumption until your gut aches. The story of chocolate goes back as far as the discovery of America. Columbus came back from America with the main ingredient of chocolate—cocoa beans—and delivered them to the Court of King Ferdinand and Queen Isabella. Around 1765 the first chocolate factory was established in New England and gained much attention and interest from cocoa bean growers, manufacturers, and consumers. Chocolate's a want for some and for others it's their livelihood.

● **Lavish Lands**
Cocoa beans are only cultivated in land no more than 20 degrees north or south of the equator.

● **The Average Danish**
Denmark consumes the most sugar per capita in the world.

● **Sweet Sales**
The chocolate industry sells $13 billion of product per year.

● **The World's Nuts**
Chocolate manufacturers use 40 percent of the world's almonds and 20 percent of the world's peanuts.

● **Essential Nutrients**
The U.S. Army food rations include three 4-ounce chocolate bars.

Idea Factory

To learn more about the chocolate industry, visit the *Introduction to Business* Web site at **www.introbus.glencoe.com**, and click on Unit 1 The Economy and You.

Chapter 1

A Look at Wants and Needs

Learning Objectives

After completing this chapter, you'll be able to:

1. **State** the differences between wants and needs.
2. **Describe** how limited resources relate to wants.
3. **Identify** business activities that are used for products and services.
4. **List** the two factors that motivate businesses.
5. **Explain** the relationship between business and you.

Why It's Important

Businesses satisfy people's basic needs all the way to their lavish wants. Competition and profit motivate these businesses to continually strive for your business.

Key Words

wants	business
needs	profit
goods	competition
services	consumer
resource	

BusinessWeek Feature Story

Paperless Page-Turners?

Gemstar Hopes Best-Selling Authors Will Make the Difference. When Stephen King released his 66-page novella *Riding The Bullet* exclusively in digital form, an estimated 400,000 computer users downloaded copies. At the same time, though cumulative sales of paperback-sized gizmos, known as e-books, barely numbered in the thousands. It was a sad contrast for the ragtag contingent of companies that have been trying to kick-start the e-book business since 1998. But industry leader Gemstar-TV Guide International Inc. learned an important lesson: authors sell books, whizbang formats don't.

Source: Excerpted with permission from "Will E-Books Be Real Page-Turners?" *BusinessWeek Online*, October 23, 2000.

An Extension Activity

Liquid crystal display (LCD) makes it possible for you to read a portable e-book, a wristwatch, a calculator, and so on. Research the science behind liquid crystal display and who manufactures most of it.

BUSINESS Online
The Full Story

To learn more about e-books, visit the *Introduction to Business* Web site at **www.introbus.glencoe.com**, and click on *BusinessWeek* Feature Story, Chapter 1.

Economics' Starting Points: Wants and Needs

Look at the tag on your shirt or the label on your backpack. You make choices about the clothes you buy and music you download. When you buy snacks from the vending machine, you choose a product based on cost, taste, brand recognition, and supply. Guess what? You've just made business decisions. New products, higher prices, and the supply of products affect your family, friends, and you.

Business in Today's World

Suppose you have $10. You could use it to buy lunch, buy a magazine, or go to a movie. What is the difference between what you want and what you need? How can you satisfy wants and needs with the money you have available? Figure 1.1 asks you to think and write about your wants and needs.

Figure 1.1 — **WANTS AND NEEDS OF YOUR SANCTUARY**

➡ You need your own "space." Studies show your bedroom is an expression of yourself.

How would you revamp your space if you could? On a separate piece of paper, write your answers to this worksheet below.

Amount to Spend	From $ _____ to $ _____
Size and Shape of Bedroom	
Color	
Theme	
Curtains	
Posters	
Doorway	(For example: bead curtains, hanging shapes, and so on.)
Closet	(For example: walk-in, organized, sliding doors, mirror, rotating clothes rack, and so on.)
Extras	(For example: private bathroom, window seat, entertainment area, sitting room, fireplace, mini refrigerator, desk, bookshelves, and so on.)

An Abundance of Wants

Wants are the things you wish you could have. Each person has wants. You might want a mountain bike, while your best friend may want a road bike. A group of people may also share the same wants. A family may want a new car, a company may want a more advanced computer system, or an athletic club may want to add a swimming pool. Although these wants are shared, they are considered *private wants*.

On the other hand, some wants are widely shared by many people. These wants are no longer considered private but become *public wants*, such as highways, drinking water, and education. For the most part local, state, and federal governments satisfy public wants.

Satisfying Wants and Needs With Goods and Services

Necessary wants are **needs**. Food, shelter, and clothing are basic needs. Whether private or public, necessary or optional, some type of good or service can satisfy most of your wants and needs. **Goods** can be physically weighed or measured. Bicycles and skates are goods, as are groceries and telephones. Goods satisfy your wants and needs for material things that you *can* see or touch.

At some point, your mountain bike may need a tune-up. Although you could try to do this yourself, it's more likely that you will take it to a bike shop for maintenance. If you pay a bike shop to repair your bike, you're buying a service. **Services** are tasks that people or machines perform. Services also satisfy some of your wants for things you *cannot* see or touch. Many services such as cutting hair or teaching guitar lessons are provided for a fee.

Not all business activities satisfy wants. People want things that cannot be valued in terms of money. For example, individuals want love and respect. In a business context wants are *not* about these intangible kinds of desires. Businesses please those wants that can be satisfied by goods and services.

Unlimited Wants, Limited Resources

Most people have unlimited wants for goods and services. In the United States, Canada, England, and Japan, the majority of consumers have satisfied their lower-order needs, so marketers promote goods and services that will appeal to higher-order needs. Take Marie Van de Mark, a young entrepreneur, who started Jam Enterprise. She created a $2 million company from making promotional items from metal. Amazon.com and A/X Armani Exchange like her products. The more money you make, the more goods

WHAT THE PUBLIC WANTS

Entertainment TV won't save your life. Political scandals don't cure a chronic cough. Sixty-two percent of Americans are tired of hyped newscasts. Instead, they want the media to spend more attention to medical research issues. **Does the media sway the public's wants and needs?**

continued on p. 9

Technology Toolkit

Listen to Your Ring, Watch Your Watch

Wristwatch cameras have been standard equipment for action heroes. Today, this "smart jewelry" is a reality for anyone. Pervasive computing inserts silicon chips in your jewelry so you can listen to the radio, phone friends, take pictures, download music, or withdraw money from your bank account.

Students in a Florida high school already use the personal computer rings to record their attendance, gain entrance to classrooms, and even pay for cafeteria meals.

Critical Thinking

What other kinds of wearable computers might enhance people's wants and needs?

or services you want. However, few have enough resources to satisfy all of their wants. A **resource** is anything that people can use to make or obtain what they need or want. Examples of resources include fuel, timber, labor, and money. The problem of unlimited wants and limited resources affects individuals, companies, and nations.

Resources limit the number of wants people can satisfy. For example, you may want a new pair of jeans and a new camera, but you may only have enough money to buy one of these things. You may also want to earn a lot of money, but you have only so much time to work between school and family responsibilities. Businesses and government are influenced by the same problem. They lack the resources to do all the things that they want to do. It is important for individuals, businesses, and nations to make the best use of limited resources.

Deciding on Your Resources. Every day you have opportunities to make choices about how you'll act, how you'll treat others, and what you'll do. You should make these important decisions carefully. People make the most of their resources by making the right choices about what to buy. The decision-making process is a step-by-step method to carefully consider alternatives that result in better choices. The decision-making process is a procedure for carefully considering alternatives and their consequences before you make a final decision. The process has these essential steps:

Step 1. Identify the problem. Whether the decision-making problem is one that occurs daily or comes up only a few times in a lifetime, this is the first step. It is often the easiest.

Step 2. List the alternatives. Take time to think through the problem, so you can come up with a good range of alternatives. Try to include all the important ones.

Step 3. Determine the pros and cons. Write down and weigh the advantages and disadvantages of each alternative. Your values and goals now become part of the decision-making process.

Step 4. Make the best decision. Determining the best alterative is the key step in the process. Rank the alternatives according to their pros and cons. After you pick a winner, ask yourself what you'll lose if you give up your second choice. Do you really want to give that alternative?

Step 5. Evaluate your decision. After you've put your decision into effect, ask yourself whether you achieved the results you expected. Would you make the same choice again?

You may not use all of the steps of the process every time you buy something. For example, when you decide to buy orange juice, you may always buy the same brand. However, many decisions need more careful thought. A bike can be an important purchase because you're likely to keep it for some time. A bike can also cost anywhere from $100 to $2,000. When you consider what type of bike to buy (mountain bike or road bike) and what brand (Gary Fisher or Trek) you'll probably use all five steps of the decision-making process.

✔ Fast Review

1. Define wants, needs, goods, services, and resources.
2. What is the difference between public wants and private wants?
3. List the steps in a decision-making process.

What Is Business?

Whether you're deciding what movie to see or what bike to buy, your wants and needs are usually satisfied by business. **Business** is any activity that seeks profit by providing goods or services to others. Businesses provide you with necessities such as food, clothing, housing, medical care, and transportation, as well as things that make your life easier and better. Businesses also provide people with the opportunity to become wealthy. For instance, take the late founder of Wal-Mart Stores, Inc., Sam Walton. In 1962 Walton opened the first store in Arkansas. Today, the company sells about $200 billion worth of goods and services. To become a successful company, it had to figure out that its customers wanted low prices and genuine customer service.

WHAT THE PUBLIC WANTS
Take a deep breath of air in an urban area and you just might get a diesel fuel-like aftertaste. According to the U.S. Environmental Protection Agency (EPA), 107 million people live in areas with high levels of air pollutants. **How will the EPA's decision to clean up big diesel trucks, buses, and diesel fuel influence some businesses?**

continued on p. 11

What Business Does

You might be surprised about all the things that happen before you see a product in the store. What happens before your favorite soft drink is available to buy? The company conducted taste tests to make sure enough people liked the flavor of the soft drink. Chances are you saw an ad for that soft drink on TV. Someone else made sure that your local grocery store had enough of the soft drink on hand so that it is available when you go to buy it.

Levi Strauss and Jacob Davis successfully responded to people's wants and needs. The two became business partners in 1873 and began selling work pants to miners, surveyors, cowboys, and other hard-working westerners. Early buyers called the denim pants "Levi's" and the name stuck. Today, Levi Strauss & Company dominates the world of manufacturing jeans.

Similar business activities happen for every product or service that is offered. A business must *organize* the people and equipment to provide the product. People within the organization *manage* the company's resources to *produce* the product. The company then *markets* the product or service by deciding where to sell it and how to advertise it. Every business uses some combination of these activities.

Businesses' Motivations

Why would a person or a business supply the goods and services you want? It comes down to turning a profit. **Profit** is the amount of money left over after a business has paid for the cost of producing its goods and services. Without profit, a company cannot survive in a competitive business world where each strives for a chunk of the market's business. Profit is the motivation for taking the risk to start a business. It's the reward for satisfying the needs and wants of consumers. A business is profitable when sales are high, and costs are kept low.

Figure 1.2

RIDING THE SEA OF CHEESES

➡Cheese lovers' tastes are changing to specialty cheeses. While cheddar and mozzarella are mainstays, sheep's and goat's milk cheeses are moving straight ahead to your nearest deli counter. **Imagine you want to become a cheese maker. What kind of cheese would you make? Why?**

A Snapshot of Dairy Product Production[1]		
CHEESE	PREVIOUS YEAR	PRESENT YEAR
American[2]	302,331	277,547
Cheddar	236,410	216,003
Swiss	17,486	18,000
Brick & Muenster	6,974	6,766
Cream & Neufchatel	38,763	42,757
Hispanic	7,271	7,264
Mozzarella	204,909	216,254
Other Italian	53,602	53,378
Total Italian	258,511	269,632
All other types	14,231	14,642

[1] Production reported in thousands of pounds.
[2] Includes cheddar, colby, monterey, jack

When consumers' wants and needs change then businesses are motivated to change along with them. In order to change with consumers' wants and needs the companies thrive on **competition**, or the contest between businesses to win customers. For example, people are very interested in buying cellular telephones. Motorola offers cell phones with access to the Internet, digital operating systems, and an FM stereo. The Finnish pioneer of wireless telecommunications, Nokia, offers you the power to personally design your own cell phone cover in the company's online studio.

When there is more than one kind of cellular phone to choose from, you can buy the cheapest one, the one that is the right size, the right shape, the right color, or has the right high-tech capabilities. Competition is a direct response to consumers' wants and needs. Figure 1.2 asks you to make a business decision based upon the consumer's tastes. Will competition and profit wager into your decision?

Business and You

Businesses make many decisions that impact you. They decide what products and services to produce. However, you also affect business. You decide what kind of products and services you want and where you will buy them. This mutual relationship relies on each partner making a decision.

You as a Consumer. A **consumer** is a person who selects, purchases, uses, or disposes of goods or services. Business is aware of your changing needs and wants. For instance, take electrical engineer Jeff Hawkins who is the original creator and designer of the Palm™Pilot, a handheld computer product. The handheld device has changed the way people communicate and organize their lives. A compact handheld computing device allows you to electronically organize your to-do list, calendar, e-mail, address book, and download software.

Businesses also affect you when they discontinue products. The decision to stop manufacturing products is often because there is a decreasing demand. When a company is slow to respond to customers' complaints and doesn't communicate very well, then customers usually find another company's product to buy. When customers behave this way the company doesn't make much money. Either the company makes some changes to satisfy its customers or the company folds.

You as a Wage Earner. Businesses affect you as a wage earner. In order to make products and provide services, businesses hire people to work. In order to produce a product, the business decides how it will be produced. For example, if Gene's Pizza decides to deliver pizzas to its customers, it needs to hire pizza-delivery drivers.

Real-World Application

part **3** of 4

WHAT THE PUBLIC WANTS

According to 81 percent of those surveyed by a team of researchers from Washington State University, learning is a lifelong pursuit for a successful career. More adults are enrolling in continuing education courses. **How are colleges and universities changing to meet this demand?**

continued on p. 13

In business today, workers have more input about how business is done. A business you work for may ask you to think of ways to improve the production process. When you're an employee, decision-making skills, quality of work, and input to problems help a business flourish. IDEO is a product-design company responsible for innovating Polaroid's I-Zone instant camera and Crest's stand-up toothpaste tube. The small company attracts passionate people who have fun and work hard as a team to produce its products every day.

✓ Fast Review

1. Define business.
2. List the business activities that happen behind every product or service.
3. How does business affect you as a consumer and as a wage earner?

Working Lifestyle

What are you doing at 10 A.M.?

Curing Children

"A lot of doctors go into pediatrics because they want to work with kids," says pediatrician Eric Lau. "Then they find you treat the parents as much as the children. When kids are sick, parents are really stressed out!"

Lau always wanted to work with kids, so when he volunteered at a hospital and became interested in medicine as a college student, pediatrics was a perfect fit for him as a career. Since graduating medical school, going through residency, and joining a small practice, he hasn't been disappointed.

Appointments at Lau's office begin at 8:45 in the morning, so by 10:00 he is diagnosing coughs, colds, and ear infections. Lau says, "It's sort of like what I expected, but you never really know what it's like until you're there.

The pace is always changing. You're faced with situations where you're not sure what's going on, but you have to make decisions. You're always thinking."

Lau is always making on-the-spot decisions, but the most rewarding aspect of his job is long-term. He says, "I treat kids, make them better, and, over the course of time, watch them grow."

Salary

The median income of physicians is about $164,000, with a range between $120,000 and $250,000 a year.

Outlook for This Career

This profession is expected to grow faster than average due to a growing population. This drives the overall growth of healthcare services.

Connecting Careers Activity

Education and training to become a doctor takes longer than any other occupation. What are the benefits of choosing a medical career path?

Health Science

CAREER PATH

Self-Discovery in Business

Before dinner you start watching the local news. A broadcast journalist talks about the price of consumer goods. A little later, the reporter mentions that a major online company filed for bankruptcy. The federal government announces a change in interest rates. What does this mean to you? What difference does it make? Will it influence your life, your friends, or your family? Do the actions of the government and businesses have any impact on you?

More than ever before, you need to understand the world you live and work in. What happens in business and government will make a difference in your life. Change comes faster and faster. Companies come and go, and new types of companies continually appear.

The Value of Knowledge

What do you need to be a wise consumer, a good employee, or a successful business owner? Everyone is a consumer. Learning how to get the most from your spending now is important, but getting the most from your future income is even more important.

When you become a business owner, manager, or employee, you'll need business knowledge. You'll probably have several jobs during your lifetime. The more education you have, the better your income. Business in today's world has all types of jobs, and you'll learn and understand the role of those jobs, which influence the millions of workers in all economies.

What Do You Like?

You may not know yet whether you would like to work for someone else or whether you would like to have your own business. Explore the world of business. Learn as much now in order to make an informed decision in the future.

If you like to work outside, for example, you could explore businesses in forestry, gardening or landscaping, ranching, or animal care. If you prefer to take risks on new ventures then being an entrepreneur may appeal to you. If you like to create ideas, you might like to be a writer or an actor. If you like to work with numbers and solve problems, you may find yourself drawn to being an accountant, an engineer, or a mathematician. Explore all the business opportunities in order to see what is available to you in order to satisfy your wants and needs.

Real-World Application

part **4** of 4

WHAT THE PUBLIC WANTS

Diversity is the core of the U.S. public. More minorities are attending college, which feed the workforce. **Why is diversity an important stimulant for the workforce?**

✓ **Fast Review** _____

1. Why is it important to understand business today?
2. How will knowledge help your career?

Summary

1. Wants are those things you wish you could have. Needs are things you need for survival, like food, shelter, and clothing. Goods satisfy your wants and needs for material things that you can see or touch, whereas services satisfy some of your wants for things you cannot see or touch.

2. Limited resources affect the number of wants.

3. Business activities include producing and distributing goods and services to consumers. Every business organizes, manages, produces, and markets a product or service.

4. Both profit and competition motivate businesses to meet wants and needs.

5. Business affects consumers by the products or services it decides to offer. You affect business by what products and services you buy. Business also affects you as a wage earner by determining the types of jobs that will be available. You also affect business by how you work.

● Using Business Key Words

In today's business world, people often use the following terms. See if you can match each term to its definition.

- **wants**
- **services**
- **needs**
- **resource**
- **goods**
- **business**
- **competition**
- **consumer**
- **profit**

1. Things we must have to survive.
2. Any activity that seeks profit by providing goods or services to others.
3. Anything that people can use to make or obtain what they want or need.
4. The contest between businesses to win customers.
5. Things we wish we could have.
6. A person who selects, purchases, uses, or disposes of goods or services.
7. Tasks that people or machines perform.
8. Material things that can be weighed or measured.
9. The amount of money left over after a business has paid for the cost of producing its goods and services.

● Review What You Learned

10. Explain how a family, a business, or a group could have private wants.
11. Who satisfies most of the public wants shared by many people?
12. Describe the difference between wants and needs. Give two examples of each.
13. Explain the major difference between goods and services. Give two examples of each.
14. Describe the problem of unlimited wants and limited resources.
15. Is time an example of a resource? Explain your answer.
16. Why is the decision-making process important to use when making choices about what to buy?
17. Describe the business activities that happen for every product or service that is offered for sale.
18. How do the decisions that businesses make affect you as a consumer?
19. How do the decisions that you make as a wage earner affect a business?

● Understanding Business Concepts

20. Give a personal example of a private want, a public want, and a need.
21. Do you think it's possible to have all your wants satisfied? Explain.
22. Think about a purchasing decision you'll have to make in the next few weeks. Use the five-step process to carefully consider your alternatives.
23. How does business provide people with the opportunity to become wealthy?
24. Describe how business decisions determine the jobs that you and other wage earners have.

● Critical Thinking

25. Why do you think Wal-Mart has been so successful?
26. What would you do if a product you like to buy was no longer offered by the business?
27. List three situations in which decision making has greatly influenced your life.
28. How have you improved the production process of something?

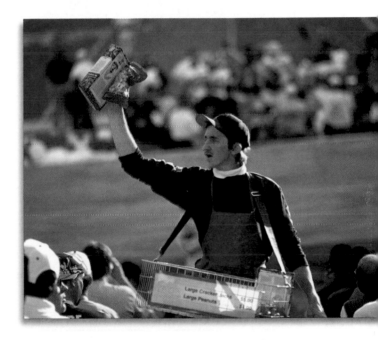

● Viewing and Representing

Examining the Image. Pair up with a partner and take turns asking each other these questions: What exactly do you see in this photo? What people and objects are pictured? Thinking about wants and needs, what do you think is going on? What would you want if you were in this situation? Would you really need it or them?

Building Academic Skills

 Grouping

List five businesses you're familiar with in your community. Identify whether the business provides goods or services? Do any provide both? For example, many hair salons not only provide the service of cutting and styling hair but also sell hair-care products, which are goods. List the kinds of decisions that the business might have made in choosing what to provide for its customers.

 Researching

Research the history of Wal-Mart. Include information about how Sam Walton became one of the richest people in America. Find out how many stores are currently located in the United States and if there are any located outside the United States. Write a two-page paper with your findings.

MATH **Budgeting**

Imagine you've been given $100 for next month's expenses. Create a budget showing how you would spend the money. Determine how much of the $100 would be spent on needs and how much would be spent on wants. Compare your budget with another member in your class.

COMPUTER TECHNOLOGY **Predicting**

Handheld computer devices, like the Palm™Pilot, are becoming very popular. Research another emerging technological device and predict when you think it will become as popular as handheld computers. Write a 100-word paragraph about the device and include a picture if possible.

Linking School to Home

Compare and Contrast. Suppose you're stranded on a small, uninhabited tropical island. Do you think your wants and needs would be different on the island than at home in your own community? Would satisfying those wants and needs be different on the island? Describe how the resources available on the island would impact your wants and needs.

Linking School to Work

Evaluating Information. Interview the manager or owner of a local small business. Find out about the sources of information he or she uses in making business decisions. Ask how he or she evaluates the information before acting upon it. Does he or she use the decision-making model described in this chapter? Write a 200-word report about the ways that person evaluates information.

E-Homework

Applying Technology

Create a Database. As a class, research all the resources that were used to build and furnish your school. Create a database of the resources used. Save this database to be used in Chapter 2.

Online Research. Using the Internet, research a business that sells a product that you use. Who started the business? When and why was it founded? Find out what resources were used to create the product the business sells. Is the product a want or need for you?

Connecting Academics

Math. At the baseball park you pay a lot if you want to buy food at the concession stand. You could satisfy your need for food and drink by bringing healthy snacks from home that cost less. If you buy a hot dog, peanuts, and soda from the concession stand it could cost you $5. Let's say instead, you bring a homemade ham sandwich, grapes, and a soft drink, and they only cost you $3. What's your percentage savings?

Social Science. When there are limited resources, you need to make decisions. Imagine you're managing the concession stands at the major league baseball park nearest to you. You need to make a profit. Here are possibilities on how to run the concession stands:

- Research concessions at ball parks and then brainstorm about your concessions.
- List the materials, equipment, and labor you'll need. If possible, use a spreadsheet program.
- Write your five steps in the decision-making process.
- What other information, if any, do you need to make an informed decision?

BusinessWeek Analyzing the Feature Story

You read the first part of "Paperless Page-Turners?" at the beginning of this chapter. Below are a few questions for you to answer about the article. You'll find the answers to these questions when you're reading the entire article. First, here are the questions:

29. What is Gemstar predicting about the wants of people who buy books?
30. How do the decisions of Gemstar and publishers affect consumers who buy books?

CREATIVE JOURNAL ACTIVITY

Plan your own pizzeria by answering these questions.

Organize: How many people will work in the restaurant? Where will the equipment be located?

Manage: Who will supervise the pizza makers? Who will make sure the pizzas are made with quality ingredients?

Produce: How will the pizzas be made? Who will make the pizzas?

Market: How will you advertise? Will coupons be given away?

BUSINESS *Online*

The Full Story

To learn more about e-books, visit the *Introduction to Business* Web site at **www.introbus.glencoe.com**, and click on *BusinessWeek* Feature Story, Chapter 1.

Economic Resources and Systems

● Learning Objectives

After completing this chapter, you'll be able to:

1. **Define** scarcity.
2. **List** the four factors of production.
3. **Identify** the differences between market and command economies.
4. **Explain** why most countries prefer a mixed economy.

● Why It's Important

Understanding economic resources and systems is essential to lessening economic problems.

● Key Words

scarcity
factors of production
natural resources
human resources
capital resources
entrepreneurial resources
economics
market economy
demand
supply
equilibrium price
command economy
mixed economy

BusinessWeek Feature Story

Poland—Goods Runneth Over

Poland Is an Inspiration for the Rest of Europe. For a newcomer, it was quite a scene. Merchants, artisans, and even bankers lined the streets to offer their products at a fair in Warsaw's Old Town on a recent Sunday afternoon. As a band played Louis Armstrong's "Wonderful World" and other tunes, prosperous-looking Poles shopped for private pension funds as well as locally made goods ranging from candies to cosmetics. What a change from a decade ago when voters ended communist rule by supporting Solidarity candidates in Poland's first competitive elections. Within months, communism had collapsed across Eastern Europe.

Source: Excerpted with permission from "Poland: A Beacon for the Rest of Europe," *Business Week Online*, June 21, 1999.

An Extension Activity

Research the brainchild behind the theories of the Communist movement. Then find out which Soviet leader modified it and lead the Revolution of October 1917.

BUSINESS *Online*

The Full Story

To learn more about Poland, visit the *Introduction to Business* Web site at **www.introbus.glencoe.com**, and click on *BusinessWeek* Feature Story, Chapter 2.

What Is Economics?

You're gearing up for a weekend trip to the boardwalk with your friends. You take out your in-line skates from the back of your closet. Just by looking at the scratches and dust on them you suppose they need a wheel rotation. Unfortunately, you don't have the parts to do it. You also don't know how to switch the wheels yourself, and you don't have enough money to get it done. You have a shortage of resources. Just as individuals have to deal with a shortage of resources, so do societies.

Factors of Production

A society might not have enough oil, doctors, or technology to satisfy the wants and needs of its people. This shortage of resources is called **scarcity**. A basic economic problem for any society is how to manage its resources. Figure 2.1 illustrates how your choices between wants and needs influence your economic situation.

To meet the wants and needs of its people, a society must produce goods and services. The means to produce them are called economic resources, or **factors of production**. Factors of production include things like the wheat that grows in the ground, the tractor that harvests it, and the labor that turns it into flour.

Figure 2.1

YOUR ECONOMIC REALITY AT A GLANCE

➡ The average American spends $7 a day on food. People spend less than half of that money on home-cooked meals. On a separate piece of paper, re-create this table below. Insert a check mark in the appropriate square based upon your eating experiences in one week.

How do your choices influence your economic situation?

Choice	Fast-food restaurant	Home-cooked meal	Eat at a friend's house
Sunday			
Monday			
Tuesday			
Wednesday			
Thursday			
Friday			
Saturday			

Natural Resources

The raw materials found in nature are called **natural resources**. Natural resources become factors of production when used to produce goods. The trees used to make paper and the fish harvested for food are factors of production. Natural resources are often basic elements that can be combined in various ways to create goods. Even synthetic or artificially produced materials are made by combining or changing natural resources. For example, nylon is a synthetic material derived from coal, water, and air.

The economy of many countries is based on its natural resources. For example, the economy of Saudi Arabia depends on its oil production. Many Latin American countries rely on their coffee crops. Other countries, such as Japan, have few natural resources and must get them from somewhere else.

Some resources, like wheat and cattle, are *renewable*. They can be reproduced. Other resources are limited, or *nonrenewable*, like coal, iron, and oil. The amount of natural resources available to a society has a direct effect on its economy.

Human Resources

To produce goods and provide services requires the work of many people. The knowledge, efforts, and skills people bring to their work are called **human resources**, or labor. Teachers, coal miners, bank managers, and farm-workers are all human resources. Whether you're a cashier or a news anchor, you're a human resource. Human resources are needed for everything from drilling oil out of the ground to selling gasoline at a service station.

Labor can be skilled or unskilled, physical or intellectual. One of the biggest problems facing many nations today is not a shortage of labor but a shortage of skilled labor. Many developing nations have plenty of human and natural resources but lack the training or technology to use them. In the United States there is a shortage of nurses, which is problematic since 78 million baby boomers begin turning 65 in a decade. A shrinking hospital staff threatens their future care as well as for all patients.

Capital Resources

Another factor of production is capital resources. Capital resources are not the same as capital, or money. **Capital resources** are the things used to produce goods and services, like buildings, materials, and equipment. They include delivery trucks, supermarkets, cash registers, and medical supplies. A Deere & Company tractor that a farmer uses to

Real-World Application

part 1 of 4

HOW THE HEARTH SAVED YOU MONEY

Homeowners are tired of paying high bills for natural gas and electricity. Midwesterners have turned to Mike Haefner, the founder of American Energy Systems, Inc., in Hutchinson, Minn. His company manufactures a hearth alternative: a corn-burning appliance.

Is corn a renewable or nonrenewable resource?

continued on p. 23

harvest wheat is a capital resource. The headquarters of IBM is a capital resource. If you're a writer or an accountant, the computer you use is a capital resource.

As the wants and needs of people change, so do the needs for capital resources. In developing nations such as Zimbabwe, there is still a great need for agricultural equipment.

Entrepreneurial Resources

To meet the changing wants and needs of people requires **entrepreneurial resources**. Entrepreneurs recognize the need for new goods and services. They improve on ways to use resources, or create and produce new ones. Henry Ford perfected the factory assembly line method of mass production. Computer industry pioneers William Hewlett and David Packard developed the programmable scientific calculator.

A key to dealing with scarcity is to develop new resources and technologies. For example, researchers at Pioneer Hi-Bred and DuPont are developing and improving insect resistant corn to protect against corn rootworm, which is a costly expense to farmers.

✓ Fast Review

1. What is scarcity?
2. What are the four factors of production?
3. What are some examples of capital resources?

Making Decisions About Production

The problem of scarcity forces societies to answer some basic economic questions. No society has enough productive resources available to produce everything people want. Every society must, therefore, make choices.

Basic Economic Questions

Rules and regulations determine choices. A society makes the choices by answering the following three economic questions: What should be produced? How should it be produced? Who should share in what is produced?

What Should Be Produced?   Every country must decide how to use its resources to meet the needs of its people. It has to determine what to produce and how much to produce. The resources used for one purpose can't also be used for something else. For example, a piece of land could be used to grow wheat or corn. It could also be used as the site of a factory, a housing development, or a park. However, the land can only be used for one of these things at a time. Deciding to use it for one purpose means giving up the opportunity to use it for something else.

Consider This...

Blood Is Thicker Than Oil
Occidental Petroleum Corp. is exploring for oil in Colombia. However, the U'wa people oppose oil exploration on the land they have lived on for thousands of years. For them, oil is the "blood of Mother Earth." The problem is more complex because the Colombian government supports the oil production, which will bring development to the country.
ANALYZE
Who has the right to the land—the U'wa people, the corporation, or the Colombian government?

How Should It Be Produced? When a society decides what to produce, it must also address other types of questions, such as what methods will be used, how many people will work on the production, and what will be the quality of the items produced? The answers to these questions depend on two factors. One factor depends on how goods are to be produced. Another important factor is the quantity of available resources. In a country where there are workers but very little capital resources, it's probable that little equipment and larger amounts of labor are used in producing goods. The opposite would be true in a country with capital resources but relatively few workers.

Who Should Share in What Is Produced? This question focuses on the concept that people can't get everything that they want because the society doesn't have enough resources. Thus, who gets the limited number of goods that are produced? Although the first two basic economic decisions are important, choosing how goods and services are distributed probably interests people most. In most societies, people can have as many goods and services as they can afford to buy. Thus, the amount of income people receive determines how many goods and services they can have. Then the question arises as to how does the society determine the income earned by each individual in that society?

HOW THE HEARTH SAVED YOU MONEY
The Countryside Multi-Fuel Corn/Pellet Stove burns corn (and it doesn't smell like popcorn). Burning corn saves the homeowner ten times more money than electricity or heating oil. **Based upon the cost savings, do you think the price of corn is high or low?**

continued on p. 25

✓ Fast Review

1. When a society chooses to use a resource for one purpose and gives up the opportunity to use it for some other purpose, what cost is involved?
2. What happens to production methods when a country discovers new ways to combine economic resources?
3. In most countries, what determines how many goods and services a person can buy?

Types of Economic Systems

Economics studies how society chooses to use resources to produce and distribute goods and services for people's consumption. Businesses may contribute to an economic system by inventing products that use available resources.

To use its limited resources effectively, every nation needs an economic system. An economic system determines how resources will be used. The primary goal of an economic system is to provide people with a minimum standard of living, or quality of life.

To answer the basic economic questions just discussed, two basic and opposing economic systems have been developed. They are commonly referred to as a market economy and a command economy.

Market Economy

In a **market economy** economic decisions are made in the market-place according to the laws of supply and demand. Mobil gas stations, Fantastic Sam's hair salons, Federal Express offices, and the New York Stock Exchange are all marketplaces. The marketplace is anywhere money changes hands.

The Market and Prices. Price plays an important role in the market economy. Price is the amount of money given or asked for when goods and services are bought or sold. If producers think the price consumers will pay for a good or service is too low, and the price does not earn them a profit, they will produce little or none of the product. If they think the price is high enough to earn a profit, they will produce the good and service.

Consumers are the ones who determine the demand of an item. **Demand** is the amount or quantity of goods and services that consumers are willing to buy at various prices. Generally, the higher the price, the

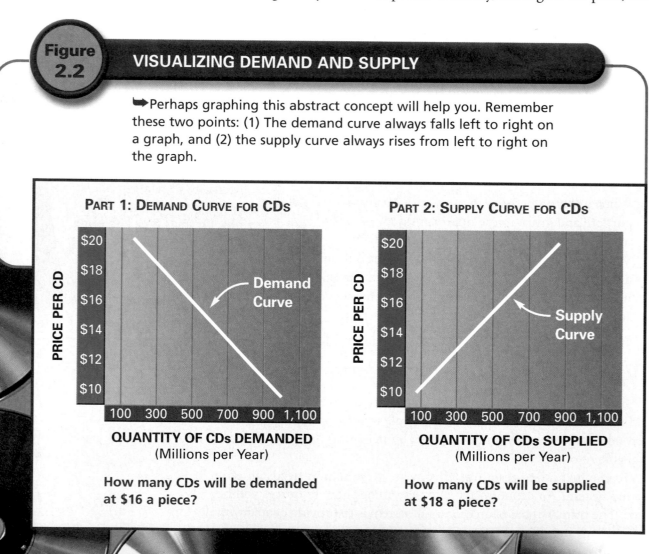

Figure 2.2

VISUALIZING DEMAND AND SUPPLY

➡️Perhaps graphing this abstract concept will help you. Remember these two points: (1) The demand curve always falls left to right on a graph, and (2) the supply curve always rises from left to right on the graph.

PART 1: DEMAND CURVE FOR CDs

Demand Curve

PRICE PER CD: $20, $18, $16, $14, $12, $10

QUANTITY OF CDs DEMANDED
(Millions per Year)

100 300 500 700 900 1,100

How many CDs will be demanded at $16 a piece?

PART 2: SUPPLY CURVE FOR CDs

Supply Curve

PRICE PER CD: $20, $18, $16, $14, $12, $10

QUANTITY OF CDs SUPPLIED
(Millions per Year)

100 300 500 700 900 1,100

How many CDs will be supplied at $18 a piece?

fewer consumers will buy an item. The opposite also applies: The lower the price, the more consumers will buy.

Suppose you walk into a store with $15 to buy a CD. The store is having a "two for one" sale on CDs. You decide to buy two CDs for the price of one. Chances are many other customers will do the same thing. This results in more CDs being sold. The sale encourages consumers to buy more.

Producers are influenced to supply goods or services by the prices in the market. **Supply** is the amount of goods and services that producers will provide at various prices. Producers want to receive a price for their goods and services that will cover their costs and provide a profit.

Suppose the price for eggs rises from $2 to $4 a dozen. The price will probably increase because egg-producing businesses will see more profits to be made at $4. At that price, producers are encouraged to produce more eggs.

Demand and supply work together. Figure 2.2 illustrates demand and supply. When the quantity demanded and the quantity supplied meet, this is called the **equilibrium price**. Equilibrium, then, is the price at which the amount supplied and the amount demanded meet.

A market economy is also called *capitalism*, or private enterprise. In a capitalist system, resources are privately owned. You can own your own home, your own land, and your own business. You decide how your business will be run, what to sell, and how much to charge. As a consumer, you decide where to live, where to shop, and what to buy. If you need shampoo, you can buy the name brand for dry, unmanageable hair, or the store brand that's on sale. Government control of the marketplace is minimal. The primary role of government is to support the marketplace by removing obstacles such as trade barriers. The United States and Japan are examples of capitalist countries.

Real-World Application

part **3** of 4

HOW THE HEARTH SAVED YOU MONEY

The corn hearth only requires a vent pipe (no chimney) installed through the wall, and it uses as much electricity as a 100-watt light bulb. **Why do you think foreign countries are interested in buying these corn-burning appliances?**

continued on p. 27

The Market's Motivations. A market economy also offers incentives, such as competition and the profit motive, to produce more. The *profit motive* is simply the desire to make more money. You have an incentive to work harder and longer if you can make more money. Businesses compete for customers by producing better and cheaper products. The constant demand for new goods and services encourages entrepreneurship.

The problem with a market economy is that owners and producers reap the most rewards. Unskilled workers and older adults are often unable to afford basic needs such as health care. In the United States, for example, the average chief executive officer makes almost 500 times as much as the average blue-collar worker. A small number of large companies can join forces to control the supply of products and manipulate prices. The profit motive can become an end in itself rather than a means to improve the product for all.

Command Economy

Many nations have a command economy. A command economy is also called a planned or managed economy. In a **command economy** a central authority makes the key economic decisions. This central authority is usually the government, or state.

There are two types of command economies. In a strong command economy, such as *communism*, the state makes all the economic decisions. The state controls all the resources for the common good. The state decides what to produce, how much, and how to distribute it. China, Cuba, and many Latin American and African countries have strong command economies.

Business Building Blocks

Math

Interpreting Line Graphs

Graphs are a quick and useful way to visually communicate information. You see these from newspaper articles to cereal boxes. Line graphs often show change over a period of time. The left side of a graph is the *vertical axis*. The bottom of the graph is the *horizontal axis*. Both axes display numbers and a label indicating what the numbers represent. Dots on the graph show numerical information. When the dots are connected, they form a line whose location and direction on the graph reveals information about change through time.

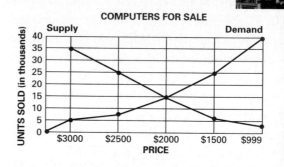

COMPUTERS FOR SALE

Practice

Use the graph to answer the following questions: How many $3,000 computers are being supplied? What is the difference between supply and demand for $3,000 computers? At what price does the supply equal the demand for computers?

How to Interpret a Line Graph

- Read the title of the graph.
- Read the label on each axis.
- Understand the numbers on each axis, including the interval used. The *interval* is the unit of measurement between numbers.
- Examine where the dots are located on the graph.
- Determine what the line(s) or curve(s) symbolize.
- Compare the line(s) on the graph to both axes to determine the graph's meaning.

In a moderate command economy, also called *socialism*, there is some form of private enterprise. The state owns major resources, such as airlines and steel, and makes the key economic decisions. However, individuals may own some businesses. France and Sweden are countries that have moderate command economies.

The primary advantage of a command economy is that it guarantees everyone an equal standard of living. The state provides you with a job, a place to live, and health care. Goods and services are distributed evenly. The state also takes care of things like utilities, transportation, and defense. There is usually less crime and poverty because everyone's needs and wants are equally met.

There are some disadvantages to a command economy. In a strong command economy since the state provides all goods and services there is little choice of what to buy. Goods that aren't considered necessities like fashion clothing and VCRs are often unavailable. Prices are fixed by the state, so there is no incentive to produce a better product. Wages are fixed by the state. If you're a highly skilled worker, like a doctor or a lawyer, you often earn the same wage as an unskilled worker. There is no incentive for entrepreneurship when you can't run your own business.

Mixed Economy

A free market economy and a command economy are great ideas in principle but don't always work in practice. In a market economy, there can be great poverty in the midst of great wealth. In a command economy, everyone is economically equal. In reality, few nations have an economy based totally on one model or the other.

Most nations have a **mixed economy**, a combination of a market and command economy. The state takes care of people's needs while the marketplace takes care of people's wants. In the United States, for example, the government provides things like defense and education. The marketplace provides things like cars, computers, and fast food. There is some government regulation of business.

In every country, one type of economy is dominant. However, most countries find a mixed economy is the best way to manage their limited resources.

Real-World Application

part 4 of 4

HOW THE HEARTH SAVED YOU MONEY
The average home using a multi-fuel corn stove will burn 150 to 200 bushels of corn a season. Imagine a command economy that only allows 100 bushels of corn per household.
How might this affect the people?

✔ **Fast Review** _____

1. What is an economic system?
2. What is the difference between a market economy and a command economy?
3. What are the advantages and disadvantages of a command economy and a market economy?

Chapter 2 Economic Resources and Systems   **27**

Global *Economy*

Demand for Oil Americans demand oil for many purposes, but mostly as a fuel for their automobiles. About 193 million vehicles burn 122 billion gallons of gasoline a year. Domestic supplies meet about half of the demand for oil. The map below shows where we get the rest.

Canada supplies 13 percent

Mexico supplies 11 percent

Caribbean Nations supply 4 percent
(Leading Sources: Virgin Islands, Trinidad and Tobago, Netherlands Antilles)

South America supplies 24 percent
(Leading Sources: Venezuela, Colombia, Argentina)

On average, a barrel holding 42 gallons of crude oil produces 21 gallons of gasoline.

**Europe supplies
7 percent**
(Leading Sources: Great
Britain, Norway, Belgium)

**Persian Gulf Region
supplies 23 percent**
(Leading Sources: Saudi
Arabia, Iraq, Kuwait)

**Asia and Oceania
supply 3 percent**
(Leading Sources: Australia,
Indonesia, Brunei)

**Africa supplies
15 percent**
(Leading Sources: Nigeria,
Angola, Algeria)

Thinking Globally

1. Which region of the world is the largest source for American oil imports?

2. What percentage of American oil imports do Canada and Mexico provide?

Summary

1. Scarcity is the shortage of economic resources such as oil, doctors, or technology.

2. The four factors of production are natural resources, human resources, capital resources, and entrepreneurial resources.

3. In a market economy all economic decisions are made in the marketplace according to the laws of supply and demand. In a command economy a central authority makes all economic decisions. In a market economy there are many incentives to produce, but owners and producers reap the most benefits. In a command economy there is economic equality, but few incentives to produce.

4. In a mixed economy, the state takes care of people's needs while the marketplace takes care of people's wants.

Using Business Key Words

On a separate piece of paper, rewrite the sentences below, using the correct term to complete each one.

- scarcity
- entrepreneurial resources
- economics
- factors of production
- market economy
- equilibrium price
- natural resources
- supply
- demand
- human resources
- command economy
- capital resources
- mixed economy

1. The raw materials found in nature are called _____.
2. Buildings, material, and equipment used to produce goods and services are _____.
3. Society's shortage of resources is called _____.
4. Economic decisions are made according to _____.

5. _____ are required to meet the changing wants and needs of people.
6. Communism is an example of a _____.
7. _____ are the knowledge, efforts, and skills people bring to their work.
8. The _____ are the economic resources used to produce goods and services.
9. A _____ can be defined by the state taking care of the people's needs while the marketplace takes care of the people's wants.
10. The amount or quantity of goods and services that consumers are willing to buy at various prices is called _____.
11. The amount of goods and services that producers will provide at various prices is called the _____.
12. The study of how society chooses to use resources to produce and distribute goods and services for people's consumption is called _____.
13. When the quantity demanded and the quantity supplied meet, this is called _____.

Review What You Learned

14. What resource problem is faced by all societies?
15. What are the four main economic resources?
16. Name the two types of natural resources and give an example of each.
17. What is one of the biggest labor problems facing many nations today?
18. What is the key to dealing with the problem of scarcity?
19. What is the primary goal of an economic system?
20. In a market economy, who owns the resources?
21. What incentives are offered in a free market economy?
22. Describe the two types of command economies.

Understanding Business Concepts

23. Select an item that you see in your classroom. List the factors of production you think were used to produce that item.
24. Are some natural resources more valuable than others? Explain.
25. Describe how a country's economy is affected by its natural resources. Provide an example.
26. What happens when human resources are scarce?
27. How do entrepreneurs help meet the changing needs and wants of people?
28. Give an example of how the concept of supply and demand has affected you.
29. Why is the profit motive considered an incentive in a free market system?
30. Why do most countries find a mixed economy the best way to manage their limited resources?

Critical Thinking

31. Think about a career you might be interested in pursuing. What capital resources would you use in that career?
32. A company produces a new toy that is liked by both children and adults. There is great demand for it. The supplier raises its price because there's no competition. The supplier cannot keep up with the demand. Some people believe the supplier is taking advantage of the public by increasing its price. Are such price increases allowed in a market system? Should the government control the price? What are other toy producers likely to do?

Viewing and Representing

Examining the Image. Look closely at the photo. Where do you focus? Step into the picture. What do you hear? What else do you see around you? Imagine you could buy the goods. Does the price seem fair? Would you buy them at the price shown? Why or why not? How does price affect the demand?

Chapter 2 Review

Building Academic Skills

 Reading Current Events

Select a current event that you have read about in the newspaper or have heard about on the news. Write a one- to two-page paper on how the event has had an impact on the U.S. economy.

 Researching Economic Resources

In a group, choose a foreign country and research the country's economic resources. Assign research topics to each member, such as:

- What natural resources are plentiful?
- What does the country produce with its natural resources?
- What kind of human resources does the country have?
- How does the country make up for the resources that are in short supply?
- What impact do entrepreneurial resources have on its economy?

Create a display of your group's findings, including graphics and photos.

 Averaging Prices

List five things you buy often. Then list all the places you can buy those items. Record the price that each store charges for each item. Do some stores charge more than others? Why do prices differ for identical products? Determine the average price of each item based on the prices you recorded.

 Researching Economic Transition

Using the Internet, find a country that is making the transition from a command economy to mixed or market economy. Prepare a report on the process, the successes, and the difficulties of the transition.

Linking School to Home

Listing Factors of Production. Select five items found in your home that you and your family use quite frequently. List the factors of production you think were used to produce each item. Ask another family member to work on this project with you.

Linking School to Work

Presentation on Technology. Technology has had a dramatic effect on the economy in the United States. Create a list of all the technology that is currently available for consumer use. How much of it was available five years ago? Ten years ago? How has it impacted the U.S. economy? Prepare a two-minute presentation to share your findings with the class.

E-Homework

Applying Technology

Categorizing Data. Using the database created in Chapter 1, categorize the resources according to whether they are natural, human, capital, or entrepreneurial. Then, convert the database into a graphical representation of each category.

Speculating on a Shortage. Research the shortage of workers in information technology. Find out what kinds of jobs are available, the types of skills needed, and the training required in order to get into this career field. Then, speculate why you think there are so many job openings in information technology.

Connecting Academics

Math. Jasmeen, a jewelry vendor at the flea market, looks at her record of prices and sales volume over the past seven months:

	Price	Number of items sold
April	$10	3,000
May	$12	2,900
June	$14	2,800
July	$20	2,500
August	$15	2,800
September	$13	3,200
October	$12	3,400

She asks you to draw a line graph showing the relationship between price and sales. Using the graph, explain to Jasmeen how price affects demand for the jewelry.

Language Arts. Get together in teams to teach one another about economic resources or economic systems. As a team, create a fun lesson plan on one of the following topics:

- Scarcity and factors of production
- The three economic questions
- Market economy
- Supply and demand
- Command economy and mixed economy

Use real-world examples in your lessons. Present the lessons.

BusinessWeek Analyzing the Feature Story

You read the first part of "Poland—Goods Runneth Over" at the beginning of this chapter. Below are a few questions for you to answer about Poland. You'll find the answers to these questions when you're reading the entire article. First, here are the questions:

33. What economic system is Poland moving toward?

34. Name a factor of production that Poland plans to use more of in the future.

CREATIVE JOURNAL ACTIVITY

Break into small groups and agree on another Eastern European country to research.

- What factors of production could this country use?
- What natural resources are available?
- What human resources do they have?

Share your findings with the rest of the class.

BUSINESS *Online*

The Full Story

To learn more about Poland, visit the *Introduction to Business* Web site at **www.introbus.glencoe.com**, and click on *BusinessWeek* Feature Story, Chapter 2.

Economic Activity in a Changing World

● Learning Objectives

After completing this chapter, you'll be able to:

1. **Identify** how economic activity is measured.
2. **Explain** how inflation and deflation work.
3. **Discuss** the four phases of the business cycle.

● Why It's Important

Economic activity affects everyday life. The history of the economy affects industries and people of today and tomorrow.

● Key Words

gross domestic product (GDP)
standard of living
inflation
deflation
budget deficit
national debt
budget surplus
business cycle
prosperity
recession
depression
recovery

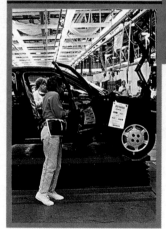

BusinessWeek Feature Story

Moving up the Ladder

From Cheap Labor to Skilled Workers. Inside his cramped, two-bedroom house, in a subdivision of identical tan- and cream-colored dwellings, José Brigido Aguirre boasts of the changes in his life. Since he moved from his small hometown to booming Ciudad Juarez on the U.S.–Mexican border, he's found employment as a technician in a factory. Thanks to a mortgage he lined up through a program funded by the government and his employers, Delphi Automotive Systems Corp. in Tory, Mich., Aguirre, 25, now supports three generations—eight people in all—under one roof on $135 a week before taxes.

Source: Excerpted with permission from "Moving up the Ladder: From Cheap Labor to Skilled Workers," *BusinessWeek Online*, November 6, 2000.

An Extension Activity

Imagine your friend from Mexico City just landed an internship with Southwest Airlines in Dallas, Texas. Your friend is a little nervous about living in a new country with new etiquette. Research business etiquette tips that he or she might use to fit in.

BUSINESS Online

The Full Story

To learn more about globalization, visit the *Introduction to Business* Web site at **www.introbus.glencoe.com**, and click on *BusinessWeek* Feature Story, Chapter 3.

The Influences on Economics

George Santayana, the American writer said, "Those who cannot remember the past are condemned to repeat it." In the realm of economics, the wealth of nations rises and falls through periods of war, recession, and prosperity. You'll remember that a major purpose of an economic system is to produce the goods and services wanted by people. You might also say that almost anyone can start a business in the U.S. economy. Measuring an economic system's activity greatly impacts everyone. Figure 3.1 illustrates how the GDP seasonally adjusts.

Figure 3.1

GROSS DOMESTIC PRODUCT

➡ The gross domestic product (GDP) is the output of goods and services produced in a country.
What percentage did the GDP increase from the end of Year 2 to the beginning of Year 3?

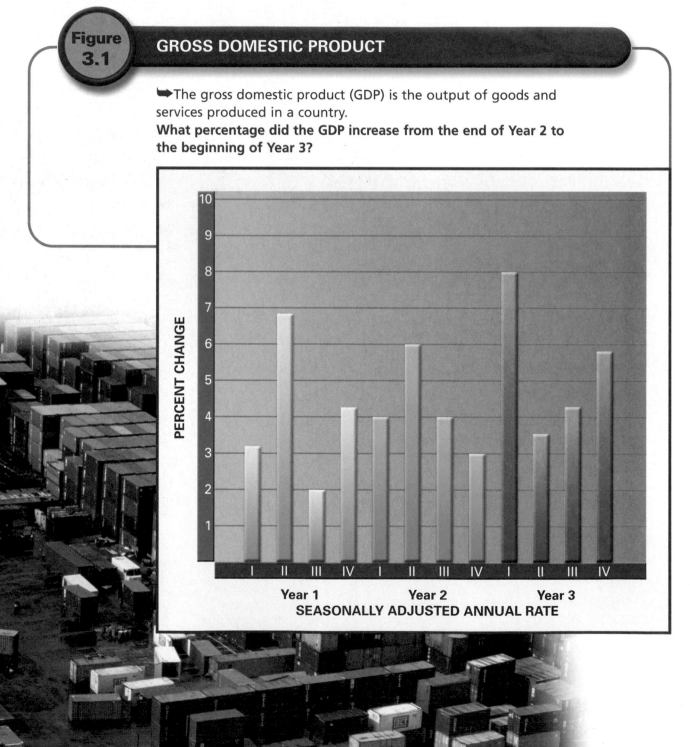

36

Measuring Economic Activity

Baseball fans know that batting averages, strikeouts, RBIs, and ERAs are figures used to measure a player's performance. Figures are also used to measure economic performance. These figures are called *economic indicators*. They measure things like how much a country is producing, whether its economy is growing, and how it compares to other countries.

Gross Domestic Product (GDP)

Goods and services that satisfy your wants and needs are the final output of an economy. They're the result of all the economic activity in the country. One way of telling how well an economy is performing is to determine how many goods and services it produces during a certain period of time.

An important measure of a country's economic health is its level of *productivity*, or how much it produces. The total value of the goods and services produced in a country in a given year is called its **gross domestic product (GDP)** (see Figure 3.1). The United States has a very high GDP compared to other countries.

To calculate the GDP, economists compute the sum of goods and services. They include four main areas:

- consumer goods and services
- business goods and services
- government goods and services
- goods and services sold to other countries

The GDP doesn't include the goods and services that aren't reported to the government, like daycare, babysitting, and mowing lawns.

The United States produces so much more than other countries that it has a higher standard of living. The **standard of living** is the amount of goods and services the average citizen can buy. In the 1990s, the GDP of the United States grew from about $5.5 trillion to almost $9 trillion. This is a sign that the U.S. economy has continued to grow over time.

Unemployment Rate

The *unemployment rate* measures the number of people who are able to work but don't have a job during a given period of time. There are different reasons for being unemployed, some more serious than others. For instance, if you just quit your job or you just graduated from school you're probably looking for work. This type of unemployment is temporary and has little effect on the economy. Another type of unemployment is seasonal. If you harvest crops or work in retail during the holiday season, you may only work during a certain part of the year.

ERAS THAT CHANGED THE ECONOMY

The Colonial Era, 1578–1776. People lived off the land. They traded some of what they produced with England, but they traded mostly among themselves. **Did colonists develop their own industries?**

continued on p. 39

A more serious type of unemployment is caused by changes in industry. New technology can replace workers or require new skills. Companies merge or restructure and "downsize," laying off thousands of workers. These types of workers can remain unemployed for a long period of time unless they're retrained or a company finds them new jobs. The worst type of unemployment occurs when the entire economy slows down. Millions of people in every industry can lose their jobs because there isn't enough work. This type of unemployment lasts until the economy recovers, which can take years.

Changes in the unemployment rate show whether an economy is picking up or slowing down. For example, in 1999, the unemployment rates in Japan and the United States were almost the same, about 4.4 percent. Between 1990 and 1999, however, the unemployment rate in the United States steadily decreased while in Japan it almost doubled. This shows that the U.S. economy was actually growing while the Japanese economy was declining.

Rate of Inflation

Another important measure of economic strength is the rate of inflation. **Inflation** is a general increase in the cost of goods and services. Inflation can happen when an economy actually becomes too productive. The more people are employed, the more people spend. As the demand for goods goes up, producers raise their prices. To pay the higher

You Make the Call

Dealing With Different Economic Systems

You're the president of a large biotechnology company that produces new vaccines for several tropical diseases. The communist government of Cuba has requested that you sell the vaccine to help stop a serious disease. Only your company has developed the vaccine. Personally, you're opposed to communist societies.

Making an Ethical Decision

1. Should you encourage other company executives to approve sale of the vaccine?
2. Does it matter if the disease is deadly? What if it wasn't fatal but caused blindness and was highly infectious?
3. If the United States doesn't allow its citizens to trade with Cuba, would you still discuss the topic with executives? If the executives want to help, how else could your company get the vaccine to those who need it?

prices, workers demand higher wages. When wages go up, producers raise prices again to pay for the higher wages, and so on. This situation might spiral out of control and lead to *hyperinflation*.

Many other factors can lead to inflation, such as the government printing too much money. When the supply of goods is greater than the demand it can result in deflation. **Deflation** is a general decrease in the cost of goods and services. When an economy produces more goods than people want, it has to lower prices and cut production. As a result, people have less money to buy goods so the demand continues to go down. This is what happened to some of the Asian nations in the 1990s. Manufacturing countries like Japan and Taiwan over-produced goods such as TVs and VCRs, which led to an economic collapse.

The United States tries to maintain a slow but steady rate of economic growth to avoid both inflation and deflation. This is done by controlling productivity and keeping a certain number of people unemployed. That way there is less risk of producers making too many goods or workers demanding higher wages.

National Debt

Countries can run up large debts. The main source of income for a government is taxes. It uses the tax money to pay for social programs like defense, education, and social security. When the government spends more on programs than it collects in taxes, the difference in the amount is called the **budget deficit**. The U.S. government ran up a huge deficit in the 1980s when it cut taxes while increasing spending on programs. To pay for the difference, the government borrows money from the public, banks, and even other countries. The total amount of money a government owes is its **national debt**. If the debt gets too large, a nation can become dependent on other nations or unable to borrow any more money. This is the case in many developing nations.

On the other hand, a situation when a government's revenue exceeds its expenditures during a one year period is a **budget surplus**. The government will probably use a surplus to cut taxes, reduce the national debt, or increase spending for certain programs. For the most part, a surplus is a rarity.

Real-World Application

part 2 of 4

ERAS THAT CHANGED THE ECONOMY

The Industrial Revolution, 1861–1914. Society transitioned from an agricultural economy to one relying on complex machinery. Farming still ruled most industry even with the invention of Eli Whitney's cotton gin. **How did factories influence the workforce?**

continued on p. 41

✔ **Fast Review** _____

1. What are some reasons for unemployment?
2. What is the difference between inflation and deflation?

The Business Cycle

Once you enter the workforce, you'll experience many ups and downs over the years. You could make a lot of money drawing cartoons for an animation studio, get laid off, and take a temporary job managing a copy shop. You could go back to school to study computer graphics, and then get a job doing special effects, or start your own business. Some of the changes you go through will be due to changes in the economy.

Economies go through ups and down as a result of wars, foreign competition, and changes in technology. Over long periods of time these changes seem to form patterns. For example, the U.S. economy went through slumps in the 1930s, the 1950s, and the 1970s. Slumps in economic activity were always followed by a new wave of productivity. This rise and fall of economic activity over time is called the **business cycle**. The business cycle has four phases—prosperity, recession, depression, and recovery. Figure 3.2 shows the ebb and flow of the business cycle.

Figure 3.2

BUSINESS CYCLE MODEL

➡ The repeated rise and fall of economic activity over time is called a business cycle.
What are the four phases of the cycle?

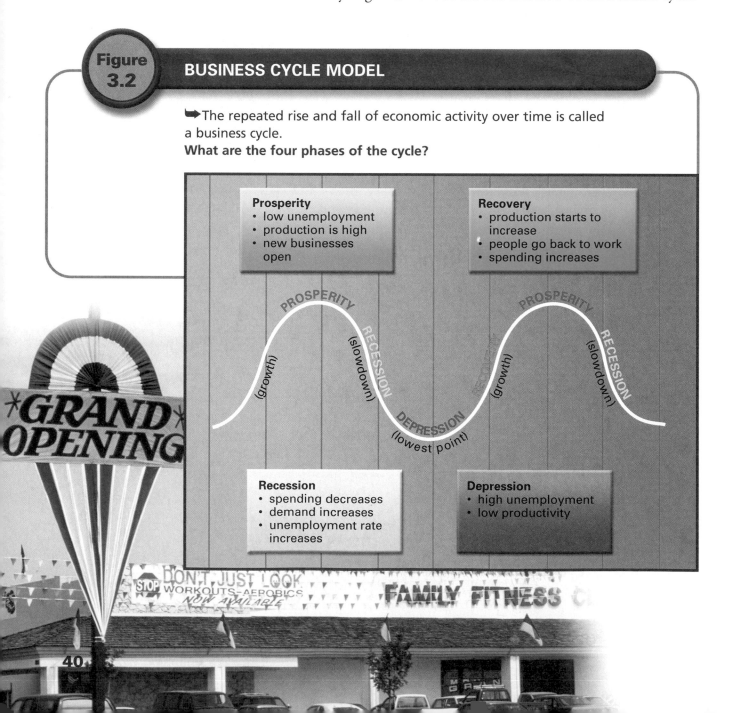

Prosperity
• low unemployment
• production is high
• new businesses open

Recovery
• production starts to increase
• people go back to work
• spending increases

PROSPERITY (growth) — RECESSION (slowdown) — DEPRESSION (lowest point) — RECOVERY (growth) — PROSPERITY — RECESSION (slowdown)

Recession
• spending decreases
• demand increases
• unemployment rate increases

Depression
• high unemployment
• low productivity

Every phase indicates changes to an economy, to industries, and to working people. Changes in the economy can affect some industries, such as the manufacturing industry or the health-care industry, as well as working people. A period of expansion or economic growth affecting the auto industry may mean more job opportunities and higher employment in that industry.

The economic ups and downs of one country can affect other countries too. In a global economy, in which several countries are trading goods and services with one another, one country's economy can affect its other trading partners. If the U.S. economy is in a period of economic expansion, the United States may purchase goods and services from other countries—promoting expansion in those countries. In today's global economy, most countries are interdependent (that is, their economies are linked together).

Prosperity

Prosperity is a peak of economic activity. Unemployment is low, production of goods and services is high, and new businesses open. This condition spreads throughout the economy. Wages are usually higher so there is a greater demand for goods to be produced. More people can buy houses, so the building industry is busier. People also want to buy more goods from other countries, so those countries benefit as well.

The 1990s was a record period of prosperity in the United States. Much of it was due to the low rate of inflation and the Internet creating new business opportunities. Prosperity, however, doesn't last. Any number of things can change. Companies produce too much, people stop buying, or inflation starts to rise.

Recession

During a **recession**, economic activity slows down. Spending decreases and so does the demand for products. Businesses produce less so they need fewer workers. The unemployment rate then increases so people have less to spend. There is a general drop in productivity and the GDP declines.

A recession can affect only one industry, related industries, or spread to the entire economy. For example, if there is a recession in the auto-making industry, it leads to a recession in industries that make parts for cars, like steel and rubber. When this happens, it's called the *ripple effect*. In the 1970s an oil shortage in the United States caused gas prices to increase. Gas is used for every kind of economic activity, from driving

ERAS THAT CHANGED THE ECONOMY
The Era of Mass Production, 1914–1995. World War I (WWI) was the first mechanized war. It created a demand for massive resources. By the end of WWI, Henry Ford had perfected the assembly line. **How did the assembly line change American society?**

continued on p. 43

to work to transporting goods to market. As a result, the price of everything went up and led to a major recession.

Depression

A deep recession that affects the entire economy and lasts for several years is called a **depression**. During a depression there is high unemployment and low productivity. It can be limited to one country but usually spreads to related countries. The state of the economy is affected by large numbers of people out of work, acute shortages, and excess capacity in manufacturing plants.

Working Lifestyle

What are you doing at 10 A.M.?

A Heritage of Life

From spring planting through autumn harvest, Tom Wall's days start at 6:30 A.M. and might not end until 11:00 P.M. It's barely 10:00 A.M. and Wall has already been at work for two-and-a-half hours. He's fed the livestock, cared for newborn pigs, and set the computerized feed mill for the babies.

Wall is a farmer. He and his father farm the land he grew up on near Morse, Iowa. Wall and his family grow corn and soybeans on 900 acres. His 2,100-hog operation is "farrow to finish," which means he raises the animals from babies until they're big enough for market.

The Wall farm isn't just a small business—the family manages several million dollars worth of assets in equipment, buildings, and inventory. He and his father provide most of the labor. In addition to farming, Wall also runs a thriving seed business from a machine-shed/warehouse/office he built on the property. He sells corn, soybean, and alfalfa seed produced by Monsanto and Garst seed companies.

"To succeed as a farmer, you have to wear a lot of different hats," Wall says. "And you have to be willing to commit the time and effort to make things work."

Salary

Full-time farmers earn between $15,704 and $32,188.

Outlook for This Career

The increasing world population will increase the demand for food. Thus the employment outlook for farmers is expected to remain steady.

Connecting Careers Activity

Research how biological career paths might influence dairy, crop growing, and livestock farmers. Write a small paragraph on the influences.

CAREER PATH

Agriculture & Natural Resources

Fortunately, depressions are rare. The stock market crash on October 29, 1929, or "Black Tuesday," marks the beginning of the Great Depression. Between 1929 and 1933, GDP fell from approximately $103 to $55 billion—a decline of nearly 50 percent. At the same time, the number of people out of work rose nearly 800 percent—from 1.6 to 12.8 million. During the worst years of the Depression, one out of every four workers was jobless. Even workers who had jobs suffered. The average manufacturing wage, which had reached fifty-five cents an hour by 1929, plunged to five cents an hour by 1933.

Many banks across the country failed. The FDIC didn't exist at the time, so depositors were not protected. To prevent panic withdrawals, the federal government declared a "bank holiday" in March of 1933. Every bank in the country closed for several days, and many never reopened.

The money supply fell by one-third. Currency was in such short supply that towns, counties, chambers of commerce, and other civic bodies resorted to printing their own money. This was used to pay teachers, firefighters, police officers, and other municipal employees.

Recovery

A rise in business activity after a recession or depression is called a **recovery**. During a recovery, production starts to increase. People start going back to work and have money to spend again. The new demand for goods and services stimulates more production and the GDP grows. Recovery leads back to prosperity as new businesses open.

A recovery can take a long time or it can happen quickly. In 1939 the United States was only beginning to recover from the depression when World War II began. During the war, the United States recovered much faster because of the demand for war production.

During a recovery businesses might start to innovate a new product or a new way of performing a task. When a business innovates, it often gains an edge on its competition, because its costs go down or its sales go up. Profits increase, business grows, and economic activity soars.

Real-World Application

part 4 of 4

ERAS THAT CHANGED THE ECONOMY
The Cyber Era, 1995–present. The Internet has changed business and consumer behaviors. Business is done anywhere in the world, 24 hours a day. **How has the Internet changed the way people do business?**

✔ Fast Review

1. What are the four phases of the business cycle?
2. How does the ripple effect impact the economy?

Summary

1. Gross domestic product, the unemployment rate, and the rate of inflation are types of economic measurements. The GDP is the total value of goods and services produced in a country in a given year. When a country produces much more than other countries it has a higher standard of living. The worst kind of unemployment occurs when the entire economy slows down. People in every industry can lose their jobs because there isn't enough work.

2. Inflation occurs when the costs of goods and services rise. When the supply of goods is greater than the demand it can result in deflation. If wages go up, producers raise prices again to pay for the higher wages then this situation might lead to hyperinflation.

3. The four phases of the business cycle are prosperity, recession, depression, and recovery. Prosperity is the peak of economic activity. During a recession, economic activity slows down. A deep recession that affects the entire economy and lasts for several years is called a depression. The rise in business activity after a recession or depression is called a recovery.

⬤ Using Business Key Words

When talking about the business cycle and economic activity, people use the following terms. See how well you know them by matching each term to its definition.

- **gross domestic product (GDP)**
- **standard of living**
- **budget deficit**
- **budget surplus**
- **national debt**
- **inflation**
- **deflation**
- **business cycle**
- **depression**
- **prosperity**
- **recovery**
- **recession**

1. The amount of goods and services the average citizen can buy.

2. Repeated rise and fall of economic activity over time.

3. A general rise in the prices of goods and services.

4. Period of severe economic decline.

5. The monetary value of all the goods and services produced in a country in a given year.

6. A general decrease in the costs of goods and services.

7. When the government spends more than it collects in taxes.

8. A time when economic activity slows down.

9. The total amount of money a government owes.

10. The peak of economic activity.

11. A rise in business activity after a recession or depression.

12. A situation when a government's revenue exceeds its expenditures during one year.

Review What You Learned

13. What do economic indicators measure?
14. What is one very important measure of a country's economic health?
15. Name three reasons people become unemployed.
16. What do changes in the unemployment rate indicate?
17. Describe hyperinflation.
18. What is the main source of income for the U.S. government?
19. What are the four phases of the business cycle?
20. What is the difference between a recession and a depression?
21. Describe the Industrial Revolution.
22. What was the impact of mass production of cars on other industries?

Understanding Business Concepts

23. Explain why you think the gross domestic product (GDP) in the United States is very high compared to other countries.
24. If many people in a country were able to afford a few food items and there was a severe housing shortage, would that country have a high or low standard of living? Explain.
25. Suppose you go to the grocery store to buy toothpaste, canned soup, and a loaf of bread. You also consider buying a can of soda, but notice the price is 20 cents higher than it was last week. The prices of the other items seem to be the same as always. Is the soda price increase an example of inflation? Why or why not?
26. Why do you think inflation would be especially difficult for retired people?

Critical Thinking

27. Do you think it's a good idea for the government to control economic growth when the inflation rate begins to increase? Why or why not?
28. The Internet has revolutionized how people do business. How has it revolutionized school and the teaching and learning process?
29. How would you rate the standard of living for a country in which all the residents have adequate housing, ample food to eat, good medical care, but in which few people have expensive cars, boats, and jewelry?
30. How might knowledge of nationwide economic statistics help you?

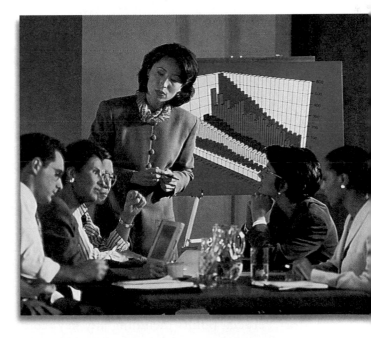

Viewing and Representing

Examining the Image. In a group of three, examine the photo and ask one another journalistic questions beginning with the words who, what, where, when, why, and how. Whose point of view is expressed here? How relevant and reliable is this picture? Discuss your reactions to the photograph.

Building Academic Skills

 Creating a Poster

In a group of three or four, create the next economic era after the Cyber Era. Describe the inventions, how people will work and go to school, and the impact on the economy. Create a poster that illustrates your new era.

HISTORY A Historic Figure

Research an American who had an impact on the U.S. economy during the Colonial Era or the Industrial Revolution. Write a two-page paper and share your findings with the class.

 A Graphic Illustration

Choose five products that you purchase frequently. Find out how prices for these products have changed since you were born. Determine if the rise in price is the result of inflation or other factors. Calculate the percentage of increase or decrease for each product. Present the data graphically.

COMPUTER TECHNOLOGY Government Databases

The federal government uses many economic indicators to measure how well the economy is doing. Among these indicators are the following: the number of building permits issued, the average workweek for production workers in manufacturing, the number of unfilled orders for durable goods, consumer installment debt, common stock prices, and unemployment claims.

Work in a group of three or four to conduct online research to retrieve government databases of three of these indicators from 1980 to the present. Present the data in chart form and analyze in a brief paragraph what the numbers indicate about the economy.

Linking School to Home

Tracking News Stories. During a two-week period, read the newspaper or watch the national news each day. Be sure to take notes if you're watching television. Write down the news story's crucial points including any key words that you just learned in this chapter. You could also clip and save any newspaper or periodical articles that apply to this assignment. Count how many articles or stories relate to the economy in the United States and in other countries around the world. Select one news story and write a 200-word essay about it.

Linking School to Work

Oral History. Interview a relative or someone in your community who lived through the Great Depression from 1929 to 1939. Find out what he or she remembers about this period in history and how it impacted life. Ask questions about the standard of living at this time. How does it compare to today's economic state? What goods and services weren't available then but are widely used today? Create an oral presentation to share your interview findings with the class. If possible, invite the person you interviewed to attend your presentation.

● E-Homework

Applying Technology

Finding Trends. Using the Internet, find the dollar amount of the current national debt. What was it ten years ago? The year you were born? Fifty years ago? Has it gone up or down?

Web Pages. Imagine you would like to do business on the Internet. You know what kind of business you want to open. You know how to create a Web page. Using the Internet, research several virtual businesses that might be considered your competition. Evaluate their sites for the following:
- Is the price of the product clearly defined?
- What process is used to place orders?
- Is the site easy to use and user friendly?

● Connecting Academics

Math. Find unemployment statistics for the following years: 1933, 1944, 1955, 1966, 1977, 1988, 1999, and the most recent year for which statistics are available. Present the information in a bar graph. Use computer software if possible. Discuss the reasons for the differences shown in the graph.

History. Did economists accurately predict the economic boom in the early '90s? Study economic forecasts one year before March 1991. Did all economists agree on the direction the economy would take? What indicators did economists use to base their predictions? Present a scorecard-type summary of economic forecasters, March 1990 to March 1991.

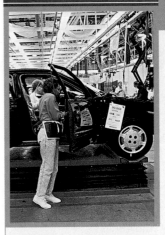

BusinessWeek Analyzing the Feature Story

You read the first part of "Moving up the Ladder: From Cheap Labor to Skilled Workers" at the beginning of this chapter. Below are a few questions for you to answer about the article. You'll find the answers to these questions when you're reading the entire article. First, here are the questions:

31. What economic era is affecting workers in underdeveloped countries? How has it affected them?

32. What helps underdeveloped countries succeed in the global era?

CREATIVE JOURNAL ACTIVITY

Research another country's economic system. Write a report discussing which economic eras have influenced it in the past. Predict its future.

BUSINESS Online

The Full Story

To learn more about globalization, visit the *Introduction to Business* Web site at **www.introbus.glencoe.com**, and click on *BusinessWeek* Feature Story, Chapter 3.

Business Ethics and Social Responsibility

● Learning Objectives

After completing this chapter, you'll be able to:

1. **Explain** business ethics.
2. **Give** reasons why ethical behavior is good for business.
3. **Define** social responsibility.
4. **Describe** the social responsibilities of businesses.

● Why It's Important

Understanding business ethics and social responsibility informs you of your rights as a consumer, employee, and citizen.

● Key Words

ethics
business ethics
sweatshops
Occupational Safety and
   Health Administration
code of ethics
social responsibility
conflict of interest
Food and Drug
   Administration
Equal Pay Act
Environmental Protection
   Agency

BusinessWeek Feature Story

Commerce Reweaves the Social Fabric

Companies Apply Money and Expertise to Social Issues. It's Futuretown, USA, circa 2020. The kids attend for-profit schools; the teachers get their technology training from computer specialists dispatched by IBM. Young teachers and other budding professionals seeking affordable housing flock to the Wal-Mart Riverview apartment complex. Elderly residents get their hearing checked at EarCare clinics funded by Abbott Laboratories, makers of the Ensure nutritional supplement for seniors. Culture vultures gawk at contemporary sculpture at the local American Express Museum of Modern Art.

Source: Excerpted with permission from "Commerce Reweaves the Social Fabric," *BusinessWeek Online*, August 28, 2000.

An Extension Activity

Some corporations offer employees the opportunity to join volunteer programs during the workweek. Find a company that encourages its employees to volunteer as an alternative to the workplace during the year.

BUSINESS Online
The Full Story

To learn more about corporate citizenship, visit the *Introduction to Business* Web site at **www.introbus.glencoe.com**, and click on *BusinessWeek* Feature Story, Chapter 4.

Who Benefits From Business?

Maybe you've heard about auto mechanics that cheat customers by making unnecessary repairs. If they get caught they might be sued, lose their business license, or even go to jail. Even if they don't face legal action, they stand to lose customers and their reputation. Businesses are active and involved in a responsible and fair way in the lives of individual employees and their communities. Their responsibility goes beyond producing goods and services, paying taxes, and providing jobs. Figure 4.1 illustrates conservation methods that help the community and environment.

ENVIRONMENTALLY FRIENDLY

➧Ethics is the set of principles by which you conduct yourself in society.

How often do you help the environment? What do you do?

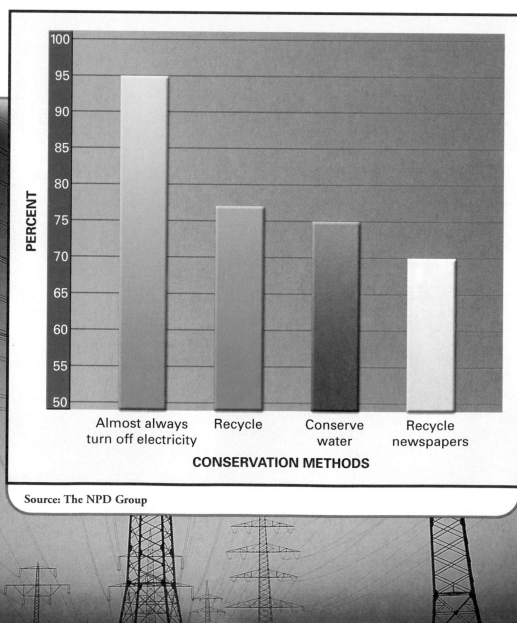

Source: The NPD Group

What Is Ethics?

Mom complains about all of the mail order catalogs and e-mail advertisements she receives. She didn't ask for them. Somehow or another her name was part of a mailing list, which was sold to these other firms. She is concerned about her privacy. Then Dad is concerned that one of his colleagues at work spends too much time writing personal e-mails instead of completing work on time. What do all of these things have in common? All of these deal with business ethics.

Ethics is the set of moral principles by which people conduct themselves personally, socially, or professionally. For example, you don't cheat on a test or steal clothing because of your personal honor and integrity. For the good of society, for example, you recycle to take care of the environment. In business, people create a code of business ethics. **Business ethics** is a set of laws about how a business should conduct itself. In general, for any business to be successful, it must operate legally and humanely.

Legal Responsibility

On March 26, 1911, 146 workers—mostly young Eastern European women—died in a fire at the Triangle Shirtwaist Factory Company in New York City. This disaster is one of the worst industrial tragedies in U.S. history. The business's inadequate exit doors and fire escapes and overcrowded factory led to the deaths of the Triangle workers, who jumped ten stories to their death or burned in the fire. This calamity sparked the nation's attention to examine **sweatshops**. Sweatshops are factories that have unsafe working conditions, treat workers badly, and pay poorly.

The U.S. government sets up independent agencies to protect society. The **Occupational Safety and Health Administration** (OSHA) is a division of the Department of Labor that sets and enforces work-related health and safety rules. Other independent agencies protect consumers, monitor broadcast communications, and address discrimination in the workplace.

Businesses that fail to follow laws are subject to fines, lawsuits, and new regulations. Most businesses police themselves by distributing codes of ethics. A **code of ethics** is a set of strict guidelines for maintaining ethics in the workplace. Professional groups such as doctors, lawyers, journalists, and teachers have their own code of ethics. Individual companies usually have their own codes as well. A code of ethics can cover everything from employee behavior to environmental safety. Businesses that regulate themselves are able to operate more freely.

Real-World Application

part 1 of 4

OFF THE BEATEN PATH

Up for a longboard surf contest at Guéthary? What about mountaineering at Yosemite? Before you surf or climb, Patagonia—the outdoors outfitter—asks you to first remember nature.

Why should a company make a vested interest in nature over its product?

continued on p. 53

Web-Spun Tunes

Millions of people use their computer's hard drive as a database of personal music selections. Using file-sharing software on the Web downloads a copy of a song. The key to this trend is "player" software. The software allows users to transform the bulky music files on their CDs into a compressed file format called MP3—a process known as "ripping." Music sharing operates on the idea of peer-to-peer computing. Every computer becomes both a sender and receiver of information.

Critical Thinking

How will artists make money if people download music?

Ethics as Good Business

Unethical business practices might affect your business in more ways than one. If you violate government regulations you can be fined or go to jail. If you violate a company code of ethics, you might be fired or lose your license. However, not all unethical practices are covered by the law and, even if they are, you may not get caught for violating the law. Even so, unethical business practices might affect your business indirectly.

Suppose you own an auto body paint shop. To increase your profits you charge top price and use the cheapest paint. One of your customers complains but you don't care because she has already paid. What's one customer, right? The fact is most businesses (especially small businesses) rely on repeat customers and word-of-mouth to get new customers. The amount you make in profits from one unhappy customer translates into a lot more in lost business.

Treating employees unethically can also backfire. Suppose you manage a small film distribution company. You hire Jaime fresh out of business school to run the office. You teach him how to use the computer system, how to deal with customers, and how the business works. You also pay him poorly, make him do all your work for you, and treat him like a doormat. The first chance Jaime gets, he quits and ends up being hired by one of your competitors. You now have to retrain a new employee to take his place. Meanwhile, your competition now has a well-trained employee, who is much more efficient.

Important Ethical Questions

Ethics involves an endless series of relationships—between buyer and seller, employer and employee, business and government, and business and society. When considering a questionable course of action, you have to ask yourself these important questions:

- Is it against the law? Does it violate company or professional policies?
- What if everyone did this? How would I feel if someone did this to me?
- Am I sacrificing long-term benefits for short-term gains?

Ethical decision making leads to more business activity and more efficient production of goods and services. Business works best when there is mutual trust between buyers and sellers.

Making Decisions on Ethical Issues

Making ethical decisions is not a quick task. It takes some real hard thinking. A derivation of the problem-solving process works well for ethical decision making. Here are some steps if you find yourself in an ethical dilemma:

1. Identify the ethical dilemma.
2. Discover alternative actions.
3. Decide who might be affected.
4. List the probable effects of the alternatives.
5. Select the best alternative.

Using this process will enable you to make a more informed ethical choice. Making an ethical decision involves more people than just you.

✔ **Fast Review** _____

1. How do companies benefit by enforcing their own codes of ethics?
2. Why does it pay to treat customers ethically?
3. What are some important ethical questions to ask?

Social Responsibility

Social responsibility is the duty to do what is best for the good of society. Business ethics focuses on decisions considered good or bad, correct or incorrect. The social responsibility of business takes into consideration all that business does or does not do to solve problems of society.

The goal of business is to make a profit. Business, however, also involves the interaction of many different people. For a business to prosper it has to offer goods and services that other people want. If you manage a supermarket you rely on your employees to do a good job. When you go to a restaurant you expect to get good service. As a member of society, you're both a consumer and a producer.

Businesses have an ethical obligation to provide safe products, create jobs, protect the environment, and contribute to the overall standard of living in society. An ethical question in business occurs whenever there's a conflict of interest. A **conflict of interest** is when a business is tempted to put profits before social welfare.

The effect of unethical behavior is not always obvious. For example, pocketing a few CDs from the store you work at might not seem like a big deal. After all, you might think, no one will miss them and they're overpriced anyway. One of the reasons CDs cost as much as they do is because people steal them. Consumer and employee theft costs businesses billions of dollars each year. To make up for their losses, businesses have to charge more for their products. As a result, everyone has to pay more.

Real-World Application

part **2** of 4

OFF THE BEATEN PATH

As the designers of a fleece jacket made from a 2-liter soda bottle, Patagonia distributes clothing and equipment that's environmentally responsible. **How does the consumer pay for a company's inventions?**

continued on p. 55

Responsibility to Customers

Customers are a business's first responsibility. Businesses should offer a good, safe product or service at a reasonable price. The **Food and Drug Administration** (FDA), a government agency, protects consumers from dangerous or falsely advertised products. Most companies obey the government's rules. Figure 4.2 asks you to analyze an over-the-counter medicine label.

For example, in 1982 Johnson & Johnson coped with a public health crisis. When people died from poisoned Tylenol capsules the company quickly responded. It alerted the public to the danger and recalled all bottles of its product at a cost of $100 million. The company put Tylenol back on the market in new tamper-proof bottles. Today, Tylenol is one of the best-selling pain medicines.

Fair competition between businesses is healthy for the marketplace, but some companies don't always play reasonably. Some companies use

Figure 4.2 OVER-THE-COUNTER MEDICINE LABEL

➥ The FDA governs advertising and labeling of over-the-counter medicines.

Analyze why FDA officials might feel that regulation of advertising and packaging labels is necessary.

unethical means to eliminate competition. One of the most common means is to conspire with other companies to control the market for a product. Together, the companies can control the supply of a product and determine the prices.

When companies overpower competition, consumers are affected. Consumers have less choice in what they can buy and how much they have to pay. When a company doesn't have to compete, its productivity decreases. This can backfire on a business. When the market changes or new markets open up, a company can find itself unprepared to compete.

For example, in the 1940s, a handful of entertainment studios controlled the film industry. They controlled the industry by owning most of the theaters. Smaller studios could make movies, but they couldn't get them shown anywhere. The government sued the big studios and forced them to sell their theaters. As a result, small studios were able to compete in the marketplace.

Responsibility to Employees

Businesses have provided work experience for those who haven't been successful in the workplace. Many of these people are public assistance recipients. The purpose of the program is to develop their skills and confidence levels necessary to continue success in the working world.

Many employees take one or more days off during the year to work on a project in the local community while still being paid. Key Bank in upstate New York has implemented this type of program. Volunteerism is another way businesses tackle societal problems.

Businesses have a social responsibility to create jobs. They are also expected to provide employees with safe working conditions, equal treatment, and fair pay. Less than one hundred years ago, however, workers had few rights.

Over the years the government has passed laws to protect workers from a range of issues, from child labor abuses to the rights of workers to organize. As the workplace has changed, the government has passed new laws. The **Equal Pay Act** (passed in 1964) requires that men and women be paid the same wages for doing equal work. More than 40 years later, however, the closing of the wage gap between men and women has been at a rate of less than half a penny a year. The Americans with Disabilities Act bans discrimination against persons with physical or mental disability. More than 50 million current or potential workers are likely to be covered by this law.

OFF THE BEATEN PATH
Patagonia believes if you bear witness to an injustice, you must take action. Become an environmental activist by writing letters to the editor of a local newspaper, shopping selectively, boycotting, and reducing personal consumption. **What are social issues you're interested in pursuing? How are businesses involved?**

continued on p. 57

Building on a Sacred Site

This activity gives you the chance to add to your portfolio. Communicate, interview, research, and write your way into a story. Choose one imaginary path, Avid Activist or Determined Developer. Follow your path's steps to complete your own story.

pick a path

Avid Activist

The Setting. A real-estate developer from Insti-House Inc., believes there is a lack of housing for retired people in town.

Rising Action. You discover the site contains historic relics from a Native American village dating back to around 1050 A.D. Additionally, an important nineteenth-century poet built a house on the site. Although the house burned down long ago, the poet's original garden still thrives. You decide to organize a committee to preserve the site's heritage.

Step 1. Present a list of various ways to preserve the site, which will be presented to the committee.

Step 2. After the meeting, you hone and tackle the first item on your list—write a letter to the editor of the local newspaper.

Determined Developer

The Setting. You're the public relations director for Insti-House, Inc. Your boss, the developer, reads the newspaper and sees all the letters to the editor protesting her real-estate development. Citizens of the community are angry. Insti-House wants to develop property on a historic site.

Rising Action. Delaying the development will cost Insti-House thousands of dollars. Its reputation is being damaged by bad publicity.

Step 1. Hoping to sway public opinion, your boss asks you to write a one-page press release outlining the Insti-House position on the development.

Step 2. Find out how you submit press releases to the local media.

Conclusion

Now it's time to reflect on your choice in the last section. Did you face a conflict of interest on any level? Take a few minutes to write in your journal about the business ethics and social responsibility of your situation.

Most companies have realized the value of treating workers fairly and have adopted codes of ethics in the workplace. For example, United Airlines has a strict policy against sexual harassment on the job. It's in a company's best interest to treat its workers fairly otherwise low morale, poor productivity, and a high turnover rate are its troubles.

Responsibility to Society

In the nineteenth and even into the twentieth century, many polluted and destructed the environment in order to profit. The lapse of judgment to keep the land, water, and air clean hurt many because the tradeoff for a higher standard of living only benefited a few. Around the middle of the twentieth century, many people were questioning whether this was a wise tradeoff. Polluting the environment became an ethical issue.

Businesses have responsibilities not only to customers and to employees but also to society as a whole. One of the biggest social issues facing businesses today is environmental responsibility. In 1970, the U. S. government created the **Environmental Protection Agency** (EPA), a federal agency that enforces rules that protect the environment and control pollution.

Some firms are very concerned about limiting the damage that they do to the environment. Companies obey the pollution standards set by the government for air, water, or land. The Body Shop places environmental concerns as an integral part of its mission. Biodegradable materials are contained in its products. An increasing number of businesses are buying recycled paper to use in their businesses.

The *Los Angeles Times*, a daily newspaper with over one million dedicated readers, uses recyclable paper and environmentally friendly soy-based ink. Car manufacturers like Honda and Toyota offer eco-cars, which reduce air pollution. Businesses that hold fast to environmental policies have better public relations.

An increasing number of businesses, especially corporations, consider social responsibility to be more important than ever. Many of them plan for their social responsibilities just like planning for production and sale of their products.

OFF THE BEATEN PATH
Patagonia responsibly takes a stand against genetically modified organisms (GMO). Its position states that companies must be held accountable if any GMO released into the environment causes damage. **What government agency has a responsibility to society?**

✓ **Fast Review**

1. Define social responsibility.
2. What is a conflict of interest?
3. What do companies adopt in the workplace to treat their workers fairly?

Chapter 4 Review

Summary

1. Ethics is the set of moral principles by which people conduct themselves personally, socially, or professionally. Businesses have a legal responsibility to do what is right for society's welfare.

2. Unethical business practices aren't only illegal but they are also bad for business. Good ethics affects a business's profits, customer base, and employee loyalty.

3. Social responsibility is the duty to do what is best for the good of society. Businesses have a responsibility to consumers, workers, and society as a whole. The FDA, Equal Pay Act, and the EPA are examples of government actions that were passed to improve societal concerns.

4. A conflict of interest is when a business puts profits before social welfare.

Using Business Key Words

Companies are expected to run their businesses responsibly. Find out if you understand what it means for companies to be both socially and ethically responsible. Fill each blank with the term that best completes the sentence.

- **ethics**
- **social responsibility**
- **business ethics**
- **Equal Pay Act**
- **conflict of interest**
- **Food and Drug Administration (FDA)**
- **sweatshops**
- **code of ethics**
- **Occupational Safety and Health Administration (OSHA)**
- **Environmental Protection Agency (EPA)**

1. The principles you live by, like honor and integrity, are called your _____.
2. Most businesses police themselves by distributing a _____.
3. _____ are factories that have unsafe working conditions, treat workers badly, and pay poorly.
4. _____ is a set of laws about how a business should behave.
5. The obligation a business has to do what is best for society is called _____.
6. An ethical question in business will occur when there is a _____ between social well-being and profits.
7. A division of the Department of Labor that sets and enforces work-related health and safety rules is called the _____.
8. The _____ (passed in 1964) requires that men and women be paid the same wages for doing equal work.
9. The _____ is a government agency that protects consumers from dangerous or falsely advertised products.
10. The federal agency that enforces rules that protect the environment and control pollution is called the _____.

Review What You Learned

11. Describe ethics.
12. Why was the Occupational Safety and Health Administration created?
13. How do most businesses police themselves?
14. Describe some of the ways unethical business practices can affect a business.
15. What are three questions you could ask yourself when considering a questionable course of action?
16. When does a conflict of interest occur?
17. What is the mission of the Food and Drug Administration?
18. What responsibilities do businesses have to their employees?
19. Name the biggest social issue facing businesses today.

Understanding Business Concepts

20. What is the difference between social responsibility and business ethics?
21. Why is it important for a business to treat its employees in an ethical manner?
22. Give an example of a conflict of interest that a business might face.
23. Why is competition important to the consumer?
24. What has the government done to protect workers?
25. How do socially responsible firms improve the quality of life for everyone in society?
26. Do you think the United States should trade with China or other countries with a poor human rights record? Why or why not?

Critical Thinking

27. Do you think most businesses act responsibly towards consumers? Can you think of a company that hasn't? Describe the company's behavior and the consequences of its actions.
28. Do you think a country has the right to impose its ethical standards on another country? Why or why not?
29. What do you think is a manager's role in setting ethical standards?
30. How do you think a business's social responsibility is measured?

Viewing and Representing

Examining the Image. What's going on in this picture? What interests or motivations are behind what's happening in this picture—both for the students and for the company? Compare what's represented in this photograph with the experience of your school and with company volunteer programs; what ways are they similar or different? Write a paragraph answering the questions.

Building Academic Skills

 Raising Money

The president of Walker Computer Company wants her company to raise $5,500 for Habitat for Humanity. She divided the employees into teams and asked each team to raise money towards the goal. There are nine teams.

- How much money should each team raise to meet the goal?
- If each group raises $300, what percentage of the goal did each collect?

 Presenting a Company

Research a business (past or present) that has demonstrated social responsibility. Describe the activities that took place and present your findings to the class.

 Desktop Publishing

Promote the idea of social responsibility. Work in groups to create a brochure outlining the service projects and activities that are available in your community. Projects could include feeding the homeless, building projects, raising money for cancer research, and so on. Use word processing or desktop publishing software to create the brochure. If possible, make copies of the brochure and distribute them in school.

HISTORY **Selecting a Law**

Select a law that the U.S. government passed to protect workers. Research the events leading up to the law being passed. Find out what impact the law has had on workers. Write a two-page paper with your findings.

Linking School to Home

Dealing With a Dilemma. At school you may have been involved in a situation that called your ethics into question. You're not alone—parents deal with dilemmas at work too. Ask your parents or other family members if they have ever been faced with an ethical issue at work. If so, find out what happened and how it was resolved. Discuss with them how they answered the important ethical questions you learned earlier in this chapter. Ask them to walk you through their steps of making an ethical decision.

Linking School to Work

Creating a Code. As a class, create a formal code of ethics for the classroom. Be sure to include the following:
- purpose of the code
- rules for classroom behavior
- rules for making ethical decisions
- consequences for breaking the code

Then, in teams of three or four, create two different ethical situations that could occur in the classroom. Role-play the situation and the resolution.

E-Homework

Applying Technology

Online Research. Using the Internet, research the code of ethics for a profession (doctor, lawyer, teacher) or a business. Read the code and choose two or three policies to share with the class.

Computer Usage. Imagine you have been hired by a small business to write a code of ethics to cover computer/technology usage. Write four or five rules that the employees of the company must follow.

Connecting Academics

Math. Rhonda, administrator for a non-profit group in Texas, has gathered data on company volunteer programs. She has tracked the number of volunteers working with schools in the area:

Year	Company Volunteers
1996	1500
1997	1530
1998	1570
1999	1600
2000	1660
2001	1740

Present the information in a line graph. Use the graph to make a prediction about how many volunteers there will be in 2010.

Language Arts. Making ethical decisions is part of being a strong leader both in everyday life and in the business world. Think of two examples when you had to make an ethical decision. Walk back through the five steps to making an ethical decision that you learned earlier. Do this for each example you come up with. For both examples, write two paragraphs detailing the situation, the possible choices, the resulting decision, and the effects of the decision.

BusinessWeek Analyzing the Feature Story

You read the first part of "Commerce Reweaves the Social Fabric" at the beginning of this chapter. Below are a few questions for you to answer about corporate citizenship. You'll find the answers to these questions when you're reading the entire article. First, here are the questions:

31. What is the main motivation for the good corporate citizenship of companies such as Prudential Insurance Co. and Merck & Co.?

32. What are some potential disadvantages for the companies that practice good corporate citizenship?

CREATIVE JOURNAL ACTIVITY

Create your own Futuretown, USA. Using poster board and magic markers, design Main Street and match corporate sponsors with the following public projects: a library, housing for seniors, a city park, and an outdoor concert arena. Explain how each company would benefit from being associated with a specific public work.

The Full Story

To learn more about corporate citizenship, visit the *Introduction to Business* Web site at **www.introbus.glencoe.com**, and click on *BusinessWeek* Feature Story, Chapter 4.

BusinessWeek Seminar

Unit 1
Global Business

What Is Today's Chinese Business Trend?

In Chapter 3, you read about the Industrial Revolution. Many workers during this historical period worked in the factories and on the railroads. China, with its 1.2 billion people and abundance of natural resources, is facing its own economic revolution. This seminar asks you to investigate China's contemporary business trend.

Factoids

Population. In 1200, Hangchow, China, was the fourth city in the world that had over a million people. (Nearly 700 years later, New York City's population reached a million people.)

Climate. The country has an extreme range of climates from its tropical south to its subarctic north.

Natural Hazards. Typhoons strike along the southern and eastern coasts about five times a year.

Geography. China is the world's fourth-largest country (after Russia, Canada, and the United States).

Downtown. China has half of the world's tallest buildings.

Greetings. A Chinese group applauds anyone introduced to the group. Applaud back.

Investigate the Images

Look at the photographic collage on the left page. What do you see? What do you think? What do you feel? The power of reading visuals is in analyzing and dissecting your observations. On a separate piece of paper, reconstruct the worksheet below in order to complete your investigation. The questions may help shape and focus your analysis.

Your Observations

1. How many photographs do you see?

2. Examine each photograph. How is each assembled in relation to the others?

3. What is the subject of each photograph?

4. Does color signify a message?

5. What issues do you take from these images?

Information

6. Summarize what you know about the photographs from your observations.

Exploring Culture

7. What do you know about China's culture—business, education, politics, and so on?

8. Where do you learn this information (for example, newspapers, TV, magazines, textbooks, films, etc.)?

Taking Aim at Global Business

● Preparation

Find out why Chinese workers are migrating from farming villages to industrial cities, and how their moves affect business trends in China.

Objective

In this *BusinessWeek* Seminar, you will:
- **Research** the media to find articles on Chinese workers' migration patterns.
- **Investigate** the topic by using a journalist's arsenal of key questions—who, what, where, when, why, and how.
- **Interview** a classmate who poses as a migrant worker.

Materials Needed

✓ Recent copies of *BusinessWeek*, the *Wall Street Journal*, or Internet access
✓ Paper
✓ Pencil
✓ Small tape recorder (if it's available)
✓ Poster board
✓ Markers

● Procedures

1. Choose a research partner.

2. Find and read a recent article written about the migration of Chinese workers. If possible, use the Internet to access the Web site of a business publication. For example, access the *BusinessWeek* Web site at **www.businessweek.com**. Click on the tab labeled "Global Business" or use the internal search engine to locate the topic.

3. Consider the following issues:
   - Why are people migrating to the cities?
   - What problems do they encounter?
   - Are the benefits worth the risks?
   - How does this affect China's economy?

4. Create a role-play in which one partner plays a newspaper reporter interviewing a migrant worker, and the other plays the worker. In your role-play, you should describe why the worker left his or her village and what his or her feelings are about living and working in a big city. Make sure to discuss living conditions in the village versus working conditions in the city. The role-play should last two to three minutes. Perform the role-play for the class.

Chart It

With your partner make two lists: "Advantages of Migrating to the City" and "Disadvantages of Migrating to the City," and list what you think are the three most important of each. As a class, reproduce the table that is below and create a comprehensive list on the board.

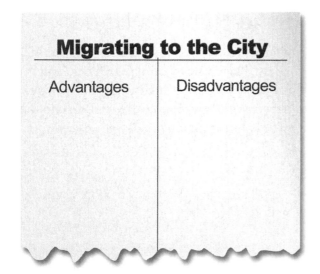

Migrating to the City

Advantages	Disadvantages

Analyze and Conclude

After studying the comprehensive list on the board, answer the questions below:

1. **Making Inference.** What is the most important reason a worker has for migrating to a city in China?
2. **Recognizing Cause and Effect.** What are the dangers of migrating?
3. **Interpreting the Facts.** How will the migration of workers influence the economy of China and, therefore, business in China?

Becoming an Informed Citizen

Congratulations, you finished the seminar. Now it's time to reflect on the decisions you made.

Critical Thinking. Why did you choose to report certain aspects of your research and not other parts of the information? Did an article's images play any part in your decision making? Or did you pick an article based on its title?

Analyzing Your Future. How will China's migration patterns affect you as a citizen of the world?

Further Exploration

To find out more about workers' migration patterns in other countries, visit the Glencoe *Introduction to Business* Web site **www.introbus.glencoe.com**.

Unit 2

Owning and Operating a Business

Go Under the Hybrid's Hood

Disappointed that it's the twenty-first century and cars still can't fly? Well, don't be. There's a new car on the block, and it's called the hybrid model. This machine is a high-tech composite of old and new technology. Honda leads eco-cars on the roadways. Learn more about this car by reading the five important Ps.

● **Pounds**
It takes about 1,000 pounds of batteries to store as much energy as one gallon of gasoline.

● **Power**
The gasoline-electric hybrid car is a cross between a gasoline-powered car and a battery-operated car.

● **Pollutants**
Hybrid cars have been traveling on Japan's roads since the late nineties.

● **Parity**
The hybrid car was created to minimize tailpipe emissions and improve mileage.

● **Passage**
An electric car can go between 50 and 100 miles between charges. A gas-powered car can go 300 miles before refueling. A hybrid car can go 720 miles before refueling!

Chapter 5

Entrepreneurship and Small Business

Learning Objectives

After completing this chapter, you'll be able to:

1. **Describe** an entrepreneurship and a small business.
2. **List** the advantages and disadvantages of an entrepreneurship.
3. **Recognize** the advantages and disadvantages of a small business.
4. **Explain** why small businesses may fail.

Why It's Important

Entrepreneurships and small businesses bring vital energy and innovation to the economy. The risks involved energize entrepreneurs and small business owners to become successful.

Key Words

entrepreneurship
virtual business
    or dot-com company
entrepreneur
risk taker
profit
small business

BusinessWeek Feature Story

Paint by Numbers

Gamblin Artists Colors Paints in Popular Hues. Martha and Robert Gamblin's work hangs in some of the world's top art museums. But don't bother looking for their names on gallery walls.

The Gamblins toil behind the scenes, manufacturing some of the world's finest oil paints. Each year, Gamblin Artists Colors in Portland, Oreg., ships more than 500,000 tubes and cans of paint in some 150 colors to artists and supply stores worldwide. Leading painters such as David Hockney and Chuck Close swear by them. "They make colors other companies just don't," says Wolf Kahn, a West Brattleboro (Vt.) landscape painter whose work is on display in museums nationwide.

Source: Excerpted with permission from "Paint by Numbers," *Frontier*, **November 6, 2000.**

An Extension Activity

Color is a science. Researchers have studied everything from how color affects brain activity to energy consumption. Study your classroom. Find out if the colors are "brain compatible."

The Full Story

To learn more about Gamblin Artists Colors, visit the *Introduction to Business* Web site at www.introbus.glencoe.com, and click on *BusinessWeek* Feature Story, Chapter 5.

The Visionaries Behind New Businesses

Imagine you inherit $2,000 and want to start a graphic design business. With the money, you purchase QuarkXpress® and Adobe Illustrator®. Next you design a business card and work hard to bring in business. Three years later a local business magazine awards you Young Entrepreneur of the Year. The award is for creating fantastic designs for the breast cancer awareness campaign. The public responded to its attractive and effective message. Your dream, hard work, and financial investment are paying off.

The Ins and Outs of an Entrepreneurship

An **entrepreneurship** is a business started by someone who notices a need for a product or service. Entrepreneurship soared in the late 1990s as entrepreneurs took their business ideas online. The Internet became the arena to sell products and services.

A **virtual business** or a **dot-com company** is a business that operates on the Internet. A dot-com company may exist only online or it may be in addition to a company's actual storefront.

Figure 5.1

ARE YOU ORIGINAL?

 ➡ Take this quiz and see if you would be a good entrepreneur.

Below are traits of an entrepreneur. Rate yourself by choosing a number that best describes you. At the end you'll add up your points to see how you fared (1 is lowest, 5 is highest).

Trait					
Need for achievement	1	2	3	4	5
Energy level	1	2	3	4	5
Willingness to take risks	1	2	3	4	5
Determination	1	2	3	4	5
Self-confidence	1	2	3	4	5
Willingness to work hard	1	2	3	4	5
Desire to "control your own destiny"	1	2	3	4	5
Enthusiasm for projects you undertake	1	2	3	4	5

Rate your score:
35–40 points = true entrepreneur
30–35 = willing to take risks and try something new
25 and under = you take fewer risks

In July 1995 Amazon.com opened its virtual doors to the world. The company wanted to change book buying over the Internet. Nearly 29 million customers later, the online e-tailer forges ahead in high-tech shopping.

It may take Amazon.com ten years before it turns a profit but the company's lead man, Jeff Bezos, accepts the challenge. What would you expect from an entrepreneur? An **entrepreneur** is a person who recognizes a business opportunity and organizes, manages, and assumes the risks of a business enterprise, with the intent of increasing the market value of the business. Every year thousands of entrepreneurs start businesses. Many entrepreneurs establish very successful companies that remain small. Many of these businesses will fail within a few years of opening. Others will go on to become giant companies. Figure 5.1 is a quiz you can take to see if you would be a good entrepreneur. You'll rate yourself based upon traits that best describe you.

Advantages of an Entrepreneurship

Entrepreneurs are take-charge, self-directed people. They want to work for themselves. Often an entrepreneur is a **risk taker**, or someone who likes to take risks.

Satisfaction From Taking a Risk and Becoming a Success. Miranda wasn't the kind of person who could sit at a desk all day. She decided this last summer when she was an administrative assistant at a news organization. Every day couriers came into her office with packages for pick up and delivery. They were constantly on the move and she liked that. She decided to leave her position and take the risk of making enough money with her own courier service. Miranda found satisfaction in taking a risk and becoming a success.

Showing Expertise and Skills. Raphael worked as an assistant restaurant manager for three years. He decided it was time to leave that restaurant and open his own establishment. One year later he opened a charming bistro in the hip, arty part of the city. The restaurant's quick success labeled him the hottest entrepreneur in the city. Starting his own business gave Raphael a way to demonstrate his expertise, skills, and self-determination. His experiences as an assistant manager gave him the skills to start his own business.

Working From Home. Briana is among the 20 percent of small business owners running a home-based business. She loves needlework. Instead of working for a large company, she started Briana's Gifts. She sells her homemade gifts at trade shows and conferences. Briana, like many entrepreneurs,

bozart
toys by artists

THE BIZ BEHIND BOZART
In the early '90s, the art market slowed down. Larry Mangel, an art dealer, decided to change his career focus and open his own business, Bozart Toys.
What makes Larry Mangel an entrepreneur?

continued on p. 73

Technology Toolkit

It's a Digital World

Entrepreneur Lane Wyrich started a multimedia production company, Xap Interactive. His company uses digital video and computer technology to create videos and movies. Digital recording marries image and sound into single pieces of data. Each piece of data is a complete image or a specific sound. Wyrich uses a computer to edit the digital data (or movie footage) to create the finished product.

Critical Thinking

Why do you think Wyrich uses digital video and computer technology?

prefers to set her own flexible schedule instead of keeping a big company's mandatory workweek.

Gaining Profit. Joseph started his own network consulting company. It was important to him that he received all the profits from his hard work. **Profit** is the money left over after a business has paid all costs of producing its goods or services. In fact, profit is one reason that many entrepreneurs start a business.

Disadvantages of an Entrepreneurship

Entrepreneurs know they are taking a risk when starting a business, and are aware that risk may result in failure. Success means working hard. A successful venture doesn't come easy to an entrepreneur.

Total Responsibility for the Business. Do you remember Miranda, the new owner of a courier service who was introduced a few paragraphs ago? She knows her business's success depends on her managerial skills. She is responsible for her employees, customer service, vendor relations, the finances, and the facility. She has a tough job. A business owner is responsible for everything.

Long Hours. Raphael works longer hours now that he owns his own restaurant. He has been working 80 to 100 hours a week to get his restaurant started. Time and effort are important pieces to making a company successful.

Financial Risks. Money is a worry for entrepreneurs. Joseph's consulting business was profitable but it struggled for the first year. Before his business became profitable he financed all costs. He was in charge of paying his employees, producing his service, and meeting his customers' needs. The main reason why entrepreneurships fail is because they run out of money.

✔ Fast Review

1. What are some characteristics of entrepreneurs?
2. What are three advantages of an entrepreneurship?
3. What are some disadvantages of an entrepreneurship?
4. What is the main reason that entrepreneurships fail?

Small Business: What You Need to Know

The Small Business Administration (SBA) defines a **small business** as an independently owned business that usually has the owner as its manager. A small business serves a limited geographic area, employs fewer than 500 people, and is not dominant in its industry. Figure 5.2 shows the different types of businesses that provide employment.

Most businesses in the United States are small businesses. There are about 25 million small businesses, and they are a vital part of our economy. Small businesses employ more than 50 percent of the total workforce in the United States. They generate more than half the nation's income. They are the principal source of new jobs. Small businesses account for about 38 percent of jobs in high technology.

Advantages of Small Business

Small businesses offer many opportunities and are easier to form than large businesses. As a small business owner you would enjoy meeting the challenges of running a business.

Being the Boss. Michelle owns Paint Your Own Pots, a small business. She said, "I want to provide a high-quality service, so I enjoy managing the store myself." Small business owners like being their own boss. An important advantage of being a small business owner is the ability to be in charge. Small business owners make their own decisions. They usually are the managers as well as the owners. Many small businesses, in fact, have no employees.

Opportunity to Offer Services Large Companies Cannot Offer.
Paco saw opportunities that large companies didn't offer. His business was small so he could respond quickly to his customers' needs. For example, Paco knows his customers so well that he can suggest products to meet their individual needs. A large company may not take the time to know its customers on a personal level.

Ease of Formation. Zach noticed how easy it was to form his own hair-cutting salon. He had worked for large businesses before and noticed how hard they were to form. Small businesses require licenses for operation. Their buildings must meet local zoning requirements. Zach found that taking the steps to start his small business took a short time.

THE BIZ BEHIND BOZART
Bozart Toys started with a business plan in '95. One year later Mangel acquired the money and produced the first toy, Marco the Magnificent.
Why do you think Mangel's company became a success?

continued on p. 75

Disadvantages of Small Business

When you're a small business owner, you're responsible for decisions. At times, life as a small business owner can create a feeling of loneliness if you're used to a workplace where people foster friendships and collaboration. Working long hours, making hard financial choices, and accepting responsibility don't always beget success.

Successful business practices are key to keeping your small business alive. About four out of five small businesses fail in their first five years. Business closings may result from many factors. Small business owners may mistake the freedom of being in business for oneself for the liberty of working or not. Other times a small business may underprice or overprice goods or services. Going into business with little or no experience and without first learning something about it may result in the business closing.

Normally, the most successful businesses are the ones that require advanced training, like dentists' offices and physicians' offices. Yet one of the businesses with the highest odds of monetary growth is manufacturing. Below are two specific causes of why a small business might not work.

Effect of Change. Styles and trends change. Consumers' tastes change. The economic system goes through ups and downs. All of these factors influence the small business. A small business owner must be aware of change and quickly adapt. If flexibility and change are not part

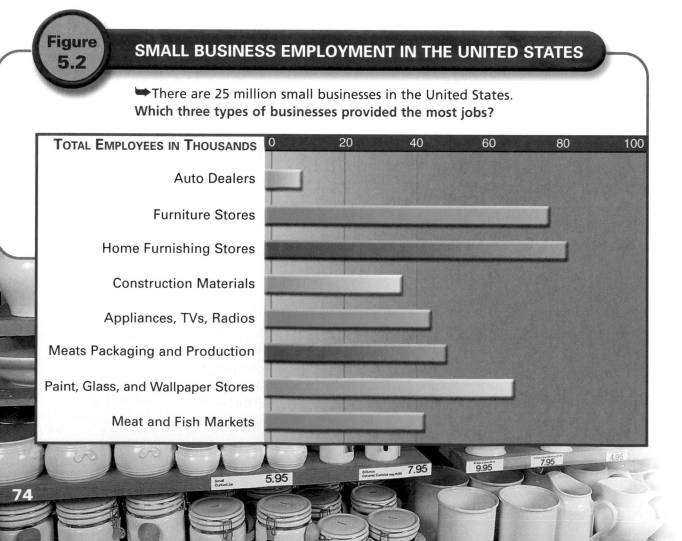

Figure 5.2

SMALL BUSINESS EMPLOYMENT IN THE UNITED STATES

➡There are 25 million small businesses in the United States. Which three types of businesses provided the most jobs?

TOTAL EMPLOYEES IN THOUSANDS

	0	20	40	60	80	100

- Auto Dealers
- Furniture Stores
- Home Furnishing Stores
- Construction Materials
- Appliances, TVs, Radios
- Meats Packaging and Production
- Paint, Glass, and Wallpaper Stores
- Meat and Fish Markets

of the business then it's likely to fail. Not being market savvy can push a small business down as its smart competitors take advantage of opportunities.

Managerial Skills Needed. A small business owner must have multiple skills. For example, Michele must handle financing, employee relations, production, customer relations, and any other area needing a decision.

Inadequate Financial Planning. To keep the business alive, owners must be financially smart. Starting with little money, spending carelessly, borrowing money without planning how to use it, and forgetting about taxes, insurance, and other business costs may result in closure. Money management helps keep a small business successfully afloat.

✓ **Fast Review** _____

1. How does the Small Business Administration define a small business?
2. Give an example of a service that a small business may offer that a large company cannot offer.
3. Which is more difficult to form: a large business or a small business?
4. Give examples of special skills that a small business owner needs.
5. List two financial reasons that small businesses fail.

Preparing for Your Own Business

Once you've decided that you want to start a business, the next step is to analyze what you want to do and find a way to do it. When you begin to plan, you start turning your daydream into reality. Careful planning from the beginning is one way to ensure the success of starting a business.

Whether you're starting up a butterfly-breeding business or a picture-hanging business, it is a good idea to develop a business plan. A _business plan_ is a written description of a new business venture that describes all aspects of the business. It helps you focus on exactly what you want to do, how you'll do it, and what you expect to accomplish. The business plan is essential for potential investors and financing agencies you'll go to for start-up funds.

Checklist for Starting a Venture

A checklist is a good way to organize your thinking when you begin planning your own business. Entrepreneurs and small business owners

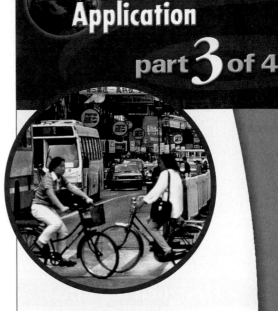

Real-World Application

part **3** of **4**

THE BIZ BEHIND BOZART
Mangel manages all aspects of Bozart. He travels to China a few times a year to ensure quality control in the manufacturing of the toys. **Identify some reasons why a small business might be hard to manage.**

continued on p. 77

On Being Your Own Boss

This activity gives you the chance to add to your portfolio. Communicate, interview, research, and write your way into a story. Choose one imaginary path, Designed for Life or Cold Comfort. Follow your path's steps to complete your own story.

pick a path

Designed for Life

The Setting. You're interested in designing attractive spaces where people live and work. The places will be inexpensive and environmentally friendly.

Rising Action. You'll design a living space or work space, organize the whole project, and supervise the actual builders.

Step 1. Draw up a business plan to present to your bank for financial backing.

Step 2. Investigate the local and state regulations about the licensing requirements for starting a contracting business.

Cold Comfort

The Setting. One winter day you were scraping the ice off your car when you came up with a terrific idea for a foolproof ice scraper. Your scraper would touch along the entire edge of the glass regardless of the curvature of the windshield.

Rising Action. Now you want to launch a company to develop, test, produce, and market your ice scraper.

Step 1. Write a business plan for the company. Include a name for your ice scraper.

Step 2. Interview a local attorney, law school professor, or experienced inventor about whether or not you should patent your invention.

Conclusion

Now it's time to write your own story and reflect on your path. Explain your business venture to a group of students. Write a few expository paragraphs that will serve as the basis of your talk. Remember, an effective expository paragraph has appropriate organization and specific details that make sense to your audience.

should keep these questions and their answers in mind as they develop and write their business plan.

Here are some questions to consider: What will I produce? Who are my main competitors? Why is my product needed? How much will my product cost to produce? How many people will I need to run the business? What physical facilities will I need? What licenses, permits, or other legal documents do I need? How much money will I need to get started?

Parts of a Business Plan

The Center for Entrepreneurial Management in New York reports that most business plans take more than five months to prepare. Yet it takes most readers, such as bank officers, fewer than five minutes to decide whether or not to read the entire document. Therefore, a business plan must be well-organized, easy to read, and follow a logical format. The essential parts of a business plan are as follows:

- The *summary* is a one- to three-page overview of the plan. Place it at the beginning of the finished proposal but write it after you complete the rest of the sections. Make sure it intrigues readers so they want to read more.
- The *company description* explains the type of company you plan to start. Will it be a manufacturing plant? A retail business? Will it provide a service?
- Expand on the company description in the *products and services* section. Describe the kinds of products you will sell or the services you will provide.
- The *marketing plan* describes your likely customers and details your competition. Indicate the marketing strategies that you plan to put into place. Include types and location of advertising.
- A good business plan also needs to include a *legal plan* that points out how you will organize your company. Will it be a sole proprietorship, a partnership, or a corporation? (See Chapter 6 for types of business organizations.)
- The *management plan and operating plan* detail the company's key personnel as well as their expertise and experience. Specify the company's daily operations, facilities, overall personnel, materials, and processing requirements.
- Of course, no business plan is complete without a *financial plan*. You should discuss the company's financial needs and financing as well as your projections for revenues, costs, and profits.

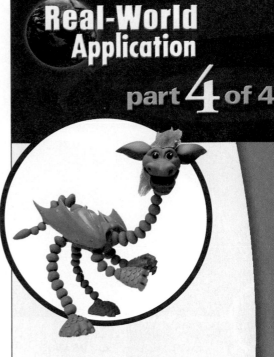

Real-World Application
part 4 of 4

THE BIZ BEHIND BOZART
The Bozart Toys Web site shows consumers its products, but other online sites and toy stores sell the toys. **What are some benefits of selling toys online?**

✓ **Fast Review** _____

1. What is a business plan?
2. Name the essential elements of a business plan.

Picture This...

What Happens When You Type a URL?

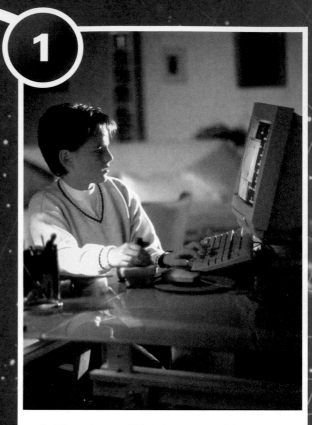

1. Type into a Web browser this Universal Resource Locator (URL): http://www.businessweek.com.

2. The Web browser communicates with a domain name server to find the **www.business week.com** Internet Point (IP) address.

3. The domain name server sends the *BusinessWeek* IP address to your Web browser.

4. Your Web browser then uses the IP address to connect to the *BusinessWeek* server and asks for the *BusinessWeek* home page.

4

5. The *BusinessWeek* server sends its home page file to your Web browser. That home page file is in HTML text.

5

```
-//W3C//DTD HTML ‹
EN" "http://www.w3.org
/TR/REC-html40/loose.dtd">
<html>
<head>
<TITLE>
Business Week Online
</TITLE>
<META name="description" la
content="Business Week mag:
```

6

File Edit View Favorites Tools Help

Back Forward Stop Refresh Home Search

Address http://www.businessweek.com/

BusinessWeek online

| BW MAGAZINE | DAILY BRIEFING | INVESTING | GLOBAL BUSINESS | TECHNOLOGY |

▶ **BW MAGAZINE**
Where layoffs are a last resort •New

▶ **DAILY BRIEFING**
AT&T and BellSouth talk merger

▶ **INVESTING**
Q&A: S&P's Ken Shea •New

▶ **GLOBAL BUSINESS**
The fallout in Europe •New

▶ **TECHNOLOGY**
OS X gets its finishing touches

BW MAGAZINE

A New World

Business and markets know how to handle conventional risk. But not these days. One word describes the near future: Uncertainty
Go to Special Report | Go to Magazine

DAILY BRIEFING

Less Global Help

A flood of funds from abroad helped finance America's amazing growth. Now the flow will likely ebb — and that may be good

6. Your Web browser changes (or formats) the HTML file to display the *BusinessWeek* home page on your screen.

Now *You* Take a Shot...

Research a Virtual Business. Remember you imagined inheriting $2,000 at the beginning of this chapter? You decide to open a savings account to hold your money. Visit a real-time online bank on the Internet. List the benefits of an online bank over a bricks-and-mortar bank.

Summary

1. An entrepreneur recognizes a business opportunity and organizes, manages, and assumes the risks of a business venture. Small businesses are vital to our economy. They employ more than half of all workers in the United States, and they're the main source of new jobs.

2. Entrepreneurs show expertise, may work from home, and gain the profit from their own work. On the other hand, entrepreneurs have to take total responsibility for the business, work long hours, and endure financial risks when they decide to start the business.

3. The advantages of running a small business include being your own boss, providing great personal service, and easy formation. A small business owner faces potential problems if he or she doesn't adapt to change and possibly lacks the managerial skills needed to successfully run the business.

4. Small businesses often fail because the owners start with little money, freely extend credit, have little business experience, don't keep adequate records, don't plan for the ups and downs of business, and haven't mastered time management.

● Using Business Key Words

Use these business terms correctly in the following sentences.

- **entrepreneurship**
- **entrepreneur**
- **virtual business or dot-com company**
- **risk taker**
- **small business**
- **profit**

1. A(n) _____ is a person who recognizes an opportunity and who organizes, manages, and assumes the risks of a business enterprise, with the intent of increasing the value of the business.

2. A person who likes to take chances is a(n) _____.

3. A(n) _____ is a business that operates on the Internet.

4. The money that is left over after a business has paid all the costs of producing its goods and services is called _____.

5. An independently owned business serving a limited geographic area is called a(n) _____.

6. A business started by someone who accepted the risk of starting and running a business is a(n) _____.

Review What You Learned

7. What do all people who start a new business do?
8. What is an entrepreneurship?
9. What is a virtual business sometimes called?
10. How does the Small Business Association (SBA) define a small business?
11. What is profit?
12. Name the advantages and disadvantages of entrepreneurships.
13. Why may an entrepreneurship fail?
14. How do small businesses help the U.S. economy?
15. Why is it important for a small business owner to be aware of consumer trends?

Understanding Business Concepts

16. Why do you think it is important that entrepreneurs be take-charge, self-directed people?
17. Why are so many people starting home-based businesses?
18. Why might it be more satisfying to run your own company than work for someone else?
19. Why does the owner of a business usually put in more hours at work than an employee?
20. Why is the need for money considered to be the most serious problem an entrepreneur faces?
21. Why do you think small businesses are able to offer services that larger companies cannot?
22. Why is it so important for small business owners to be able to keep adequate financial records?

Critical Thinking

23. Why do you think some virtual businesses or dot-com companies fail?
24. What skills and attributes do you think a successful entrepreneur needs? Why?
25. Explain the difference between being self-disciplined and self-motivated.
26. A checklist is a good way to organize an entrepreneur's thinking when beginning to plan a business. What questions might be on the entrepreneur's checklist?

Viewing and Representing

Examining the Image. With a partner, examine this picture. What kinds of questions does this image seem to answer? Are the questions personal, creative, analytical, or informational? How effective is the image itself for drawing viewers or readers into the issue? Write a brief story based upon your perceptions of this image. Share your story with the class.

Building Academic Skills

 Oral History

Brainstorm and write questions in order to conduct an interview with someone who is an entrepreneur or a small business owner. Prepare questions that will get the interviewee to tell how his or her life changed as the result of being an entrepreneur or small business owner. Present the interview to the class. Discuss how the interviewees' stories compare with the information in the text.

 Journalism

Pick a partner to produce a newsletter that describes the successes and failures of the small businesses in your community. Some topics might include funding, laws, economic trends, consumer wants and needs, time management, risk management, help wanted ads, technology, and so on.

COMPUTER TECHNOLOGY **Charting Growth**

The hottest market for small businesses isn't across a great ocean. It's right here in the United States. Currently, the combined buying power of U.S. minority groups totals $1.3 trillion, or some 20 percent of the country's purchasing power. The Commerce Department estimates that the spending power of non-whites will reach $4.3 trillion, or 32 percent by 2045. In a database program, create a chart or graph to show this likely purchasing power.

 Calculating Closings

In the city of Orange, 187 new businesses opened in 2000. By 2001, 15 percent of businesses were no longer in operation. How many were open in 2001? One year later, another 12 percent were considered discontinued. How many businesses were still open in 2001?

Linking School to Home

Investigate Product Loyalties. Create an inventory of the products and services you and your family use that are produced by small businesses or entrepreneurs. Categorize them by family member. Then interview each family member, and find out why he or she purchases the products and services from the small business or entrepreneur. Compile your results and share them with the class.

Linking School to Work

Portfolio Project. Research the requirements for setting up a small business in your community. Investigate areas such as government regulations, financing, and the costs of leasing space and buying equipment. The local chamber of commerce might direct you in your research. Write a report with your findings.

E-Homework

Applying Technology

Electronic Survey. Use word processing software to create a survey that can be sent to local small business owners and entrepreneurs in your community. Through the survey, find out what technology skills they currently possess and what type of skills they think they'll need in the future. If possible, send out the surveys using e-mail. As a class, compile the results using a spreadsheet or database software.

High-Tech Callings. Research the technology classes that are available in high schools, technical centers, and colleges in your community. As a class, brainstorm a list of businesses that could be started by someone who has technology skills.

Connecting Academics

Math. Joaquin wants to start his own business for renting bikes at the park. He begins researching the age of his hometown's residents. He learns the following:

0–5 years of age	960 residents
6–11	1,840
12–18	4,500
19–35	8,225
36–60	2,960
Over 60	2,960

Construct a bar graph to present this information. Use computer software if possible.

Language Arts. You want to strengthen your entrepreneurial qualities. Complete the following steps to learn more about other entrepreneurs and yourself:

- **Reading.** Go online or to the library to read articles and books about entrepreneurs and entrepreneurial activities.
- **Writing.** Write about individuals you know who are entrepreneurs. Did this person overcome obstacles to achieve success?

- **Watching.** Find films about athletes, businesspeople, or others who achieved success.
- **Practice.** Find case studies that involve goals, creativity, and risk taking.

BusinessWeek Analyzing the Feature Story

You read the first part of "Paint by Numbers" at the beginning of this chapter. Below are a few questions for you to answer about the Gamblins. You'll find the answers to these questions when you're reading the entire article. First, here are the questions:

27. What motivated the Gamblins to take the risk of starting a new business?
28. How does Gamblin Artists Colors use technology in its small business?
29. What's the purpose of the special line of paints the company recently introduced?

CREATIVE JOURNAL ACTIVITY

What are your hobbies or interests? List business ideas related to your hobbies. How can you reap the benefits of your talents?

BUSINESS *Online*

The Full Story

To learn more about Gamblin Artists Colors, visit the *Introduction to Business* Web site at **www.introbus.glencoe.com**, and click on *BusinessWeek* Feature Story, Chapter 5.

Business Ownership and Operations

Learning Objectives

After completing this chapter, you'll be able to:

1. **Name** business ownerships.
2. **Compare** the ownerships.
3. **Describe** alternative ways to do business.
4. **Identify** types of businesses.

Why It's Important

You need to understand business ownerships and operations before starting a business.

Key Words

sole proprietorship
unlimited liability
partnership
corporation
stock
limited liability
franchise
nonprofit organization
cooperative
producer
processors
manufacturers
intermediary
wholesaler
retailer

BusinessWeek Feature Story

Selling Out, Staying On

Grow Your Business by Selling It. Like any other mountain biker at a crossroads, Steve Christini, 28, relies on experience to choose the best path. In deciding which way to go in selling his mountain bike company, he relied on something else: a cold calculation of the chances Christini Technologies Inc. could ever, on its own, become the big, successful bike manufacturer he dreamed of.

Source: Excerpted with permission from "Selling Out, Staying On," *BusinessWeek Online*, November 6, 2000.

An Extension Activity

After a few teenagers saw your skateboard, they wanted to know where you got it. Fortunately, you and your friends made it. You all decide to manufacture a few of the new skateboards. One friend is the designer, and the other is going to handle marketing. They've asked (and you've agreed) to find investors. How do you go about finding financial investors?

BUSINESS Online

The Full Story

To learn more about Christini's business, visit the *Introduction to Business* Web site at **www.introbus.glencoe.com**, and click on *BusinessWeek* Feature Story, Chapter 6.

Organizing a Business

Suppose you're a whiz at computer graphics or car repair and want to go into business. How do you want to set it up? Do you want to own and operate it yourself or go into business with a friend? Do you want to run your own multinational corporation? Starting a business is a real challenge. However, it's possible to lower the risk. Careful planning and analysis might help you bring your business right into focus. Consider your own skills, abilities, and potential market for your product or service. Describing your choice and the reasons for it is an important part of your business plan.

Types of Business Ownership

As your business expands, you might want to change the form of ownership. You have three different ways you can own a business: sole proprietorship, partnership, and incorporation.

Figure 6.1

GENERATIONS OF FAMILY-OWNED BUSINESSES

➡Family-owned businesses are sometimes kept in the family for more than one generation.
What percentage of families have had their family-owned businesses for two or more generations?

- 1%
- 5%
- 11%
- 83%

- 1 Generation
- 2 Generations
- 3 Generations
- 4 or more Generations

Look for the Label.
Buy Small Business.

Small Business Works

Sole Proprietorship

A **sole proprietorship** is a business owned by only one person. It's especially suitable if you want to start a business that offers a specific product or service, like a car repair shop. Most bookstores and floral shops are sole proprietorships. So are most farms and home-based businesses. About three-quarters of all businesses in the United States are sole proprietorships. Figure 6.1 shows how many generations of family-owned businesses have been passed on.

Owning your own business is great. First of all, it's easy to start. Depending on the local laws, you might need only a license or permit to start a sole proprietorship. Second, you get to be your own boss. You can come and go as you please and run the business as you see fit. Third, you get to keep all the profits from the business yourself. Finally, the taxes are usually low because you only have to pay them on your personal profits.

On the other hand, there are disadvantages to running your own business. First, you have to pay for everything yourself. You have to buy your own supplies, pay for advertising, rent office space, and pay taxes. You might have to use your personal savings or borrow money from the bank to start your business or keep it going. A lot of sole proprietorships fail because they run out of capital.

You might also lack business skills. You might know everything about car repair but nothing about record keeping or tax preparation. You might need to hire an office manager or accountant to help you run your business.

A serious disadvantage to owning a sole proprietorship is that you have **unlimited liability**, or full responsibility for your company's debts. If you lose more money than you make, you have to make up the difference. You could lose your personal savings, your property, and even your car if your business has debts it cannot repay.

Partnership

Starting a sole proprietorship may sound risky to you. It might seem to be too much work for one person. If you don't have enough money to start a sole proprietorship, you could go into business with a partner. You could bring the idea and your partner could find the money. A **partnership** is a business owned by two or more persons who share the risks and rewards. More owners can contribute to the business. All partners who share in the business have good reason to work hard for its success, since they share the rewards. Like the income of a sole proprietorship, the income of a partnership is taxed only once.

To start a partnership you need to draw up a partnership agreement, which is a contract that outlines the rights and responsibilities of each

Real-World Application

part 1 of 4

CAUTION: LOW-FLYING FISH
Nestled between the Waterfront on First and Pike, you'll find Seattle's famous Pike Place Market. Merchants, travelers, and regulars have frequented this open-air market since 1907. In 1973 the Pike Place Merchants Association (PPMA) became officially incorporated as a nonprofit membership organization. **What's the aim of joining forces and starting an organization?**

continued on p. 89

partner. If you decide to start a car repair business with your friends, Thelma and Ray, you need to agree on certain things. For example, how much money will each of you invest, and how will you share the profits? You also need to specify how to share the work and how to end the partnership. If Ray decides to leave the business, the partnership legally ends. Your partnership agreement should provide a way to buy Ray's share of the business so the business can continue.

There are several advantages to a partnership. Like a sole proprietorship, you might need only a license to start and have to pay taxes only on your personal profits. Unlike a sole proprietorship, it's easier to obtain capital. Each of your partners can contribute money to start the business. Banks are often more willing to lend money to partnerships than sole proprietorships.

Your partners can also bring different skills to the business. You might be best at fixing cars, Thelma at running the office, and Ray at getting new customers. The business can run more efficiently and each partner has an incentive to do a good job.

There are several disadvantages to a partnership. You not only share the risks with your partners, you also share the profits. You might not get along with Ray or Ray might decide to leave the business. In that case, you have to end the partnership and reorganize the business.

You also share unlimited legal and financial liability with your partners. If one partner makes a bad decision, all partners are equally responsible. A bad decision by one partner can result in the business losing money. All partners are responsible for debts that result from the person's bad decision. If Ray loses the company money by buying bad equipment, you have to share the debt. If Ray does something really

You Make the Call

Going Solo or Partnering Up?

It was raining one Thursday last November, so you and your best friend, Jeremiah, decided to try an experiment. You cooked up some packaging "peanuts" on your mother's stove and discovered they turn into a gummy matter that works wonders to cure a leaky faucet. You decide you'd like to sell some of this caulking material, which you'll call "Peanut Better." Jeremiah hears you talking to your business teacher about the new business and says he wants to be a partner.

Making an Ethical Decision

1. What are the advantages and disadvantages of "going solo" in a business venture?
2. How can having a partner help launch and grow a business? Are there any drawbacks?
3. Since Jeremiah was involved in the initial experiment, do you have an obligation to invite him to be a partner? What if he had been the one who decided to start the business without you?

stupid, like buying stolen equipment, you could end up sharing a jail cell with him.

Corporation

Suppose your car repair business has grown and you want to add more shops or buy new equipment. You need more capital but you don't want to borrow more money or bring on new partners. What you can do is form a corporation.

A **corporation** is a business owned by many people but treated by law as one person. It can own property, pay taxes, make contracts, and be sued just like a person. However, it exists separate from its owners.

To form a corporation, you need to get a corporate charter from the state your headquarters is in. A corporate charter is a license to run a corporation.

To raise money, you can sell **stock**, or shares of ownership in your corporation. The new owners (or stockholders) pay a set price for each share. For each share of common stock, the stockholder gets a share of the profits and a vote on how the business is run.

You also must have a board of directors who control the corporation. They don't actually run the day-to-day business operations of the company but they hire officers to do it. You get to pick the first board of directors, but each year the stockholders get to vote on them.

A major advantage of a corporation is its **limited liability**. If your company loses money, the stockholders lose only what they invested. Since your corporation exists separately from you, if it goes out of business you can't have your personal property or savings taken away from you.

Another advantage is that the corporation doesn't end if the owners sell their shares. As long as your business makes money, you can continue the company by reselling the shares. You can also raise more capital at any time by selling new shares.

A disadvantage of a corporation is that you often have to pay more taxes. The federal government and some state governments tax corporate profits. The owners are taxed on their income from the corporation. The corporation itself has to pay taxes. The government also closely regulates corporations. It's more difficult to start a corporation than a sole proprietorship or a partnership and running it can be much more complicated.

Real-World Application

part **2** of 4

CAUTION: LOW-FLYING FISH
At 86 Pike Place, you'll find the world-famous fish-flingers at Pike Place Fish. In 1965 John Yokoyama purchased it because he needed the money to make his car payments. **What's the benefit of going into business for yourself?**

continued on p. 91

✔ Fast Review

1. What are some of the advantages of a sole proprietorship?
2. What is the difference between a sole proprietorship and a partnership?
3. If a partner makes a bad business decision, what responsibility do the other partners have?
4. What are the disadvantages of a corporation?

Alternative Ways to Do Business

You might find it easier to start a business with the help of an established company. You could also start a business by pooling your resources with other businesses. Maybe you're more interested in providing a service to your community than you're into making a profit. Franchises, cooperatives, and nonprofit organizations offer you other ways to do business.

Franchise

A **franchise** is a contractual agreement to sell a company's products or services in a designated geographic area. You probably have several franchises in your neighborhood, such as Taco Bell. If you decide to open a Blockbuster video store, you're the franchisee. Blockbuster, the existing or parent company, is the franchisor.

To run a franchise you have to invest money and pay the franchisor an annual fee or a share of the profits. In return, the franchisor offers a well-known name and a business plan. It provides management training, advertising, and a system of operation. You can operate a franchise yourself, as a sole proprietor, as a partnership with someone else, or even as a corporation.

An advantage of opening a franchise is that it's easy to start. You can rely on the proven methods and product of the parent company. The name of the parent company can be a big draw for customers. When someone wants to rent a video, they often go to the nearest Blockbuster store.

The disadvantage of running a franchise is that the franchisor is often very strict about how the business is run. Your business must operate like every other franchise. You might be limited in what products or services you can offer your customers. If you want to start a business but lack business know-how, however, you might want to choose a franchise.

Nonprofit Organization

Not everyone goes into business just to make a profit. You might want to start a business whose main purpose is to help children, the poor, local artists, or animals. A **nonprofit organization** is a type of business that focuses on providing a service rather than making a profit. The Children's Television Workshop, the American Red Cross, and Meals on Wheels are nonprofit organizations. Private hospitals, schools, and museums can also be set up that way.

Like a corporation, a nonprofit organization has to register with the government and might be run by a board of directors. Because it doesn't make a profit, however, it doesn't have to pay taxes. Instead of investors, nonprofit organizations rely on government grants and on donations from businesses and individuals. Donors don't receive dividends like investors, but they can deduct their donations from their taxes.

Consider This...

Manufacturing Products

Compaq Computers and Cisco Systems don't build their own products anymore. These companies rely on Flextonics, a company that specializes in manufacturing electronics, to build their equipment. This allows Compaq and Cisco to focus on creating new products. Flextonics has grown into a global contractor that produces $10.5 billion a year in electronic gizmos.

ANALYZE

What do Compaq Computers and Cisco Systems give up when they rely on an outside manufacturer?

Cooperative

A **cooperative** is an organization owned and operated by its members for the purpose of saving money on the purchase of certain goods and services. For example, Ocean Spray is a cooperative of cranberry growers. A cooperative is like a corporation in that it exists as a separate entity from the individual businesses. You also need a government charter to start one. Like a corporation, a cooperative can also sell stock and choose a board of directors to run it.

With a cooperative, small farmers, book dealers, or antique merchants can pool their resources. They can save money by buying insurance, supplies, and advertising as a group. They can share factory facilities and warehouse space. Cooperatives also pay less in taxes than regular corporations do. Other examples of cooperatives are Ace Hardware and Welch's.

✓ Fast Review

1. What are some examples of franchise businesses?
2. What types of assistance does the franchisor give a franchisee?
3. How is a nonprofit organization like and unlike a corporation?
4. What are some advantages of a cooperative?

Types of Businesses

After school you go to a fast-food restaurant with some friends to get a hamburger. Before you take a bite out of that burger you might stop to consider how much work it took to get it to you. Selling it over the counter is the tip of the iceberg. Before that the food had to be grown, processed, manufactured, refined, transported, and stored by different types of businesses.

There are many different types of businesses and different ways to classify them. One way is to group them by the kind of products they provide:
- producing raw goods
- processing raw goods
- manufacturing goods from raw or processed goods
- distributing goods
- providing services

Producers

A **producer** is a business that gathers raw products in their natural state. Raw goods are materials gathered in their original state from natural

Real-World Application

part 3 of 4

CAUTION: LOW-FLYING FISH
Pike Place Fish didn't become world famous by advertising. (Instead a Spike Lee Levi's commercial, NBC's *Frasier*, and MTV's *Real World* helped expose the market.) Pike Place prides itself on interacting with the people. The staff wants to give each person a memorable experience.
Can a business have a contractual agreement with its customers?

continued on p. 93

resources such as land or water. A farmer who grows wheat in Kansas is a producer. So is a miner who digs for iron ore in Minnesota and a petroleum worker who drills for crude oil in Alaska. Industries that are producers include agriculture, mining, fishing, and forestry. Business firms that perform activities of this sort are producers of raw goods.

Processors

Most of the time we don't use raw goods in the same form they're found in nature. **Processors** change raw materials into more finished products. They're involved in the processing of raw goods. Processing goods are made from raw goods that may require further processing. For example, wheat is turned into flour, crude oil into gasoline, and iron ore into steel. Paper mills, oil refineries, and smelting plants are types of businesses that process raw goods. Their products, processed goods, are made from raw materials that may require further processing.

Working Lifestyle

What are you doing at 10 A.M.?

The Fast-Paced Circle

"Just when you become an expert on a system, everything changes again and you start learning all over again," says Sunny Kim. This applications specialist for 21st Century Insurance tries to balance a fast-paced career, her family, and attending continuing education courses.

"It's a vicious cycle of knowledge," Kim says. "There's always a challenge to learn a new system and to be aware of how things might change." That's why it's especially important to specialize in one area. Then together with a team of other technology specialists, they interact and contribute to the company's information network.

At 10 A.M. Kim and the other system experts discuss the tasks for the week. Today it's about data storage—they're the ones who will continue creating the "paperless processing" environment. Information never stops. She makes it seamlessly arrive on time for the company to utilize.

Salary

The median income for an applications specialist is $40,000, with a range between $38,000 and $50,000.

Outlook for This Career

This job group is expecting rapid growth among all computer-related occupations.

Connecting Careers Activity

What other occupations require working in a fast-paced environment?

CAREER PATH

Manufacturers

Manufacturers are businesses that make finished products out of processed goods. They turn raw or processed goods into finished goods that require no further processing and that are ready for the market. A bakery makes bread out of flour. An automotive plant makes cars out of steel, glass, and plastic. A furniture factory makes tables out of lumber. Many of the leading businesses in the United States are manufacturers; others are producers and processors. Boeing, Pepsi Co, General Electric, Procter & Gamble, and Eastman Kodak are examples of leading manufacturers in their industry.

Intermediaries

An **intermediary** is a business that moves goods from one business to another. It buys goods, stores them, and then resells them. A **wholesaler**, also known as a distributor, distributes goods. Wholesalers buy goods from manufacturers in huge quantities and resell them in smaller quantities to their customers, usually other companies. The clothing wholesaler, for example, may buy thousands of jackets from several manufacturers. The wholesaler then divides the large quantities into smaller quantities and sells them to retailers. A **retailer** purchases goods from a wholesaler and resells them to the consumer, or the final buyer of the goods. It's another type of business that moves goods. Service stations, record stores, and auto dealers are examples of retailers.

Service Businesses

Service businesses provide services rather than goods. Goods are material products such as cars, CDs, and computers. Services are the products of a skill or an activity such as hairstyling and car repair. Some service businesses meet needs, such as medical clinics and law firms. Some provide conveniences, such as taxi companies and copy shops. Newspapers and Internet services, such as Yahoo!, give us access to information. Service businesses employ about three-quarters of the workforce and are rapidly increasing in numbers.

CAUTION: LOW-FLYING FISH
Yokoyama has such a strong desire to empower other business leaders that he's formed a consulting team. His commitment to his people and his customers is one model other businesses are learning in corporate training videos. **What area does Pike Place Fish focus on other than fish?**

✓ Fast Review

1. What is the difference between a producer and a processor?
2. What does a manufacturer do with raw or processed goods?
3. What does an intermediary do?
4. Give examples of service businesses.

Chapter **6** Review

Summary

1. Three types of business ownership are sole proprietorship, partnership, and corporation.

2. Each type of business ownership has its advantages and disadvantages. A sole proprietorship is easier to start than a partnership or corporation. On the other hand, it's easier to obtain capital if you're in a partnership rather than a sole proprietorship. Corporations are more difficult to start than sole proprietorship and partnership.

3. A franchise, nonprofit organization, and cooperative are alternative ways of doing business.

4. Producers, processors, manufacturers, intermediaries and service businesses are types of businesses that treat products differently.

● Using Business Key Words

Complete each sentence with the correct term.

- **sole proprietorship**
- **partnership**
- **corporation**
- **intermediary**
- **cooperative**
- **unlimited liability**
- **limited liability**
- **nonprofit organization**
- **wholesaler**
- **processors**
- **manufacturers**
- **franchise**
- **producer**
- **retailer**
- **stock**

1. A _____ is a business organization with two or more owners who share the risks and rewards.
2. Shares of ownership in a corporation are called _____.
3. A _____ buys and resells goods.
4. A business owned by one person is called a _____.
5. A business that is treated by law as a separate entity is a _____.
6. Businesses that change raw goods into more finished products are called _____.
7. _____ turn raw or processed goods into finished products.
8. _____ is full legal and financial responsibility for a business.
9. _____ is financial responsibility only for what the owners of a corporation have invested.
10. A contractual agreement to sell a company's products or services in a designated geographic area is a _____.
11. A business whose main purpose is to provide a service rather than to earn a profit is called a _____.
12. _____ is a group of small businesses banded together into a type of corporation.
13. A _____ is a business that gathers raw products in their natural state.
14. A type of business that buys goods in large amounts and resells them to other businesses in smaller lots is called a _____.
15. A type of business that buys goods from wholesalers or manufacturers and sells them directly to the public is called a _____.

Review What You Learned

16. List four advantages of a business organized as a sole proprietorship.

17. How many people must be involved in a partnership? Is there a limit on the number of partners a business can have?

18. Sole proprietorships and partnerships both have unlimited liability for their business debts. What does that mean to the owners?

19. What happens when a partner leaves the business or dies?

20. What is the major advantage of a corporation? Explain your answer.

21. Describe the differences between producers, processors, manufacturers, and intermediaries.

22. What is another name for an intermediary?

23. Currently, service businesses employ what percentage of the workforce?

Understanding Business Concepts

24. What do you consider to be the biggest disadvantage of a sole proprietorship?

25. Why would two or more people decide to form a partnership instead of forming a sole proprietorship with one of them as the owner?

26. There are more sole proprietorships than partnerships or corporations in the United States. Why do you think so many businesses are organized this way?

27. What is the major way a corporation is different from a sole proprietorship or partnership?

28. Give three examples each of raw goods and processed goods.

29. Think of one of your favorite food products. Describe the raw materials that make up the food, how it might have been processed and then manufactured into the food you enjoy.

Critical Thinking

30. Which of the types of businesses described in this chapter would have the easiest time obtaining money to expand their business? Why?

31. Why do many people believe that profits on sales of finished goods are much higher than they actually are?

32. Describe the steps involved in making a hamburger.

33. Have you ever purchased a defective product? Did you exchange or return the product? Do you think the defective product cost the producer money? Why or why not?

Viewing and Representing

Examining the Image. Describe the contents of this photograph. What does the photographer want the viewer to think or feel? If you and your family ran a wholesale bait business, would you run it as a sole proprietorship or as a corporation? Why? What kind of wholesale business would you be interested in running?

Building Academic Skills

LANGUAGE ARTS — Profiling an Owner

Interview a local sole proprietor about what he or she enjoys and finds difficult in running his or her own business. Discuss the advantages and disadvantages of a sole proprietorship with the owner, then write a profile of the business owner.

COMPUTER TECHNOLOGY — Charting and Comparing

Suppose you have $1,000 to invest. Check the stock listings in your newspaper and choose one or more corporations in which to invest your money. Follow the daily progress of your own stock in the newspaper for one week. Then use graphing software to create a graph showing whether your stock went up or down in value. Compare your stock selection with others in your class.

MATH — Percentage

The neighborhood bakery makes bread, cakes, cookies, and pies. At the end of the day, all the leftover products are reduced by 75 percent. What will the reduced prices be for the following:

Bread	$3.49
Chocolate cake	$6.99
One dozen sugar cookies	$3.99
Apple pie	$4.75

Social Science — Research

In a group, prepare a bulletin board or a large chart tracking the route of an item from raw material to the consumer product. On the display, showcase the country or countries that have been a part of the process.

Linking School to Home

Inventory and Interview. Create an inventory of the products and services you and your family use that are produced by small businesses or entrepreneurs. Categorize them by family member. Then, interview each family member and find out why he or she purchases the products and services from the small business or entrepreneur. Compile your results and share them with the class.

Linking School to Work

Guest Speakers. Invite local businesspersons representing sole proprietorships, partnerships, and corporations to serve on a panel discussion in your class. Ask them to share:
- advantages and disadvantages of each type of business ownership
- how they got their start
- qualities they feel are important to the success of the particular type of business ownership they represent

Have questions ready when the panel members arrive. Be sure to thank them for their time.

E-Homework

Applying Technology

Convenient Technology. Computers, personal digital assistants, pagers, and cell phones are tools routinely used in the business world today. Explain whether this technology is as critical to the sole proprietor as it's to a corporation with many stockholders.

Creating a Database. Compile a database of local businesses in which you include fields for the name, address, the telephone number, and the category of business—producer, processor, manufacturer, or intermediary. Use the local Yellow Pages to locate the information. Try to find at least one business in each category and include a minimum of ten businesses. Print out your database. If you can't find a local business in one of the categories, explain why you think this might be so.

Connecting Academics

Math. Draw a circle graph to give a visual representation comparing percentages of the forms of ownership of small businesses. Use the following statistics: corporations 22 percent, partnerships 7 percent, and sole proprietorships 71 percent. Color your graph. What is the most popular form of business ownership? What might be the reason for this?

Language Arts. What interests you most? Choose a form of business ownership or a type of business—from producers to service businesses—to research important details. Create a visual display connected to your chosen topic. Present an oral report to your class.

BusinessWeek — Analyzing the Feature Story

You read the first part of "Selling Out, Staying On" at the beginning of this chapter. Below are a few questions for you to answer about Christini's business. You'll find the answers to these questions when you're reading the entire article. First, here are the questions:

34. What made Christini's business idea suitable for a sole proprietorship?

35. What disadvantage of sole proprietorships was behind Christini and other sole proprietors' decisions to sell their company?

CREATIVE JOURNAL ACTIVITY

An alternative form of business to a sole proprietorship or corporation is a franchise. What questions do you have about how a franchise is run?

BUSINESS Online
The Full Story

To learn more about Christini's business, visit the *Introduction to Business* Web site at www.introbus.glencoe.com, and click on *BusinessWeek* Feature Story, Chapter 6.

Organizational Structures

Learning Objectives

After completing this chapter, you'll be able to:

1. **Explain** how businesses organize for management.
2. **List** three levels of management and compare their responsibilities.
3. **Name** the four functions of management.
4. **Analyze** if a managerial position is for you.

Why It's Important

Understanding business organization and management is key to knowing how a company is run.

Key Words

management plan
organizational chart
line authority
centralized organization
decentralized organization
departmentalization
top-level managers
middle managers
operational managers

BusinessWeek Feature Story

A Fruitful Relationship

Tiny Plumtree and Giant P&G Both Benefit From Agreement. The drops from a leaky pipe in the ceiling were heavy, and loud—enough to make everyone at the meeting in Plumtree Software Inc.'s tiny San Francisco conference room edgy. Especially Dan Gerbus. The Procter & Gamble Co. executive flew into San Francisco that morning to meet Plumtree's managers for the first time. He wondered if P&G, with an annual revenue of $38 billion, was crazy to trust a multimillion-dollar software project to a company with only ten customers, and led by executives who just three years before had been hashing out a business plan in a Berkeley (Calif.) boarding house.

Source: Excerpted with permission from "A Fruitful Relationship," *BusinessWeek Online*, November 20, 2000.

An Extension Activity

Why do you think Procter & Gamble hired an outside firm to get it "wired" as opposed to keeping the project in-house?

BUSINESS *Online*

The Full Story

To learn more about business organizations, visit the *Introduction to Business* Web site at **www.introbus.glencoe.com**, and click on *BusinessWeek* Feature Story, Chapter 7.

Organizing for Management

Suppose you've created your own comic book and want to start a comic book company. Do you want to produce comic books or market and distribute them as well? Do you also want to produce cartoons, video games, and action figures based on your comic books? Either way, you'll need some type of organization.

As a successful business owner, you'll want to accomplish your goals. Your business needs some form of organization that identifies who is responsible for which tasks. Usually a manager directs and coordinates the activities of the workers and deals with any problems that might arise.

Managerial Structures

Any business that employs more than one person needs a management plan. A **management plan** divides a company into different departments run by different managers. Managers direct workers, coordinate activities, and solve problems that might occur. Figure 7.1 asks you to examine how a management plan helps nature. Companies use an **organizational chart** to show how the business is structured

Figure 7.1

WATERFOWL MANAGEMENT PLAN

➡️Fifty-three percent of the original 221 million wetland acres found in the United States has been destroyed. The waterfowl depend upon the wetlands. The North American Waterfowl Management Plan is a joint venture to preserve migratory birds and their habitats.
How might this management plan save the habitat?

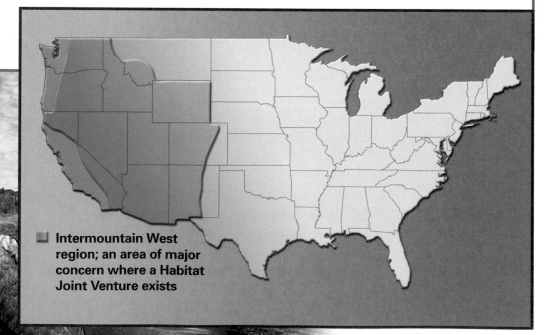

■ Intermountain West region; an area of major concern where a Habitat Joint Venture exists

and who is in charge of whom. In some companies, one person is in charge, and in others, several people might be in charge.

One way to organize management is called **line authority**. The managers at the top of the line are in charge of those beneath them, and so on. **Centralized organization** puts authority in one place, with top management.

Pretend you'd like to run all aspects of your comic book company yourself but it's too much for one person. **Decentralized organization** gives authority to a number of different managers to run their own departments. For example, you might have one person run the production department and another person in charge of marketing.

Formal Structure

Formal structures are usually departmentalized. **Departmentalization** divides responsibility among specific units, or departments. Departments can be organized by what they do, what they make, or by region.

Your comic book's distribution department, for example, is responsible for shipping your product. If your company also produces cartoons and advertisements, you might have a separate department for each. Suppose your company markets comic books nationwide. You'll need managers to run offices in different parts of the country. The Coca-Cola Company markets Coca-Cola® not only in the country but also throughout the world. In each country they have a regional manager who knows his or her market best.

Informal Structure

Smaller businesses can be run more informally. If a business doesn't need a big marketing or distribution network, it doesn't need a lot of managers. The employees can be more flexible and share the duties.

Suppose you decide to publish comic books over the Internet with a couple of partners. One partner is better at computer graphics and the other is better at writing. You can work on projects alone or collaborate on each other's projects. Each week you meet with your partners to plan work on your projects. The informal structure works better for you than having one person in charge.

Real-World Application

part **1** of 4

THE UNMANAGEMENT STYLE OF GORE
W. L. Gore & Associates, Inc., makers of GORE-TEX®, breaks all the corporate rules with its organizational structure. Bill and Vieve Gore created the lattice organization.
How do you suppose a lattice organization is run?

continued on p. 103

✔ **Fast Review** _____

1. How does a centralized organization differ from a decentralized organization?
2. Give an example of departmentalization.

Levels of Management

Every aspect of business has to be managed from setting goals to meeting them. Your long-range goal is not only to produce comic books. You also want to produce cartoons, video games, and action figures. You'll need managers to run each division and oversee the day-to-day operations of each division. Most businesses have three levels of managers: top-level managers, middle managers, and operational managers.

Top-level managers are responsible for setting goals and planning for the future. They have titles like president, vice president, and chief executive officer (CEO). Top management usually consists of a small group of people, or even one person. Lucasfilm Ltd., which produced the *Star Wars* movies, has several different divisions. However, George Lucas alone runs the company.

Middle managers carry out the decisions of top management. They include plant managers, regional managers, and department heads. They're responsible for planning and controlling an operation. The person in charge of development for your video game department is a middle manager.

Operational managers are responsible for the daily operations of the business. Supervisors, office managers, and crew leaders are types of operational managers. Their duties include overseeing workers and meeting

Business Building Blocks

Communication

Developing Teamwork

In business, collaboration is key. Working in a team requires flexibility, creativity, good communication, and shared goals. In fact, those characteristics also describe *improvisation*—to arrange something offhand. To accomplish a goal in a company, people must work together.

Practice

1. You and three others are "actors" in an improvisational skit.
2. You can only communicate by asking questions. You and other actors are trying to decide whether or not to check into a sleazy hotel for your vacation.
3. Two actors will communicate at a time. If one makes a statement rather than asking questions, he or she must step aside and the next person takes over immediately.
4. After five minutes, analyze how you and your fellow actors developed communication skills.

Tips on "*Improv*ing" Your Teamwork

- Working as a team is better than working separately.
- Listen to each other as you brainstorm for solutions.
- Engage in problem solving while creating and offering solutions within constraints.

deadlines. The supervisor of your accounting department is an operational manager.

✓ **Fast Review** _____

1. What are three levels of management?
2. Which of the three levels is most involved in the day-to-day supervision of employees?

Managerial Functions

To meet the goals of your company you need good management. A good manager doesn't just pass on orders. A good manager has four different functions: planning, organizing, leading, and controlling.

Some decisions are routine, such as setting deadlines. Some are risky, such as marketing a new product. Sometimes long-term goals have to be changed because of short-term problems. Managers need to make decisions at all four levels.

Planning

Good planning requires setting realistic goals. Suppose your comic books are a big success and you want to branch off into cartoons, video games, and toys. You can't expect to produce them overnight and have them sell well. First, you need to see if there's a big enough market for them. You have to find out what kind of technology to use, and how long it will take to produce them.

Long-range planning involves top-level management deciding how the company should perform. As part of the planning process, management must answer the following key questions:

- What must be done?
- Who will do it?
- How will the work be grouped?
- Who supervises whom?
- Who makes decisions about the work to be done?

These questions are applied and answered when you get together with your management team. The team decides your plan to market a variety of products is too ambitious. You decide on a more realistic plan of only producing a cartoon show. If the show is a big success, then you can consider producing video games and action figures.

Organizing

To organize a business plan you need to assign managers different tasks and coordinate their activities. One manager is in charge of video production and one is in charge of marketing. Another manager is in charge

Real-World Application

part **2** of 4

THE UNMANAGEMENT STYLE OF GORE
The Gore corporate culture has no chain of command, no pre-determined channels of communication. Instead, the staff communicates directly with each other. There is no hierarchy. **What are the benefits of such a management style?**

continued on p. 105

of the budget. Each manager needs to organize his or her department and know what the other managers are doing. Your production manager has to decide whether to set up a small studio or hire an existing one overseas. Your marketing director has to do some research to decide whether your cartoons will sell well in the United States or Japan. Both managers need to know how much money they have in the budget to carry out their tasks.

You also need to determine who makes decisions and who answers to whom. Can some managers make decisions for themselves or do they have to report to you? Figure 7.2 demonstrates the managerial functions in a graphic organizer.

Leading

Good management also requires good leadership. There's more to leading than just giving orders. You have to create a vision of your company to inspire your employees. You need to set standards, such as deadlines and sales quotas, so your managers know their goals. You need to communicate with them to provide guidance and resolve conflicts. Some employees might need training. Others might be self-motivated and work better on their own.

Figure 7.2

MANAGEMENT FUNCTIONS

➡Managers carry out four different functions.
Which function involves coordinating resources?

PLANNING
Setting objectives and making long- and short-term plans for meeting the objectives.

ORGANIZING
Obtaining and coordinating resources so that a business's objectives can be met.

CONTROLLING
Setting standards for work, evaluating performance, and solving problems that prevent certain tasks' completion.

LEADING
Influencing, guiding, and directing people under one's management to carry out their assigned tasks.

You especially want to encourage your employees. Most companies offer incentives such as pay raises and promotions. Some companies, like Intel and Wal-Mart, offer stock options and profit sharing to their employees so they feel like they have a stake in the company. The primary objective of a good manager is to help each person in the company work to his or her potential.

Controlling

Controlling means keeping the company on track and making sure all goals are met. You have to keep track of the budget, the schedule, and the quality of the product. You also have to monitor your employees and review their performance. Suppose your first cartoon comes in ahead of schedule and it looks great. You might want to reward your production manager with a pay raise or a day off.

On the other hand, sometimes things don't go according to plan. Your first cartoon just came in over-budget and it looks awful. You need to find out what went wrong and fix it. You might have to fire your production manager or find a new studio.

Controlling also involves monitoring customer satisfaction. Your marketing manager can measure the success of your cartoon by studying sales charts and ratings. You might find out your show did well on television but did poorly on video. If your show was more popular with adults than children you might want to come up with a new marketing plan.

✓ **Fast Review** _____

1. What are the four functions of management?
2. What is a manager's objective in leading?

Real-World Application

part **3** of 4

THE UNMANAGEMENT STYLE OF GORE
Gore hires associates (not employees) to work on general projects. Within the guidance of sponsors (not bosses) a team is formed. **What are some challenges a Gore team might encounter?**

continued on p. 107

Is Being a Manager for You?

Most managers begin their career as a company employee and are promoted after they have gained experience and have shown certain qualities.

- *Ability to perform varied activities.* Managers usually have many tasks to perform at one time. Managers have to plan their time and decide which tasks are the most important at any one time.
- *Ability to work under pressure.* A manager often has to solve many small problems in a fairly short time. For example, a supervisor may have to organize next week's work schedule, solve a production problem, and train two new employees—all in the same workday. Also included might be attending one meeting, writing seven letters, and skimming four industry periodicals.

Writing for Business

Assess and Reorganize

This activity gives you the chance to add to your portfolio. Communicate, interview, research, and write your way into a story. Choose one imaginary path, Hired Consultant or Personnel Director. Follow your path's steps to complete your own story.

pick a path

Hired Consultant

The Setting. The vice president of operations at a tractor-manufacturing company has called you, a consultant. She needs your help in reorganizing the company's managerial positions.

Rising Action. You've never consulted on this type of job before, but you need the money so you cannot turn it down.

Step 1. Call or write to the personnel department of a large corporation. Ask for information about the company's organizational structure.

Step 2. Create a graphic illustration of how the different managerial levels relate.

Step 3. Using this graphic as a model, write brief job descriptions for each managerial position as it relates specifically to the tractor-manufacturing company.

Personnel Director

The Setting. You're the personnel director at a tractor-manufacturing corporation. The company wants to open a manufacturing plant in northern Mexico.

Rising Action. You know the company needs to address issues about global growth. You need to consider the company's organization, wages, and working conditions as they relate to Mexico.

Step 1. Read recent articles about the globalization of American corporations.

Step 2. Prepare a memo to your boss, the vice president of operations. The memo outlines your recommendations about offering fair wages and working conditions abroad.

Step 3. Lastly, explain in the memo how your recommendations benefit the corporation as well as its employees.

Conclusion

Now it's time to reflect on your choice. Take a few minutes to write a note to your teacher about the path. Briefly explain why you chose it and what you learned from researching and writing it. Attach this note to your assignment.

- *Effective communication.* Every manager has to communicate well. Communicating might be done on the telephone, by fax, or e-mail, in individual or group meetings, or in a written report or a letter. Listening is also an important part of communication. Most of a manager's day is spent interacting with other people.
- *Interpersonal skills.* Managers work with people and need human relations skills, or skills in dealing with people. For example, a manager may be asked to resolve conflicts among employees.
- *Ability to gather and use information.* Managers must be aware of the events and forces in the global market that affect their business. For example, some managers read local and national newspapers daily. They may also use online services to access international news relating to their company's various markets or products.

If you were offered a job with management responsibilities, would you take it? To help you decide, consider some of the advantages and disadvantages.

Advantages

Managers usually earn more money than employees in non-management jobs. People become managers because they're leaders, and good leaders are respected. So, being a manager has prestige. Because managers are leaders, they have more influence than other employees on how the company is run. That is, managers have more authority than other employees do in planning, organizing, directing, controlling, and evaluating company resources. Managers have varied duties and make decisions about many kinds of things. Managers also have greater control over their time and how they'll spend it.

Disadvantages

Managers get the blame when things go wrong, even if another employee caused the problem. Managers are also often targets for criticism. When managers do make mistakes, they can be more costly than other employees' mistakes because their decisions affect many workers. Managers get a lot of pressure to do things right the first time. Finally, some managers feel their relationship with lower-level employees is different than their relationship with fellow managers. Employees are often careful of what they say or do when their manager is around for fear of jeopardizing their jobs.

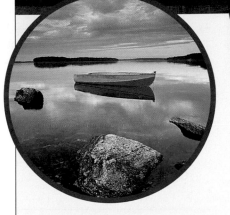

Real-World Application

part **4** of 4

THE UNMANAGEMENT STYLE OF GORE

At Gore, everyone will try to be fair, committed, and encourage freedom. Associates are to consult with one another before taking action that might be "below the waterline" and cause serious damage to the company.

What does this saying mean?

✓ **Fast Review** _____

1. What are five qualities or skills a manager should have?
2. What are the advantages and disadvantages of being a manager?

Chapter 7 Review

Summary

1. Businesses may be organized with authority focused in one place (centralized) or with authority in a number of units (decentralized).

2.

LEVEL OF MANAGEMENT	RESPONSIBILITIES
Top-Level Manager	Set goals and plan for the future.
Middle Manager	Carry out decisions of top management. Planning and controlling an operation.
Operational Manager	Oversee daily operations of business. Manage staff. Meet deadlines.

3. Managers plan, organize, lead, and control.

4. Successful managers are able to carry out varied tasks, perform under pressure, communicate effectively, relate to people, and grasp and use information. Managers have prestige, influence, and power; however, they usually experience a lot of pressure too.

Using Business Key Words

When discussing management and how businesses are organized, it's helpful to know the following terms. Match each term with its definition.

- centralized organization
- middle managers
- decentralized organization
- management plan
- operational managers
- organizational chart
- line authority
- departmentalization
- top-level managers

1. Managers who carry out the decisions of top management.
2. A business plan that divides a company into different departments run by different managers.
3. Authority lies in one place.
4. Authority lies with several different managers.
5. Supervisors, office managers, and crew leaders are examples of this type of manager.
6. Plant managers, regional managers, and department heads are examples of this type of manager.
7. A way of organization that subdivides responsibilities by specific units.
8. A chart that shows how a business is structured and who is in charge of whom.
9. An organizational structure in which managers at the top of the line are in charge of those beneath them.

Review What You Learned

10. What is line authority, and how does it look on an organizational chart?
11. Who has the decision-making authority in a decentralized organization?
12. Describe the three different ways in which departments are organized.
13. What are the primary responsibilities of top-level managers?
14. What is the difference between middle managers and operational managers?
15. Name the four managerial functions.
16. What does good planning require?
17. Describe the function of leading and how it affects a manager's job.

Understanding Business Concepts

18. What are some of the differences between a business that has a formal organization and one that is informally organized?
19. Why do managers at all levels need to communicate well?
20. Describe the management function of organizing.
21. What is the primary objective of a good manager?

Critical Thinking

22. Would you choose to work in a formally or informally structured organization? Explain why.
23. Describe the ideal manager that you would like to work for someday.

24. Amazon.com and Toys "Я" Us decided to work together to sell toys over the Internet. What decisions would executives from each company have to consider in order to successfully complete this alliance?
25. Business organizations that are run by women are more likely to:
    a. Grow quickly.
    b. Take financial risks.
    c. Place less emphasis on who is in charge.
    d. Or all of the above.

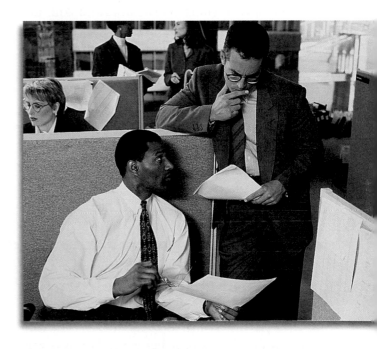

Viewing and Representing

Examining the Image. Team up with a partner. What details do you see in this photograph? What people and objects are shown? Decide whether the organization shown is centralized or decentralized. Explain your reason. Do you feel you would enjoy working in this organization? Why?

Building Academic Skills

Brainstorming

Work with a partner and imagine that one of you is the manager and the other is an employee. Choose two business situations that a manager must be able to deal with. Each of you should take the role of the manager in one of the situations you chose. After you have acted out the situation, discuss the skills you used. Draw up a list of the management responsibilities and skills that you and your partner think are important for handling the situations you examined.

COMPUTER TECHNOLOGY Creating a Graphic

Using computer software, create an organizational chart of the administration of your school. Explain what type of organization it has.

HISTORY Decision Making

Top-level managers make major decisions and establish company objectives. For example, top-level managers at Coca-Cola® decided several years ago to introduce a "new Coke" with a slightly different recipe. It was a disaster. Consumers didn't like it. So top management decided to bring back the original, calling it "Coca-Cola® Classic." Research a similar top-level management decision. In a short paragraph, summarize the management decision and its effect(s) on the company.

Exploring Math Skills

Working in groups of three or four, create a list of all the math skills that are needed by managers at each level. Give a detailed explanation of how each skill would be used on the job. As a class, combine the lists.

Linking School to Home

Family Members' Workplace. Ask a family member how his or her workplace is organized. How is the management structured? Create a poster summarizing your findings.

Linking School to Work

Functions of Management. Interview a manager from a local business to find out how he or she uses leadership skills to manage people and resources on the job. Use the following questions as a guide when you interview the manager:
- What must be done?
- Who will do it?
- How will the work be grouped?
- Who supervises whom?
- Who makes decisions about the work to be done?

Also, ask the manager what percentage of his or her time is spent on each of the four functions of management (i.e., planning, organizing, leading, and controlling). Then, using the information you have obtained, write a 250-word report.

E-Homework

Applying Technology

Pie Chart. Using the information you obtained from the Linking School to Work activity, create a pie chart demonstrating the percentage breakdown of the four management functions for the manager you interviewed. Title the chart and include the company name, product, and manager's title. Also, carefully label the sections of the chart. Write a short caption for the chart explaining the percentage breakdown. Print out the finished product.

Organization Chart. Work in small groups. Imagine you start a greeting card company. Decide what functions your team members will perform, taking into account the talents and interests of individuals. Will your company be structured formally or informally? Make a chart using presentation software to show how you organized your company. Present your chart to the class.

Connecting Academics

Math. You're a delivery manager at Blue Bag Bakery, a wholesale bakery. The bakery employs two drivers and owns two trucks. Each truck can deliver up to 175 crates of bread a day. The bakery usually has orders for 340 crates a day from local supermarkets, schools, and hospitals. A new supermarket is opening soon and you expect orders to increase 225 percent. How many trucks and drivers will you need to cover your new deliveries?

Math. Fran, merchandise manager for Blue Bag, is planning her department's yearly budget. Fran is in charge of three employees, each earning $350 a week. Fran earns $500 a week. The business pays social security taxes of 8.15 percent on employee earnings for social security taxes.

How much money does Fran need to enter in her department's budget to cover salaries and taxes for the year?

BusinessWeek Analyzing the Feature Story

You read the first part of "A Fruitful Relationship" at the beginning of this chapter. Below are a few questions for you to answer about Plumtree and Proctor & Gamble's business organizations. You'll find the answers to these questions when you're reading the entire article. First, here are the questions:

26. How do Plumtree and Proctor & Gamble's business organizations differ?
27. What management skills did Gerbus of P & G use to make the alliance with Plumtree a success?

CREATIVE JOURNAL ACTIVITY
What kind of organization would you like to work in? Should it have a formal or informal structure? Write a short description of the ideal business environment for you.

BUSINESS Online
The Full Story
To learn more about Plumtree and Proctor & Gamble's business organizations, visit the *Introduction to Business* Web site at **www.introbus.glencoe.com**, and click on *BusinessWeek* Feature Story, Chapter 7.

Chapter 8

Leadership in Management

Learning Objectives

After completing this chapter, you'll be able to:
1. **Describe** the difference between a manager and a leader.
2. **Name** the qualities needed to be a leader.
3. **Identify** the three styles of leadership.
4. **Illustrate** the advantages of working in teams.

Why It's Important

Managers need to recognize leadership qualities and leadership styles that motivate employees to be creative and productive.

Key Words

leadership
initiative
human relations
integrity
autocratic leadership
democratic leadership
free-rein leadership
delegating
self-managed teams

BusinessWeek Feature Story

The Boss in the Web Age

Communicate, Comprise, Think Globally—And Do It Fast. Ask a chief executive officer what the job will be like in the year 2020, and the CEO is apt to give the reply, "Who knows?" With the drop-dead pace of technological upheaval, it's hard enough to scope out the business landscape three months from now, let alone two decades. But by the time today's ambitious, twenty something dot-com entrepreneurs reach middle age and settle into the role of running multibillion-dollar operations, the corner office will hardly be recognizable.

Source: Excerpted with permission from "The Boss in the Web Age," *BusinessWeek Online,* August 28, 2000.

An Extension Activity

Vision motivates people by providing them a direction toward goals. Give an example from your life when a leader inspired you. How did this person's inspiration influence you?

BUSINESS *Online*

The Full Story

To learn more about business leadership, visit the *Introduction to Business* Web site at **www.introbus.glencoe.com**, and click on *BusinessWeek* Feature Story, Chapter 8.

The Future of Leadership

You've probably been in a group situation where one person wants to take charge. That person might want to lead for the wrong reasons—to order everyone else around or for personal gain. Others often play "follow the leader" because they just want to be told what to do. There's more to leadership than just being in charge. The business world is faced with many challenges in the twenty-first century. The expanding vision of global business and technology affects organizations, people, and production. Management is focusing on turning individuals into cooperative team members to create and follow through with the company's vision.

Leadership Qualities

In management, **leadership** means providing direction and vision for a company. Test your leadership knowledge in Figure 8.1. Being a manager isn't the same thing as being a leader. Managing is a job. Leading is a skill. Managers focus on specific tasks and make sure the work gets done. They give orders and carry out orders. Leaders have vision. They see the big picture and never lose sight of their goal. They manage others by inspiring them rather than ordering them.

It's possible to be a good manager but not a good leader. Sometimes a good leader isn't even the person in charge. For example, Warren Sapp of the Tampa Bay Buccaneers football team is a defensive lineman and not the

Figure 8.1	WHAT DO YOU KNOW ABOUT LEADERSHIP?

➡Respond to these statements about leaders as "true" or "false." They show some of the perceptions people sometimes have about leadership. **How would you respond to each statement?**

You are born a leader.	T	F
Only top-level and middle managers can be leaders.	T	F
A leader is a "boss."	T	F

Rate your score:
All three statements are false.

quarterback. He is often considered the team's leader because of his energy, experience, and commitment to the team. Ideally, the person in charge is also a leader. To be both a good manager and a good leader takes several qualities.

Motivation

Motivation means three different things. It means having **initiative**, or the desire to take action and get things done. Someone with initiative doesn't wait to be told what to do but takes action. In business, initiative is the main quality of an entrepreneur. Good leaders also motivate others to get things done. They often do this by inspiring others with their energy, enthusiasm, and charisma, or charm.

Most importantly, motivation means having a goal, whether it's to create the best video game or to make the best skateboard ever. A true leader is motivated by a vision and inspires others with it. Civil rights activist and theologian Martin Luther King, Jr. delivered powerful speeches like "I Have a Dream," which built a vivid picture of the future with his language. One year later Congress passed the Civil Rights Act of 1964. The same year King received the Nobel Peace Prize, an outstanding award for his peace efforts.

Confidence

To lead others you also need to inspire their confidence. The best way to do this is by having self-confidence. Self-confidence means more than acting sure of yourself. It means actually knowing what you're doing. To lead you not only need a goal, but some idea of how to reach it. The more others are convinced that you know what to do, the more confidence they'll have in you.

A confident leader is also a decisive leader. Suppose you run a student magazine and it comes back from the printer with a big mistake on the cover. You could put it out as is, remove the covers, or send it back to the printer. The longer you take to decide, the more you'll look like you have no confidence in your judgement. You can get advice from your workers, but then you need to make a decision. If your decision turns out to be wrong, you take responsibility for it. People have more confidence in a leader who is willing to make mistakes and learn from them.

Communication

A leader must be good at **human relations**, or the ability to communicate with people. Even if you have a vision and the confidence to carry it out, you can't lead others if you can't communicate with them. To motivate others, you need to be able to explain what your goals are

Real-World Application

part 1 of 4

LEADING THE PACK
Ancella Livers is a confirmed people-watcher. As a manager for the nonprofit Center for Creative Leadership in Greensboro, North Carolina, she trains managers and executives. **What do you think her role is as a corporate trainer?**

continued on p. 117

to them. Many leaders use gestures, draw pictures, or tell stories to communicate their ideas. President Ronald Reagan relied a lot on body language and described scenes from movies to inspire people.

To communicate with people, a leader also needs to be a good listener. By listening to people you can understand them better and get them more involved. You need to listen to people to be informed about what they're doing, what their strengths and weaknesses are, and what they need to do a better job. You can often benefit by listening to other people's ideas and getting their advice. When Bill Clinton ran for president the first time, he traveled the country by bus and held town council meetings to find out what people wanted.

Integrity

Integrity is the most highly valued quality in a leader. **Integrity** means holding to principles like honesty, loyalty, and fairness. In order to lead, you need to set a good example. If you're willing to sacrifice the quality of your product to make a bigger profit, people aren't going to have much faith in your vision. You can't expect your employees to have good work habits if you show up late for work, leave early, and miss deadlines. A leader who tries to cover up mistakes or blame them on employees isn't going to inspire loyalty or confidence.

President Harry Truman had a sign on his desk that said, "The Buck Stops Here." That meant that he took full responsibility for whatever

You Make the Call

Ghostwrite

Ms. Fernandez is the chief executive officer (CEO) of a sunglass manufacturer. She is scheduled to speak at a national trade show. You know Ms. Fernandez isn't a very good public speaker. You're an employee in the communications department of the company, so she asks you to *ghostwrite* a speech for her. (Ghostwriting means to write anonymously for another person who is then recognized as the author of a speech or book.)

The speech is so good, however, that a major publisher asks Ms. Fernandez to expand it and publish it as a how-to book. She asks you to ghostwrite the book. Only her name will be on the cover.

Making an Ethical Decision

1. Is it appropriate for Ms. Fernandez to ask you to write the book without being at least a co-author?
2. Is it appropriate for you to write a book without informing readers about who wrote it?
3. What if the book became an international bestseller—would that change your answers? If so, why?

happened, rather than "passing the buck" to someone else. President Truman might be considered an inspiring leader. He evoked confidence, though, because everyone knew they could trust him. If you lose the confidence and respect of people, you can't lead them.

Developing Leadership Skills

Some people say leaders are born and not made. The exact opposite is true. A person with charisma, like the star athlete or coolest kid in class, is often mistaken for a natural born leader. Charisma, however, doesn't make somebody a good leader. President Truman and President Richard Nixon had little charisma but were effective leaders.

Even the shiest person can become a leader. You're not born with self-confidence, vision, and the ability to communicate. These qualities are learned through knowledge and experience. You can learn leadership skills in a number of ways:

- There are many books, videos, and courses on leadership. Some colleges even offer a degree in leadership.
- Work with someone who has leadership ability and study what he or she does. It could be a teacher, a coach, or a relative.
- Join a club, a team, a drama group, or a community organization to develop communications skills.
- Take the initiative at school, at work, or in club activities. Volunteer for projects or activities that give you an opportunity to lead.

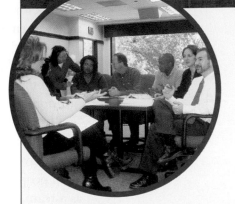

Real-World Application

part 2 of 4

LEADING THE PACK
Many successful managers and executives aren't born leaders. In fact, Livers says, leadership is a skill that most of us learn.
What leadership quality do you want to learn?

continued on p. 119

✓ **Fast Review** _____

1. What is the difference between being a manager and being a leader?
2. Why is integrity an important trait for a leader?

Styles of Leadership

Different leaders have different styles. Some rule with strict discipline and watch your every move. Some are easy going and leave you alone to do your work. Figure 8.2 asks you to test your communication skills. Many leaders use more than one style depending on whom they're managing. There are three basic styles of leadership: autocratic, democratic, and free rein.

Autocratic Leadership

Autocratic means self-ruling. An **autocratic leadership** is when you like to run everything yourself and answer to no one. You make all the decisions without consulting anyone. When you give orders you expect them to be obeyed without question. Autocratic leaders assume people don't like to work, that they avoid responsibility, and that they have to be watched all the time. They usually control their workers through fear and intimidation. Henry Ford was a classic autocratic leader. He went so far as to hire secret police to spy on his managers to make sure they were doing what he told them.

The biggest problem with autocratic leaders is that people don't like to work for them. The leader's lack of trust in his or her employees doesn't inspire them to be creative. These leaders rarely give credit to their employees so there is little room for initiative. They get people to work hard as long as they're around, but once they leave workers are less productive. If something happens to an autocratic leader, there is usually no one in a position to take over the business.

An autocratic leader is useful in situations where it's important to obey orders without question. Fire fighters, combat troops, and police often have to deal with emergencies where there's no time to consult. Such people are specially trained to work that way, however, and to work as a team. An autocratic style rarely works in a business setting.

Figure 8.2

HOW GOOD ARE YOUR COMMUNICATION SKILLS?

➥ Evaluate yourself on your communication skills.
Do these traits apply to you?

1. **People often don't get what I'm saying.**
2. **I find it easy to see things from someone else's point of view.**
3. **I pretend to listen even if my mind drifts away.**
4. **When I am wrong, I am not afraid to admit it.**
5. **I tend to jump to conclusions.**
6. **I try to put myself in the other person's shoes when we are talking.**
7. **It upsets me if someone disagrees with me.**
8. **When I work with others, I try to do my fair share of the work.**

Rate your score:
If you answered that traits 2, 4, 6, and 8 apply to you, you're on the road to being a good communicator. Traits 1, 3, 5, and 7 are characteristics you may need to work on.

Democratic Leadership

Democratic leadership means that managers and employees work together to make decisions. Everyone meets, discusses a situation, and listens to everyone's opinion. New ideas are encouraged in this workplace environment. As a democratic leader you still make the final decisions, but you explain your reasons to everyone.

A democratic leader assumes that people aren't lazy and want to work. By giving them more responsibility, workers will be more productive and creative. If they don't have someone looking over their shoulders all the time they will take initiative in their work. By showing your workers you have confidence in them, they're more likely to have confidence in you.

Henry Ford's autocratic style almost ruined his company. General Motors, on the other hand, chose a more democratic style. Alfred Sloan, the chairman of GM, broke the company up into divisions and gave his managers the power to make decisions. As a result, GM started selling more cars than Ford.

Free-Rein Leadership

Free-rein leadership requires the leader to set goals for your managers and employees and then leave them alone to get the job done. This style shows the most trust and confidence in workers. Another name for this type of leadership style is *hands-off leadership*. That doesn't mean you just put other people in charge and leave them alone. You have to deal with the big decisions and keep your managers informed. You also have to be available to them if they have questions or if any problems occur.

Giving managers and employees the power to run things and make decisions is called **delegating**. There are several reasons for a leader to delegate:

- You don't have the time to run everything yourself.
- You can focus on more important work.
- It gets your employees more involved.
- It gives your employees a chance to develop their own potential.

There are also reasons not to delegate. You shouldn't delegate if you're doing it because you're lazy, don't have confidence, or don't want the responsibility. That is not leadership. You also don't want to delegate power to managers who are irresponsible. Who you choose to delegate power to is a test of your leadership skill. Hiring employees who are experienced, reliable, and knowledgeable about the goals leads to success.

Real-World Application

part 3 of 4

LEADING THE PACK
Today is the second day of training 20 top executives, several of whom are from Fortune 500 companies. Livers asks her students to think of a lesson from childhood that has played out in their adult lives. Livers leads her class in a discussion of how such a childhood role might affect leadership as an adult. **Executives in this workshop are investing time into what resource?**

continued on p. 121

✔ Fast Review

1. In what situations is an autocratic style of leadership useful?
2. Give reasons for a manager to delegate authority.

Business Building Blocks

Communication

Making a Group Succeed

Building a workable team isn't always an easy task, because everyone is different. Here is an exercise on creative teamwork:

Practice

Get-to-Know Bingo requires that each student takes an active part.

1. Each person takes a piece of paper and creates a 4 x 5 bingo card with 20 enclosed boxes.
2. Inside each box, write a different characteristic. (Examples: Grew up in another state, is fluent in another language, sang in a choir, is afraid of spiders, and so on.)
3. Ask each student questions. When you discover a characteristic about another player, mark that box on your card with a "X."
4. You must finish the game with a bingo on your card.

Tips for Teamwork

- Make the team's goals your top priority.
- Continue to communicate with team members outside of meetings.
- Respect the other members of your team.
- Try to inspire others to get involved.

Leadership in Teams

Only 20 or 30 years ago autocratic leadership was the main style used in most American companies. As companies learned the value of giving workers more power they started using a more democratic or free-rein style. Today, the trend is to go even further. Many companies have been putting workers on **self-managed teams**, or work groups that supervise themselves. The role of the manager is being replaced by the role of the team leader.

Self-Managed Teams

The use of self-managed teams started in Japan and came to the United States later. American companies had emphasized people working as individuals on separate jobs. Decisions were left up to managers. Japanese companies had stressed people working in teams and making decisions as a group. The Japanese method was such a success that American companies started copying them.

American companies also had too many managers running things. Every decision had to go through several managers before anything could get done. It slowed things down and was very costly. By letting teams manage themselves, companies were able to get rid of many managing jobs and replace them with a team leader.

In a self-managed team, the leader is a team player rather than a boss. The leader doesn't have to answer to an upper management so the team is freer to get the job done.

A team leader makes decisions with the team rather than alone. This person learns a range of jobs rather than just one. The team usually works on a single project, like designing a video game. This way the project is more goal-oriented rather than task-oriented.

The Organization of Self-Managed Teams

Self-managed teams are organized in two ways: (1) each team member has a special skill or (2) the team selects one team leader. Let's examine the first type of team. Each member of the team might have special skills. For example, Dexter might be an expert in game theory, Pablo a whiz at computer graphics, and Allison skilled at storytelling. The members of your team might also be from different departments. For example, Pablo actually designs the game while Dexter deals with the budget, and Allison handles the marketing. Self-managed teams get to work on their own, but everyone is expected to produce results.

The second type of self-managed team appoints a team leader. The team leader might be appointed by a top manager or selected by the team. At W. L. Gore & Associates, Inc. (creator of GORE-TEX® fabric), there are no hierarchies, bosses, and titles. Its team approach encourages and fosters creativity and opportunity.

A team leader isn't always a manager as much as a team captain. If you're a team leader, your job isn't to give orders but to motivate your team and get the members to work together toward a shared goal.

The idea behind self-managed teams is that the whole is greater than the sum of its parts. Self-managed teams have many advantages:

- They're more goal-oriented than task-oriented.
- They're faster and more efficient.
- Team members have a chance to learn each other's jobs and obtain new skills.
- It simplifies the decision-making process.
- Team members learn to participate and cooperate with each other.
- Self-managed teams learn to solve their own problems.

Real-World Application

part **4** of **4**

LEADING THE PACK
In addition to teaching managers leadership skills, Livers also coaches executives on an individual basis over a period of time. After observing an individual in a variety of settings and under various conditions, Livers presents her observations and offers suggestions for improvement.
Why is it important to seek self-improvement?

✔ **Fast Review** _____

1. What effect are self-managed teams having on management?
2. What are some advantages of self-managed teams?

Summary

1. Being a manager isn't the same thing as being a leader. A manager manages projects, people, and situations in a company. A leader has a vision, which inspires others.

2. Leaders need vision, motivation, confidence, integrity, and the ability to communicate.

3. The three basic styles of leadership are autocratic, democratic, and free rein. An autocratic leader likes to rule everything and answer to no one. One person at the top makes decisions. Firefighters, combat troops, and police often work with an autocratic leader when time is of the essence. A democratic leader means managers and employees work together to make decisions. Equal responsibility instills creativity and productivity in the people involved. Lastly, free-rein leadership, or hands-off leadership, allows the leader to set goals and let people work alone to get the job done.

4. Today's leadership trend is toward self-managed teams. The team-oriented approach allows workers to be more goal-oriented, efficient, analytical, creative, productive, and self-reliant.

● Using Business Key Words

To be a successful manager, you must be a leader, an effective communicator, and a team player. Fill each blank in the following sentences with the term that best completes each sentence.

- **initiative**
- **free-rein leadership**
- **autocratic leadership**
- **democratic leadership**
- **delegating**
- **human relations**
- **self-managed teams**
- **integrity**
- **leadership**

1. Some managers make decisions without consulting their employees. This type of leadership is called _____.

2. Some managers ask employees for suggestions and discuss alternatives with them. This type of leadership is called _____.

3. A leader shows great _____ if she or he has the desire to take action and get things done.

4. Leaders often engage in _____ if they don't have time to run everything themselves or to get employees more involved.

5. A leadership style in which managers allow employees the freedom to decide how to do their work is called _____.

6. Providing direction and vision is called _____.

7. The ability to communicate with others is called _____.

8. Holding to the principles like honesty, loyalty, and fairness is called _____.

9. _____ is when work groups supervise themselves.

Review What You Learned

10. Which leadership style is considered the best?

11. What is the key to the modern workplace?

12. Name two disadvantages of working in teams.

13. Explain how nonverbal actions are considered a form of communication.

14. What happens if managers and employees don't communicate well?

Understanding Business Concepts

15. Compare the three leadership styles.

16. Why do you think most managers use a mixture of leadership styles? Do you think it might be confusing to employees? Why or why not?

17. Have you ever worked as part of a team on a class project? What were the advantages and disadvantages of working this way?

18. Explain the flow of communication.

19. How has technology, especially the Internet, changed the way people communicate? Has it made a difference for you? Explain.

Critical Thinking

20. Imagine you're the manager of an ice cream store near your high school. You have five employees—a bookkeeper with ten years of experience, two college students who have worked with you for six months, and two high school students who just started last week. What leadership style(s) do you think you'll use with your employees? Explain your answer.

21. Keep a log of the number and kinds of communication skills used during one day at your school.

22. More companies are adding a new type of executive to its hierarchy: the chief knowledge officer (CKO). How do you think a CKO would benefit a company?

23. Between now and the year 2020, chief executive officers (CEOs) are more likely to:
   a. Be women and minorities.
   b. Stay in their jobs for shorter periods of time.
   c. Place greater emphasis on teams and consensus.
   d. All of the above.

Viewing and Representing

Examining the Image. Draw a sketch of this photograph. Include every detail. What's the main idea? What messages and emotions are team members expressing? Invent names for the members of this self-managed team. Write a brief story on your perceptions of the image. Share your story with the class.

Building Academic Skills

 ### Historic Leadership Styles

In a group of three or four, research the way business was conducted 100 years ago. Examine a variety of issues including leadership styles, employee rights, methods of communication, advertising techniques, and products and services available. Write a two-page paper with your findings and share with the class.

COMPUTER TECHNOLOGY Netiquette

E-mail is a very popular form of communication. Netiquette is network etiquette, or the "dos and don'ts" of online communication. Research netiquette on the Internet and create your own list of ten rules you should follow when communicating in this way. Create a poster of your rules and display in your class.

 ### Percentage of Sales Goal

Your manager at the Burger Barn wants each employee to sell $350 worth of hamburgers and fries during his or her shift. Yesterday your sales totaled $325. Today your sales totaled $400. Determine the percentage you achieved above or below the goal for yesterday and today.

LANGUAGE ARTS Oral Presentation

Locate and read an article on one of the following topics: effective leadership styles, teamwork, skills needed for management, or effective communication skills. Prepare a summary and present it orally to the class.

Linking School to Home

Analyzing Big Business. Think about the U.S. government as the manager of a very large corporation. Brainstorm examples of the leadership style(s) the government uses, whether or not teamwork is utilized, and the way information is communicated to the masses. Consult your parents and family members for their thoughts. Share your opinions with the class.

Linking School to Work

Observations. If you're employed, observe the activities of your manager for a one-week period. Answer the following questions:
- What type of leadership style does your manager use with you? With others in the organization?
- Does your manager organize his or her employees into teams? If so, how effective do you think they are?

Present your findings to the class. (Note: If you aren't employed, observe the activities of a particular teacher or friend for one week.)

E-Homework

Applying Technology

Emoting Emoticons. *Emoticons* are type-written pictures of facial expressions used in e-mail to communicate emotions, like happy, sad, mad, and so on. Using the Internet and other resources, create a list of emoticons.

Leadership Assessment. Use the Internet to research the three leadership styles. If possible, locate an online leadership assessment and try to determine your own leadership style.

Connecting Academics

Math. You're the CEO of Tropic Aquaria, a rapidly expanding company. You've been managing purchasing but you need to spend more time planning company goals. Purchasing takes 10½ hours a week during a five-day workweek. The employee needs to concentrate on purchasing two days a week. Before you delegate the purchasing workload to an employee, you must look at your staff's schedule. Their work hours are:

Maya	6:30 A.M. to 12 noon
Susan	8:15 A.M. to 3:00 P.M., with an hour lunch
Kele	11:45 A.M. to 5:30 P.M., with a half-hour lunch

Which employee would you assign to purchasing? How many hours a week does this person have left to work on other tasks?

Language Arts. You work at Tropic Aquaria. Tropic Aquaria runs many self-managed teams. You're on a team assigned to plan and make a pamphlet describing how to run a successful work team. Work with a small group and create a pamphlet with helpful tips and guidelines.

BusinessWeek Analyzing the Feature Story

You read the first part of "The Boss in the Web Age" at the beginning of this chapter. Below are a few questions for you to answer about Sylvia Chen and Xcelerent Software Inc. You'll find the answers to these questions when you're reading the entire article. First, here are the questions:

24. What leadership style is best demonstrated by Chen's actions? Give examples to support your argument.
25. How important is communication in regard to one of Xcelerent's new programs?

CREATIVE JOURNAL ACTIVITY

Interview a business or civic leader in your community. Find out how communication and teamwork affect his or her work. What are other keys to success? Report back to the class.

BUSINESS Online
The Full Story

To learn more about business leadership, visit the *Introduction to Business* Web site at **www.introbus.glencoe.com**, and click on *BusinessWeek* Feature Story, Chapter 8.

Chapter 9

Technology's Impact on Business

Learning Objectives

After completing this chapter, you'll be able to:

1. **Explain** how technology influenced business industries.
2. **Describe** the three aspects of the e-workforce.
3. **List** specific examples of e-commerce.
4. **Analyze** the advantages and disadvantages of e-commerce.

Why It's Important

Knowing how technology has influenced business sheds light on new and future industries.

Key Words

e-workforce
digital workflow
start-ups
e-commerce
e-tail
multi-channel retailer
bricks-and-mortar
clicks-and-mortar
e-tickets

BusinessWeek Feature Story

Zen and the Art of Net Start-ups

Banana Republic's Founders Try to Work Their Magic Online. Mel Ziegler remembers the exact moment he figured out the Web. It was 18 months ago when his doctor recommended he take fresh ginseng. Unsure of where to get the stuff, the 55-year-old Zen enthusiast turned to the Web. A quick search led him to a small ginseng farmer in Wisconsin. Ziegler marveled at how he could instantaneously communicate with the farmer in Wisconsin while sitting at his computer in Mill Valley, Calif. He also began to wonder how he and his wife, Patricia, co-founders of Banana Republic and the Republic of Tea, might use the medium for business themselves.

Source: Excerpted with permission from "Zen and the Art of Net Start-ups," *BusinessWeek Online*, October 16, 2000.

An Extension Activity

What challenges do businesses face today as they go to the Internet to extend their markets?

BUSINESS *Online*
The Full Story

To learn more about online start-ups, visit the *Introduction to Business* Web site at **www.introbus.glencoe.com**, and click on *BusinessWeek* Feature Story, Chapter 9.

www.sephora.com

The Cyber Age

Michael Furdyk and his partners sold MyDesktop.com for more than $1 million. Their Web site began just for fun as a help line to explain how the Internet works. What's unusual about this story? Furdyk is only 17 years old and hasn't yet graduated from high school. Furdyk is no fluke. A small but growing number of teenagers are starting online businesses. Eight percent of all teens, about 1.6 million in the United States are making at least some money on the Internet.

Technology's Influence on Business

Thomas Edison said his greatest discovery was discovering what people could use. His inventions include the light bulb, the phonograph, and the movie camera. These made the power, music, and film industries possible. Figure 9.1 rates the top technologists over the past century.

Technology refers to the tools and machines people have invented to make life easier. Inventions like the radio and the television entertain and inform us. The telegraph and then the telephone made it easier to communicate with each other. Trains, cars, and airplanes made it easier to get around.

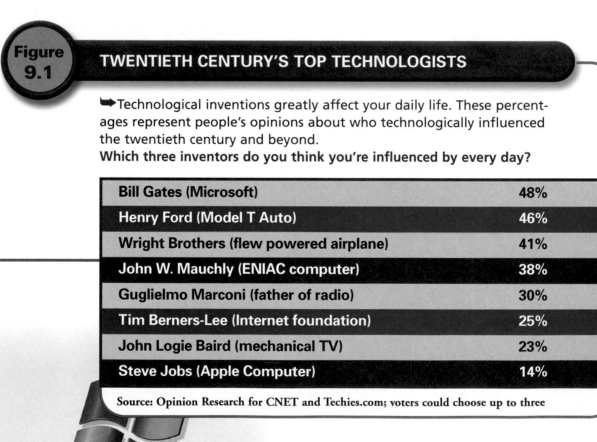

Figure 9.1

TWENTIETH CENTURY'S TOP TECHNOLOGISTS

➡Technological inventions greatly affect your daily life. These percentages represent people's opinions about who technologically influenced the twentieth century and beyond.
Which three inventors do you think you're influenced by every day?

Bill Gates (Microsoft)	48%
Henry Ford (Model T Auto)	46%
Wright Brothers (flew powered airplane)	41%
John W. Mauchly (ENIAC computer)	38%
Guglielmo Marconi (father of radio)	30%
Tim Berners-Lee (Internet foundation)	25%
John Logie Baird (mechanical TV)	23%
Steve Jobs (Apple Computer)	14%

Source: Opinion Research for CNET and Techies.com; voters could choose up to three

Microsoft
Windows xp

Perhaps the most common technology staple today in businesses is the computer. They electronically store thousands of files, which saves time, labor, and office space. Scanners read the prices of products and record sales instantly, making business move much faster. Accounting and bookkeeping computer software programs help organize, plan, and control businesses operations. The film industry uses digital technology to edit film as well as enhance the colorful images and create animated scenes.

Technology in the Past

Even the simplest invention, like the plow, had a huge impact on business. Before the plow was invented, people had to dig in the earth with hand tools. It took forever to plant a field of corn or wheat. The plow made it possible for one person to do the work of 50 in the same amount of time. More corn could be planted which meant more corn could be produced. This meant hiring more people to harvest the corn, selling more corn in the market, and building a corn selling business.

Plows were so useful that making them became a big business. Companies specialized in making plows and other farm tools. Woodworkers and metalworkers were needed to make parts for them. General stores could make money selling them. There was a constant demand to produce new and more efficient tools. John Deere invented a better plow in 1838 and started his own business. Today, Deere & Company is one of the leading makers of farm tools in the world.

Since the plow, countless new inventions have changed the way we live, work, and do business. Steam engines, blast furnaces, and boilers provided ways to produce greater power and made factories possible. The automobile made it possible to transport goods faster. Auto making became a major industry and created new demands in other industries like steel, rubber, glass, and oil. New roads needed to be built, creating a boom in construction. The construction industry created new jobs in trucking, mechanics, and engineering.

A STAKE IN A STEAK
Is it elegant and tender? Firm and hearty? Or what about light and joyous? A cut of meat has more flavor and character than you'd think. Just ask someone at Omaha Steaks, a fifth-generation owned and managed company in Omaha, Nebr. Its new e-commerce site gives you direction your local meat market might not.
Why is it important to take chances in business, particularly when launching a Web site?

continued on p. 131

Modern Technology

In the past 50 years electronics revolutionized business and society. Today, the economies of many countries such as Japan and Taiwan are based on manufacturing electronics. There is a never-ending demand to make electronic goods smaller, faster, cheaper, and more powerful.

Around 1945 a computer took up an entire room and could barely do a math problem. Now a microchip stores billions of bits of information.

Computers were first used only by the military. Now, the computer is an important business tool. It can electronically store thousands of files, saving time and office space. The computer also created a boom in nearly all business industries.

✔ **Fast Review** _____

1. Explain how the plow changed business.
2. How does the computer help businesses?

E-Workforce

A desk jockey with dry, red eyes is sitting in front of a computer at work. Other workers in the office are in front of computers wearing eyestrain eyeglasses. Down a few more cubicle rows another worker rubs the back of her neck. This is a portrait of today's electronic workforce, or e-workforce.

Working Lifestyle

What are you doing at 10 A.M.?

Piecing Together Footage

"I created a career out of skateboarding by filming and editing local skateboarders' 'sponsor me' tapes," says Wing Ko. The homemade videotapes helped the local skateboarders become pros and got Ko's foot in the door of the industry. Today Ko makes money by skate shops selling his videos.

As a self-employed, skater guru, Ko enjoys the life of being his own boss. That requires pounding the pavement all the time to find projects and understand the relationship between art and business. "This is the hardest skill because they're a lethal combination," says Ko, who studied filmmaking at Columbia College in Chicago.

At 10:00 A.M., Ko is either driving to the editing studio or trying to wake up skateboarders to coordinate video shoots. He recommends, "Love what you do because it makes life easier."

Salary

The median income of a photographer and video editor is $20,940, with a range between $15,250 and $30,820.

Outlook for This Career

This highly competitive and creative field is expected to experience steady growth.

Connecting Careers Activity

What other careers do you need a "good eye" for creativity and imagination? Do these appeal to you?

Arts, A/V Technology & Communications

CAREER PATH

E-workforce is when people work with computers while doing business. According to the Bureau of Labor Statistics more than 70 million people use computers daily.

Employment

Technology created a boom in many industries. It created new markets for products like printers, fax machines, video games, cellular telephones, and modems. New products are constantly being invented, developed, and manufactured by various companies. Innovation means more jobs and more people learning new skills. In every office environment, coworkers like to know they have one technology whiz in their company in case something malfunctions. Technology makes people work easier and faster. Its speed saves time and creates new jobs.

Digital Workflow. Placing hard copies of documents on a digital platform, like CD-ROMs or a database has greatly influenced time efficiency. People have access to a broad range of information more quickly than ever before. A library's catalog and sets of encyclopedias are available in digital format. This places information at your fingertips in an instant.

By switching information to a digital format, there is less paper involved. A **digital workflow** links all the steps in a process digitally. For example, digital workflow has greatly influenced the publishing and printing industry. Authors, editors, marketing, manufacturing, and archiving can work together in a seamless electronic pace. Each department's step in the process of creating a book, journal, or newspaper is linked electronically.

Technology Centers. The high-tech industry can be found in practically any city, but it's heavily populated in various technology centers, like California's Silicon Valley, New York's Silicon Alley, Oregon's Silicon Forest, and Austin's Silicon Hill. Next in line is New Mexico. Computer chip manufacturer Intel Corp. already built a facility in Rio Rancho, New Mexico.

New Jobs. One fraction of the high-tech industry is the Internet. It has created a demand for new jobs such as software writers, online writers, and Web page designers. Companies are now able to post job opportunities on their home page, on a newspaper's online classified section, and partner with an Internet job service, like Monster.com.

Real-World Application

part 2 of 4

A STAKE IN A STEAK
Not sure how to properly thaw the filet mignon before Sunday dinner? Omaha Steaks takes pride in its customer service, which is available seven days a week by e-mail or by telephone. More than 1,800 Omaha Steaks employees work to achieve 100-percent-guaranteed service and quality of its products. **Name two things that make Omaha Steaks a success.**

continued on p. 133

✓ Fast Review

1. How has the computer created demands for related products?
2. Name an industry that manages a digital workflow?

Virtual Business

The ease of doing business online has created a boom in new businesses, or **start-ups**. This type of business is called a virtual business. (Virtual business was introduced in Chapter 5.) Vocational schools, universities, colleges, and community centers offer technology training or degrees for people interested in expanding their job skills. These skills will make you very attractive to an employer.

Technology transports your mind to new places in the world. While it would be nice to order a fresh, glazed donut and hot chocolate over the Internet and receive it in five minutes, well, technology isn't there. However, if you don't have a donut shop in your town but still want to purchase donut mix and hot chocolate powder, then you just might be able to purchase these over the Internet.

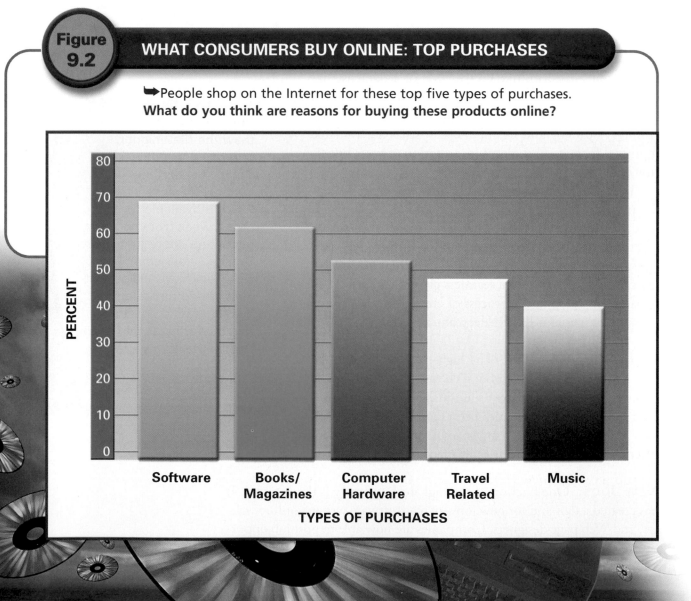

Figure 9.2

WHAT CONSUMERS BUY ONLINE: TOP PURCHASES

➡People shop on the Internet for these top five types of purchases. What do you think are reasons for buying these products online?

Bar chart showing PERCENT (y-axis, 0–80) vs. TYPES OF PURCHASES (x-axis): Software ≈69, Books/Magazines ≈62, Computer Hardware ≈53, Travel Related ≈47, Music ≈40.

E-Commerce

Electronic commerce, or **e-commerce**, has made it possible for businesses to directly reach customers anywhere in the world. Everyone hooked up to the Internet is a potential customer. This hasn't only changed the way products are sold, it has changed the way all business activities are conducted. E-tail and e-ticket are two specific examples of e-commerce.

E-Tail. In Chapter 5 you read about dot-com entrepreneurs. Remember Jeff Bezos? He's the entrepreneur of Amazon.com, a clicks-and-mortar company. As a matter of fact, Amazon.com is a well-known and trusted e-tailer. **E-tail** is electronic retail. The business sells products over the Internet. The main activity of e-commerce is buying and selling goods and services. Figure 9.2 shows you what consumers buy most online. Any company can go online to sell any product.

JCPenney, a major department store, sells products in stores, by mail, and online. This type of company is called a **multi-channel retailer**. It uses several means to sell products. Businesses often call their stores and warehouses **bricks-and-mortar**, referring to building materials. Businesses that also use the Internet are called **clicks-and-mortar** operations.

E-commerce makes it easier to send catalogs of e-tailers' products to consumers. This is especially useful for companies that do a lot of mail-order business, like Land's End. Putting catalogs on the Internet rather than shipping them by mail saves a lot of money in printing and mailing costs.

How does e-tail benefit you as a consumer? Here are the advantages:

- *Convenience.* You can shop at home without going to the store. The Internet is never closed, so you can shop 24 hours a day, 7 days a week. If you don't have access to transportation and you need or want an item, you can buy it online, because it's convenient.

- *Choices.* The number of companies selling products online gives you more choice and lets you compare prices easier. Some online companies allow you to download music, computer games, or preview movies trailers. Look for Web sites that compare and contrast goods, like ZDNet.com. Before buying a new or used car, the Internet has many useful sites to explore all elements of the transaction.

A STAKE IN A STEAK
Poultry, gourmet foods, seafood, veal, and lamb aren't typically online consumers' top purchases. Originally, the Web site was another avenue to sell its products just as it did with mail-order catalogs, direct marketing, and retail stores. Omaha Steaks attributes increased sales over the past two years to the Web site. **Why do you think sales increased?**

continued on p. 135

Writing for Business

Designing Function or Form

This activity gives you the chance to add to your portfolio. Communicate, interview, research, and write your way into a story. Choose one imaginary path, A University's Home Page or Bricks vs. Clicks. Follow your path's steps to complete your own story.

pick a path

A University's Home Page

The Setting. You finally decided to quit your job as a telemarketer and become a freelance Web designer.

Rising Action. The University of Texas has asked you to submit ideas for the design of its new Web site.

Step 1. Using a computer design program or paper, design UT's home page. Look at the Web sites of several colleges and universities for ideas of useful subcategories you could turn into links, including admissions, programs of study, and student life.

Step 2. Use the school colors in your design. Write UT's brief mission statement. Use at least one photograph and other design elements.

Bricks vs. Clicks

The Setting. You support Bookwell, a local independent bookstore, by volunteering to organize its public poetry readings and live acoustic music night on Wednesdays. You work during the day as a Web designer for a design firm.

Rising Action. Your boss has asked you to design a Web page for the firm's new account, Super Books, an online bookstore.

Step 1. You're worried the Super Books e-commerce site will decline the sales at Bookwell. Research how independent bookstores are coping with the advent of mega-online stores.

Step 2. After you've taken a position on whether or not you want to design the Web site, write a letter to your boss, which outlines your position.

Conclusion

Now it's time to write your own story, and reflect on your path. Create and revise a thesis statement for your path. A successful statement does several things: In one sentence it presents the main idea that you'll develop in your paper; it explains your perspective on the topic; and it prepares readers to see how you arrived at your perspective.

On the other hand, there are disadvantages to e-tail. These include:

- *Buying power.* It's easy to overspend. If you're not careful you can order things by mistake.
- *Other charges.* Since most products bought online are delivered by mail, you have to pay shipping charges and usually tax. The exchange and return policies may be pricier than in a store.
- *Immediacy.* While shopping online is convenient, you still have to wait for most products to be delivered. (Unless, of course, you live in New York City. Barnes & Noble online will deliver a book you ordered on the same day.)
- *Relying on observation.* It's hard to know for sure whether you like a sofa unless you sit down and try it. The same can be said for clothes, CDs, or books. Online buying requires you to rely on pictures and descriptions instead of actually touching things yourself.

E-Ticket. With more than 70 million people signed onto the Internet in the United States alone, businesses are finding that customers want to buy services online as well goods. Using their computers, people can now purchase **e-tickets**, or electronic tickets. E-tickets are available for concerts, museums, airlines, movies, and amusement parks.

Some people find purchasing an e-ticket is easier and cheaper than visiting an actual store. For example, a travel agency may charge you a $8 to $25 fee for handling your airline ticket. If you buy a ticket from an online virtual business travel agency you may only be charged $1.

On the other hand, if an airline lost your e-ticket in its system you might be required to buy another ticket. An e-ticket makes it more difficult to transfer to another airline if your flight is cancelled. Due to this, it's often better to have paper tickets. The do-it-yourself attitude to making travel arrangements isn't great news for travel agents. Jupiter Communications estimates that online travel sites will account for 62 percent of online bookings, where as travel agencies will sell 20 percent of conventional ticket sales. E-business in travel is nearly a $70 billion a year industry. There are always precautions you should take when purchasing a ticket online. Always write down the amount of the ticket and the date when you purchased it.

A STAKE IN A STEAK
Omaha Steaks felt its Web site had to be fluid, easy to use, and navigable otherwise customers might lose patience. Shopping online is a convenient, time-saving activity that's complete with a click of a mouse. **What have been your experiences with online shopping?**

✔ **Fast Review** _____

1. How does e-commerce differ from e-workforce?
2. What is a multi-channel retailer?

Summary

1. Technology refers to the tools and machines people have invented to make life easier. Often they inform us and are entertaining. Technology affects business by saving labor, increasing production, and creating new industries.

2. The e-workforce involves people using technology and learning new skills to work it. Part of this includes working with a digital workflow. People have access to a broad range of information more quickly then ever. The growth of technology centers attracts droves of people trying to jump aboard the tech industry's workforce. The new tech jobs might be anything computer related from graphics to database management to quality control. High-tech jobs on the Internet are only a fraction of the entire e-workforce.

3. E-commerce, or electronic commerce, is business done using the Internet. E-tail and e-tickets are two specific examples of e-commerce. People buy many goods online. Consumers buy software, books/magazines, computer hardware, travel tickets, and music the most often online.

4. E-tail has its advantages and disadvantages. On the one hand, buying online is convenient and offers you many choices. On the other hand, it's easy to overspend, you might have to pay for additional charges, products aren't always immediately delivered, and you must rely on observation.

● Using Business Key Words

Technology has dramatically changed the way industry and consumers do business. Match each term below with the correct statement.

- **e-commerce**
- **e-tickets**
- **multi-channel retailer**
- **clicks-and-mortar**
- **bricks-and-mortar**
- **e-tail**
- **start-ups**
- **digital workflow**
- **e-workforce**

1. Short for electronic tickets.
2. The use of both the Internet and buildings, such as stores and warehouses, to do business.
3. Business conducted on the Internet, or electronic commerce.
4. A company that uses several means to sell products, such as retail stores, mail-order catalogs, and the Internet.
5. Businesses that are starting up.
6. People who work with computers while doing business.
7. Linking all the steps in a process digitally.
8. Electronic retailing, or selling, on the Internet.
9. The stores and warehouses that businesses use; referring to the building materials.

Review What You Learned

10. What does the term clicks-and-mortar mean?
11. What is the major reason e-commerce is so popular with consumers?
12. Why is it so convenient to shop online?
13. Describe the disadvantages of e-commerce to consumers.
14. How has e-workforce shaped employment?
15. Give an example of e-commerce.
16. What are three advantages of e-commerce to business?
17. Give two examples of technology that changed business before the invention of computers.

Understanding Business Concepts

18. How does technology change the world of business?
19. Have you ever purchased something online? If so, describe the experience, any problems that occurred, and whether or not you would do it again.
20. Describe how an online company might function as an intermediary.
21. Name two companies that could be described as multi-channel retailers.
22. How can consumers create financial problems for themselves by shopping online?
23. Explain why e-commerce sellers build customer profiles.
24. Do you, as a consumer, feel more loyalty to online companies than bricks-and-mortar businesses or the other way around? Give examples.
25. What trends do you see happening in the e-workforce in the upcoming years?
26. Give an example of digital workflow in your school or work.

Critical Thinking

27. Do you think it's possible for a retailer to be successful as a bricks-and-mortar business but unsuccessful in the online world? Explain why or why not.
28. Are there any products you would never buy online? Explain your answer.
29. Why do you think small business owners are likely to use e-mail, banner ads, and other online tactics to get their message out?
30. Eight percent of all teens, about 1.6 million in the United States, are making money on the Internet. Why are more teens than ever becoming online entrepreneurs?

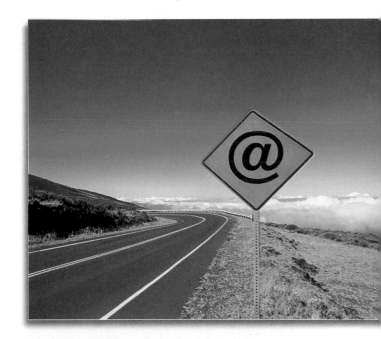

Viewing and Representing

Examining the Image. Looking at the photograph, list at least ten things that come to mind. How will the technology influence businesses and consumers in the next three years?

● Building Academic Skills

 Creating a Pamphlet

Work with a partner to create a pamphlet for consumers to use when planning to shop online. Include the advantages and disadvantages of shopping online and suggestions for how consumers can protect themselves from potential problems. Also include a list of reputable Web sites for the beginner. If possible, use the computer to make the pamphlet and distribute to students in your school.

 Online Merchant

Select an online merchant and evaluate the Web site for the following information:
- user friendliness
- type of product or service
- payment procedures
- return policy

HISTORY Illustrating History

Choose a type of technology, other than the computer, and research its history. Describe when it was invented, who invented it, how it is used, and its prospects for the future. Create a poster illustrating the technology's history and display it in your classroom.

MATH Graphing Growth

Recent reports estimate that over 16 million people logged onto the Internet for the first time last year. Conduct research to determine the growth of the Internet over the last ten years. Graph your results.

● Linking School to Home

Online Shopping. Research the e-commerce sites that allow consumers to grocery shop online. Although this service is not available in all communities, it's a fast-growing service. Find out how the prices compare on ten products that you and your family purchase frequently. Then ask your parents or other family members if they would ever grocery shop online. Have them explain why or why not.

● Linking School to Work

Local E-Commerce. Interview a manager from a local business to find out how e-commerce has impacted his or her business. Ask the following questions:
- Has e-commerce helped or hurt the business?
- How is business conducted differently now that e-commerce is a viable option for consumers?
- Are there any plans to add e-commerce as another channel of distribution?

Report your findings to the class.

E-Homework

Applying Technology

Distance Learning. Using the Internet, research online high schools and universities such as the Florida Online High School or the University of Phoenix. Write a two-page paper describing online education. Do you think there is a future for online learning? Is it for you? Why or why not?

Online Survey. Conduct a survey of the online service providers used by the students in your class. Find out which provider they use, their level of satisfaction, any problems that occur, and the monthly cost. Create a chart showing the results. If possible, conduct the survey with all the students in your school and compare your results.

Connecting Academics

Math. In a year, half of Dell Computer's sales, $16 billion, came from e-commerce. Overall, corporate and government customers account for 75 percent of its sales. The rest of Dell's sales are to consumers. For the year, what is the total dollar figure of Dell's sales to consumers?

Computer/Technology. Tomorrow, you're in charge of a power meeting to plan your company's use of CD-ROMs, databases, and the latest storage technology to place information quickly and easily at the fingertips of employees. You know that an agenda is a powerful tool for successful meetings. Use the Internet to research current ideas on agendas for successful meetings. Create the agenda for your meeting tomorrow using software suitable for this task.

BusinessWeek Analyzing the Feature Story

You read the first part of "Zen and the Art of Net Startups" at the beginning of this chapter. Below are a few questions for you to answer about online start-ups. You'll find the answers to these questions when you're reading the entire article. First, here are the questions:

31. Are the founders of ZoZa.com planning to sell exclusively online or as a multi-channel retailer?

32. Why is this strategy important?

CREATIVE JOURNAL ACTIVITY

Research an online e-tailer of your choice. How many different products is it offering through its site? Is it selling exclusively online or through multiple channels? Summarize your findings in a one-page report.

BUSINESS Online
The Full Story

To learn more about online start-ups, visit the *Introduction to Business* Web site at **www.introbus.glencoe.com**, and click on *BusinessWeek* Feature Story, Chapter 9.

Unit 2
Small Business

Discovering Small Business

In Chapter 5 you read about the advantages and disadvantages of entrepreneurship. An entrepreneur is a person who recognizes a business opportunity and organizes, manages, and assumes the risks of a business enterprise. Many of the topics in other chapters of this unit are also important for an entrepreneur to know. For example, an entrepreneur needs to know how to organize a new business and how to create a management plan (Chapter 7). Knowing how technology will affect a new business is another important consideration of the entrepreneur.

Factoids

What Qualifies as Small?

BusinessWeek classifies public, small companies with sales between $25 million and $1.5 billion.

Employee Loyalty.

Almost 80 percent of employees working for small companies say that they're very loyal to their companies. In contrast, only 48 percent of those who work for companies with more than 1,000 employees say they're very loyal.

Path for Retiring Entrepreneurs.

When they retire, older entrepreneurs may close down full-scale operations. However, many plan to stay in business. Some will work as consultants and others will start part-time businesses with only themselves to manage.

Employment Opportunities.

Twenty-two percent of small businesses plan to expand their workforce in the near future.

Capital Expenditures.

Two-thirds of small businesses reported recently spending money on new buildings or upgrading current buildings.

Investigate the Images

Look at the collage on the left page. What do you see? What do you think? What do think the images represent? The power of reading visuals is in analyzing and dissecting your observations. On a separate piece of paper reconstruct the worksheet below in order to complete your investigation. The questions may help shape and focus your analysis.

Your Observations

1. How many photographs do you see?

2. Examine each image. How is each assembled in relation to one another?

3. What is the subject of each photograph?

4. Does color signify a message?

5. What issues do you take from these images?

Information

6. Summarize what you know about the photographs from your observations.

Exploring Culture

7. How does the emphasis on individual achievement in U.S. culture contribute to the success of entrepreneurs in this country? Can you think of activities offered at your school that may foster individuality or an entrepreneurial spirit?

8. How do television shows affect your view about entrepreneurship and small business ownership? What messages do these shows give you about having or starting a small business?

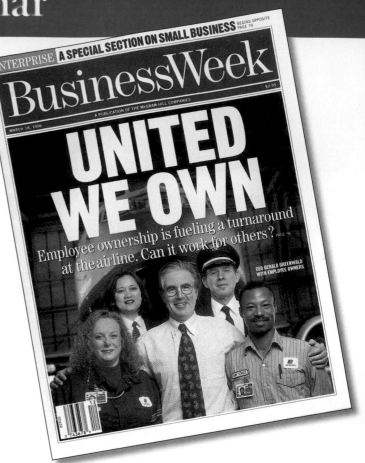

Taking Aim at Small Business

● Preparation

Research an idea for a new business, test market it, and decide how to structure your new company.

Objective

In this *BusinessWeek* Seminar, you'll:

- **Research** a new business idea.
- **Create** a business plan for your idea.
- **Present** your ideas to a group of potential investors.
- **Analyze** the potential of your business and make changes based on feedback from your classmates.

Materials Needed

✓ Notebook paper
✓ Flip chart paper
✓ Construction paper
✓ Pencils
✓ Pens
✓ Markers

● Procedures

1. Brainstorm about products or services that your classmates or community may want or need. Here are a few ideas:
   - Sell a product that is labeled with the school mascot (for example, pencils, plastic cups, or pennants).
   - Offer a tutoring service to students in a specific subject before midterms and final exams.
   - Offer a car wash.

2. Research your idea using one of the following techniques.

- Investigate the competition. How does the competition differ from what you plan to do? What would you do similarly? How are they pricing their product or service? How do they get it to their customer?
- Survey your intended customer. Write a one-page questionnaire to find out more about your customer.

3. Write a two-page business plan. See Chapter 5 for the elements of a business plan.

4. Summarize your business plan on four sheets of flip chart paper. Be creative in how you illustrate your idea.

5. Present your business idea to your classmates. Make sure to include what you would like them to do. Are you looking for financial investment? Employees? Customers?

Chart It

Find out what your classmates think of your business idea by asking them the following questions.

Strengths	What do they like about your plan? What are its best elements?
Weaknesses	What about the business idea seems unrealistic or difficult?
Opportunities	What changes do they recommend to increase the potential of the business? What opportunities did your plan miss?
Threats	Who do they see as your competition? What other obstacles will you need to overcome to make your business a success?

Create a SWOT analysis. SWOT is an acronym that stands for **s**trengths, **w**eaknesses, **o**pportunities, and **t**hreats. Companies use the SWOT analysis as a technique that evaluates a company's internal strengths and weaknesses and its external opportunities and threats. Together as a class, use your SWOT table to discuss the information.

Analyze and Conclude

After creating the SWOT table, answer the questions below:

1. **Decision Making.** What new things did you learn that would help make your business idea more successful? What changes do you need to make to your plan based on the discussion with your classmates? Were there any suggestions that you won't add to your plan?

2. **Negotiating to Arrive at a Decision.** Share your revised plan with the classmates, who made suggestions that you plan to implement. Do they support your plan more?

3. **Reasoning.** If you were to move forward, would you start over with a new idea or move forward with what you have created?

Becoming an Informed Citizen

Congratulations, you finished the *Business-Week* Seminar. Now it's time to reflect on the decisions you made.

Critical Thinking. What are the essential skills and talents you need to be an entrepreneur? How is entrepreneurship different from what you expected? How is it similar?

Analyzing Your Future. Do you think you would prefer starting your own business or working for someone else?

Further Exploration
To find out more about an entrepreneurship and small business, visit the Glencoe *Introduction to Business* Web site, **www.introbus.glencoe.com**.

Unit 3

Groups Affecting Business

A Model Material

It's early morning on a California boardwalk. You see a surfer riding the leftover wind swell. You also notice someone managing a small radio-controlled plane. What do the surfboard and this plane have in common? Balsa wood. Grown internationally and imported, it's a raw material used for boat and raft building, surfboards, and model airplanes.

● **The Raw Material**
Deep in a Costa Rican jungle grow a few balsa trees, which are valued for their strength and buoyancy.

● **Before Harvesting**
Balsa, a common name for a tropical tree or corkwood, grows to the height of about 70 feet. They grow for at least four years.

● **Free-Market Competition**
The Costa Rican government has begun business transactions with the U.S. government to ensure its share in the global market.

● **Imported to the United States**
The United States imports nearly $96 million worth of tropical wood from Latin America.

● **U.S. Exports to Costa Rica**
The best prospects for U.S. agricultural exports to Costa Rica include: (1) soybeans, (2) corn, (3) wheat, (4) rough rice, (5) fresh fruit, (6) processed fruit/vegetables, and (7) snack foods.

Business in a Global Economy

Learning Objectives

After completing this chapter, you'll be able to:

1. **Explain** why nations need to trade with each other.
2. **Describe** how currency exchange works.
3. **State** the advantages of protectionism and free trade.
4. **Name** types of trade barriers.
5. **Identify** some of the major trade alliances in the world today.

Why It's Important

Global trade doesn't just influence business, it also affects all the countries and people of the world.

Key Words

multinational corporation
imports
exports
exchange rate
balance of trade
protectionism
tariff
quota
embargo
free trade

BusinessWeek Feature Story

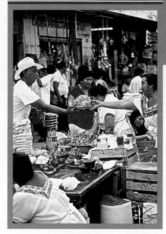

The Bumpy Road to Global Trade

A Trade Mission Can Put Your Company on the Map. Mary Ellen Mooney, co-owner of $15 million Mooney Farms, was a woman with a mission. She had joined "Baja 2000," a trade tour to Mexico, with one overriding goal: to sell her sun-dried tomato products up and down the coastline they call the Mexican Riviera.

There were problems from the start. First, the bus carrying about 20 California entrepreneurs in food-related businesses spent 45 minutes waiting in Tijuana for one of the organizers. As the bus edged southward along the coastal road, the group was dismayed to see the rugged seascape marred by haphazard lean-tos, ancient trailers, and windblown trash.

Source: Excerpted with permission from "The Bumpy Road to Global Trade," *BusinessWeek Online*, October 9, 2000.

An Extension Activity

What are some problems businesses may face if they try selling their goods or services to another country?

BUSINESS
Online

The Full Story

To learn more about global trade, visit the *Introduction to Business* Web site at **www.introbus.glencoe.com**, and click on *BusinessWeek* Feature Story, Chapter 10.

Global Producers and Consumers

You may not know it but you're a part of the global marketplace. You might buy clothes made in Taiwan. Turnover your alarm clock, is there a sticker that reads, "Made in Indonesia"? In the future, you might work for a French company in the United States or for an American company in Paris. During the last 20 years, the United States and other nations have greatly relied on one another's goods and services to stay prosperous. The global marketplace exists anywhere business crosses national borders. Most countries don't produce everything their citizens want. A country might not have the necessary resources, it might not have the technology, or perhaps it's not interested in making the product. However, countries can satisfy their citizens' wants and needs by buying goods in the global market. A consumer, citizen, employee, and business leader of the twenty-first century must have an understanding of international trade and business in order to be an informed decision maker.

Figure 10.1 — MAJOR EXPORTS AND IMPORTS OF THE UNITED STATES

➡Look at the graph to see what products the United States imports and exports.
Name the product that the United States exports more than it imports.

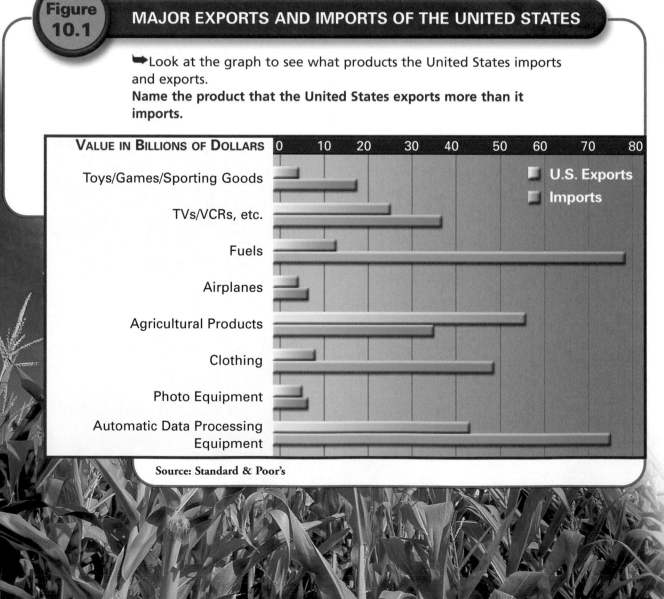

Source: Standard & Poor's

The Global Marketplace

A company that does business in many countries and has facilities and offices in many countries around the world is a **multinational corporation**. The global marketplace works much like a shopping mall or a supermarket. You go to the store to buy things you need that you can't make yourself, like bread or jeans. In Figure 10.1, notice what products the United States imports and exports. More than likely, you've purchased more than one of these products before.

No matter how much a country produces, it can't make everything itself. The United States is rich in resources—human, natural, and production—but it still needs things from other countries.

Specialization

Specialization builds and sustains a market economy. Few people produce all of the goods and services that they need. Instead, individuals concentrate their activities in a particular area or field, such as being a carpenter, a doctor, or an administrative assistant. Each worker's money buys goods and services that others have specialized in producing. With specialization, everyone is dependent on each other for goods and services.

Countries also specialize and trade some of the items that they produce, in order to gain other countries' goods and services. For example, the United States, Japan, and Germany are the world's top automobile producers. They have the resources—materials, technology, factories, and labor force—needed to produce a large volume of cars. Actually, these countries have a comparative advantage in producing cars—meaning that this is a strong area of production compared to other ways they could use their resources. Other countries could become major producers of cars. Many of them have decided that they have a comparative advantage in producing something else, leaving auto production to such countries as the United States, Japan, and Germany. Money gained from the sales of the cars to other countries is then used to buy items that those other countries produce.

The kinds of resources available to a country often influence what it specializes in producing. For example, a major industry for Colombia is the production of coffee. The climate, soil, and environmental conditions are right for it to produce coffee. Few nations in the world have a climate suitable for raising large amounts of coffee. The United States could raise coffee, but would require a costly controlled environment.

Real-World Application

part **1** of 4

CULTURAL CUISINE

What's for dinner you ask? If Peggy and Andrew Cherng have their way, they'll make sure Chinese food is on your weekly dinner menu. The owners of Panda Restaurant Group are among other business owners interested in serving ethnic food from across the world to your grumbling stomach. The Cherng's founded and built Panda Express, the largest Chinese restaurant chain in history. **In the global marketplace, what is the importance of specialization?**

continued on p. 151

Therefore, Columbia has a comparative advantage in producing coffee. The United States doesn't have that comparative advantage.

A country with little money or advanced technology but a large population might specialize in manual labor. This means the wages are probably low. In a number of highly populated countries in Asia, such as South Korea and Taiwan, one of their specializations is the assembling of color televisions, videocassette recorders, and computer components sold around the world. Without trade each nation would try to produce the items that it needs and wants, some of which wouldn't be very natural or efficient for them to produce. Similarly, you couldn't specialize in doing one type of job, such as teaching, fixing cars, and building houses unless you had the opportunity to get other things that you need and want from others.

Countries specialize in producing certain goods and services. By specializing, countries can sell what they produce best so they can buy the products they need from other countries. Many countries don't have the capital resources to manufacture goods but have valuable natural resources. Kuwait specializes in producing oil. Some countries like Israel and Ireland rely a lot on their culture to attract tourism. The United States has a wide range of resources so it can specialize in many products such as wheat, cars, and movies.

Types of Trade

The United States buys pepper from India, bananas from Honduras, and coffee from Columbia. These products are called imports. **Imports** are goods and services that a country buys from another country. The

You Make the Call

Global Ethics

You're the buyer for a large department store chain that sells clothing at reasonable prices. Many underdeveloped countries manufacture clothing that the company sells. These manufacturers pay their employees low wages and they work in hot warehouses.

Making an Ethical Decision

1. What are the benefits and drawbacks of a global economy for the United States?
2. What are the benefits and drawbacks of globalization for people living in underdeveloped countries?
3. How can underdeveloped countries break into world markets?
4. Should prosperous, industrialized nations monitor labor issues in other countries? If so, how? If not, who should monitor these issues?

United States also sells wheat and corn syrup to places like Mexico and Australia. These products are exports. **Exports** are goods and services that one country sells to another country. One country's exports are another country's imports.

Imports and exports aren't the only types of trade between countries. Countries can invest in other countries by building factories there. Nations also exchange human resources, like doctors, managers, and engineers. Tourism, military aid, and loans are other types of trade. Countries also export cultural products like movies and music. A movie can involve several types of trade. It can be produced by an American company, filmed in Mexico with a Mexican crew, and shown in theaters all over Europe.

Currency

Countries don't directly trade with each other as if swapping clothes for computers. They have to pay for each other's products with *currency*. Currency is another name for money. Just as different countries use different languages they also use different currencies. Americans use dollars, Mexicans use pesos, and the Japanese use yen.

If a tourist from Japan wants to buy something from you, you expect to get paid in dollars, not yen. This means the tourist exchanges his or her yen for dollars at a bank first. The same goes for companies that do business with other countries. If an American company wants to import cheese from a French producer it has to pay for it in euros. To do that, the company has to change dollars into euros on the *foreign exchange market*. The foreign exchange market is made up of banks where different currencies are exchanged.

Exchange Rates. Different currencies have different values compared to each other. The price at which one currency can buy another currency is called its **exchange rate**. For example, one American dollar is worth a certain number of Mexican pesos or Japanese yen. Exchange rates change from day to day and from country to country. One day the value of the American dollar might go up compared to the Mexican peso, but down compared to the Japanese yen. How much the currency of a country is worth depends on how many other countries want to buy its products. If every country wants TVs and VCRs from Japan they'll need Japanese yen to buy them. The increased demand for the yen makes its value increase. If no one wants products from Japan, the value of the yen decreases.

CULTURAL CUISINE
Cherng created the Panda Express concept in 1983 when he modified his cuisine to fit into the shopping mall's food court atmosphere in Glendale, Calif. Instead of rice and egg rolls, he adapted the recipes of his late father, Ming-Tsai, an international chef. Tender orange-flavored chicken and tofu dishes topped off the menu. Now, the fast-food chain is in Japan and Puerto Rico, as well as the United States.
As a restaurant owner, what kinds of things might you import and export?

continued on p. 153

Prices. A company follows the change in exchange rates to find the best prices for products. When the value of a country's currency goes up compared to another country's, it has a *favorable exchange rate*. When it goes down, it has an *unfavorable exchange rate*. A country with a favorable exchange rate can buy more of the other country's products. If American dollars go up compared to French euros, it will take fewer dollars to buy French cheese. It also means that American products will cost more for the French to buy. The United States might import more French cheese, but the French might import fewer American TVs. Some countries choose to lower the value of their currency to bring in more business. (It's like putting everything in a store on sale.) When this happens it costs less to buy products from that country. Other countries can build factories and hire labor more cheaply there.

Balance of Trade

A country wants to have more money coming in than going out. The difference in the value between how much a country imports and how much it exports is called its **balance of trade**. When a country exports more than it imports, it has a *trade surplus*. That means it has money left over to buy more products. When a country imports more than it exports, it has a *trade deficit*. That means it is in debt.

A country can have an unfavorable balance of trade with one country and a favorable balance with another. For instance, the United States has a favorable balance with Brazil but an unfavorable balance with France. Overall the United States imports far more than it exports so it has a large trade deficit. Until the 1980s, the United States had a trade surplus. By the year 2000, it had run up a trade deficit of about $330 billion. This changed mostly because of competition from other countries.

✓ Fast Review

1. Give examples of how countries specialize based on the types of resources they have.
2. Name types of trade between countries other than imports and exports.
3. Why would a country want to devalue its currency?

Global Competition

In the global marketplace, countries benefit from buying one another's products. Countries compete to make the same products. The United States, Japan, and Germany all specialize in making cars. China and the Ukraine both produce steel.

Global competition often leads to *trade disputes* between countries. At the heart of most trade disputes is whether there should be limits on trade or whether trade should be unrestricted. There are two opposing points of view: free trade and protectionism.

Protectionism

Protectionism is the practice of putting limits on foreign trade to protect businesses at home. Most countries sell what they produce at home so they often want to keep out foreign competitors. They also have reasons not to share what they produce with other countries. Here are some of the reasons in favor of protectionism:

- Foreign competition can lower the demand for products made at home.
- Companies at home need to be protected from unfair foreign competition.
- Industries that make products related to national defense, like satellites, aircraft, and weapons, need to be protected.
- The use of cheap labor in other countries can lower wages or threaten jobs at home.
- A country can become too dependent on another country for important products like oil, steel, or grain.
- Other countries might not have the same environmental or human rights standards.

Trade Barriers. To limit competition from other countries, governments put up *trade barriers* to keep foreign products out. For example, the United States and Brazil both produce sugar, but Brazil can sell it in the United States for less. The U.S. government can protect sugar producers at home in three different ways—with a tariff, a quota, or an embargo.

A **tariff** is a tax placed on imports to increase their price in the domestic market. By adding a tax on Brazilian sugar, the United States can make it more expensive than American sugar. A **quota** is a limit placed on the quantities of a product that can be imported. If the United States allows only a small amount of Brazilian sugar into the United States, Americans still have to buy American sugar. An **embargo** is when the government decides to stop an import or export of a product. Embargoes are rare and usually used against another country for political or military reasons.

Real-World Application

part **3** of 4

CULTURAL CUISINE
Beside the Cherng's, investors also estimate that the next big thing in dining is Chinese food. With a hot marketplace comes competition. Panda Express competitor P.F. Chang's China Bistro chain is launching Pei Wei, a similar fast-food service. The pressure to remain successful has the Cherng's looking at business expansion plans. **By expanding operations domestically and internationally, how does this affect the economies involved?**

continued on p. 155

Free Trade

Economic or foreign policy often determines which countries trade with other countries. Globalization stirs up the controversy about what kind of foreign trade policy to uphold. Supporters of **free trade** believe there should be no limits on trade. All countries should be free to compete anywhere in the world without restrictions. Free trade offers several benefits:

- It opens up new markets in other countries. There are 250 million potential customers in the United States but 6 billion worldwide.
- It creates new jobs, especially in areas related to global trade like shipping, banking, and communications.
- Competition forces businesses to be more efficient and productive.
- Consumers have more choice in the variety, price, and quality of products.
- It promotes cultural understanding and cooperation between countries.
- It helps all countries raise their standard of living.

Trade Alliances. As the economy becomes more global, the trend among countries is toward more free trade. To reduce limits on trade more countries are forming *trade alliances* with each other. In a trade alliance, several countries merge their economies into one huge market. (See Figure 10.2.) For example, NAFTA (North American Free Trade Agreement) combined the economies of the United States, Canada, and

Figure 10.2

MAP OF TRADE ALLIANCES IN THE WORLD

➡The European Union (EU) is the oldest and best-known economic community formed to promote free trade among the members of the community and to foster common economic policies.
What nations make up the European Union?

NAFTA

EU

ASEAN

Mexico. As a result, it is easier for the United States to buy oil from Mexico and to sell its cars there. Free trade is good in general, but it's not painless. NAFTA was controversial specifically because some workers would be displaced when trade barriers were lowered. Opponents predicted that some high-paid American jobs would be lost to Mexico. Proponents predicted that trade among all three nations would increase dramatically, stimulating growth and bringing a wider variety of lower-cost goods to everyone, protectionists and free traders alike.

With trade alliances, instead of countries competing against other countries, whole areas of the world compete against each other. Some of the major trade alliances in the world today are:

- NAFTA (includes the United States, Canada, and Mexico)
- European Union (EU) (Austria, Belgium, Denmark, Finland, France, Germany, Great Britain, Greece, Ireland, Italy, Luxembourg, the Netherlands, Portugal, Spain, and Sweden)
- Association of Southeast Asian Nations (ASEAN) (Indonesia, Malaysia, Philippines, Singapore, Thailand, Brunei, Vietnam, Laos, Myanmar, and Cambodia)

International Business and Finance Affects Everyone

Understanding international business and finance has become increasingly important for the consumer, wage earner, investor, citizen, and business leader. Citizens should understand international trade in order to make decisions in the polling booth: Does a candidate support or oppose free trade? Investors need to understand international trade when investing in companies both here and in other countries. Which firms will be successful in generating international business and which will not? What will the exchange rate be for the dollar in six months if you decide to sell a particular foreign stock?

An understanding of international business helps you understand why goods and services are at particular prices. You'll also be able to understand why you can buy more goods in some countries than in others. The business leader of tomorrow will have a good grasp of international business and finance.

CULTURAL CUISINE
The Cherng's have their eyes set on expanding the business instead of selling out to a mega company. They want to keep it in the family. Their business vision includes opening 10,000 stores. Currently there are 423 Panda Express outlets, employing over 5,000 people. Outlets are franchised, owned by financial investors, and owned by the Cherngs.
How might Panda Express change domestic culture?

✓ Fast Review

1. What is a trade war?
2. What are some of the major trade alliances in the world today?

Summary

1. Countries need to trade with each other because they cannot produce everything themselves.

2. The currency exchange market is made up of different currencies from around the world. To trade with one another countries have to convert their currency into foreign currency.

3. Countries use trade barriers to protect businesses at home from foreign competition. Free trade opens up new markets, creates jobs, gives consumers more choice, and promotes cooperation between countries.

4. Three types of trade barriers are tariffs, quotas, and embargoes.

5. Major trade alliances include NAFTA, EU, and ASEAN.

• Using Business Key Words

Technological advances, trade alliances, and changes in trade barriers have created a global economy. Match the following terms with their definitions to find out how much you know about the global marketplace.

- **imports**
- **protectionism**
- **exports**
- **tariff**
- **exchange rate**
- **quota**
- **balance of trade**
- **embargo**
- **free trade**
- **multinational corporation**

1. Products made in one country and sold in another.
2. A fixed limit, set by the government, on the import of a product.
3. A complete ban on a product or all the products from another country.
4. A view that there should be limits on foreign trade in order to protect business at home.
5. Products one country buys from another country.
6. A special tax on goods made in one country and sold in the United States.
7. The price at which one currency can buy another currency.
8. The difference in value between how much a country imports and how much it exports.
9. A view that all countries should be free to compete anywhere in the world without restrictions.
10. A company that does business in many countries and has facilities and offices in many countries.

Review What You Learned

11. Where is the global marketplace?
12. What are imports? What are exports?
13. Define the foreign exchange market.
14. How is the value of a country's currency determined?
15. Why does a country want to export more than it imports?
16. Why does global competition often lead to trade disputes?
17. What is the difference between protectionism and free trade?
18. Define a tariff, a quota, and an embargo.
19. Which trade alliance does the United States belong to?

Understanding Business Concepts

20. How are consumers and producers dependent on other countries?
21. The United States specializes in wheat, cars, and movies. Name some other goods and services that you think the United States specializes in producing.
22. Is it possible for one country to have a favorable balance of trade with one country and an unfavorable balance of trade with another? Explain.
23. Do you think companies in the United States need to be protected from unfair foreign competition? Why or why not?
24. Give an argument for and against having tariffs on imports.
25. Trade barriers can work both ways. Describe why this can be a problem.
26. How does free trade provide consumers with more choices?
27. Name three products you have purchased recently that were imported into the United States.

Critical Thinking

28. Should the United States trade with any country that produces the goods and services that we need and want, regardless of that country's political beliefs? Why or why not?
29. Suppose a country can produce everything its people need at less than it would cost to import these items from other countries. Should that country trade with other countries? Explain.
30. If a product shipped from the United States to Japan is considered a U.S. export, then what is it considered in Japan?
31. Protectionism in Japan may help certain segments of the economy, such as rice farmers or autoworkers, but it doesn't help Japanese consumers. Why would this be?

Viewing and Representing

Examining the Image. With a partner, look closely at this picture. Compare this scene in Bangkok with a typical business district you'd expect to see in a city near you. What's the same, and what's different?

Chapter 10 Review

Building Academic Skills

Social Science — International Business

Understanding how other countries conduct business is important in the global marketplace. Choose a country and research the business and social etiquette that you would need to know and understand before doing business in that country. If possible, include the following:

- Non-verbal communication and gestures
- Verbal communication
- Cultural do's and don'ts
- Dining out
- Business attire
- Gifts and greetings
- Business negotiations

Create a poster of your findings and display in your classroom.

Computer Technology — Graphics Software

Conduct online research to determine how and to what extent your state participates in global trade. Use graphing software to create pie charts that show (1) the percentage breakdown of the products exported to other countries and (2) the percentage breakdown of export income as a portion of state resources.

Math — Graph It

NAFTA created a total market of nearly 374 million people: 27 million live in Canada, 255 million live in the United States, and 92 million live in Mexico. Graph this data in a format that would best explain it.

Language Arts — Interview and Report

Use the local telephone directory to locate a business in your community that imports products. Interview the person directly involved with purchasing the products. Compare your findings with the others in your class.

Linking School to Home

Locating International Products. Create a list of international products that you and your family enjoy. Using a world map, locate the countries where the products were produced. Then, determine whether or not a similar product is made in the United States. If it is, what makes the international product more attractive to purchase?

Linking School to Work

Charting Exchange Rates. Choose one of the countries from the list you developed in the *Linking School to Home* activity. Research the country's currency and the current rate of exchange. As a class, create a chart that combines all the countries, their currency, and exchange rates. Then, invite someone from a local bank that deals with currency exchange to speak to the class. Prepare questions ahead of time and include the following:

- Is there a cost involved when exchanging currency? If so, what is that cost?
- When traveling to another country, is it better to exchange currency before going to the country? If not, why not?
- How are imported and exported products affected by the exchange rates?

E-Homework

Applying Technology

Internet Search on Trade Alliances. Use the Internet to research one of the trade alliances discussed in this chapter. Find out which countries are involved, when the alliance began, why it was formed, and the impact of the alliance on the rest of the world.

Creating an Advertisement. Imagine you work for a business that exports their products to customers all over the world. Select one of the countries your company markets to and use the computer to create an advertisement for a product your company produces. Research the language, design, and colors that would be appropriate in the advertisement.

Connecting Academics

Math. Next week you'll take an exciting biking trip in Thailand. You have $850 for your trip. When your plane arrives in Bangkok, you'll convert your U.S. dollars to Thai baht. The service charge for exchanging currency is a flat rate of 185 baht. Using the exchange rate below, how many baht will the clerk give you?

1 U.S. dollar = 45.3 Thai baht

History. Research trade barriers and find facts that interest you. Visualize a picture representing global trade barriers. Draw the picture you see. Include at least three types of trade barriers in your picture. Use pencil, markers, watercolors, or collage techniques. Make the picture realistic or abstract, but be prepared to explain your artwork.

BusinessWeek Analyzing the Feature Story

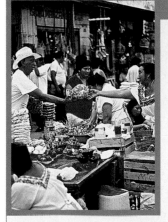

You read the first part of "The Bumpy Road to Global Trade" at the beginning of this chapter. Below are a few questions for you to answer about trade alliances and Mooney Farms. You'll find the answers to these questions when you're reading the entire article. First, here are the questions:

32. Which trade alliances make it possible for Mooney Farms to sell its sun-dried tomatoes on the Mexican Riviera?
33. What benefit of free trade is Mooney Farms trying to take advantage of by attending the "Baja 2000" trade tour?

CREATIVE JOURNAL ACTIVITY

Mooney improvised and set out on her own. Take a few minutes and think of a situation in your life when you had to improvise. How did you cope? What did you learn? Write it down in your journal.

BUSINESS Online
The Full Story

To learn more about global trade, visit the *Introduction to Business* Web site at **www.introbus.glencoe.com**, and click on *BusinessWeek* Feature Story, Chapter 10.

Chapter 11

The Role of Government in Business

Learning Objectives

After reading this chapter, you'll be able to:

1. **Describe** ways government protects business.
2. **Name** some of the services the government provides.
3. **Explain** why the government collects taxes.
4. **State** the ways the government promotes business.

Why It's Important

Government rules promote and regulate the actions of business. The laws influence the production, selling, and pricing of goods and services.

● Key Words

interstate commerce	breach of contract
intrastate commerce	copyright
oligopoly	patent
monopoly	trademark
trust	revenue
antitrust laws	subsidies
contract	tax incentives

BusinessWeek Feature Story

Should Europe Be More Like America?

The Right Economic Model for the Old World Is the Subject of Great Debate. Economists gathered in Davos, Switzerland, for the World Economic Forum say Europe won't achieve American-style growth rates of 5 percent-plus until governments speed up deregulation, liberalize labor markets, and make deep structural reforms. Only then will Europe be more like the United States. "We're already more flexible and less regulated than many observers think," says Ferdinand Piëch, CEO of Volkswagen, the German automaker. "What we need isn't more liberal labor laws but lower taxes to boost our competitiveness. We should also improve the way the [European Union's] single market functions."

Source: Excerpted with permission from "Should Europe Be More Like America?" *BusinessWeek Online*, January 29, 2001.

An Extension Activity

When a nation experiences an economic slowdown, what does this mean?

BUSINESS *Online*

The Full Story

To learn more about the European economy, visit the *Introduction to Business* Web site at **www.introbus.glencoe.com**, and click on *BusinessWeek* Feature Story, Chapter 11.

How Government Affects Business

Suppose there were no traffic laws or you had to pay the fire department to put out the fire burning in your house. The roads would be chaos and your house would burn down by the time your credit card cleared. That's why government is needed. If you're looking for a street address in an unfamiliar city, you might go to a police officer for directions. If you're looking at a product's label, you might check for FDA approval. In each case, a government agency has helped make your life a little easier.

The government created traffic laws to protect drivers and courts to protect the rights of individuals. It has also created laws to regulate

Figure 11.1

GOVERNMENT REGULATIONS

➦Government regulates these four aspects of the economy.
Which one do you think has side effects on our environment?

REGULATING PRODUCTION PROCESS

PROTECTING COMPETITION

REGULATORY FUNCTIONS OF GOVERNMENT

PROTECTING CREATIVE PROPERTIES

PROTECTING BUSINESS AGREEMENTS

business. Government agencies regulate everything from the quality of the food you eat to how products are advertised. Their job is to protect both business and the public from unfair, unsafe, and unethical business practices.

One of the government's roles is to foster economic success. The economic health of a nation depends on the success of individual businesses. To promote this economic growth, local, state, and national government pass laws to both promote and regulate business.

Government as Regulator

There are three different levels of government—federal, state, and local. The federal government runs the country, state governments run individual states, and local governments run cities and counties. Each level of government oversees a different level of business. The federal government focuses on business that takes place across all states, or **interstate commerce**. State governments focus on **intrastate commerce**, or business within each state.

The government regulates these four aspects of the economy: (1) protecting competition, (2) protecting business agreements, (3) protecting creative properties, and (4) regulating the production process. Figure 11.1 illustrates these four ways in which the government intervenes in economic activity.

Protecting Competition

When a small number of companies control the market without actually forming a trust, this is called an **oligopoly**. In the 1800s a few large companies took over major industries and wiped out the competition. A company that controls an entire industry is called a **monopoly**, which means "one seller." Since a monopoly doesn't have to compete with other companies it can charge anything it wants for a product. It would be like one shoe company owning all the stores in the country. You would have no choice of what to buy or how much to pay.

Rival companies can also form a monopoly by banding together into a **trust** and agree not to compete with each other. In the 1800s, John D. Rockefeller gained a monopoly on oil. By 1890 there was a sugar trust, a steel trust, a bank trust, and even a tin can trust.

To prevent monopolies and promote competition, the U.S. government passed a series of antitrust laws. **Antitrust laws** allow the government to break up monopolies, regulate them, or take them over. This hasn't always stopped companies from competing unfairly. In the 1940s

Real-World Application

part 1 of 4

GOVERNMENT IN YOUR DAILY LIFE
When you travel on a highway, you're using a resource financed by federal and state money.
List some roadways or highways in your community that need work. Does the city have any plans to repair them?

continued on p. 165

the government sued a group of studios for trying to take over the film industry. In the 1990s the government sued Microsoft for trying to wipe out its competition.

The government created the Federal Trade Commission (FTC) to regulate interstate trade. Its job includes setting standards for honest advertising. For example, if a company makes false claims about its product or another company's product, it can be sued.

Protecting Business Agreements

One of the most basic ways the government protects business is by enforcing contracts. A **contract** is a legal agreement between two or more parties to conduct business. It can be written, verbal, or even done with a handshake. A rental agreement, a car insurance policy, and even the warranty on a CD player are all types of contracts.

A contract protects all the parties that agree to it. If you take out a student loan and refuse to pay it back later, the lender can take you to court. If your CD player breaks down before the warranty has expired and the company refuses to fix or replace it, you can sue them. When one party fails to live up to the terms of a contract it is called a **breach of contract**. It's important to make a contract and read the terms of it before you do business. For example, suppose you're in a band that plays at a coffeehouse and the manager refuses to pay you. If you didn't have a contract with the manager, there's nothing you can do about it.

Protecting Creative Properties

The government has laws protecting the right to own creative properties. Creative properties are things like inventions and artwork. If you write a great story or invent a time machine and don't legally register it, someone can steal your idea from you. You can protect your property by getting a copyright, patent, or trademark.

A **copyright** gives artists the sole right to own their creations, such as plays, photos, music, paintings, and books. If you own the copyright to a story you wrote, anyone who wants to print it, make a movie out of it, or use it in any way has to get your permission. A copyright usually last until 70 years after the artist has died. That means if a studio wants to use a song by Moby in a movie, it has to pay him for it.

A **patent** gives you the sole right to own an invention. Even the simplest inventions need to be patented. George de Mestral patented his invention, Velcro, in 1955 and made millions of dollars. Thomas Edison owned over 1,000 patents. A **trademark** is a brand name, trade name, trade characteristic, or a combination of these that is given legal protection by the federal government. Familiar trademarks include Frito-Lay's *Doritos®*, Kellogg's *Rice Krispies Treats®* cereal, and *VISA®*.

Consider This...

Limits on Competition

The merger between America Online (AOL) and Time Warner is the largest media merger in history. The new company is worth $110 billion. The Federal Trade Commission was concerned that the new AOL-Time Warner would limit competition. To avoid this, they required Time Warner to open its broadband pipes to competing Internet service providers.

ANALYZE

What are the advantages of the AOL and Time Warner merger?

Regulating the Production Process

The fourth way the government intervenes with economic activity is by regulating the production process. The government tries to stop industrial pollutants with regulations. These regulations limit the amount of waste that factories can discharge into the environment. As a result of federal budget cutbacks, environmental regulations are often not enforced. Then it is up to the state and local communities to take responsibility for regulating pollution to the water and air.

✓ **Fast Review**

1. What is the difference between interstate and intrastate commerce?
2. What are the ways the government can deal with a monopoly?
3. What kinds of properties are protected by copyrights?

Government as Provider

In many cases, when you want something you can save your money and then buy it. However, you can't buy some things. For example, you can't buy highways, bridges, or water treatment plants. The government provides these along with a large number of other goods and services. Who decides which goods and services the government should provide? Where does the money to pay for them come from? Who decides how much the government should spend?

The role of government in business isn't limited to passing and enforcing laws. It also takes an active role. It provides important services, conducts business itself, and acts as a partner to business. These activities are carried on at every level of government.

In a democratic system, people make their collective wants known through their elected officials. These officials try to satisfy as many of the people's wants as possible. However, the officials must also consider public welfare. Satisfying the wants of many different groups of people as well as providing for the public welfare can be difficult, because the government's funds are limited. Most government funds come from taxes that people and businesses pay. Government officials, including those you elect to office, determine how much money will be spent.

GOVERNMENT IN YOUR DAILY LIFE
Your school probably receives some form of aid from the local, state, or federal government.
List the issues your local board of education recently passed. What did it want to spend money on?

continued on p. 167

People pay for government-provided goods and services through taxes. You probably pay sales tax when you buy a book, video game, or CD. For some goods, such as gasoline, taxes are included in the purchase price. If you have a job, taxes are deducted from your wages.

The idea behind taxes is to pay for public goods and services and to share the cost among many people. (Figure 11.2 illustrates the average workday that goes to paying taxes.) Some people may not receive direct benefits from their tax money. For instance, some people may never need to call on the fire department, but the fire department has value for everyone in the community. Families without children don't directly use the community's schools, but the entire community benefits from having better-educated children and adults.

People who use public goods and services generally don't directly pay the full cost. For example, those who use city parks and libraries usually pay little to no entrance or membership fee. The admission charge for a public museum is rarely enough to cover the museum's costs. The charges people pay for public health services generally are far below the costs. Government uses the taxes it collects from all the people to make up the difference between the actual costs of such goods and services and the amount of those goods and services used.

Government spending decisions directly affect how resources are allocated. If the government spends its revenues on projects such as

Figure 11.2 WORKING FOR TAXES

➡During an average eight-hour workday, nearly three hours of your workday goes to paying federal, state, and local taxes. This comparative chart shows where people work the most and least for taxes.
Name some ways in which the government uses the money you earn for projects or services on your community.

Connecticut	**3:09**
New York	**3:09**
Washington, D.C.	**3:01**
New Jersey	**3:01**
Alaska	**2:17**
Mississippi	**2:21**

Source: Tax Foundation

missile systems in rural areas rather than on social welfare programs in urban areas, economic activity is stimulated in rural areas as resources are shifted there. The allocation of resources can be affected indirectly as well. In agriculture, the decision to support the prices of milk, grains, or peanuts keeps the factors of production working in those industries.

Government spending also influences the distribution of income, or the way in which income is allocated among families, individuals, or other designated groups in the economy. The incomes of needy families, for example, can be directly affected by increasing or decreasing transfer payments.

Incomes are affected indirectly when the government decides where to make expenditures. The decision to buy fighter planes from one factory rather than from another has an impact on the communities near both factories. Many businesses not linked to either company will feel the effects when workers are laid off or get new jobs and alter their spending habits. These situations are not merely hypothetical. The military base closings of the 1990s had a devastating impact on incomes in local communities that had come to depend on the military installations.

On the positive side, government can provide temporary income support for selective groups. In 1999, for example, the Department of Agriculture purchased millions of pounds of pork in an attempt to support low pork prices for farmers.

Providing Public Services

The government is the single largest provider of services in the country. Business offers goods and services to individuals on demand to make a profit. The government provides services to the public as a whole for the good of society. It spends the most on transfer payments, like welfare and unemployment compensation.

Many of the services the government provides are necessary for the protection of the public, such as the military, police, and fire department. Other services promote social welfare, like parks, and libraries. The government also provides public education, roads, courts, post offices, and countless other services. Every time you go to a park, take a bus, or mail a letter, you're using a government service.

The cost of providing all these services is enormous. To pay for them, the government has to raise money. The money the government takes in is called **revenue**. The government's main source of revenue is taxes, which is money collected from businesses and the public. Each level of government collects different kinds of taxes for different kinds of services. Federal income tax is used to pay for national highways, defense, and social security.

GOVERNMENT IN YOUR DAILY LIFE
Many goods that you buy are produced in accordance with local, state, and federal regulations.
Has your family ever bought a product that was recalled by the manufacturer because it didn't meet government regulations? What was it?

continued on p. 169

Local taxes are used to pay for streets, libraries, and parks in your community. All three levels (local, state, and federal) of government fund public education.

Providing Work

The government is the single largest employer in the country. The federal government alone employs over three million people. Employees are needed to run the daily operations of government from courthouse clerks to mail carriers. Public officials from your local mayor to the President of the Unites States are public employees. The government pays all members of the army, navy, and air force. Other public employees include teachers, bus drivers, police, trash collectors, and fire fighters.

Working Lifestyle

What are you doing at 10 A.M.?

A Celebration of Urban Design

Walt Disney Corporation launched the successful town called Celebration, Fla. Creating and designing this central Florida town was no Mickey-Mouse project. Just ask Brian Shea.

Shea is a partner in the New York City architectural planning and urban design firm, Cooper, Robertson, & Partners. As part of the team of creative minds that designed Celebration, Shea focused on fitting the 5,000-acre planned community into its natural surroundings.

He asks his receptionist to hold a ten o'clock call as he fine tunes a drawing. Shea's professional tools are rather simple: tracing paper, soft pencils, ink pens, and Magic Markers. He uses hard-line tools, such as a T-square and triangle if transferring a drawing to a computer. As a designer, he endlessly manipulates paper and pencil and thinks analytically about a project.

Salary

A typical urban planner is expected to earn a median base salary of $39,137.

Outlook for This Career

Employment of urban and regional planners is expected to grow about as fast as the average for all occupations. Non-governmental initiatives dealing with historic preservation and redevelopment will provide additional openings.

Connecting Careers Activity

Imagine you've been asked to consult on the design of an urban community. What would be the four major cornerstones (i.e., what services, businesses, or activities might be needed)?

CAREER PATH — Architecture & Construction

For people temporarily out of work, the government provides unemployment insurance. It offers welfare benefits and job training programs for people who have trouble finding work. Social Security provides insurance by taking certain amount of money out of your paycheck and setting it aside for your future retirement.

Assisting Business

The government is also the single largest consumer of goods and services. It has to buy computers, furniture, and supplies for schools and government offices. To maintain the military it has to buy uniforms, food, ships, aircraft, and weapons. The government buys most of its equipment directly from businesses or has it specially made, such as military aircraft and fire trucks. The government also hires businesses to build courthouses, schools, and roads.

The government promotes and assists business in a number of ways. The Small Business Administration (SBA) offers different kinds of loans to aspiring small-business owners. The government also lends money to big businesses that are in financial trouble. For example, when Chrysler Corporation was on the verge of bankruptcy in 1980, the government lent it $400 million to bail it out. The government even lends money to help foreign countries build up their economies in order to create new markets for American goods.

To protect American businesses from unfair foreign competition, the government sets up trade barriers (as discussed in Chapter 10). In same cases, important businesses like corn or steel have to lower the cost of their products to compete with foreign companies. The government helps them out by giving them subsidies. **Subsidies** are payments the government gives to businesses to make up for their losses.

To encourage socially responsible behavior, government offers businesses reductions in taxes, or **tax incentives**. For example, oil companies that lower the amount of pollution they cause are rewarded with lower taxes. Tax breaks are also given to companies that conserve energy or use alternate sources of fuel. Both loans and tax breaks are offered to businesses that do community development. Community development can consist of donating profits to local schools or setting up a business in a poor area to create jobs.

Real-World Application

part **4** of 4

GOVERNMENT IN YOUR DAILY LIFE
If you own property, buy goods, or earn an income, you probably pay taxes that help pay for many government activities.
What is the amount of state tax you pay for clothing or food?

✔ **Fast Review** _____

1. What are some services the government provides for the public?
2. Name different types of government workers.
3. What kinds of goods does the government buy from businesses?

Summary

1. Government protects business competition, agreements, and creative rights.

2. Public protection, public education, roads, courts, and social welfare are examples of government services.

3. The government collects taxes to pay for the services it provides.

4. Government assists businesses with loans, subsidies, and tax breaks.

Using Business Key Words

The government has a major impact on business in the United States. Find out how much you understand the impact by completing the sentences below.

- **antitrust laws**
- **intrastate commerce**
- **copyright**
- **oligopoly**
- **monopoly**
- **breach of contract**
- **interstate commerce**
- **patent**
- **trademark**
- **subsidies**
- **tax incentives**
- **trust**
- **contract**
- **revenue**

1. The federal government focuses primarily on _____, or business activities that cross state boundaries.
2. Business activities within the state are called _____.
3. A legal "right" that prevents copying or use of an invention is called a _____.
4. _____ control a market and prevent unfair competition.
5. If a large company controls a market's prices, then it has a _____ on the market.
6. A _____ provides protection for authors of books, plays, software, movies, and for other kinds of artists.
7. When a group of companies band together to form a monopoly and eliminate competition, they create a _____.
8. A _____ controls an industry by a small group of companies.
9. A _____ is upheld between two parties. It can be written, verbal, or even done with a handshake.
10. If a party fails to live up to the terms of a contract, this is a _____.
11. Kleenex® is an example of a _____.
12. _____ is government or business income.
13. The government gives businesses _____ to encourage certain activities.
14. The government gives a business _____ to make up for the business's losses.

Review What You Learned

15. Explain the government's role as regulator.

16. Why was the Federal Trade Commission established?

17. Explain the government's role as protector of individuals.

18. Define a patent, a copyright, and a trademark.

19. For what purpose does the government use the taxes it collects from the public?

20. What types of products and services are provided by the local government?

21. Why might each state government spend its money differently?

22. What is the number-one expenditure for the federal government?

23. Why would the government lend businesses money?

Understanding Business Concepts

24. Why do you think our government wants businesses to succeed?

25. Does competition improve the quality of products or services that consumers purchase? How?

26. If the only two businesses that sell television sets in a small town agree to sell their products at the same price, does that action create a monopoly? Why or why not?

27. List five trademarks you see used in your community.

28. For what purposes do you think your state uses the money it collects through sales tax?

29. Do you agree with the federal government's spending priorities? Explain your answer.

Critical Thinking

30. Do you believe the U.S. government looks out for the common welfare of all the people in the country? Why or why not?

31. When a business is required by U.S. law to install pollution control equipment, who ultimately pays for the cost of the equipment?

32. Make a list of people in your community who help pay for the cost of public goods and services but don't directly use them.

33. How do people in a democracy acknowledge their social wants so that the government can help satisfy these?

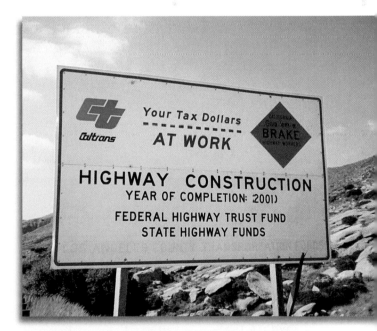

Viewing and Representing

Examining the Image. Find every last detail in this photograph. Ask yourself these questions: What do you think's important here? Which taxes are being used? Can you give examples of government-funded work that's going on in your area?

Building Academic Skills

 Compare and Contrast

In a group of three or four, make a list of ways to increase competition among businesses. Make a second list of ways to decrease competition. Compare your lists with those of the other groups in your class. Circle the items that are regulated by the government. Use your lists as the basis for a class display showing the advantages and disadvantages of government regulation of business.

 Determine Percentage

In groups of three or four, contact your local city or county government. Ask for a copy of the budget from last year and this year. Determine the percentage increase or decrease of the income and expenses for the city or county government. Evaluate the expenses and decide if there are any services that could be eliminated if necessary. Justify your decisions.

HISTORY **Researching Antitrust Laws**

Research the antitrust laws of a market-driven country (other than the United States). Write a two-page paper comparing the similarities and differences to the antitrust laws in the United States.

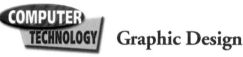 **Graphic Design**

Using the computer, design a trademark or logo for a business in your community that you frequent. When creating the design, consider the fact that the trademark or logo could be used on billboards, signs, letterhead, business cards and packaging. Display your completed work in the classroom.

Linking School to Home

Local Businesses. Make a list of all the businesses within a two-mile radius of your home. Use the phone book and newspaper ads to determine the following:

- Which businesses sell products made outside the United States?
- Are there more businesses selling imported products than products made in the United States?

Linking School to Work

Analyzing Student Government. Compare your school's student government to the federal, state, and local government. Then, answer the following questions:

- How does your school's student government look out for the common welfare of all the students within the school?
- What is the role of the student government?
- Has the student government created any rules or regulations that all students must follow? If so, how are they enforced?
- Does the student government have any money to spend? If so, where do they get it? What do they spend it on?

● E-Homework

Applying Technology

Government Laws. Using the Internet, research four laws that the government has created to protect individuals. Research one in each of the following categories: (1) environmental protection, (2) consumer protection, (3) employee protection, and (4) general welfare protection.

Copyrighting Music. Imagine a friend has just written a piece of music that will be performed at the next California Music Festival. You suggest she publish the piece. Using the Internet, help her find information about copyrighting music. Research the following:
- What is the procedure for copyrighting music?
- How should your friend register her music with the copyright office?
- What specific laws protect the original works of musicians?

● Connecting Academics

Math. You're an event coordinator for A to Z National Conventions. You work from 8:30 A.M. to 5:00 P.M. Tomorrow you're calling: an acrobatic team in New York, a specialty caterer in California, a display designer in Hawaii, a master magician in Colorado, and a video producer in Texas. You assume the companies you're calling are open between 9:00 A.M. and 5:00 P.M. Taking into account time zone differences, make a list of the times you might call each vendor.

History. Choose a local manufacturer. Complete the following steps to learn more about government services and government regulations in business:
- **Investigate.** Find at least five services provided by government.

- **Explore.** Research and then list three activities regulated by government to protect workers, consumers, and the company.

BusinessWeek Analyzing the Feature Story

You read the first part of "Should Europe Be More Like America?" at the beginning of this chapter. Below are a few questions for you to answer about the European economy. You'll find the answers to these questions when you're reading the entire article. First, here are the questions:

34. How do the economists who gathered in Davos, Switzerland, view deregulation in Europe?

35. What type of government reform are European business leaders interested in?

CREATIVE JOURNAL ACTIVITY

Research *BusinessWeek Online* for one of the major regulatory agencies listed in the chapter. What information is available on the site?

BUSINESS *Online*
The Full Story

To learn more about the European economy, visit the *Introduction to Business* Web site at **www.introbus.glencoe.com**, and click on *BusinessWeek* Feature Story, Chapter 11.

Chapter 12

Money and Financial Institutions

Learning Objectives

After completing this chapter, you'll be able to:

1. **Describe** the functions and characteristics of money.
2. **Explain** the services that banks offer.
3. **Name** the types of banks.
4. **Identify** the functions of the Federal Reserve System.

Why It's Important

Understanding the way money and financial institutions work is crucial to understanding the economy.

Key Words

monetary system
money
financial institution
bank account
deposit
withdrawal
interest
electronic funds transfer (EFT)
collateral
mortgage
safety-deposit box
Federal Reserve System

BusinessWeek Feature Story

The Euro: Back From the Depths

The Ups and Downs of the Euro. The chilly December markets were merciful to at least one person—Wim Duisenberg. As late as October, the European Central Bank chief's days seemed numbered as the euro fell against the U.S. dollar. Then, in late November, the currency began climbing. On Christmas Day, it hit 93 cents in thin Tokyo trading. The level stuck. As of December 28, it was holding around 93.10 cents. That's 13 percent above its low of 82.25 cents reached on October 26.

Source: Excerpted with permission from "The Euro: Back From the Depths," *BusinessWeek Online*, January 8, 2001.

An Extension Activity

The Federal Reserve System is the centralized banking organization in the United States. Who is its chairperson, and what do you think he or she does?

BUSINESS Online
The Full Story

To learn more about the euro, visit the *Introduction to Business* Web site at **www.introbus.glencoe.com**, and click on *BusinessWeek* Feature Story, Chapter 12.

Money and Banking

Although there are places in the world where money and banks play only a small role in the local economy, it's hard for us to imagine life without them. Money enables people and businesses to buy and sell goods and services around the world with easy efficiency. Banks and the banking system play an extremely important role in managing money and controlling and simulating the economy.

The History of Money

The monetary system makes business much easier. In the **monetary system** goods and services are indirectly exchanged using money, which can then be exchanged for other goods and services. **Money** can be anything that people accept as a standard for payment. Modern society uses coin, currency, checks, and credit cards. In other times and places people have used shells, stones, corn, parrot feathers, and even gopher tails for money. Figure 12.1 illustrates why items might or might not be good sources for money.

Figure 12.1

WOULD THESE ITEMS BE ACCEPTABLE AS MONEY?

➡Imagine what business would be like without money. If you worked in a fast-food restaurant, it might pay you in food. *Bartering* is exchanging one product for another. American Colonialists engaged in this way of doing business.
Explain why or why not these items could serve as money. On a piece of paper, re-create this table and check the appropriate box(es) for each that applies.

ITEM	FUNCTION		
	Durability	Portability	Divisibility
Hammer			
Hamburger			
Bushel of oats			
Rocks found on the ground			

Functions of Money

Money has three basic functions. First of all, it's a *medium of exchange*. Whether you buy a soda or sell a corporation, money changes hands. Without money, people would be forced to *barter*—trade goods or services directly for other goods or services. Barter is a clumsy method of exchange. Suppose you've grown an extra bushel of tomatoes. You'd like to use tomatoes to get new CDs. In the barter system, you'd have to find someone willing to accept tomatoes for CDs. If you have particular CDs in mind, you might have to make several trades to acquire something the CD owner would accept. You could spend a lot of time bartering for things you need. With money, however, the exchange becomes easy—you sell your extra tomatoes for money. You then exchange the money for the CDs you want. In a system that uses money, both buyers and sellers agree on exchanging money. Money itself is not a good or a service but a means of exchanging goods and services. It's a medium in that it's used between people to make business easier, just as radio is a medium that makes communication easier.

Money also functions as a *standard of value*. A standard is a fixed means for measuring the weight, amount, size, or value of something, like a yardstick or a scale. Money provides a means for measuring the value of goods and services. As a standard of value, money makes it possible to set a fixed value on a product and to compare the costs of different products. In the United States, the standard used is the dollar.

Finally, money functions as a *store of value*. That means it holds its value over time and can be stored or saved. You can also accumulate money over time to increase your wealth.

Characteristics of Money

Practically all over the world, paper money and coins are common forms of money. For money to carry out its functions, it must have several characteristics. No matter what form it takes, all money shares these characteristics.

Money must be stable in value. To be used as money, an item must be *scarce*. If the supply of an item is overly plentiful, it loses its value and cannot serve very well as money or a store of value since it would have little worth. People would lose faith in its value as a medium of exchange.

Money must be *accepted*. People have to be willing to take money in exchange for goods and services. Before accepting it, people must have

Real-World Application

part 1 of 4

HOW BANKS CREATE MONEY

The Federal Reserve System (Fed) is the central bank of the government in the United States. Suppose Region Bank sells a government bond to the Fed and receives $1,000. This is $1,000 in "new" money because the Fed creates it by writing a check. **How does the Fed create money?**

continued on p. 179

faith that the item used as money has value and will continue to hold its value. If people don't have faith in the value of their money, they may use something else like gold or diamonds. To be valuable, money must be acceptable.

Money should be *divisible* into parts. Suppose you have $20 but spend only $4.50 on a sandwich. Since money is divisible, the cashier can give you $15.50 in return. A money system using coins and bills of different values makes that possible.

Finally, money has to be *portable* and *durable*. Coins made of metal and bills made of strong paper can last a long time, can be used over and over again, and are easy to replace.

✓ **Fast Review**

1. What is the monetary system?
2. How is money a standard of value?
3. What are some of the characteristics money must have to be useful?

Business Building Blocks

Math

Understanding Interest

Simple interest, compounded annually, is a percentage of the amount borrowed. The amount borrowed is called the *principal*. Compound interest may be computed daily, monthly, or yearly.

How to Compute Interest

Simple Interest. Imagine you borrow $1,000 for 3 years at a rate of 10 percent per year. Here's how to find out the amount you owe at the end of three years.

Step 1. Convert the interest rate percent to its decimal equivalent.
(10% = $^{10}/_{100}$ = .10)

Step 2. Use this formula: interest = principal x interest rate x time

Principal	x	Decimal Interest Rate	x	Time	= Interest
$1,000	x	.10	x	3	= $300

At the end of 3 years, the cost of the loan would be $300. Since you also must pay back the principal, you owe the lender $1,300.

Practice

Find the simple interest on a $2,000 loan at 12 percent interest for 5 years.

Banking

Banks manage money, move it around, and maintain a supply of it. A system of banks makes it possible to keep your money in a safe place and get access to it wherever you go. The banking system is the main type of **financial institution**, or organization for managing money, in our economy. Banks offer people a variety of financial services.

Storing Money

One of the primary services banks provide is storing money for customers in bank accounts. A **bank account** is a record of how much money a customer has put in to or taken out of a bank. The money put in a bank is called a **deposit**, and the money taken out is called a **withdrawal**. Keeping your money in a bank prevents you from losing, spending, or having your money stolen too easily.

The two main types of accounts are *checking accounts* and *savings accounts*. Checking accounts are used for storing money in the short term so you can draw on it easily if you want to go shopping or pay a bill. Banks usually charge a fee for checking accounts to pay for the cost of maintaining them. Savings accounts are used for storing money over a long period of time. An advantage of a savings account is that it earns more interest than most checking accounts. **Interest** is a rate the bank pays you for keeping your money there. For example, if a bank pays you 5 percent interest per year on a $1,000 savings account, you'll have earned $50 after one year.

Real-World Application

part **2** of 4

HOW BANKS CREATE MONEY

The government requires a bank to keep a certain percentage of a deposit on hand, let's say 20 percent. With a 20 percent reserve requirement, the bank must hold how much money in reserve if it lends out $1,000?

continued on p. 181

Transferring Money

Every single business transaction involves the transfer of money. Banks make it easy to transfer money from one person or business to another. For example, suppose you have a paycheck for $85 from the store where you work. You take the check to your bank, and they give you $85 cash for it. The bank then transfers the money from the store's bank account to the bank's cash account. You could also deposit the check into your bank account, in which case the store will transfer the amount from the store's account into your account.

Today more banks are using **electronic funds transfer (EFT)** to move money around. With EFT, money is transferred from one account to another through a network of computers. Instead of writing a check, your employer can use EFT to deposit your paycheck into your account electronically. You can also use EFT to pay your phone bill, withdraw money from your account, or buy movie tickets.

Lending Money

The money you deposit in a bank makes it possible for the bank to lend money to other customers. Just as the bank pays you interest on your savings, customers have to pay the interest on the money they borrow from the bank. The interest earned by the bank is then used to pay the interest on savings accounts and to cover the bank's expenses.

Most bank loans require some form of collateral. **Collateral** is something valuable you put up for a loan, such as a car or a coin collection, so that the bank can take it if you fail to pay back the loan. There are four main types of loans banks offer to businesses and individuals:

Figure 12.2

HOW BANKS DO BUSINESS

➡Banks are businesses that provide financial services to make a profit.
What would happen to a bank's profits if deposits suddenly decreased?

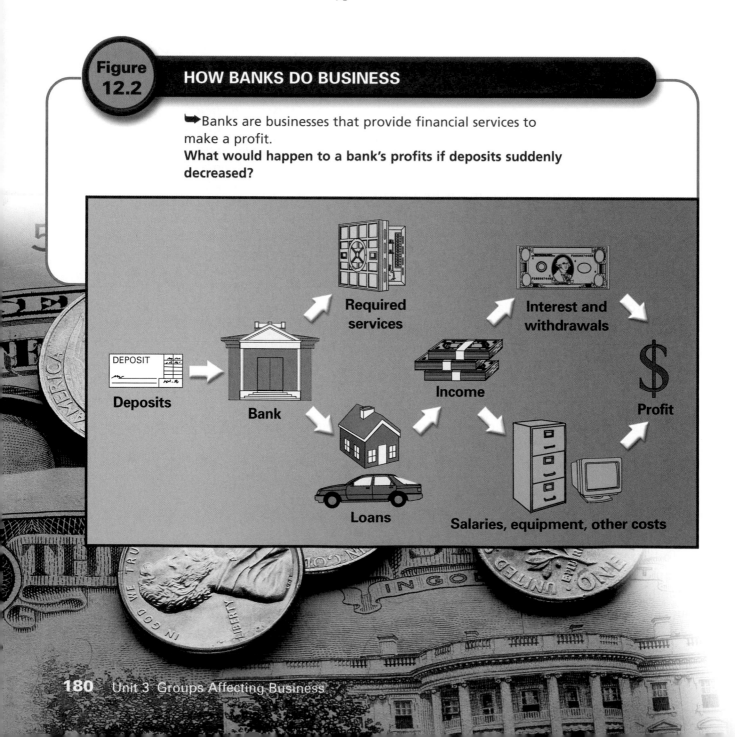

- A *mortgage loan* is a loan used to buy real estate, such as a house or an office building. A **mortgage** is a deed to give the lender the property if the loan is not paid back.
- A *commercial loan* is a loan made to businesses to buy supplies and equipment.
- An *individual loan* is a loan made to an individual to pay for personal items like a car, home repairs, or a vacation.
- A *line of credit* is an amount set aside by a bank for preferred customers that is available on demand. For example, a bank can issue a customer a $15,000 line of credit that can be used any time for any purpose.

Other Financial Services

Banks offer a variety of other services. Many of them provide financial advice on managing and investing your money. Not only can you store your money in a bank but you can also store valuable items, such as jewelry and certificates in **safety-deposit boxes** . Many banks offer credit cards such as MasterCard or Visa. Banks also manage *trust funds* such as an inheritance.

✔ Fast Review

1. What are the three main functions of a bank?
2. How does an EFT work?
3. What are the types of loans a bank offers?

Types of Banks

Banks operate on a state, national, and international level. There are strict rules for starting one because banks handle so much money. To open a federal or a state bank, you have to meet special requirements and apply for a charter from the federal or state government. You must also prove you have enough capital to start a bank. In the United States there are three main types of banks. Figure 12.2 illustrates how banks do business in order to make a profit.

Commercial Banks

Most of the banks in the United States are commercial banks. Commercial banks offer the entire range of services discussed such as checking and savings accounts, loans, and financial advice. They are often called *full-service banks*. They are like businesses in that they operate to make a profit. To make a profit they usually charge much more interest on the money they lend than the interest they pay on savings accounts.

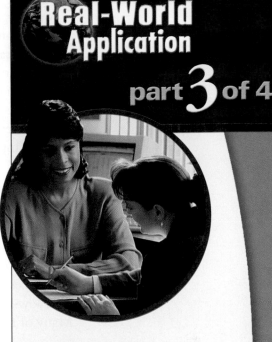

Real-World Application

part **3** of 4

HOW BANKS CREATE MONEY
Suppose you want to buy a new mountain bike. The bank loans you $800. The bank must keep in its reserve 20 percent of a new deposit.
How much money does the bank need to keep in the bank? How much can the bank lend?

continued on p. 183

Savings and Loan Associations

Savings and loan associations were originally set up to offer savings accounts and home mortgage loans. Their purpose was to encourage people to save money and make it easier to buy a home or start a business. To do this they charged lower interest on loans and paid higher interest on savings. In the 1980s about 20 percent of savings and loans failed. The government passed new regulations allowing them to charge higher interest rates and offer more services like credit cards. As a result, most savings and loans today are more like commercial banks.

Credit Unions

Credit unions are nonprofit banks set up by organizations for their members to use. Many companies, labor unions, and professional groups have their own credit unions. Credit unions offer members a full range of services, including credit cards, checking accounts, and loans. They offer low-interest loans and pay high interest rates on savings accounts. Many of them also pay interest on checking accounts.

Other Financial Institutions

There are types of financial institutions other than banks that offer some of the same services. *Mortgage companies* provide loans specifically for buying a home or business. *Finance companies* offer short-term loans to businesses, but at much higher interest rates than banks charge. *Insurance companies* not only provide protection against things like fire and theft, but also offer loans to businesses. *Brokerage firms* that sell stocks and bonds, may also offer a wide range of financial services to its customers.

You Make the Call

Home Equity

You and your family are moving to a new town and you're looking for a house to buy. There's one house everyone likes that's by a creek and on a wooded lot. The realtor mentions that next year a multiplex housing complex for low-income families will be built down the road.

Making an Ethical Decision

1. What are the most important financial issues that people should consider when buying a home?
2. What are the advantages of living in neighborhoods that are economically mixed?

1. What are the types of banks?
2. How is a credit union different from a commercial bank?
3. Name some financial institutions other than banks that offer similar services.

The Federal Reserve System

The **Federal Reserve System** (or Fed) is the central banking organization in the United States. Congress set up the Fed in 1913 to end the periodic financial panics during the 1800s and early 1900s. It consists of 12 Federal Reserve district banks, 25 branch banks, and about 5,000 member banks. The Fed is run by the Board of Governors, which is headed by a chairperson. It supervises the Federal Reserve district banks and regulates activity of the member banks.

HOW BANKS CREATE MONEY

The bank treats the $640 as a new deposit. Eighty percent of $640 (or $512) might be lent again. The process continues, with each new deposit giving the bank new funds to continue lending.
How does the money supply expand?

Functions of the Fed

The Fed has six functions. These functions are as follows:

- *Clearing checks.* This transfers funds from one bank to another when you write or deposit a check.
- *Acting as the federal government's fiscal agent.* The Fed spends and distributes money to Federal Reserve member banks and commercial banks. It also tracks the deposits and holds a checking account for the U. S. Treasury.
- *Supervising member banks.* It regulates state banks that are members of the Federal Reserve System.
- *Regulating the money supply.* The primary responsibility of the Fed is to determine the amount of money in circulation. This affects the amount of credit and business activity in the economy.
- *Setting reserve requirements.* Regulating the money supply is the most important function of the Fed. By law, banks are required to keep a certain percentage of their deposits in reserve. This percentage determines the amount of money in circulation.
- *Supplying paper currency.* The Fed is responsible for printing and maintaining the nation's paper currency.

✔ **Fast Review** _____

1. What is the Fed?
2. Name the six functions of the Fed.

Global *Economy*

A Brief History of Money
Over the centuries such items as cattle, salt, large stones, seashells, metals, beads, tea, coffee, tobacco, fishhooks, and furs have served as money. Some of the more important developments in the history of money are described here.

Two Bits
Do you know why people sometimes call a quarter "two bits"? The origin of this term dates back to colonial times. The American colonists used Spanish silver dollar coins called pieces of eight. Each coin was divided into eight pieces— or bits—so that it could be broken to make change. Four bits was equal to half a dollar, while two bits equaled a quarter.

Rings and Ingots
Perhaps as early as 2500 B.C. the people of ancient Egypt and Mesopotamia—the land between the Tigris and Euphrates Rivers— were using gold and silver as money. The money took the form of rings, small ornaments, and ingots, or bars.

The First Coins

The Lydians, who lived in what is now western Turkey, probably made the first coins during the 600s B.C. These coins were made of electrum, a mix of gold and silver, and were stamped with pictures of gods or emperors. The Greeks, Persians, and Romans adopted Lydian coining techniques and, in time, the use of coins spread throughout much of Western Europe.

The First Paper Banknotes

The Chinese may have begun to make coins around the same time as the Lydians. These coins were made of bronze and often had holes in them so that they could be carried on a string. The Chinese also began using paper banknotes—printed on paper made from mulberry bark—in the 800s A.D.

Cowrie Shells

Cowrie shells have been used as money throughout Asia, Africa, and Oceania. The cowrie was still in use in some African countries as recently as the mid-1900s. The name for Ghana's monetary unit, the cedi, comes from the Ghanaian word meaning "cowrie shell."

Thinking Globally

1. Where did the use of coins develop?

2. What developments in the history of money took place in China?

3. How is the history of money in Africa reflected in the currency of Ghana?

Summary

1. Money functions as a medium of exchange, a standard of value, and a store of value. The characteristics of money include scarcity, acceptability, divisibility, portability, and durability.

2. Banks offer a variety of financial services including storing money, transferring money, and lending money.

3. The three main types of banks are commercial banks, savings and loan associations, and credit unions.

4. The Fed has six basic functions. Its most important function is regulating the money supply.

● Using Business Key Words

Understanding these business terms will help you understand the banking institution. Match the terms below with their definitions.

- **monetary system**
- **deposit**
- **Federal Reserve System**
- **bank account**
- **mortgage**
- **interest**
- **electronic funds transfer (EFT)**
- **money**
- **withdrawal**
- **safety-deposit box**
- **financial institution**
- **collateral**

1. Something to place valuables in at the bank.
2. The money banks pay to depositors for use of their funds.
3. Sums of money placed in accounts in the bank.
4. Responsible for controlling the amount of money in circulation.
5. The process of moving money from one account to another through the use of computers.
6. Goods and services are indirectly exchanged through this medium.
7. Anything accepted as a standard form of payment.
8. Taking money out of the bank.
9. An organization for managing money.
10. Records how much money a customer has put in or taken out of his or her bank.
11. Something of value you put up for a loan.
12. A deed that states if you can't pay back your loan, the lender has right to take certain things.

Review What You Learned

13. Describe the three functions of money.
14. What are the two characteristics that dollars must have to be accepted as money in our society?
15. Why must money be portable?
16. How does a debit card work?
17. What is the bank's primary source of income?
18. Why does the government require banks to keep a certain percentage of their deposits on hand?
19. Compare the three different types of loans—mortgage, commercial, and individual.
20. How does the Federal Reserve control the amount of money in circulation?
21. Describe the characteristics of a credit union.
22. What is the central banking organization of the United States?
23. What happened when the government deregulated the banking industry?

Understanding Business Concepts

24. Why does money need to be divisible? Give an example.
25. Banks pay depositors for leaving their money in savings accounts. Why?
26. Explain how a bank makes a profit by providing loans to its customers.
27. Compare an individual loan with a line of credit. What are the similarities and differences?
28. Describe how banks help to eliminate money.
29. What other financial institutions, besides banks, savings and loans, and credit unions offer financial services?

Critical Thinking

30. What do you think would happen if all the depositors of a bank requested their deposits at the same time?
31. How can the Federal Reserve use the reserve requirement to slow the economy's growth?
32. Find out how currency is printed and what security measures are taken to avoid counterfeiting. What steps would you take to suggest minimizing counterfeiting?
33. Why do you think coins have been a more desirable form of money than paper currency throughout U.S. history?

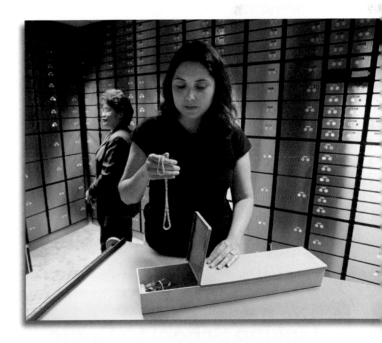

Viewing and Representing

Examining the Image. Get ready. For 15 seconds, look closely at the photograph. Then cover it up with a piece of paper. List everything you remember. What did you remember first? Are you surprised at how much information your mind captures in a short time? Do you think that images are powerful? Write a paragraph on your findings and answers.

Building Academic Skills

 Showing Interest

In groups of three or four, call three banks, credit unions, or other financial institutions and find out how much interest they pay on a regular savings account. Create a table to show the results of your research. If possible, use computer software to create the table. Then, as a class, combine your results. Determine which savings institution in your community provides the best interest rate.

LANGUAGE ARTS **Personal Essay**

Team up with three classmates to form a bank. Open your bank with a deposit of $20,000 in pretend game money. Invite classmates to play the role of business and individual customers in your bank. Determine the interest rate you will charge on loans and pay on deposits. Decide what you need to do to place $200,000 into the classroom economy. Remember the following may affect your decisions:

- Your bank must keep 10 percent of each deposit on reserve.

- You'll need to pay salaries, rent, and other costs.
- You'll compete for customers with other banks in your classroom.

Write a 300-word report that explains how your bank works.

 Researching the Fed

Use e-mail to contact the nearest Federal Reserve System branch bank. Request general information about the Federal Reserve System and particular information about the Federal Reserve System branch. Share the information you receive with your classmates.

HISTORY **Other Nations' Banking**

The Bank of England was used as the model for forming and organizing our Federal Reserve System. Choose the central bank of two other nations to research. Identify their main functions and responsibilities and compare them to the Federal Reserve. Prepare a three-minute oral report to share your findings with the class.

Linking School to Home

Interviewing and Charting. Interview your parents or other family members to find out why they chose the financial institution(s) they currently use. Ask them about the services offered, location, quality of customer service provided, and interest rates. Create a chart showing the features that helped make their decision.

Linking School to Work

Local Advertisements. Collect various financial institutions' advertisements from local newspapers. Using the advertisements, list the services provided by each one of the institutions. Create a chart showing the services. Then, as a class, combine the charts. Evaluate the financial institutions based on the services provided and select one that you think is the best. Invite someone from that institution to speak to your class about their institution and the services they provide.

E-Homework

Applying Technology

Banking Decisions. Discuss how technology has affected where people do their banking. Include online banking in your discussion.

Digital Cash. Although cash and checks are still very common methods of paying for goods and services, various access cards are becoming more and more popular. Use the Internet to research stored value cards and digital cash. Write a two-page paper sharing your findings. Present your opinion on whether or not you think cash and checks will soon be an outdated way of doing business.

Connecting Academics

Math. Assume you live in a country where a silver coin is the currency. The weight of one silver dollar is 0.94 ounces. Compute the total weight of the silver dollars you would have to carry to purchase the following: a television set, a round trip plane ticket to Tokyo, and a new sports car.

Computer/Technology. Diagrams often help clarify information in a textbook. Create a diagram indicating the relationship between banks, bank accounts, deposits, withdrawals, interest, electronic fund transfer (EFT), and safety-deposit boxes.

BusinessWeek Analyzing the Feature Story

You read the first part of "The Euro: Back From the Depths" at the beginning of this chapter. Below are a few questions for you to answer about money. You'll find the answers to these questions when you're reading the entire article. First, here are the questions:

34. What characteristic of money is the main concern of this article?

35. How does globalization affect currency in different countries?

CREATIVE JOURNAL ACTIVITY

Research the current value of the dollar against the currencies of three different countries. See if you can find out what these currencies were worth in dollars last week. How about last year? Create a chart with your results. Which country's economy has the most potential?

BUSINESS Online
The Full Story

To learn more about the euro, visit the *Introduction to Business* Web site at **www.introbus.glencoe.com**, and click on *BusinessWeek* Feature Story, Chapter 12.

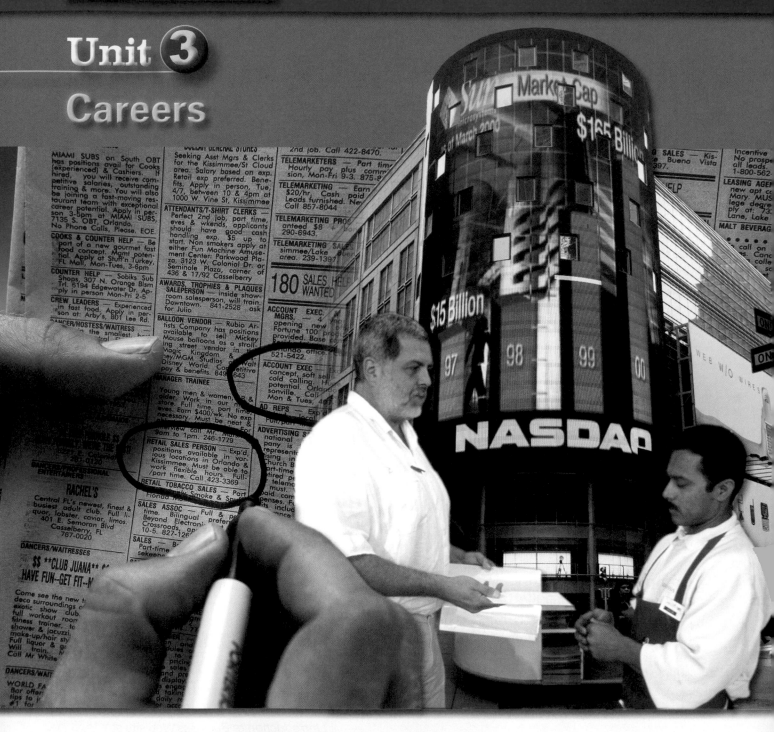

Unit 3
Careers

Discovering Business Careers

In Chapter 11 you read about the impact of government on a business. One of the ways government affects business is by influencing the economy through policies established by the Federal Reserve, the central banking system of the United States. The Federal Reserve cuts the interest rates that banks charge one another in an effort to strengthen the economy by making borrowing money more affordable for businesses. When businesses can't afford to borrow money, businesses can't grow and workers lose their jobs.

Investigate the Images

Look at the collage on the left page. What do you see? What do you think? What do think the images represent? The power of reading visuals is in analyzing and dissecting your observations. On a separate piece of paper reconstruct the worksheet below in order to complete your investigation. The questions may help shape and focus your analysis.

Your Observations

1. How many photographs do you see?

2. Examine each image. How is each assembled in relation to the other?

3. What is the subject of each photograph?

4. Does color signify a message?

5. What issues do you take from these images?

Information

6. Summarize what you know about the photographs from your observations.

Exploring Culture

7. What do you know about unemployment in this country? How does it affect your community? What about your family?

8. Do you think the media objectively reports why businesses layoff employees? Why or why not? Is the news the source of all truths?

Factoids

Mandatory Vacation. When the economy weakens, some businesses shave dollars off the payroll by forcing people to take unpaid vacation.

Keeping Your Options Open. Cisco Systems lays off 6,000 employees. This San Jose, Calif., company is allowing those terminated the chance to collect one-third of their severance package, plus benefits and stocks if they work for a local nonprofit organization. These individuals are first in line for Cicso's rehire once the economy recovers.

Looking for Opportunities. Users visited Monster.com over two million times in a month.

Job Stability. Seventy-four percent of working adults express some kind of concern about job security.

Employee Development. U.S. companies spend an average of $700 per eligible worker on employee training.

Taking Aim at Careers

Preparation

In this seminar, you'll research three different jobs and decide which job, if any, would withstand slower economic times.

Objective

In this *BusinessWeek* Seminar, you'll:

- **Research** three different career opportunities available.
- **Participate** in a job fair, in which each member of your class will set up a display of the jobs he or she has researched.
- **Discuss** with your classmates which three jobs are most likely to withstand an economic downturn.

Materials Needed

- ✓ Recent business news publications, such as the *New York Times* and *BusinessWeek*
- ✓ The business and classified advertisement sections of your local newspaper
- ✓ Notebook paper
- ✓ Posterboard
- ✓ Construction paper
- ✓ Pencils
- ✓ Pens
- ✓ Markers

Procedures

1. Identify three jobs that interest you.

2. Research these three jobs. Consult the *Occupational Outlook Handbook*, which should be available in your school or local library.

3. Research business and economic trends. Use the Internet to access *BusinessWeek Online* at **www.businessweek.com**.

4. Write a brief report for each of the three jobs you have identified. Each report should describe the job, the training and education required, and the future outlook for that job.

5. Create a poster or brochure that promotes the positive aspects of each job. You'll use them to create interest in the jobs you've researched.

6. As a class, stage a job fair. Set up a display for the jobs you have researched. Visit others students' displays. Write down any concerns you have about a particular job.

Chart It

Discuss with the class which jobs seem both interesting and secure during economic downturns. Were many of the same jobs presented by different classmates? Make sure you understand what makes one job more secure than another.

As a class, vote for the three jobs most likely to withstand an economic downturn. As a class reproduce the table that is below and create a comprehensive list on the board.

Jobs to Withstand an Economic Downturn		
Most Interesting Jobs	Most Secure Jobs	Jobs Both Interesting and Secure (Explain)
1.	1.	1.
2.	2.	2.
3.	3.	3.
4.	4.	4.
5.	5.	5.

Analyze and Conclude

After voting for the top three jobs, answer the questions below:

1. **Decision Making.** What were the top three jobs? Of those three, which job is most interesting to you? Why? What makes one job more secure than another?

2. **Negotiating to Arrive at a Decision.** Do you have to choose between interest and security in a job?

3. **Reasoning.** From all the jobs you have learned about, through your own research and the job fair, which job are you most likely to pursue? Why?

Becoming an Informed Citizen

Congratulations, you finished the *Business-Week* Seminar. Now it's time to reflect on the decisions you made.

Critical Thinking. What are the essential elements you look for in career? Is it straightforward? Or creative? What are some ways you can start to pursue your interests in this career?

Analyzing Your Future. How will the state of the economy affect your career?

Further Exploration

To find out more about job trends during economic downturns, visit the Glencoe *Introduction to Business* Web site, **www.introbus.glencoe.com**.

Unit 4

Marketing to the Consumer

A Hunting They Will Go

Don't look now, but the Cool Hunters are watching you. Cool Hunters are market researchers who try to spot the next big trend in teen culture, whether it's mood rings, skater slang, or pocket TVs. They hang out at malls, parks, schoolyards, dance clubs, and basketball courts, studying teens and taking notes. They sell their information to big corporations that use it to design products, logos, and ad campaigns for teens.

● **It's the Real Thing**
During its first year in business, the Coca-Cola Company sold 25 bottles of coke.

● **It's That One Commercial Again, With That Cool Music**
According to one survey, the average American sees more than 20,000 television commercials each year.

● **Synchronized Watches**
In ads that show a watch or a clock, the time displayed is usually 10:10.

● **Have a Nice Day**
The Smiley Face, which has been used in countless ad campaigns, sold more than 50 million buttons at the height of its popularity, and was even issued as a postage stamp. It was designed in 1963 by Harvey Ball, who was paid $45 for it.

● **Soap Box**
Daytime TV's soap operas got their name from soap companies, who originally sponsored them.

Marketing in Today's World

BusinessWeek Feature Story

Can Marvel's Heroes Save the Day?

Marvel Treats Its Characters Like Brands to Maximize Profits With Savvy Deals. For a few days in June, Marvel Enterprises saw its lethargic share price jump from $4 to $7, then tumble back to $4. It's easy to see what caused the brief excitement. Marvel owns the fantasy comic-book property *The X-Men* and anticipation of the major motion picture's premier was building. In fact, *The X-Men* film—from 20th Century Fox—was a pretty big summer hit, raking in $150 million at the box office. Too bad Marvel hasn't been able to capitalize on the runaway success of its cool mutant X-Men characters.

Source: Excerpted with permission from "Can Marvel's Heroes Save the Day?" *BusinessWeek Online*, September 6, 2000.

An Extension Activity

In Chapter 6 you were part of a start-up company manufacturing new skateboards. You found financial investors. Now your friends ask you to plan the company's channel of distribution. What is your plan?

BUSINESS Online
The Full Story

To learn more about Marvel's marketing plan, visit the *Introduction to Business* Web site at **www.introbus.glencoe.com**, and click on *BusinessWeek* Feature Story, Chapter 13.

Marketing Essentials

Marketing a skateboard requires a different strategy than marketing diamond earrings. Each item appeals to people of different ages, genders, and income ranges. Every holiday season more gadgets, toys, and clothes hit the stores. Behind a product is a company's intense research, development, and marketing. To successfully market a product, a company has to understand what people want to buy and why they want to buy it.

Basics of Marketing

It all comes down to knowing your market. **Market** is a group of customers who share common wants and needs, and who have the ability to purchase the product. There's more to marketing than just selling a product. **Marketing** is the process of creating, promoting, and presenting a product to meet the wants and needs of consumers. Marketing involves

Figure 13.1

U.S. GAME CONSOLE MARKET

➡Fun and Games. A market can be described as the people who are potential customers of a product, as well as by the classification of a product in a category.
Which company that makes game consoles interests you most? What does it do to grab your attention?

- Sony
- Nintendo
- Sega
- Others

0.1%
21.4%
21.5%
57%

a number of stages from studying what people want to buy to designing a product's package. For example, you might be part of the $7 billion market who buys video game consoles (see Figure 13.1). Businesses need to know their customers' wants and needs in order to make a profit. This is known as the **marketing concept**.

Businesses want you to buy their product so they perform detailed research on markets (like teenagers) to find and analyze potential customers in their market. This is called **target marketing**. Later on in this chapter, you'll read how marketing decisions are made based upon target marketing.

Functions of Marketing

There are seven functions of marketing. Each aspect is important to the entire function.

Distribution. This involves moving goods and services from one place to the end user. Trucks, trains, airplanes, and ships are possible transportation methods.

Financing. Money is necessary to keep any business afloat. Businesses decide if customers can pay with credit or other payment options.

Marketing Information Management. Making an informed decision requires good research and development. Companies conduct market research to learn more about their market. (Market research is discussed in more detail later on in this chapter.)

Pricing. Marketers have to figure out what price to charge for a product so the company makes a profit. Marketing needs to consider the impact of distribution, because each time a product goes through another channel of distribution the price goes up. (You'll read more about channels of distribution later in the chapter.)

Product/Service Management. Obtaining information, developing, and maintaining products helps marketers decide how to respond to market opportunities.

Promotion. Communication through any type of media gets a business's product out and into the hands of the public.

Selling. Retailers or the business-to-business market provides customers or industrial users with goods and services. A popular trend in today's marketing world is **relationship marketing**. Companies use

BEYOND STREET-SKATERS
Vans Inc., the maker of slip-on sneakers for maverick teens who like to skateboard, is about being market smart. The last thing its audience wants is to be beaten over the head with slick advertisements. That would be the fastest way to losing loyalty.
Name some qualities about the teen market. What do you want and need?

continued on p. 201

Technology Toolkit

Online Whiffs of Wonder

Is that scent coming from...your computer? Well, DigiScents, Inc., is developing a digital scent device called the iSmell. DigiScents has indexed thousands of odors based on their chemical structure. Each scent is a digitized file, which can be embedded in Web content or an e-mail message. The computer user hooks up iSmell to a computer and requests a scent with the click of a mouse.

Critical Thinking
How might online odors help businesses sell their products?

this strategy to build customer relations. In a competitive world, this keeps a company aware of how it's meeting its customers' wants and needs.

Marketing Mix

Even before a product appears on the market, marketing specialists have to consider a number of questions. Who will the product appeal to? How much should it cost? Where should it be sold? What's the best way to tell people about it? The four elements of marketing—product, place, price, and promotion—are called the **marketing mix**, or the *four Ps*.

Product. Marketing is used first to find out if there is a demand for a product. Then it is concerned with how to present a product to the customer to make it as appealing as possible. How to package a product is a major element of marketing. Packaging includes the design, color, size, and even brand name of a product. Books and CDs rely a lot on cover designs to attract buyers.

Place. Marketers have to figure out where to sell a product to get it to the right customers. One of the first things they have to consider is *where to sell* a product. For example, a company is much more likely to sell snowshoes in Maine than in Texas.

Then marketers have to consider in *what kind of location* to sell their product. Does the product need to be at a fast-food restaurant or gas station? Does the product need to be in a large department store or a boutique?

The *placement* of the product in a store is equally as important. When you first enter a store you'll see featured products on display stands. At checkout counters, you'll find key chains, candy bars, and other small items you might want to buy at the last second.

Price. To determine the price of a product a marketer considers three questions: (1) how much are customers willing to pay, (2) is the price competitive with other products, and (3) can the company make a profit? The amount of money a company has to make on a product to pay for its costs is called the **break-even point**.

Promotion. Promotion consists of making customers aware of a product. The most familiar form of promotion is advertising, which will be covered in the next chapter. There are, however, many other means companies use to promote a product. One way is to offer discounts in the form of coupons, rebates, and sales. Fast-food restaurants offer package deals with free toys.

Another way companies promote their products is through public relations, or *publicity*. Publicity is a kind of free advertising. It consists mostly of news stories on TV, in newspapers, or in magazines. For example, companies like Sony and Microsoft benefit from news articles about the latest in high-tech products. Celebrities go on talk shows and appear on magazine covers to promote their new movie or CD. Big companies sometimes stage *media events*, like a big party or an awards show, to promote the company or one of its products.

✔ **Fast Review**

1. What is marketing?
2. What are a few functions of marketing?
3. Name the marketing mix, or the four Ps.

Market Research

Have you ever been approached by a marketing researcher while you were shopping at the mall? Market researchers commonly ask shoppers to take a few minutes to answer questions, taste a new food, or watch a new commercial.

Companies do **market research** to gather and study information about consumers to determine what kinds of goods and services to produce. Figure 13.2 (see the next page) breaks down who uses market research the most. Marketing experts keep track of consumers using surveys, sales figures, databases, and the census. Marketers analyze and categorize their markets by demographics. **Demographics** are facts about the population in terms of age, gender, location, income, and education. Once marketers know the demographics of a market, companies can start developing products to fit that particular group.

Product Development

The demand for products changes constantly. Fads and fashions go in and out of style. New technology replaces old technology. A company's ability to create a new product or a slight variation of an already successful one is important to increasing sales.

There are seven steps in developing a new product. You could use these to develop a car, dish soap, a book, or even clothing. New products invigorate the marketplace. Let's look at the seven important steps.

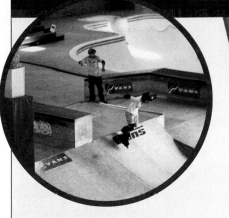

Real-World Application

part **2** of **4**

BEYOND STREET-SKATERS
It's no longer just about the shoes. Instead of mass advertisements, Vans integrates its products into lifestyles. The company built skateboard parks from West Orange, Calif., to Houston, Tex., for skateboarders.
Describe the marketing mix of these skateboard parks.

continued on p. 203

Generating Ideas. Soda cans and leftover sandwich wrappers litter a conference table. A group of coworkers brainstorm for creative ideas for the company's new product line. One writes down the group's creative ideas on an interactive SMART Board™. People from the company's development department, the market research staff, and even outside market researchers are generating ideas for a new creative product. Collaboration is key to this step.

Screening Ideas. Once the team puts together a final list of creative ideas for the product, they're evaluated. How do these ideas fit the company's mission and the company's strategy? Does the new product compete with one of the company's existing products? If the product's concept is risky, the company might ask consumers about the creative concept. Consumers would identify what they liked or disliked about

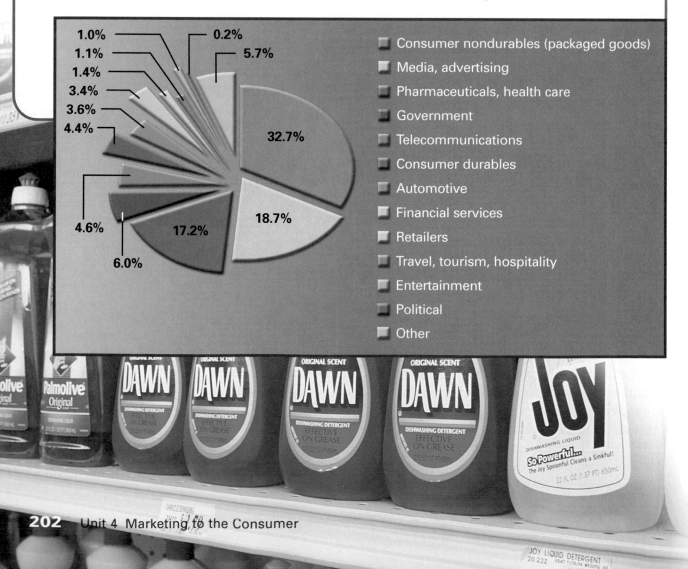

Figure 13.2
MARKETING RESEARCH REVENUES BY INDUSTRY GROUPS

➥Client industry groups for marketing research spend over $3 billion annually.
Why does the government spend money on marketing research?

- 1.0%
- 1.1%
- 1.4%
- 3.4%
- 3.6%
- 4.4%
- 4.6%
- 6.0%
- 17.2%
- 18.7%
- 32.7%
- 5.7%
- 0.2%

■ Consumer nondurables (packaged goods)
■ Media, advertising
■ Pharmaceuticals, health care
■ Government
■ Telecommunications
■ Consumer durables
■ Automotive
■ Financial services
■ Retailers
■ Travel, tourism, hospitality
■ Entertainment
■ Political
■ Other

the concepts. Their responses are crucial as to whether or not the company continues with a proposed product.

Developing a Business Proposal. Once the creative idea passes the screening process, one or two of the ideas are developed into a business plan. (This business plan has many of the same parts and pieces as the business proposal you read about in Chapter 5.) The written proposal provides answers about the market, potential sales, costs, profit potential, market trends, the competition's products, and the level of risk.

Developing the Product. Now that the company's appropriate managers and decision makers are in favor of the product, a prototype is made. This is a model of the actual product. It's used to test ideas. If any aspects of the prototype need to be changed this is the stage to make those changes. A company might experience delays in finalizing the product as it is tested. The government requires extensive testing during various stages of product development. Any one of the testing stages may delay the product.

Test Marketing the Product. Once the product is fully developed, the product might be test marketed. The goal is to collect customers' responses. Sometimes, though, the cost of test marketing a product isn't in the budget. Also, testing may leave time for the competitor to produce a similar product. Then both products may enter the market at the same time.

Introducing the Product. The product passed the market test. Now it's ready for the marketplace. Publicity is used to introduce the product. The costs of doing this are often high. The company has a small amount of time in the market before competition produces a similar product.

Evaluating Customer Acceptance. Once the product is introduced, marketers track customers' responses. The reports answer key questions which inform companies' research and development. Who are their best customers? What new products are they buying? How often do customers buy the new product?

Real-World Application

part 3 of 4

BEYOND STREET-SKATERS
Innovating shoes has made Vans a reputable business pioneer. The latest is its snowboard boots but it decided against designing inline skates. For its hard-core skateboarders, inline skating isn't in their interest. Why do you think Vans didn't try marketing inline skates?

continued on p. 205

✔️ **Fast Review** _____

1. What's the purpose of market research?
2. Name the seven steps in developing a new product.

Channels of Distribution

Marketers have to decide how and where customers will buy their goods and services. (This is the *place* step of the marketing mix that you learned about earlier.) A good marketing strategy includes a distribution plan.

To make this decision, marketers must decide on their channel of distribution. A **channel of distribution** is a particular way to direct products to consumers. Producers use a specific channel to move goods to their final user. **Direct distribution** occurs when the goods or services are sold from the producer directly to the customer; an intermediary isn't involved. **Indirect distribution** involves one or more intermediaries.

The biggest impact distribution has on marketing is how it affects the price of products. Each time a product goes through another channel the cost of marketing it increases. Wholesalers, retailers, truck companies, and warehouses all have to cover their own expenses and make a profit. Therefore, the cost of distributing a product has to be added to its price, which makes it hard for some companies to compete. Let's take a closer look at the channel members of distribution.

Channel Members

Moving the product from manufacturer to the final user is an intermediary, or a go-between. Intermediaries can include distributors, wholesalers, retailers, and today, even the Internet.

Distributors. This kind of intermediary represents a single manufacturer in a geographic area. Cosmetics, cars, furniture, and shoes are sold through distributors.

Wholesalers. A **wholesaler** receives large shipments of products from many different producers. They break the shipments into smaller batches for resale. A company that makes canned peas may sell a truckload of its peas to a wholesaler. The wholesaler, in turn, will sell a few cases of peas to several local supermarkets.

Retailers. A **retailer** sells goods directly to the customer. This is the final stop in the channel of distribution. When you buy something in the supermarket, drugstore, or department store, you're dealing with a retailer.

Some manufacturers or service providers go directly to the customer. The Internet encourages producers to distribute their products themselves. A virtual business (as you learned in Chapter 5) allows customers to order online. This cuts down on the role of intermediaries, and can cut costs and increase profits to the producer.

BEYOND STREET-SKATERS
The founders of Vans wanted to manufacture shoes and sell them directly to its customers. Over 30 years later, Vans has sold its products through its own retail stores as well as independents.
Do you show product loyalty? If so, what are these brands? Why?

✔ **Fast Review** _____

1. Channels of distribution are classified in which two ways?
2. How does distribution affect the prices of products?
3. What are the major types of intermediaries?

Summary

1. The functions of marketing include distribution, financing, marketing information management, pricing, product and service management, promotion, and selling. The four elements of the marketing mix are product, place, price, and promotion.

2. Market research is important to study the customers' wants and needs and buying behavior. A product goes through seven developmental steps. These include: generating ideas, screening ideas, developing a business proposal, developing the product, test marketing the product, introducing the product, and evaluating customer acceptance.

3. A product has to go through channels of distribution to get from producers to consumers.

● Using Business Key Words

People who market goods and services use the following terms. See how well you know them. Match the word to its definition.

- **target marketing**
- **market**
- **marketing**
- **break-even point**
- **wholesaler**
- **demographics**
- **marketing mix**
- **direct distribution**
- **indirect distribution**
- **retailer**
- **marketing concept**
- **channel of distribution**
- **market research**
- **relationship marketing**

1. The study of population.
2. Analyzing consumer wants and providing goods and services to meet those wants.
3. A way to direct products to consumers.
4. Product, price, promotion, and place—the activities that go into selling a product to consumers.
5. The gathering of information that businesses can use to determine what kinds of goods and services to produce.
6. A group of customers who share common needs and wants.
7. Businesses need to know their customers' wants and needs in order to make a profit.
8. A popular trend in today's marketing world.
9. Detailed research on a particular segment of the population.
10. The amount of money a company has to make on a product to pay for its costs.
11. Goods and services are sold from producer directly to the customer.
12. Delivering goods and services with one or more intermediaries.
13. Receives large shipment of products from many different producers.
14. Sells goods directly to the customer.

Review What You Learned

15. During what marketing function is relationship marketing a consideration?
16. Describe each function of marketing.
17. What are the four Ps?
18. What's the purpose of market research?
19. Marketers analyze and categorize their markets by this.
20. Describe the seven important steps in developing a new product.
21. Why are channels of distribution important?
22. Describe the difference between distributors and wholesalers.

Understanding Business Concepts

23. Which of the four marketing factors do you think is the most important? Explain why.
24. Describe a situation when low pricing does not mean low quality. Give an example that you have personally experienced.
25. List a product that you think might not have been sold for a long time because of the marketplace's lack of interest.
26. Have you ever purchased something based on an interesting marketing campaign? Explain.
27. What information do you like to have included with a product that you buy?
28. What could market researchers learn about a group of people by studying the foods they bought in the last year?
29. Explain how the Internet is a channel of distribution.
30. Why do you think companies try to design easily recognizable logos?

Critical Thinking

31. How might products and services designed to meet customers' wants and needs vary between countries?
32. Some companies plan special events to draw publicity for a new product. What kind of event could a shoe company hold to attract publicity for a new line of athletic shoes?
33. Collect several magazines. Based upon the advertisements, describe which demographic the magazines cater to?

Viewing and Representing

Examining the Image. Carefully observe the photograph and write what you see. What do you already know about the time period and the people shown in the picture? What can you conclude about what is happening in the photograph? What is being promoted here? Is more than one thing being promoted? What picture of the world is being presented? Are the people or other things here being depicted with accuracy, with bias, or with exaggeration? Write your answers.

Building Academic Skills

HISTORY Sociological Decisions

In a group, conduct a survey of other students, teachers, family members, and people in the community to find out what factors are most important in their buying decisions. Use the survey to determine:

- Which stores they shop in most frequently.
- What types of advertising they pay the most attention to.
- What factors are most important to them when making decisions about convenience goods and services, shopping goods and services, and specialty goods and services.

Tabulate your results and create a chart to display your findings.

MATH Pricing

Your boss has asked that you price the new shipment of leather jackets that have just arrived. She wants the jackets to be priced 11.5 percent lower than the store across town. If the jackets sell for $129.99 at the other store, what price will you sell the jackets for at your store?

LANGUAGE ARTS Analyzing and Creating

Using magazines or newspapers, find advertisements that appeal to different demographic categories. Mount the ads on poster board and write a paragraph explaining how each ad appeals to the particular demographic category.

COMPUTER TECHNOLOGY Designing a Flier

Imagine you've been hired to create a publicity event for a shoe store that plans to introduce a new line of athletic shoes. Using a word processor, write a one-page paper about the event you'll create. Using publishing software, create a flier that you could use to promote your event. Display the flier in your class.

Linking School to Home

Mini Survey. During the next two weeks, save all the advertising and promotional material that comes in the mail for you and your family. Categorize each one based on the type of product being advertised. Conduct a mini-survey among your family and friends. Find out whether or not they would buy the products based on the advertising material that has been sent to your home.

Linking School to Work

Promoting a Product. If you're employed, choose a product sold by your company and determine the following:

- The pricing strategy utilized by your company.
- The marketing approach used to sell the product.
- The channel(s) of distribution used to direct the product to the consumer.

If you're not employed, choose a product sold at school.

E-Homework

Applying Technology

Online Want Ads. Use the Internet to research the entry-level advertising positions available online. Find out where the job is located, the starting salary, duties and responsibilities, and education required. Write a paragraph summarizing your findings.

Surveying E-tailers. Select three stores that you shop in regularly that also have a presence on the Internet. Log on to their Web sites and evaluate their Web pages in order to answer these questions:

- Is the site attractive and user friendly?
- What types of products are sold online? Are they different from the products sold in the stores? How?
- What security measures are in place to protect online buyers?

Write a one-page paper describing the site you liked the best and why.

Connecting Academics

Math. You're manager of the sweatshirt department at Trends, a clothing manufacturer. Trends plans to produce 25,000 sweatshirts. The sweatshirts will be sold to stores for $16 each. The cost of manufacturing and marketing each sweatshirt is $10. How many sweatshirts must your department sell at $16 to reach the break-even point?

Language Arts. Working in a team of three, find and read several articles on marketing, market research, or relationship marketing. Together, create a one-minute news report titled, "Marketing Fast Facts" on topics from the articles.

BusinessWeek Analyzing the Feature Story

You read the first part of "Can Marvel's Heroes Save the Day?" at the beginning of this chapter. Below are a few questions for you to answer about Marvel Enterprises. You'll find the answers to these questions when you're reading the entire article. First, here are the questions:

34. What product does Marvel Enterprises plan to use to become the leading entertainment company in the world?
35. How is Marvel planning to change its pricing strategy with movie studios?

CREATIVE JOURNAL ACTIVITY

Break into small groups. You're a product team for Marvel Enterprises. Using one of its characters, come up with a new product to sell. How will you price it? How will you promote it? Where will you sell it? Write your ideas in a marketing plan and then present your ideas to the Marvel Board of Directors (i.e., your class).

BUSINESS Online
The Full Story

To learn more about Marvel's marketing plan, visit the *Introduction to Business* Web site at **www.introbus.glencoe.com**, and click on *BusinessWeek* Feature Story, Chapter 13.

Chapter 14

Advertising: The Art of Attracting an Audience

Learning Objectives

After completing this chapter, you'll be able to:
1. **Identify** the different types of media that can be used to advertise products.
2. **List** advantages and disadvantages for each type of advertising media.
3. **Name** factors in the cost of advertising.

Why It's Important

Businesses rely on advertising to get your attention and to promote their products. Advertising pays for many of the costs of TV, radio, newspapers, and magazines.

Key Words

advertising
mass media
direct-mail advertising
transit advertising
infomercial
webcast
cyber ads
pop-up ads
banner ads
screen ads

BusinessWeek Feature Story

Yahoo! and Pepsi: "Fusion Marketing" in Prime Time

The Portal's Approach to Advertising. The slot most coveted by advertisers on Super Bowl Sunday isn't during the pregame show, or right before the start of the celebrity-studded half-time extravaganza. It won't be during the game at all. This year, the crème-de-la-crème of TV commercial positioning will be those precious three minutes between the end of the National Football League's championship game on CBS and the beginning of the network's second *Survivor* series: "The Australian Outback."

Source: Excerpted with permission from "Yahoo! and Pepsi: "Fusion Marketing" in Prime Time," *BusinessWeek Online*, January 26, 2001.

An Extension Activity

Why do companies hire models, actors, or other celebrities to sell products?

BUSINESS *Online*
The Full Story
To learn more about "fusion marketing," visit the *Introduction to Business* Web site at www.introbus.glencoe.com, and click on *BusinessWeek* Feature Story, Chapter 14.

O

HE OPRAH
MAGAZINE

CREATIVE SOLUTIONS
Making connections
Finding answers
Reviving your spirit

WE GATHER TOGETHER
A Classic Thanksgiving Dinner

AFTER SHOCK
Comfort in the face
of disaster

Confronting Issues With Images

A corporation just might be watching you. What you buy. How you act. Anything that pushes your buttons is of interest to corporations that have something to sell. What they sell you is a product through an image. Buying a product when there's an image attached—that somehow it'll make you better looking or cooler—is exactly what the company wants you to do. This way you help their profits.

Advertising Media

Advertisements are everywhere you look. You see them on TV, in movie theaters, on the streets, at checkout counters, in magazines, on the Internet, and on T-shirts. The average person sees hundreds of ads each week. In a world with so many choices for essentially the same product, advertisers use their wit, wisdom, and originality to get consumer's attention. Often companies with deep pockets gobble up the market share by spending the most on advertising campaigns. **Advertising** is the paid, nonpersonal form of communication that businesses use to

Figure 14.1

CATCHY SLOGANS

➡Advertising slogans have become so well known in many cases that people all over the country recognize them. Here are ten slogans from advertisements.
How many of the products or services can you name?

1. "It keeps going, and going, and going . . ."
2. "Plop, plop, fizz, fizz, oh what a relief it is . . ."
3. "Doesn't your dog deserve _____?"
4. "It's the real thing!"
5. "Don't leave home without it."
6. "Reach out and touch someone."
7. "Wouldn't you really rather have a _____?"
8. "Mmm mmm good . . ."
9. "Tastes so good cats ask for it by name."
10. _____ is the place for the helpful hardware folks."

promote their products. Creating and using a catchy advertising slogan over and over again is one way a company sells a product (see Figure 14.1).

Most ads consist of short messages designed to attract your attention, identify a product, and tell you something about it. They are sent using one or more types of mass media. **Mass media** are means of communication such as TV, radio, and newspapers. The type of medium an advertiser uses depends on the market it wants to reach.

Print Media

Print media uses writing and pictures to communicate. It includes newspapers, magazines, signs, and billboards. In fact, the age of advertising began with the invention of the printing press in the fifteenth century. Fliers could be mass produced and put in newspapers or posted in public places. It's still one of the most popular means of advertising.

Newspapers. Newspapers are the main advertising medium in the United States. More than 50 percent of adults in the United States read newspapers. Advertisers can target people within a certain area. This is especially useful for neighborhood businesses like hair salons and restaurants. Newspapers usually come out daily, which allows businesses to run an ad several days at a time or once a week. Advertisers can also place ads quickly and update them easily.

The cost of printing an ad is fairly cheap. Newspaper ads often include coupons that can be clipped out, so the ads can have a life beyond the newspaper. On the other hand, most people throw their newspapers away after they read them, so an ad's lifespan is usually short. Ads have to compete with news, sports, comics, editorials, and other features for attention. Many readers simply ignore the ads. Since most newspapers are printed in black and white and use recycled paper and soy-based ink, the actual ad design is less intricate than in glossy magazines.

Magazines. Most magazines are national in scope and appear every week (such as *Time*) or every month (such as *Vanity Fair*). People from around the country can see the same ad in an issue of the magazine. Many magazines also offer regional editions for different parts of the country. Special-interest magazines like *Teen* and *Sports Illustrated* make it possible to reach target markets on a large scale. For example, makers of computer software can reach the right market by placing ads in magazines like *PC*.

BATHED IN BLUE
Who doesn't love a sale? The ad promises 40 percent off for that beach towel. "Excellent," you think. And you throw two into your cart as a blue police light flashes.
What store are you in?

continued on p. 215

Technology Toolkit

Pushing the Limits

Advertisers reach people with push technology (also known as webcasting, channeling, niche casting, and narrowcasting). The Massachusetts Institute of Technology (MIT) students called their push product fishWrap®, which refers to the old expression, "Yesterday's news wraps today's fish." This personalized news service is tailor-made for its users, who fill out a personal profile when they subscribe.

Critical Thinking

How might push technology work against companies that try pushing their products to the marketplace?

People take their time to read magazines and often save them, so magazine ads have a much longer lifespan than newspaper ads. Since people tend to look at magazines more than once, they might see the same ad several times. Most magazines are printed in color with much higher quality ink and paper than newspapers. For these reasons the ads often look more attractive.

Magazines are so broadly circulated they're of little use to local advertisers. Another disadvantage is that magazines take longer to prepare so ads are placed weeks or even months in advance. They can't be easily changed or used to promote a limited offer.

Direct-Mail Advertising. **Direct-mail advertising** consists of ads sent by mail to people's homes. It's the biggest advertising medium after TV and newspapers. Direct mail allows advertisers to reach a specific target market. A business can put together a mailing list of customers who live within a certain area, belong to a certain age group, or buy certain kinds of products. It can then mail ads only to people who might be interested. For example, a college student might receive ads in the mail for backpacks, credit cards, or "spring break" specials.

Direct-mail advertisers can use a variety of formats—letters, fliers, postcards, and catalogs—and include coupons or free samples. Internet servers such as America Online (AOL) send out free trial CDs through the mail. Direct mail can also be used to make sales by including order forms.

The cost of sending ads through the mail can be very high. Mailing lists have to be constantly maintained and updated. Only 1 percent of people who receive ads in the mail actually respond. Direct mail is often referred to as "junk mail" because people who receive direct-mail advertising often throw it out without ever looking at it.

Directory Advertising. Directory advertising, which consists mostly of phone books, is especially useful for local advertisers. They can list their number and display an ad under a heading for the type of product or service they offer.

The cost of a directory is usually very cheap. Phone books are used in almost every home, in all areas, and kept for at least a year. They help local businesses by making it easy for consumers to find them on demand.

A disadvantage of directory ads is that they have to compete with numerous similar ads. Directory ads are so brief—often consisting of little more than a name, address, and phone number—that they have no way to stand out. Which business a person calls is often randomly picked. Most ads run can't be used to advertise prices, sales, and they can't be easily updated.

Outdoor Advertising. The most common form of outdoor advertising is a billboard. Most billboards are very large and placed near highways where they're highly visible. They can be seen many times by thousands of drivers. A billboard is usually placed for several months. They're useful for local businesses and businesses that cater to travelers, such as fast-food stands, motels, and radio stations.

The main disadvantage of billboards is that people often drive by them too quickly to notice. If you see the same billboard often enough you also begin to ignore it. Billboards are banned in some states, such as Maine and Alaska, because they detract from the scenery. In many urban areas like Los Angeles, billboards are restricted along freeways because they distract drivers too much.

Transit Advertising. Transit advertising uses public transportation, such as buses and trains to display ads. **Transit advertising** usually consists of posters placed on the sides of buses, in subway stations, inside trains, and at airports. They're most common in urban areas where public transportation is used more often. For this reason, they're useful for advertising things like concerts, public events, and local TV.

Broadcast Media

Broadcast media (primarily TV and radio) are the most effective means of advertising. Over 98 percent of all homes in the United States have at least one TV and almost every American owns a radio. The popularity of broadcast media makes it possible for advertisers to reach a mass audience. Figure 14.2 illustrates the amount of money corporations will spend to get their product out there.

Television. Television has an advantage over any other media because it combines sounds, images, and motion. Advertisers can be more informative, entertaining, or creative with TV ads. Some ads are so effective that they become part of our everyday language.

TV ads can be shown on national, local, or cable stations to reach any kind of market. Advertisers can also reach target markets by showing ads during certain types of shows. Ads for an animated movie are shown during Saturday morning cartoons and ads for an action movie are aired during *Monday Night Football*.

bluelight always
the best values always

was 8⁹⁹ **4⁹⁹**

BATHED IN BLUE
Kmart is known for its Blue Light Special. That infamous voice over any one of its store's P.A. systems that calls, "Attention Kmart shoppers!," was started in 1965 by a store manager in Fort Wayne, Ind.
What do you think was the impetus behind this creation?

continued on p. 217

Most TV ads are 30- or 60-second "spots." Another type of TV ad is the infomercial. An **infomercial** is a TV program, usually 30 minutes long, made to advertise a product. It is often set up like a talk show with a live studio audience and a celebrity guest who demonstrates the product.

The biggest disadvantage of TV ads is that they can be very expensive to produce. Advertisers also have to pay to broadcast an ad during a TV show. The more popular a show is, the more it costs to air an ad during it.

Radio. Like TV ads, radio ads can reach a very wide audience. Radio ads may not be as effective as TV or even magazine ads, because they can't use images. They can, however, use music, dialogue, and sound effects creatively to get an audience's attention.

Radio stations broadcast within certain areas so they're a good medium for local advertising. They also specialize in certain types of programs: talk

Figure 14.2

BIG SPENDERS

➡This chart shows the five companies who spent the largest sums of money on advertising in a recent year. General Motors Corporation, for example, spent about $2.9 billion on advertising.

Think about the advertisements for these five companies. In what media have you seen their advertisements? Why do you think their spending for advertising is so extensive?

COMPANY	SPENDING FOR ADVERTISING (APPROXIMATE AMOUNTS)
1. General Motors Corporation	$2.9 billion
2. Procter & Gamble Company	1.7 billion
3. Daimler/Chrysler AG	1.5 billion
4. Philip Morris Companies, Inc.	1.4 billion
5. Ford Motor Company	1.2 billion

Source: Data reported in the 2001 edition of *The World Almanac and Book of Facts*, published by World Almanac Books.

shows, news, classical music, rock, or country-western music. Advertisers can reach people on the move—when driving or even jogging with a Walkman®.

Webcasting. Webcasting is a new broadcast medium made possible by the Internet. A **webcast** is like a TV or radio broadcast but it's sent and received over the Web. A webcast usually consists of a live broadcast made by a Web camera (or "cam") crew hired to film a specific location or event. For example, many radio stations now use Web cams so audiences can both see and hear the station. To promote its products, a clothing company can broadcast a live fashion show on the Internet. Marketers can also use webcasting to promote concerts, sports, or other events by broadcasting them live over the Internet.

Cyber Ads

Cyber ads are ads on that appear on the Internet. They're different from webcasts in that they're displayed like magazine ads rather than broadcast like TV ads. The three main types of cyber ads are pop-up ads, banner ads, and screen ads. **Pop-up ads** appear for a few seconds when you first log onto the Internet or when you click on a site. **Banner ads** are displayed across the top or bottom of the screen and remain there. **Screen ads** appear at the left or right of the screen and can be printed for future reference. To get to the advertiser's Web site you simply click on the ad.

Cyber ads have many of the advantages of different types of print media. They can be sent directly to people on mailing lists and can include order forms like direct-mail ads. Like directory ads, consumers can look up a business easily by logging onto the Internet. Cyber ads can even be displayed in public (like billboards) on large computer screens. They have an added advantage in that they can use sound effects and animation.

BATHED IN BLUE
Recently Kmart developed a $30 million campaign to modify the Blue Light Special tradition. The idea is that every hour on the hour, Kmart will select one item and drastically reduce its price for 20 minutes. The blue light will go off and a song like Johnny Cash's "Blue Train" will play.
Why does Kmart go to such creative lengths?

continued on p. 219

✔ Fast Review

1. What are some of the differences between newspaper and magazine ads?
2. What are some disadvantages of outdoor ads such as billboards?
3. Name places where you would see transit ads.
4. What are some advantages of advertising on the radio rather than on TV?
5. What are the three biggest media for advertisers?
6. What advantages do print and cyber ads share?

Advertising Rates

The amount of money it costs to display or broadcast an ad is separate from the amount it costs to actually produce an ad. News and entertainment media pay for much of their costs by selling advertising space. The advertising rates are determined by several factors: the size of the ad, the number of people it reaches, how often it appears, when it appears, and where it's placed.

Print Media

Newspaper and magazine rates are based on circulation, or the number of people who read them. An advertiser usually pays a rate for every

Business Building Blocks

Distinguishing Between Relevant and Irrelevant Information

Information bombards you. On the job, you'll have to figure out what information is necessary, or *relevant*. Other information is *irrelevant*. Irrelevant information may be very interesting, but has no significant connection to your work. To be successful in the business world, you need to know how to distinguish relevant from irrelevant information.

Relevant information will define, explain, illustrate, or offer cause-and-effect relationships concerning the main topic you're exploring. Before gathering information, write down what you need to know. If someone gives you irrelevant information, ask questions that will redirect his or her focus to what's important. If you're reading, learn to sort out irrelevant information from that which is important and useful.

Analysis

Practice

Read the following case study. Decide what information is necessary for the main character to know, and write that information on a piece of paper.

Case Study: Examine the Information

You go to a local store to buy an inexpensive CD player so you can listen to music on the bus. You're especially interested in a feature you saw advertised in the morning newspaper. You're looking for one with the anti-roll feature. The clerk grabs off the shelf a model that's on sale. He says all the cool color CD players are on sale. These also come with three free CDs that are in the bin over there. You ask him how the anti-roll feature works on the model in your hand. He says it doesn't have it. The clerk says that the CD players in the corner have that mechanism, but they're not on sale.

1,000 people a newspaper or magazine reaches. Advertising in a local weekly newspaper costs a fraction of an ad in a large daily newspaper. An ad in a national magazine can cost thousands of dollars.

Newspaper and magazine ads are sold by the inch on the page. Ads can be small display ads, half-page ads, or full-page ads. Ads that appear on the front or back cover of a magazine cost more than ads inside the magazine. Whether an ad is in black and white or color also affects the cost.

Broadcast Media

The cost of radio and TV ads depends on the size of the audience. The cost to advertise on a national network is much more expensive than on a local station. The cost also depends on what time of day an ad is broadcast. An ad in *prime time* costs more than an ad aired at midnight. For radio, prime time on weekdays is during the morning or afternoon hours when most people are driving. TV prime time on weekdays is between 8:00 and 11:00 P.M. when most people are home. Advertisers also pay more for special events like the Oscar® Awards or the Super Bowl. During the Super Bowl, a single 30-second ad costs about $2 million.

Radio and TV advertisers usually pay for ads that are 10, 30, or 60 seconds long. They also pay more to show an ad several times a day. Sometimes an advertiser buys ads on different stations to be broadcast at the same time or buys a combination of radio and TV ads. Advertisers often hire media consultants and ad agencies to put together advertising packages for them.

The Internet

The cost of Internet advertising is based on the size and format of ads. Advertisers can buy pop-up ads, banner ads, screen ads, or ads in other formats. Ads can be large, medium, or small. The length of time an ad runs also affects the price. Like newspaper and magazine ads, Internet advertisers pay a certain amount for every 1,000 people that receive the ad. The number of people who click on a Web site determines this.

Real-World Application part 4 of 4

BATHED IN BLUE
In the discount store arena, competition is fierce. Kmart is vying for customers just like its main competitors Target and Wal-Mart. Each needs its own image. Kmart has an alliance with Martha Stewart to help distinguish itself from the crowd. **How will Martha Stewart Everyday® help Kmart?**

✓ **Fast Review** _____

1. What factors determine media costs?
2. On what day and what time might a film studio advertise an adult, action movie?

Global *Economy*

Worldwide Advertising
Each year the United States spends over $450 billion on advertising. The map below shows advertising expenditures for five countries whose economies are at different levels of development.

Russia

Category	Spending ($millions)
Television	718.4
Radio	123.0
Print*	1,130.5
Outdoor**	58.7
Point of Purchase	374.6
Promotions***	2,773.0
Direct Mail	314.5
Other	4,117.0
Total	*$9.6 billion*
% of World Total	*10.1%*

Egypt

Category	Spending ($millions)
Television	119.7
Radio	4.8
Print*	188.4
Outdoor**	9.8
Point of Purchase	46.8
Promotions***	727.9
Direct Mail	30.3
Other	128.4
Total	*$12.6 billion*
% of World Total	*1.3%*

Kenya

Category	Spending ($millions)
Television	15.2
Radio	0.2
Print*	24.0
Outdoor**	1.2
Point of Purchase	2.0
Promotions***	88.7
Direct Mail	5.5
Other	11.5
Total	*$1.5 billion*
% of World Total	*0.16%*

Vietnam

Category	Spending ($millions)
Television	15.5
Radio	0.8
Print*	24.4
Outdoor**	1.3
Point of Purchase	0.8
Promotions***	79.7
Direct Mail	7.2
Other	10.2
Total	*$1.4 billion*
% of World Total	*0.15%*

Singapore

Category	Spending ($millions)
Television	129.7
Radio	67.0
Print*	204.2
Outdoor**	10.6
Point of Purchase	261.6
Promotions***	535.7
Direct Mail	66.3
Other	244.6
Total	*$15.2 billion*
% of World Total	*1.6%*

*newspapers and magazines
**billboards, etc.
***coupons, give-aways, etc.

Thinking Globally

1. What is the largest category of advertising for each country?

2. Which of the expenditures for specific countries surprised you the most? Explain your answer.

Summary

1. Advertising is a paid, nonpersonal form of communication that businesses use to promote their products. Advertising media include print, broadcast, and the Internet.

2. Print media like newspapers, magazines, direct-mail advertising, directory advertising, outdoors advertising, and transit advertising are all highly visible in today's culture. Constant advertising makes consumers almost immune to its effect. Companies spend millions of dollars hoping you pay attention to their ad. You can find them on newsstands, sent to your home, on the side of buses, or on billboards. Broadcast media like TV, radio, and webcasting offer many advantages and disadvantages as well. While TV is highly visual and reaches national markets, it's also very expensive to produce. Radio reaches a wide audience and is good for local advertising. Lastly, people find cyber ads helpful or annoying. The use of sound effects and animation might capture your attention while surfing the Internet.

3. Advertising rates depend on the length of an ad, when it appears, where it appears, how often it appears, and the number of people it reaches.

● Using Business Key Words

There are many ways to attract an audience in order to sell a product. See how well you understand the terms that businesses use when they want to pass along information about their products. Match each term with its definition.

- **advertising**
- **cyber ads**
- **transit advertising**
- **infomercial**
- **webcast**
- **screen ads**
- **mass media**
- **direct-mail advertising**
- **pop-up ads**
- **banner ads**

1. A nonpersonal way of communicating with the public, using a mass medium.
2. Ads on the Internet.
3. Means of mass communication such as TV, radio, and newspapers.
4. A Web site that uses the Internet to broadcast information.
5. A television program that sells a product.
6. Internet ads displayed on the right or left of the computer screen and that can be printed.
7. Advertising that uses public transportation to display ads.
8. Advertising sent to people's homes by mail.
9. Internet ads that are displayed across the screen like billboards.
10. Internet ads that appear briefly when a user logs on or clicks on a site.

Review What You Learned

11. What does mass media include?
12. How does advertising serve you as a consumer?
13. What are the advantages and disadvantages of using newspapers as an advertising medium?
14. How can direct mail be personalized?
15. Explain how outdoor advertising and transit advertising are similar.
16. How is an infomercial different from a television commercial?
17. What percentage of adults read the newspaper?
18. Describe the difference between a banner ad, pop-up ads, and screen ads.
19. How are advertising rates determined for newspapers and magazines?
20. Describe how webcasting works.

Understanding Business Concepts

21. Are you more likely to read ads in newspapers or magazines? Explain your answer.
22. Name a special purpose magazine that you or one of your friends enjoys reading. What products are advertised in that magazine? Do you purchase any of those products?
23. How often do you use the yellow pages? Explain your answer.
24. Why do you think television ads are expensive compared to other media?
25. Describe your favorite television ad and your favorite radio ad. Explain why you like them.
26. Why does the future for advertising on the Internet look very promising?

Critical Thinking

27. Choose a product that is marketed specifically to teenagers. What type(s) of media is used to advertise this product?
28. How do you think cable television has changed television advertising?
29. If response rates are very low with online advertising, why do some advertisers continue to use it?
30. Will a prime-time television slot always guarantee an advertiser the best results in selling a product? Why or why not?

Viewing and Representing

Examining the Image. Glance at this ad. Write down your immediate impressions in your journal. Ads are meant to elicit emotion. How do you feel? Does the ad make you feel jealous, angry, cool, good, bad, etc? Take a longer look. When you study the ad do you feel any different? Do you want to buy the product? What background knowledge do you bring to this ad?

Building Academic Skills

 ### Producing a Radio Ad

Work with a partner to create a radio ad for one of your favorite products. Write a 30-second script and use music or other sound effects to enhance the ad. If possible, tape record the ad and play it for your class. Ask your classmates how effective they think the ad would be.

COMPUTER TECHNOLOGY ### Design a Banner Ad

Design a banner ad to promote a product on your favorite Web site. Consider the audience who will see the ad when you plan your design. Use the text, color, and graphic elements you think will make your banner ad the most effective.

 ### Historical Perspective

Choose one of the mass media that is described in the textbook. Research the history of the medium to find out:
- When it first started.
- How it has changed over time.
- The future of the medium.

Report your findings in a one- or two-page paper.

MATH ### Calculating Discounts

You receive a coupon in the mail for a 15 percent discount on a digital camera. You receive another coupon that offers a rebate of $100 on the same camera. If the camera costs $595, would you use the coupon or take the rebate?

Linking School to Home

Analyzing an Infomercial. With your family or group of friends, watch an infomercial. Answer the following questions:
- How long was the infomercial?
- Did a celebrity talk and demonstrate the product? If so, did the celebrity make you want to buy the product?
- Was there a toll-free number for customers to call in when ready to buy?
- What day and time did the infomercial air?
- Who in your family liked the infomercial? Who did not? Explain why.

Linking School to Work

Analyzing Ads. Collect a print advertisement from your place of employment. Evaluate the headline, text, illustrations, and design for its effectiveness. Describe the audience the ad is attempting to reach. Then, redesign the advertisement for a different market. If you're not working, choose an advertisement from a place you would like to work.

E-Homework

Applying Technology

Tracking Ads. Keep a log of all the advertisements for computer technology you see during a one-week period. Include all forms of mass media. Which media is used most frequently? Which advertisement did you like the best? Share your findings with your class.

Searching for Bot. Use the Internet to research "bots" or Internet robots. What are their uses? Do you think they could change the way we shop on the Internet? Why or why not? Explore a bot site and describe its function.

Connecting Academics

Math. A local candy company spent $45,000 on advertising last quarter. Radio ads comprised 7 percent of the total ads. How much money did it spend on radio ads?

The company sells a product for $3.10, but marketing costs are 48 percent of the selling price. How much is the actual marketing cost for this product?

Language Arts. Earlier in this chapter you learned about webcasting, also known as channeling, niche casting, or narrowcasting. Think of it as a personalized audio-visual clipping service. Give examples of specific webcasts. Find information about the effectiveness of webcasts. Do you feel webcasts are an effective method of advertising? Why or why not? Justify your conclusion using the information you found.

BusinessWeek Analyzing the Feature Story

You read the first part of "Yahoo! and Pepsi: "Fusion Marketing" in Prime Time" at the beginning of this chapter. Below are a few questions for you to answer about Pepsi's advertising strategy. You'll find the answers to these questions when you're reading the entire article. First, here are the questions:

31. What are the advantages to Pepsi in its Super Bowl advertising strategy?

32. What is a disadvantage of spending money on TV advertising during the Super Bowl?

CREATIVE JOURNAL ACTIVITY

Pay attention to the ads you see on television, hear on the radio, or see on billboards. What kinds of businesses advertise with each? Which medium do large, multinational companies use? Which medium is used by smaller businesses? Write a one-page report describing what you have learned.

BUSINESS Online
The Full Story

To learn more about "fusion marketing," visit the *Introduction to Business* Web site at **www.introbus.glencoe.com**, and click on *BusinessWeek* Feature Story, Chapter 14.

Unit ④ Technology

Discovering Technology in Marketing

In this unit, you learned marketing's four Ps: product, price, promotion, and place. You also learned that advertising is one form of promotion. So, how does a product become a household name on the Internet? In the late 1990s the dot-com companies boomed, but just a matter of years later they went bust. While Internet traffic has an ebb and flow, it's here to stay. Companies still look to technology as a pertinent avenue to get their product out in front of consumers. This seminar explores marketing a product using technology.

Factoids

High Speed. BMW commissioned film directors John Frankenheimer, Ang Lee, and Guy Ritchie to each create five-minute films for its advertising campaign. The edited 30-second versions were available as TV spots, but the entire films were only available at **www.BMWfilms.com**. It did this because most Net surfers are men, whose income is $75,000 a year; this is its target audience.

Big Budgets. According to PricewaterhouseCoopers, U.S. advertisers spent $8.2 billion online, $1.8 billion on outdoor advertising, and $11.2 on cable-TV ads.

Online Hours. The average Web user spends 16.5 hours online a week at home and at work.

A Developing Medium. The top U.S. advertising companies spend less than 1 percent of their budget on the Web.

Bang for Your Buck. The average banner ad costs $10,000 to make compared to a TV spot's cost of $340,000.

Investigate the Images

Look at the photographic collage on the left page. What grabs your attention at first? Is it the color or the words? The power in reading visuals is in analyzing and dissecting your observations. On a separate piece of paper, respond to the questions listed below. These questions might help sharpen the focus of your visual mind.

Your Observations

1. How many photographs do you see?

2. Examine each photograph. How is each assembled in relation to one another?

3. What is the subject of each photograph? Is place or location the subject?

4. Does color signify a message?

5. What issues do you take from these images?

Information

6. Summarize what you know about the photographs from your observations.

Exploring Culture

7. Does a product's advertising create a mood or place that persuades you into buying the product?

8. Do you feel a company has ever knowingly targeted you as a consumer? Which company and what was your reaction (i.e., did you purchase something, act differently, change your beliefs, etc.)?

Taking Aim at Technology

Preparation

Research how a company succeeds or fails when using technology to market its products. Then discover if other advertising methods might be more suitable for a product.

Objective

In this *BusinessWeek* Seminar, you'll:

- **Research** the media to find articles about a business that used the Internet to market and advertise its product.
- **Select** a product to study.
- **Create** a new Web page for this product.
- **Evaluate** the product's success story.

Materials Needed

- ✓ Copies of recent business news publications, such as the *Wall Street Journal* and *BusinessWeek* or Internet access
- ✓ Paper
- ✓ Posterboard and markers
- ✓ Copies of publications you can cut up
- ✓ Audiotape recorder or video camera (optional)
- ✓ Web page designing software (optional)
- ✓ Graphic design software (optional)

Procedures

1. With three other students, find and read articles about online businesses' successes and failures.

2. Choose a product to study. This might be an existing product or one you create.

3. Submit a one-page typed paper summarizing the story.

4. Create a new Web site for your product.
   - Each member is responsible for one Web page. Study the basic set up of Web pages. At least have a home page and three other linking pages.
   - Create the Web page with design software or create the design and place it on posterboard. The posterboard will show each page on your Web page. What is the function of each page, and how will it look?

5. Present your Web site to the class. Describe your product, and why you chose to market it the way you did.

Chart It

How do even small companies without big advertising budgets stay alive amid giant corporations? What keeps a company afloat in a competitive marketplace? Create a graphic organizer to brainstorm the answers to this question. As a class, reproduce something like this graphic below.

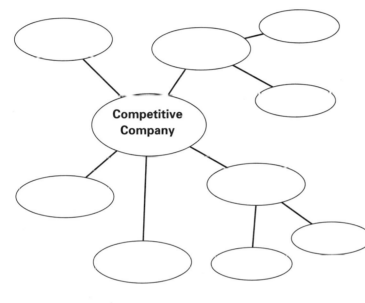

Competitive Company

Analyze and Conclude

After creating the graph, answer the following questions:

1. **Acquiring and Evaluating Information.** What are some common traits companies adhere to when marketing and advertising a product?

2. **Selecting Technology.** Is the Internet considered the end line for reaching out to a new marketplace? Why or why not?

3. **Maintaining and Troubleshooting.** In your opinion, what is the most effective way to market and advertise a product? Is it using the Internet, other technologies, print ads, etc.? State your reasons.

Becoming an Informed Citizen

Congratulations, you finished the seminar. Now it's time to reflect on the decisions you made.

Decision Making. Why did you choose your particular product? What interested you about it and why?

Analyzing Your Future. It's a competitive world and in time you're going to be vying for a job you really want. In order to impress future employers, you want to create a personal Web page. What personal qualities will you highlight on your Web page? How will you market yourself to differentiate yourself from the other applicants?

Further Exploration

To find out more about using technology to market and advertise products, visit the *Introduction to Business* Web site at **www.introbus.glencoe.com**.

The Human Resources Advantage

When in Rome...

In a global business environment, international diplomacy is no longer just for diplomats. If you're doing business in China, for instance, there are things you need to know just about exchanging business cards. When someone hands you a business card, you should accept it with both hands. Never put it away without looking at it first and never put it in your back pocket.

● **You Just Volunteered for What?!**
In Bulgaria, nodding your head up and down means NO and shaking it back and forth means YES.

● **Put to Rest That Power Grip**
It's customary in France to exchange a quick, light handshake rather than a long, firm one.

● **Keep Your Feet on the Ground**
Be careful about crossing your legs when you sit down in Turkey. It's considered very insulting to expose the bottoms of your feet to someone.

● **Be Sure to Wear Clean Socks**
You might take off your shoes when entering Japanese homes and restaurants.

● **The Right Rules**
Since the left hand is considered unclean in Egypt, use your right hand when eating and touching things.

● **Care for More Warthog?**
Don't be surprised if at a South African home or restaurant, you're served ostrich, hippo, giraffe, or warthog.

BUSINESS Online

Idea Factory

To learn more about business cultures, visit the *Introduction to Business* Web site at **www.introbus.glencoe.com**, and click on Unit 5 The Human Resources Advantage.

Chapter 15

Human Resources Management

Learning Objectives

After completing this chapter, you'll be able to:

1. **Give** examples of how businesses find new employees.
2. **Name** ways employees are oriented, trained, and evaluated.
3. **List** the ways an employee's status might change.

Why It's Important

To get the most out of its workforce, a business has to find the right employees, properly train them, and evaluate their performances.

Key Words

human resources management
job description
compensation
recruitment
orientation
on-the-job training
group training
performance appraisal
promotion
transfer
separation

BusinessWeek Feature Story

Online Benefits

New Application Service Helps Businesses Manage Human Resources Online.
CardStore.com, an Emeryville (Calif.) online retailer with about 35 employees, is in a hiring frenzy. So you might expect to find the company's human resources manager, Rhonda Mae Botello, buried in forms for payroll, health coverage, taxes, and the like. She's busy all right, but not with paperwork. When a new worker comes on board, Botello simply logs onto the Web, surfs over to eBenefits.com, and enters the new name and start date.

Source: Excerpted with permission from "New Application Service Helps Businesses Manage Human Resources Online," *BusinessWeek Online*, April 24, 2000.

An Extension Activity

CardStore.com wants to be the industry leader in personalized communication like postcards and posters. Even before it satisfies its customers, whom must it satisfy first? How?

The Full Story

To learn more about online human resources, visit the *Introduction to Business* Web site at **www.introbus.glencoe.com**, and click on *BusinessWeek* Feature Story, Chapter 15.

Employees: The Key to Success

A business's human resource is the people who work for it. These employees provide the skills, knowledge, labor, and experience needed to make a business productive. According to Henry Ford, "You can take my factories, burn up my building, but give me my people and I'll build the business right back up again."

Figure 15.1

WANT AD

➡ This job description lists the duties and responsibilities of a records assistant.
What qualifications must a person have for this position?

JOB DESCRIPTION
Title: Records Assistant
Reports to: Office Manager

Positions Supervised: None
Position Function: Provide support services to customers and maintain complete and accurate records.

Duties/Responsibilities:
1. File tickets and pull originals to prevent duplication.
2. Handle the billing process, including handling problems with processing.
3. Enter data into computer system.
4. Gather and prepare information on appeals and process the necessary paperwork for each case.
5. Assign duties and assist part-time staff as necessary.
6. Perform other related duties as assigned.

Minimum Qualifications:
Education: High school education with accounting and computer classes
Experience: Over three (3) months through one (1) year of office experience

Additional Preferred Qualifications:
Education: None
Experience: None

This description is intended to indicate the level of difficulty and the kinds of duties required of the position. It is not intended to limit the right of any supervisor to assign, direct, and control the work of the employee under his/her supervision. Where appropriate, directly related experience/education beyond the minimum stated may be substituted at the discretion of the Human Resources Department.

Finding Employees

Managing human resources isn't the same thing as supervising workers. **Human resources management** is the process of finding, selecting, training, and evaluating employees. The first step in this process is finding the right person for the job.

Job Description

If you're a human resources manager trying to fill a job you have to begin by writing a job description. A **job description** is a detailed outline of the duties, qualifications, and conditions required to do a specific job (see Figure 15.1). For example, if the job is for a graphic artist you need to say if it involves working with a supervisor, meeting deadlines, creativity, or using a computer. The job might also require someone with a certain amount of experience or education.

You also need to say if the job is part-time, full-time, permanent, or temporary. The job might need someone for only 20 hours a week or full-time for only a few months. Anyone who might be interested in the job will want to know what kind of compensation it offers. **Compensation** is how much the job pays and the benefits offered. Does the job pay minimum wage or $25 an hour? Does the company offer health insurance, sick leave, and paid holidays? Can a part-time position turn into a full-time position? A good compensation package is important to attract the most qualified people.

Employee Benefits. Employers need to meet your needs as an employee. You might evaluate a job opportunity based on the benefits package. Pay attention to the health care, retirement benefits, and specific needs of your family. Remember, it's important to look out for your own present and future needs. Let's take a closer look at different types of benefits.

People are living longer than ever before. Retirement programs are important to consider. A company's *pension plan*, a retirement plan that is funded at least in part by an employer, is important. Some plans provide you with a fixed amount of money. If you work for a business with a profit-sharing plan, it makes an annual contribution to your retirement fund each year. The third type of plan is a 401(k). You decide what portion of your check is set aside from each paycheck to go into your 401(k) fund. Your employer will often match a percentage of your contribution.

HUNTER HEADS HEADHUNTERS
From her third-floor corner office with a mountain view, Sharon Hunter helps connect corporations with top-level professionals and executives looking for new jobs.
Has anyone ever helped you get a job before?

continued on p. 237

Job Recruitment

To find the best people for a job a human resources manager has to recruit them. **Recruitment** means actively looking for qualified people to fill a job. Figure 15.2 illustrates qualities that certain positions might want you to exhibit. If you work for a large enough company, you start by looking for people who already work there. If no one is qualified, interested, or available, then you look outside the company.

One way to recruit people is by placing ads in newspapers, in magazines, at schools, or on the Internet. For example, to find a graphic artist you can post an ad for the job at an art school. You can also put an ad in an art magazine or trade paper. There are many Internet sites such as Monster.com that match people with certain skills to businesses looking for people with those skills. Employment agencies, employees' recommendations, or conventions are also ways to find qualified people.

The Selection Process

Companies want the best-qualified person for the job, the one most likely to succeed. Population trends are changing the pool of applicants. For example, the workforce is getting older. In relation to other age groups, fewer young people are entering the workplace. "Baby Boomers," workers aged 40 to 55, now are a larger share of the population. Workers are staying on the job longer. Retirement is no longer expected of all people who reach a certain age.

In the past, more men than women were in the paid workplace, but that has changed, too. An increase in the number of women in the workplace brought about a change in business practices. Childcare is a critical issue. As more men and women work, they must have care for their

Figure 15.2

WANTED QUALITIES IN AN APPLICANT

➡️Here is a list of jobs that recently appeared in a local newspaper.
Match a position to the qualification.

POSITIONS	QUALIFICATIONS
Part-time receptionist	Computer skills
Office assistant	Pleasant personality
Bank teller	Trained and licensed
Hair stylist	Detail oriented
Telesales associate	Pleasant voice

236

children. Family issues receive more attention as the percentage of women in the workplace increases.

What can you do to increase your chances of getting the job you want in the future? You must convince the employer that you're the best person for the job. Early in this course, you learned that a first impression is very important. What will impress a prospective employer? You must look like a person who's exactly what the employer is looking for. A neat appearance, poise, and confidence will help. You must have the skills needed for the job. The job description gives a clear picture of what the job requires. It will be your task to convince an employer that you can do everything in that job description well.

Human resources managers often say that prospective employees' lack communication skills. They want employees who can communicate well in writing and orally. You can begin to build your communication skills now. Inevitably, you'll have to give a presentation in front of a group. Learning how to give speeches is an excellent skill to possess. Accept opportunities to speak and learn how to perform in front of others in order to meet that requirement for selection by a business.

You live in a global economy. Business firms of all sizes do business around the world. Employees must know how to do business in other countries. What if you were to find a job with a company that does business in Brazil? How could you find out what are acceptable business practices in Brazil? Get acquainted with what other countries do. Read about international business customs (see the Unit 5 opening content and Chapter 16). Check the Internet for information about international business. You may find knowledge about other countries to be a selling point for you someday.

After recruiting enough people, you have to decide which one to hire. There are four steps to selecting the right person or *candidate* for the job. First, each candidate has to fill out an *application* listing his or her job experience, education, skills, and references. Then you *interview* the candidates to get more detailed information about them and see how they communicate. The next step is *testing* the candidates to make sure they have the right skills. Finally, you check out their *references* to make sure they went to school or worked where they claimed.

Real-World Application

part **2** of 4

HUNTER HEADS HEADHUNTERS
Hunter is president of Management Recruiters of Boulder, a "head-hunting" company that scouts talented professionals in the fields of radio frequency engineering, information technology, and construction.
What is the purpose of a headhunter?

continued on p. 239

✔ Fast Review

1. What are some of the ways a human resources manager can recruit people for a job?
2. What kind of information does a job description contain?
3. What are the four steps in selecting a candidate for a job?

Developing Employees

Suppose you decided to hire Gayle for the graphic artist job. Even if she has lots of experience working for other companies she needs to adjust to her new job and might have to learn some new skills. You also need to keep track of how she's doing her job. To develop Gayle as an employee she needs to be oriented, trained, and evaluated.

Orientation

Orientation is the process of helping new employees adjust to a company. The first step in orienting Gayle is taking her on a tour of the building and introducing her to other employees. She might go to a group orientation session and watch a video about the company. She'll receive a manual that explains everything from how the company is organized to the office's safety rules. She'll also need to read the company's code of ethics describing the company's goals and appropriate behavior.

Training

New employees usually need some training to learn the specific job they were hired to do. For example, Gayle might have to learn how to use a new computer graphics program, like Adobe Illustrator®. She can get either group training or on-the-job training. **On-the-job training** involves learning a new job by actually doing it. This is usually done under the guidance of a supervisor. Gayle's supervisor might demonstrate the program for Gayle, watch her use it, and give her feedback.

In small businesses, employees often must be able to do several jobs. In larger companies, too, a worker may have to fill in for a coworker who is absent. To be sure employees can fill in for each other,

You Make the Call

A Great Balancing Act

Thirty years ago, most law students and lawyers were men. Today, many law schools enroll more women than men. The law firm you work for needs another attorney on its staff. You're on the hiring committee.

Making an Ethical Decision

1. Do you try to hire a woman because women were discriminated against until fairly recently?
2. Do you try to hire a man because today fewer men are being trained as lawyers?
3. Do you ignore gender as an issue in hiring?

managers use job rotation. In job rotation, employees move from job to job—or rotate—for several hours, days, or weeks at a time until they learn the various tasks. Job rotation is also used to prevent boredom and keep morale high. If an employee has a variety of work experiences, the work is more interesting. Job rotation helps managers make more effective use of the company's human resources. If someone is absent or leaves, others know how to handle the tasks.

With **group training** an instructor or manager teaches Gayle how to use the program with a group of other employees like a class. This allows Gayle to learn the program in a more relaxed way and to share ideas with other employees. The company might also provide her with a course on videotape or CD. In recent years, many companies have begun using courses available on the Internet to train employees. Companies also send employees to institutes and conferences to learn new skills for the job.

Evaluating Employees

After Gayle is oriented and trained her performance needs to be monitored. This is usually done every three or six months with a performance appraisal. A **performance appraisal** is an evaluation of how well she's doing her job. This might consist of Gayle sitting down with her manager to go over her strengths and weaknesses, listen to any complaints, and suggest improvements. The appraisal is used to determine whether Gayle should get a raise, a promotion, or new training.

✔ **Fast Review** _____

1. How might a new employee be oriented at a company?
2. What are some of the ways a company can train a new employee?

Real-World Application

part 3 of 4

HUNTER HEADS HEADHUNTERS
Management Recruiters tries to link corporations to people. It's a fun but challenging job. Yesterday, for instance, one of its clients—a satellite subscriber company—rejected a candidate that Hunter felt was right for the job. Why might a company pass over a qualified applicant for a job?

continued on p. 241

Employee Turnover

A human resources manager needs to keep track of changes in the status of employees, or employee turnover. For example, Gayle might be promoted to a better position, transferred to another department, or fired. As a result, she might need to be reoriented, retrained, or replaced.

Promotion

A **promotion** is a move to a higher-level job with more authority, responsibility, and pay. Promotions are merit-based and encourage performance. If Gayle is doing a great job, she might be promoted to a managing position. She might also be promoted on the basis of *seniority* after working for the company for a certain length of time.

In promotions, it is important to consider not only how an employee performs in the current job, but also how he or she will adapt to the new one. An organization that does not consider this becomes subject to the Peter Principle. The Peter Principle states that it is possible for employees to be promoted until they reach a level at which they can no longer perform.

Suppose a management position opens up in the Quarkville Advanced Physics Laboratory. Michelle Grayson is selected for the job based on her performance as a senior scientist. When she becomes lab chief, it is clear that she has poor management skills.

The laboratory has gained a mediocre supervisor and lost an excellent

Working Lifestyle

What are you doing at 10 A.M.?

Helping Patients Cope

Maya Bhaumik is a psychiatric social worker at a large hospital. Her department helps nearly 100 patients whose afflictions include anxiety, stress, eating disorders, schizophrenia, Alzheimer's, and senility. "You see people come in the depths of depression or abuse," says Bhaumik. "You try to help them feel better and go on with their lives."

Typically at 10:00 A.M., Bhaumik facilitates group therapy for 10 to 15 in-patients. In the sessions, she talks with patients about what brought them to the hospital. They assist other patients and help themselves find new coping skills. In addition to excellent communication skills, Bhaumik's duties require strong organizational skills, deductive reasoning, and the ability to keep calm in the face of stress.

Bhaumik's position requires considerable education and experience. Bhaumik, who specialized in child psychology in India, has earned numerous degrees in the United States, including a masters in social work and a Ph.D. in psychiatric social work. She works hard to follow the latest trends, treatments, and theories in psychology.

The unique challenges of Bhaumik's profession might be overwhelming if not for her positive attitude. "You have to keep perspective and not lose hope—especially in the face of tremendous problems," she says. "You need to keep your optimism and believe in the goodness of people."

Salary

Median annual earnings of social workers are $30,590, with a range between $24,160 and $39,240.

Outlook for Career

This profession is expected to grow faster than average due to a growing and aging population, which drives the overall growth of health care services.

Connecting Careers Activity

Name career occupations that might seek a psychologist to discuss job-related issues.

CAREER PATH Human Services

working scientist. It is unlikely that Michelle will be considered for further promotions, based on her performance. She has "risen to her level of incompetence." This can be avoided by considering the aptitudes and interest of candidates for promotion, in addition to performance in their current job.

Transfer

A **transfer** is a move to another job within a company at the same level and pay. Gayle might be transferred because another department needs her, her job has been eliminated, or she needs new training. An employee is usually transferred because the company moves or opens a new office. If Gayle works for a company that has offices around the world, she might be transferred to a foreign country if she speaks the language.

Separation

The final way in which an employee leaves a position is through separation. **Separation** means leaving a company for any reason. Gayle might quit, resign, or retire.

Separation may be voluntary or involuntary. A voluntary separation occurs when an employee resigns. This separation process usually involves an exit interview. An exit interview pinpoints why an employee is leaving, such as a noncompetitive pay structure.

Involuntary separations include layoffs and terminations. If the company is losing money and needs to *downsize*, or reduce the number of employees, Gayle might be *laid off*. Layoffs occur when there isn't enough work for all employees. For example, factory layoffs may follow a cut in production. Layoffs are often temporary and Gayle could be brought back if conditions improve. If the layoff is permanent, the company might help her find another job.

Gayle could be fired, or *terminated*, for being late all the time, doing a poor job, or breaking company rules. This is the last resort. Training, counseling, and disciplinary action are all solutions to personnel problems. However, if these fail, termination is necessary. In addition to upsetting employees, it wastes company resources and time invested in hiring and training that individual. Instead of terminating an unproductive employee, the company L.L. Bean will reassign the worker to a less stressful work site, with a lower volume of sales.

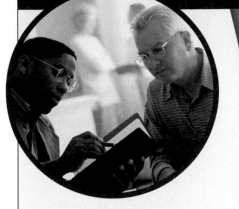

HUNTER HEADS HEADHUNTERS
Executive recruiters need to stay ahead of the game. They need to know trends in the field, whether a company is struggling, is laying off employees, or is looking to expand.
What kind of qualities do you think an executive recruiter needs to exhibit when working with clients and candidates?

✔ **Fast Review** _____

1. What is the difference between a promotion and a transfer?
2. What are the reasons an employee might separate from a company?

Summary

1. Human resources management is the process of finding, selecting, training, and evaluating employees. Human resources managers recruit employees from within the company and through ads, employment agencies, and recommendations.

2. Employees are often oriented to a new workplace by touring the building, attending group orientation sessions, and reading a company manual and code of ethics. Employees receive training on-the job or in group training. Periodic monitoring and performance appraisals are ways to evaluate employees.

3. The status of an employee changes as a result of promotion, transfer, or separation.

Using Business Key Words

Understanding these terms will help you become a better employee and one day, maybe a better employer. Fill each blank in the following sentences with the term that best completes the sentence.

- **compensation**
- **human resources management**
- **on-the-job training**
- **job description**
- **separation**
- **recruitment**
- **transfer**
- **group training**
- **orientation**
- **performance appraisal**
- **promotion**

1. A(n) _____ lists the duties and responsibilities of a job.
2. _____ is the process of helping new employees learn about and adjust to the company.
3. _____ occurs when a new employee works with a supervisor who demonstrates the job.
4. A(n) _____ is an evaluation method in which a manager shares information with the employee about how he or she is doing on the job.
5. Companies offer _____, which is pay and benefits.
6. The process of organizing all the aspects of recruiting, selecting, orienting, training, and developing employees is called _____.
7. Instead of training employees individually, many companies hold _____.
8. When an employer is actively looking for qualified people it is a form of _____.
9. A _____ occurs when an employee retires or resigns.
10. Moving to another job within a company at the same level and pay is called a _____.
11. When you receive a _____ it means more authority, responsibility, and pay.

Review What You Learned

12. What are some of the ways you can obtain information about job openings?
13. What are some of the ways human resources managers seek new employees?
14. What population trends have led to a change in the pool of job applicants?
15. How has an increase in the number of women in the workforce brought about a change in business practices?
16. Why is orientation important for new employees?
17. What are some of the different ways employees are oriented to their new workplace?
18. Describe the difference between on-the-job training and job rotation.
19. What do managers do after their workers are oriented and trained?

Understanding Business Concepts

20. Why is a job description important when a company is looking for a new employee?
21. Who would you use as a reference when you apply for a job? Explain why.
22. How does the global economy affect employees in the United States?
23. On your first day of this class, did your teacher conduct an orientation? Explain what he or she did to help you learn about and adjust to the class.
24. Why is job rotation so important?
25. What skills and attitudes do you think you have that human resources managers would want? What skills and attitudes do you need to build in order to get and keep a job? Explain your answers.

Critical Thinking

26. What are the advantages of recruiting applicants for new positions from within the company?
27. Read the local classified ads. Which jobs seem to have the most openings? Can you find any clues about what businesses want and how you can prepare for the workplace through those advertisements? Explain.
28. List two questions to be asked if you were applying for a job at a fast-food restaurant.
29. What are five leadership traits that a human resources manager might have?

Viewing and Representing

Examining the Image. In a group of three, examine the photograph and ask each other journalistic questions beginning with the words who, what, where, when, why, and how. What's important in this picture? How do you think the new employees are feeling? Discuss your reactions to the photograph.

Building Academic Skills

 Keyboarding

Select a job, research its requirements, and write a job description for it. Then write a newspaper want ad for the job. Use word processing software to attractively format both items and print out the results.

 Calculating Benefits

If the new employee orientation workshop costs the company $565 per employee, how much will the company spend during a 12-month period if they train 136 new employees?

 Writing About Apprenticeship

One form of on-the-job training that has existed for hundreds of years is called apprenticeship. Write a 250-word paper on the history of the apprenticeship program. Include information about the current status of these programs.

Preparing for an Interview

Human resources managers struggle with issues such as drug use, theft in the workplace, sexual harassment, and cultural diversity. In groups of five or six, choose one of the issues and research it using the library and the Internet. If possible, interview local business managers about the ways they deal with the issue.

Linking School to Home

Researching Jobs. Survey your family members and friends about their current jobs. Ask them the following questions:
- How did you hear about the job?
- Did you have to fill out a job application?
- Did you have to interview for the job?
- Do you have a written job description?
- How is your performance evaluated?
- What types of training programs are available for employees?

Compile your results and share the information with your class.

Linking School to Work

Role-play. In teams of two, role-play the following situation that might occur at an employee's performance appraisal. One student will play the part of the manager and the other student will play the part of the employee.

Situation: When Joan first started working at the company, she worked faster and more accurately than any other employee. During the last few months however, she has frequently been late to work and her work isn't as accurate as it should be. Her manager Helen, discusses the situation with Joan during her performance appraisal.

In the role-play, attempt to resolve this problem.

E-Homework

Applying Technology

Online Job Search. Create a list of ten Web sites that are dedicated to career and job searches.

Exchange Rates. Since companies of all sizes conduct business around the world, employees often have to understand how to figure exchange rates. Locate an Internet exchange-rate calculator online and convert a US $1 to Japanese, Canadian, German, and English currency.

Connecting Academics

Math. You're a human resources representative for a local biomedical company. To hire and keep good research workers, your company wants to offer a competitive salary compared with other companies in your area. You research other companies' salaries and find the following:

Company A	$60,100 (Annual Salary)
Company B	$45,900
Company C	$64,000
Company D	$58,500

What is the average salary (rounded to the nearest one hundred dollars)?

Social Science. Working in a team of three, choose one of the following topics related to human resources management: candidate selection, recruitment, developing employees, employee orientation, training, performance appraisal, or employee turnover. Together, find and read several articles on your chosen topic. Members of your team become the experts on this topic. Form an ask-the-experts panel. The rest of the class asks questions on your topic and listens attentively to the answers.

BusinessWeek Analyzing the Feature Story

You read the first part of "Online Benefits" at the beginning of this chapter. Below are a few questions for you to answer about online application service providers (ASPs). You'll find the answers to these questions when you're reading the entire article. First, here are the questions:

30. What are some of the advantages of using online application service providers?
31. What are some of the disadvantages?

CREATIVE JOURNAL ACTIVITY

Visit the Web sites for eBenefits.com, **www.ebenefits.com** or Employease Inc., **www.employease.com**. Write in your journal about surprising findings.

BUSINESS Online
The Full Story

To learn more about human resources, visit the *Introduction to Business* Web site at **www.introbus.glencoe.com**, and click on *BusinessWeek* Feature Story, Chapter 15.

Chapter 16

Culture and Diversity in Business

Learning Objectives

After completing this chapter, you'll be able to:

1. **Explain** how cultural differences affect doing business internationally.
2. **Define** the characteristics of a corporate culture.
3. **Describe** the effect of population changes on business.
4. **Identify** ways in which government and business deal with diversity.

Why It's Important

To succeed in the workplace, know a company's corporate culture and diversity issues.

Key Words

culture
business
  etiquette
corporate
  culture
hierarchy
bureaucracy
diversity
stereotype
baby boom generation

discrimination
ageism
Equal Employment Opportunity Act
Americans with Disabilities Act (ADA)

BusinessWeek Feature Story

Anthropologists in the Corporate Jungle

Their Special Skills of Observation Figure Out How Humans Work Together.
When your company's culture is famously dysfunctional because of warring tribes, what can you do but call in an anthropologist? The idea sounded good to Motorola, which hired one of these professional observers of human behavior two years ago, during what's now regarded as a remarkable turnaround period for the company.

Source: Excerpted with permission from "Anthropologists in the Corporate Jungle," *BusinessWeek Online*, September 20, 2000.

An Extension Activity

No one lives or works the exact same life. Hence we're all individuals. When you think about it, there are a lot of codes of conduct that need to be upheld in order to get along with people. Give examples of rules you need to follow in order to get along with all kinds of people.

The Full Story

To learn more about corporate culture, visit the *Introduction to Business* Web site at www.introbus.glencoe.com, and click on *BusinessWeek* Feature Story, Chapter 16.

The Importance of Culture in Business

When you think of the word culture, you might think of fine art, pop culture, or even subculture. The word can have several different meanings. In general, culture is the beliefs, customs, and attitudes of a distinct group of people. A group's **culture** is often defined in terms of its dress, food, language, and art. On a deeper level it can be defined in terms of a group's history, geography, and religious beliefs. It can refer to an entire country or ethnic group, but it can also refer to a specific social group or institution. How comfortable are you with diversity? Take the brief quiz in Figure 16.1 to find out.

The global economy creates a diverse culture for business. As companies trade globally, they must be aware of different cultural and business practices. Otherwise, they will not win customers. Rules for etiquette, business customs, and personal interaction are different in other cultures. In some countries, business people get acquainted before they discuss business. In other countries, it's all right to get to the point immediately. Knowing how to properly approach people from different cultures makes you smarter and more considerate.

Figure 16.1

THE DO'S AND DON'TS OF DIVERSITY

➡What do you think and do about diversity? These questions are a sample of ways you can demonstrate acceptance of differences among people.

Take this brief quiz to see if you value diversity.

Do you:
1. Try not to stereotype people?
2. Respect others' opinions even when you disagree?
3. Value and respect others regardless of gender, age, race, income, or other characteristics they may have?
4. Think about cultural differences when you communicate with others who are not from the same background as you?
5. Believe your way is not the only way?
6. Believe that all workers can contribute?
7. Try to be helpful to all people you work with?

Cultural Mores

In business, culture has two important meanings. In the broad sense, it refers to the culture of other countries with which companies have to do business. Specifically, it refers to the standards of a particular company.

Culture in a Global Economy

Companies that trade with other countries must be aware of differences in language, currencies, laws, and even systems of measurement. They must also be aware of differences in eating habits, customs, and the way people do business. In the United States it's common to point at or touch someone to make a point. In some countries pointing at or touching another person is considered rude. Americans like to eat quickly and whenever they feel like it. In other cultures, people eat only at certain hours and like to take their time. Failure to understand the culture of a country where you're doing business can ruin a deal or lead to a marketing disaster.

Marketing Abroad. To successfully market products in another country, you need to be aware of differences in language and customs. For example, when Pillsbury translated "Jolly Green Giant" into Arabic, the phrase became "Intimidating Green Ogre." Coca-Cola changes the amount of carbonation and sugar in its products to suit the tastes of different countries.

Workers Abroad. Companies doing business in other countries need to be aware of cultural differences in the workplace. When the Walt Disney Co. opened Euro Disney, French workers objected to greeting everyone with a smile, shaving, and other conditions. As a result, 3,000 workers quit.

American managers have had to adjust to working in Islamic countries, where it's customary to stop work five times a day to pray. In some cultures, workers are used to managers making all the decisions. If an American manager asks them for their opinions, they think the manager doesn't know what to do. This may be a sign of weakness on the manager's part.

Business Etiquette. What is considered acceptable social behavior and manners in business, or **business etiquette**, differs from country to country. In the United States, receiving a gift from a business partner could be seen as a bribe. In Japan, it's a custom and there are many rituals involved. For example, it's polite to refuse the gift once or twice

Real-World Application

part **1** of 4

DIGGING FOR KNOWLEDGE

Archaeologist Patricia Crown has been secluded in Harvard University's archaeological collections room for two hours. A professor of anthropology at the University of New Mexico, Crown is visiting Harvard to study pottery made by people who lived a thousand years ago in southwestern pueblos. She is interested in how the production and distribution of goods has changed over time.
What does an archaeologist do?

continued on p. 251

before accepting it. Before getting down to business in India it's customary to have tea. In Mexico, throwing documents on a table during a meeting is an insult. To convince partners in other countries you can do business in their country, you first need to show them you know and respect their customs.

Many companies avoid cultural problems by hiring local managers in countries where they do business. Companies also train their own managers to live and work in other countries. As more companies trade globally, there is an increasing demand for people who have studied other languages and cultures.

Corporate Culture

A business must be aware of diversity in its own company, too. Workers come from different backgrounds, cultures, and experiences that affect the company's culture. A company's **corporate culture** is its shared values, beliefs, and goals. It can be defined formally through a company code of ethics, a written manual, and the orientation process. It can also be defined informally through dress codes, work habits, and social activities. The cultures at McDonald's and Disney, for example, stress customer service and family values. Employees are expected to be clean-cut and greet each customer with a smile. Kinko's and Ben & Jerry's, on the other hand, stress worker satisfaction and concern for the environment.

A founder, such as William Hewlett of Hewlett-Packard, who stressed a people-first culture, can influence a company's culture. Region and tradition can also play big parts. A banker at an old Wall Street firm in New York is expected to wear a suit and tie. At a high-tech company on the West Coast, like a dot-com company in San Jose, a worker might wear a T-shirt and shorts to work.

Formal Culture. A company's culture affects the way it's organized and does business. In a formal culture, there might be a strict **hierarchy**, or chain of command, with one person at the top who makes all the decisions. There might be several levels of management, or **bureaucracy**, below. To make changes or pass down decisions can be very complicated and time consuming. Job titles are very important as indicators of power and status within a company. Dress codes and work hours are strictly enforced.

Informal Culture. At a company with an informal culture, employees are encouraged to make decisions on their own rather than going through layers of management. They're allowed to dress casually and have more flexible work hours. In some cases they can even work at home. Job titles aren't as important as creativity and teamwork. At Kingston Technology the founders of the company sit in cubicles so they can interact with employees and be available to them. At Southwest Airlines, the head of the company has all his employees call him by his first name.

Consider This...

Columbia Lighthouse for the Blind

The Columbia Lighthouse for the Blind (CLB) in Washington, D.C. trains thousands of people for jobs as technical specialists. Tools such as voice software and braille output devices let people with visual impairments function efficiently in an office environment. The key is to educate business leaders about the extent and availability of assistive devices.

ANALYZE

How can assistive technology enhance company diversity?

Few companies have a culture that is entirely formal or informal. Within the same company there are often different cultures. In the entertainment industry, for example, executives and artists have their own cultures. Executives are called "suits" and artists are called "creatives."

✓ Fast Review

1. What are two ways companies can avoid cultural problems with another country?
2. Name ways a company defines its corporate culture.
3. What are some characteristics of a formal corporate culture?

Diversity in the Workplace

Why change? Global trade isn't the only place where companies must be aware of diversity. Diversity is a feature of people in the workforce. You know that no two people are alike. Your friends have a variety of backgrounds, skills, and viewpoints. In the workplace, you'll find your coworkers are a diverse group. Your success on the job will depend on how well you work with and for people who are different from you.

Diversity in the workplace also means differences in skills, work habits, and approaches to tasks. People with the same assignments will carry them out in different ways. There is often more than one way to do a job. How are people different now, and what will the workplace be like in the future?

Companies not only have to deal with the cultural differences of people in other countries. They also have to deal with a variety of people with different backgrounds and identities, or **diversity**, in the workplace. People are diverse in terms of age, gender, ethnicity, and individual needs. People also differ in terms of education, marital and parental status, income, and religious beliefs.

There is a tendency to stereotype people who are different in some way. To **stereotype** people is to identify them by a single trait or as a member of a certain group rather than as individuals. In fact, no two people are alike. Everybody has special skills, knowledge, and experience. Dealing with diversity doesn't mean ignoring the differences between people. It means understanding and appreciating those differences.

The Impact of Diversity on Business

The population of the United States has become more ethnically diverse. For example, the fastest growing groups in the country are

Real-World Application

part **2** of 4

DIGGING FOR KNOWLEDGE
Harvard's collection of ancient pottery is stored in floor-to-ceiling drawers. Crown examines crudely made pottery. She is studying how people in different societies learn a skill and produce goods.
Does society rank people based upon their job titles?

continued on p. 253

Hispanics and Asians. Between 1990 and 2000, the Hispanic population grew by almost 60 percent. In California and Texas, Hispanics are no longer classified as a minority. Ten percent of Americans were born in other countries.

The population is also getting older and living longer. The 76 million babies born in the United States between 1946 and 1964 are called the **baby boom generation**. They control $2.6 trillion and have about 51 percent of the wealth in the country. The older baby boomers will turn 65 in 2011 and the number of Americans over 65 will nearly double in 2030.

Other population changes are taking place. The number of families with single parents is now around 30 percent. Changes like these have a far-reaching effect on business.

Changes in the Workplace. As the population has become more diverse, so has the workplace. (See Figure 16.2.) In the last few years about 85 percent of the people who entered the workforce were women and members of ethnic minorities. There are greater numbers of women,

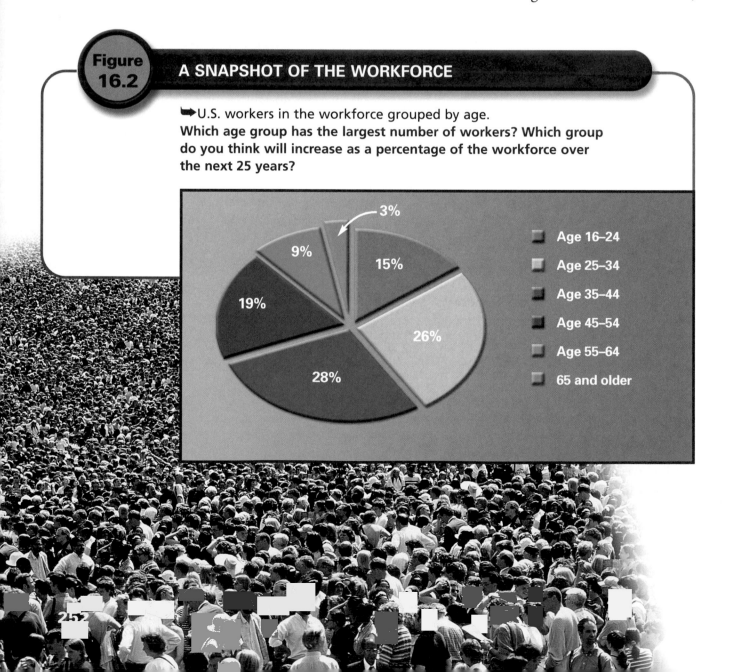

Figure 16.2

A SNAPSHOT OF THE WORKFORCE

➡ U.S. workers in the workforce grouped by age.
Which age group has the largest number of workers? Which group do you think will increase as a percentage of the workforce over the next 25 years?

- 3%
- 9%
- 15%
- 19%
- 26%
- 28%

- Age 16–24
- Age 25–34
- Age 35–44
- Age 45–54
- Age 55–64
- 65 and older

Asians, Hispanics, and African Americans in management positions.

The youth labor force (ages 16 to 24) is expected to grow more rapidly than the overall labor force for the first time in 25 years. Meanwhile, people are working more years than ever before. In the workplace, many people are coming into contact for the first time with people of different ages, ethnic backgrounds, and abilities. Within the next 50 years, groups now considered ethnic minorities will make up half the population. As a result, the workplace will become even more diverse.

Changes in the Marketplace. A more diverse population also means a more diverse marketplace. With more jobs, women and ethnic groups have more spending power and a larger share of the market. Companies that used to target only white males now target many groups. For example, sportswear companies will run ads in both English and Spanish and separate ads for women, African-Americans, and Asians. Baby boomers aren't only one of the largest groups, they also spend more than any other group. As they get older, the market for health and recreational products will increase to suit their changing needs.

Managing Diversity

Human resources managers manage diversity. They seek to find ways to make the company an inclusive organization. This leads to greater productivity and a competitive advantage. Workers know that a good diversity management program is a mark of a company that's good to work for. It's a good recruiting tool for new workers.

Diversity management programs have a broad objective. Their goal is to help all employees find a place in the company and help the company achieve its objectives. The workplace includes people with all kinds of backgrounds. Companies with diversity management programs recognize that people with different characteristics are good employees. Their goal is to create an inclusive, respectful environment. They want to draw on the strength of the diversity of their workers. What unique contributions can each worker bring to the company? How will they use their abilities, backgrounds, and skills? Diversity programs try to answer these questions. Up until the 1970s, white males dominated business in the United States. In general, people tend to hire other people most like themselves. Excluding someone on the basis of age, gender, or ethnicity is called **discrimination**. Changes in the laws and in company policies have done much toward correcting the problem.

DIGGING FOR KNOWLEDGE

In modern industrial society, most children learn in school from a teacher who tells them information and answers questions. In historic Pueblo societies, however, children learned from family members.

How will elders influence the future of the U.S. workforce?

continued on p. 255

Laws Against Discrimination. It might surprise you that workers over the age of 40 were often fired or denied jobs in the past in favor of younger workers. This form of discrimination is called **ageism**. To protect older workers, the U.S. government passed the *Age Discrimination in Employment Act*. A few years later, the **Equal Employment Opportunity Act** was passed to strengthen laws protecting workers from discrimination on the basis of gender, ethnicity, or other aspects of identity. People with individual needs, such as people with physical disabilities, often couldn't work simply because buildings lacked proper access or equipment. In 1990, the **Americans with Disabilities Act (ADA)** was passed requiring businesses to provide facilities such as wheelchair ramps.

Diversity Programs. Most company codes of ethics have rules against discrimination. This, however, isn't always enough. Many employees still have trouble working with people who are different. To deal with diversity in the workplace, most companies now offer diversity training programs. American Express, for example, uses employee

Business Building Blocks

Interpreting Points of View

You have your own point of view. If you hope to succeed in business, you'll have to recognize and be sensitive to the points of view of your coworkers, suppliers, and customers. A company that is active in the global marketplace must carefully consider whether its products will appeal to people in countries with different cultural and social viewpoints.

Practice

The following case study describes the marketing of products in a country whose cultural or social points of view differ from those in the United States. Explain how you would change

Analysis

the marketing strategy to take into account the potential customers' point of view.

Case Study

2-B-Me sells blue jeans by suggesting that its denim designs bring teenagers freedom, power, and popularity. The company hopes to expand its market to several countries that emphasize respect and obedience to elders. Teenagers in these countries spend most of their time outside of school with their families. Parents in this country chaperone and monitor the lives of their teenage children.

networking to bring together people from different groups. Corning and IBM have seminars on diversity. Other companies hire consultants or use diversity-training manuals. The goal of these programs is to promote trust and cooperation among workers of different backgrounds so they work more effectively together.

Diversity training increases acceptance of diversity by breaking down stereotypes, which reflect ignorance. People who have never worked with people with physical disabilities, for example, may assume that these workers are less capable. People who have never worked with people from other countries often make incorrect assumptions about the way foreigners think and act.

To bring together all of the people who work for them, managers must avoid stereotyping. They must create a work environment in which prejudice is not tolerated and diversity is welcomed and respected. Employees need to feel that they are valued and respected for who they are. Managers should always be sensitive to the backgrounds of their workers, and should foster a diverse and understanding corporate culture.

Benefits of Diversity. Why is diversity important? Instead of banishing people based upon diversity, differences are celebrated. Now, companies have programs to provide opportunities to employees. They recruit, develop, and retain more diverse employees. In turn, those employees are an asset in dealing with diverse clients and customers. Businesses that promote diversity in the workplace have discovered many benefits:

- Diversity reduces possible conflicts between workers.
- A diverse workforce offers a broader range of ideas and ways of looking at things.
- Greater diversity in the workplace helps a company better understand and serve the needs of a more diverse marketplace.
- It creates a greater sense of morale among employees and commitment to company goals.

Studies show that companies that value diversity have increased productivity and efficiency, lower turnover rates, less absenteeism, and fewer legal costs from employee grievances.

DIGGING FOR KNOWLEDGE
Pueblo women have made and decorated their families' clay pots, which stored and served food. Crown has discovered that as Pueblo pottery started to become a trade item a thousand years ago, the method of producing it also began to change. To increase output, women often made and completed most of the decoration on pots and then allowed their children to finish the decoration. **Understanding other cultures gives you a greater appreciation for what?**

✓ Fast Review

1. In what ways are people diverse?
2. How have changes in the population affected business?
3. Name some of the laws against discrimination.
4. What is the goal of diversity training programs?

How Do You Get a Passport?

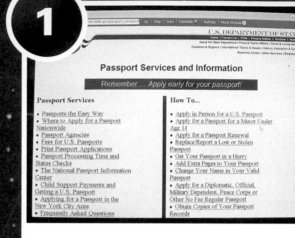

Passport Services and Information

Remember.... Apply early for your passport!

Passport Services
- Passports the Easy Way
- Where to Apply for a Passport Nationwide
- Passport Agencies
- Fees for U.S. Passports
- Print Passport Applications
- Passport Processing Time and Status Checks
- The National Passport Information Center
- Child Support Payments and Getting a U.S. Passport
- Applying for a Passport in the New York City Area
- Frequently Asked Questions

How To...
- Apply in Person for a U.S. Passport
- Apply for a Passport for a Minor Under Age 14
- Apply for a Passport Renewal
- Replace/Report a Lost or Stolen Passport
- Get Your Passport in a Hurry
- Add Extra Pages to Your Passport
- Change Your Name in Your Valid Passport
- Apply for a Diplomatic, Official, Military Dependent, Peace Corps or Other No Fee Regular Passport
- Obtain Copies of Your Passport Records

1. To apply for a passport, get application Form DSP-11 from a passport agent, the U.S. Postal Service, or download it from the U.S. State Department Web site at **http://travel.state.gov**.

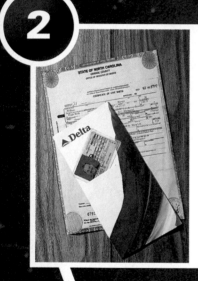

2. You need proof of U.S. citizenship, such as a certified birth certificate or naturalization certificate, and proof of identity, such as a driver's license or current student ID.

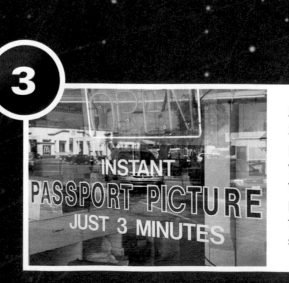

INSTANT PASSPORT PICTURE JUST 3 MINUTES

3. Get two 2″ × 2″ photos of yourself for your passport from a fast-photo service.

4. You must apply for a passport *in person* at any passport office, including federal, state, and local government offices, many post offices, and some libraries.

5. You'll receive your passport in the mail within six weeks, so apply for a passport well in advance of traveling.

6. Your passport will be checked and stamped whenever you enter or exit a foreign country.

Now *You* Take a Shot...

Protecting Yourself Abroad
Suppose you're traveling abroad. What precautions can you take and what should you do in case your passport is lost or stolen? (Note: You can find out by looking up travel tips in a travel guide or on the Internet.)

Summary

1. To do business in another country successfully, a company must be aware of differences in cultural customs as well as differences in language, laws, and currencies.

2. A company's corporate culture can be formally defined by a code of ethics, a manual, and the orientation process or informally defined by dress codes, work habits, and social activities.

3. As a result of changes in the population, the workplace and the marketplace are becoming increasingly more diverse.

4. Laws, company codes of ethics, and diversity training programs protect and encourage diversity in the workplace.

Using Business Key Words

Understanding the diverse business cultures that exist in the world is essential for success in business. See how many terms you know by matching each term with the correct statement below.

- **culture**
- **business etiquette**
- **corporate culture**
- **hierarchy**
- **bureaucracy**
- **diversity**
- **stereotype**
- **baby boom generation**
- **discrimination**
- **ageism**
- **Equal Employment Opportunity Act**
- **Americans with Disabilities Act (ADA)**

1. The acceptable social behavior and manner in business.
2. A company's shared values, beliefs, and goals.
3. A law protecting against discrimination of workers on the basis of gender, ethnicity, or other differences.
4. A formal chain of command.
5. The beliefs, customs, and attitudes of a distinct group of people.
6. Identifying someone by a single trait or as a member of a certain group rather than as an individual.
7. A variety of people with different backgrounds and identities.
8. Discrimination on the basis of age.
9. People born between 1946 and 1964.
10. A law requiring businesses to provide facilities for people with special needs.
11. Excluding someone on the basis of age, gender, ethnicity, or other aspect of identity.
12. A formal organization consisting of many levels of management.

Review What You Learned

13. Describe how a company defines its culture formally and informally.
14. Provide an example of how a U.S. product has been adapted for sale in another country.
15. What are the fastest growing segments of the United States population?
16. Describe how the labor force in the United States has changed over the last several years.
17. Explain how changes in demographics can mean changes for businesses.
18. How do companies define diversity?

Understanding Business Concepts

19. Explain why it's important for companies, especially those who trade globally, to be aware of different cultures and business practices.
20. How do human resources managers manage diversity?
21. Describe what you think you'll be doing in 15 years. How will your consumer needs be different than today?
22. Name an industry in your community that might be affected by a population that's living longer.
23. Describe your own workplace diversity. What talents, skills, and characteristics do you have that might be seen as valuable to an employer?

Critical Thinking

24. The corporate culture is the setting in which workers operate. Describe your classroom culture. What classroom rules, work habits, and activities help shape how you work, act, and deal with problems?

25. If you had the opportunity to become an exchange student in another country, what would you do to learn about the culture of that country?
26. Would you feel comfortable in a formal or informal company culture? Compare the advantages of each organizational model.
27. How could a manager's openness to suggestions influence coworkers' loyalty? Would this vary in other cultures?

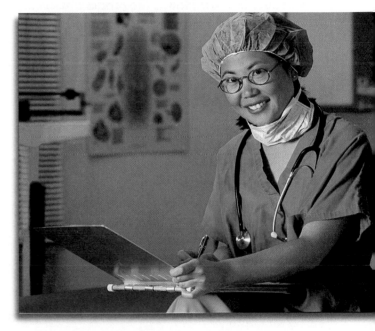

Viewing and Representing

Examining the Image. Study this photograph. What does the photographer want you to think and feel? What do you consider others would think and feel looking at this photograph—a baby boomer, a grade-school student, a person with a physical disability, a person with a different ethnic background, and so on? How do you think diversity benefits the workplace?

Building Academic Skills

 Adapting to Customs

Research a major U.S. corporation that conducts business in another country. Find out how the corporation had to adapt to the customs and cultures of the other country. What adaptations to the products had to take place before the product could be sold? How is the product marketed? Are there local managers in the other country? Present your findings orally to your class.

COMPUTER TECHNOLOGY **Influences on the Workplace**

Interview someone who works in a formal corporate culture. Find out the following information:
- How long has he or she been working in this environment?
- What are the advantages and disadvantages?
- What technology is essential in order to perform his or her job?
- How often does communication with a supervisor occur?

- Would he or she recommend this culture type to others?

Use a word processing program to write about your findings. Share this with the class.

 Visualizing Your Future

Think ahead to when you'll be 60 years old. Create a poster that visually describes what you will be doing. Will you be working? Will you be retired? What activities will you be involved in? What products and services will you buy? How will you financially provide for yourself? Display your poster in your classroom.

MATH **Creating a Chart**

Using the statistics from the latest U.S. census, create a pie chart that shows the diverse segments of our population. Then, create another graph that shows the diverse segments of your state's population.

Linking School to Home

Examining Diversity. Religious beliefs, geographic location, parental status, marital status, work background, and income are considered elements of diversity. Acknowledging diversity and treating everyone fairly are assets in dealing with clients, coworkers, and customers. Diversity is a description of variety. Determine the diversity in your own family or group of friends. What differences in gender, age, race, abilities, skills, and education are there? Write a one-page paper explaining how these differences are an asset to your family or friends.

Linking School to Work

Diversity Training. Businesses have defined diversity. They promote nondiscrimination in the workplace. Their programs are intended to assist all workers to collaborate, trust, and work together in the workplace. Contact the human resources department of a business in your community. Ask about the diversity training and programs that are offered at their company. Find out when they began, who participates, what type of information is included, and how the training has improved their business.

E-Homework

Applying Technology

Online Research. Using the Internet, research the Web sites of several major corporations. See if you can find one with an informal corporate culture and one with a formal corporate culture. Then write a paragraph explaining why you chose each site.

Creating a Model. Using your imagination, create a three-dimensional model of a piece of technology that would be beneficial to a telecommuter. (Create something that hasn't yet been invented.) Write a paragraph explaining how it works and present your project to your class.

Connecting Academics

Math. In 1988 Shoshana founded Workplace Solutions, a training company specializing in diversity awareness in the workplace. Shoshana immigrated to the United States 24 years prior to founding her company. In the year 2002, Shoshana celebrated her fifty-fourth birthday. What year was Shoshana born? How old was she when she immigrated? Is Shoshana part of the baby boom generation?

Social Science. Watch three or four TV shows showing people of different ethnic backgrounds in work situations. How did the different characters behave? Did their actions follow an ethnic stereotype? What cultural differences did you see? Did you see any evidence of discrimination? Did you see people using special skills to work better together? What were they?

BusinessWeek — Analyzing the Feature Story

You read the first part of "Anthropologists in the Corporate Jungle" at the beginning of this chapter. Below are a few questions for you to answer about Kath Fell. You'll find the answers to these questions when you're reading the entire article. First, here are the questions:

28. Why did Motorola hire anthropologist Kath Fell?
29. What role did diversity play in the strategies Kath Fell asked Motorola to implement?

CREATIVE JOURNAL ACTIVITY

You're an anthropologist who observes nonverbal behavior. The assignment is to observe others at a distance—across the ball field, the other side of the cafeteria, the other end of a corridor, and so on.
- What repeated rituals, such as saying goodbye, do you see?
- Can you interpret people's feelings by their body language?

Write your observations in your journal.

BUSINESS Online
The Full Story

To learn more about corporate culture, visit the *Introduction to Business* Web site at **www.introbus.glencoe.com**, and click on *BusinessWeek* Feature Story, Chapter 16.

Using Resources of Find the Right People

In Chapter 15, you read about how businesses find employees. A business isn't successful without the right people. In order to find the right people for the job, businesses have to be resourceful to seek out candidates. In this seminar you and a partner will develop a business and research different ways to look for employees.

Factoids

A Non-Question. An employer should never consider your economic status part of a decision whether or not to extend a job offer.

Those Who Lie. Twenty-four percent of job applicants misrepresent work or personal experience.

Proper Questions. The federal Equal Employment Opportunity Commission publishes guidelines listing proper and improper questions for employers to ask prospective candidates.

An Agreement. A job application is considered a legal document.

Necessary Training. More than 52 percent of companies utilize diversity training. By 2010, women and minorities will comprise 70 percent of the new candidates in the workforce.

Investigate the Images

Look at the photographic collage on the left page. What grabs your attention at first? Is it the color or the words? The power in reading visuals is in analyzing and dissecting your observations. On a separate piece of paper, respond to the questions listed below. These questions might help sharpen the focus of your visual mind.

Your Observations

1. How many photographs do you see?

2. Examine each photograph. How is each assembled in relation to one another?

3. What is the subject of each photograph? Is place or location the subject?

4. Does color signify a message?

5. What issues do you take from these images?

Information

6. Summarize what you know about the photographs from your observations.

Exploring Culture

7. You want to work for a particular company, but it's in a hiring freeze. Does this deter you or do you still pursue the company?

8. A good photograph will hold you captive as you interpret what you see. Think of an interview in much the same way. The employer is the viewer and you're the subject. How will you portray yourself? What kind of things will you reveal about yourself to the employer?

Taking Aim at Careers

● Preparation

Determine two specific jobs needed for your business and the qualifications for those jobs.

Objective
- **Decide** on a business you're interested in starting.
- **Identify** ways to look for employees for job openings at your business.
- **Create** and write job descriptions and application forms.
- **Role-play** a job interview, with a fellow classmate as the job applicant.

Materials Needed
- ✓ Copies of recent news publications, such as the *Wall Street Journal* and *BusinessWeek* or Internet access
- ✓ Paper, pencils, pens, markers
- ✓ Posterboard
- ✓ Props for a job interview (e.g., file folders, interview attire, table or desk, and chairs)

● Procedures

1. Choose a research partner.

2. Imagine that you're business partners in a start-up. The two of you need to decide on a business. Type a one-page description of your business that includes the name, your product (good or service), location, and reason for starting this particular business.

3. You need to hire a manager and an entry-level employee for the business.

4. Research the different ways employers look for employees.

5. Using your research in No. 4, choose two or three ways to look for a manager and entry-level employee. Consider the following:
   - Describe the qualification of each position.
   - How important is it to find the right person for the job? Or how much money are you willing to spend to find an employee for each position?

6. Write up a formal job description for each.

7. In front of the class, role-play an interview for one of the two positions. Then explain to the class how you found this particular person.

Chart It

With your partner, re-create this chart below on a separate piece of paper. List all of the ways you discovered that employers look for employees. Then indicate which methods would work best for the workers your business needs. Lastly, share your chart with other students and, as a class, create a comprehensive chart on the board.

Types of Workers	Methods for Finding Employees		
	Executive Search Firms	Classified Ads	
Executives, VP for Engineering, VP Marketing, etc.	X		
Middle Management, Chief Engineer, Editorial Director, etc.	X		
Engineers, Marketers, Editors, etc.	X	X	
Entry Level, Administrative Assistants, Receptionists, Clerks, etc.		X	

Analyze and Conclude

After considering your research and studying the comprehensive list on the board, answer the questions below:

1. **Allocating Time.** Is there one method that reaches more potential candidates than any other? If so, what is it? If not, why not?

2. **Improving and Designing a System.** Which method(s) would you use to find an employee? Why?

3. **Responsibility.** When it's your chance to find a job, how will you go about finding one?

Becoming an Informed Citizen

Congratulations, you finished the seminar. Now it's time to reflect on the decisions you made.

Participating as a Member of a Team. Discuss the process of deciding on a business to start and the qualifications of each employee. How did you rule out the qualifications your employees shouldn't have? Describe your selection process.

Analyzing Your Future. Before you enter the job market, sit down and take a personal inventory of your skills, qualities, and qualifications. Based upon these factors, what kind of job will you pursue?

BUSINESS Online

Further Exploration

To find out more about employment resources, visit the Glencoe *Introduction to Business* Web site at **www.introbus.glencoe.com**.

Unit 6

Managing Financial and Technological Resources

You Ought to Be in Pictures

Today, flying through the air has never looked more real in the movies. Thanks to computer-generated characters, the manipulation of pixels is replacing stunt doubles and actors in movies. Digital tape costs much less than film and provides better sound and image quality; you can edit it using a desktop computer system. With the development of ever more affordable digital movie cameras, it is possible for anyone to make a movie.

● **Careful Where You Step**
The original King Kong was only 18 inches tall and made out of a metal skeleton covered with foam rubber and rabbit fur.

● **What's My Motivation?**
In the 1985 *Young Sherlock Holmes* movie, a knight steps out of a stained-glass window. This first fully computer-generated effect lasted for 30 seconds and took 6 months to complete.

● **And the Best Vactor Oscar for 2050 Goes to...**
"Vactors" or "synthespians" are digitally-generated virtual actors.

● **Hair-Raising**
In the movie *Toy Story*, Sid, the sadistic kid next door, had 15,977 computer-generated hairs.

● **The Cost of a Creation's Tools**
According to Jim Blinn, a pioneer in computer animation, "The cost of the basic tools of my trade—of making images with a computer—has gone from about $500,000 to about $2,000."

BUSINESS Online

Idea Factory

To learn more about technology's influences, visit the *Introduction to Business* Web site at **www.introbus.glencoe.com**, and click on Unit 6 Managing Financial and Technological Resources.

Chapter 17

Managing Business Finances

Learning Objectives

After completing this chapter, you'll be able to:

1. **Explain** the three important aspects of financial planning.
2. **Name** the responsibilities of a financial manager.
3. **Identify** different types of budgets for managing business finances.
4. **Describe** the types of financial records businesses use.

Why It's Important

Every large or small business has to have a financial plan, a budget, and financial records to manage its financial resources.

Key Words

financial plan
asset
financial forecast
accounting
financial manager
budget
fiscal year
owner's equity
income statement
balance sheet

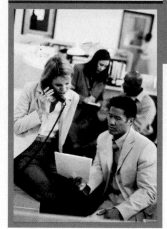
An Extension Activity

What are some major concerns a start-up company might have within its first year of business? Create a table with the pros and cons of a start-up.

The Full Story

To learn more about a company's search for funding, visit the *Introduction to Business* Web site at **www.introbus.glencoe.com**, and click on *BusinessWeek* Feature Story, Chapter 17.

Aspects of Financial Management

Suppose that some day you want to run your own small business, such as an Italian restaurant. How much money will you need to open it? Are your expenses more than your income? Will you need to borrow money to expand your operation? To run a business successfully you need to manage its finances. This involves putting together a financial plan, budgeting, and keeping track of your income and expenses.

A new business, whether large or small, needs financing. Its owner must manage the company's finances well to avoid failure. Software packages for business plans can help. They guide a person in planning a new business and tracking its finances. Take the personal inventory in Figure 17.1 to assess your career's financial future.

Figure 17.1

WHAT'S YOUR FINANCIAL ID?

➡️Your personality can help guide your future. On a separate sheet of paper, write ten of the following characteristics that best describe you. Find out if you're a persuader, communicator, or an individualist. How will this influence your financial future? **Take this financial quiz to see.**

a. I like meeting people.	k. I have perseverance.
b. I'm friendly.	l. I'm persuasive.
c. I try to avoid conflict.	m. I'm cautious.
d. I like to spend time alone.	n. I'm ambitious.
e. I like to talk.	o. I like to feel in control.
f. I'm sensitive.	p. I like to plan.
g. I'm interested in other people.	q. I like organization.
h. I'm upbeat.	r. I like to be the center of attention.
i. I'm enthusiastic.	s. I let other people do what they want.
j. I like to be active.	

Score 3 points for each of these character traits: a, b, e, g, h, i, j, k, l, n, or r.
Individualist: If you scored 6–12 points, you might enjoy a career and hobbies that give you independence.
Communicator: If you scored 15–21 points, you might enjoy activities where you're a team player working toward a common goal.
Persuader: If you scored 24–30 points, consider a career in sales or another field where you can influence people.

Managing a business requires accurate, up-to-date financial information. Managers use that information to evaluate their company's financial health and to plan for the future. A business may need additional money to grow or expand. It can seek a loan or additional money from investors. Lenders or investors must have accurate financial information to decide whether or not to risk their money with the company.

Financial Planning

The first step in financial management is drawing up a financial plan. A **financial plan** is an outline of your expenses, needs, and goals, and how you expect to meet them. It works like a game plan, a road map, or an outline for a paper. The plan helps you keep your business on track and determine what its financial state is at any given time.

You need a financial plan to tell you how much money you'll need to start out and to operate your restaurant once it's running. This includes all expenses from buying equipment to paying for deliveries. You also need the financial plan to explain how you're going to cover those expenses. Do you plan on borrowing money, using your savings, or making enough profits? A financial plan must include a way of keeping records on income and expenses. The Small Business Administration can help you come up with a financial plan.

An entrepreneur starting a new business must also plan for finances. Your start-up needs how much money? A business needs to make how much money in order to cover its costs? Until it reaches that point, a new business relies on savings or cash reserves to meet its expenses. In order to keep the business running, how much money does it need for expansion? The entrepreneur must find adequate funding. Otherwise, the business risks closure because of a lack of money.

Assets Needed

First, you need to identify your assets. Any property or item of value that your business owns is an **asset**. Cash, equipment, buildings, supplies, inventory, and land are all examples of assets. Researching your options is important before buying any major asset. Analyze and compare the price of each different item. Once your analysis is complete you'll want to purchase the item. You want to know you're getting the best item for your money. Take this careful approach with each asset.

A SOLID FOUNDATION
Miranda Wright's office is full of art created by Alaska Natives and occupies the corner of a new building overlooking the Chena River. Wright's the executive director of the Doyon Foundation headquartered in Fairbanks, Alaska. The foundation was created in 1989 by Doyon, Limited, which is a regional corporation established by Congress under the Alaska Native Claims Settlement Act. The company owns 12.5 million acres of land, making it the largest private landowner in North America.
For any business, what is the first step to financial management?

continued on p. 273

Purchasing Assets

Purchasing your assets is the second step in your financial planning. Before you purchase your items, you'll want to determine the method you'll use to purchase the items. You may want to answer a few of the following important questions: Can you purchase the items with available cash? Do you have to borrow money—either through using credit or a loan—for part or all of the purchases?

Before you can answer these questions, once again you'll need to carefully analyze your financial situation. Investigate all sources of credit and loan. This step is important in effective financial management.

When you're a business owner you might want to purchase items that are beyond your means. You may not have enough cash and you might not be able to afford everything you want. It's important, therefore, to look carefully at the needs of your business. If you're working with limited resources, you need to make decisions based upon your needs and how you'll pay for them, whether with cash or credit.

Accounting Requirements

Recognizing the financial records you need to keep is the third important step in financial planning. A **financial forecast** is an estimate of what business conditions will be like in the future. If you're just starting a restaurant business you might not make a profit for a year. To meet

You Make the Call

The Qualified Volunteer

Your daughter plays softball with a local club and you're a member of the club's board of directors. Like you, the treasurer is a volunteer parent. The club has grown recently and now operates with professional coaches and a $100,000 annual budget. You feel it's time to hire an accountant, but the treasurer insists he can do the job just fine. Several club parents have questioned whether a volunteer who isn't an accountant should be handling that much money.

Making an Ethical Decision

1. In what ways is this nonprofit really more like a business than a club?
2. What can an accountant provide that a parent volunteer cannot?
3. In what ways would ethical questions arise under the current system? How would hiring an accountant help address those ethical issues?
4. How would you tactfully convince the treasurer to step down from his role in handling the budget? Are there other roles that a volunteer treasurer could still fulfill within the club?

any unexpected expenses that might come up, you need to keep cash or savings on hand.

A forecast also includes planning for changes in the economy that might affect your business. For example, if the cost of energy is going up, you can expect to pay more to operate your equipment. To play it safe, it's best to be conservative and estimate your income on the low side and your expenses on the high side.

With current up-to-date financial information, you can make informed, reasonable decisions. This information is used for analyzing financial statements, controlling cash, and paying debts. Remember that thousands of small businesses close each year because of poor financial management.

✓ Fast Review

1. Why is financial planning important to a business?
2. What are examples of assets?
3. Describe the three steps of a financial plan.

Accounting

Accounting is the systematic process of recording and reporting the financial position of a business. Accounting records and reports help a business operate efficiently. To have a profitable business you need to track how much the business earns and spends. Figure 17.2 on page 274 outlines the common sources and uses of funds in a business.

The person in charge of a business's financial planning, funding, and accounting is the **financial manager**. As a financial manager you have three important responsibilities. First, you have to manage the funds and make sure the business is meeting its financial obligations. You need to pay your cook and waiters a weekly salary. *Cash reserves*, or savings, have to be kept on hand to pay for operating expenses like deliveries. If your business borrowed money you need to make sure the loans are paid on time.

Second, you have to find sources for additional funds. For your business to grow you'll need more money. If the restaurant makes a profit, the money can be used to buy new equipment or hire more workers. If the restaurant isn't making money you might have to borrow from investors or from a bank.

The third responsibility is planning long-range financial goals. Where do you want your business to be in five years? Do you want to open a chain of restaurants throughout the country? Do you want to market your own line of frozen dinners in grocery stores? A financial plan outlines the information you need to make decisions for the future.

A SOLID FOUNDATION
The Doyon Foundation promotes the health, education, social, and economic development and well being of Alaska Natives. Wright, who is Athabaskan, guides the foundation's blanket program.
Name some long-range goals the Foundation might have.

continued on p. 275

Budgeting

A **budget** is a written plan of what you expect your income and expenses to be over a certain period of time. It helps you predict how much money you'll need and helps control your spending. You need to compare it periodically to your actual income and expenses to avoid financial problems. There are three main types of budgets: start-up budget, cash budget, and operating budget. Let's take a closer look at each.

Start-up Budget. A start-up budget is a plan for your income and expenses from the time you start the business to when it makes a profit. To start a restaurant you need to buy equipment and supplies, rent property, and hire workers. To pay for everything you might use your savings or borrow money from a bank. If you need to borrow money, the lender will want to see a detailed start-up budget. Most new businesses don't make a profit during the first year so you also need to plan for covering your own personal expenses.

Cash Budget. A cash budget is a plan for the actual money you expect to spend and earn on a daily, weekly, or monthly basis. This includes paying waiters' salaries, utility bills, and rent regularly. A cash budget tells you how much money is needed on hand at all times for day-to-day transactions.

Operating Budget. An operating budget is a plan for how much you expect to spend and earn over a given period of time, usually six

Figure 17.2 — COMMON SOURCES AND USES OF FUNDS IN A BUSINESS

➡A budget is a written plan of what you expect your income and expenses to be over a certain period of time. This helps control your spending.
What are some uses of funds for a company? List at least four.

SOURCES OF FUNDS	USES OF FUNDS
Revenues	1.
Profits	2.
Loans and Credits	3.
Owner's Equity	4.

months or a year. It covers the total amount of regular transactions as well as other operating expenses such as advertising, taxes, and new equipment. The operating budget tells you how much money you need to keep your business running over the long term. It gives a picture of the finances and becomes a "road map" for the company.

✔ Fast Review

1. What are some of the expenses a start-up budget includes?
2. What is the main difference between a cash budget and an operating budget?

Financial Records

To keep track of how your restaurant is actually doing financially, you need to keep accurate written accounts. Your accounts tell you how well you're sticking to your budget and what your profits or losses are during a certain period. As a result, you might decide to cut costs, borrow more money, or expand your business. Your investors and creditors also want to see your financial accounts now and then.

An accounting period may be one month, three months, or one year. If the reports are for one year, the accounting period is a **fiscal year**. At the close of a fiscal year, you have to prepare reports to show your business's finances. Then you have to summarize the year with an income statement and a balance sheet. There are many business software programs you can buy that not only set up budgets, but also keep financial records.

Financial Statements

Accounting records keep track of money coming into and going out of your business. They provide a system for recording, classifying, summarizing, and interpreting financial data. The records show all daily transactions. Every sale, payment, or purchase is a transaction. Accounting records sort out the transactions to show what your business owns, how much money it takes in, and how much it owes to others.

Any amount your business owes is a *liability*. When you buy anything from a supplier, such as food products, you usually buy it on credit. The amount you owe to the supplier is a liability, or a claim against your restaurant's assets. Any debts you owe banks or investors are also claims against the assets of your restaurant. Their claim is called the **owner's equity**. Owner's equity is equal to the total assets of the business minus

Real-World Application

part 3 of 4

A SOLID FOUNDATION
Each year the Doyon Foundation asks Alaska Native artists to submit work that can be adapted for use as a blanket design. Profits from sale of the blankets go to the Doyon Foundation's college-bound student scholarship fund. At the beginning of the year, the Foundation predicts how much money it will need. **What helps it control its spending?**

continued on p. 277

the total liabilities. The relationship between a company's assets and the claims against those assets is expressed by an equation:

Assets = Liabilities + Owner's Equity

Assets should always appear on the left side of the equation. Liabilities and owner's equity always appear on the right side of the equation. The two sides of the accounting equation must always balance. This is only logical since the value of the assets must equal the claims (of owners

Working Lifestyle

What are you doing at 10 A.M.?

A Patient Account

Accounting is like fly-fishing for Jon Louvar. You're working alone in the middle of a swiftly moving current. Sometimes you slip and you end up downstream. Fortunately, if you learn the lesson and remember the mistake, you're more likely to catch the big prize next time. Both accounting and fly-fishing require patience, strategy, and risk.

Louvar uses analytical strategy to help run Trompeter Electronics, Inc., in Westlake Village, Calif. As an accounting supervisor, he uses accounting (the language of business) to track annual sales over $100 million and an inventory of more than 8,000 parts. He analyzes the company's performance and then helps its executives set and achieve corporate goals.

During a ten o'clock meeting this morning, Louvar will meet with Trompeter's controller and chief financial officer to help set the company's monthly goals. "Our overall goal is to increase value," he says, "and we try to accomplish this by identifying technological trends."

Louvar asks questions like a journalist and analyzes the answers like a mathematician. For example, did profit margins change due to an increase in energy or suppliers' costs? The engineers came up with a perfect design, but is the company manufacturing it efficiently and economically?

"You've got to be willing to attack a problem from a lot of different angles and analyze things through comparison. When you're able to understand the whole system and can explain how it all fits together—that's very satisfying," he says as he finishes his mid-morning cup of coffee.

Salary

A typical accounting supervisor earns a median base salary of $76,948, with a range between $64,494 and $91,617.

Outlook for This Career

Employment of accountants and auditors will grow faster than average.

Connecting Careers Activity

Examine your hobbies and interests. What occupations could you pursue that require you to utilize your talents?

CAREER PATH

Business & Administration

and others) against those assets. Every business transaction that takes place in the company affects this basic accounting equation.

Income Statement. The **income statement** is a report of *net income* or *net loss* over an accounting period. If your restaurant's total revenue, or earnings, is greater than its total expenses, it has a net income. If its expenses are greater than its revenue, then it has a net loss. As the owner of the restaurant, you must be sure that the revenue is enough to cover expenses. The income statement, however, isn't a complete picture of the financial health of your restaurant. A balance sheet provides more information.

Balance Sheet. A **balance sheet** is a report of the financial state of your business on a certain date. It includes a report of assets, liabilities, and the owner's equity. The left side of the sheet lists all your assets and the right side lists all your liabilities and equity. When added up, the two sides must be equal, or balanced. A balance sheet is like a photograph of your business's finances at a specific moment.

Business managers use the information in financial statements for decision making. They're responsible for decisions about budgets, ways to cut costs, and tax planning. Stockholders, employees, banks, and investment companies want to know about the financial condition of the business, too. They can compare the most recent statements with earlier statements and evaluate the business.

Whether a business is large or small, one person is usually responsible for financial management. In a small business, the owner may be responsible. Accounting managers have three important financial responsibilities: manage company funds, find sources for additional funds, and determine long-range goals for the company.

The owner or managers must manage the funds and be sure the company meets its financial obligations. Are payments made on time? Does the company have enough money to pay all its operating expenses? Wages and salaries must be paid on time. Cash reserves must be on hand for operating expenses. As a company grows, where will it find additional funds? The owner or managers must find those sources. If the company is profitable, it might use them for expansion. If it must borrow money, the owner or managers are responsible for repaying the loans on time.

Real-World Application

part **4** of 4

A SOLID FOUNDATION
The blanket project depicts some elements of the three traditional Athabaskan clans: Water, Copper, and Caribou. The Doyon Foundation has already raised $40,000 to support students. **What does the Doyon Foundation use to track the money coming in and going out?**

✔ Fast Review

1. What's the purpose of financial records?
2. Explain the difference between total assets and total liabilities.

Summary

1. A financial plan outlines a business's expenses, needs, goals, and how to meet them. Financial planning includes figuring out the assets that are needed, purchasing assets, and being knowledgeable of accounting requirements.

2. A financial manager is responsible for managing a business's funds, finding resources for additional funds, and planning long-range financial goals.

3. The three main types of budgets are start-up budgets, cash budgets, and operating budgets.

4. Businesses keep track of their financial records by using financial statements like income statements and balance sheets.

Using Business Key Words

Keeping accurate financial records is crucial to running a successful business. See how many of the following financial terms you know by filling in the blank with the word that best completes the sentence.

- **financial plan**
- **owner's equity**
- **financial manager**
- **financial forecast**
- **fiscal year**
- **asset**
- **income statement**
- **budget**
- **accounting**
- **balance sheet**

1. _____ is equal to the total assets of the business minus the total liabilities.
2. An estimate of the future business climate for the company is called a(n) _____.
3. The systematic process of recording and reporting the financial position of a business is called _____.
4. A report of the financial state of a company on a certain date is called the _____.
5. The _____ charts incoming and outgoing funds and outlines uses of the funds.
6. Cash, items to sell, equipment, buildings, and land are each an example of a(n) _____.
7. An accounting period for a company is a(n) _____.
8. A report of the net income or loss over an accounting period is the _____.
9. The person in charge of a business's financial planning, funding, and accounting is called a(n) _____.
10. A written plan of what you expect your income and expenses to be over a certain period of time is called a(n) _____.

Review What You Learned

11. What do managers do with the financial information they receive about their businesses?
12. Why is good management of finances critical for a new business?
13. What is a start-up budget? How is it different from a cash budget?
14. What are the purposes of accounting records?
15. Which report furnishes more information—the income statement or the balance sheet? Explain.
16. In a small business, who's usually responsible for the financial management?

Understanding Business Concepts

17. How do banks and other financial institutions use the financial information about a business?
18. What kind of information is included in a forecast?
19. Explain how an operating budget is a "road map" for the company.
20. How are liabilities created?
21. Explain why the income statement is an incomplete picture of the financial health of a company.
22. Why is a financial forecast important to a company?
23. Name the responsibilities of a financial manager. Briefly explain how each responsibility impacts the business.
24. If you tracked your own cash budget, how much do you expect to spend and earn on a weekly basis?
25. Why is it important that both sides of the equation must balance?

Critical Thinking

26. Do you think a business could operate without financial management? Why or why not?
27. What skills, knowledge, and interests do you have that would make you a successful finance or accounting employee?
28. What might happen to a business that only analyzes its finances twice a year?
29. What might happen if a company doesn't have enough cash reserves?

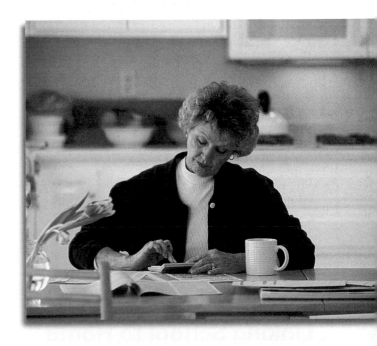

Viewing and Representing

Examining the Image. Team up with a partner. What details do you see in this photograph? What people and objects are shown? Discuss whether or not you have performed this task yet. If not, what do you need to get started?

Building Academic Skills

HISTORY — History of Accounting

The accounting system provides a common language for all businesses to speak. Research the history of accounting and answer the following questions:

- Where and when did accounting get its start?
- What was the impact of the Industrial Revolution on the system of accounting?
- How did the advent of computers change the accounting process?

COMPUTER TECHNOLOGY — Creating a Spreadsheet

Select a business you would like to open. Using a spreadsheet program, create a 12-month budget for the business. Estimate all the income and expenses you'll have for the first year. Then, choose a partner in your class and review each other's budgets. Offer suggestions and make any necessary corrections.

MATH — Evaluating Financial Conditions

Work in teams to find and review the annual reports for three different companies. In each report, find the following:

- The value of the corporation's assets
- The value of its liabilities
- The value of the owner's equity
- Add the liabilities and the owner's equity. Do they equal the assets?

Evaluate the financial condition of each company. Choose the company you think is in the best financial condition. Write a group report explaining your decision.

LANGUAGE ARTS — Writing a Memo

Research two or three different financial software programs that a business might use. Compare the features, costs, and the type of computer needed to run the software. Then, write an imaginary memo recommending one of the programs. Be sure to justify your recommendation.

Linking School to Home

Creating a Budget. Managing personal finances is very similar to managing business finances. First, create a personal financial statement and include your assets and liabilities. Second, create a budget for the next six months showing all your income and expenses. Third, set some financial goals for your future.

Linking School to Work

Interviewing a Financial Manager. In groups of three or four, interview a business financial manager or accountant. Ask about:

- The long-range business plans for the company.
- How financial forecasting is used.
- The software used for the financial management of the company.
- The most common financial mistakes businesses make.

  Write up the interview as a group.

E-Homework

Applying Technology

Researching Requirements. Use the Internet to research the education and certification requirements for the following careers:
- Bookkeeper
- Accountant
- Certified Public Accountant
- Financial Manager
- Controller

Creditable Web Sites. Create a list of ten Web sites that a financial manager might find valuable.

Connecting Academics

Math. Tran, an entrepreneur, wants to earn $42,000 in profits. His research shows that the average net profit for his type of business is 15 percent. To bring in $42,000 in profits the business will need annual sales of $280,000. Tran used the following formula:

Annual Income Desired ÷
Percentage of Average Annual Net Profit =
Total Yearly Sales Volume
($42,000 ÷ 0.15 = $280,000)

Find the total yearly sales volume for the following examples:

Annual Income	Percentage of Average Annual Net Profit
$30,000	0.08
$55,000	0.20

Computer/Technology. Working in groups of four, choose an extracurricular activity (e.g., the football team, band, debate team, theatre, etc.). Select an appropriate computer program and enter the activity's anticipated expenses and income for the entire school year. You'll maintain records of the income and expenses on a weekly basis, perform calculations, and provide reports.

BusinessWeek Analyzing the Feature Story

You read the first part of "Scrutiny on the Bounty" at the beginning of this chapter. Below are a few questions for you to answer about BountySystems's search for funding. You'll find the answers to these questions when you're reading the entire article. First, here are the questions:

30. What does BountySystems's CEO Lon Otremba say about the search for funding?

31. How did Allen Davis find venture-capital funding, and what are the names of the three main companies that invested in BountySystems.com?

CREATIVE JOURNAL ACTIVITY

Break into small groups and create a start-up budget for a new company. Consider the different expenses you might incur including rent, utilities, salaries, and office expenses. How much income will you need to meet expenses?

BUSINESS *Online*
The Full Story
To learn more about BountySystems's search for funding, visit the *Introduction to Business* Web site at **www.introbus.glencoe.com**, and click on *BusinessWeek* Feature Story, Chapter 17.

Technology Advancements in the Workplace

● Learning Objectives

After completing this chapter, you'll be able to:
1. **Describe** the role of information technology in business.
2. **Name** different ways technology has changed the workplace.
3. **Identify** how businesses share knowledge.

● Why It's Important

The advent and progression of businesses using technology has changed the workplace in numerous ways, often making it more efficient and productive.

● Key Words

information technology (IT)
telecommuting
wearable computers
computer-aided design (CAD)
expert system
Internet
Web browser
intranet
extranet
hacker
cookies

BusinessWeek Feature Story

Korea Is Leaving Japan in the Digital-Age Dust

Korea's Big Leap to the Net Has Helped Recharge Its Economy. It's only a two-hour flight from Tokyo, but Seoul seems to be in another universe altogether when it comes to embracing the Digital Age. With South Korea's economy back on the fast track, its information technology sector in overdrive, and its citizenry going online in droves, South Korea is leaving out-to-lunch Japan in the dust.

Source: Excerpted with permission from "Korea Is Leaving Japan in the Digital-Age Dust," *BusinessWeek Online*, August 8, 2000.

An Extension Activity

Why might one country embrace technology and another country might not?

BUSINESS
Online
The Full Story

To learn more about information technology in Korea, visit the *Introduction to Business* Web site at **www.introbus.glencoe.com**, and click on *BusinessWeek* Feature Story, Chapter 18.

Utilizing Technology to Manage Information

The information revolution is here, and data and research are firmly planted in many companies' networks. Data is the raw, unanalyzed, and unsummarized facts and figures. Businesses thrive on collecting, analyzing, and sharing information. In the 1990s businesses started approaching information differently. They shifted to using new technology and new methods of collecting and analyzing information.

The Role of Information Technology

Today, three-quarters of employees work with information on a daily basis. The rest of the workers use information for decision making in their jobs. **Information technology (IT)** is hardware and software for creating, processing, storing, and communicating information.

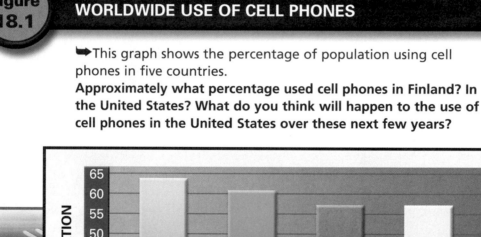

Figure 18.1

WORLDWIDE USE OF CELL PHONES

➡This graph shows the percentage of population using cell phones in five countries.
Approximately what percentage used cell phones in Finland? In the United States? What do you think will happen to the use of cell phones in the United States over these next few years?

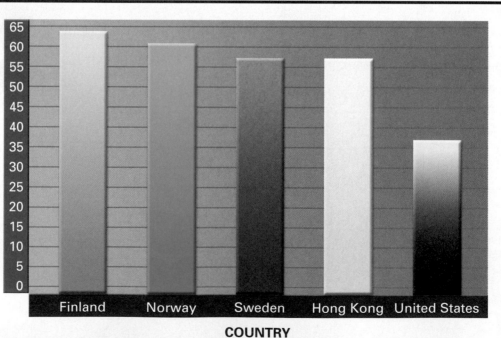

Computers are an important part of information technology. So are other tools. The telephone, for example, has been in use for many years. Faxes send information through the telephone system. Wireless technology has led to cell phones (see Figure 18.1). Wireless technology is used in other devices, too. For example, computers and printers might communicate with each other without cables.

Computers that design and produce products have made a difference in manufacturing. Wearable computers provide on-the-spot information and directions. Millions of employees stay at home and work. Others have their own businesses in their homes. Information technology makes all of these innovations possible.

Even if you don't realize it, computers affect you. Appliances are computerized. You use computers for your schoolwork. You may know people who process information in their jobs.

Changes in the Workplace

When computers were first used in business, employees only used the computer at work. Now mobile computers and communications technology allow workers to work from home. They can stay in touch with their offices through technology.

New technology is changing the workplace. Wearable computers, manufacturing technology, and all kinds of specialized software packages make a difference.

Telecommuting. Does working in your pajamas at home sound inviting? The Gartner Group, a market research firm, estimates that about 29.7 million Americans frequently work from home. (This is about 22 percent of the labor force.)

Telecommuting is a work arrangement that allows employees to work away from the workplace. Employees stay in touch with the workplace using computer and communications technology. Some are full-time telecommuters, and others are part-time. Some telecommuters don't go to the office at all. They work at home instead of traveling to a regular workplace. Others work in a center. Center-based telecommuting uses office space close to home. The employee works at the center without direct supervision.

Telecommuting has advantages. Workers like having less commute time. They like the freedom to schedule their work with flexible hours. Employers often have found that the quality of telecommuters' work improved. Some telecommuters are absent or sick less often than when they worked full-time at the company.

Real-World Application

part 1 of 4

ENGINEERING SOLUTIONS

Barb Sines is a "people person." She is outgoing, likes to work in teams, and she's a good manager and problem solver. Sines is an industrial engineer—someone who works on the "people side" of machines: equipment, production, and business.

How has automation changed the workforce?

continued on p. 287

Dr. R2D2?

Two California companies, Intuitive Surgical, Inc., and Computer Motion, Inc., have designed and tested robotic devices that can perform surgery on the heart, gall bladder, and digestive tract. Doctors using these devises now can perform surgery through incisions no wider than a pencil. The surgeons use handgrips and a foot console to control three robotic arms that carry the camera and instruments. Less pain, faster recovery, and tiny scars are the end results.

Analyze

Who do you think benefits more from robotic surgery: the doctors or the patients? Explain.

A major problem with telecommuting is the lack of contact with other workers. Many telecommuters don't like to be isolated from other workers. Some people have too many distractions at home and can't get their work done. For employers, a major problem is supervising an employee at a remote site. They also have to have more equipment. Offices already have computers and communications equipment. Buying more equipment for the telecommuter at home adds costs for the employer.

Wearable Computers. In many industries you might use **wearable computers**. They're small, lightweight computers that workers carry with them. They use head mounts, with a processor attached by cable. These computers understand and record speech.

A worker can check information on a miniature display screen. They get what they need from the wearable computer while walking or working with their hands. For example, equipment engineers check maintenance manuals stored on the computer. Farmers can collect and record data and search for information while out in the field.

Technology in Manufacturing. Computers have made a difference in design and manufacturing. **Computer-aided design (CAD)** is software for designing products with a computer. CAD is a powerful tool for planning and design.

When CAD and computer-aided manufacturing (CAM) programs are used together, companies can custom design and produce products. With CAD, engineers can design without paper. They can change designs quickly and easily.

Manufacturing plants now are partly or wholly automated. Robots and computer-controlled machine tools do the work. They can do hard jobs that were done in the past by people. In the plants, highly skilled workers with technical training direct these robots and machine tools.

Expert Systems. An **expert system** is computer software that stores and uses knowledge that a human expert would have on the same subject. Expert systems are used in many businesses. For example, software that checks for problems in an automobile analyzes them like an expert would. In the medical field, an expert system compares hundreds of symptoms to help a doctor identify an illness. Airlines use expert systems to find the best use of an airport's terminal gates.

Expert systems protect data and databases. The computer's expert system can identify possible problems. Many credit card companies use expert systems to prevent fraud. The software uses pre-stored data to imitate the decisions that a human expert would make.

Electronic Information Transfer. Electronic information transfer gives businesses information quickly and easily. Many companies electronically transfer paychecks to employees' bank accounts. A national sales manager uses electronic mail to transmit sales figures to regional managers. The vice president for development faxes a report to the company's overseas offices. A bank officer in New York City authorizes electronic transfer of funds to a bank branch in London. All of these people use technology to transfer information electronically.

Consumers use electronic information transfer, too. The automated teller machine (ATM) at a bank is a familiar tool. The ATM process uses a terminal, the bank's network, a computer, and transaction processing software. An ATM user has an ATM account, an ATM card, and a personal identification number (PIN).

The Internet makes it possible to transfer information electronically. With Internet access and software, a consumer can transact business online. Banking online is a growing technology. Trading on the stock market electronically from a home computer is commonplace. Paying bills through your home computer is routine. More and more consumers are using electronic transfer services.

Virtual Training. Virtual training allows learners to simulate a real situation through a computer. A computer-run flight simulator allows pilots to learn how to fly aircraft. The simulator includes a room with cockpit controls and a video screen that shows pilots the results of their actions. The entire room is movable, with its motion controlled by a computer.

Schools use computer-based science labs. Students conduct science experiments, complete with mistakes, from a computer keyboard. They use a menu to choose chemicals to combine and in what amounts. They are safe—no danger of explosion if they make a mistake.

Virtual reality is used in training. The computer recreates physical places and actions that seem real to people. A computer with specially designed technology creates the feeling of being in space. The senses of sight, sound, motion, and touch give the illusion of real objects or places.

The user views events from inside a head-mounted display in a helmet. Inside the helmet, two miniature television screens show slightly different images to each eye. These screens imitate human eyes and show the user three-dimensional viewing. A data glove is the input device. The data glove relays the movements of the user's hand to the computer.

ENGINEERING SOLUTIONS

Sines, the vice president and general manager of Rockwell Automation, is in charge of the company's graphical terminals, which control automated production lines in many industries worldwide.

How might Rockwell Automation use an expert system?

continued on p. 289

Analyzing Sci-Fi

This activity gives you a chance to add to your portfolio. Communicate, interview, research, and write your way into a story. Choose one imaginary path, Searching for Sci-Fi Gizmos or Dissecting Technology. Follow your path's steps to complete your own story.

pick a path

Searching for Sci-Fi Gizmos

The Setting. You've just finished reading Jules Verne's famous novel, *Twenty Thousand Leagues Under the Sea*. Verne combined his knowledge of science with his ability to tell a good adventure story. Now you want to write one of your own.

Rising Action. Think about several challenges that technology might solve.

Step 1. Consider what those technological innovations must do and how they can meet the challenge. Using your common sense, your knowledge of technology and mechanics, and your imagination, write a description of two such possible devices.

Step 2. Add a paragraph describing how you would market these devices to people who were skeptical about their potential effectiveness.

Dissecting Technology

The Setting. Writers have presented their ideas about the future. George Orwell's novel, *1984*, described a totalitarian society of the future. In 1938, actor Orson Welles performed a radio version of H.G. Wells's *War of the Worlds* that convinced listeners aliens had landed on earth.

Rising Action. You're interested in how the media portrays technology.

Step 1. Read a science-fiction novel or watch an old science-fiction movie. Is the futuristic technology believable? Has the problem been solved by other technology? Is the technology believable because it was based on an actual scientific principle?

Step 2. Write your arguments and descriptions in a one-page essay.

Conclusion

To determine the precise relationship of events, it's important to look at the connections between events and their causes or consequences. For example, many causes may lead to one effect. In other cases, one event can have several effects. How does a cause-and-effect relationship affect your story? In your journal, explain why certain events are connected to other events.

The information is processed and sent to the headset. As a result, the user can "reach into" the three-dimensional scene. The sensitive data glove allows surgeons to practice medical operations without real patients.

✓ Fast Review

1. Define information technology.
2. List the pros and cons of telecommuting.
3. How might CAD improve a manufacturing plant?
4. The ATM is an example of which type of technological change?

Sharing Business Knowledge

The virtual frontier is about deciphering which information to keep and which to ignore. Knowledge management is the key to time efficiency and production. A company needs to learn how to manage and use the knowledge to stay competitive. New technologies allow a business to communicate with vendors, suppliers, and customers.

The Internet

The Internet is a way businesses are establishing and keeping relationships with their customers. The **Internet** is a collection of tens of thousands of connected computer networks. The Internet isn't owned or controlled by any one person. The closest thing to an Internet manager is the Internet Society (ISOC) in Reston, Va. This professional, nonprofit organization leads the future of the Internet with constructive insight, leadership, and monitoring new technologies. The ISOC runs Internet conferences around the world.

The Internet was made *user friendly* by the creation of the World Wide Web (or the Web). So, what's the difference between the Internet and the Web? The Web is a means of accessing, organizing, and moving through information on the Internet. Therefore, the Web is part of the Internet. The Internet is really a large library full of information except it's not very organized.

Web Browser. A **Web browser** is a program that makes it easier for you to search and retrieve information on the Web. Netscape® and Microsoft Internet Explorer are two of the most widely used Web browsers. The inclusion of design, graphics, and sound on the Web makes it more enjoyable to *surf* for information.

ENGINEERING SOLUTIONS

The plant produces graphic display terminals that perform real-time machine control. "The concept is similar to the touch-screens we use at automatic bank machines," Sines says. Over the noise of production, she talks with several line workers. She is trying to figure out how to improve their work conditions. **Could virtual reality exist in a production environment? Why or why not?**

continued on p. 291

Other Types of Links

A company may want to give its employees information but deny the public access to this information. An **intranet** allows a company to connect employees with Internet-like technology, but it's closed to public access. The employee handbook, benefits package, employee directory, code of ethics, and announcements may be included on a company's intranet.

There is another type of link that companies use called the **extranet**. This is a semiprivate network that allows more than one company to access the same information. It allows different companies to share information and to collaborate. A company may also use the extranet to manage and communicate with customers, vendors, suppliers, and other organizations by secure Web sites.

Managing the Threats

With the advent of technology, danger looms. Anyone using a computer or network needs be aware of hackers. Take the quiz on Figure 18.2 to see what you think about privacy and security in technology.

Figure 18.2

WHAT DO YOU THINK ABOUT PRIVACY AND SECURITY?

➡What do you think about privacy and security in technology? **Answer true or false for each of these six statements and give a reason for your response.**

1. No one should have access to another's personal information on the Internet without permission.
2. Web sites shouldn't track users.
3. A user should never enter personal information on an Internet site.
4. Children are especially at risk when they access Internet sites.
5. Users must take responsibility for the security of their computers.
6. Antivirus software is a necessity, and a user must purchase updates frequently.

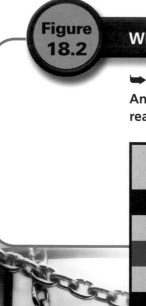

A **hacker** is a person who breaks into computer systems for illegal purposes and vandalizes Web sites, hard drives, and government agencies. Last year there were over 22,000 hacker attacks against the U.S. Defense Department. Each attempt costs the government $1 million.

Privacy Issues

You probably enter personal information into the computer often and don't think about what could happen to that information. Software tools allow companies to track you online. Web sites often send **cookies** to your computer. Cookies are pieces of information about a computer user, which are stored on your hard drive and accessed by a server when the user connects to a Web site. Every time you visit a Web site, even if you don't buy anything, your personal information can be stored.

You can buy software to protect yourself, and it's a good investment. You can use software to protect your e-mail. The software can code your e-mail messages or automatically destroy them after a given time. You can route your e-mail through a secure site. You can use software to protect information about your Web browsing so it isn't shared with site operators.

Virus. A virus is a big problem for computer users. A computer *virus* is a program that infects computer files by copying itself into those files. A virus may do little harm, or it may destroy your files. Every user needs antivirus software to protect the computer. New viruses are created every day, so the software must be updated regularly.

Firewall. Other software packages can protect computer systems. You can buy personal firewall software for your computer. A *firewall* is a software program that acts as a security wall between your computer and the Internet. It protects your personal information on the Internet.

ENGINEERING SOLUTIONS

"If a machine breaks down or we get a new production unit or we decide to revamp our team approach—I can be called in to help," Sines says. "That's my job—to solve problems, to help other engineers, corporate managers, and employees work as a team, and in the process, to add value to the product."

Time efficiency and quality production are examples of what?

✓ Fast Review

1. What are some ways you can protect personal information on your computer?
2. What is the purpose of antivirus software?
3. Describe the Internet.
4. What are two other types of links a business might use as a form of communication?

Picture *This...*

Why Do They Call It a Cell Phone?

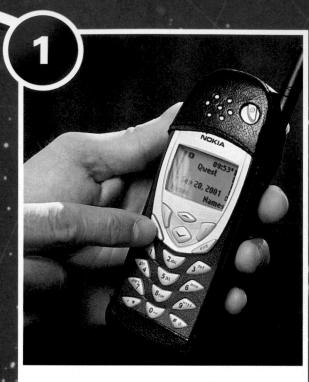

1. When you turn on a cell phone, it transmits a signal.

2. The signal is picked up by the Mobile Telephone Switching Office (MTSO), the central office of the phone company, or service carrier, you use.

3. The MTSO identifies which part of the city—or cell—you're in and routes your signal to its transmitter, or base station, within that cell.

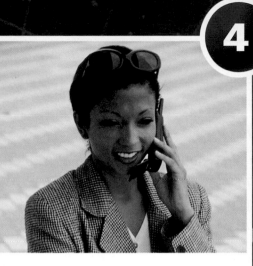

4. The base station then connects your call to its destination.

5. If you're using a cell phone in a moving vehicle, as you move from one part of the city to another—or from one cell to another—the MTSO switches your signal to the next base station.

Now *You* Take a Shot...

Integrated Technology
A built-in clock, calculator, and address book in one device is yesterday's wristwatch. Today technology continues to integrate several electronic devices into one. Stop by an electronics store and check out the latest cell phone technology. What are some of the things you can do with a cell phone other than make a call?

Chapter 18 Review

Summary

1. Information technology allows business employees the capability to create, process, store, and communicate information.

2. Telecommuting, wearable computers, technology in manufacturing, expert systems, electronic information transfer, and virtual training are technological advances that have changed the workplace.

3. The Internet, intranet, and extranet are all ways businesses communicate with one another.

Using Business Key Words

It seems like each day technology dramatically changes the workplace. See how ready you are for the technologically savvy workplace by completing the sentences below, with the following key terms.

- **information technology (IT)**
- **Internet**
- **expert system**
- **Web browser**
- **cookies**
- **telecommuting**
- **wearable computers**
- **intranet**
- **extranet**
- **hacker**
- **computer-aided design (CAD)**

1. A work arrangement called _____ allows employees to work away from the workplace.
2. A powerful tool for planning and design is called _____.
3. Computer software that stores and uses knowledge that a human would have on the same subject is _____.
4. A collection of tens of thousands of connected computer networks is called the _____.
5. Hardware and software for creating, processing, storing, and communicating information is called _____.
6. A program that makes it easier for you to search and retrieve information on the Web is called a(n) _____.
7. Small, lightweight computers that workers carry with them are called _____.
8. A program that allows a company to connect employees with Internet-like technology, but is closed to public access, is called the _____.
9. A program that allows more than one company to access the same information is called the _____.
10. Pieces of information about a computer user, which are stored on your hard drive, and accessed by a server when the user connects to a Web site are called _____.
11. A person who breaks into computer systems for illegal purposes is called a _____.

Review What You Learned

12. Describe the advantages and disadvantages of telecommuting.

13. What happens when CAD and CAM programs are used together?

14. What types of businesses use expert systems?

15. Explain how an ATM terminal works.

16. How are consumers using the Internet to transact business online?

17. How is virtual reality used to train pilots?

18. What is a PIN and how is it used?

19. What does the Internet Society do?

Understanding Business Concepts

20. Describe a job you think could be done through telecommuting.

21. Can you think of a local business where a robot could be used to complete a job or part of a job? Explain.

22. Why do you think electronic information transfer is becoming so popular?

23. Have you every played a virtual reality game? If so, describe your experience. If not, describe what you think it would be like.

24. Do you think people will be able to replace their keyboarding skills with speech recognition technology? Explain your answer.

25. Explain why technology is just a tool.

26. Name a few industries that use expert systems. What's the purpose of these systems?

27. What's the difference between the Internet and the Web?

Critical Thinking

28. Do you think it's good that people can be in touch with their workplace all day, every day? Explain why or why not.

29. What are some problems with too many people using the Internet?

30. Which office occupations might be downsized with these technological changes?

31. Hypothesize about the fastest-growing occupations that use technology. How do these generate new openings in the information-technology world?

Viewing and Representing

Examining the Image. What's happening in this photograph? Write a product summary based upon your perceptions of each device. Share the summaries with the class.

Building Academic Skills

 Research Emerging Technology

Research a piece of emerging technology and write a 250-word paper on the impact it might have on the business world.

 Creating an Oral Presentation

Research virtual reality and find out:
- When it first emerged
- Who was the first to use it
- Equipment needed
- Examples of how it might be used in the future

Create an oral presentation to share your findings with the class.

 Needed Math Skills

In a group of three or four, choose five different information technology related careers. Research the math skills that are needed to be successful in those careers.

COMPUTER TECHNOLOGY **Targeting Technology**

Interview someone who uses a computer system in his or her business. Does this person have any problems running the system? Has technology given him or her any problems while trying to run the business? Did technology solve any problems? How? Write your findings in your journal. Be thorough about how the business solved any technological problems.

Linking School to Home

Brainstorm About Managing Information. Never before has there been more information available to you with the click of a mouse. Using your time efficiently means knowing what information to keep or discard. Explain to your family and friends how important it might be to protect your company information from other competitors. Brainstorm with them and come up with several ways to keep your information secure. Create a guide to share with others about how a company can create privacy.

Linking School to Work

Technology Affects Business. As mentioned earlier in this chapter, three-quarters of employees work with information on a daily basis. If not working directly with information, then you might be using it to make decisions. Interview a small business owner in your community to learn about how technology has changed the way his or her business operates. What changes have been made based on information technology? What expenses were incurred? What changes are planned for the future?

E-Homework

Applying Technology

Creating Your Ideal Work Space. Imagine you have the opportunity to work from home. Create a picture of your ideal home office and include the technology tools you'll need in order to do your job.

Researching Wearable Computers. Visit a computer store in your community or online. Research the wearable computers that are described in the text. Select one that you think would help you in school and write a paragraph about it.

Connecting Academics

Math. You're tired of working for other people. Now is your chance to break away and start your own consulting company. In order to find investors in your business idea, you've got to conduct a lot of research. You want your business to be national in scope so it can't be limited to just your local community. Technology has influenced the way business is done around the world. Find statistics about the increased use of a particular type of technology used in business. Draw a graph of your findings.

Language Arts. You work for Ads Etc., which needs to hire six temporary designers. There's no office space so Twyla, your boss, asks you to research the advantages of having these designers telecommute. Write a business memo or e-mail to Twyla outlining the advantages. Include two things Ads Etc. will need to do to protect information when setting up the communication between the off-site designers and the company.

BusinessWeek Analyzing the Feature Story

You read the first part of "Korea Is Leaving Japan in the Digital-Age Dust" at the beginning of this chapter. Below are a few questions for you to answer about South Korea. You'll find the answers to these questions when you're reading the entire article. First, here are the questions:

32. How much of South Korea's economic growth was based on info-tech spending and investment?
33. What theories do South Koreans have for their success in entering the Digital Age in comparison to Japan's?

CREATIVE JOURNAL ACTIVITY

Write how a country's lack of attention to technology might influence it. How would it differ from a technologically advanced country?

To learn more about information technology in Korea, visit the *Introduction to Business* Web site at **www.introbus.glencoe.com**, and click on *BusinessWeek* Feature Story, Chapter 18.

Chapter 19

Basics of Computers

Learning Objectives

After completing this chapter, you'll be able to:

1. **Describe** the parts of a complete computer system.
2. **Name** the different hardware components of a computer.
3. **Identify** measurements for computer memory and storage.
4. **Explain** the various software programs available to businesses.

Why It's Important

For every kind of business task, from accounting to graphic design, there is a software program available.

Key Words

personal digital assistant (PDA)
scanner
hardware
random access memory (RAM)
byte
software
desktop publishing
spreadsheet program
database
groupware

BusinessWeek Feature Story

A Powerful Shareware Rival to Mighty Microsoft

Idea Keeper Is an Everything-Software Program. Idea Keeper is shareware for the Macintosh at its best. This little, inexpensive program is nearly as powerful as Microsoft Word. It can even do some things that mighty Word can't, such as automatically stripping out the weird formatting of e-mail text. Not a bad trick for a program that costs only $15. For starters, Idea Keeper looks different. You're not greeted with a word processor's traditional blank page at startup.

Source: Excerpted with permission from "A Powerful Shareware Rival to Mighty Microsoft," *BusinessWeek Online*, May 3, 2000.

An Extension Activity

How does technology affect productivity and efficiency? Research ten facts then write a one-page report.

BUSINESS Online
The Full Story

To learn more about Idea Keeper, visit the *Introduction to Business* Web site at **www.introbus.glencoe.com**, and click on *BusinessWeek* Feature Story, Chapter 19.

Communicating Through Computers

Scouting out aisles filled with software in your neighborhood office-supplies store may be mind-boggling. Whether you're looking for crossword puzzle software to create your own games or you're looking to update your computer software, the choices are endless. Before you buy the best product for your needs it's a good idea to know the basics about computers—both the software and the hardware.

You might take computers for granted. People depend on them to handle work of all kinds. When your parents pay a bill, a computer records the payment. You can use your computer to pay the bill electronically. In that case, your computer communicates with the computer at the business you're paying. Computers of all sizes and types run appliances, cars, calculators, and other devices. They're everywhere.

The Speed of Communication

Computers have increased the speed of communication. While there's the initial expense of the computer equipment you need, you save time and increase productivity down the road. As Benjamin Franklin said,

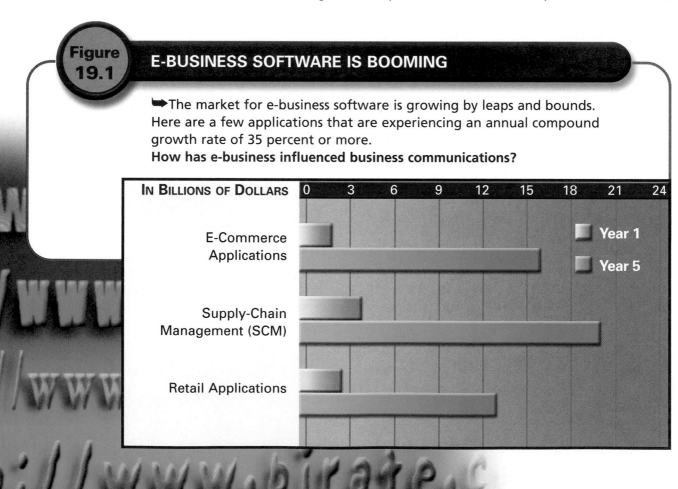

Figure 19.1

E-BUSINESS SOFTWARE IS BOOMING

➡The market for e-business software is growing by leaps and bounds. Here are a few applications that are experiencing an annual compound growth rate of 35 percent or more.
How has e-business influenced business communications?

IN BILLIONS OF DOLLARS 0   3   6   9   12   15   18   21   24

Year 1
Year 5

E-Commerce Applications

Supply-Chain Management (SCM)

Retail Applications

"Time is money." Businesses can access data, send e-mail, or make bank deposits in the blink of an eye. As technology continues to change, businesses keep finding more and more uses for computers (see Figure 19.1).

In the workplace, computers handle just about every kind of task for businesses. Handheld devices track appointments, telephone numbers, addresses, and other data. The personal computer (PC) is an essential tool for the workplace. Businesses of all sizes use PCs to record information and keep track of those records. Entrepreneurs and small business owners rely on computers as much as large corporations do. In fact, they couldn't get along without them.

Types of Computers

Business and its employees are constantly on the move. With laptop computers, cellular phones, and pagers you can do business anywhere you go. A **personal digital assistant (PDA)** is a hand-held computer you can use as an address book, an appointment book, and a voice recorder. You can even use a PDA to go on the Internet. The Palm™ Pilot and Compaq iPAQ Pocket PC are two different types of PDAs.

In the workplace, the desktop computer can perform countless different tasks. It can be used to type reports, analyze sales records, prepare taxes, deposit checks, store files, and send e-mail. In large companies, computers are linked to each other through either a central computer called a *mainframe* or a *network computing system*. This allows the computers to share files, data, printers, and e-mail within the company.

There are also different types of computers for different types of jobs. In retail stores, computerized cash registers automatically record the prices of items using a scanner. A **scanner** is a device that reads images, such as price codes, and records or transfers the information. Most car repair shops can now tell what's wrong with your car by hooking it up to a diagnostic computer. Film studios use special computers to produce sound and visual effects for movies.

Parts of a Computer System

Regardless of how many parts and pieces make up a computer, it's controlled by programmed instructions. These instructions give the computer guidance. A complete computer system consists of four parts: software, people, data, and hardware.

Software tells the computer what to do. It's a set of electronic information consisting of complex codes to make the computer perform

Real-World Application

part **1** of 4

WEAVING A NETWORK
Amiel Dunn is on the trail of two mysteries. Dunn is a senior network analyst for Howard University in Washington, D.C. Several years ago, he and the rest of a small staff created the school's sophisticated computer network, which links students, faculty members, and staff into one system. **What do you use a computer for?**

continued on p. 303

Technology Toolkit

Reading Your Palm

Pocket-size and smart—this is a hand-held computer, or a personal digital assistant (PDA). This complements (not replaces) your personal computer. If you record an appointment in your PDA, you need to upload it to your laptop. If you write a memo on your desktop computer and want to revise it during a trip, you'll need to transfer it to the PDA. This communication between a PDA and a PC is *data synchronization,* or *syncing.* A cable or infrared light syncs the information.

Critical Thinking

How could competing software companies try to monopolize the hand-held computer market?

tasks. In order to make the computer operational, people need to be the users. Whether you're designing, building, or using a computer, it requires your attention.

As discussed in Chapter 18, computers make sense of all the data. The computer alters and moves the data into comprehensible information. Data may be letters, sound, graphics, or numbers.

The physical components of a computer system are called the **hardware**. It includes a processor, memory, input and output devices, and storage devices. Each computer system uses these main elements. Here's a closer look at each important piece of the whole.

Processors. The *processor* is the brain of a computer. It transforms the data into usable information for the user. The processor interprets and carries out instructions for the user. It performs calculations and logical comparisons at extremely high speeds. One of the advancements in computers over the last several years has been higher and higher processor speed. It's located in the central processing unit (CPU) of personal computers. In a personal computer the processor usually consists of chips. These are small pieces of silicon or other material with electronic circuits. The data passes through these pieces of silicon to other areas to complete the instruction in the computer.

Memory. The computer's *memory* can be thought of as a kind of scratch pad. The computer uses memory to hold all of the data and instructions required during operation. The most common type of memory is called **random access memory**, or RAM. When a computer saves information, the first place it goes is to RAM. As long as your computer is on, the information remains in this temporary memory for the computer to use quickly. As soon as you turn off the computer, RAM loses information. For that reason, storage is a very important part of a computer system.

Memory's capacity is measured in bytes. A **byte** is the amount of memory it takes to store a single character. With the advance of science and technology research and production, the number of bytes per computer can increase. The most common units of measurement for computer memory and storage are as follows:

Kilobyte (KB)	1,000 bytes
Megabyte (MB)	1 million
Gigabyte (GB)	1 billion
Terabyte (TB)	1 trillion

Input and Output Devices. Without the input and output of information a computer would be useless. Input devices accept data and instructions. Examples of input devices include a keyboard, mouse, touchpad, joystick, digital camera, and microphone. The output device returns the processed data back to the user or to another computer system. Examples of output devices include a computer monitor, printer, fax machine, and speakers.

Storage Devices. *Storage devices*, such as hard drives, floppy disks, and CD-ROMs, all save and hold information. Computer storage devices save all the bits of information you and your computer use. You can think of storage devices as file cabinets in which you can keep information. The hard drive is like a huge filing cabinet. It has space for all the work you want to do and it stores all the data you need to carry out your instructions. The hard drive is sealed inside a box in your computer. As technology advances, hard drives have more and more capacity, too.

Portable storage devices are also popular methods to store information, since the hard drive is sealed inside the computer. You can easily move these from machine to machine. ZIP disks are widely used to store information permanently. Small diskettes (only three-and-a-half inches in diameter) can hold hundreds of files. You can think of a hard drive as a filing cabinet. Think of a diskette as a file folder. It can hold lots of information, but not nearly as much as a hard drive.

Diskettes cannot hold some of the complex software programs needed for the work that powerful computers can do. ZIP disks and CD-ROMs also can store data, and they have much greater capacity. Most software programs sold to consumers now are stored on CD-ROMs.

✓ Fast Review

1. What four parts complete a computer system?
2. The hardware of a computer is comprised of these four categories. Name them.

Real-World Application
part 2 of 4

WEAVING A NETWORK

A network is a combination of computer hardware and software that allows people to share resources immediately and across long distances. It's a complex system that occasionally can develop glitches. Dunn's first mystery occurred when some network users received a momentary "error" message. Trying to solve this particular type of mystery can be frustrating because it doesn't last long enough to pinpoint.
How have you handled a computer's error message?

continued on p. 305

Computer Software

Computers are just machines. Sometimes people are in awe of them, but they cannot do anything without instruction from human beings. As discussed earlier in this chapter, **software**, or a computer program, is a set of instructions that tell computers what to do. Some software programs tell a computer how to calculate numbers or arrange words.

Other software programs are custom-made for special uses, such as preparing taxes or designing a house. For every kind of business activity there are software programs available. Without software a computer is just a collection of parts. Since software is so essential, software development is a career field with great opportunity. Anything a computer does must have software instructions.

Word Processing Programs

What if you want to send 30 letters to members of a club? Or you would like to send an announcement about a meeting? Having to write 30 letters is a lot of work. When you have written the letters, you still have to prepare envelopes. Word processing software prepares letters, announcements, and envelopes with ease.

Word processing is one of the most popular types of software for business. Businesses of all sizes and types create documents, and word processing software makes document creation easy. Documents are created and then edited and printed. Users find word processors important in the step of revising documents. The editing features make it possible for a user to make multiple changes easily.

Word processing programs, such as Microsoft® Word, are the most commonly used type of computer software. If you have a computer you've

You Make the Call

Portable Phones, Portable Privacy

As the vice president of production for a biotechnology company, business travel is a weekly occurrence. While waiting for a flight you overhear a woman talking on a cell phone behind you and realize she's the chief executive officer (CEO) of your biggest competitor. She's talking about important information regarding an experiment. Everyone in the biotech industry knows that whoever discovers the answer first will reap millions of dollars worth of profit from the patent. The CEO has just mentioned something that could be the final piece to the research puzzle for your company.

Making an Ethical Decision

1. Are you eavesdropping on privileged information? If so, should you walk away until you're out of earshot?
2. Should you tell the CEO you overheard her conversation?
3. Is someone who uses a cell phone in a public place entitled to the same privacy as someone who uses it in a workplace?

probably used a word processing program to write a school paper. It allows you to use your computer like a typewriter but with many added features. For example, you can type over words, rearrange paragraphs, change margins, and check your spelling with ease.

Some programs combine word processing with graphics so you can do desktop publishing. **Desktop publishing** consists of writing, designing, and laying out documents on your computer like a professional publisher. With desktop publishing, you can produce high-quality reports, newsletters, presentations, and magazines.

Spreadsheet Programs

A **spreadsheet program** is a computerized worksheet. Sales figures, quantities, prices, and production costs can be easily listed and compared. With a click of a button, information can be changed instantly. If the dates or costs change, you can enter the new data in one place, press a key, and your spreadsheet will automatically update the list for you. Two of the most popular spreadsheet programs are Lotus® 1-2-3 and Microsoft® Excel. Figure 19.2 on page 306 is an example of a spreadsheet program.

Accounting Programs

All businesses need to keep accurate, up-to-date accounting records. With an accounting software package, you can keep records, prepare reports, and even write checks on the computer. The software handles all financial transactions. You can use it to keep payroll accounts, send out bills, and do your taxes. With a keystroke you can find out what your profits or losses are at any given time. Peachtree® and QuickBooks® are two programs you can use.

Database Programs

A **database** is a collection of information usually kept in a list. It can consist of a list of names, supplies, products, or schedules. With database software, a list can easily be updated, changed, or rearranged. You can print out part of a list or display it any way you like. The same list can be used at different times for different purposes. For example, an employee database can be used to keep track of workers' hours, wages, vacations, or benefits.

Databases are also used to keep track of inventory and sales. Sales records can then be used to make long-range forecasts. The ability to

Real-World Application

part **3** of **4**

WEAVING A NETWORK

Dunn uses a Macintosh, a PC, and several laptops to troubleshoot network problems at the university. The laptops are especially important because they allow him to "communicate" with the larger machines. "The laptop is like a screwdriver," Dunn says. "I actually take it to the computer on campus where I think the problem has developed, plug in the laptop, and then use it to find and fix the problem."

Explain how you might troubleshoot a computer glitch.

continued on p. 307

search large amounts of data at great speed to find specific information is an important part of making sound business decisions. Corel Paradox® is an example of a database manager.

Graphics and Presentation Programs

Presentation software is used to produce professional presentations. With it you can take data from spreadsheets and put it in the form of graphs, charts, or figures for visual presentations. You can do layouts for a slide show and arrange them in any order. Special effects such as shadows, backgrounds, and textures can be added to make them more interesting. Sound effects, animation, and video clips can be added to make a presentation even more effective. Among the most popular presentation and graphics programs are Microsoft PowerPoint® and Harvard Graphics.

Figure 19.2

HOW A SPREADSHEET PROGRAM WORKS

➡A spreadsheet program is the equivalent to how an accountant's worksheet works. Programs that automate bookkeeping tasks show you how to budget and save money.
How could you use spreadsheet software?

Microsoft Excel - BUDGET.XLS

File Edit View Insert Format Tools Data Window Help

Librarian

	A	B	C	D	E	F	G
1	Acct #	Account Description	YTD	June	May	April	March
2							
3	Subcontractors & Services						
4	201	Telecommunication Serv	$2,616	$436	$7,200	$436	$436
5	202	Design Consultants	$1,625	$500	$375	$375	$0
6	203	Photo/Video Services	$830	$45	$325	$45	$325
7	250	Graphic Services	$2,561	$765	$95	$375	$95
8	251	Photo/Stats	$2,228	$568	$755	$0	$755
9	252	Typesetting	$1,483	$388	$325	$195	$325
10	253	Printing Services	$5,667	$951	$849	$325	$849
11	254	Legal & Accounting	$780	$130	$130	$130	$130

Communications Software

Communications software makes it possible for computers to communicate with each other. You need it if you want to send a file to another computer. You also need it to send and receive e-mail. Businesses also use communications software to access databases, accounts, and other shared files. With some programs, you can receive faxes and voice mail directly on your computer. Microsoft® Outlook and QUALCOMM® Eudora are two popular communication programs.

Groupware

As discussed in Chapter 8, the trend in business is toward self-managed teams. **Groupware**, or project management software, makes it easier for team members to work together on the same project. The program is run on a network so all members of the team can access it. It can be used to track costs, schedules, resources, and tasks. It can also compute the best way to complete tasks, manage resources, and meet deadlines.

The program can also create graphs and charts to guide workers on a project. A builder, for example, can use the program to plan a construction project. The software can help the builder to complete the project within the estimated budget and schedule. By planning the entire project for the workers, the software makes it possible to complete the project more efficiently. Lotus® Notes is an example of a groupware program available.

Web Page Programs

The World Wide Web is an important part of businesses reaching the world. Web pages make it possible for businesses to market their products. Macromedia® Dreamweaver and SiteRack are the two most popular Web page programs.

Real-World Application

part 4 of 4

WEAVING A NETWORK
Dunn's colleagues tell him that they've located a computer on campus where someone is trying to hack into another PC somewhere in the Midwest. Dunn begins working on the day's second mystery—tracking down a culprit using the computer network he helps keep tied together.
What do you do to manage computer threats?

✓ **Fast Review**

1. What can you do with desktop publishing?
2. What kinds of information might be kept in a database?
3. What are some special effects you can produce with presentation software?
4. What kind of software is useful for managing team projects?

Summary

1. Software, people, data, and hardware are the four parts to a complete computer system.

2. Hardware is comprised of the processor, memory, input and output devices, and storage devices. The processor is the brain of the computer. The memory holds the data and is measured in bytes. Input devices accept data and instructions. Output devices return the processed data back to the user or to another computer system.

3. The following is a list of the most common units of measurement for computer memory and storage:

Kilobyte (KB)	1,000 bytes
Megabyte (MB)	1 million
Gigabyte (GB)	1 billion
Terabyte (TB)	1 trillion

4. Business software programs exist for accounting, spreadsheets, databases, communications, and Web design. Businesses can use desktop publishing and graphics software to produce high-quality reports and presentations.

Using Business Key Words

Match each of the following key words with its definition. Then, using magazines, newspapers, and the Internet, find a picture that represents each word.

- **scanner**
- **software**
- **random access memory (RAM)**
- **spreadsheet program**
- **hardware**
- **byte**
- **desktop publishing**
- **database**
- **personal digital assistant (PDA)**
- **groupware**

1. The physical components of a computer system.
2. Used by accountants to calculate revenue, expenses, net income, etc.
3. Sets of instructions that tell computers what to do.
4. A collection of related records.
5. A small scanning device that allows a printer to read printed product codes.
6. A hand-held computer you can use as a personal organizer.
7. This is the most common form of memory.
8. This is project management software.
9. Software that consists of writing, designing, and laying out documents on your computer.
10. Memory is measured in this.

Review What You Learned

11. Why is software development a career field with great potential?
12. What's the heart of a computer?
13. Name two examples of portable storage devices.
14. What types of documents do businesses create using word processing software?
15. Describe elements of a publication produced with desktop publishing.
16. Name the four types of information that can go into a spreadsheet.
17. How does a business utilize a spreadsheet program?
18. What are some examples of the ways businesses use electronic databases?
19. What does communication software allow us to do?
20. What does project management software allow us to do?

Understanding Business Concepts

21. Explain why storage is such an important part of a computer system.
22. Create a list of ten business tasks that computers can perform.
23. Why do you think word processing software is one of the most-used software programs for business?
24. How do you think your school might use databases?
25. How do you think your school might use presentation software?
26. Explain why you think communication software has become a necessity for businesses and consumers.
27. Imagine you're on the planning team for this year's prom. Describe how project management software might be useful for your team.

Critical Thinking

28. Do you think it's possible to run a successful business today without using a computer? Explain why or why not.
29. Describe how you could use word processing, spreadsheet, database, communication, presentation, and project management software to enhance your schoolwork.
30. How can you avoid losing information you may have saved on a business's network?
31. What steps would you take to share important project information with coworkers?

Viewing and Representing

Examining the Image. Looking at the photograph, list details that you see. Who do you think benefits from handheld computers? What new computer-related inventions have there been in the last few years?

Building Academic Skills

 Online Bill Pay

Research an electronic bill paying service. Answer the following questions:
- How much does it cost?
- What features are available?
- How is security handled?
- How are problems resolved?
- What are the requirements to enroll?

Preparing a Cost Estimate

A local business owner has asked you to prepare a cost estimate for a new computer system. The owner will use the computer in every aspect of her business—communication, accounting, marketing, and project management. Using the newspaper, magazines, and the Internet, prepare the estimate. Be sure to include software and a printer.

 Composing a Letter

You work as an administrative assistant for a cookie company. Your boss has asked you to write a form letter to your customers describing the new cookie that will be on the market next week. Compose and word-process the letter.

 Historical Timeline

In a group of three or four, create a timeline that shows how computers have been used in the workplace. Begin with the early 1950s. Add pictures and graphics to add interest to your timeline. Display in your classroom.

Linking School to Home

Creating a Chart. Take a survey of your family and friends. Find out what types of software they use to make their lives easier. Create a chart that shows the name of the software, the tasks it performs, and how often it is used.

Linking School to Work

Researching Handheld Computers. PDAs are becoming more and more popular in the workplace. Research one brand of these handheld devices and find out the following:
- Cost
- Business features
- Personal features
- How it interfaces with a desktop computer Share your results with the class.

E-Homework

Applying Technology

Designing a Letterhead. Design is about line, value, shape, color, and texture. There is no precise formula for design, unlike grammar that requires parts of speech to perfectly interlock into meaning. Think about a designer's basic ingredients for this assignment. Create a letterhead logo and business card for an imaginary business. Use clip art and interesting fonts that will make your business appealing.

Creating a Database. Sport occupies a vast majority of people's time. Whether they're watching a little league game, rooting for a major league team, or buying team memorabilia, sport is part of culture. Now, this is your chance to research and calculate a sports team of your interest. Create a database of your favorite sports team. Include players' names, colleges, years in the league, and game statistics.

Connecting Academics

Math. Daily newspapers across the country have special technology sections. The advent of new gadgets always gets attention. Research major newspapers' archives to find information about trends in personal digital assistants (PDAs). Create a bar chart or circle chart representing the trends.

Language Arts. Break into groups. Find photographs and graphics from newspapers and magazines representing computers being used in the workplace to process information. Create a poster.

BusinessWeek Analyzing the Feature Story

You read the first part of "A Powerful Shareware Rival to Mighty Microsoft" at the beginning of this chapter. Below are a few questions for you to answer about Idea Keeper. You'll find the answers to these questions when you're reading the entire article. First, here are the questions:

32. What are some benefits of Idea Keeper in comparison to traditional word processing software?

33. What are some disadvantages of Idea Keeper compared to word processing software?

CREATIVE JOURNAL ACTIVITY

Go to the Web site for *PC World* or *PC Magazine* and research new business software. How much of it is shareware in relation to software? Did you find any other software that's a hybrid of word processing, spreadsheet, or presentation software? Write a one-page report summarizing your findings.

BUSINESS Online
The Full Story

To learn more about Idea Keeper, visit the *Introduction to Business* Web site at **www.introbus.glencoe.com**, and click on *BusinessWeek* Feature Story, Chapter 19.

Unit 6
Technology

Applying Technology to New Business Ideas

In Chapter 19 you learned about technology's impact on the way you live. Not only does technology influence the workplace, culture, and business, but it also influences the environment, health, and science. In this seminar you'll work in a group to develop or refine a product that uses technology to improve health or to better a quality of life.

Factoids

Living in a Bubble. A couple builds what is believed to be the nation's first antimicrobial home near Simi Valley, Calif. It's engineered to stop the growth of fungus, mold, and bacteria.

A Slow, Constant Zap. Researchers hope to use low-radio frequency waves instead of chemicals to control zebra mussels in intake pipes at power plants.

Ending a Tragedy. Child malnutrition in Latin America is expected to end by 2010 with agricultural investments of $140 million.

A Promising Pledge. Microsoft promised $58 million over the next five years to help President Vicente Fox's initiative called "e-Mexico" to get 98 percent of the country online. The Internet will help Mexico's education and health sectors.

A Photograph That Stays With You. For $895 you can get a full-body computed tomography (or CT) exam, which is a scan of your internal body. The scan can detect future health problems that might not be diagnosed right away.

Investigate the Images

Look at the photographic collage on the left page. What grabs your attention? Is it the color or the words? The power in reading visuals is in analyzing and dissecting your observations. On a separate piece of paper, respond to the questions listed below. These questions might help sharpen the focus of your visual mind.

Your Observations

1. How many photographs do you see?

2. Examine each photograph. How are they assembled in relation to one another?

3. What is the subject of each photograph? Is place or location the subject?

4. Does color signify a message?

5. What issues do you take from these images?

Information

6. Summarize what you know about the photographs from your observations.

Exploring Culture

7. What aspect of your daily life is influenced by technology? Does it create stress in your life?

8. How, where, and on whom should scientists and doctors perform experimental medical research?

Taking Aim at Technology

● Preparation

Discover how a business uses technology to enhance a product's form and function, and decide the benefits of applying technology to it.

Objective
- **Research** a product that uses technology.
- **Examine** a marketable idea for a product, and explain why it's beneficial or desirable.
- **Create** a marketing plan for your product, and create a model that describes the benefits of using technology.

Materials Needed
✓ Copies of recent news and technology publications such as *Yahoo! Internet Life, BusinessWeek,* or a major newspaper.
✓ Paper, pencils, pens, markers
✓ Posterboard
✓ Materials for product mock-up or sketches

● Procedures

1. With two other students, find and read articles about applying new technologies to daily living. Possible topics include home networking, interconnected appliances, and robotics. Use the Internet to access business or technology publications or sections of the newspaper.

2. Brainstorm ideas for products that use new technologies. Either create a new product or refine a product's function that you read about.

3. As a group, submit a one-page, typed paper describing your product and answering these questions:
   - What is your product?
   - What new technology is being used?
   - How would it be used in daily living?
   - Who is your market? Who would buy this product?

4. Review what you learned in Chapter 13 and create a marketing plan. Decide which media—Internet, television, radio, magazines, newspapers, etc.—would advertise your product most effectively. Decide, too, how you would distribute your product.

5. Display a mock-up or drawing of your product and explain how it works. Present your product and marketing plan to the class.

Chart It

With your group compile a list of reasons for using new technology in everyday life. Use the information presented by the class and found during your research. On a separate sheet of paper, draw a pie chart that describes how your group ranks the reasons for using technology in daily living. Compare your pie chart with other groups.

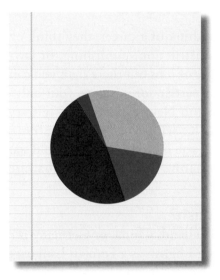

Analyze and Conclude

After considering your research and the other groups' charts, answer the questions below:

1. **Participating as a Group.** Which is the most popular reason (within your entire class) for using new technology?

2. **Teaching Others.** In your group's opinion, which is the most popular reason for using new technology?

3. **Applying Technology to a Task.** Name three other reasons for using new technology in daily living.

4. **Selecting Technology.** What do you think is the greatest benefit for using new technology? Give your reasons.

Becoming an Informed Citizen

Congratulations, you finished the seminar. Now it's time to reflect on the decisions you made.

Knowing How to Learn. Why is it important to think about technology on a larger scale than just how it affects a business and a workplace?

Analyzing Your Future. Knowing the importance of health and technology in your daily life, what are some possible career opportunities that might be available to you in the future?

BUSINESS Online

Further Exploration

To find out more about using technology in daily life, visit *Introduction to Business* Web site at **www.introbus.glencoe.com**.

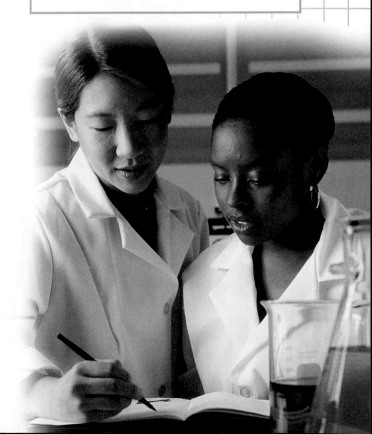

Unit 7

Career Planning in a Global Economy

Wanted: A Cool Job

When most people think of a career, they think of something like business, construction, publishing, or law. There are, however, more types of jobs out there than you can imagine. If you want to be an artist, for instance, your only option isn't to move into a loft in New York and slowly starve. You could get a job carving ice sculptures, designing film sets, or doing police sketches. If you like animals, you could start a pet day-care. Find more jobs at **www.cooljobs.com** and **www.jobs.net**.

● **How Is Your English?**
You could live in Thailand, China, or Germany certified as a TEFL (Teaching English as a Foreign Language) instructor. You don't even need to know a foreign language.

● **Shop Till You Drop**
Market research companies hire a mystery shopper to shop at stores and evaluate the quality of goods and services.

● **Paid to Play**
Software companies have game testers, who test new games they're developing for technical glitches and level of difficulty.

● **Watch Out Where You Land**
Smokejumpers, the commandos of firefighting, fly into fire areas and parachute in to control and "mop-up" fires.

BUSINESS
Online

Idea Factory

To learn more about the jobs and careers,
visit the *Introduction to Business* Web site at
www.introbus.glencoe.com, and click on
Unit 7 Career Planning in a Global Economy.

Developing a Career Plan

Learning Objectives

After completing this chapter, you'll be able to:

1. **Explain** the difference between a career and a job.
2. **Describe** a personal inventory.
3. **Name** ways to find out about your career options.
4. **List** the things you can do to get prepared for a career.

Why It's Important

There's no better time than the present to start planning a career. There are positive steps you can take toward reaching a career goal.

Key Words

career	profession
career	trade
planning	apprenticeship
aptitudes	journeyworker
skills	internship
career	shadowing
counselor	career ladder
networking	entry-level job

BusinessWeek Feature Story

Can Your Nerves Take a Dot-Com Job?

The New Frontier of Career Opportunities. How much personal risk you can and should tolerate is a very subjective matter. Simply stated, you should not sign up for a tech start-up situation where you would be highly uncomfortable. You may be in a situation where you are outside your normal comfort zone. If you're a first-time tech start-up prospect, then the tech start-up will definitely push your comfort envelope. However, in today's economy, taking calculated risks is becoming more necessary than ever.

Source: Excerpted with permission from "Can Your Nerves Take a Dot-Com Job?" *BusinessWeek Online*, September 8, 2000.

An Extension Activity

Depending on your path in life, money will always be an issue—too little, too late, too much, and so on. Do you equate a career choice with making a lot of money? Or not? What are the advantages and disadvantages of taking career risks?

BUSINESS Online
The Full Story

To learn more about taking career risks, visit the *Introduction to Business* Web site at **www.introbus.glencoe.com**, and click on *BusinessWeek* Feature Story, Chapter 20.

Three Steps to Planning a Career

The auditorium is a mass of mortarboards and gowns from your view in the balcony. Your sister is graduating from high school, and this fall she will attend a nearby state university. Your mother keeps encouraging her to study her interests, like painting and writing. As you lean on the balcony's railing, trying to find your sister in the crowd, you start drifting into your own career daydream. You've always liked taking apart circuit boards and dissecting bugs in the summer. Yet you've always been interested in history. As a sophomore in high school, it's never too soon to start planning.

Choosing a career is a very important decision that each person has to make. The decision will affect the rest of your life. But what's a career? How is it different from the job you do after school or on weekends or vacations? Unlike simply getting a part-time job or doing work during a vacation, a career involves preparation, such as education or training, as well as specialized skills or abilities. A wise career choice

Figure 20.1

MAJOR TYPES OF APTITUDES

➡These aptitudes are used to a certain degree in every job, but some aptitudes are especially important in particular jobs.
What aptitude does a person have who listens well to others and can work well with a variety of people?

APTITUDE	EXPLANATION	EXAMPLES OF OCCUPATIONS
Mechanical	Ability to work well with your hands	Copier Technician, Carpenter
Math	Ability to work with numbers	Retail Sales Associate, Insurance Underwriter
Communication	Ability to express yourself in speech and in writing	Writer, Customer Service Representative
Human Relations	Ability to understand and get along with people	Supervisor, Health-Care Worker
Problem Solving	Ability to apply the reasoning process to problem situations	Manager, Systems Analyst
Kinesthetic	Ability with physical coordination	Exercise Trainer, Professional Athlete
Artistic	Ability to create or re-create forms of expression	Dancer, Architect, Designer

may require more of you, but will provide more to you in return. Your choice affects the amount of money you will earn but more importantly, it affects the amount of satisfaction that you can gain from your work. It's a good idea to choose work that is satisfying since you'll be spending a lot of time earning a living.

Step 1: Deciding What You Want to Do

When you leave school you'll have to work for a living. You have a choice of whether to get a job or whether to pursue a career. A job is something you do to make money. A **career** is an occupation or field in which you work over a long period of time. To pursue a career takes time, training, experience, and most of all, planning. **Career planning** consists of assessing your potential, analyzing your options, and preparing for the future. The first step in choosing a career is taking inventory of your interests, abilities, goals, and values (see Figure 20.1). The second step is analyzing your job options, and the third step is researching a career.

Interests

What do you enjoy doing? Your answer to this question will tell a lot about your interests. Many people's hobbies are their interests. For example, cooking, writing stories, hiking, and playing musical instruments are all hobbies. Each one might suggest a possible occupation. You might also consider what subjects and activities you enjoy at school. If you like to do science experiments or write articles for the school newspaper, you may find that one of those interests could lead to a career.

As you talk with people, read about jobs, and see workers in action, you'll probably be drawn to a few choices. To narrow your choices, you need detailed information about specific jobs. Keep the following questions in mind when looking at specific occupations or careers:

- What tasks do people in the position typically perform? What are their responsibilities? Do they work with information, people, machines, tools, or a combination of these? Do they perform a variety of tasks, or do they do the same thing over many times?
- What qualifications were necessary to secure the position? These are the requirements for specific jobs, such as education, training, experience, and special skills.
- Which skills do people in the position use? Are these skills learned on the job, or must workers already have these skills to apply for the position?

Real-World Application

part **1** of 4

THE WRITE BUSINESS
As a freelance and newspaper staff reporter for the last ten years, Larisa Brass has written about the world of business in Tennessee. She's a business reporter for the *Knoxville News-Sentinel*, where she specializes in technology and telecommunications reporting. Brass got her start in high school.
What activities do you do now that could turn into a career?

continued on p. 323

- What personal and physical characteristics are necessary? What type of personality is best for the position? Do the tasks require problem-solving skills or good manual dexterity?
- Is any previous work experience required or preferred? If so, what kind?
- What are the wage levels for the position? What are the opportunities for advancement?
- What is the outlook for this occupation? How will technology affect it and will the product or service being produced become less or more in demand? What are the advantages and disadvantages of the occupation?

Abilities

After you have considered what you like to do, ask yourself what you're good at doing. Identifying the things that you do well will help you choose a career. Every person has certain skills and aptitudes. Aptitudes are very different from skills. **Aptitudes** are talents that come naturally. **Skills** are abilities developed through learning and experience.

If you're good at figuring out how to fix things, you probably have mechanical aptitude. You need more than aptitude, however, to repair a personal computer. To fix a computer, you would need to develop skills through the study of electronics. You might want to pursue a career in art if you have an aptitude for it, but you will also need to acquire skills working with different materials.

Goals and Values

When you choose a career, it's important to consider whether it will give you the satisfaction that you want. Most of us have similar values, but we put them in vastly different orders of importance. The occupations that you choose should relate to what you value or think is important for your life. Keep in mind that your values could well change during your life. At this point, though, you should make choices based on the values that you hold right now.

If you place great emphasis on freedom and independence, you might want to become an entrepreneur and start your own business. On the other hand, many people prefer working for others. They value the security of having someone else in charge as well as the steady income and benefits. If you place a high value on helping others, you might consider a career in teaching, social work, or health care. You might want to be an artist and also make a lot of money. Since artists often don't make very much money, you have to decide which goal is more important to you.

Consider This...

A Home Run Career Decision

Steve Sclafani dreamed of a career in major league baseball. As a star second baseman at the University of Pennsylvania, he thought he might have a shot. The pro scouts thought otherwise. Instead, he founded Baseball Factory, which specializes in getting high school players onto college teams. It does it by holding "showcase" games so talented high school players can perform for college coaches.

ANALYZE

How did Sclafani morph his talents into a business?

✔ **Fast Review**

1. What is the difference between a job and a career?
2. What is the difference between an aptitude and a skill?

Step 2: Analyzing Your Job Options

The second step in planning a career is figuring out your options. What kinds of jobs will be in demand in the future? What kinds of skills will you need? Where can you get information? Before deciding on a career, you need to find out where the jobs are and how to find them.

The Job Market

The job market changes along with changes in population, technology, and other factors. For example, as a result of the boom in computer technology, there's a great demand for computer experts. In contrast, the demand for typists, bank tellers, and office workers is much less. The popularity of desktop publishing has resulted in little demand for typesetters and paste-up workers. Almost any career you want to pursue will require computer skills.

As the population increases, there will be an increased demand for workers in construction and engineering. More workers will be needed to design and build houses, roads, and bridges. The demand for nurses and teachers will increase. Health care is expected to be one of the biggest areas of growth. There will be a greater demand for physical therapists, speech therapists, and medical assistants.

Sources of Career Information

Investigating the job market can be overwhelming. After all, there are thousands of different occupations from which to choose. However, career information is plentiful and simple to use if you know how to find it.

Asking Career Counselors. One of the best ways to get information is by speaking to a career counselor. A **career counselor** is a person trained to provide information and guidance on choosing a career. A career counselor can also help you learn more about your interests and abilities. For example, if you've done public service or played on a team, a counselor might recognize leadership or organizing skills you've shown. A counselor can inform you about what careers might suit you and advise you on what classes would prepare you best for these careers.

Your school probably has a career or guidance counselor. If you're interested in going to a community college or a university, a counselor there can help you make long-range plans. Your teachers might also be able to suggest careers that would use the abilities and interests you have shown in class.

Networking. Another way to get information is by networking. **Networking** consists of meeting and talking to people in different

THE WRITE BUSINESS
"I revived our high school newspaper," she says, "and discovered that journalism was my thing." After studying journalism in college, Brass worked for one year at a small newspaper in Oak Ridge, Tenn.
Imagine a career you're interested in. What steps can you take today to learn more about the career?

continued on p. 325

occupations to find out what they do and to make connections. By talking to people you can learn about what their job involves, how they got it, what their training was, and whether you'd like it. Most people are happy to talk about what they do. You can start by talking to relatives, family friends, and local business owners. Some companies have open houses and give tours of their facilities. If you're interested in a job someone told you about ask that person for career-planning advice.

Researching Careers. Figure 20.2 illustrates the most widely used job search methods. You can find information about careers at your school library or public library. For example, the *Occupational Outlook Handbook (OOH)* describes more than 300 occupations. It lists the fastest-growing job fields and gives addresses of places to write for more information. The *OOH* is also available on CD-ROM and on the Internet. The *Encyclopedia of Careers and Vocational Guidance* describes over 1,500 jobs including educational requirements, employment outlook, and opportunities for experience.

A simple way to learn what the market is for certain types of occupations is by looking in the want ads of a newspaper. You'll usually find plenty of listings for engineers, teachers, and nurses. Business magazines and journals are a good source of information on changing job trends.

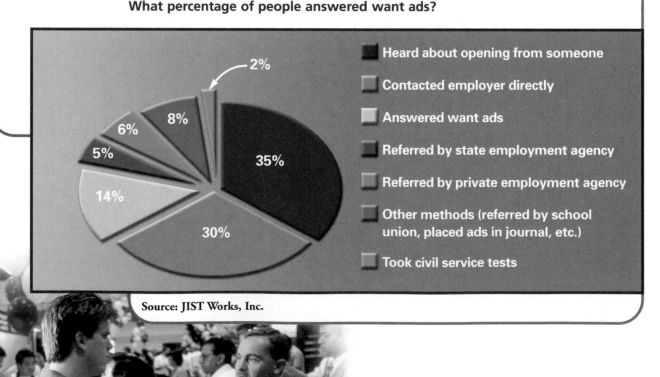

Figure 20.2

JOB SEARCH METHODS

➡ Most job searchers don't find employment with just traditional search methods.
What percentage of people answered want ads?

- Heard about opening from someone
- Contacted employer directly
- Answered want ads
- Referred by state employment agency
- Referred by private employment agency
- Other methods (referred by school union, placed ads in journal, etc.)
- Took civil service tests

35%
30%
14%
5%
6%
8%
2%

Source: JIST Works, Inc.

You can find a lot of information on the Internet by checking out the Bureau of Labor Statistics or job Web sites such as **www.monster.com**. For other sources of information, you can attend career days and job fairs that might be held at a local school or community center.

✓ Fast Review

1. Name some areas where there's expected to be an increased demand for workers.
2. What are sources you can use to research careers?

Step 3: Researching a Career

At this point in your life you might not be able to decide what kind of career you want to pursue. There are numerous ways to research careers. During the course of your lifetime, you might also change careers more than once. Whether you know what you want to do or not, however, you can increase your options with education and experience. The more skills you acquire, the better your chances of having the career you want and the more money you're likely to make.

Education

Most jobs today require at least a high school education. To pursue a career, you'll probably need some form of advanced education. There are different types of schools to choose from depending on whether you want to go into a profession or a trade. A **profession** is a field that requires a high level of education, such as law, medicine, or architecture. A **trade** is a field that requires a high level of manual or technical skill, such as carpentry, mechanics, or computer programming.

To pursue a profession, you have to study at a college or university for many years and get an advanced degree. If you want to learn a skill, you can go to a trade, technical, or vocational school. These types of schools prepare you for a specific occupation, emphasize hands-on training, and help you find a job afterward. Most schools offer students some form of financial aid, or money to help you pay for your education. Your career counselor or the financial aid officer at a school you'd like to attend can tell you what types of aid you can get.

Experience

In planning for a career, gaining experience is as important as getting an education. If you don't plan on going to college, or you want to

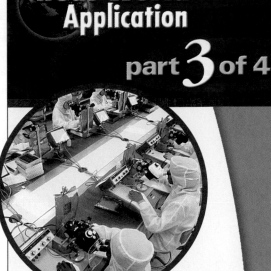

Real-World Application

part **3** of 4

THE WRITE BUSINESS
Brass is trying to meet a deadline for a story about local high-tech start-up companies. "This part of Tennessee is a Silicon Valley wannabe," she says. "With the University of Tennessee and National Laboratories nearby, technology companies should be attracted to the area."
Is your career plan contingent upon living in a particular region?

continued on p. 327

enhance your education, there are a number of ways you can gain work experience.

Apprenticeship. An **apprenticeship** consists of learning a trade by working under the guidance of a skilled worker, such as a chef, a plumber, or an electrician. Many apprenticeship programs are available through labor unions and trade schools. You can also find out about them through your state employment office. An apprenticeship can last from two to five years. During the program, an apprentice might not make very much money. As an apprentice's skills increase, however, so does the pay. An apprentice who completes a program is called a **journeyworker**, or skilled craftsperson, and can make very high wages.

Internship. An **internship** is a program that provides hands-on experience for a beginner in an occupation, usually as a temporary, unpaid trainee. Most internships are offered to students through colleges or on the Internet. Internships are available in almost every type of business and profession, such as marketing, film production, and law. If you're

Working Lifestyle

What are you doing at 10 A.M.?

The Sweet Life

Kate Jansen's mother taught her cooking skills but her passion for fare took her to Italy for 11 months. There she studied the fine art of making pastries and Italian cuisine. In 1993, Jansen decided to open her own business, and she and her partners—a bread baker and a financial expert—launched Firehook Bakery.

Today Jansen is one of the finest pastry chefs in Washington, D.C. By 10:00 A.M. she already has been working for 4 hours, supervising her staff of 15, and checking orders.

Even an embassy order for chocolate raspberry truffle cakes doesn't cause Jansen to overlook her regular customers. She chats with them while folding the cake boxes for a noon delivery.

Salary

In large cities, pastry chefs can earn an average salary between $44,000 and $65,000 per year.

Outlook for This Career

The food service industry is expanding. People increasingly want fine, unprocessed food. The outlook for this occupation is very good.

Connecting Careers Activity

List other occupations that contribute to making a pastry come to life.

CAREER PATH Hospitality & Tourism

interested in going into broadcasting, you can start by getting an internship at a TV or radio station. Internships allow you to learn how a business works from the inside and can lead directly to a job.

Other Types of Experience. You can also gain valuable skills and experience by doing volunteer work. If you're interested in learning broadcasting but can't get an internship, you can volunteer to work at a local TV or radio station. By volunteering for community service, you can learn organizing and leadership skills. If you plan on starting your own business some day, you can volunteer to work at a family or local business. Even if you don't intend to go into that particular line of business, you can learn how a business is run.

Your school might have a cooperative work or earn-and-learn program. In this type of program, business and community leaders, teachers, and students work together to plan students' work experiences and educational goals. Studies have shown that students with such work experiences have great success getting their first job. In some cases, you may be able to shadow a person in a certain business or trade. **Shadowing** means following a person throughout a workday to see what a job involves. Some schools provide shadowing experience for students.

The Career Ladder

You can't expect to go from broadcasting school or an internship at a TV station to landing a job as the anchor for the national news. You have to move up the **career ladder**, or through different job levels within an occupation. You might have to start out with an **entry-level job**, or a beginning career job. For example, if you want to become a newspaper reporter, you might have to start out as a fact checker. You climb the ladder to better positions as you gain more skills, knowledge, and experience.

You might not like the idea of borrowing money to pay for college, taking a low-paying entry-level job, or working as an unpaid intern. Building a career, however, takes time and patience. Keep in mind that people who obtain the right skills and education end up earning a lot more money in the long run. The time and money you spend preparing for a career is an investment in your future.

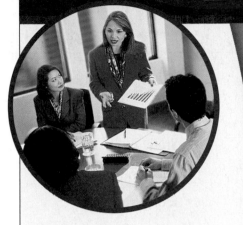

Real-World Application

part 4 of 4

THE WRITE BUSINESS
Brass says her favorite stories have focused on the impact of venture capital on local technology start-ups. She explores what's happening in the area, why the growth of local technology-based industries hasn't met expectations, and what's needed to change that situation. **How can you take your experiences and apply them to a career plan?**

✔ **Fast Review** _____

1. What is the difference between a profession and a trade?
2. What are some ways you can gain work experience?
3. Where can you find out about apprenticeship programs?

Summary

1. A job is something you do to make money. A career is a lifetime occupation that takes time, training, experience, and planning to pursue.

2. A personal inventory consists of assessing your interests, abilities, goals, and values.

3. You can find out about your career options by:
   - Studying the job market.
   - Meeting with a career counselor.
   - Networking.
   - Doing research.

4. You can prepare yourself for a career by going to a college or trade school or getting experience through an apprenticeship, internship, volunteer work, or school program.

Using Business Key Words

The following terms will help you understand how to plan and decide on a career plan. Match each term to its definition.

- career
- entry-level job
- career ladder
- career counselor
- aptitudes
- networking
- profession
- shadowing
- apprenticeship
- career planning
- journeyworker
- skills
- trade
- internship

1. An occupation or field in which a person works over a long period of time.
2. The mobility possibility from an entry-level position to one at the top of the field.
3. A program that provides hands-on experience for a beginner in an occupation, usually as a temporary and unpaid trainee.
4. Learning a trade by working under the guidance of a skilled worker.
5. Accompanying an employee throughout his or her workday to see what the position involves.
6. A field that requires a high level of manual or technical skill, such as carpentry, mechanics, or computer programming.
7. A skilled craftsperson who has completed an apprenticeship.
8. Talking to people about their jobs.
9. Abilities developed through training and experience.
10. Assessing one's potential, analyzing one's options, and preparing to pursue a career.
11. A person who provides career advice.
12. Ability that comes naturally.
13. A field that requires a high level of education, such as law, medicine, or architecture.
14. A beginning career job.

Review What You Learned

15. How is a career different from a part-time job?

16. Name the three steps of a good career plan.

17. Explain the difference between interests and abilities.

18. How does technology play an important role in the workplace?

19. Name three sources of career information.

20. What is a career ladder?

21. Describe a cooperative work program.

22. What is an apprentice? In what occupations are most apprentices found?

23. What should the criteria for evaluating a career be based upon?

24. How can you prepare for a career while still in high school?

Understanding Business Concepts

25. List three of your interests and three of your abilities. Do any suggest a possible occupation? Explain.

26. Why are guidance counselors and teachers especially helpful in matching your aptitudes to possible careers?

27. Review the list of common aptitudes located in the chapter. Choose two and explain why they're important to you.

28. What's the advantage of networking?

29. What's an entry-level position? Give an example of such a position, and describe what types of jobs it might lead to within the same career field.

30. Why is the money you spend on education like investing in yourself?

31. Create a list of criteria that is important to you when you evaluate a career.

Critical Thinking

32. Choose a job you're interested in pursuing. What three qualifications do you think you would need for it?

33. Describe your personal career goals. What steps will you take to ensure you achieve those goals?

34. Describe ways people move up the career ladder.

35. How does the economy affect career choices?

Viewing and Representing

Examining the Image. Look closely at the photograph. Use your five senses to step into the photograph. What do you hear? What else do you see around you? Imagine you're doing this work. Is this the type of job you want? Would this job fit your aptitudes and skills? Would you make the best use of your abilities and skills in this career?

Chapter 20 Review

Building Academic Skills

 Essay Writing

Work in groups of four. Brainstorm a list of ten careers. For each career write the interests, abilities, values, and goals you think would be relevant. Then divide into pairs. Interview your partner about his or her interests, abilities, values, and goals. Suggest one or two careers from your group's list that you think would be suitable for your partner. Then switch roles. Write a brief essay about the career your partner suggested for you and why you think it might or might not be suitable for you.

 Preparing a Plan

Select a career cluster and determine the skills and knowledge necessary for it. Devise a personal plan to achieve competency in that career cluster. Use word processing software to prepare a copy of your plan.

MATH **Average Salaries**

Choose two careers that interest you. Research the average salaries for those careers. Research the education requirements and costs to obtain the skills necessary to be successful in the careers. Prepare a chart of your findings.

Social Science **Studying Abroad**

Understanding the world outside the borders of the United States is becoming a very marketable skill for many career fields. Student exchange programs and overseas internships are two ways to gain experience abroad. Research opportunities to live and work overseas. Write a two-page paper with your findings and explain whether or not you would like to take advantage of an overseas experience.

Linking School to Home

Diagraming Career Paths. Interview a family member about his or her career ladder. Create a diagram that shows the jobs your family member has had. Then connect the skills, experience, education, and leadership roles that led to advanced positions on the ladder. If you prefer, interview a teacher, neighbor, or mentor instead.

Linking School to Work

Finding Programs. Compile a chart of the programs in your school and community that link school to work. Be sure to ask the guidance counselors and teachers to help you. Include names, addresses, telephone numbers, and contact people. Then, as a class, compile all the charts. Prepare a document that can be shared with other students in your school.

E-Homework

Applying Technology

Career Sites. Use the Internet to research the various career planning Web sites available. Create a list of the ten best sites and explain why you think they would be a valuable resource to someone who is planning and making career decisions.

Jobs in Technology. Research the entry-level jobs in the field of technology. Choose two you might be interested in finding out more about. What are the educational requirements of the two jobs selected? Do you have an interest in either one? Why or why not?

Connecting Academics

Math. The *Occupational Outlook Handbook (OOH)* contains descriptions of more than 300 broad categories of occupations in 11 occupational grouping. It lists the fastest-growing job fields and provides addresses of places to write for more information. The *OOH* is also available on CD-ROM and on the Internet. The *Occupational Outlook Handbook* puts the average weekly salary range for a career at $750 to $900. Laticia earns the minimum of this range and then receives a 5 percent raise. What is her new weekly salary?

Language Arts. Send an e-mail or letter introducing yourself to someone working in a career that interests you. Describe why you're interested in the career and request an information interview. Include a list of six questions for the person.

BusinessWeek Analyzing the Feature Story

You read the first part of "Can Your Nerves Take a Dot-Com Job?" at the beginning of this chapter. Below are a few questions for you to answer about working at a tech start-up. You'll find the answers to these questions when you're reading the entire article. First, here are the questions:

36. What values or goals would you need to take a job with a tech start-up?

37. What is one way to minimize the risk of working for a tech start-up?

Creative Journal Activity

List three skills you currently have. Now list three more that you would like to have. Choose three jobs you might consider as a career. Do any of these jobs match the six skills?

BUSINESS Online
The Full Story

To learn more about taking career risks, visit the *Introduction to Business* Web site at **www.introbus.glencoe.com**, and click on *BusinessWeek* Feature Story, Chapter 20.

Chapter 21

Getting a Job

Learning Objectives

After completing this chapter, you'll be able to:
1. **Name** the employability skills.
2. **Describe** how to prepare a résumé.
3. **List** sources of information about job openings.
4. **Explain** the job application process.

Why It's Important

Most employers follow similar procedures when they have job openings to fill. Once you know the procedures you can move through the steps with confidence.

Key Words

qualifications
employability skills
body language
résumé
reference
employment objective
job lead
referral
employment agencies
cover letter
job interview

BusinessWeek Feature Story

Asking the Right Questions

Companies Rely on a Variety of Techniques to Interview Candidates. During a job interview six months ago, Roopea Mehendale Foley came up with a well-reasoned analysis. That's one reason why she's now vice president for product development in the New York City based e-commerce outfit, Dash. The company didn't hire a consultant or use a formal personality test, however. It turned to the time-honored approach of using probing questions, getting Foley to solve puzzles, and react to real-world situations.

Source: Excerpted with permission from "Asking the Right Questions," *BusinessWeek Online*, October 13, 2000.

An Extension Activity

How can you prepare for brainteasers an interviewer may ask you to solve? Ask any of your family members or friends who have been at a job interview some of the difficult questions the interviewer asked.

The Full Story

To learn more about job interviews, visit the *Introduction to Business* Web site at **www.introbus.glencoe.com**, and click on *BusinessWeek* Feature Story, Chapter 21.

On Becoming a Producer in Society

Club sports and student government never really interested you. You're bored after school and tired of not having any money to buy the latest CD, jeans, or tennis shoes. One day on your way home from school you see a want ad in the local pizzeria's window. You look past the sign into the shop and see a cook gracefully tossing dough in the air. You walk inside, ask the manager for an application, and take it home to fill it out.

Employability Skills

You need to know what employers look for when they hire a new employee. Different jobs require different **qualifications**, or education, skills, and work experience to do a particular job. What's important for one job might be less important for another. Employers look for

Figure 21.1

MEDIAN EARNINGS OF FULL-TIME WORKERS

What is the annual difference in earnings of a high school dropout and a high school graduate?

Source: Bureau of Labor Statistics.

more than just job qualifications, however. They also consider a person's character, personality, and ability to work with others. All these factors combined are called **employability skills**.

Level of Education

For most jobs, employers want applicants to have at least a high school diploma. High school dropouts have fewer job opportunities, especially if they have no previous work experience. On the whole, the level of education of workers in our country has risen. The more skills and education you have, the wider the job market will be for you. Figure 21.1 illustrates the average income gap between high school dropout and earning an advanced degree.

Required Skills

Employers expect workers to have certain basic skills for practically any job. Employees must be able to read well enough to function in their jobs. They must be able to communicate with others and do simple math problems. Basic computer skills, such as entering or accessing data on a computer, are also necessary. An employee must be able to follow instructions and be able to work well with others.

Work Experience

Many employers look for people with some work experience. Sometimes employers even require that potential employees have a certain number of years of experience. Experienced workers have proven skills and a familiarity with the job. They need less training to take over a new job. This, of course, can be a problem if you're looking for your first job. That's why it's important to get some kind of experience either through a school program, volunteer work, or even helping out at a family business. Some jobs require little or no experience. The more skill and experience a job requires, however, the better it pays.

Character and Personality

Though skills are important, employers also look for employees who have certain character traits. Employers value honesty, dependability, and hard work. They also want employees who have a good attitude toward work, a desire to do the job well, and the ability to get along

AN ILLUSTRATIVE VISIONARY

"Find something you love to do and do it. If you work hard at a career you really like, the money will take care of itself," says Gary Kelley, a graphic artist. "Freelance graphic art is a life without structure. I go to my studio six days a week, and more often than not, four of those days will be very different from one another." **What kind of skills would you need to be a freelancer?**

continued on p. 337

Technology Toolkit

E-Résumés

E-mailing your résumé through the Internet presents special challenges. Send your résumé as a text-only document on a PC and then paste it into a message. Don't send it as an attachment—the company you're sending it to may not be able to open it. After you've e-mailed your résumé, send a hard copy through the mail. E-mailed documents sometimes lose their formatting, such as boldface and italics. Companies now use computers to scan résumés so fancy typefaces and graphics don't scan well.

Critical Thinking

Companies often use computer programs to look for key words in résumés. How can you find out what those key words are?

with other workers. Research shows that the main reason people lose their jobs is because of a poor attitude and difficulty working with others. An employer can learn about these traits in several ways.

Body Language. Your **body language**, or nonverbal communication, often says more about you than your spoken or written words. Posture, eye contact, facial expression, and gestures can either add to or take away from the impression you make. For instance, if you seem fidgety or bored during an interview it looks like you have a short attention span or aren't really interested in the job.

School Records. Employers might check school records for information. Good grades show motivation and a willingness to apply yourself to a task. Employers usually check attendance records. Even if you don't have the best grades, good attendance and punctuality indicate that you're reliable and will show up for work on time.

Extracurricular Activities. Extracurricular activities are social activities that you take part in outside of school. They indicate extra effort on your part, as well as possible leadership ability. For example, taking part in team sports shows an ability to work with a group. Any volunteer work you do shows a sense of commitment and responsibility. What you're doing now, in and out of school, is creating a record that your future employers will want to see.

✓ Fast Review

1. What are the employability skills employers look for when considering a job applicant?
2. What are things an employer can look at to learn about your character?

Beginning Your Job Search

Before you begin looking for a job, you need to discover which jobs you would like most and which you would be able to do best. You should avoid limiting your search to one type of job. Some jobs require little or no experience. Other jobs require work experience. Still others might require certain skills.

Preparing Your Résumé

One of the first steps in finding a job is preparing a résumé. A **résumé** is a summary of your skills, education, and work experience (see Figure 21.2). Its purpose is to persuade potential employers to grant you an interview. The beginning of a résumé includes personal information such as your name, address, and telephone number. Some people also include a fax number or an e-mail address.

Your education and work history tell an employer about your abilities and work ethic. Be sure to include volunteer work you've done, such as working on a school fundraiser. If you have a good school record as well as experience related to the job, an employer is more likely to be interested in hiring you.

The appearance of your résumé makes the first impression on an employer. If it's disorganized and chock-full of grammatical errors, your chances of getting an interview are slim. Therefore, be sure the résumé is neatly formatted and that the information is presented clearly. Check your grammar and spelling before sending it.

Reference. A **reference** is a person an employer can contact to find out about your experience, education, and character. A reference could be a teacher, former employer, or other adult. Job and school references are used to verify that you worked and went to school where you claimed. Personal references are used to testify to your character. Before using people as references, be sure to get their permission.

Employment Objective. Résumés might vary in content, but usually include an **employment objective**. This is a statement of your career goals or interest in a business. You might state that you're interested in a career in the field, are working your way through school, or think you can learn a lot from the job. Your statement should be brief and to the point.

AN ILLUSTRATIVE VISIONARY
Today he is at the top of his profession, a world-renowned graphic artist whose illustrations grace magazine, book covers, posters, and postcards. **How might your extracurricular activities turn into something more, like a job?**

continued on p. 339

Looking for Openings

You're not aware of all of life's opportunities until you start looking for them. How do you go about finding a job? You need to get a **job lead**, or information about a job opening. Job leads can come from several sources.

Your Network. Your network consists of people you know, such as friends, relatives, neighbors, and members of groups to which you belong. They're often the best source of job leads. They might be able to tell you about better job openings or openings that aren't advertised.

If you're interested, they can also give you a **referral**, a personal recommendation to an employer or other job lead.

Your School. Your school might have a work placement office. Someone there can help you look for job leads. Employers frequently post job openings there. Your school might also have a cooperative education or work experience program. Besides helping you plan your career, these programs can help you find a job. You can talk with your guidance counselor and teachers about the kind of job you'd like to have.

Want Ads. Recruitment advertisements in newspapers can be useful in several ways. First, you can find out quickly if any jobs are listed in which you might be interested. You can also get a good idea about how much certain jobs pay and what skills or education are required. You can search local and national databases on the Internet for jobs. The databases

Figure 21.2 — A SAMPLE RÉSUMÉ

➡A résumé tells a prospective employer four things—who you are, what you want to do, what you have done, and what you can do. **Why was it a good idea for Peter Cortez to list his activities?**

PETER A. CORTEZ

| 134 North Avenue | Telephone: 317-555-2492 |
| Indianapolis, IN 46268-1452 | E-mail: pcortez@aol.com |

| **OBJECTIVE** | To secure an office position, with potential for growth. |
| **EDUCATION** | Northwest High School
Will graduate June 14, 20XX |

Related Coursework

Accounting	Math With Business
Algebra	Applications
Computer Applications	Microcomputer
Cooperative Office Education	Keyboarding
Introduction to Business	Personal Finance

| **WORK EXPERIENCE** | September 2000-present
Part-time Office Assistant
Cameron's Business Supply |

Responsibilities

Maintain company files as directed.
Key-enter data for reports, correspondence, and monthly customer billings.

SPECIAL SKILLS	Working knowledge of Lotus 1-2-3, MS Word, MS Excel. Speak and write Spanish fluently.
ACTIVITIES	Vice President of local chapter of Business Professionals of America. Tutored middle school students in math at Hispanic center.
REFERENCES	References will be provided upon request.

338

are updated often and usually provide detailed descriptions of jobs.

Local Businesses. Some businesses post job notices on bulletin boards in supermarkets or in shopping malls. You can also call a company's personnel office to see if they have jobs open. You might find help-wanted signs in businesses' windows. Sometimes you can find a job by walking around your local business district and asking business owners if they're hiring.

Employment Agencies. Services that help people find jobs are called **employment agencies**. These can be public or private. Public agencies are usually run by the state or local government and might be connected with the unemployment office. They often offer tests to help you identify what kind of job you'd like and for which you'd be qualified. The Federal Job Information Center has regional agencies that can give you information about government job openings. Private employment agencies, such as temp services, charge for their services. If you contact an agency, be sure to find out if they charge a fee.

✔️ **Fast Review** _____

1. What is the purpose of a résumé?
2. What is the difference between a job or school reference and a personal reference?
3. Name four ways you can look for jobs at local businesses.

Contacting Potential Employers

You've prepared a résumé and found several interesting job openings. How do you go about applying for the jobs? The process includes several steps: the cover letter, job application, employment testing, and the interview.

Cover Letter

You should always include a cover letter with your résumé. A **cover letter** is a one-page letter that tells the employer about you and why you're applying for the job. It should be specifically addressed to the employer. For example, if you're applying for a job at a video store, your cover letter should include the name and address of the store, and the title and name of the manager. Like your résumé, the cover letter also needs to make a good impression. Your cover letter should be properly formatted and free from errors (see Figure 21.3).

Real-World Application
part 3 of 4

AN ILLUSTRATIVE VISIONARY
Kelley is waiting for a phone call from one of his clients, *Rolling Stone* magazine. He began the day by doodling. "I often start by doing a thumbnail sketch of my ideas using pencil and tracing paper," says Kelley from his studio. "As a graphic artist, you can think until you're blue in the face, but until you actually put something on paper, you're not making progress." **How can you use your free time to research job opportunities?**

continued on p. 341

Job Application

Most employers ask a job applicant to fill out an application form (see Figure 21.3). Like your résumé, this form presents you to a potential employer so you should carefully follow the directions. Provide the information requested and write neatly. The process will be easier if you have your résumé and list of references with you since you often have to include this information on the application. Begin by answering each question. Don't leave any blanks. If a question doesn't apply to you, write "not applicable," or N/A as the shorthand.

Figure 21.3 — JOB APPLICATION ESSENTIALS

PETER A. CORTEZ

134 North Avenue
Indianapolis, IN 46268-1452

Telephone: 317-555-2492
E-mail: pcortez@aol.com

May 12, 20XX

Ms. Marcia Chisholm
Director of Human Resources
Oakland Insurance Company
One Acorn Park
Indianapolis, IN 46244-7777

Dear Ms. Chisholm:

When I read the description for the position of eligibility specialist at your company, I just knew that I was the person for the job. I have the technical and computer skills you require as well as the math and written communication experience you desire. As you review my résumé, you will see that my education, work experience, and activities have prepared me to be a successful addition to your company.

I will graduate from high school in June. Working as an eligibility specialist at your company will continue to develop the skills I have gained from school and work. I know I am the right person who can do the job for you. I will call you next week to arrange an appointment, or you may reach me at 317-555-2492 after 3:00 P.M.

Sincerely,

Peter A. Cortez

Peter A. Cortez

Enclosure

➡**Part 1** A cover letter introduces you to a prospective employer. It should be tailored to the position you're interested in.
What should accompany the cover letter?

EMPLOYMENT APPLICATION

AN EQUAL OPPORTUNITY EMPLOYER
Oakland Insurance Employment Policy forbids discrimination based on age, citizenship status, ethnicity, disability, marital status, national origin, race, religion, sex, sexual orientation, or veteran status.

NAME *Cortez* (LAST) *Peter* (FIRST) *A.* (MIDDLE INITIAL) DATE *May 22, 20XX*

ADDRESS *134 North Avenue* (STREET) *Indianapolis* (CITY) *IN* (STATE) *46268-1452* (ZIP)

PHONE NO. *(317) 555-2492*   SOCIAL SECURITY NO. *032-32-2712*

In case of emergency notify *Emilio Cortez, 134 North Avenue, Indianapolis, IN 46268*

Position desired *Eligibility Specialist*   Salary desired *Negotiable*

EDUCATION	Name and Address of School	Dates Attended From	To	Date Graduated	Major Area of Study
Elementary	Valley Elementary School Indianapolis, IN 46266	Sept. 1989	June 1997	June 6, 1997	N/A
High School	Northwest High School Indianapolis, IN 46244	Sept. 1997	June 2001	June 14, 2001	N/A
College	N/A	N/A	N/A	N/A	N/A
Other	N/A	N/A	N/A	N/A	N/A

List all foreign languages you can write and speak fluently. *Spanish*
List all computer applications you can use. *Lotus 1-2-3, MS Word, MS Excel*
EMPLOYMENT: List most recent employer first. Use extra sheet if necessary.

Name and Address of Employer	Dates Employed From	To	Position	Reason for Leaving
Cameron's Business Supply 193 Troy Street, Indianapolis, IN 46244	Sept. 2000	Present	Part-time office assistant	need full-time job
N/A	N/A	N/A	N/A	N/A
N/A	N/A	N/A	N/A	N/A

REFERENCES: Do not list relatives or former employers.

Name	Address	Telephone	How long known
John Durkee	54 East Border Road Indianapolis, IN 46268	555-6014	4 years
Amanda Freymann	1037 Crawford Drive Indianapolis, IN 46268	555-3744	7 years
William Council	468 Center Street Indianapolis, IN 46244	555-9468	3 years

Are you currently employed? *Yes*   Date available for work *June 16*

To the best of my knowledge all of the foregoing is true and given voluntarily. I authorize Oakland Insurance to contact my references, including previous employers, to confirm credentials.

Peter A. Cortez
SIGNATURE

➡**Part 2** Most employers ask potential employees to fill out application forms. It's important to read the directions carefully and fill out the form neatly and completely.
How many computer applications is Peter able to use?

Employment Testing

When you apply for a job you might be asked to take a test to see if you have the proper skills. For example, if you apply for a job as an office assistant your computer skills might be tested. If you apply for a job where you have to make deliveries, you might have to take a driving test. If you want to work for a bank, you'll probably have to take a math test. Jobs for the government or in law enforcement often require drug tests and lie-detector tests.

Job Interview

A **job interview** is a formal face-to-face discussion between an employer and a potential employee. It's an exchange of information about the nature of the job and your qualifications for it. Keep in mind these few things about the interview:

- *Do some homework about the job.* Find out as much as you can about the company in advance.
- *Be on time.* If you're late, an employer will think you're careless about being on time for work and meeting deadlines. If you can't be on time, call and inform the interviewer.
- *Wear appropriate clothes.* Dress neatly and in a style appropriate for the job you're seeking.
- *Put your best foot forward.* Be courteous and cooperative during the interview. Make eye contact and beware of your body language.
- *Ask questions about the job.* You need to learn if the job is right for you. Ask about the pay and benefits. Asking questions also suggests that you're interested in the job.
- *Don't expect an answer right away.* The employer might have other people to interview and need time to make a decision.

You should also follow up after the interview. Call or write a letter thanking the interviewer. This shows you're still interested in the job and allows you to add anything you forgot to mention in the interview. If you don't hear from the interviewer, call back in a few days.

Real-World Application

part **4** of **4**

AN ILLUSTRATIVE VISIONARY

Kelley is trying to capture *The Great White Hope* on paper. It's going to be presented by the famous Washington, D.C. theater, Arena Stage. He goes to the library to look for images from around 1915. He wants to get the design's details—boxing rings, clothing, ropes, and boxing shoes—right. In order to impress the client, his art must connect the whole story from beginning to end.

What are some things you need to do in order to impress a potential employer?

✓ Fast Review

1. What's the purpose of a cover letter?
2. Name different kinds of tests you might have to take for different kind of jobs.
3. Why should you follow up after a job interview?

Picture This...

Getting Ink on Paper

1. The computer sends information, such as the page format, font, text, and images to the printer to tell it what to do.

2. A laser beam inside the printer draws the letters and images in light pulses onto a rotating drum called the photoreceptor, which works like photo paper.

3. The printer then coats the drum with toner—a kind of ink made of fine powder and plastic—that sticks to the laser image using static electricity.

4. The paper is fed into the printer and picks up the toner as it rolls across the drum.

Paper Exit

Toner Hopper

Laser Unit

Photoreceptor Drum Assembly

Fuser

Paper Tray

©2001 HowStuffWorks

5. The paper then passes through the fuser, or a pair of heated rollers, which melts the plastic in the toner so it sticks to the page.

Fuser

Photoreceptor Drum

Toner Roller

©2001 HowStuffWorks

6. When the paper comes out of the printer, it is still hot from the fuser.

Now *You* Take a Shot...

Not All Laser Printers Are Created Equal

Laser printers are better than inkjet or dot-matrix printers, but there are still big differences between various laser printers. Stop by a computer appliance store and have a consumer service representative demonstrate some laser printers for you. What are the different types of features they offer and how do they differ in quality?

Summary

1. Employability skills include education, job skills, work experience, character, personality, and ability to work with others.

2. A résumé is a summary of your skills, education, and work experience. It includes references and an employment objective. Make sure you proofread your résumé very carefully before sending it to an employer.

3. You can find out about job openings through your personal network, your school, want ads, local businesses, and employment agencies.

4. The job application process includes writing a cover letter, filling out an application, taking a test, and interviewing for a job.

● Using Business Key Words

Are you ready for the world of work? There are many employability skills that will help you succeed in a job. See how ready you are by choosing the term below that best completes each of the following sentences.

- **body language**
- **qualifications**
- **employability skills**
- **referral**
- **résumé**
- **job lead**
- **employment agencies**
- **reference**
- **cover letter**
- **employment objective**
- **job interview**

1. Organizations set up to help people find jobs are called _____.

2. A(n) _____ may be a teacher, former employer, or other adult who can assess your personal and work habits.

3. When you send your résumé to a prospective employer, you should also send a _____.

4. A(n) _____ is a statement that tells the prospective employer about your motivation and interest in their business.

5. Qualities that employers look for in a person they want to work for them and the techniques for letting an employer know you have the qualities are called _____.

6. A document that highlights your job qualifications is called a(n) _____.

7. Nonverbal communication, such as posture, eye contact, facial expression, and gestures is called _____.

8. Information about a job opening is called _____.

9. _____ is (are) the education, skills, and experience required for doing a particular job.

10. A personal recommendation to an employer or other job lead is a _____.

11. A formal face-to-face discussion between an employer and a potential employee is a(n) _____.

● Review What You Learned

12. What are the basic skills many employers expect workers to have?
13. Why do many employers look for people with work experience?
14. What is the No. 1 reason why people lose their jobs?
15. What do your extracurricular activities indicate to a potential employer?
16. What is the purpose of a résumé?
17. Before you use someone as a reference, what should you do?
18. What people could you use as a reference?
19. What services do public employment agencies provide?
20. Why is it important to be on time for a job interview?

● Understanding Business Concepts

21. Which character traits do employers want their employees to have? Which one do you think is the most important? Explain your answer.
22. What might be a disadvantage of using a private employment agency?
23. Why might you be asked to take job-related tests when applying for a job?
24. When you're interviewing for a position, why is it important to ask questions about the job or the company itself?
25. Should you expect to be offered a job immediately following an interview? Why or why not?
26. Why is it important to write a thank-you letter after the interview?

● Critical Thinking

27. Do you have a good attitude? Explain. Then, name three things you could do to improve your attitude at home, school, and work.
28. Why is it important to find out as much as possible about a position before you're offered the job?
29. How much does your personality play in working with other coworkers?
30. What are some ways to ensure that your résumé is correct before sending it to an employer?

● Viewing and Representing

Examining the Image. Working with a partner, challenge each other to find important details in this photograph. Ask each other these questions: If you were doing this, what skills would you be using? Could you use these skills in a job? In an interview, you could be asked to give examples of your skills. If you were working as a volunteer like this, what examples could you give to demonstrate your skills?

Building Academic Skills

 Researching and Graphing

Conduct online research to gather data on the annual and lifetime earnings for workers with varying levels of education. Create a spreadsheet of the information you find. Then, use software to graph the information. Print your spreadsheet and graphs.

LANGUAGE ARTS **Role-Playing**

Read the following scenario about Pat (see below). With a partner, develop a role-play in which a friend helps Pat maintain a positive attitude at work. Feel free to add details about Pat and the work situation. Present your role-play to the class.

Scenario: Pat works in a hotel cleaning rooms and making beds. The wages for this job are low, but sometimes guests leave tips. The hours of the job are 8 A.M. until 4 P.M. or until all the rooms are clean. Pat can walk to work and the hotel provides free lunches for its workers. The job takes hard work, cleaning and organizational skills, and could lead to a cleaning supervisor's job. Although other workers do the same tasks, they work alone. Pat seldom talks to fellow workers, because everyone is busy. Pat is frequently bored and lonely at work.

 Labor Laws

Research the child labor laws in your state. Write a two-page paper and include the following information:
- When and why the laws were passed.
- The number of hours per week a child is allowed to work.
- Activities that can't be performed by minors on the job.
- Allowable exceptions (students who are enrolled in work experience programs, youth apprenticeships, and so on).

 Writing a Survey

In a group of four or five, survey several local retail and fast-food businesses in your community. Find out what kind of math skills they're looking for when hiring employees. Then, create a handout of workplace math problems. Create an answer key as well. Provide copies of the handouts for classmates who want to practice their math skills before they apply for a job.

Linking School to Home

Interviewing and Presenting. Interview two relatives or friends who are working. Find out what kind of training they had when they began working. Have they received training on the job and what new skills have they developed? How have their job responsibilities and opportunities changed since they first started their jobs? Have they changed jobs? Make an oral presentation to your class with your findings.

Linking School to Work

Creating an Information Card. Create a small document you can carry in your wallet with all the pertinent information necessary to complete a job application. Obtain sample job applications to use as a resource for this activity.

E-Homework

Applying Technology

Reading the Want Ads. For a period of two weeks, study the jobs that are advertised on the Internet and the local newspaper. What conclusions can you draw about the kinds of jobs offered in your area, the salary range for various jobs, the benefits available, and the qualifications or work experience required? Are there any differences between the jobs advertised on the Internet and those advertised in the newspaper? Write a 250-word summary of your findings.

Résumé Software. Use the Internet to research the résumé writing software available. Locate at least three different products and compare them for the following:
- Cost
- Features offered
- Minimum computer specifications
- Technical support provided

Based on your research, which product would you purchase? Why?

Connecting Academics

Math. You have two job offers. Job A salary is $2,400 a month and requires a daily 48-mile round-trip commute. Job B is closer to home and the salary is $1,920 a month. You'll be working five days a week. Taking into account the current price of gas and your car's gas mileage, how much will the commute to Job A cost you each month? Which job will benefit you most?

Language Arts. Break into groups of three. Select an interviewer, a job candidate, and an observer. Conduct a mock job interview for one of the following positions: grocery store clerk, lifeguard, or newspaper delivery person. After ten minutes, the observer provides feedback to the interviewer and interviewee. What questions were most relevant? What answer gave the best information? Now switch roles and conduct the next interview. Repeat until everyone has been in each role.

BusinessWeek Analyzing the Feature Story

You read the first part of "Asking the Right Questions" at the beginning of this chapter. Below are a few questions for you to answer about job interviews. You'll find the answers to these questions when you're reading the entire article online. First, here are the questions:

31. What characteristics are these employers looking for in job applicants?

32. Are interviewers looking for one correct answer?

CREATIVE JOURNAL ACTIVITY

In a group of four, create a job interview checklist. Include insights your classmates have gained from their own interview experiences.

BUSINESS *Online*
The Full Story

To learn more about job interviews, visit the *Introduction to Business* Web site at **www.introbus.glencoe.com**, and click on *BusinessWeek* Feature Story, Chapter 21.

Career Options in a Global Economy

In this unit you learned about how to develop a career plan and gain skills that will help you reach your career goals. Getting the job you really want takes careful research, detailed planning, and smart follow-up. In this seminar, you'll investigate career opportunities in other parts of the world.

Investigate the Images

Look at the photographic collage on the left page. What grabs your attention first? Is it the color or the words? The power in reading visuals is in analyzing and dissecting your observations. On a separate piece of paper, respond to the questions listed below. These questions might help sharpen the focus of your visual mind.

Factoids

Communicating Around the World. English is the language for international business, finance, and technology.

Worldly Vision. Marriott selects trainees from the Braille Institute in Anaheim, Calif., to attend its Pathways program, which trains persons with visual impairments for a career in its international reservation center.

Speak Up. Toastmasters International is a nonprofit organization that helps members become better public speakers.

Know Your Culture. Prove you've got credentials and keen insight into the U.S. psyche if you're looking at a company overseas. This may make you more qualified than the country's natives.

Overseas Opportunities. There are more than 300,000 corporate American employees working overseas. The international assignments usually last between two and four years.

Your Observations

1. How many photographs do you see?

2. Examine each photograph. How are they assembled in relation to one another?

3. What is the subject of each photograph? Is place or location the subject?

4. Does color signify a message?

5. What issues do you take from these images?

Information

6. Summarize what you think about the photographs from your observations.

Exploring Culture

7. Imagine you're in an interview for an international position. The interviewer asks you to describe U.S. culture. What is your response?

8. Give an example of a company that has changed U.S. culture. How were people influenced by this company or its products?

Taking Aim at Global Business

● Preparation

Research international employment opportunities that sound interesting based upon your own career interests.

Objective

- **Investigate** jobs in countries outside the United States.
- **Decide** on an international career, and create a plan for achieving that career goal.
- **Analyze** classmates' responses and create a final document.

Materials Needed

✓ Copies of recent business news publications such as the *Wall Street Journal* or *Business-Week*, or business sections of international news publications, such as the *New York Times*.

✓ Access to the Internet and your local or school library.

✓ Paper, pens, pencils

● Procedures

1. Research international job opportunities. First, you might want to look into various business opportunities in different countries. Try *BusinessWeek Online*, **www.monsterboard.com**, or **www.coolworks.com** as references.

2. Select an international career. Recall your career interests. Try to match your career interests and your knowledge about the jobs you're interested in with international businesses or consumers in other countries.

3. Create a plan for achieving that career goal. Develop two or three short- and medium-term goals that you'll need to reach to achieve your long-term international career goal.

4. Submit a written or typed report that describes your international career goal. List the steps you need to take to achieve that goal. Be specific.

5. Present your international career goal to the class. Describe your career goal and explain your plan to achieve that goal. Using a world map, identify your international career location.

Chart It

After the presentations have been given, as a class re-create on the board a chart like the one below. It lists career paths and countries to live in. Use X's to show which places students want to go for certain careers. Then, make a separate list of the different reasons classmembers gave for wanting to go to a particular area.

Examples of Countries With Opportunities					
Career Goals	England	Japan	Brazil	South Africa	Pakistan
Nurse		X		X	X
Engineer		XXX		X	
Import/ Export Entre- preneur					X
Teacher	X	X	X	X	X
Minister				X	

Analyze and Conclude

After considering the chart, identify the classes' international career goals and locations, and then answer the questions below:

1. **Interpreting and Communicating Information.** What's the most popular choice of country among classmembers? Why is that country more popular than any other?
2. **Organizing and Maintaining Information.** Is there any special relationship between particular career goals and places? If so, please explain.
3. **Reasoning.** Were you influenced by the choices of other classmates when choosing an international location? Why or why not?

Becoming an Informed Citizen

Congratulations, you finished the seminar. Now it's time to reflect on the decisions you made.

Seeing Things in the Mind's Eye.
What does working internationally teach you?

Analyzing Your Future.
As the U.S. economy motions for more free trade among industries, how might this influence your career options and moves?

BUSINESS *Online*

Further Exploration
To find out more about international employment opportunities, visit the *Introduction to Business* Web site at **www.introbus.glencoe.com**.

Unit 8

Buying Goods and Services

Recycling in the Cyber Era

Where do old computers go when they die? About 500 million computers will become obsolete within the next few years. Ninety-seven percent of the materials in a computer are recyclable. While 70 percent of all major appliances are recycled, only 6 percent of computers are. Many computer companies will recycle old computers. Contact Electronics Industries Alliance at **www.eiae.org** for more information about recycling computers.

● **...And It Makes a Nice Paperweight**
French and British companies have come up with a way to make nuclear waste easier to transport and store—by turning it into glass.

● **Save a Tree**
China throws out 45 billion pairs of chopsticks each year, which is equal to about 25 million trees.

● **Go Shower**
The average bath uses up about 20 gallons of water. The average shower uses up about 13 gallons.

● **Where Wildlife Thrives**
Rainforests take up only 7 percent of the world's dry land, but are home to 50 percent of the world's plants and animals.

● **When Tossing the Soda Can**
It takes the same amount of energy to make 20 cans out of recycled aluminum as it does to make 1 new aluminum can.

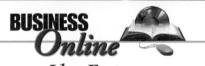

Chapter 22

Making Consumer Decisions

Learning Objectives

After completing this chapter, you'll be able to:

1. **Describe** choices consumers make when buying goods and services.
2. **Identify** types of stores where consumers can make purchases.
3. **List** ways to be a smart consumer.

Why It's Important

As a consumer you have the issue of making your money go as far as possible. If you want to get the most for your money, you have to learn how to make good consumer decisions.

Key Words

brand name
generic products
comparison shopping
unit price
promotional sale
clearance sale
loss leaders
impulse buying
warranty

BusinessWeek **Feature Story**

Dead Letter?

Stamps.com and E-Stamp Struggling for Online Buyers. A little over a year ago, two California start-ups thought they had an irresistible sales pitch: Buy stamps on the Web and you'll never have to stand in line at the post office again. Investors loved the idea. After going public in June 1999, Stamps.com's stock soared fourfold to $48 a share—even before it had sold its first stamp.

Today, Stamps.com and E-Stamp are taking an unexpected licking. Both set out to sell their products to small and home-office customers that don't use postage meters—a potential market of nearly $22 billion in annual sales.

Source: Excerpted with permission from "Dead Letter?" *BusinessWeek Online*, October 23, 2001.

An Extension Activity

When you want to buy a product and more than one company offers similar versions of the same product, how do you decide which one to buy? What factors influence your decision?

BUSINESS
Online
The Full Story

To learn more about online buyers, visit the *Introduction to Business* Web site at **www.introbus.glencoe.com**, and click on *BusinessWeek* Feature Story, Chapter 22.

Buying Goods and Services

When you shop, making choices isn't always easy, especially when you have so many options. Tennis shoes. Jeans. Shirts. Skirts. Sweaters. The malls are filled with tantalizing trends. Even at the grocery store you have thousands of options of different products on sale. Even small neighborhood stores have several hundred different products from which you can choose. In addition, there are many places to look for the best buy.

Consumer Choices

Being a consumer—a person who selects, purchases, uses, and disposes of goods and services—is difficult when you have many choices. If you had unlimited money, you could buy whatever you wanted. People can't do that, though. They have to stretch their dollars to meet their wants and needs.

What to Buy

The first problem of being a consumer is deciding what to buy. Usually you must decide which item has the highest priority for you at any one time, such as a CD or new shoes. After you decide what goods or

Figure 22.1 — MAKING A BRAND DECISION

➡Generic brands usually cost less than brand-name products. Fresh, frozen, and canned are choices for many food products. When would you buy each of these different vegetable products?

COMPARISON OF VEGETABLE PRICES		
DESCRIPTION	**COST**	**WEIGHT**
Generic brand (canned)	49 cents	1 lb.
Brand name (canned)	69 cents	1 lb.
Fresh	99 cents	1 lb.
Frozen (packaged)	79 cents	1 lb.

services you want, you must then select from various choices. You can choose to buy either a brand-name product or a generic product. A **brand name** is a word or name on a product that helps consumers distinguish it from other products. Familiar brand names include Nike, Reebok, Healthy Choice, Campbell's, Coke and Pepsi.

On the other hand, **generic products** are plainly labeled, unadvertised, and sold at lower prices. Most generic products are either medicines or grocery items, such as aspirin, paper towels, and peanut butter. On the average, generic products cost 40 percent less than name-brand products. The main reason they cost less is because the producers spend so little on marketing and advertising. Despite the difference in cost, they are often the same quality as brand-name products. Figure 22.1 illustrates a comparative chart on making a brand decision.

When to Buy

Prices for many items change during different times of the year. Postponing a purchase or planning a purchase in advance can save you a lot of money. For example, if you plan on buying a car or a computer, the prices usually go way down shortly before the new models are released. If you want to own a nice raincoat or wool sweater, you can get one for much less during the summer when it's out of season. You might be tempted to buy yourself a few things while shopping for others during the holidays. If you wait until after the holidays, however, you can usually get the same items for less when the stores have big sales to clear out their remaining stock.

Where to Buy

Along with choosing what to buy, you also have to decide where to shop. Do you want to go to a well-known department store, an outlet mall, or a warehouse store? Do you want to stay home and shop online? There are three reasons consumers choose where they shop: the kinds of goods and services sold, the prices, and the convenience.

Department Stores. Department stores sell a wide variety of goods, such as clothing, furniture, appliances, and sporting goods. Because department stores offer name brands and customer services, their prices are often higher than other types of stores. Macy's and Marshall Field's are examples of department stores.

Discount Stores. Discount stores sell a wide variety of goods like department stores but at lower prices. They can sell for less because they

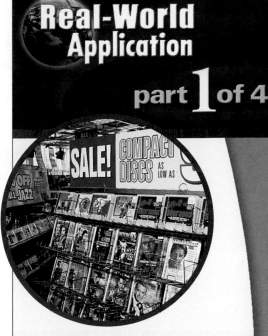

HOW ARE YOU SWAYED?
Has a catchy advertisement ever lured you into a store? Businesses want your business so they'll use advertisements to hook you. Here's a test: You see a sign that reads "CD Bargain Bin. Regular $7.95, on sale for $5.95."
Is this statement rational or emotional?

continued on p. 359

offer few services and stock merchandise in large quantities. Kmart is an example of a discount store.

Off-Price and Outlet Stores. These types of stores carry well-known brand names at bargain prices. They're able to offer large discounts because the items they sell have minor flaws, are out of season, or have been discontinued. T.J. Maxx, Stein Mart, and Loehmann's are examples.

Limited-Line Retailers. Limited-line retailers, or specialty stores, sell a large assortment of goods in one product line or a few related lines. They often sell clothes, sporting goods, or home appliances. Foot Locker and Ace Hardware are two examples.

Superstores and Hypermarkets. These stores are like supermarkets but sell items such as books, hardware, and clothing as well as

---

What are you doing at 10 A.M.?

Houses That Help the World

Lilia Abron and her 130 employees at PEER Africa apply scientific knowledge and business know-how to help black South Africans build houses that are affordable, energy-efficient, and environmentally friendly. At 10 A.M., these three factors keep this environmental engineer's mind busy.

Poor housing and inefficient energy use created severe environmental problems in parts of Africa, including dangerous air pollution, deforestation, and water shortages. PEER Africa's designs tackle both the human and the environmental problems.

Abron's Washington-D.C.-based company has grown to include offices in ten cities and projects in four African countries. Although Abron's company isn't in the construction business, it helps builders apply good engineering and scientific principles to the building process.

Salary

The median income for environmental engineers is $57,262.

Outlook for This Career

The overall employment for engineers is expected to increase as fast as the rest of other occupations.

Connecting Careers Activity

You're entering the century of advanced scientific research. How will new technologies and research benefit the economy and your career path?

CAREER PATH

---

groceries. Like supermarkets, they're also self-serve. Kroger, Meijer, and Safeway operate superstores.

Warehouse Stores. Warehouse stores typically are about the size of a football field. They carry a huge selection of food and nonfood items at low prices and in bulk quantities. They sometimes require customers to become members of the store by paying a membership fee. Costco and Wal-Mart's Sam's Wholesale Club are examples of warehouse clubs.

Showroom Retailers. These stores sell from showrooms where they display samples of their products. Customers visit the showroom and select from the samples. They fill out an order form and the orders are filled from a backroom warehouse. Best Products and Service Merchandise are examples.

Shopping at Home. You can also shop without ever leaving your home by ordering products through home shopping channels, through mail-order catalogs, or on the Internet. Some retail stores, such as Crate & Barrel and Eddie Bauer, also send out catalogs. Many companies sell items only through the mail or on the Internet. Because money doesn't change hands directly, you usually have to buy products by filling out an order form and providing a credit card number.

What to Pay

The number of choices in any store gives you a wide range of prices. Some people think the most expensive item is always the best quality. In fact, the least expensive item or the one in the middle might be the best buy for you. On the other hand, it's often worth paying more for higher quality. If you want to buy a new TV, it might be worth paying more for one that lasts five years instead of paying less for one that could burn out in two years.

Checking the price and quality of a product in more than one store is called **comparison shopping**. Comparison shopping is most important when you're making a major purchase, such as a car or a computer, because the difference in cost can be so much. (See Figure 22.2 on page 360, which illustrates comparison shopping.) For smaller purchases, you need to consider the cost of the time and energy you spend comparison shopping in contrast to the money you might save. If you spend $2.35 on transportation to save $1.50 on an item, you're losing money.

Some products come in so many different sizes it can be hard to determine which is the best buy. That's why it's important to look at the unit price of an item. The **unit price** is the cost of an item for a

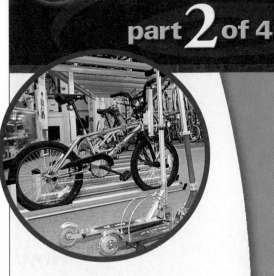

HOW ARE YOU SWAYED?
You've saved up enough money from your part-time job to buy a scooter. At a sporting goods store, an advertisement next to the $50 scooter you want says, "We match prices." You remember a friend talking about a superstore that carried one style.
What do you do next?

continued on p. 361

standard unit of measurement, such as an ounce. Peanut butter, for example, often comes in three or four different-sized containers. If you're looking for the best buy, it helps to know that Brand A costs 17.3 cents per ounce and Brand B costs 19.9 cents per ounce. Many stores list the unit price under the posted cost of an item. If not, you can calculate the unit price of an item yourself by dividing the total price by its weight, volume, or number. For example, if a 12-pack of soda costs $3.60, dividing $3.60 by 12 tells you that each costs 30 cents.

✓ Fast Review

1. Why do generic products cost less than brand-name products?
2. When is a good time to shop for a product like a car, a computer, or an item of clothing?
3. What are ways you can shop at home?
4. How can you calculate the unit price of an item?

How to Be a Smart Consumer

As a consumer, you have to decide what's really a bargain for you. You can become a smart consumer by planning in advance. Start by checking

Figure 22.2

CHECKLIST FOR COMPARISON SHOPPING

➡ When you're comparison shopping, check for various products' features.

When you examine an item of clothing for quality, what should you look for?

Price	Keeping within a certain price range is important to most people.
Features	Check the characteristics of the product to see that they meet your needs.
Quality	How well is the product made? How will it perform its job? How long will it last?
Convenience	What labor-saving and time-saving features does the product have? Is the store location convenient for you to shop at?
Warranty	Does the product have a warranty? Is it a full warranty or a limited warranty? Exactly what protection do you have if it's defective?

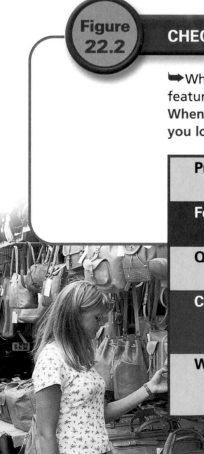

to see what the good buys are. Newspapers and magazines include advertising that can help. Big stores often send out their own advertisements.

Study Advertisements

U.S. companies spend about $135 billion a year on advertising. To be a wise consumer, you should learn how to read advertisements. Most advertisements are one of two types. *Rational advertising* attempts to convince you with facts and information. It tries to persuade you that you should choose a specific product because it's the best one for your purpose. On the other hand, *emotional advertising* appeals to your feelings. Emotional advertising might suggest, for example, that if you buy something, you'll be the most popular person in town.

When you look at advertising, decide whether it gives you useful information. An ad that simply says "The best buy in town!" won't necessarily help you become a smarter consumer. On the other hand, an ad that says "9 oz. Sparkle-Plenty Toothpaste, $1.99" might be very helpful. If you know that Sparkle-Plenty Toothpaste is good, and that it usually sells for $2.79 for 9 ounces, you know the sale is a good buy.

Read Consumer Publications

Magazines such as *Consumer Reports* and *Consumers Research Magazine* give detailed information about goods that have been tested and rated by them. If you're considering buying an expensive item, such as a used car, you can learn about any car's gas mileage, brake system, and repair record.

Consumer magazines examine and rate everything from bottled iced-tea beverages to travel agencies. Many specialty magazines, such as those for photographers or hikers, rate equipment like cameras or hiking boots. Libraries and online services are good places to find these sources of consumer information.

Shop at Sales

Some shopping experts say that the average consumer can save up to 15 percent by taking advantage of sales. Stores might use two different kinds of sales. A **promotional sale** is one that gives you a special buy on a new product or a product that's in season. It's usually held at a time when consumer buying is down, such as in January after the holidays. A store might also have a **clearance sale** to clear out goods that are going out of season or are no longer profitable in order to make room for new merchandise. Clearance sales often mark the end of a season.

HOW ARE YOU SWAYED?
Sunday morning after you read the comics you turn to the newspaper's pull out advertisement section. You're looking to buy a new DVD player. A few stores have them on sale. One ad reads: "The best buy in town. Sale ends today!"
Is this statement rational or emotional?

continued on p. 363

During sales, look for products that are advertised as selling at a loss or below cost. These advertised specials are called **loss leaders**. Even though a store doesn't make any money on these products, the low prices bring customers into the store in hope that they'll buy other things.

Use Shopping Lists

It's fairly easy to fall into the trap of impulse buying when you don't have a firm idea about what you want before you enter a store. Have you heard of impulse buying? **Impulse buying** is purchasing things on the spur of the moment. It can ruin your budget and result in buying things you really don't need.

To cut down on unplanned buying, use a shopping list. It might keep you from making unnecessary shopping trips because you forgot

Business Building Blocks

Communication

Developing Listening Skills

In business, good communication spells success. Active listening is an important part of good communication. You can learn and improve active listening.

Practice

Use the following checklist to become an active listener. On a separate sheet of paper, answer each question in the box with these ratings: **A** (Always), **F** (Frequently), **S** (Sometimes), or **N** (Never).

Rate your score:

Answered mostly A and F = great listening skills

Answered mostly S and N = listening needs improvement

Each week choose two of these questions. Practice the skills indicated in the questions. Keep notes about your active listening.

Checklist for Active Listening

When you're listening, do you:
- ☐ Fidget?
- ☐ Ignore distracting things?
- ☐ Keep your eyes on the speaker?
- ☐ Concentrate on what the person is saying?
- ☐ Pick out the important ideas and think about how they're related?
- ☐ Summarize the ideas in your head?
- ☐ Take notes to help you focus and remember?
- ☐ Ask the person to repeat or explain something that isn't clear to you?
- ☐ Avoid interrupting before the speaker is finished talking?
- ☐ Avoid thinking of what you'll say next?
- ☐ Pay attention even if the person doesn't interest you?

something you need. A shopping list might save you money as well, because you have decided ahead of time what to buy and you resist buying on the spur of the moment.

Resist Pressure and Gimmicks

Some salespersons use high-pressure tactics to try to get you to buy what they're selling. They can be very persuasive. You should always ask yourself if what the salesperson is saying is true, if you need the product or service, and whether you can afford it.

Sales gimmicks, such as "free prizes" or "super low prices" are meant to grab your attention and get you into the store or draw you into buying something. For example, you might get a notice in the mail that says you've won a "free" prize. However, after reading carefully, you realize you won't receive the prize unless you buy something else. You should always closely examine any deal or bargain that seems too good to be true.

Read Labels and Warranties

Before buying a product, read the label. You might find information on the label that will make you decide not to buy the product. For example, a sweater that needs to be dry-cleaned presents you with the problems of extra expense and inconvenience. You might want to look around for a machine-washable sweater. If you're in the market for fruit juice, you should read the food label for the contents. You might discover that what you thought was 100 percent fruit juice consists mostly of corn syrup.

Many items, such as cars and CD players, come with warranties. A **warranty** is a legal document that states the rights and responsibilities agreed to by the consumer and the store or the manufacturer. Full warranties state that the seller will repair a product that doesn't work, usually free of charge. It could also offer to replace the product or refund your money. Full warranties are usually good for a stated time period, such as 90 days or one year. Limited warranties cover only certain parts of a product.

HOW ARE YOU SWAYED?
The last item on your family's grocery list is orange juice. There are oodles of choices. One label reads: 100 percent fruit juice; 8 ounces gives you 75 percent of your daily requirement of Vitamin C.
Is this statement rational or emotional?

✔ Fast Review

1. What is the difference between rational advertising and emotional advertising?
2. What two consumer magazines are good sources of information about products?
3. Why do stores have clearance sales?
4. What is the difference between a full warranty and a limited warranty?

Picture This...

Where Do Those Coupons Go?

1. After you hand your discount coupons to the cashier, the cashier scans them and puts them in the cash register drawer.

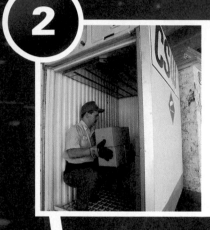

2. Each week all the store's coupons are put in bags and sent to the store's company headquarters.

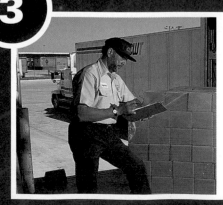

3. At the head-quarters, bags of coupons from all the company's stores are put into boxes and then shipped to a clearinghouse.

4. At the clearinghouse, the coupons are sorted out, often by hand, according to the product manufacturer and then added up.

5. The sorted coupons are then sent out to the various manufacturers with an invoice, or bill, for the value of the coupons.

6. The manufacturers reimburses the store by sending a check for the value of the coupons.

Now *You* Take a Shot...

Average Savings
Go through a coupon mailer or flyer for a local grocery store. Add up the face value of at least 20 coupons. Divide the total by the number of coupons that you added together. What is the result? The figure should tell you the average savings you get from a coupon.

Summary

1. When you shop, you have choices about what to buy, when to buy, where to buy, and what to pay.

2. You can buy from a number of different types of stores, order from a catalog, or buy online. Your choice of store depends on the type of product, the price, and the convenience.

3. Smart consumers study advertisements, shop at sales, use shopping lists, read consumer publications, resist gimmicks and pressure from salespeople, and read labels and warranties.

Using Business Key Words

Part of being a good consumer means understanding the terms connected with buying goods and services. See how well you know them. Match each term to its definition.

- **brand name**
- **clearance sale**
- **generic products**
- **loss leaders**
- **comparison shopping**
- **impulse buying**
- **unit price**
- **warranty**
- **promotional sale**

1. A price expressed in a standard measurement, such as per ounce, for the same product.
2. A sale to move goods that are going out of season or that are no longer profitable.
3. Purchasing things on the spur of the moment.
4. Activity in which a consumer checks the price and quality of a product in more than one store.
5. A sale that gives you a special buy on a new product or a product that is in season.
6. Products that have plain labels, lower prices, and no brand name.
7. Products that are sold below cost in order to bring customers into the store.
8. A legal document that states the rights and responsibilities agreed to by the consumer and the store or manufacturer.
9. A word, picture, or logo on a product that helps consumers distinguish it from other products.

Review What You Learned

10. How do generic products differ from brand-name products?
11. Describe the differences between department stores and discount stores?
12. Why are off-price and outlet stores able to offer large discounts?
13. Why are consumers willing to pay higher prices at stores like White Hen Pantry Inc. and 7-Eleven?
14. How much money do U.S. advertisers spend per year on advertising?
15. Describe rational advertising.
16. What kind of information will you find in consumer publications?
17. Compare a promotional sale with a clearance sale.
18. What problems can occur if you fall into the trap of impulse buying?
19. Why is it important to read the label before you buy a piece of clothing?

Understanding Business Concepts

20. Of all the places where consumers can buy goods and services, which do you think will have a bright future? Do you think any will become less popular in the next ten years? Explain your answers.
21. List some advantages and disadvantages of shopping online.
22. Why is unit pricing important in getting the best buy?
23. In many grocery stores, racks in front of the checkout lanes have a wide range of "convenience" goods on display. Why do you think those products such as candy, magazines, razor blades, and chewing gum are displayed in that way?
24. When does it make sense to buy certain products in large quantities?

Critical Thinking

25. Bring some labels, tags, seals, or packaging from various products to class. List the information you find on those items. Which type of information is helpful? Which is not?
26. Using newspapers and magazines, find two examples of rational advertising and two examples of emotional advertising. Mount them on a poster and display in your class.
27. What useful information could you find in an advertisement other than price and quality?

Viewing and Representing

Examining the Image. Choose one small area of this photograph and imagine you can zoom in on that area. Write a short description of the area. Read your description to a partner. Can your partner find the area in the actual photograph? What's the overall message of the photograph to consumers? Discuss possible messages with your partner.

Building Academic Skills

 Creating a Database for Comparative Shopping

Select a big-ticket item that you're interested in purchasing. Use database software to create a database of stores in your area that stock the item you're interested in purchasing. Include names, addresses, telephone numbers, prices, and any other information you determine to be relevant to the purchasing decision. Print out the database and use the information to analyze the best place to purchase the item you want.

 Writing a Research Paper

Before the advent of department stores, convenience stores, and online shopping networks, there were trading posts and general stores. Conduct research on the ways people in the United States shopped in the 1800s and the early 1900s. Write a 250-word paper with your findings.

MATH **Analyzing the Cost Savings**

Five ounces of toothpaste cost $2.09. Eight ounces cost $2.69, and 9 ounces cost $2.88. Which is the best buy?

LANGUAGE ARTS **Devising a Survey**

In groups of three or four, devise a shoppers' survey. Include questions such as these in your survey:
- Do you use a shopping list?
- Do you compare unit prices?
- Do you buy large, economy-sized products?
- Do you wait for sales?
- Do you read consumer publications?

Each group member can survey shoppers at a different store. Tally your survey results and then write a profile of typical consumer behavior in your community.

Linking School to Home

Smart Shopping. Visit a grocery store and choose five items that are available as generic products. Record their prices. Find brand-name versions of the same items and record their prices. Calculate the unit prices of the brand-name items and the generic items. Make a chart showing how much money your family might be able to save by buying generic products.

Linking School to Work

Categorizing Your Community. Using the yellow pages and local newspapers, create a chart of the types of places to shop in your community. Use the categories found in this chapter. If possible, list at least three examples of each type of store. Include the address of each store in your chart.

E-Homework

Applying Technology

Membership Fees. Using the Internet, research the cost of joining a warehouse club like Costco or Sam's Club. Find out the membership terms, cost, and whether or not you can purchase items online.

Product Research. Choose a product you are thinking about purchasing in the next few months. Using the Internet, find as much information as possible about the product that would help you make an informed decision about purchasing. Use online consumer publications as resource sites.

Connecting Academics

Math. Shantha is shopping for two pounds of basmati rice. Annapurna Grocery sells basmati rice for $1.39 a pound. Foodstuffs sells 8-ounce packages for 99 cents. Grocerola sells a 32-ounce package for $2.89. Calculate the unit price in ounces for each choice so you can advise Shantha which store offers the best price.

Language Arts. Adar, your boss at the consumer protection agency, comes to your desk and says, "Here's your project for this week. Make an eye-catching poster which gives ten tips on how to make good consumer decisions. Illustrate each tip with drawings, magazine cut-outs, or photos."

Math. At Super-Market, Maria found milk on sale for $2.99 a gallon. Other stores were selling milk from $3.09 to $3.39 a gallon. Why might Super-Market have a lower price?

BusinessWeek Analyzing the Feature Story

You read the first part of "Dead Letter?" at the beginning of this chapter. Below are a few questions for you to answer about E-Stamps. You'll find the answers to these questions when you're reading the entire article. First, here are the questions:

28. Why have the sales of online stamps been so much lower than expected?

29. What strategies are E-Stamps and Stamps.com planning to try to appeal to consumers?

CREATIVE JOURNAL ACTIVITY

Research a product or service that you buy on a regular basis. Where can you buy it? How do you predict what most people pay (cash or credit) for it? How often is this product or service offered at a discount? Why do you think this is the case? Write a one-page report of your results.

BUSINESS Online
The Full Story

To learn more about online buyers, visit the *Introduction to Business* Web site at **www.introbus.glencoe.com**, and click on *BusinessWeek* Feature Story, Chapter 22.

Chapter 23

Consumer Rights and Responsibilities

Learning Objectives

After completing this chapter, you'll be able to:

1. **Name** the seven rights of consumers.
2. **List** the basic responsibilities of a consumer.
3. **Explain** how you can conserve resources.
4. **Describe** ways you can learn consumer skills.

Why It's Important

As a consumer, you have rights about the safety and the quality of the products you buy. Along with those rights, you also have responsibilities to choose and use products wisely.

Key Words

consumer rights
consumer movement
product liability
bait and switch
fraud
pollution
conservation
recycling
boycott

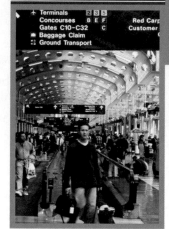

BusinessWeek Feature Story

A Dogfight Over Net Travel Info?

Airlines and Online Travel Giants Aren't Happy With the Small Dot-Coms Gathering Airfare Info. When Web surfers hunt for cheap travel deals at search engine Qixo, they get a wealth of airfare information from 19 separate travel sites. That helps customers find cheaper fares with less effort. Just one problem: Qixo never bothered to ask Travelocity or Expedia for permission to mine their sites. In fact, Qixo CEO Daniel S. Ko has partnership deals with only seven of the sites his company scours, most of them hotel resellers.

Source: Excerpted with permission from "A Dogfight Over Net Travel Info?" *BusinessWeek Online*, November 30, 2000.

An Extension Activity

Before the advent of booking travel arrangements online, consumers continually approached travel agencies. To date, Web surfers have spent more than $12 billion on online travel purchases. How might this affect travel agencies?

BUSINESS Online

The Full Story

To learn more about online airfare information, visit the *Introduction to Business* Web site at **www.introbus.glencoe.com**, and click on *BusinessWeek* Feature Story, Chapter 23.

Being a Smart Consumer

Your new boss just handed you a paycheck for two week's worth of work. It's Friday night and you're ready to go shopping with your friends. All of the new summer clothes are in the stores and there's one item you've had your eye on. When you get to the mall, you talk your friends into going to the clothing store so you can buy the shirt. The store's got your size. You plan on wearing it tomorrow when you and your friends go to the movies. Saturday arrives and you put it on, look in the mirror, and notice a hole in the shoulder. The good news is that as the owner of the new shirt, you've got rights.

The Consumer Bill of Rights

In 1962, President John F. Kennedy outlined what he called the Consumer Bill of Rights. The bill said that every person has these four basic **consumer rights**—the right to be informed, the right to choose, the right to safety, and the right to be heard. These rights received a lot of attention from the **consumer movement**, a movement to pass laws protecting consumers from unfair and unsafe business practices. Over the years, three more rights were added—the right to have problems corrected, the right to consumer education, and the right to service. Figure 23.1 asks you to match the scenarios to the appropriate consumer right.

Figure 23.1

WHAT ARE YOUR CONSUMER RIGHTS?

➡ The government outlines consumers rights.
On a separate piece of paper, match the statement to the consumer right.

1. An automaker recalls its new model that has malfunctioning seat belts.	Right to be informed
2. The over-the-counter medication label mentions pregnant or nursing women should not use it.	Right to choose
3. The advertisement for the new home-theater system tells the consumer the total cost and interest rate.	Right to safety
4. Your local electronics store displays three highly similar and competing computers.	Right to be heard
5. The department store replaces your new shoes since the soles are coming loose.	Right to have problems corrected
6. *Consumer Reports* compares washing machines.	Right to consumer education

The Right to Be Informed

Consumers can make wise decisions only if they have the information they need. As a consumer, you have a right to accurate information. For example, customers weren't always told in the past how much interest charges would add to the cost of an item, such as a car or house bought over time. Some businesses hid the interest charges in long, complicated agreements. According to consumer laws, companies must clearly list interest charges.

Businesses are also required to give you certain information about their products. Drug companies must list the minerals and vitamins in vitamin pills. Clothing manufacturers must list the fibers used in materials. Packaged foods must list all ingredients starting with what they contain the most. For example, if you buy a bran muffin that lists sugar, flour, and vegetable oil before bran, that means it contains more of those ingredients than it does bran.

The Right to Choose

Consumers can choose from a wide variety of goods and services, because the United States has a market economy. Businesses compete with each other to sell their products to consumers. They try to offer new products, the lowest prices, the highest quality, or the best service to get you to choose their products. Competition means choice. When one company controls the market, it has a monopoly. If only one company produces television sets, you could buy only the models it sells and only at the prices it sets. Lack of competition hurts the consumer.

The federal government has the power to keep markets competitive. It can use antitrust laws to stop monopolies from forming or to break up them. Sometimes the government will prevent a large company from buying a smaller company if it might lead to control of the market.

The Right to Safety

You have a right to products that are safe to use. Federal laws ensure that clothing, food, toys, and other items won't harm consumers. The legal responsibility that manufacturers have to make a safe product is called **product liability**. Before new drugs are sold to the public they must be tested extensively and proven safe. Tools and appliances must have safety devices for your protection. Products that might be dangerous if used improperly must have instructions for correct and safe operation.

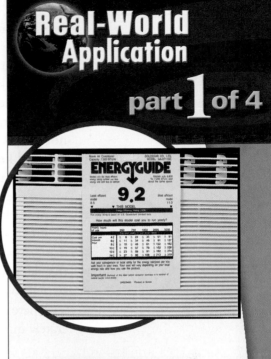

Real-World Application

part 1 of 4

GUIDE TO BETTER LIVING

Americans *waste* as much energy as two-thirds of the world's population consumes. When buying household appliances, ask your family to purchase them with the highest-energy efficiency stickers. Look for a yellow and black Energy Guide label on the product. This could save your family about $400 per year in energy bills.

How much money could your family save in five years if you used energy-efficient appliances?

continued on p. 375

The Right to Be Heard

Consumers who have complaints about products or services have a right to be heard. Suppose you buy a bike helmet from a sporting goods store. After wearing the helmet a few times, you find that the strap under your chin keeps coming loose. If you let the store know you're not happy with the helmet, it might be able to fix or replace the helmet. Businesses rely on satisfying their customers in order to stay in business. If you're not happy, they generally want to hear about it so they can fix the problem and keep you as a customer.

There are always some businesses that don't operate in the best interests of the consumer. They might place a high price tag on an item and then mark it down to make it look like the item is discounted. They might also try a tactic known as **bait and switch**. This consists of advertising an item at a low price to lure you into the store. Once you're there, the salespeople tell you they're out of the item and try to get you to switch to a more expensive item.

There are a number of laws to protect consumers from **fraud**, or deliberately misleading business practices. You can turn to various government

Working Lifestyle

What are you doing at 10 A.M.?

Searching for Blight

From tree to table, walnuts from Summers' Farms in California are among the finest quality in the world. The farm foreman, Paul Stanfield, has supervised the raising of walnuts on the farm for 16 years.

"We're delivering a crop of walnuts to the co-op at 10:00 A.M. today," Stanfield says. "We can't deliver walnuts in the shell that are more than eight percent moisture, so we dry them in a bin."

Stanfield can determine certain other qualities about the crop, including the presence of walnut blight. "We're looking to produce the biggest, prettiest walnut inside the shell," he says. "Blight can affect the meat, but to the trained eye, blight is apparent on the hull even in the disease's early stages."

Salary

A typical quality inspector earns $36,820, with a range between $28,540 and $48,670.

Outlook for This Career

Employment of inspectors and compliance officers will grow as the public continues to demand for a safe environment and quality products.

Connecting Careers Activity

Name other industries that need inspection officers. Do any of these industries interest you?

CAREER PATH — **M**anufacturing

or consumer organizations for help if you have a problem. You will learn about those organizations in the next chapter.

The Right to Have Problems Corrected

Sometimes products don't work properly after you buy them. Usually if you take a defective item back to the store with your receipt, the business will replace the item or refund your money. Many large businesses have customer service departments to handle consumer problems. If a business refuses to correct a problem, you can write to the manufacturer to find out how to get the problem resolved. Communicating your problem clearly, concisely, and courteously will speed up the solution.

The Right to Consumer Education

Consumers have the right to learn how a market system works. You should be able to get the best value and the greatest satisfaction for your money. When you decide to buy an item, you should know that different stores might charge different prices. You can comparison shop to find the best buy. Check the information required by law on labels and fact sheets about the products you buy. Schools and colleges offer consumer education classes. Magazines such as *Consumer Reports* and consumer organizations provide consumers with information so they can make educated choices.

The Right to Service

Customers have a right to be treated in a respectful and courteous manner. This is the case whether you're being served in a restaurant, by a salesperson, or by a repair department. You have the right to expect fast delivery of goods or services and that they meet the standard of quality a business claims. You also have the right to be served without discrimination on the basis of your race, gender, income, or age. If you ever feel you're not being treated fairly by a salesperson, you should complain to the person's manager. Sometimes just asking to speak to the manager changes the person's attitude right away.

GUIDE TO BETTER LIVING

Cars are responsible for 25 percent of the greenhouse effect. Avoid using the car whenever possible. Instead use public transportation, walk, or bike. Encourage your local government to construct bike lanes for bikers and sidewalks for pedestrians.
How will this help everyone?

continued on p. 377

✔ Fast Review

1. How are the ingredients in packaged foods listed?
2. What is a manufacturer's legal responsibility to make a safe product called?
3. What is bait and switch?
4. Name some sources of consumer education.

Your Responsibilities as a Consumer

Along with rights come responsibilities. As a consumer, you have the responsibility to educate yourself. If information about a product is available, you have the responsibility to read that information and to use the product the way it is intended. Figure 23.2 asks you how a newspaper's headlines should make you a responsible consumer.

The Responsibility to Be Informed

Responsible consumers know what they're buying. Whenever you shop for food, read the labels for nutritional facts. They can tell you how much salt, sugar, fat, and protein a product contains. When you shop for clothes, read the labels to find out what materials they contain and how they should be washed. If you toss your new wool sweater into the dryer because you didn't read the label and it comes out the size of a dog sweater, you have only yourself to blame.

Before making a major purchase you should always do some homework. Read the Fact Sheets from the *Consumer Product Safety Commission.* The Fact Sheets tell how a product is rated on safety, performance, and value. You can

Figure 23.2

HOW YOU CAN TAKE ACTION

➡The local newspaper runs these stories.
As a consumer, what is your responsibility after reading these headlines?

FDA Alerts Public to Possible Health Risk Associated With Certain Candy Lollipops From Mexico

Allergy Alert Issued on Mint Chocolate Chip Ice Cream

Half-Gallon Cartons May Contain Pistachio Nuts

POISON

TREATMENT

also find out information on the Internet. Consumer organizations and most manufacturers have sites for consumers.

The Responsibility to Choose Carefully

Responsible consumers make comparisons to find the best product or service at the best price. Which electronics company offers the best guarantee? Which cars have the best record for reliability? Which computer will best fit your budget and your needs? Taking time to make comparisons pays. You can examine the options and prices and then make an educated choice.

Pollution. One of the most serious concerns facing consumers is the effect that buying patterns have on the environment. Individuals have a right to drink pure water, breathe clean air, and live in a healthful place. However, the environment is threatened with all kinds of **pollution**, or contamination of air, water, and land. Pollution is caused by waste from products as well as the ways we use those products. A large share of air pollution comes from exhaust fumes from vehicles. Consumers (and producers) must do their part to cut down on pollution.

Conserving Resources. At one time, it seemed that the United States had boundless resources. Over the years, however, the population has grown and people have increased their demands for all kinds of resources. Now people and businesses have learned that they must conserve resources. **Conservation** is the process of preserving, protecting, and planning the management of resources. Every consumer should be aware of the limited supplies of resources and adjust their consumption accordingly.

Recycling. Part of conservation is learning to avoid waste. You can help by reducing, reusing, and recycling materials in your daily life. Why not recycle! **Recycling** involves collecting products for processing so that they can be used again. Many cities have programs to collect products made of paper, plastic, metal, and glass for recycling. Unfortunately, many cities have a hard time persuading consumers to recycle. It's the responsibility of all consumers to reduce the use of disposable materials, reuse products when they can, and recycle materials to reduce waste.

The Responsibility to Use Products Safely

The government has passed many laws to make products safe. However, consumers must follow the instructions given by the manufacturer for the

GUIDE TO BETTER LIVING
Ground water is used at a rate of 25 percent greater than the rate of replenishment. Volunteer to wash the family car instead of taking it to the carwash. By shutting off the hose between soap and suds, you can save 150 gallons of water.
Hand washing a car is an example of which consumer responsibility?

continued on p. 379

Seeing the Big Environmental Picture

This activity gives you the chance to add to your portfolio. Communicate, interview, research, and write your way into a story. Choose one imaginary path, The Recyclable Plan or The Science of Garbage. Follow your path's steps to complete your own story.

pick a path

A Recyclable Plan

The Setting. During the Great Depression many people lost their jobs and often struggled to obtain necessities, including food. Almost everyone was forced to live with fewer consumer goods such as new clothing and cars.

Rising Action. Research the various ways recycling is done in your community. Call your local government offices to find out how organizations help recycle materials in your town.

Step 1. Make a chart that shows what items are recycled by various local organizations. Do they throw away items that could be recycled? Make a list of these items.

Step 2. Now brainstorm ideas about how you could develop a business to recycle these items and materials. Also write several sentences about how you would convince local residents to pay you to recycle these things.

The Science of Garbage

The Setting. The University of Arizona Bureau of Applied Research in Anthropology has conducted research on garbage. The researchers interview people about what they believe they throw away and then compare those beliefs to what is actually thrown away in certain communities.

Rising Action. Research the various ways your family recycles.

Step 1. Write down everything you think your family throws away during a week. Include numbers of items (for example, one empty box of tissues and two broken lightbulbs).

Step 2. Then keep a log and record what actually is thrown away, including food, packaging materials, and items that could be reused or recycled. Talk to your family about what you have discovered.

Conclusion

Now it's time to write your own story, and reflect on your path. Reducing waste, reusing consumer goods, and recycling materials are part of daily life and your future. One way to understand the overall direction of environmental conservation is to construct a timeline. Start with the beginning dates of recycling. Identify the major turning points. Then insert details and look at the big picture. Share your timeline.

safe use of products. You must read the label of a cold remedy to find out the recommended dosage. You should use common sense when handling or storing chemicals or electrical devices. You can have safety problems if you buy products from an unreliable source. If you know it's unsafe, contact a consumer protection agency about the product.

The Responsibility to Speak Out

A responsible consumer can help improve the policies and products of the businesses where they shop. Most of all, you can let the company know if you don't approve of its products or policies. You also have a responsibility to report unfair, unsafe, and illegal business practices. Reporting those practices helps protect other consumers from problems. There are actions you can take as a consumer. If you object to a company's policies or products, you can **boycott**, or refuse to buy, a company's goods or services.

The Responsibility to Seek Remedy

Part of being a good consumer is getting the best value for your money. You have a responsibility to seek remedy for a defective product. If you plan to exchange an item or get a refund, it's your responsibility to bring with you the item, the receipt, and any warranties or guarantees that came with the item. If the store can't solve the problem to your satisfaction, you should write to the manufacturer or contact a consumer organization for help.

The Responsibility to Learn Consumer Skills

Find information to help you make consumer decisions. It's a bit overwhelming to think of researching every purchase you make. However, you can follow a few simple tips:
- Read information on labels and packages.
- Compare prices at different stores and look for sales.
- Pay attention to the media to become aware of illegal practices.
- Read consumer information publications.
- Attend classes or workshops on consumer issues and problems.

Real-World Application

part **4** of 4

GUIDE TO BETTER LIVING
Next time you're done with lunch don't just throw everything into the garbage: Recycle it. If your school doesn't have recycling bins for plastic, glass, and aluminum in the lunchroom, ask your teachers or write a letter to the editor about starting a recycling program. **What consumer responsibility are you demonstrating by trying to improve the environment?**

✓ **Fast Review**

1. Why is it important to read product labels?
2. Would you choose not to buy a manufacturer's products for ethical reasons?
3. What are three things you can do to conserve resources?
4. Do you have a responsibility to report illegal business practices?

Chapter 23 Consumer Rights and Responsibilities **379**

Summary

1. Consumers have seven basic rights—the right to choose, the right to be heard, the right to be informed, the right to safety, the right to have problems corrected, the right to consumer education, and the right to service.

2. Consumers have a responsibility to be informed, to choose carefully, to use products safely, to speak out, to seek remedy, and to learn consumer skills.

3. Consumers can conserve resources by saving energy, avoiding waste, and recycling.

4. Consumers can learn consumer skills by reading labels, comparing prices, listening to and reading local media, reading consumer publications, and attending classes or workshops.

Using Business Key Words

When dealing with consumer rights and responsibilities, it's important to know the following terms. See how well you know them. Complete each sentence with the correct term.

- **bait and switch**
- **recycling**
- **pollution**
- **boycott**
- **conservation**
- **consumer rights**
- **consumer movement**
- **product liability**
- **fraud**

1. The consumer group decided to _____ the food-processing company because of its policy towards workers.
2. The practice of advertising a lower-priced item to lure customers to the store and then attempt to get the customers to buy a higher-priced item is called _____.
3. A large share of air _____ comes from exhaust fumes from cars.
4. _____ involves collecting products for processing so that they can be used again.
5. The process of preserving, protecting, and planning the management of resources is called _____.
6. The right to choose, the right to be heard, and the right to be informed are three examples of _____.
7. The _____ protects consumers from unfair and unsafe business practices.
8. Manufacturers have a legal responsibility to make a safe product and this is called _____.
9. A deliberately misleading business practice is called _____.

Review What You Learned

10. What are your basic consumer rights?
11. Why might the government try and prevent a large company from buying a smaller company?
12. Where would you go first if you had a problem with an item you purchased?
13. If a business refuses to correct a problem for you as a consumer, what should you do next?
14. What do consumers do with the information they receive from magazines like *Consumer Reports?*
15. What responsibilities do you have as a consumer?
16. Why is the conservation of resources so important?
17. How can responsible consumers help improve the policies and products of the businesses where they shop?

Understanding Business Concepts

18. What is the difference between consumer rights and consumer responsibilities?
19. How does a market economy affect the consumer?
20. Describe an environmental problem around your community. List your responsibilities to help solve the problem. What actions could be taken?
21. Why is safely using products a consumer responsibility?
22. As a consumer, how can you make sure you get the best value for your money when you make a purchase?

Critical Thinking

23. Compile a list of sources for consumer information in your city or local area.
Then describe how a person could use each of the sources.
24. What measures could your community take to conserve resources?
25. Imagine a company is dumping hazardous waste into a reservoir just outside of the city limits near a state park. What are some actions you can take to stop this company from its behavior?
26. A growing number of organizations are aimed at teaching kids the virtues of giving. KidCredits is a Web site that allows 8- to 13-year-olds to donate up to $10 to charity. The donation is based on pre-approved amounts charged to a parent's credit card. What might be the goal of this site?

Viewing and Representing

Examining the Image. Can you think of public persons who represent consumer rights and responsibilities? What are the benefits of a celebrity being the voice and face of an issue? Would a celebrity or public person persuade you to take action for his or her cause just because of fame or status?

Building Academic Skills

 Developing a Survey

As a team, develop and then conduct a survey to determine the awareness of environmental issues by local businesses and community members. Your survey could include some of the following information:

- What conservation methods are used?
- Do you recycle? What items?
- Did consumers' wishes influence your conservation measures?

Compile your team's findings in a written report and share it with the class.

COMPUTER TECHNOLOGY **Building a Table**

Survey five different local stores (department, hardware, computer, clothing, books, shoes, and so on) regarding their returns policy. Then use word processing software to compile the information in an attractive table. Print out the results of the survey and share it with the class.

 LANGUAGE ARTS **Writing a Letter of Complaint**

Suppose you bought a defective DVD player from the local electronics store. You spoke with the manager and asked for a replacement. She refused to replace your player. Write a letter to the manufacturer asking for a replacement and expressing your concern about the store's return policy.

MATH **Studying a Product Label**

Bring a food label to class. Read the label and answer the following questions:

- What is the serving size?
- How many servings per container?
- How many calories per serving?
- How many grams of fat per serving? How many milligrams of sodium per serving?
- What percentage of your daily value of vitamin A does the product contain? Vitamin C? Calcium?

Linking School to Home

Sharing Consumer Tips. Ask your family and friends to share their consumer tips with you. Find out how they make wise decisions about the products and services they purchase. Compile their tips and share them with your class.

Linking School to Work

Interview and Report. Interview a local businessperson to find out how he or she ensures the business caters to the rights of consumers. Prepare your questions in advance, and include questions similar to these:

- How does your business inform consumers?
- What choices does your business offer?
- How does your business ensure safe products?
- Describe the customer service.
- How does your business correct problems? Write a report of the businessperson's responses.

E-Homework

Applying Technology

Comparison Shopping. Using the Internet, select a product you plan to purchase soon. Find several different online sites that sell the product and then comparison shop. Which site offers the best value for the money?

Presenting Your Consumer Rights. Do you think other students at your school know about their rights as consumers? Why is it important to know your rights? How can knowledge help you? Inform others with your arsenal of consumer rights and responsibilities material. Using presentation software, create a presentation outlining your consumer rights. Then, give the presentation to other classes in your school.

Connecting Academics

Math. Miguel saw an ad for Mundane biking shorts for $19.99. He went to Ibex Cycle Shop to buy a pair. Kristin, the salesperson, told Miguel that Ibex was out of Mundane shorts but that Mountain King biking shorts were priced at $27.99 and were on sale for 30 percent off. Kristin also said, "Mountain King shorts are really a much better product." Calculate the sale price of Mountain King shorts. Was Ibex trying to use the bait-and-switch tactic on Miguel?

Language Arts. Give three examples of times you or a member of your family has taken responsibility as a consumer—that is the responsibility to report unfair, unsafe, or illegal business practices, or the responsibility to seek remedy for a defective product. Give a short presentation of your examples. What was the outcome? Would this person take action again?

BusinessWeek | **Analyzing the Feature Story**

You read the first part of "A Dogfight Over Net Travel Info?" at the beginning of this chapter. Below are a few questions for you to answer about Qixo and Orbitz. You'll find the answers to these questions when you're reading the entire article. First, here are the questions:

27. Qixo's business model depends upon what consumer rights?
28. Why is the justice department investigating Orbitz, the big airlines, and travel companies' competing sites?

CREATIVE JOURNAL ACTIVITY

Divide into groups. One team represents the airline companies and travel sites and the other team represents Qixo. Prepare your arguments showing how your side benefits consumers. Conduct a short debate.

BUSINESS *Online* **The Full Story**

To learn more about Qixo, visit the *Introduction to Business* Web site at **www.introbus.glencoe.com**, and click on *BusinessWeek* Feature Story, Chapter 23.

Chapter 24

Protecting Consumers

● Learning Objectives

After completing this chapter, you'll be able to:

1. **Describe** what consumers can do when they have problems with products.
2. **Identify** groups and individuals that act as consumer advocates.
3. **Explain** how government protects consumers.
4. **Name** ways in which businesses help and inform consumers.

● Why It's Important

As a consumer, you're empowered by the establishment of resources and organizations.

● Key Words

refund
small claims court
consumer advocates
consumer reporter
grade labels
recall
legal monopolies
licenses
Better Business Bureau (BBB)

BusinessWeek Feature Story

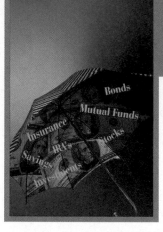

He's Raring to Fight for Fund Investors' Rights

An Industry's Clean Reputation. Do mutual fund investors need a consumer advocate? Mercer Bullard thinks so. And just who is Mercer Bullard? A 39-year-old former Securities and Exchange Commission attorney, Bullard is the founder and CEO—and still the only employee—of Fund Democracy. He hopes to make Fund Democracy a force for change in the mutual fund world. He has already ruffled feathers in the industry and among his former colleagues at the SEC.

Source: Excerpted with permission from "He's Raring to Fight for Fund Investors' Rights," *BusinessWeek Online*, November 17, 2000.

An Extension Activity

List some TV programs you've seen that revealed businesses' shaky professional practices. Which businesses do you think need an objective watchdog to make sure they're not engaging in any misguided practices? How did the businesses change?

BUSINESS Online

The Full Story

To learn more about consumer advocate Mercer Bullard, visit the *Introduction to Business* Web site at www.introbus.glencoe.com, and click on *BusinessWeek* Feature Story, Chapter 24.

Protecting Consumers From Unsafe Products

You'll probably have trouble with a product at some point. There are things you can do yourself. There are many agencies, organizations, and individuals who work to promote the health, safety, and honest treatment of the public. Legislators at the local, state, and national levels have passed laws that establish rules and regulations to protect and inform customers. In addition to government agencies, there are many non-governmental organizations that work on behalf of consumers. Even businesses themselves offer avenues for consumer complaints and concerns.

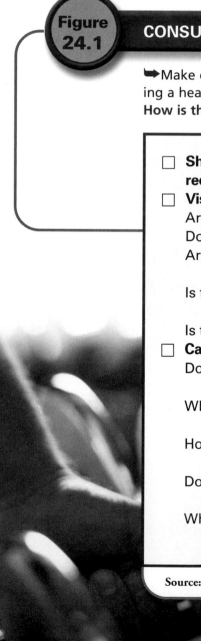

Figure 24.1

CONSUMERS' CHOICES REQUIRE CAUTION

➡ Make exercising more than a New Year's resolution. Before joining a health club, carefully consider your options.
How is this information useful to the consumer?

- ☐ **Shop around. Ask friends, coworkers, and doctors for recommendations.**
- ☐ **Visit the club at the time of day you will use it.**
  Are the hours convenient?
  Does the club have facilities and services that suit your needs?
  Are the equipment, exercise areas, and locker rooms clean and well-maintained?
  Is the facility overcrowded? Does the club limit new membership to prevent future crowding?
  Is the atmosphere friendly?
- ☐ **Carefully consider the contract.**
  Does the contract list all services and facilities? All oral promises should be written down.
  What is total cost and payment schedule, including enrollment fees and finance charges? Do some services cost extra?
  How long is a membership term? A short-term membership is usually best in case you find yourself unmotivated or the club closes.
  Does the contract allow for a tryout period? Will the trial fee be applicable to longer-term membership?
  What are your cancellation and refund rights if you move, become disabled, or the club closes?

Source: Better Business Bureau

Your Power as a Consumer

You have a role as a consumer. You also have power as a consumer (see Figure 24.1). Every time you buy a good or service, you send a message to the company that you like its product. If enough people support the product, the company will continue to produce it. You and other consumers are responsible for the company's success or failure.

On the other hand, suppose that few consumers buy an item. Eventually, the company will discontinue the item because it isn't profitable. The business's choice to discontinue the item affects your choices. You have fewer items from which to choose. Whenever you visit a store, you send a message that the location is convenient for you. If a business finds its location doesn't attract customers, it might move to a more convenient location. You have a voice in what's sold and where stores are located.

Customer Satisfaction

Although an informed consumer can usually avoid problems, they sometimes do occur. Suppose you buy a printer that turns out to be defective. The first thing you should do is take it back to the store. In most cases, the problem is simply a bad part that an inspector missed and isn't the fault of the store or the salesperson. The store will usually give you a **refund** (return the cost of a product to you), fix the item, or replace it. Businesses are generally willing to offer refunds or replacements to satisfy an unhappy customer.

Legal Action

Sometimes a business might refuse to satisfy a customer. For example, you take your faulty printer back to the store and they refuse to refund your money, or you pay someone to fix your bike and they don't do the job right. In that case, you can take them to small claims court. **Small claims court** settles cases involving relatively small amounts of money. In most states, a consumer can go to small claims court with little cost and without a lawyer. The size of claims varies from state to state but can be as low as $25 or as high as $5,000.

Real-World Application

part 1 of 4

THE TRUTH ABOUT FRENCH FRIES
Idaho Spuds. Depending on your favorite grease-to-salt ratio, these thinly cut potatoes, with crispy outer edges and meaty middles, are a craving for many. Nearly a decade ago, a few fast food restaurants listened to the public's concern about fries' impact on cholesterol.
Name one way restaurants made this favorite fast-food side order healthier?

continued on p. 389

✓ **Fast Review**

1. If you return a faulty product to a store, what are the three things the store might do to satisfy you?
2. What is the range of claims in small claims court?

Consumer Organizations

Groups and individuals that work to protect, inform, and defend consumers are called **consumer advocates**. Many groups are private, nonprofit organizations. Some test products and report their findings. Their information is usually available in magazines. Most of these organizations also have their own Web sites. They help consumers become better informed.

Consumer Federation of America

There are a number of national consumer organizations. The Consumer Federation of America (CFA) is one of the largest. Since 1968 it has worked to inform the public and government about consumer issues. It has more than 50 million members in over 260 groups. The members study federal laws that affect consumers. When Congress considers consumer bills, the Federation lets its members know. It works to promote laws that help consumers. Its six major areas are financial services, utilities, product safety, transportation, health care, and food safety.

Working Lifestyle

What are you doing at 10 A.M.?

Four-Car Carrier

"I drive what they call a four-car carrier," says José Guzman. "Usually by 10:00 A.M., I'm picking up my third car from a body shop and getting ready for my fourth."

Guzman drives for a national auto salvage business that works mostly with insurance companies. He explains, "We take a car, check to see if it's totaled, then sell it. Most of our sales are for recycling."

Before Guzman began driving trucks, he worked at his employer's impound yard as a forklift operator and shipping manager. He applied for a Class B driver's license and transferred to a driving position in order to make more money. "My dad used to be a truck driver and he taught me," explains Guzman. "All my life I've been driving big trucks."

Patience and safety, Guzman says, are key to good driving. "It's tiring after a while, especially dealing with traffic. I have to be patient."

Salary

The median hourly earnings of truck drivers is $11.67, with a range between $8.80 and $15.57 an hour.

Outlook for This Career

The occupation is expected to grow at a steady rate.

Connecting Careers Activity

Competition is high for good wages and favorable work schedules. What constitutes a favorable work schedule to you? Does that matter when choosing a career?

CAREER PATH

Transportation, Distribution & Logistics

National Consumers League

The National Consumers League also works on behalf of consumers' rights. It's the nation's oldest nonprofit consumer group. Membership is open to anyone. It provides government, businesses, and other agencies with the consumer's point of view. One of its services is a national fraud information center. It also monitors the Internet to prevent consumer fraud.

Consumers Union

Consumers Union is the nonprofit publisher of the magazine *Consumer Reports*. Consumers can subscribe to the magazine, which reports on consumer products. Consumers Union tests products in its laboratories and reports the findings in its magazine. The magazine doesn't advertise products or allow its findings to be used in advertisements. Consumers Union also testifies before government agencies on consumer concerns.

Major Appliance Consumer Action Program

Some industries have consumer assistance panels. The Major Appliance Consumer Action Program (MACAP) is an active panel. MACAP helps consumers solve problems with large appliances such as washers, stoves, and freezers. Most major appliance dealers are members of MACAP. If a company doesn't respond to a consumer's problem with an appliance, MACAP will help.

Radio and Television

Local radio and TV stations in many cities use the power of the press to help consumers with problems. They often have a **consumer reporter**, who reports on issues important to consumers, such as product safety, testing, and shopping. The reporter might feature one consumer's problem with a local business and visit the business to try to resolve the problem. The chance that the problem will be featured on radio or TV is often enough to get a company to settle the conflict.

Real-World Application

part 2 of 4

THE TRUTH ABOUT FRENCH FRIES
Give just the fry facts folks. McDonald's U.S.A. believes in sharing its nutritional and ingredient information. In any one of its stores you'll find posters, wallet-sized cards, and brochures offering the facts. A description of its french fries is in compliance with the U.S. Food and Drug Administration.
What's the purpose of providing nutritional facts?

continued on p. 391

✔ Fast Review

1. What is *Consumer Reports'* policy about advertising?
2. If you have problems with a new stove or washer, what organization can help you?

Government Organizations

Many federal, state, and local governments provide consumer information. They publish materials to help consumers with their buying decisions and problems. They also pass laws to protect consumers.

Federal Agencies

Consumers can order publications from government agencies. The Consumer Information Center in Pueblo, Colorado is a good source for those materials. Some of the booklets are free and others have a small fee. Consumers can order by mail, phone, or the Internet. These booklets give advice to help consumers decide what and where to buy.

Many federal agencies have been set up to protect consumers. The Federal Trade Commission (FTC) enforces laws about business practices. The U.S. Department of Agriculture (USDA) inspects foods such as meat and gives them **grade labels** that indicate the level of quality. Meat, for example, might be graded as "prime" or "choice." You can use the

Figure 24.2

THE IMPORTANCE OF LABELS

➥Labels provide information to consumers.
If you were buying a pair of gloves, what are three types of information on the label you would find helpful?

100% polyester
Machine wash lukewarm
Tumble dry low
Do not use bleach or water softener
Do not press, iron, or steam
One size fits all   Made in China

⚠ WAR
Children Can Be K[
by Passenger Air Bag
The back seat is the safest place for children 12 and under.
Make sure all children use seat belts or child seats.

grade labels as a guide in choosing what to buy. (Figure 24.2 illustrates how labels on products inform consumers of what they're getting.) The Food and Drug Administration (FDA) tests and approves all drugs before they can be offered to consumers. The National Highway Traffic Safety Administration can order automakers to **recall**, or take back and repair or replace cars with defective parts.

State Agencies

Each state has a consumer affairs division. In some states, the attorney general's office handles consumer affairs. These offices help consumers with their problems and enforce consumer laws. State governments work to prevent unfair practices such as false advertising. States have laws about credit card interest rates, health care businesses, banking and mortgage rates, and other consumer services. Each state agency provides consumer information for the areas they regulate.

Public Utilities. Public utilities are **legal monopolies**, or companies that are allowed to operate without competition. A state public utilities commission regulates the rates charged by electric, gas, and water companies. In some areas, they also regulate local telephone services. The commission protects consumers from unfair prices for their gas, electricity, or water.

If a utility plans a rate increase, the commission usually holds a public meeting where consumers and consumer groups can speak out. The commission listens to all sides before ruling on a rate increase. A state insurance commission controls and approves insurance rates in the same way.

Licenses. If you need someone to fix your plumbing or do your taxes, how do you know if they're qualified? To prevent people from practicing occupations they're not qualified to do, states issue **licenses**, or legal permits to conduct business. Doctors, teachers, roofers, hair stylists, architects, and even professional wrestlers are required to have a license. To get a license, a person usually needs special training and has to pass a test. When you hire someone to provide a special service, you should first check to see if that person has a license.

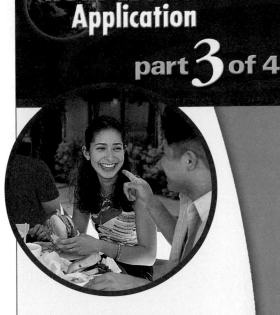

Real-World Application

part **3** of 4

THE TRUTH ABOUT FRENCH FRIES
A recent study shows that teenagers consume almost a third of the total vegetable intake required through two high-fat, low-nutrition foods: french fries and potato chips. Do you know what's exactly in that food you're eating? To find out more about fast-food restaurants' nutritional offerings, visit their Web site.
As a consumer, how often do you study nutritional labels? Why or why not?

continued on p. 393

✓ **Fast Review** _____

1. What does the U.S. Department of Agriculture do to protect consumers?
2. How does a state public utilities commission protect consumers?
3. What are some occupations that require a license?

The Business Community

The business community also provides consumers with information. For example, most products come with product labels, which you can read. Often they tell you about the product in detail. If you shop for clothing, the label tells you about the fabric, how to care for the item, and where the product was made. Food labels tell you about nutrition and how to use the product.

Customer Service Representatives

Customer service representatives can answer questions or help you with problems. Most businesses have a customer service representative. When you buy a product, the package often lists the address, telephone number, or Web site for a customer relations representative. If you have a question or a problem, you can contact the representative. The company might also provide you with consumer booklets about its products at little or no cost.

Business Building Blocks

Customer Service

Have you ever wanted to buy something in a store and the salesperson wasn't around? Or maybe you have worked as a salesperson and had to deal with cranky customers. For a business to succeed, everyone involved needs to be treated with respect.

Practice

Look at the tips in the box and write down how you would respond in the following situations:

1. You sell cars. A man comes in to buy a used car. After he introduces himself, do you address him by his first name?
2. You're the only person working behind the counter at a

Analysis

convenience store. Two lines form and one customer complains that you served someone else before her.

Tips for Good Customer Service

- Pay attention to what's happening around you.
- Look for clues. How are people interacting?
- When someone is acting inappropriately, ask yourself what might be motivating such behavior.
- Keep lines of communication open.
- Everyone deserves respect.

Some companies have specialists to help you select the best product for your needs. For example, if you want to buy a new furnace, a specialist will help you select the right one. The specialist plans the installation and checks to be sure that your furnace works properly after it's installed.

The Better Business Bureau

Local businesses support the **Better Business Bureau (BBB)**, a well-known organization that helps consumers. The BBB is a nonprofit organization that collects information on local businesses and handles complaints. If a consumer has a complaint about a local business, the BBB will try to help. It also shares information about problems that consumers have had and distributes consumer publications. The BBB doesn't enforce laws and it won't recommend one local business over another.

Advertising

Advertising can be a good source of consumer information. Although businesses use ads to promote their products, they also use them to tell consumers as much about their products as possible. Ads tell you not only how much a product costs, but also what kinds of features it offers. For example, an ad for a computer will tell you how much memory it has, what type of processor it uses, and what kinds of drives come with it. You can use the information in ads to compare products and decide which one best suits your needs.

Magazines

Some commercial magazines are good sources for consumer information. They include articles or guides to help you choose products. If you want to buy a household appliance, for example, you can compare different brands featured in the guides. *Good Housekeeping* features consumer information and endorses products with a "seal of approval." Specialty magazines on cars, computers, sports, and travel can give you information about certain types of products.

Real-World Application
part 4 of 4

THE TRUTH ABOUT FRENCH FRIES

Are you one of the average Americans who eats 30 pounds of french fries in one year? No matter what restaurants deep fat fry fries in, there is still medical evidence that the fatty cooking substance increases consumers' risk of heart disease. One company, Proctor & Gamble, developed a calorie-free fat replacer called Olestra.
How might this affect the consumer? What if Olestra caused unpleasant side effects?

✔ **Fast Review**

1. What is the Better Business Bureau (BBB)?
2. How can advertising be used as a source of consumer information?

Summary

1. Consumers who have problems with a product can return products, go to small claims court, or seek help from consumer groups.

2. Consumer advocates, organizations, and reporters protect, inform, and defend consumers. The Consumer Federation of America (CFA), National Consumers League, Consumers Union, Major Appliance Consumer Action Program (MACAP), and the Better Business Bureau (BBB) are examples of consumer organizations.

3. Federal and state government agencies protect consumers by regulating business, enforcing laws, inspecting food, testing drugs, requiring licenses, and informing consumers.

4. Businesses help and inform consumers through customer service representatives, advertising, and magazines.

Using Business Key Words

An informed consumer is a smart consumer. See how smart you are by matching the following terms with their definitions.

- **consumer advocates**
- **grade labels**
- **consumer reporter**
- **legal monopolies**
- **refund**
- **small claims court**
- **recall**
- **licenses**
- **Better Business Bureau (BBB)**

1. Champions on the side of consumers' rights.
2. Labels that indicate the quality of a food.
3. Companies that are allowed to operate without competition.
4. Someone who provides information on consumer problems and then tries to resolve them.
5. To return the cost of a product.
6. A court that settles cases involving relatively small amounts of money.
7. An order to take back or repair defective products.
8. A legal permit to conduct business, usually issued by states.
9. A nonprofit organization that collects information on local businesses, handles complaints, shares information about problems that consumers have had, and distributes consumer publications.

Review What You Learned

10. Name four sources of help for consumers who have experienced problems with products they have purchased.
11. What is your role as a consumer?
12. Which consumer organization is one of the largest? Describe its main function.
13. What do grade labels indicate?
14. How do state governments protect consumers?
15. What services does the Better Business Bureau (BBB) provide?

Understanding Business Concepts

16. The new CD you purchased skips two of your favorite tracks each time it plays. What should you do?
17. Which consumer organization monitors the Internet to prevent consumer fraud?
18. Why do you think large companies have entire departments devoted to customer service?
19. Why do you think the need for consumer protection has grown over time?
20. Some people believe that the government should not be so involved in consumer protection. What do you think? Explain your answer.

Critical Thinking

21. Some people argue that consumers are intelligent enough to make wise choices when buying goods and services and don't need all the protection that's provided. Others say that consumer affairs offices and government agencies are necessary. Choose a partner and debate the topic.

22. Why do you think manufacturers of food, drugs, and cosmetics are required to have their products checked by the Food and Drug Administration?
23. One way government protects consumers is by requiring people practicing certain professions to be licensed. What kinds of professions need licenses in your state?
24. Name a few types of complaints that might be taken to small claims court.

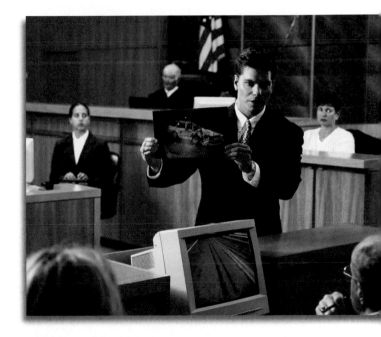

Viewing and Representing

Examining the Image. Write down your impressions of this picture in your journal. How do you feel? Does the picture make you feel tense, angry, good, bad, etc? Have you, or anyone in your family, been to small claims court? If not, use your background knowledge. How are your judgements formed based upon events you've never experienced? What is your thought process? Write about the experience.

Building Academic Skills

 Oral Presentation

Select one of the national consumer information organizations discussed in the text. Research how, when, and why it got started. Prepare a two-minute oral presentation and share your findings with the class.

 Writing a Critique

Choose an advertisement for a product or service from your local newspaper. Note any special claims, incentives, or time limits. Contact the seller/supplier/vendor to verify the information in the advertisement. Using word-processing software, write and print out a one-paragraph critique of the advertisement from the point of view of the consumer.

 Calculating a Rate Increase

Contact one of the public utilities in your community. Find out what the rates are for the utility service. Also, find out the last time the rates were changed. Determine the percentage increase (or decrease) of the rate change.

Researching Products

Study an issue of *Consumer Reports* or *Consumers' Research Magazine*. List the types of products that are reported. Write a summary of the kinds of information provided about each product and indicate how you might find more information about the products.

Linking School to Home

Watching Consumer News. With your family, watch or listen to a consumer news program. Write a paragraph about the specific complaint, how it was resolved, and whether or not you would purchase the product. After seeing or hearing the report, do you make a decision right away? If not, why? Also discuss with your family how the media influences your decisions to purchase something or not. Where else do you get your information in order to make an informed, educated decision?

Linking School to Work

Choosing a Product. Work in teams of four or five students. Choose a product that a team member or family member has found unsatisfactory. Prepare a short presentation showing how to file a complaint about the product or service. Be sure your presentation includes:

- A description of how to approach the business where the goods or services were purchased.
- A sample letter describing the problem and a possible solution.
- A private, state, local, or federal consumer advocate or agency that might handle the complaint.

E-Homework

Applying Technology

Online Ordering. Using the Internet, locate the Consumer Information Center. Order one of the free publications that interests you. If it's impossible to order one, then choose one you would like to order.

Creating a Database. Create a database of the various ways consumers can obtain information. Include company or agency names, addresses, phone numbers, and any other pertinent information. Print out the database and share the information with your classmates.

Connecting Academics

Math. As you read earlier, the Better Business Bureau is a nonprofit organization that helps consumers collect information on local businesses and handles complaints. The 150 Better Business Bureaus in the United States handle ten million consumer questions a year. One third of these questions is about retail businesses, one third is about home improvement companies, and one quarter is about service firms. The remaining portion is about other types of businesses. Draw a pie chart of this data. Include the actual number of consumer questions in each category.

Math. The display failed on your one-month old camera so you exchanged it for a new one at the electronics store. After just six weeks the flash on your new replacement camera stopped working. Now what action could you take to solve your problem? If that failed, what further action could you take?

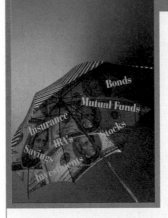

BusinessWeek Analyzing the Feature Story

You read the first part of "He's Raring to Fight for Fund Investors' Rights" at the beginning of this chapter. Below are a few questions for you to answer about consumer advocate Mercer Bullard. You'll find the answers to these questions when you're reading the entire article. First, here are the questions:

25. What are the main goals of Fund Democracy?
26. In Bullard's opinion, how is government's ability to advocate for mutual fund investors limited?

CREATIVE JOURNAL ACTIVITY

Select a product that you or your family may want to buy in the near future. Go ahead and research different brands of this product on the *Consumer Reports* Web site or by reading back issues of the periodical at your local library. Decide which brand is best for you based on price and features.

BUSINESS *Online*
The Full Story

To learn more about consumer advocates, visit the *Introduction to Business* Web site at **www.introbus.glencoe.com**, and click on *BusinessWeek* Feature Story, Chapter 24.

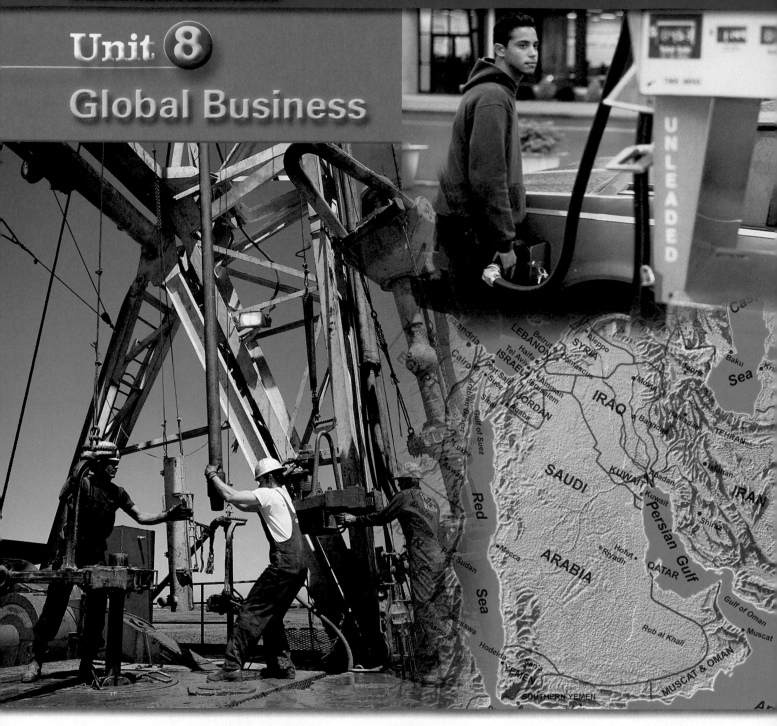

Unit 8
Global Business

Understanding OPEC

In this unit you learned about making wise consumer decisions. You learned that a smart consumer needs plenty of information in order to buy a product or service. Take, for example, crude petroleum oil. It affects the prices of many other consumer products, like gasoline, heating oil, plastics, and synthetic fabrics. In this seminar you'll discover how the Organization of Petroleum Exporting Countries (OPEC) helps you as a consumer.

Factoids

Barrels of Money. OPEC pumps about 40 percent of the world's oil. Its average crude basket price per barrel is about $23.

Piece of the Income. Oil accounts for less than 10 percent of Mexico's exports, whereas in OPEC countries, it can account for 90 percent of a government's income.

Market Maneuver. In 1911, the U.S. courts broke up the Pacific Coast and John D. Rockefeller's Standard Oil Company monopoly.

Buy and Sell. The oil exploration industry has the most publicly traded companies on the stock market.

Clogged Drains. Restaurants improper disposal of cooking grease harms a city's sewers as it coagulates, blocks, and hardens leading to spills.

Investigate the Images

Look at the photographic collage on the left page. What grabs your attention? Is it the color or the words? The power in reading visuals is in analyzing and dissecting your observations. On a separate piece of paper, respond to the questions listed below. These questions might help sharpen the focus of your visual mind.

Your Observations

1. How many photographs do you see?

2. Examine each photograph. How are they each assembled in relation to one another?

3. What is the subject of each photograph? Is place or location the subject?

4. Does color signify a message?

5. What issues do you take from these images?

Information

6. Summarize what you know about the photographs from your observations.

Exploring Culture

7. How might the increased cost of crude oil affect automakers? If the price of gas became too high, how would they lure consumers' into buying their product?

8. In your daily life, how often and how much oil and gas does your family consume? Can you think of conservation methods to use less?

Taking Aim at Global Business

● Preparation

In this seminar, you'll research OPEC and the current price of crude oil.

Objective

- **Choose** a petroleum-based product to research.
- **Explain** how knowing about this product affects consumer decisions.
- **Create** a model of the relationship between the price of your chosen product and the price of oil.

Materials Needed

✓ Copies of recent business news publications, such as the *Wall Street Journal,* the *New York Times,* and *BusinessWeek*

✓ Access to the Internet and your local or school library

✓ Paper, pens, and pencils

✓ Posterboard and markers

● Procedures

1. With a partner, research OPEC. Use the *Reader's Guide to Periodical Literature*, your local or school library's CD-ROM database, or the Internet to find out the basics about OPEC.

2. Write a brief report about OPEC that answers the following questions:
   - Which countries started OPEC?
   - When was it started?

- What is its purpose?
- What countries make up OPEC today?
- What have crude oil prices been for the past two to five years?

3. Choose a product made from oil and research this product. (Suggestions include gasoline, automotive oil, heating oil, and plastics.)
   - Find out how your chosen product is made, and what part oil plays in its production.
   - Research the prices for your product. If possible, find prices for the past two to five years.

4. Present your report to the class.

Chart It

Using the price information obtained from your research, create a graph that shows the relationship between the price of crude oil and your product. Draw your graph on poster board to use in your presentation to the class.

EXAMPLE:

Crude Oil Prices

PRICE PER BARREL — $50, $40, $30, $20

YEAR — 1950, 1960, 1970, 1980, 1990

Becoming an Informed Citizen

Congratulations, you finished the seminar. Now it's time to reflect on the decisions you made.

Interpreting and Communicating Information. If you were standing at the pump to buy gas for your family car, what factors would you consider when choosing a kind of gasoline?

Critical Thinking. What do you think would happen if OPEC disbanded?

BUSINESS Online

Further Exploration
To find out more about consumerism, visit the *Introduction to Business* Web site at **www.introbus.glencoe.com**.

Analyze and Conclude

Study the graph that you created in Chart It. Then answer the questions below.

1. **Acquiring and Evaluating Information.** What is the relationship between crude oil prices and the price of your product?
2. **Interpreting and Communicating Information.** Does understanding this relationship affect any consumer choices you make or will make? If so, how? If not, why not?
3. **Reasoning.** How does understanding OPEC help you make wiser consumer purchases?

Unit 9

Credit

The Price of Debt

Not good on your word to pay back money? In the good old days, if you couldn't pay back your debts you were thrown into debtor's prison. The cells were generally small, overcrowded, unheated, filthy, and disease-ridden. A debt as little as 50 cents could put you in prison. To get out, you not only had to pay back your debt, but the cost of your imprisonment as well. When debtor's prisons became too overcrowded, the government enacted bankruptcy laws.

● **That's the Way the Money Goes**
The children's song *Pop Goes the Weasel* is about borrowing money from a pawnshop. "Pop" is slang for pawn, and "weasel" is slang for coat.

● **I Owe U**
The major credit card companies pay some universities millions of dollars for the right to market their credit cards on campus. They often offer free gifts, such as T-shirts and flashlights, to students who apply for a card.

● **Check Please**
The first credit card appeared in 1951 in the United States. Twenty-seven restaurants in New York accepted the Diners Club credit card.

● **Don't Leave Home Without It**
Financier Eli Broad, who charged a Roy Lichtenstein painting for $2.5 million to his American Express platinum card, was the biggest credit card purchase ever made.

Chapter 25

What Is Credit?

Learning Objectives

After completing this chapter, you'll be able to:

1. **Describe** the nature of credit.
2. **Explain** the advantages and disadvantages of using credit.
3. **Name** the places where you can get credit.
4. **List** the three main types of charge accounts.
5. **Identify** the different types of credit cards.

Why It's Important

You'll probably use credit some day. When you do, it will be helpful to know what credit is and the types of credit you can use.

Key Words

credit
creditor
debtor
interest
consumer credit
commercial credit
credit rating
charge account
revolving account
installment loans

BusinessWeek Feature Story

Tapping Teens' Plastic Potential

Beware of Being Hooked. The next time you're out shopping, standing in line behind teenagers, don't expect them to fish out a few wadded twenties as payment. If credit card companies have their way, more teens will be using their own cards, complete with their names embossed on the pieces of plastic, to buy everything from the latest must-have pair of jeans to movie tickets.

Credit card company representatives have been signing up card members on college campuses for years. But in a new twist on the concept of plastic and young people, several credit card giants, including American Express and Visa International, have developed cards specifically for the high school set and younger.

Source: Excerpted with permission from "Tapping Teens' Plastic Potential," *BusinessWeek Online*, January 11, 2001.

An Extension Activity

Have you ever been approached by a company to sign up for a credit card? How did you handle the offer? Was it a tempting offer? Or did you leave it behind? Explain your situation.

BUSINESS Online
The Full Story

To learn more about teen credit cards, visit the *Introduction to Business* Web site at **www.introbus.glencoe.com**, and click on *BusinessWeek* Feature Story, Chapter 25.

The Nature of Credit

Buying an item now and paying for it later can be an easy and convenient way to make a purchase. Consumers use credit to buy everything from a tank of gasoline to a new car. How does buying on credit work? What are the advantages and disadvantages of using credit?

Figure 25.1

WHAT IS YOUR CREDIT IQ?

➥Do you know how to use credit wisely?
On a separate piece of paper, write the letter that best describes your answer to the following questions.

1. I pay any bills I have when they are due _____.
   a. always   **b.** most of the time   **c.** sometimes

2. If I need more money for my expenses, I _____ borrow it.
   a. never   **b.** sometimes   **c.** often

3. If I want to see a copy of my credit report, I can contact _____.
   a. a credit reporting agency
   b. a bank
   c. the principal at my school

4. If I default (don't pay) on a loan, it will stay on my credit report for _____.
   a. 7 years   **b.** 2 years   **c.** 6 years

5. If I have serious problems, I should _____.
   a. contact my creditors to explain the problem
   b. contact only the most persistent creditors
   c. not contact my creditors and hope they will forget about me

6. I can begin building a good rating by _____.
   a. opening a savings account and making regular monthly deposits
   b. paying most of my bills on time
   c. opening a checking account and bouncing checks

Scoring: Give yourself 3 points for each "a," 2 points for each "b," and 1 point for each "c." Add up the number of points.
   6–9 points = learn more about credit before you're in debt
   10–13   = you're off to a good start; be sure you know about the pitfalls of opening a credit account
   14–18   = you know a lot about credit and use it wisely

Source: *How to Be Credit Smart* (Washington, DC, Consumer Education Foundation, 1994).

Credit: The Promise to Pay

Credit is an agreement to get money, goods, or services now in exchange for a promise to pay in the future. When buying on credit, you're delaying the payment for the item. (Learn to see if you might use credit wisely by taking the quiz in Figure 25.1.)

The one who lends money or provides credit is called the **creditor**. The one who borrows money or uses credit is called the **debtor**. Credit is based on the creditor's confidence that the debtor can and will make the payments. In other words, credit is a matter of trust.

Creditors charge a fee for using their money, which is called **interest**. The amount of interest is based on three factors. One of them is the interest rate, which is a percentage of the total amount borrowed. A second factor is the length of the loan. The longer you take to pay off a loan, the more interest you have to pay. The third factor is the amount of the loan. The larger the amount, the more the interest. The amount of interest varies from one provider to the next. It's important to shop around for credit because creditors may charge different rates.

Who Uses Credit?

Many people use credit today. To a great extent it has replaced money as a means of making purchases. Credit is used practically everywhere. You'll probably use credit in the future to buy CDs, eat at restaurants, or take out a student loan. The type of credit used by people for personal reasons is called **consumer credit**.

Businesses often use credit for the same reasons that consumers do. They might need to borrow money to buy goods or pay salaries. Manufacturers borrow money to buy raw materials, new machinery, factories, or trucks. Credit used by business is called **commercial credit**. When businesses borrow money, however, they often pass along the cost of interest to consumers by charging higher prices on their products.

The federal government uses credit to pay for many of the services and programs it provides to its citizens. For example, during World War II, the federal government used credit to finance military spending. State and local governments use credit to pay for such things as highways, public housing, stadiums, and water systems.

Advantages of Credit

The main advantage of credit is that it's convenient. You can shop and travel without carrying large amounts of cash. You don't have to worry

Real-World Application

part 1 of 4

BEFORE YOU SAY YES, COMPUTE IT!
You may be eligible for credit as soon as you begin working at a job. You may think it's a great idea to open charge accounts—after all, you can get things you want right away. There is an important drawback, however: finance charges. **How does credit work?**

continued on p. 409

about getting cash before you go to the store or having it lost or stolen. Instead of saving for an expensive item, like a car or computer, you can get it and use it right away. Credit is especially useful in an emergency. If you lose your job, you can use credit to pay for food and rent. If your car breaks down and you don't have the cash to fix it, you can use credit. Without credit, you couldn't buy some things. To order airline tickets over the phone or shop on the Internet, you need a credit card.

Buying on credit enables you to establish a credit rating. A **credit rating** is a measure of a person's ability and willingness to pay debts on time. A good credit rating tells other lenders that you're a responsible borrower and a good credit risk. Credit also helps you keep track of your spending. Whenever you buy something on credit, it goes on your credit card bill so you have a record of your expenses.

Finally, credit contributes to the growth of our economy. If you use credit, you can buy more goods and services. Since so many consumers make credit purchases, businesses must hire more workers and produce more goods to keep up with the demand.

Disadvantages of Credit

Since credit is so convenient to use, it can also be easy to misuse. With credit, it's tempting to buy things you can't afford, buy too much, or buy things you don't need. Advertising and salespersons constantly urge you to buy more things. You might find it hard to resist a clothes sale or splurging on a new DVD player.

Items also cost more when you use credit instead of cash because of the interest. The more items you charge and the longer you take to pay off your credit cards, the more you pay in interest.

As credit card bills pile up, you might have trouble paying them. After awhile, you may reach your credit limit, the point where you can't charge any more. Late or missed payments lower your credit rating, which will make it difficult for you to get credit in the future. According to a recent report, half of all people with credit problems are between the ages of 18 and 32. Always remember when you use credit that it's not money you own, it's money you owe!

✓ Fast Review

1. What is the difference between a creditor and a debtor?
2. What is commercial credit?
3. Name the disadvantages of using credit.

Types of Credit

Credit is available from many different sources. These sources provide different types of loans for varying lengths of time. Loans can be short-term (one year or less), medium-term (one to five years), or long-term (more than five years). The risk a creditor takes in lending money or selling on credit is the most important factor in determining the cost of credit. Businesses and banks lose up to $1.5 billion per year in credit card fraud alone. Consumers who have a good credit rating will usually pay less interest than those who have a poor rating. In general, the lower the risk, the lower the costs of obtaining credit.

Charge Accounts

One of the most common types of short-term and medium-term credit is the **charge account**. Dealers or stores generally offer these. Customers who have charge accounts at a store can use their credit to buy now and pay later. When the bill arrives in the mail, the customer can pay some of the total amount owed or the entire amount. There are three main types of charge accounts: regular, revolving, and budget.

Regular Charge Accounts. These accounts require that you pay for purchases in full within a certain period, usually 25 or 30 days. If the bill is paid on time, you don't have to pay interest. If you don't pay the entire bill, interest is charged on the amount that hasn't been paid.

Revolving Charge Accounts. A **revolving account** allows you to borrow or charge up to a certain amount of money, such as $3,000, and pay back a part of the total or the entire balance for each month. Interest is charged on the unpaid amount.

Budget Charge Accounts. These accounts let you pay for costly items in equal payments spread out over a period of time. Many of these are medium-term loans for up to five years. Each payment includes part of the total due on the item plus interest. Large home appliances, cars, and furniture are often bought this way.

Credit Cards

Credit cards are like charge accounts but some can be used in many different places. Those issued by banks, for example, can be used in different stores, including companies that sell on the Internet. Some of the cards have annual fees, which might range from $25 to $80. Credit card companies earn money from the interest they charge. Interest rates vary a lot. You can find credit card rates on the Internet at various Web sites. There are three basic types of credit cards: single-purpose, multipurpose, and travel and entertainment. Figure 25.2 illustrates two credit card companies that are vying for your business. Which would you choose?

BEFORE YOU SAY YES, COMPUTE IT!
At first, you may think finance charges aren't very high. If you buy a TV and DVD player for $1,000 with your credit card, you may be paying a finance charge of 1.5 percent per month. That's $15.00 interest each month. $1,000 x 1.5 percent = $15.
What if you don't pay off that $1,000 before next month?

continued on p. 411

Single-Purpose Cards. These cards can only be used to buy goods or services at the business that issued the card. Single-purpose cards operate like revolving charge accounts. Each month you receive a statement listing all the purchases you made in the past 30 days. You can pay part or the entire amount you owe. Credit cards issued by oil companies are examples of single-purpose credit cards. There is no annual fee for single-purpose cards.

Multipurpose Cards. These cards are also called bank credit cards because banks issue them. Multipurpose cards work like a revolving charge account. These cards may be used at many different stores, restaurants, and other businesses all over the world. MasterCard® and VISA® are examples of multipurpose cards.

Travel and Entertainment Cards. These cards usually work like regular charge accounts. You must pay the full amount due each month. Cards such as American Express® and Diners Club® are examples. They are accepted worldwide for purchases connected with travel, business,

Figure 25.2

HOW DO YOU CHOOSE A CREDIT CARD?

➡No matter what your age is, credit card companies hound you to sign up and spend. Before you accept a company's offer, carefully consider your options. Look at the comparative chart below.
If you wanted to get a credit card, which one would you consider? Why?

Credit Card A	Credit Card B
• No annual fee	• No annual fee
• Offers a fixed 8.90 percent APR (for the first 6 months of purchases; then 15.49 percent)	• An interest-free grace period of at least 25 days (if you pay your entire monthly balance)
• Eligible for 14 round-trip e-tickets	• A free customized credit card
• Eligible for calling card (free 10 minutes per month for 1 year)	• Accepted at more than 18 million locations
• Customer service available 24 hours a day	• Toll free customer service 24 hours a day

and entertainment such as restaurant and hotel bills, car rentals, and airline tickets. Often they have an annual fee, which is higher than a multipurpose card.

Banks and Other Financial Institutions

Financial institutions, such as banks, savings and loans, and credit unions offer many types of loans. They usually have the lowest rates on their loans. They do place more demands on the borrower, however, which can make it more difficult to get a loan. For example, these financial institutions only want to lend money to people with good credit ratings. Many credit unions only lend money to credit union members and employees in a certain business or field (such as a teachers' credit union).

Single Payment Loan. As the name suggests, the debtor pays back this type of loan in one payment, including interest (at the end of the loan period). Many farmers secure single payment loans in the spring to pay for their seed and fertilizer. They then pay back the loan in the fall after they have harvested their crops.

Installment Loan. Student loans, personal loans, and home improvement loans are types of **installment loans**, or loans repaid in regular payments over a period of time. The debtor receives the loan money for a certain period, such as two years. Over that period, the debtor makes equal monthly payments, which cover the amount of the loan and the interest.

Mortgage Loan. A mortgage loan is a form of an installment loan only it's written for a long period, such as 15 to 30 years. Over the period of the loan, the debtor makes regular payments (usually monthly). Some loans require *collateral*, which is something of value the bank can take if you don't make the required loan payments. Cars, houses, and boats are used as collateral when you borrow money to finance them.

Seller-Provided Credit

Many stores provide credit for their customers. Clothing, furniture, appliance, boat, hardware, and car dealers are among those who offer credit for customers. Generally, seller-provided credit is extended for less than one year, up to five years. One of the reasons they provide such credit is to make it easier for consumers to buy their products and to not go elsewhere.

BEFORE YOU SAY YES, COMPUTE IT!
What if you buy other items and increase your credit card debt? If your credit card charges 1.5 percent per month, you would be paying 18 percent per year in finance charges: 1.5 percent x 12 months = 18 percent.
How much would it cost you to keep an unpaid balance of $1,000 on your credit card bill for a year?

continued on p. 413

Consumer Finance Companies

You can have trouble borrowing from banks or other financial institutions if you don't have a steady job or if you have a poor credit rating. Consumer finance companies specialize in loans to people who might not be able to get credit elsewhere. Their loans usually range from less than one year, up to five years. The cost of a loan from a consumer

Business Building Blocks

Communication

Locating and Verifying Information

When you work, you rely on your colleagues and others for many different reasons. This is especially true when you need information to complete your own projects.

You can find or verify information in many ways. Some information, like last year's sales figures, will be available from your own company. To obtain other information you may have to rely on reference books, interviews, and the Internet.

Make sure the sources you use are reliable and up-to-date. Check the copyright date of books or the issue date of periodicals. Verify your information whenever possible by cross-checking with another source.

Practice

How can you be certain you're getting accurate, up-to-date information? Read the Information Source Guide in the box for recommendations. Use it to figure out how to find the following information:

1. Population of your town or city.
2. Number of cars your favorite car manufacturer sold last year.
3. Names and addresses of two companies that manufacture a product or provide a service in a career field that interests you.

Information Source Guide

Newspapers. The *New York Times* and *Wall Street Journal*.

Magazines. Consult the *Reader's Guide to Periodical Literature* for general interest magazines. Search specialized indexes, such as the *Business Periodicals Index*, too.

Directories. Specialized directories may have exactly the information you need. The *Thomas Register of American Manufacturers*, for example, is published annually.

Atlases. An atlas can be a great source for certain kinds of facts and figures. Even old editions can be useful if you're doing historical research.

Internet. The amount and type of information can change daily, so keep up-to-date by consulting the "last time modified" clause on a Web page.

The U.S. Government. The Government Printing Office publishes free or inexpensive information about many subjects.

finance company is higher than the cost of a loan from other sources since this loan involves a greater risk.

The interest rate a consumer finance company charges varies from state to state and can be more than 20 percent, which is quite high. Before securing a loan from a consumer finance company, check to see if you can secure a comparable loan from a bank, savings and loan, savings bank, or credit union. Also, check out whether you can get a better deal on a credit card where you're eligible.

Payroll Advance Services

Many people have difficulty making their paychecks stretch from one payday to the next. If you don't have any savings and an unexpected expense occurs, you might look for a short-term loan until payday.

Pawnshop Loan. This type of loan is based on the value of something you own. For example, you could pawn your bicycle for an amount of money that's less than the bike is worth. You receive a ticket for the item and can redeem, or buy back, your bike within a certain period of time for the loan amount plus a service charge. The service charge is like interest. If you don't redeem it, the pawnshop sells your bike. Generally, the cost of this type of loan is very high.

"Borrow Until Payday" Loan. Some businesses provide very short-term loans, usually for 5 to 14 days. The cost of this kind of loan is especially high. In some cases, it could be 1,000 percent when you calculate it on an annual basis. This kind of loan isn't permitted in some states and limited in others by a maximum fee or loan amount allowed.

A payday loan is made without a credit check, but you must have proof of a checking account and employment. It's strongly recommended that you don't use this source of credit. People with poor credit ratings are most likely to use this service because they can't get a loan anywhere else.

BEFORE YOU SAY YES, COMPUTE IT!
Many credit cards demand a minimum monthly payment, but they don't require you to pay the balance, are otherwise known as revolving credit.
How might revolving credit impact your credit card bill and finances charges?

✓ Fast Review

1. What is the most important factor for a creditor in determining the cost of credit?
2. What are the three types of charge accounts?
3. What is the difference between a single payment loan and an installment loan?
4. What three types of loans usually cost the most?

Summary

1. Credit is an agreement to get money, goods, or services now by promising to pay later. Creditors charge a fee (interest) for using their services.

2. Using credit is convenient, useful in an emergency, helps you establish a credit rating, helps you keep track of your spending, and contributes to the growth of the economy. It also costs more, can lead to overspending, and, if handled improperly, may lower your credit rating.

3. Credit is available through charge accounts, credit cards, banks, businesses, consumer finance companies, and pawnshops.

4. The three main types of charge accounts are regular, revolving, and budget.

5. The three basic types of credit cards are single-purpose, multipurpose, and travel and entertainment.

Using Business Key Words

Consumers use credit to make purchases every day. It's a convenient way to buy something, but it's something you need to learn to use wisely. See how well you know these credit terms. Complete each sentence with the correct term.

- **credit**
- **charge account**
- **creditor**
- **revolving account**
- **debtor**
- **consumer credit**
- **installment loans**
- **interest**
- **commercial credit**
- **credit rating**

1. A (n) _____ lends money or provides credit.

2. A form of credit account, which allows one to borrow or charge up to a certain amount of money and pay back a part of the total each month, is called a(n) _____.

3. Loans repaid in regular payments over a period of time are called _____.

4. Credit used by businesses to buy goods, pay salaries, or buy property is called _____.

5. The _____ is the one who borrows the money or uses the credit.

6. Credit used by consumers for personal purchases is called _____.

7. _____ is the opportunity to obtain money, goods, or services now in exchange for a promise to pay in the future.

8. Creditors usually charge _____, or a fee for using their money.

9. Some factors that determine a person's _____ are income, current debt, and debt history.

10. A short-term credit arrangement provided by a store or company to purchase their product is called a _____.

Review What You Learned

11. What is the cost of using credit?
12. What are the factors that determine a person's credit rating?
13. How does credit contribute to the growth of the economy?
14. Why does it often cost more to purchase an item on credit than it does when you purchase the item with cash?
15. What is the difference between a short-term, medium-term, and long-term loan?
16. Who usually borrows money from consumer finance companies?
17. Explain the differences between a regular charge account, a revolving charge account, and a budget charge account.
18. MasterCard® and Visa® are examples of what type of credit cards?
19. Why is it strongly recommended that you not use a "borrow until payday" loan as a source of credit?
20. How can offering credit become a disadvantage to a business?

Understanding Business Concepts

21. Why do people like to buy on credit?
22. Describe two situations in which cash is more convenient. Next, describe two situations in which credit is the better choice.
23. Why is it important to take care of your credit rating?
24. Why do consumer finance companies have higher finance charges than other places?
25. Why do credit card companies try so hard to persuade you to use their card?
26. If people use credit, does that mean they have money problems? Explain.
27. How do businesses use credit to help sell their products?

Critical Thinking

28. "Everyone would gain if there were no consumer credit. Consumers would benefit because goods and services could be sold at a lower price. The lower price means the businesses would sell more goods and services." Do you agree or disagree with these statements? Explain.
29. What types of consumers would benefit from a travel and entertainment credit card? Explain.
30. What are your thoughts on the pros and cons of credit?
31. What trends in credit have you noticed?

Viewing and Representing

Examining the Image. In a group of three, examine the photograph and ask one another questions about the content. What's important in this photograph? Discuss your ideas about using credit.

Building Academic Skills

LANGUAGE ARTS — Writing About Credit

Keeping a business financially stable is a requirement in order to stay open. As you've learned in this chapter, a business relies on lenders for credit to help continue expanding its company. The media continually reports on businesses' financial situations. Bring in several newspaper articles and advertisements that show uses of credit by consumers, businesses, and the government. Write a paragraph for each explaining who benefits the most from these examples of credit.

MATH — Analyzing the Cost of Credit

In a group, research the cost of credit from each of the sources listed below. Use newspaper and radio advertisements or make phone calls to local creditors to gather the information. Then rank them in order, from the lowest interest rates to the highest interest rates.

- Consumer finance company
- Revolving charge account
- Travel and entertainment credit card
- Credit union
- Commercial bank

COMPUTER TECHNOLOGY — Surveying Students

Create a survey to find out what the students in your school know about credit. Ask questions like (1) what is credit?, (2) do you have a credit card?, and (3) if so, what do you use it for?

Add at least five other questions to the survey. Compile the results using a spreadsheet program. Print your results.

Social Science — A Collective Discussion

In a group, discuss whether you agree or disagree with the following statements. Try to come to consensus. Record the reasons for the group's opinions. Share your opinions with other groups.

- The use of credit is usually justified for necessities but not for luxuries.
- The best way to minimize the cost of credit is to borrow at the lowest available interest rate and repay the loan in the shortest possible time.
- A good credit rating is a valuable thing to have, so a consumer should protect that rating.
- It's best to shop for credit just as you would shop for any major purchase.

Linking School to Home

Analyzing Advertisements. During the next two weeks, save all the advertisements and junk mail that come to your home, which try to persuade you and your family to become a user of their credit cards. Log the promotional offers that are advertised. Conduct a mini-survey among your family and friends and find out whether or not they would choose one of the cards based on the advertising material that has been sent to your home.

Linking School to Work

Comparing Credit Cards. Obtain a credit card application from two different retail stores or gas stations. As a group, compare the applications and list the similarities and differences. Be sure to examine the interest rates and repayment procedures. Create a table in a word processor or a spreadsheet. Discuss your findings with the class.

E-Homework

Applying Technology

Comparing Credit Cards. Use the Internet to research interest rates and credit lines of multi-purpose credit cards. Find examples of at least four and compare their rates, repayment terms, and the application process.

Flexible Credit. Some small business owners only need small loans. Banks, however, usually prefer to make loans of $50,000 or more. Heather McCartney needed $5,000 to give her ethnic-themed cookie cutter business a boost. She got the cash from a nonprofit micro-lender called Count Me In for Women's Economic Independence. Go to the Internet to find out more about this nonprofit organization.

Connecting Academics

Math. A generally accepted consumer credit scoring scale, The Fair Isaac Company (FICO) score, ranges from about 350 to 900 points. A good score is often considered 600 or greater. Banks and other companies may not give credit to people with scores below 600. List whether or not the following people are likely to receive credit:

Sam	300 credit score
Jill	590
Tina	480
Guillermo	600

Social Science. Working in a team of three, choose one of the following topics: what is credit, advantages and disadvantages of credit, types of charge accounts, types of credit cards, or types of loans. Together, research your chosen topic. Imagine members of your team are customer service representatives at a local credit information organization. Now you're ready to take client calls (i.e., classmates voicing issues and asking customer-oriented questions).

BusinessWeek Analyzing the Feature Story

You read the first part of "Tapping Teens' Plastic Potential" at the beginning of this chapter. Below are a few questions for you to answer about teen credit cards. You'll find the answers to these questions when you're reading the entire article. First, here are the questions:

32. How do teen credit cards differ from normal credit cards?

33. According to marketing experts, what are the credit card companies' motives for promoting the cards to teens?

CREATIVE JOURNAL ACTIVITY

Consider the consumer advantages and disadvantages of having a teen card. Create a poster illustrating your points.

BUSINESS *Online*
The Full Story
To learn more about teen credit cards, visit the *Introduction to Business* Web site at **www.introbus.glencoe.com**, and click on *BusinessWeek* Feature Story, Chapter 25.

How to Get and Keep Credit

Learning Objectives

After completing this chapter, you'll be able to:

1. **Name** the five factors creditors use to consider credit worthiness.
2. **Identify** the types of credit you can use.
3. **Explain** some of the costs involved in paying for credit.
4. **Describe** how to maintain a good credit rating.

Why It's Important

Credit can enhance your life if used properly, or it can cause major problems if used improperly.

Key Words

credit bureau	finance
credit limit	charge
cosigner	variable rate
down payment	cash
principal	advance
secured loan	grace period
unsecured loan	garnishment
annual percent-	of wages
age rate	repossess

BusinessWeek Feature Story

Majoring in Debt

Many College Students Aren't Ready for Plastic.
Daniel Peña graduated from the University of California at Riverside last year with a degree in biology—and almost $10,000 in credit-card debt. He had used his three Visas, two MasterCards, and one Discover card to charge books, a computer, video and stereo gear, restaurant meals, and clothing. "I couldn't even make the minimum payment each month," says Peña, 24, who abandoned plans to go to medical school to take a job in computers. "It's going to take me a few years of living frugally before I'm debt-free."

Source: Excerpted with permission from "Majoring in Debt," *BusinessWeek Online*, September 25, 2000.

An Extension Activity

It takes time to build a good credit history. You can begin by applying for a department store or gas station credit card. These are easier to qualify for. Why do you think it's important to pay your credit card bills on time?

BUSINESS Online
The Full Story

To learn more about credit cards, visit the *Introduction to Business* Web site at **www.introbus.glencoe.com**, and click on *BusinessWeek* Feature Story, Chapter 26.

Getting Credit

Credit card applications bombard just about everyone's mailbox weekly. The average college student has about three credit cards and is $1,843 in debt. You should try not to use credit if you can, but sometimes it's unavoidable. You might need to get a student loan or finance a car. You might want to keep a credit card around for convenience or for emergencies. If you do decide to get a credit card, there are several things you need to know.

Figure 26.1 — CREDIT APPLICATION

➡The information you put on a credit application gives the creditor information about where you live and work. It allows the creditor to access financial information about you from a credit bureau. **How old must you be to apply for this credit card? How do your choices influence your economic situation?**

CREDIT APPLICATION

PLEASE TELL US ABOUT YOURSELF
Your entries must consist of alpha-numeric characters only (e.g., characters such as "*", "$", and "#" will not be accepted in some fields).

First Name: _Jody_   M.I.: _S_   Last Name: _Meir_
SSN: _320_ - _46_ - _3555_   Home Phone: _123_ - _456_ - _7890_
Address Line 1: _26 Elmwood Drive_
Address Line 2: _____
City: _Des Moines_   State: _IA_
Zip Code: _50313_ - _____
(You must be a U.S. resident to apply. No P.O. Boxes please)

Lived There: _2_ years _0_ months
Date of Birth: _03/12/1989_ (MM/DD/YYYY)
(You must be 18 or older to be considered for a First USA credit card)

Dependents: _0_
(Excluding yourself)

Mother's Maiden Name: _Greer_

E-mail Address: _—_

If you provide us with your e-mail address, when you become a First USA Card-member, we'll keep you informed about upcoming special values via e-mail.

PLEASE TELL US ABOUT YOUR JOB
(If retired, note previous employer. If self-employed, note nature of business.)

Employer: _ABC Supplies_   Position: _Clerk_
Worked There: _1_ years _3_ months
Work Phone: _800_ - _555_ - _0987_

PLEASE PROVIDE SOME FINANCIAL INFORMATION
**Alimony, child support, or separate maintenance income need not be revealed if you do not wish it to be considered as a basis for repaying this obligation.

Annual Household Income: $ _16,000_ .00
Please select the type(s) of bank account(s) you have: _Checking_
Select Residence: _Rent_   Monthly Rent or Mortgage: $ _600_ .00

2ND CARDHOLDER
Yes, please send a second card at no extra cost for:

First Name: _—_   M.I.: _—_   Last Name: _—_

Picking a Credit Card

The main consideration in choosing a credit card is the cost of credit, which will be discussed later. Besides costs there are other features to consider. Who accepts the card? What is the amount you can charge to meet your needs? Can you use the card to get cash? Some cards offer benefits such as rebates or refunds on a percentage of how much you charge. Other cards offer free travel or contributions to a charity after you charge a certain amount.

Applying for Credit

To open a credit or charge account, you'll have to fill out an application form. Figure 26.1 is a sample of a credit application you might fill out. The form asks for information about where you live, where you work, and what other credit you've received. It'll also ask questions about your income and how much savings you have. If a company accepts your application, you'll receive a security agreement. The agreement explains how interest will be charged on the account. When you sign your name on it, you agree to follow the rules described in the agreement.

Your Credit Worthiness: The Five Cs

Before creditors give you a charge or credit account, they want to make sure you're worth the risk. There are several factors they consider, which are usually referred to as the "five Cs of credit."

Capacity. One of the first things creditors consider is your capacity to pay. If you already have a large amount of debt, creditors will be unlikely to give you more credit. To determine your ability to pay, they'll check to see whether you have a job, how much you make, and how long you've been employed.

Character. Creditors want to know what kind of person you're before they lend money to you. They might ask for *credit references* from businesses or people you've borrowed from in the past who can testify to your reliability.

Credit History. The creditor then checks with a **credit bureau**, an agency that collects information about you and other credit consumers. Your credit bureau report tells whether you pay your bills on time or have failed to pay debts. It also indicates the amount of debt that you have.

Real-World Application

part **1** of 4

ROAD TRIP TO MARFA
You might know the trilemma of teenagers—a little money, no car, and you need a vacation. This summer you and your friends want to go to the West Texas desert to see the Ghost Lights of Marfa, the small, unidentifiable lights in the sky. You've been working a part-time job during the school year and saved money for a car. Your dad says he'll help pay for half of the car. He suggests you get a credit card to help finance your future purchase. **How creditworthy do you think you are?**

continued on p. 423

How Smart Is Your Card?

A smart card is a small plastic card that contains a computer. It carries information on an imbedded chip. People can use smart cards to buy items online, to enter a theater, or even to buy their school lunches. You decide to add an account to your card, like your favorite clothing store. You can get rid of any account whenever you want. After graduating from high school you won't want that school lunch account anymore.

Thinking Critically
How is a credit card different from a smart card?

Capital. Your capital is how much you have beyond what you owe. It includes cash, savings, investments, and possessions. Creditors want to know if you have enough capital so that if you lose your job, you can still pay them back with savings or by selling something.

Collateral. Collateral is like capital in that it consists of property or valuables. Unlike capital, collateral is used as security for a loan. If you fail to pay back a loan, the creditor can take whatever you put up as security, such as a house, car, or boat.

Your Credit Limit

The creditor will take into account all these factors to decide how much you can borrow. The maximum amount you can spend or charge on a credit account is your **credit limit**. If you have a $1,000 credit limit, you won't be able to charge more than that amount. If you pay your bills regularly, the creditor will often increase your credit limit.

Cosigners

If you have no credit history, a poor credit rating, or no collateral, you can still get a credit card or loan by having someone cosign it for you. This person, a **cosigner**, is responsible for a loan if you don't make the payments. A cosigner might be a relative or a close friend who not only knows you, but also knows you can be relied on to pay your debts.

✓ Fast Review

1. What kinds of things can be used as collateral for a loan?
2. What is a credit limit?
3. What is the responsibility of a cosigner?
4. List the five Cs of credit.

Using Credit

Credit cards and charge accounts are convenient ways to make inexpensive purchases. For expensive items, such as cars, furniture, and appliances, many consumers spread out the cost over a period of months or even years by taking out a loan. Loans from banks usually cost less in interest than credit cards or other sources of credit.

Installment Loans

If you buy a car or large appliance in an installment plan, you might have to make a down payment. The **down payment** is a portion of the total cost that you pay when you purchase a product. The **principal** is the amount of money you still owe and on which the interest is based. For example, if you buy a used car for $5,000 you might be required to pay $1,000 up front and pay the rest in installments. The $1,000 is the down payment and the remaining $4,000 is the principal.

Cash Loans

Cash loans can be obtained from banks, credit unions, savings and loans, and finance companies. A cash loan can be used to purchase an item anywhere and is paid back like an installment loan. Bank credit cards, such as VISA®, are another source of cash loans. In this case, the payments are billed on a monthly credit card statement. The interest charged for cash loans varies widely. Some people get cash loans from their credit cards because they're unable to get a cash loan from the other sources.

Secured and Unsecured Loans

When you receive an installment loan or a cash loan, you must sign a written agreement to repay the loan within a certain period of time. If the loan is backed by collateral, it's called a **secured loan**. If not, then it's called an **unsecured loan**. Because of the increased risk, the interest charges on an unsecured loan are often higher than on a secured loan.

✓ **Fast Review** _____

1. If you make a $500 down payment on furniture that costs $2,000, what is the $1,500 that you still owe called?
2. What is the difference between a secured loan and an unsecured loan?

Paying for Credit

Before you take out a loan or apply for a credit card, you should figure out the costs to see if you can afford it. Different cards have different interest rates. There are also different types of fees and other charges you might not have realized.

Real-World Application
part **2** of 4

ROAD TRIP TO MARFA
Lately you've been doing more chores around the house even before your dad asks you. While this shows responsibility it's not going to convince a credit card company you're worth its risk. You have no credit history and the credit card company needs evidence that you're good on your promise to pay.
What can you do to get that credit card?

continued on p. 425

Annual Percentage Rate

What's the best way to gauge the cost of credit? Look at the **annual percentage rate (APR)**. This percentage rate determines the cost of your credit on a yearly basis. For example, an APR of 18 percent means that for each $100 you owe, you pay $18 per year or $1.50 per month. The amount of interest you pay in a year depends on the interest rate, the total length of the loan, and the amount of the loan.

Finance Charges

According to law, each lender must indicate the APR and the finance charge of a loan. The **finance charge** is the total amount it costs you to finance the loan stated in dollars and cents. It includes the interest and any other charges, such as an application fee. This law was passed so consumers would have a way to compare prices for credit. Figure 26.2 illustrates how these charges might appear on your credit card statement each month.

Figure 26.2

SAMPLE OF A CREDIT CARD STATEMENT

➡ Credit card statements are required to show certain pieces of information, such as the APR, periodic rate, method of calculating the finance charge, and the finance charge. **What is the periodic and annual interest rate on this account? How much interest was charged for this billing cycle?**

Credit Is U
America's Credit Card Company

Account Number:	000 000 0
Payment Due Date:	2-19-01
Minimum Payment:	236.08
Total Amount Due:	1,124.17
Amount Enclosed:	_____

Cardmember Name:
Tim Gray
1562 W. Wells Way
Lakeland, FL 33803

Mail Payment to: PO Box 00000000
Newark, DE 19716

Detach and mail this portion with your check or money order to the address above.
Do not staple or fold.

Account Number	Billing Date	Payment Due Date	Days in Billing Period
000 00 0	01-25-01	02-19-01	32

Date	Reference Number	Description	Amount
1-14-01	01010101	CD Haven	22.30
1-21-01	02020202	Pizza, Etc.	8.33

Credit Line $7,500   Credit Available: $6,336

Previous Balance	- Payments & Credits	+ Finance Charge	+ Purchases	= New Balance	Minimum Payment
1,072.30	.00	21.24	30.63	1,124.17	236.08

The finance charge is determined by applying a periodic rate of	Which is an ANNUAL PERCENTAGE RATE of	To that part of the balance subject to finance charge of up to	Balance computation methods shown on reverse side
.05754% Daily	21.00%	Entire Balance	Method 2

Purchases, returns, and payments made just prior to billing date may not appear until next month's statement.

Inquiries: Send inquiries (not payment) to: PO Box 222, Denver, CO 80202
Notice: See reverse side for important information.

424

For example, the used car you want costs $5,000. You don't have enough money, so you make a $1,000 down payment and pay the other $4,000 in installments. The installments cost you $160 a month for 36 months. Your total cost on the car comes to $6,760. The extra $1,760 you pay ($6,760–$5,000) is the finance charge, or the amount you pay in interest.

Changes in Interest Rates

It's important to note whether or not the interest rate will change on a credit card or loan. With a **variable rate**, the rate changes as interest rates in the banking system change. For example, banks might change the rate they charge for home loans to adjust for inflation. With a *fixed rate*, the interest rate always remains the same.

You should beware of introductory rates creditors offer. In many cases, a credit card might offer a low introductory rate like 3 percent. After a few months, however, the rate might jump up to 20 percent. If you charged some big items and didn't pay off your card before the rate changed, you're stuck with a much higher interest rate than you expected.

Fees

In some cases, you have to pay an application fee for a card to cover the cost of a credit check. Some companies charge an annual fee to use their card that can range from $20 to $80 or more per year. There is often a separate fee for a cash advance. With a **cash advance** you borrow money on a credit card rather than use it to make a purchase. A late or missed payment fee is charged when you miss a payment or don't make a payment on time. This fee can be a lot and is added to the balance you owe. Fees are charged in addition to interest and added to the total amount interest is calculated on.

Grace Period

The **grace period** is amount of time you get to pay off a debt without having to pay interest charges. If you pay the total amount you owe by the due date, you won't be charged any interest. This is the one case where credit doesn't cost money. Cards also have a grace period for making a late payment before extra interest is charged or the card is cancelled.

Fast Review

1. Why should you beware of low introductory interest rates?
2. What are some types of fees credit cards charge?

Real-World Application

part 3 of 4

ROAD TRIP TO MARFA
After the credit card application process and the company's approval, you're ready to go car shopping with dad. Two test drives and a mechanic's assessment later, you've found your first car. The car costs $4,000. You've got a $3,000 down payment between you and your dad.
When using credit to pay for the balance, what types of fees do you need to remember?

continued on p. 427

Keeping Credit

Someday you might want to get a loan for a major expense, such as a house or a business. You also might want to increase your credit limit or apply for another credit card. To continue using credit or to get new credit, you need to maintain a good credit rating. If you always make your payments on time, you'll probably have an excellent credit rating. If not, your credit rating will be poor. Creditors are happy to extend credit to people with a good rating, but refuse those with a poor rating.

Your Credit Burden

You need to consider how much credit you can afford. Experts in personal finance say that you shouldn't use more than 20 percent of your income for credit payments. Suppose you get your first full-time job for $2,000 a month. After taxes are taken out, you bring home $1,500. You already have two monthly loan payments—$120 for a student loan and $160 for a car payment. You see a new entertainment system you just can't resist and could get it by paying $50 a month over three years. Can you afford it? No. Twenty percent of your income is $300. Your total payments each month would be $330, which is more than 20 percent.

You Make the Call

A Little Garnishment on That?

You're a financial advisor in Springville. One of your clients, Sophia Rocca, has two young children and works at the local ice cream shop. She has a fairly high credit card debt, has bounced several checks, and her work is seasonal. With your help, she is trying to reorganize her finances and start saving money to go to a two-year technical college.

Rocca wants to buy a used car. She brings you a contract for a loan to look over. The used car salesman is also one of your clients. You notice clauses in the contract that indicate if she is late with one repayment of the loan, the lender/car salesman can either repossess the car, demand full payment of the loan, or garnish Rocca's wages. You have faith that Rocca will pay despite her past financial problems.

Making an Ethical Decision

1. Who is your client in this situation?
2. What choices does Rocca have?
3. What advice would you give her? What explanation would you provide for that advice?

Making the Minimum Payment

Each credit card statement always includes a *minimum payment* you have to make on a bill. For example, if you owe $2,000 on a credit card, you might have to make a minimum payment of $50 each month. Many people think they can get by just making the minimum payment. To pay off a credit card debt of $2,500 at 18.9 percent interest, however, it would take over 30 years if you only make the minimum required payment. The total interest would be more than $7,800. You should always pay more than the minimum payment and pay off a debt as soon as possible.

Overextending Your Credit

One problem that could occur is that once you reach your credit limit on a card, you might be tempted to use another credit card. The more credit cards you have, the more you might be tempted to make impulse purchases. You can quickly reach the credit limit on several cards. If this happens, eventually you can't charge any more on your cards and it becomes a struggle just to make the minimum payments on them each month. Additionally, you wouldn't have credit available for emergencies.

Credit Problems

Do you have trouble making even the minimum monthly payment on your credit card bills? Do you receive second or third payment due notices from creditors? If so, these are two warning signs that you might be in financial trouble. Late payments, missed payments, too much credit, and other problems can give you a bad credit rating. If you want to borrow money to buy a house or a car, you might have a hard time because creditors consider you too much of a risk.

Misusing credit can also lead to more immediate problems. Some credit contracts allow the creditor to take all or part of your paycheck if you miss a payment. This is called **garnishment of wages**. If you put up something valuable as collateral on a loan, such as a car, a creditor has the legal right to **repossess** it, or take back the collateral. The creditor then sells the car to someone else to obtain the money you still owe.

ROAD TRIP TO MARFA
You and your friends are heading south on Highway 17 to Marfa. The gas gauge points ever closer to empty and you're all hungry. There's not much around in the vast flat landscape, so you decide to stop at this one roadside gas station and diner. You pay for your bill with a credit card. The waitress processes your card and it comes through as rejected.
What are the keys to keeping your credit intact?

✔ Fast Review

1. What is the highest percentage of your income that personal finance experts say you should spend on credit payments?
2. What is garnishment of wages?

Picture This...

How a Magnetic Strip Is Read

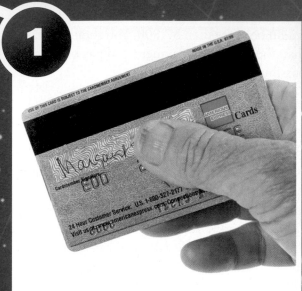

1. Your credit card has a magnetic stripe on the back of it, which stores tiny bits of encoded information.

2. As you "swipe" or insert your card in a machine, the machine's head reads the information on the magnetic stripe.

3. The machine sends the information to the cash register, or point of sale (POS) terminal.

4. The POS terminal contacts a credit card database via modem to verify the information on the card.

5. The database sends back a message to the POS terminal accepting or rejecting the card.

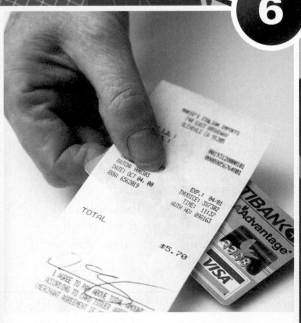

6. If the card is accepted, the cashier completes the transaction.

Now *You* Take a Shot...

Don't Try This on a Credit Card
The strip on the back of a credit card is like a piece of videotape. Get an old videotape and an ordinary refrigerator magnet. Wipe the magnet across a segment of the videotape and then play that portion of the tape. What happened? Why do you think this happened?

Summary

1. The "five Cs" creditors use to consider a borrower's credit worthiness are capacity to pay, character, credit history, capital, and collateral.

2. The types of credit you can use include installment loans, cash loans, secured loans, and unsecured loans.

3. The costs of credit include an annual percentage rate (APR) and different types of fees. The total cost of credit for a purchase is called the finance charge.

4. To maintain a good credit rating, you should spend less than 20 percent of your income on credit payments, make more than the minimum payment each month, and avoid overextending your credit.

Using Business Key Words

When establishing and using a credit card, it's important to know the following terms. Match each term to its definition.

- **credit bureau**
- **credit limit**
- **cosigner**
- **down payment**
- **finance charge**
- **principal**
- **annual percentage rate (APR)**
- **secured loan**
- **grace period**
- **unsecured loan**
- **repossess**
- **garnishment of wages**
- **variable rate**
- **cash advance**

1. A loan that is backed by collateral.
2. A loan that is not backed by collateral.
3. An agency that collects information about you and other credit consumers.
4. This determines the cost of your credit on a yearly basis.
5. The amount of money owed and upon which the interest is calculated.
6. The number of days available to pay a credit card balance without having any interest charged.
7. An initial portion of the total cost paid with cash or with a check.
8. Someone who agrees to make payments on a loan if you fail to do so.
9. The cost of credit stated in dollars and cents.
10. A type of loan where the rate changes as interest rates in the banking system change.
11. The maximum amount you can spend or charge on a credit account.
12. The legal right to take back collateral.
13. Something you get when you borrow money on a credit card rather than use it to make a purchase.
14. When a creditor takes all or part of your paycheck if you miss credit card payments.

Review What You Learned

15. How can credit make your life easier?

16. Why is it important to comparison shop when you enter the credit market?

17. Why do creditors look at the amount of collateral you have before deciding whether or not to loan you money?

18. What do creditors use your credit rating for when deciding whether or not to loan you money?

19. Why is the interest rate charged on an unsecured loan often higher than that charged on a secured loan?

20. What does the law require a lender to provide to a consumer when he or she is considering borrowing money?

21. What should you consider when looking at the cost of a credit card?

22. What is a secured credit loan? Who are they marketed to?

23. Explain the three ways finance charges are calculated on unpaid credit card balances.

24. What is one of the primary causes of debt problems?

Understanding Business Concepts

25. When a person uses credit, is he or she really borrowing money? Explain your answer.

26. "The real benefit of credit cards comes when a consumer pays his or her bill in full each month." What does this mean?

27. Would you be willing to cosign on a loan for your best friend? Why or why not?

28. What is the best way for consumers to compare interest rates?

29. Why is making the minimum payment on credit card bills a bad idea?

Critical Thinking

30. Survey a number of adults on their opinions about buying expensive items. Do they favor using credit for such purchases? For what types of items would they pay cash only? Write a summary of your survey.

31. What criteria would you use in choosing a credit card?

32. Do you agree that you should always pay off a debt as soon as possible? Why or why not?

Viewing and Representing

Examining the Image. Make a list of everything you see in this photograph. Describe what you think is happening in this picture. Has anyone ever asked you for a loan? What factors made you decide to say yes or no? If you loaned money, how and when would you expect the person to repay the loan?

Chapter 26 Review

Building Academic Skills

 Investigating Credit

As a group, choose a high-priced item such as a used car, a sound system, or a computer system that would probably be purchased on credit. Each team member should investigate the terms of credit from a different credit source, such as commercial banks, credit unions, or savings and loans. Consider these questions:

- Is credit available from the seller?
- Is a down payment required?
- What is the annual percentage rate?
- What would the monthly payments be?

Make a chart of the information that you and your team have gathered. Use the chart to decide which source offers the best credit terms. Write a paragraph describing your group's decision.

 Determining Finance Charges

Select two different credit card applications in local stores or banks. Check their monthly finance charges and their annual percentage rates. Using the information from each of the applications, determine for each of the cards how long it would take to pay off $700 if you made a $75 payment each month. What would you pay in finance charges for each of the cards? Create a table to compare the numbers and write a short paragraph explaining which card you would choose and why.

 Creating a Spreadsheet

Many installment loans require a percentage of the total price as a down payment. Use spreadsheet software to set up a spreadsheet to compute the down payment for each of the items in the table below.

Item	Price	Required Down Payment	Amount of Down Payment
CD Player	$ 295	10%	$
Color TV	298	10%	
Electric Stove	489	20%	
Desk and Chair	263	15%	
Used Car	5,495	25%	
Sofa	995	17%	

HISTORY **Oral Presentation**

Research the history of consumer credit in the United States. Find out when and why it started. Then, give an oral presentation with at least one visual aid.

Linking School to Home

Composing a Letter. Imagine a family member or a friend received his or her credit card statement and it contained an error. Help write a letter to the credit card company requesting a correction. Compose the letter using a word processor.

Linking School to Work

Write About a Credit Counselor. Research the career of a credit counselor. Find out what the job entails, the skills the counselor should have, what education is required, and the salary range for an entry-level counselor. Investigate the certification offered by the National Foundation for Consumer Credit. Write a one-page paper with your findings.

E-Homework

Applying Technology

Multimedia Presentation. Unfortunately, a majority of young people are in debt. There are plenty of professionals out there with books and advice on debt management. Use the Internet to research information about debt or debt management. Create a computerized presentation of your findings.

Searching for Consumer Credit. Use the Internet to locate Web sites that provide consumer credit information. Select five sites you think are the best and explain why.

Connecting Academics

Math. The safe debt load—the debt a person can take on after accounting for all necessary expenses—is often estimated by subtracting total expenses from after-tax income and dividing the difference by three. Devon's annual take-home pay is $23,980. This year he estimates $4,800 for housing, $4,900 for food, $1,280 for transportation, and $950 for clothes. What is Devon's safe debt load?

Math. Imagine you've charged a lot on your credit cards. You're earning a good salary and you feel it's up to you to become more financially responsible. What is your plan of action to become debt free?

Social Science. Many items can be bought with cash, with installment payments, or with a credit card. Decide what you think is the best way to purchase each of the following items: a swimming pool, a bag of groceries, a car, a pair of shoes, a refrigerator, books for school, a sofa and chair, and a CD player. Give reasons for each option that you choose.

BusinessWeek Analyzing the Feature Story

You read the first part of "Majoring in Debt" at the beginning of this chapter. Below are a few questions for you to answer about credit cards. You'll find the answers to these questions when you're reading the entire article. First, here are the questions:

33. Why are consumer advocates concerned about college kids having and using credit cards?

34. What is one common trick that credit card companies use?

CREATIVE JOURNAL ACTIVITY

Visit the financial center of the *BusinessWeek* Web site. Explore different credit card types, and compare the features of each. Interview an adult to learn more about what credit card he or she uses and why.

BUSINESS Online
The Full Story

To learn more about credit cards, visit the *Introduction to Business* Web site at **www.introbus.glencoe.com**, and click on *BusinessWeek* Feature Story, Chapter 26.

Chapter 27

Your Credit and the Law

● Learning Objectives

After completing this chapter, you'll be able to:

1. **Explain** how government protects credit rights.
2. **Name** federal laws that protect consumers.
3. **Identify** consumers' credit rights.
4. **Describe** credit problems.

● Why It's Important

To maintain a good credit rating you have specific rights and protections under the law.

● Key Words

usury law
Consumer Credit
   Protection Act
truth-in-lending disclosure
Equal Credit Opportunity Act
Fair Credit Reporting Act
Fair Credit Billing Act
collection agent
Fair Debt Collection
   Practices Act (FDCPA)
credit counselor
consolidation loan
bankruptcy

BusinessWeek Feature Story

Credit Cards: Entrepreneurs Are Tapping Them More Than Ever

Small Businesses to Qualify for Credit. When Paul Baum started his computer hardware company in 1991, he did what new entrepreneurs have long done: He whipped out his credit cards for instant financing.

Seven years later, he's still plunking down plastic—4 cards now, down from a high of 15, with credit lines totaling more than $2 million. Says Baum, CEO of Rumarson Technologies Inc. in Kenilworth, N.J.: "I've never had a bank loan." He has a $1.8 million bank credit line, which charges ¼-percentage point over the prime rate the moment he taps it. Still, he prefers his cards because by paying the balance every month, the financing is free.

Source: Excerpted with permission from "Credit Cards: Entrepreneurs Are Tapping Them More Than Ever," *Business Week Online*, December 14, 1998.

An Extension Activity

What concerns might you have in using credit as opposed to cash? Create a table with the pros and cons of using credit.

The Full Story

To learn more about the use of credit cards, visit the *Introduction to Business* Web site at **www.introbus.glencoe.com**, and click on *BusinessWeek* Feature Story, Chapter 27.

Continuing Your Creditworthiness

If you have more than one credit card, it's important not to accumulate more debt after you pay off your cards. It's not advisable to have more than one credit card open with no balance. Before you get into trouble you may want to close the accounts.

While credit is widely used, relying on credit has created certain problems. Billing mistakes, unfair credit charges, and misleading claims are just a few problems that consumers face. The government has passed laws to protect consumers from credit abuses. See Figure 27.1 to see where consumers can go if they have a complaint.

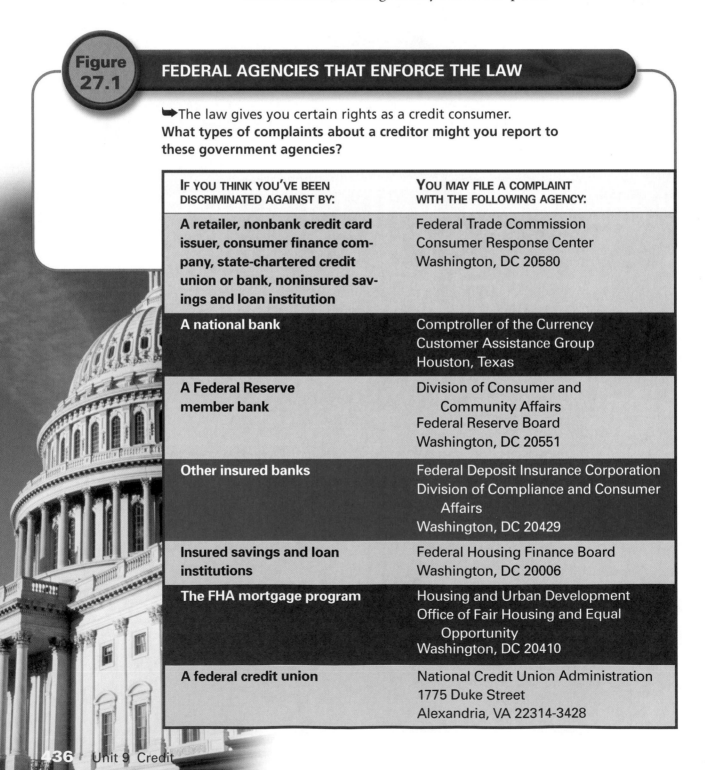

Figure 27.1

FEDERAL AGENCIES THAT ENFORCE THE LAW

➡The law gives you certain rights as a credit consumer.
What types of complaints about a creditor might you report to these government agencies?

IF YOU THINK YOU'VE BEEN DISCRIMINATED AGAINST BY:	YOU MAY FILE A COMPLAINT WITH THE FOLLOWING AGENCY:
A retailer, nonbank credit card issuer, consumer finance company, state-chartered credit union or bank, noninsured savings and loan institution	Federal Trade Commission Consumer Response Center Washington, DC 20580
A national bank	Comptroller of the Currency Customer Assistance Group Houston, Texas
A Federal Reserve member bank	Division of Consumer and Community Affairs Federal Reserve Board Washington, DC 20551
Other insured banks	Federal Deposit Insurance Corporation Division of Compliance and Consumer Affairs Washington, DC 20429
Insured savings and loan institutions	Federal Housing Finance Board Washington, DC 20006
The FHA mortgage program	Housing and Urban Development Office of Fair Housing and Equal Opportunity Washington, DC 20410
A federal credit union	National Credit Union Administration 1775 Duke Street Alexandria, VA 22314-3428

Protecting Your Credit Rights

To protect consumers, both the federal and state governments control and regulate the credit industry. Most states, for example, have set a maximum on the interest rates that may be charged for certain types of credit. A law restricting the amount of interest that can be charged for credit is called a **usury law**.

Concern about consumer problems has also resulted in the passage of a series of federal laws. Among other things, these laws help inform consumers about the costs of credit. They also set rules and regulations concerning the credit application process, credit history information, privacy, and debt collection.

Consumer Credit Protection Act

At one time, consumers who bought with credit didn't know how much the credit would cost. To make comparing credit costs easier, Congress passed the **Consumer Credit Protection Act**, also known as the Truth in Lending Law. It requires creditors to inform consumers about the costs and terms of credit and it protects consumers if their credit cards are lost or stolen.

Truth-in-Lending Disclosure. The most important part of the Consumer Credit Protection Act is the requirement that all costs of borrowing be made known to the consumer. **Truth-in-lending disclosure** provides the costs that a creditor gives to a borrower. Costs must be expressed in two ways. One is the dollar cost of credit, or the total finance charge. The other is the annual percentage rate (APR). A truth-in-lending disclosure shows the total finance charge so the borrower can determine whether buying on credit is worth the extra cost.

In addition, the disclosure shows the APR so the borrower can compare it with interest rates at various banks, credit unions, and finance companies. The truth-in-lending disclosure also states the credit terms and conditions. For instance, what happens if a payment is late? Is the finance charge reduced if the loan is paid off earlier than agreed? If so, how much is the finance charged reduced? Is there a penalty for paying off the loan ahead of time?

Advertising Credit. Another important condition in the Truth in Lending Law involves the advertising of credit. An advertisement must

Real-World Application

part 1 of 4

IDENTITY CRISIS: PROTECT YOURSELF
Experts say that nearly half-a-million people are victims of identity theft each year. Identity theft is the fastest growing type of robbery. Thieves steal your identity and then they start opening credit cards and charging away. Federal law limits consumer liability to $50 for credit card fraud. **How might this affect your credit history?**

continued on p. 439

tell the number of payments, the amount, and the period of payments if the amount of the down payment is given. In other words, if an advertisement offers credit at $10 down and $2 a week payment, the number of weeks must also be given.

Protecting Card Owners. Finally, the Truth in Lending Law protects credit card customers. If your card is lost or stolen and is used by someone else, your payment for any unauthorized purchases is limited to $50. Some credit card companies don't make you pay the $50 if you report the loss immediately. Also, credit card companies aren't allowed to send cards to consumers who didn't request a credit card.

Equal Credit Opportunity Act

When you apply for a loan or a credit card, you must provide certain information. This information is used to determine whether you're a good credit risk. The **Equal Credit Opportunity Act** says that the application can be judged only on the basis of financial responsibility. No person can be denied credit on the basis of gender, age, ethnicity, or religion. It allows only three reasons for denying credit: (1) low income, (2) large current debts, and (3) a poor record of making payments in the past.

The Equal Credit Opportunity Act also requires that all credit applicants be informed of whether their application has been accepted or rejected within 30 days. Any person who is denied credit must be given a written statement listing the reasons why.

Fair Credit Reporting Act

When you apply for and use credit, the information goes into a file at one or more credit bureaus. As you learned in Chapter 26, a credit bureau is an agency that collects and maintains information about the paying habits of consumers. Figure 27.2 on page 440 provides a checklist for building and protecting your credit history. Lenders rely heavily on credit reports when they consider loan applications.

A credit file includes personal, employment, and financial information. In the past, there was concern about the accuracy of credit file information. Inaccurate or false information was often included in a file. For these and other reasons, the **Fair Credit Reporting Act** was passed.

Right to Know. The Fair Credit Reporting Act gives you the right to know what's in your credit file. If incorrect information is found, it must be removed from your file after the situation is examined. If there's disagreement between you and the business that made the statement, you have the right to have your version of the situation placed in your file.

For example, suppose you stopped payments on a stereo system because you believed it was defective and you informed the store of your concerns. The store where you bought the system might report that you missed a payment. Both your version and the store's version must be included in your credit file if no agreement is reached.

Right to Be Notified. The Fair Credit Reporting Act also states that you must be notified when an investigation is being conducted on your credit record. If you're denied credit, insurance, or a job because of a credit report, you must be given the name and address of the credit bureau that provided the report.

Right to Privacy. The privacy of the information in your credit file is important. According to the law, only authorized persons can see a copy of your credit report. People can legally obtain your credit report when you apply for additional credit, a job, or insurance.

Fair Credit Billing Act

Every month millions of credit card and charge account customers receive their monthly statements. Most of the time these bills are correct, but sometimes a billing error can occur. An error might be due to a computer problem. There might be an incorrect amount for a charge. The **Fair Credit Billing Act** requires creditors to correct billing mistakes brought to their attention. The law also requires that consumers be informed of the steps they need to take to get an error corrected.

Notify the Creditor. The first step in correcting errors is to notify the creditor in writing. In the letter, you must give your name, account number, an explanation of the error, and the amount of the error. The creditor must either correct the error or explain in writing why the account is correct. If the creditor made the mistake, you don't have to pay any finance charge on the amount in error. If there was no error, you might have to pay a fee for any late payments.

Stop Payment. The Fair Credit Billing Act permits consumers to stop a credit card payment for items that are damaged or defective. Before stopping payment, however, you must attempt to return the item to the place where you bought it. A creditor that fails to follow the rules that apply to correcting any billing errors will automatically give up the amount owed on the item in question and any finance charge on it, up to a combined total of $50. This is true even if the bill is correct.

Real-World Application

part **2** of 4

IDENTITY CRISIS: PROTECT YOURSELF
If you believe that an identity thief has accessed your bank account, close the account immediately. If your checks are stolen or misused, stop payment on them.
What do you think you should do if your debit card is lost or stolen?

continued on p. 441

Fair Debt Collection Practices Act

A **collection agent** is a person or business that has the job of collecting overdue bills. This agent might contact consumers who get behind in their credit payments. At one time, collection agents could use almost any method they chose to collect overdue bills. They could call

Figure 27.2

WHAT IF YOU'RE DENIED CREDIT?

➥Write the wrong. The law requires credit card companies to correct inaccurate or incomplete information in your credit report.
Is it best to request changes of incorrect information by letter rather than by phone?

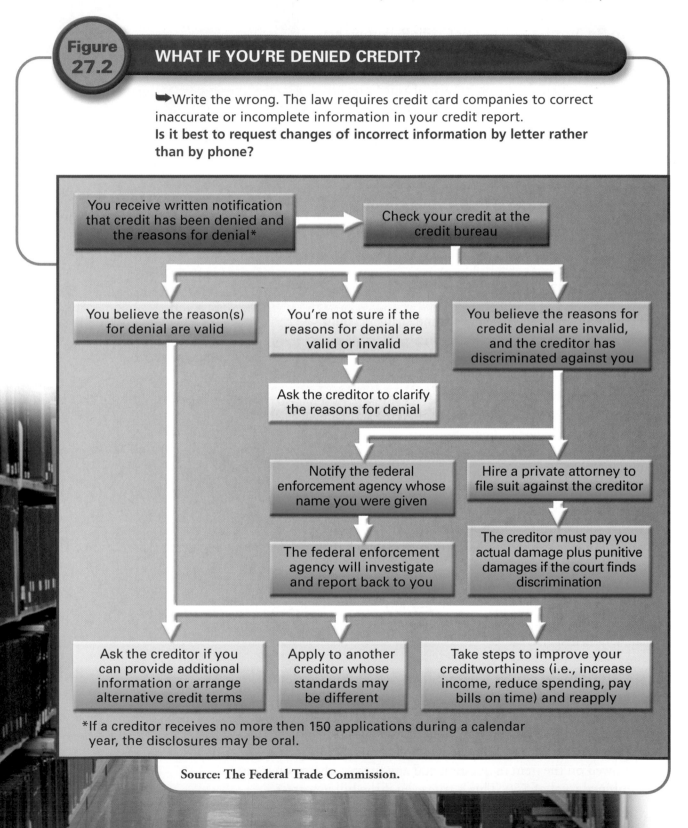

You receive written notification that credit has been denied and the reasons for denial* → Check your credit at the credit bureau

You believe the reason(s) for denial are valid

You're not sure if the reasons for denial are valid or invalid

You believe the reasons for credit denial are invalid, and the creditor has discriminated against you

Ask the creditor to clarify the reasons for denial

Notify the federal enforcement agency whose name you were given

Hire a private attorney to file suit against the creditor

The federal enforcement agency will investigate and report back to you

The creditor must pay you actual damage plus punitive damages if the court finds discrimination

Ask the creditor if you can provide additional information or arrange alternative credit terms

Apply to another creditor whose standards may be different

Take steps to improve your creditworthiness (i.e., increase income, reduce spending, pay bills on time) and reapply

*If a creditor receives no more then 150 applications during a calendar year, the disclosures may be oral.

Source: The Federal Trade Commission.

late at night, use threats of jail or seizing property, and even try to collect more than was owed. They could show up at your workplace and harass you for the money. The **Fair Debt Collection Practices Act (FDCPA)** made all of these practices illegal.

The FDCPA protects consumers from collection agents in several ways. First, collection agents must identify themselves to the people whose bills they're trying to collect. They can't tell others about the debt. This is considered a violation of privacy and is forbidden by the law. They can't contact a person at work if the employer doesn't permit it. If they use the phone, they can't keep calling all the time or pretend to be someone else. Finally, they can't state the amount of a debt on a postcard that a neighbor or someone else might see.

Enforcing the Laws

The federal government has established numerous agencies to regulate business activities. One agency is the *Federal Trade Commission (FTC)*. In addition to protecting competition, the FTC is responsible for enforcing the laws on credit. The FTC also helps consumers with credit problems. It handles complaints about being denied credit unfairly, being overcharged on a bill, or being bothered by collection agents. Several other federal government agencies deal with specific credit matters.

On the state level, you can contact your state banking department about credit problems. A consumer protection division of your state attorney general's office deals with complaints that other government agencies might not handle. Many city and local governments also have consumer credit protection agencies.

✔ **Fast Review** _____

1. What does the usury law do?
2. In what two ways must the costs of credit be expressed in a truth-in-lending disclosure?
3. What are the only three reasons a person can be denied credit according to the Equal Credit Opportunity Act?
4. Name the three rights the Fair Credit Reporting Act guarantees.
5. What does the Fair Debt Collection Practices Act prevent collection agents from doing?

IDENTITY CRISIS: PROTECT YOURSELF
Lost credit cards are a key element in credit card fraud. Make sure the vendor returns your card after a purchase. Unreturned cards can find their way into the wrong hands. It's also a good idea to keep a record of your credit card number. You should keep this record separate from your card. **If someone does steal your credit card, by federal law, how much are you responsible to pay?**

continued on p. 443

Handling Your Credit Problems

What can you do when you have a credit problem or when you've gone too far in your use of credit? Of course, it's best to avoid a credit problem in the first place. If you're already in trouble, however, there are ways to deal with your problem.

Credit Counseling

If you can't meet your payments, the first thing you should do is contact the creditor. Talk to the credit manager and try to work out a plan that will make your payments easier. Consumers who are unable to work out their own credit problems or who repeatedly have problems with credit should talk to a **credit counselor**. Credit counselors help consumers with their credit problems. They can help you revise your budget, contact creditors to arrange new payment plans, or help you find other sources of income.

Consolidating Debts

Another possible solution is to get a consolidation loan. A **consolidation loan** combines all your debts into one loan with lower payments. For example, suppose you have to make monthly payments on several credit cards, student loans, and a car. You can consolidate all your debts into one monthly payment. There are two problems with a consolidation loan, however. First, it usually has a high interest rate because people

You Make the Call

Collection Protection

A year ago, you launched a very successful catalog sales business that offers specialty children's clothing, Bubble Bee Knees. It even has its own credit card. Lately, however, you've gotten complaints from credit card customers. It seems the credit card company uses a recorded message to repeatedly call customers who don't pay their monthly bills.

Making an Ethical Decision

1. Does the credit card company have the right to call customers whose payment is overdue?
2. How does the Fair Debt Collection Practices Act protect customers?
3. Is a credit card company that uses recorded messages rather than live callers to collect late payments following the spirit of the law? Why or why not?

who get such loans are considered poor credit risks. Second, because there is only one monthly payment, you might feel that the credit problem is under control and start charging new purchases.

Bankruptcy

The last resort is to declare **bankruptcy**. This is a legal process in which you're relieved of your debts, but your creditors can take some or all of your assets, such as a car, savings, or business. Individuals or businesses can declare bankruptcy. When bankruptcy is declared, the debtor, the creditor, and a court-appointed trustee come up with a plan to repay the debt on an installment basis. You should avoid bankruptcy because it gives you a bad credit record. Recent changes in the law have also made it harder to declare bankruptcy.

Credit Services

Some companies will provide credit even if your credit rating is poor or if you have been denied credit in the past. Their interest rates or fees are much higher than banks, credit unions, or even finance companies. They might also require some form of collateral. Loans that offer a credit line for the value of a house require the house as collateral. The cost of the loan is often so high that borrowers end up losing their homes.

Others charge a fee to "clean up" your credit rating but they're seldom able to restore a bad credit rating. Accurate reports of missed payments or bankruptcy can't legally be removed from your credit report. If your credit rating has been unfairly damaged by inaccurate information, you can work with a credit agency or bureau to correct the errors.

There are also some very good credit companies that provide quality services for consumers. The Better Business Bureau will give you a complaint history if it already has a name. Also, the Chamber of Commerce will give you names of businesses, but it doesn't recommend one over another. Many reputable credit counselors offer their services at a very low fee.

IDENTITY CRISIS: PROTECT YOURSELF

Surfing the Internet is as typical as watching television and talking on the telephone. Increasing numbers of consumers shop, invest, and bank online. Before shopping online, sharpen your "fraud sensors."

How can you make sure all online transactions are secure?

✓ **Fast Review**

1. What are two problems with a consolidation loan?
2. What effect does declaring bankruptcy have?

Summary

1. Federal and state governments have passed laws to help consumers with credit problems. Federal agencies, including the Federal Trade Commission, enforce federal credit laws.

2. Federal laws that protect consumers include the Consumer Credit Protection Act, the Equal Credit Opportunity Act, the Fair Credit Reporting Act, the Fair Credit Billing Act, and the Fair Debt Collection Practices Act.

3. Consumers have the right to be informed of the terms and costs of credit, to know what's in their credit files, to have billing mistakes resolved, and to be protected from collection agents.

4. If you have credit problems, you can get credit counseling, get a consolidation loan, or declare bankruptcy.

Using Business Key Words

Credit is used every day in the United States. Laws have been written to protect consumers who use credit. Understanding the legal aspects of credit is important. See how many of these terms you know by matching each one with the correct statement below.

- **usury law**
- **Consumer Credit Protection Act**
- **truth-in-lending disclosure**
- **credit counselor**
- **collection agent**
- **consolidation loan**
- **Equal Credit Opportunity Act**
- **Fair Credit Reporting Act**
- **bankruptcy**
- **Fair Debt Collection Practices Act (FDCPA)**
- **Fair Credit Billing Act**

1. Person who has the job of collecting debts that are overdue.
2. Law designed to limit rates consumers can be charged for credit.
3. A document that informs consumers about all the costs of borrowing money.
4. A person who helps people with credit problems.
5. A loan that combines all of a person's debt.
6. A legal process in which some or all of the assets of the debtor are distributed among the creditors.
7. A law, also known as the Truth in Lending Law, that requires creditors to provide information about credit to consumers and protects consumers if their credit cards are lost or stolen.
8. A law against denying credit on the basis of gender, age, ethnicity, or religion.
9. A law giving people the right to know what is in their credit file at credit bureaus.
10. A law requiring creditors to correct billing mistakes brought to their attention.
11. A law that protects debtors from unfair methods or practices used by collection agents.

Review What You Learned

12. What problems do some people face because of their reliance on credit?
13. What should you do if you suspect there is an error on your credit card statement?
14. If your credit card is stolen and you report the loss immediately, what is the dollar amount of unauthorized charges that you'll be responsible for?
15. What is the purpose of a usury law?
16. How does a truth-in-lending disclosure help consumers compare credit costs?
17. Which act gives you the "right to know" what is in your credit file?
18. What is the responsibility of the FTC?
19. How does a credit counselor help people with their credit problems?
20. Why is bankruptcy a last resort for a consumer with debt problems?

Understanding Business Concepts

21. A person may be denied credit only if he or she has a low income, owes large sums of money, or has a poor credit record. Why do you think the Equal Credit Opportunity Act allows credit to be denied for these reasons? In what other ways does the act protect consumers?
22. You have applied for credit at a department store. The store has denied you credit because of your credit rating. Since you know that you have always paid your bills on time, what action should you take?
23. For a fee, you can receive a copy of the information in your credit file at the credit bureau. Why would you want to check your credit record?
24. How can the truth-in-lending disclosure help protect consumers from credit problems?

Critical Thinking

25. The Truth in Lending Law requires that consumers be given complete credit cost information in advertisements that mention credit sales. Decide whether each of the following credit information blurbs is complete. Explain your answers.
    * $20 down, $43 a month
    * Finance charge is $10 a month, 18.15 APR
    * $35 down, $14 a month for 2 years
    * Payments for 52 weeks and only $15 down payment
26. Do you think the federal government should have to pass so many credit protection laws? Shouldn't people take responsibility for themselves?

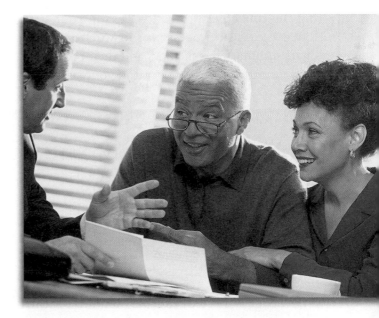

Viewing and Representing

Examining the Image. Team up with a partner. What details do you see in this photograph? What do you think these people are discussing? Discuss how life would be without credit protection under the law. What would be the effect on individuals? On businesses?

Building Academic Skills

 Contacting a Local Credit Counselor

As a team, contact a consumer credit counseling service in your area. Find out when it first began providing services. How have the requests for services changed over the years? Are there more requests or fewer requests? Then, find out if the service has copies of any educational materials about using credit wisely. If possible, obtain a copy.

COMPUTER TECHNOLOGY **Research and Chart the Law**

Use e-mail to contact your state consumer protection agency. Retrieve information regarding the consumer protection laws in your state. Then use word processing software to create a chart summarizing the laws and their provisions. Print out the chart and post it in your classroom.

LANGUAGE ARTS **Organized List of Agencies**

Using the local telephone book, compile a list of all the agencies that provide consumer credit protection for people in your community. Organize the list according to local, state, and federal agencies.

 Percentage Increase

Unfortunately, many people view bankruptcy as an easy way to solve their money problems. The total number of personal bankruptcies has risen over the past 40 years. Records indicate that there were approximately 180,000 bankruptcies filed in 1960 and 1,460,000 filed in 1999. What was the percentage of increase in bankruptcies during that time?

Linking School to Home

Stories Behind the Laws. Interview your family members and find out what they know about the credit protection laws. Ask them specifically about the Truth in Lending Law, the Equal Credit Opportunity Act, and the Fair Debt Collection Practices Act. If your family members' knowledge is limited, educate them. Ask them if they think the three reasons for denying credit under the Equal Credit Opportunity Act are fair. Would they add any others? Why or why not?

Linking School to Work

Role-Playing. You're a small business owner and some customers are behind in their payments. How might the Fair Debt Collection Practices Act affect your business attempts to collect the payments? Work with a partner to role-play a situation where a consumer with credit problems is confronted by you, the business owner.

E-Homework

Applying Technology

Internet Puzzle. Create an Internet scavenger hunt about managing credit, avoiding credit problems, and the laws designed to protect consumers. Locate Web sites that would be appropriate and provide clues for the players of your game.

FTC Web Site. Explore the Federal Trade Commission's Web site. Is the site user-friendly? What major topics are found on the site? Are there any links for children or students?

Connecting Academics

Math. States regulate the maximum annual interest rate that may be charged for credit cards. In Connecticut the maximum is 19.8 percent. In New Jersey it's 30 percent. Marika maintained a credit card balance of $750 for a year. If she lived in Connecticut, what is the amount of finance charge owed? What about in New Jersey?

Language Arts. You applied for a charge account at Rogers and Hall Department Store. The store turned down your application. You ask for an appointment with its credit department manager. Describe what preparation you'll make for the meeting. What documents will you take with you? How will you convince the manager that you're a good credit risk?

Language Arts. You're a credit counselor and your friend is seeking advice on a credit problem. After your friend explains the problem, you outline several strategies for dealing with it based on your education and experience. Explain some basic approaches on how your friend can handle the problems.

BusinessWeek Analyzing the Feature Story

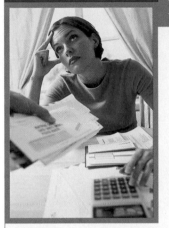

You read the first part of "Credit Cards: Entrepreneurs Are Tapping Them More Than Ever" at the beginning of this chapter. Below are a few questions for you to answer about the use of credit cards. You'll find the answers to these questions when you're reading the entire article. First, here are the questions:

27. Why are entrepreneurs using credit cards rather than more conventional funding options?

28. What is one of the risks of using credit cards to fund a business idea?

CREATIVE JOURNAL ACTIVITY

Break into groups with two other students. You're the product team for a credit card company that's launching a new card specifically aimed at small business owners. Create an advertisement for the card using the medium of print, video, or radio. What message will be most compelling to your target market? What are the advantages of using a credit card for entrepreneurial funding? Present your ad to the class.

BUSINESS Online
The Full Story

To learn more about the use of credit cards, visit the *Introduction to Business* Web site at **www.introbus.glencoe.com**, and click on *BusinessWeek* Feature Story, Chapter 27.

Using Credit to Start a Small Business

In Chapter 25 you learned about credit and the different places to get credit. Many, if not most, new businesses need credit to get started, and they need credit to keep their businesses growing. In this seminar you'll research how a person might use credit to start up a business.

Investigate the Images

Look at the photographic collage on the left page. What grabs your attention first? Is it the color or the words? The power in reading visuals is in analyzing and dissecting your observations. On a separate piece of paper, respond to the questions listed below. These questions might help sharpen the focus of your visual mind.

Your Observations

1. How many photographs do you see?

2. Examine each photograph. How are they assembled in relation to one another?

3. What is the subject of each photograph? Is place or location the subject?

4. Does color signify a message?

5. What issues do you take from these images?

Information

6. Summarize what you know about the photographs from your observations.

Exploring Culture

7. Federal and state laws prohibit banks or lending institutions from discriminating against clients based on ethnicity or gender. What options do you have if you've been discriminated against?

8. Minority-owned banks often focus on relationship building. Why might a first-generation immigrant entrepreneur choose to use this particular bank over another one when seeking start-up funds?

Factoids

Bigger Fish to Fry. Owners of Wahoo's Fish Taco received a $1.5-million line of credit from Merrill Lynch in order to expand its market in Southern California. It's competing for market share in fresh Mexican food, the fastest growing segment in the restaurant business.

Caller, You're on the Air. Due to dwindling federal funds, public radio broadcasting depends on corporate underwriting and fund-drive pledges to keep them thriving with news and entertaining programs. Have you supported your local public radio station today?

Learn the Language. It's tough to get a business loan if you don't know English or if you aren't familiar with American business practices. Anyone interested in starting a company must put together a business plan, tax returns, and personal financial statements, which can be a daunting task.

Coping with the Slowdown | Why You Can't Get DSL

THE RESOURCE FOR ENTREPRENEURS

Frontier

Minority Mergers

Big companies are suggesting—and sometimes insisting—that small suppliers team up to win major contracts

P&G brought together Woodrow Hall (left) and Robert Johnson

Taking Aim at Small Business

Preparation

Research how people use credit and other types of funding to start up a small business.

Objective

In this *BusinessWeek* Seminar, you'll:

- **Research** how small businesses raise money through credit.
- **Contact** the Small Business Administration (SBA) for information.
- **Create** a chart that describes some of the different SBA loans.

Materials Needed

- ✓ Copies of recent business news publications such as *BusinessWeek* or *Frontier*
- ✓ Access to the Internet and your local or school library
- ✓ Paper, pens, pencils
- ✓ Posterboard and markers

Procedures

1. With one or two partners, find and read articles about how small businesses raise money through credit. One resource is the "Small Business Guide" accessible at the *BusinessWeek* Web site on the Internet at **www.businessweek.com**.

2. Write a one-page report on your research.

3. Contact the SBA to request information on loans available to small businesses. You can access SBA information on the Internet at **www.sba.gov**. Then click on the link "Financing Your Business." You can also find the SBA office nearest you by calling 1-800-U-ASK-SBA or by looking in your local telephone directory under "United States Government."

4. After you've compiled information from the SBA, write a report that answers these questions:
   - What is the SBA?
   - How does the SBA help small businesses acquire loans?
   - What are three different SBA loan programs? How do they compare to one another?

Chart It

Using the information about loan programs from the SBA, create a chart that compares them. The chart should include the name of the program, purpose of the program, collateral required, maturity, interest rates, maximum loan amount, and eligibility.

Name of Loan Program	Program No. 1	Program No. 2	Program No. 3
Purpose of Loan Program			
Collateral			
Maturity			
Interest Rates			
Maximum Loan Amount			
Small Business Eligibility			

Analyze and Conclude

After studying your research and your chart, answer the questions below:

1. **Interpreting and Communicating Information.** What is the biggest difference between the three loan programs?

2. **Decision Making.** How are the three programs similar?

3. **Creative Thinking.** Which loan would you choose if you were starting a new business and why?

Becoming an Informed Citizen

Congratulations, you finished the seminar. Now it's time to reflect on the decisions you made.

Critical Thinking. Why do you think there are so many loan programs available?

Exercising Leadership. Imagine a group of your friends want to start a business, but they know nothing about starting up a company. They look to you for guidance since you're the only one who has taken this business course. Where do you tell them to start with their plan? What kinds of advice do you give them?

BUSINESS Online

Further Exploration

To find out more about small businesses and finding funding, visit the Glencoe *Introduction to Business* Web site at **www.introbus.glencoe.com**.

Unit 10

Money Management

Tiptoe Through the Tulips

Tulips are closely associated with Holland, but in 1550 they were unknown in Europe. A Dutch botanist brought home a tulip bulb from Turkey and the flower caught on like wildfire. People overvalued tulips bulbs and started investing in them like stocks. At the height of the tulip frenzy, a single bulb sold for as much as $10,000. People borrowed large sums of money or mortgaged their homes and businesses to buy them. In 1637 when the tulip market crashed, tulip investors felt that financial crunch.

● **The British Are Coming**
Wall Street, home of the New York Stock Exchange, gets its name from a wall built in 1653 by Dutch colonists to protect themselves from English invaders.

● **How Do Your Future Finances Look?**
The Psychic Investor and The Wall Street Psychic use methods such as tarot cards, astrology, numerology, clairvoyance, and candle magic to predict the stock market.

● **The Day the Value Dropped**
The biggest drop in stock market history wasn't "Black Monday," October 28, 1929, when the Dow Jones fell 13 percent and the Great Depression began, but October 19, 1987, when the Dow Jones fell 519 points in one day, or 22.6 percent.

BUSINESS Online

Idea Factory

To learn more about trading stocks, visit the *Introduction to Business* Web site at **www.introbus.glencoe.com**, and click on Unit 10 Money Management.

Chapter 28

Planning a Budget

Learning Objectives

After completing this chapter, you'll be able to:
1. **Explain** how budgeting is helpful.
2. **List** the five steps in planning a budget.
3. **Name** different types of income and expenses.
4. **Describe** how a computer is used in budgeting.

Why It's Important

Budgeting techniques help you keep track of where your money goes so that you can make it go further.

Key Words

money management
budget
income
gross pay
deductions
net pay
withholding
expenditures
fixed expenses
variable expenses
budget variance

BusinessWeek Feature Story

Why Higher Rates Aren't Denting Consumers' Spirits

Tight Job Market Keeps Households Right on Spending. You would think that consumers might have become more wary of financial conditions by now. After all, the Dow Jones Industrial Average is off 8 percent this year, and the tech-oriented Nasdaq has plunged by nearly a third since mid-March. Moreover, mortgage rates have risen by a full point in the past six months. But so far, consumers have just shrugged, as if to say, "So what?"

With consumer confidence through May as high as ever, it's clear that the labor markets are the major force shaping overall household attitudes and buying behavior.

Source: Excerpted with permission from "Why Higher Rates Aren't Denting Consumers' Spirits," *BusinessWeek Online*, June 12, 2000.

An Extension Activity

How does the job market affect your household? Ask a parent how the outlook for the economy affects how your family spends its money.

The Full Story

To learn more about personal budgeting, visit the *Introduction to Business* Web site at www.introbus.glencoe.com, and click on *BusinessWeek* Feature Story, Chapter 28.

Money Management

Andre Becker is a 22-year-old single man who works as a radiology technician. He shares an apartment with two other roommates. When Andre decided to make up a budget, he thought carefully about his lifestyle. He doesn't spend much money on clothes for work. There is little transportation expense because the bus is just down the street from his apartment. On the weekends he likes to go out with his friends to restaurants, otherwise he eats meals at home. How would your lifestyle description be different from Andre's? How would it be the same?

Lifestyle Costs

Money is a limited resource. Most people want more goods and services than they can buy with their money. **Money management** is the process of planning how to get the most from your money. With planning, you can figure out how to use the money you have to buy the things you really want or need. Figure 28.1 illustrates how the average household spends its money.

A **budget** is a plan for using your money in a way that best meets your wants and needs. It's like a road map or guide that you set up and

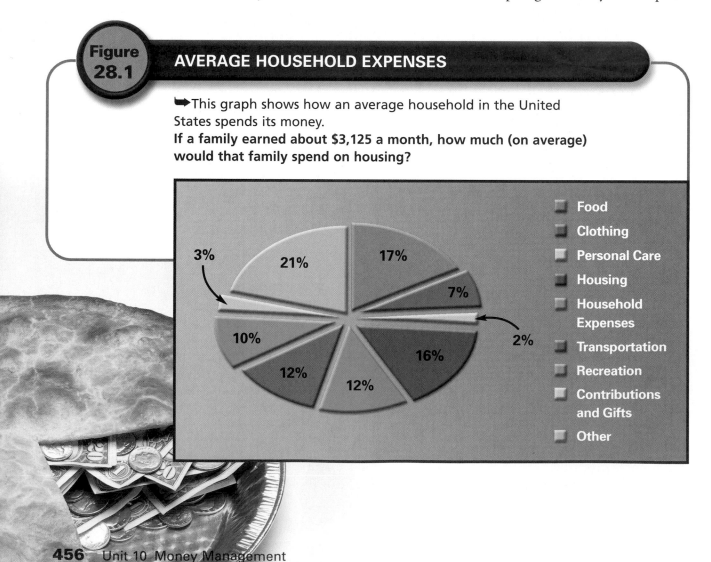

Figure 28.1

AVERAGE HOUSEHOLD EXPENSES

➡This graph shows how an average household in the United States spends its money.
If a family earned about $3,125 a month, how much (on average) would that family spend on housing?

- Food
- Clothing
- Personal Care
- Housing
- Household Expenses
- Transportation
- Recreation
- Contributions and Gifts
- Other

3% 21% 17% 7% 10% 12% 12% 16% 2%

try to follow. A budget includes a record of your expected income, your planned expenses, and your planned savings over a certain period of time. You avoid wasting money on things that aren't very important to you, because you decide in advance how you'll use your money. A good budget helps you set priorities for spending and saving and keeps track of how you're managing your money.

Planning a budget is easier if you divide the process into five steps: Set your goals, estimate your income, estimate your expenses, plan for savings, and balance and adjust your budget as needed.

Set Goals

As you prepare to set your monetary goals, you have to consider several questions: What do I want to accomplish in the next month? The next year? The next five years? What is important to me? Are my goals practical? It's useless to set a goal of buying a new computer in one year if your total income for the year is less than the cost of the computer. A budget should help you decide which goals you can meet with the amount of money you have.

Estimate Income

Knowing how much money you have available is an important step in the budgeting process. Your **income** is the actual amount of money you earn or receive during a given time period. If you get a weekly allowance, that's income. Wages you earn as a stock clerk at a supermarket or tips you get waiting tables are income. Any interest you earn on a savings account or money from investments is also part of your income.

Gross Pay. If you have a job, you may remember your surprise when you got your first paycheck. Your **gross pay**, the total amount of money you earned for a specific time, may have seemed like a lot of money. For example, if you worked 20 hours a week at $6.50 an hour, your gross pay was $130 for the week.

Net Pay. You don't get to keep all of your gross pay, however. Your gross pay is reduced by various **deductions**, or amounts that are taken out of your pay before you receive your paycheck. Deductions include things like taxes, health insurance, retirement, and union dues. Your take-home pay, or **net pay**, is your gross pay minus deductions. For example, if your gross pay is $200 a week and 20 percent is taken out in deductions, your net pay is $160 a week.

THE STRIVING ARTISTS
Austin, Tex. In a bare-bones, big room at Audio Arts Studio, musicians Barry Whittaker, Jason Lee, Will Tabanou, and Mark David get ready for their recording session. Their band, The Agency, is recording a demo CD. Before they stepped foot into the studio, they negotiated a fee to use the space.
In order to negotiate a fee, what did they have to know first?

continued on p. 459

Other Income. If your net pay is the only income you have to consider, it's easy to figure your total income. If you're budgeting for a family and other members contribute to the total income, include their take-home pay in the budget. Don't count on gifts or unusual income, however. If part of your income is from tips, don't overestimate how much you expect to receive in tips. To stay within your budget, use a figure that's lower than what you think you'll receive. Think conservatively.

Taxes. Full-time workers pay several kinds of taxes, which are deducted from their paychecks. **Withholding**, or subtracting taxes from a paycheck to be forwarded to the government, may include federal, state, and local income taxes. In addition, the worker's contribution to social security is withheld. These taxes reduce the amount of take-home pay. Employers are responsible for forwarding the taxes that are withheld to the government units that assessed them.

Workers who don't have all taxes withheld from their paychecks must budget for payment of those taxes. Self-employed persons, for example, pay their taxes directly to the government. They must budget for those payments on a regular basis.

Business Building Blocks

Math

Determining Averages

If you've ever figured out your average grade for a series of math tests, you're familiar with an *average*, or mean. An average is a single number used to represent a group of numbers. The average, or mean, of two or more numbers is the sum of the numbers divided by the number of items added.

Practice

First, review the rules and examples for computing an average (mean) in the box. Then complete this problem: You want to buy a new pair of jeans before visiting your friend in Chicago. At the local mall you visit six different clothing stores. Each store charges a different price for a pair of jeans: $25.95, $24.50, $27.95, $24.36, $26, and $29.95. What is the average price?

Review on Computing an Average

Over the years, Sam has earned the following hourly wages: $4.75, $6.68, $7.36, and $10.19. What is Sam's average hourly wage?

Step 1. Add up the different wages.
$4.75 + 6.68 + 7.36 + 10.19 = $28.98

Step 2. Divide the total by the number of different wages.
$28.98 ÷ 4 = $7.24.

Estimate Expenses

Money you make is called income. You have to plan for a variety of expenses. Food, rent, and clothing are called **expenditures**. You must plan for rent, food, transportation, and any unexpected expenses, such as medical visits. You also have to take into account the rising costs of some expenses, such as gas. If a budget doesn't include all estimated expenses, real problems might arise. There are two basic types of expenses you have to consider: fixed and variable.

Fixed Expenses. **Fixed expenses** are expenses that occur regularly and that are regularly paid. They include such things as rent, insurance, and car payments. The amount of a fixed expense might change from time to time, but it's usually about the same over long periods. You can't reduce or avoid fixed expenses without creating problems.

Variable Expenses. **Variable expenses** are expenses that fluctuate. They include expenses such as food, long-distance phone charges, entertainment, and gifts. The amounts for these expenses usually vary from month to month. A good way to begin estimating your expenses is to look at how much you paid for similar items in the past. The more expenses you track, the easier it's to estimate expenses for your budget.

Plan for Savings

A budget isn't complete without a regular plan for savings. Not only will savings make it possible for you to meet future wants, but they're also a protection. Savings protect you against expenses that you didn't budget for, that are higher than you expected, or that are completely unexpected. You also need a savings plan if your long-term goal is to buy a new computer or take a vacation.

Balance and Adjust the Budget

The most difficult step in the budgeting process is balancing and adjusting the budget. The total estimated income for a period—usually a month or a year—should equal the total estimated expenses. The difference between how much you planned to spend and how much you actually spent is the **budget variance**. If total expenses are greater than total income, you have to make some changes in the budget. You must either decrease your expenses or increase your income. You might need

THE STRIVING ARTISTS
After recording six songs they run out of money. Whittaker takes out more student loans and continues balancing art school and work. The rest of the guys continue working full time. Each spends his monthly income on food, clothing, rent, and entertainment. **These things are examples of what?**

continued on p. 461

to move into an apartment with lower rent or cut down on your phone or electricity usage. You might need to add a part-time job or try to find a higher-paying job to meet your expenses.

✓ Fast Review

1. What is the difference between gross pay and net pay?
2. Give some examples of deductions.
3. What types of taxes are often withheld from a paycheck?
4. Give examples of variable expenses.
5. What is a budget variance?

Working Lifestyle

What are you doing at 10 A.M.?

An English Teacher Sets the Stage

At 6:45 A.M. Susanna Barkataki grabs a toasted bagel on her way out the door and drives to her old high school. Though she hasn't grown any taller since she was a student, she now walks the halls as an English teacher. Now, she's on the other side of the desk, with the grade book and a tattered copy of *Catcher in the Rye* at her side.

By 10 A.M. Barkataki sets the stage by asking the students to open their journals and respond to some wacky question like "Will the sun rise tomorrow? How do you know? What would you do if it didn't?" Students laugh, occasionally roll their eyes, and then start writing. Barkataki uses the students' responses as a starting point for the theme of the day's class. Other times she sets up a day's theme by asking critical thinking ques-

tions, which require them to use their interpretive skills.

Barkataki has a passion for books, ideas, and language. "I'm doing what I love," she says, even at the end of a day of teaching. "My students discuss great ideas and bring a fresh perspective. I'm constantly asking them to look deeper into literature by connecting these universal themes to their lives and our world."

Salary

A typical high school teacher earns a median income of $43,761, with a range between $37,519 and $54,571.

Outlook for This Career

Employment of teachers is expected to grow faster than other occupations. Teaching positions in rural and urban locations are especially plentiful.

Connecting Careers Activity

Imagine you are a high-school teacher six years from now. What one value, or one book, would you teach? List at least ten good questions you would ask the students.

CAREER PATH

Education & Training

A Sample Budget

Let's follow the steps that a young couple, Michael and Nora Kemal, used to set up a budget. They want to plan their spending so they can get the most for their money. They decided to set up a monthly budget and an annual budget.

Step 1: Setting Goals

First, they drew up a list of their goals, both short-term and long-term. They decided which of their wants were most important to them. Setting goals is the first step in developing a spending plan that will meet as many of their goals as possible.

Step 2: Estimating Income

Next, the Kemals estimated their income for the year. They wanted to know how much money they would have available during the planning period. Michael, a salesperson, earns a gross annual income of $19,000. Nora is a management trainee and earns $21,500 a year. Michael and Nora included only their take-home pay as income. Although they earn a total of $40,500, their take-home pay is only about $31,200. They used that amount in their planning, since that's the amount they actually have to spend.

If the Kemals had an income from investments or rental properties, they would include this income in their budget. They don't have a large savings account. Most of their savings have gone to rent a new apartment. They don't, therefore, include interest from their savings account in their budget. When they have built up their savings again, they may be able to add interest income to their estimated total income.

Step 3: Estimating Expenses

Next, the Kemals estimated their expenses for the planning period. They kept a record of actual expenses for the past several months. Then they made a list of planned expenses and savings for the year. The list included their fixed expenses like rent, variable expenses like food and clothing, and money to put in their savings account.

Step 4: Planning for Savings

When Michael and Nora prepared their budget, they took their goals into consideration. Their savings budget reflects their goals. To begin saving for a vacation, they're cutting their entertainment expenses.

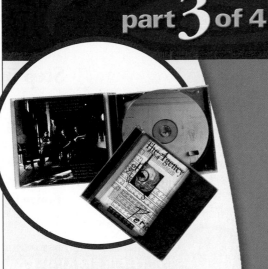

THE STRIVING ARTISTS
Five months later and armed with greener pockets, they head back into the studio to finish recording their demo. Tabanou uses his sound engineering skills to finalize each track's mix. Whittaker applies his talents to the CD artwork. Between the prepress shop and manufacturing costs, The Agency forks over another $1,700 for production costs.
Name some of their estimated expenses in order to finish the CD.

continued on p. 463

Michael and Nora know that to save money, they need to have a regular, systematic plan. The Kemals' budget is shown in Figure 28.2.

When they developed their budget, Michael and Nora had to be sure that the total income figure was the same as the total for planned expenses and savings. If their planned expenses and savings had been more than their income, they would have had to cut some expenses or find some other source of income.

Step 5: Balancing and Adjusting the Budget

After their budget was prepared, the Kemals kept records of their actual expenses. They organized their expenses into various categories, such as car expenses, rent, and entertainment. After they had estimated annual expenses and income, the Kemals developed a monthly budget. They divided the yearly figures by 12 to estimate how to manage their money from one month to the next. At the end of each month, Michael

Figure 28.2

THE KEMALS' FAMILY BUDGET

➡A budget should be broken down into annual and monthly amounts for each category.
Identify how much the Kemals spend on insurance payments.

BUDGET	Annual	Monthly
Income (after taxes)	**$ 31,200**	**$ 2,600**
Fixed Expenses		
Rent payments	7,800	650
Insurance payments	1,200	100
Loan and credit card payments	2,220	185
Variable Expenses		
Food	4,800	400
Utilities (heat, phone, electricity)	1,920	160
Car repair/transportation	1,860	155
Contributions/gifts	720	60
Health and personal care	1,140	95
Travel	600	50
Entertainment	900	75
Clothing	2,040	170
Household (furniture, supplies)	3,000	250
Savings	3,000	250
Total Expenses	**$ 31,200**	**$ 2,600**

and Nora totaled their actual expenses for each item. They then compared these totals with their budgeted amounts to see if they were keeping within their budget.

Balancing the Budget. When they compared their monthly budgeted amounts with their actual expenses, the Kemals found that they spent less than they had budgeted for food, utilities, car expenses, and entertainment. On the other hand, they spent more than their budgeted amounts for health care, clothing, and household expenses. Even with these differences, Michael and Nora had money left at the end of the month. Their total expenses were close to their total income for the month. They were living within their budget.

Adjusting the Budget. After looking at their actual expenses, the Kemals decided to make some changes in their budget. They chose to reduce the amount budgeted for food. They decided not to decrease the other budgeted amounts, since their utility bills or car expenses may be higher in the future. They increased the budget for clothing and household expenses, the two main areas in which their expenses were more than the budgeted amounts. They increased those two items by the amount they reduced the food budget. The Kemals have adjusted their budget according to their needs.

Using a Computer for Budgeting

Many people have computers in their homes. Several kinds of software programs are available for setting up and maintaining a household budget. With a computerized budgeting program, you can store your budgeted amounts and enter your expenses as they occur or at the end of the month. The computer can give you a quick analysis of total expenses, including amounts that are over and under the budget.

In addition, the computer can help with "what if" situations. For example, what if Nora Kemal's income increased by ten percent? With their computer, the Kemals can easily find out how much more they could save each month. What if their rent went up by $50 a month? What if they also wanted to save for a new computer? How much more would they have to cut their entertainment and travel expenses to buy the computer in one year? By using a computer, the Kemals could quickly see how such changes would affect their budget.

THE STRIVING ARTISTS
After spending $3,200 on studio time, $355 on practice space, $200 on artwork, and $1,500 on manufacturing the CDs, The Agency has a finished product. With the CD in hand and the motivation to break into the Los Angeles music scene, this Texas foursome decides to make a new budget called "relocation expenses."
How might they have to adjust their budget in order to move to a bigger city?

✓ **Fast Review** _____

1. What is the Kemals' gross income and net income?
2. How did the Kemals use their annual figures to come up with a monthly budget?

Global *Economy*

A Day on the Town

First, you go downtown to meet a friend for lunch. Later, a friend invites you to a movie. On the way to the theater, you stop and buy gasoline for your car. Check the map below to see what your day might cost in various cities around the world.*

Vancouver, Canada

Trolley fare, one way	$ 1.90
Lunch, per person	7.05
Gasoline, one gallon	1.70
Movie ticket	6.47

Chicago, U.S.A.

Subway fare, one way	$ 1.50
Lunch, per person	8.74
Gasoline, one gallon	1.36
Movie ticket	6.29

Rio de Janeiro, Brazil

Subway fare, one way	$ 0.28
Lunch, per person	13.58
Gasoline, one gallon	2.08
Movie ticket	8.11

*All prices have been converted to U.S. dollars.

Berlin, Germany

Subway fare, one way	$ 2.60
Lunch, per person	11.76
Gasoline, one gallon	3.86
Movie ticket	6.35

Moscow, Russia

Subway fare, one way	$ 0.22
Lunch, per person	22.70
Gasoline, one gallon	1.59
Movie ticket	7.63

Mumbai, India

Subway fare, one way	$ 0.10
Lunch, per person	7.53
Gasoline, one gallon	2.16
Movie ticket	1.07

Tokyo, Japan

Subway fare, one way	$ 1.60
Lunch, per person	20.16
Gasoline, one gallon	4.58
Movie ticket	20.00

Johannesburg, South Africa

Subway fare, one way	$ 0.85
Lunch, per person	10.14
Gasoline, one gallon	1.93
Movie ticket	7.78

Sydney, Australia

Subway fare, one way	$ 1.79
Lunch, per person	9.88
Gasoline, one gallon	2.16
Movie ticket	8.23

Thinking Globally

1. In which city would your day on the town cost the most? The least?

2. Look at the prices for Mumbai. How do you think most people get around the city—by car or by public transportation? Why?

Summary

1. A good budget helps you set priorities for spending and saving and keeps track of how you're managing your money.

2. The five steps in planning a budget are setting goals, estimating income, estimating expenses, planning for savings, and adjusting the budget as needed.

3. Gross pay is the total amount of money you earn; net pay is the amount you take home after deductions. Fixed expenses are expenses that must be paid regularly; variable expenses are expenses that change and you have some control over.

4. Computer software can help you set up, maintain a budget, and predict how changes will affect your budget.

Using Business Key Words

When you're trying to manage your money, it's important to know the following terms. See how well you know them by completing each sentence with the correct term.

- **budget**
- **net pay**
- **gross pay**
- **budget variance**
- **fixed expenses**
- **income**
- **money management**
- **deductions**
- **withholding**
- **variable expenses**
- **expenditures**

1. _____ are expenses that fluctuate and over which you have no control.

2. Your _____ is your gross pay minus deductions.

3. An important part of managing money is making a plan, or a _____.

4. Your _____ is the total amount of money you earn for a specific time.

5. _____ are expenses that occur regularly and that must be paid regularly.

6. Taxes, insurance payments, retirement contributions, and union dues are examples of _____.

7. The process of planning how to get the most from your money is called _____.

8. Your _____ is the actual amount of money you earn or receive during a given time period.

9. Money subtracted from a paycheck for taxes is called your _____.

10. Clothing, food, and rent are examples of spending money on _____.

11. The difference between planned, or budgeted spending, and actual spending is called _____.

Review What You Learned

12. What is money management?
13. What is the purpose of a budget?
14. What are the three categories of items that should be included in a budget?
15. Should a budget ever be changed? Why or why not?
16. What is the difference between fixed expenses and variable expenses? Give an example of each.
17. Why is it important to save part of your income on a regular basis?
18. How can using a computer help in budgeting?

Understanding Business Concepts

19. Your friends spend money like water. Sometimes you wonder how they afford to buy nice clothes and shoes. Has it ever occurred to you they might be living above their means? Perhaps they're living off credit? What do people's spending habits say about them? How should a budget relate to your values and goals?
20. When you make a budget, why is it best not to include gifts or unusual income?
21. What is a good way to estimate your expenses from month to month when you are preparing a budget?
22. What is the most difficult step in the budgeting process? Explain why.
23. Did the Kemals follow the five steps as they prepared their budget? Explain.

Critical Thinking

24. In planning a budget, why is it important that the figure for take-home pay (not gross pay) be used for income?
25. Examine your own fixed and variable expenses. Which are higher? Explain why.
26. Kareen, a friend who started working full-time, got her first paycheck last week. Explain Kareen's withholding.
27. Do you think a computer is useful in keeping a budget? Explain why or why not.

Viewing and Representing

Examining the Image. Look at the picture. How does it make you feel? Imagine you have a million dollars. What would you do to manage a million dollars? Make a list of how you would allocate the money to yourself, your family, and any other purposes.

Building Academic Skills

 Writing Down Goals

What are your goals for the future? Write a description of where you see yourself living and what you see yourself doing in ten years. Then, write a short plan describing the money management techniques you'll use in order to meet your goals.

Preparing a Personal Budget

Select a postsecondary institution (e.g., technical school, community college, or university) that you would like to attend after high school. Obtain information on tuition and other fees. Add to these amounts the costs of food, shelter, clothing, books and supplies, transportation, and any other items you believe are part of the cost of the education you would like to receive. Estimate the total cost of the education. Then, estimate how you'll pay for the education. Include income from parents or relatives, loans, scholarships, personal savings, and part-time employment. Prepare a budget for the length of time that will be needed to finance and complete your education.

 Spreadsheet Software Application

Prepare a personal budget with your information above and present it in spreadsheet form.

Comparing Budgets

In groups, obtain a copy of the budget for your school, school district, local government agency, or other public entity from ten years ago. Then, obtain a current copy. Compare the budgets. Has income increased or decreased? Have the expenses increased or decreased?

Linking School to Home

Interviewing. The accessibility to personal finance software makes it easier for everyone to become personally empowered by controlling his or her own finances. Interview someone who uses technology to record and organize his or her budgets and other financial records. Ask for an explanation of how the technology has affected the way he or she handles money and budgets for expenditures. How much does this person estimate he or she saved by adhering to a budget? Write a one-page paper with your findings.

Linking School to Work

Creating a Workshop. Unfortunately many people are working to just pay their bills instead of learning how to reevaluate their personal financial situation. Become an investor in your future by learning how to budget, which is one step closer to financial freedom. In groups of four or five, create a workshop based on the five steps in this chapter. Present the workshop in class and ask your fellow students to critique it. Make any changes that are necessary and offer the workshop to other students, faculty, and community members.

● E-Homework

Applying Technology

Personal Finance Software. Using the Internet, locate examples of free software that can be used for budgeting and/or money management. Choose the best one you can find and share the Web site with your class.

Researching Social Security. One of the deductions from your paycheck is to the Social Security Administration. Log onto the Web site for the Social Security Administration (**www.ssa.gov**). Find out what benefits are paid for through this fund.

● Connecting Academics

Math. Collect from magazines pictures and prices of three big-ticket items you'd like. For each item, figure out the equivalent cost in movies (at $7 per movie) and the equivalent cost in eating out (at $9 per meal). For example, if a stereo costs $350, its cost-equivalent is 50 movies. If you gave up one movie a week, how long would it take to save enough money to purchase each item? If you gave up eating out twice a month, how long would it take to save enough money to purchase each item?

Social Science. To become wealthy and self-reliant, you must be a savvy investor. You need to decide if purchasing the latest gadget or an expensive meal is more important than a larger goal like buying a car, going to college, or investing in your retirement plan. A big boost to your self-worth comes from managing your money. Make a realistic spending plan for this week and stick to it. By keeping to your plan and knowing you're in control of your money, you'll build your self-esteem. It's evidence that you can set and achieve a goal.

BusinessWeek · Analyzing the Feature Story

You read the first part of "Why Higher Rates Aren't Denting Consumers' Spirits" at the beginning of this chapter. Below are a few questions for you to answer about personal budgeting. You'll find the answers to these questions when you're reading the entire article. First, here are the questions:

28. Why does the Federal Reserve care about household spending?

29. How would personal budgeting help consumers who spend at a faster rate than their incomes grow?

CREATIVE JOURNAL ACTIVITY

Create a budget based on your weekly allowance or earnings from part-time work. How much money do you want to spend on entertainment or eating out? What percentage would you like to save for a special purchase?

The Full Story

To learn more about personal budgeting, visit the *Introduction to Business* Web site at **www.introbus.glencoe.com**, and click on *BusinessWeek* Feature Story, Chapter 28.

Chapter 29

Checking Accounts

● Learning Objectives

After completing this chapter, you'll be able to:

1. **Identify** types of checking accounts.
2. **Describe** some of the major services that banks provide.
3. **Name** the ways checking transactions are recorded.
4. **Explain** how to reconcile a checking account.

● Why It's Important

Paying with checks is the most common medium of exchange.

● Key Words

demand deposits
interest-bearing account
signature card
overdrawing
overdraft protection
stop payment
debit card
check register
endorsement
bank statement
canceled checks
bank reconciliation
outstanding checks

BusinessWeek Feature Story

The Dynamo of E-Banking

Inside Scandinavia's Successful Internet Bank. Five years ago, lunchtime queues at the dozen teller windows of the Nordea bank branch in Helsinki's financial district would have stretched to a half-hour. But shortly after noon on a recent Monday, only four tellers serve customers—and even then, no lines. The reason for the change? Simple: Nearly two-thirds of Nordea's Finnish clients bank on the Internet. "There's nothing more natural than banking with your computer," says Bo Harald, Nordea's director of electronic banking.

Source: Excerpted with permission from "The Dynamo of E-Banking," *BusinessWeek Online*, April 16, 2001.

An Extension Activity

What might be a big hurdle for an upstart like an online bank? Visit an online bank to see what kind of transactions can be made online. What would make you become a customer of an online bank?

BUSINESS *Online*
The Full Story

To learn more about e-banking, visit the *Introduction to Business* Web site at **www.introbus.glencoe.com**, and click on *BusinessWeek* Feature Story, Chapter 29.

The Basics of a Checking Account

You've learned about money, banking, and the Federal Reserve. This information should help you get the "big picture" of banking and banking services. As part of the federal government, the Fed oversees and establishes financial policy for banks that serve the public. Now it's your

Figure 29.1 — TYPES OF CHECKING ACCOUNTS

➡This chart shows the different types of checking accounts available at one bank.

Which type of account requires the smallest amount of money to open?

	Basic Checking	Unlimited Checking	Deluxe Checking
Minimum opening deposit	$50	$250	$500
Requirements for no monthly service fees and no transaction charges	Not available	$750 minimum daily balance—OR—$1,500 monthly average balance	$1,500 minimum daily balance—OR—$3,000 monthly average balance
Monthly service fee	None	$6	$10
Item charges (No charges for deposits)	35 cents on each withdrawal transaction—check, automatic payment, or ATM	None	First 50 withdrawal transactions—check, automatic payment, or ATM—free; 25 cents each additional withdrawal transaction
Interest earned	None	2.5 percent if minimum balance is maintained throughout statement period	2.5 percent if average minimum balance is maintained throughout statement period
Bank credit card available	Yes, $1.50 monthly fee	Yes, $1.50 monthly fee	Yes, no charge
Debit card available	No	Yes, $50 annual fee	Yes, no annual fee
Overdraft protection available	Yes, $250 maximum, $2.50 monthly fee	Yes, $500 maximum, $2.50 monthly fee	Yes, $1,000 maximum, no monthly fee
Returned and overdraft items	$25 per item/ Maximum: three items per quarter	$25 per item/ Maximum: three items per quarter	$25 per item
Stop-payment charges	$20 per item	$20 per item	$20 per item

chance to find out the basics about checking accounts, whether or not you have one now or in the near future.

You may already know that banks offer savings and checking accounts. However, banks also offer other services such as credit cards, loans, financial planning services, and investments. The Federal Reserve System, the central banking authority in the United States, regulates many of these services. As part of federal government, the Fed oversees and establishes financial policy for banks that serve the public. In this chapter you'll learn how you, as a consumer, can use checking account services offered by banks and other financial institutions.

Opening an Account

One of the most important services banks provide is the convenience of checking accounts. It's hard to imagine how businesses would function without the convenience of checks. About 85 percent of all U.S. households have checking accounts. Figure 29.1 illustrates the types of accounts often available. With a checking account, a customer deposits money in an account and receives a book of checks. The checks can then be used to pay for purchases anywhere. Checking accounts are sometimes called **demand deposits** because each check a customer writes is an order to the bank to release money from the account on demand. The check is paid to the payee, the person or business indicated on the check. Checks are the most common medium of exchange. They're more widely used than cash or credit cards.

Types of Accounts

Most banks offer several types of checking accounts. Before opening a checking account, a wise consumer investigates all the kinds of accounts available, as well as their advantages and costs. The customer service representatives at banks can answer questions about account services, fees, and charges. You might also want to ask other people about their experience with different banks and different types of accounts. Shop around and compare financial institutions and what they have to offer.

Regular Account. A regular checking account is designed for customers who write a few checks each month and don't keep a minimum amount of money in the account. If a customer can afford to keep a minimum balance—ranging from $50 to $500—other options are available. Withdrawals from a checking account include checks the customer

Real-World Application

part **1** of 4

WHERE DOES THAT CHECK GO?
Just in the United States, an estimated 70 billion checks are written each year. Every day people write and hand over 270 million checks for some kind of transaction. As you stand in line at the grocery store perusing a glossy magazine and gazing at the tabloids' headlines, you notice your mom writing a check for the groceries.
What do you think the grocery store does with her check?

continued on p. 475

has written, automatic deductions (such as car payments), and automated teller machine (ATM) withdrawals.

Some accounts do require a minimum balance. If the balance falls below the minimum, a service charge is deducted from the account. A $7 or $8 charge every month can take quite a bite out of your funds. Usually this can be reduced or eliminated by having your pay directly deposited. A service charge is a fee for the paperwork the bank does to maintain the account. This charge might be a flat fee, such as $5 or $10 a month. In addition, the bank might charge an individual fee for each check paid from the account.

Interest-Bearing Account. In addition to regular checking accounts, most banks offer interesting-bearing accounts. An **interest-bearing account** is a checking account that earns interest on your account's balance. It usually has a minimum balance requirement with an unlimited number of checks allowed each month. The minimum balance might be much higher than for a regular checking account, and could run from $1,000 to $10,000.

Joint Account. You might also open a joint account, an account shared by two people who are equally responsible for the account. They are often used by married couples or for businesses with more than one owner. With a joint checking account, either person can write checks on the account.

Signature Card

Once you decide what type of account you want, you have to fill out a signature card. A **signature card** is a record of your signature used by the bank to verify your identity. The bank can check your signature card when one of your checks is presented for payment. If the signature matches, the check will be cashed. If it doesn't match, the bank won't cash the check. This helps prevent other people from cashing your checks.

The signature you put on your card is the same one you have to use when you sign your checks. For example, if you sign your card with your middle initial rather than with your full name, you have to sign your checks the same way. If you're opening a joint account, both owners of the account have to sign the signature card. You also have to provide your address, phone number, and the name and address of your employer on the card. The bank then assigns you a checking account number and issues you a book of checks.

Consider This...

Online Bill-Paying

CheckFree provides the online bill-paying functionality for the majority of the United States' largest banks. It works with the banks that want to provide online bill paying for their customers. CheckFree has little competition since others don't want to build the required complex computer system.

ANALYZE

What other vendors could CheckFree build relationships with in order to be successful?

✔ **Fast Review** _____

1. What is an advantage and a disadvantage of an interest-bearing checking account?
2. What is the main purpose of a signature card?

Account Services

Banks offer various services for checking accounts. Some of these services are offered as protection to the consumer. Other services are designed to make banking more convenient.

Overdraft Protection

One risk of having a checking account is writing checks for more money than you have in your account, or **overdrawing** your account. If you write a check to someone without enough funds to cover it, the bank returns the check to the person. Your account is then charged a returned check fee. Some banks charge $20 or $25 for each returned check. The business you wrote the check to will probably also charge a fee.

Some banks offer a service to protect a customer from this problem. **Overdraft protection** is a line of credit for overdrawn checks. If you write a check for more than you have in the account, the bank will cover the check up to a certain amount. The amount can vary from hundreds to thousands of dollars. You pay a service fee for the overdraft protection and interest on the overdrawn amount until it is repaid.

Stop Payment

There might be a time when you want to stop the payment on a check. A **stop payment** is an order for a bank not to cash a particular check. For example, you might have misplaced a check, sent a check for a wrong amount, or sent a check to the wrong address. If you wish to stop the check, contact the bank immediately. If the check hasn't yet been processed, the bank won't cash the check. As with other services, banks charge a fee to stop payment on a check.

Debit Cards

Many banks also offer check cards, or debit cards. A **debit card** is like a credit card but money is taken directly from your checking account when you use it rather than charging the amount to a credit account. A debit card can be used almost anywhere a credit card can, such as a movie theater or grocery store. You don't pay interest on the purchase because it is used as a kind of check rather than a credit card. Debit cards are often referred to as ATM cards.

Real-World Application

part 2 of 4

WHERE DOES THAT CHECK GO?

Everyone doesn't hold a checking account at the same bank. This means the grocery store's bank probably isn't the same as your family's bank. So the grocery store's bank must verify your mom's check before it can convert her check to cash. This is often when checks go to an intermediary bank.
What do you think an intermediary bank does?

continued on p. 477

Technology Toolkit

Your Eyes Say It All

Bank United was the first bank in the United States to use iris recognition at ATMs. Iris recognition technology identifies a user through the appearance of the iris—the colored part of the eye. The iris is a more accurate identity marker than fingerprints. Here's how it works: Your iris is photographed and it's compared with a previously taken image of your eye. The match enables access to your account information. Bank United provided secure financial transactions in the blink of an eye.

Thinking Critically
How might iris recognition benefit large corporations?

Online Checking

Banks and other financial institutions offer a broad range of ways to handle your money. Banking technology offers customers quick and easy handling of their checking accounts through online banking. Online banking allows you to check your accounts, transfer money, or pay bills at any time of the day. With online banking, your checking account information is available to you from your home computer 24 hours a day, 7 days a week. To use online checking, you need access to the Internet, an ID, and a password. Online checking is less expensive for banks, so service fees are often lower than a traditional account.

For online checking, you can use an Internet browser on your computer. With personal finance software, you can store information about your transactions for your records. You can pay your bills online if you choose, saving the cost of mailing your checks. Often banks offer the option of scheduling automatic payment of your bills from the checking account, too.

✓ Fast Review

1. What happens if a customer has insufficient funds in a checking account to pay a check?
2. How is a debit card different from a credit card?

Account Records

An advantage of a checking account is that it enables you to keep records of your financial transactions. There are various types of checking account records that you keep yourself or that your bank provides for you. With these records, you can keep track of your income and expenses.

Writing a Check

There are usually three people, or parties, named on a check. The party to whom the check is written and who is cashing the check is the *payee*. The party who wrote the check and is paying the money, or drawing it from an account, is called the *drawer*. The third party is the *drawee*, the bank or financial institution where the drawer has an account.

When you write a check, record the check number, the amount of the check, the date, and the name of the payee in your check register. Your **check register** is your checkbook log where you keep track of all your checking transactions. If you don't record the check immediately, you might forget some of the information. Some checks also have a line where you can write the purpose of the check. If you're writing a check to a utility, loan, or insurance company, you should use the line to write your account number with the company.

Depositing a Check

To deposit a check in your account you need to fill out a deposit ticket. The deposit ticket lists the amount of cash and checks as well as the total amount you're depositing. After you make the deposit, record it in your check register. Many ATM machines don't require a deposit ticket and you can use the ATM receipt as a record of your transactions.

To deposit or cash a check requires an **endorsement**, or the signature of the payee on the back of the check. To endorse a check, follow these rules for your protection:

- Endorse the check on the back (on the lines printed for the endorsement). Don't write below those lines.
- Use a black pen so your signature can't be erased.
- Sign your name exactly as it's written on the front of the check.
- If you're depositing a check rather than cashing it, write "For Deposit Only" above your signature. That way, if the check is lost or stolen, it can only be used for depositing in your account.

Bank Statements

Periodically, usually once a month, banks issue a bank statement. A **bank statement** is the bank's record of all the transactions in your checking account (see Figure 29.2). It includes a record of all withdrawals, deposits, interest, and fees. It also includes a record of all **canceled checks**, or checks you've written that have been cashed. Your canceled checks are proof that the money has been paid to the payees.

WHERE DOES THAT CHECK GO?

Now the intermediary bank needs to identify the paying bank. It knows this by looking at the routing number on the bottom left-hand corner of your mom's check. **What's the purpose of the routing number?**

continued on p. 479

✔ **Fast Review** _____

1. What are the three different parties on a check?
2. Why should you write "For Deposit Only" on the back of a check?

Bank Reconciliation

Bank reconciliation is the process of seeing whether your records agree with the bank's records for your account. To reconcile is to bring into agreement, or balance. You can usually reconcile your account by using a form on the back of your bank statement. If the bank statement shows a different balance than your check register, you should reconcile the two records.

Balancing Your Checkbook

The first step to reconciling your account is to see whether the bank has processed all your checks and deposits. With the bank statement and your check register, you can identify your **outstanding checks**, or checks that have been written but haven't yet been cashed. The total dollar amounts of outstanding checks should be subtracted from the balance shown on the bank statement.

Figure 29.2

SAMPLE BANK STATEMENT

➡ Michael and Conchetta Chung received this bank statement. **What were the totals for checks written and deposits for the month?**

STATEMENT

FIFTH NATIONAL BANK

Michael and Conchetta Chung
121 Bayside Road
Fall River, OH 42119-0120

Account Number: 211-37-065

Date of Statement: 3/31/04

PREVIOUS BALANCE	CHECKS AND CHARGES	NO. OF DEPOSITS	NO. OF CHECKS	DEPOSITS AND CREDITS	BALANCE AT THIS DATE
535.80	1,011.15	1	7	814.20	338.85

CHECKS AND OTHER CHARGES		DEPOSITS AND OTHER CREDITS	DATE	BALANCE
Beginning Balance				535.80
Check No.	Amount			
106	50.00		3/13	485.80
107	75.00		3/19	410.80
109	120.00		3/23	290.80
		814.20	3/24	1,105.00
111	58.25		3/25	1,046.75
112	23.90		3/26	1,022.85
114	650.00		3/28	372.85
115	28.00		3/28	344.85
Service Chg.	6.00			338.85

Please examine your statement at once. If no error is reported in 10 days, the account will be considered correct and vouchers genuine. All items are credited subject to final payment.
C – Certified Check   S – Service Charge   CR – Overdraft   R – Returned Check

If you have made any deposits that haven't been recorded on the bank statement, those deposits should be added to the bank statement balance. If the bank charged any service fees, you may not have recorded them in your check register. The service fee should be subtracted from the balance in your check register. If your account earns interest, add the interest shown on the bank statement to your check register.

After you have recorded outstanding checks and unrecorded deposits on the bank statement, and service fees and interest earned in your check register, the balance on the bank statement and in your check register should be the same, or should agree. If they agree, you've reconciled (or brought into agreement) your check register balance with the bank statement balance.

Finding Errors

Sometimes bank reconciliation isn't that easy. You may follow all of these steps and still find a difference between your records and the bank statement. If your balance still differs from the bank's balance, you can follow these steps to find the problem.

- Check your own account records to see whether you wrote the correct amount for each check and deposit.
- Check all your additions and subtractions. You may find mistakes in your arithmetic.
- Check to see whether you carried the correct balance forward for each new page of your check register.
- Recheck to see that you have correctly identified all of the outstanding checks and deposits that haven't been processed by the bank.
- Check the bank's additions and subtractions. Are all canceled checks and deposits listed on the bank statement? If you find a mistake in the bank's figures, report it immediately.

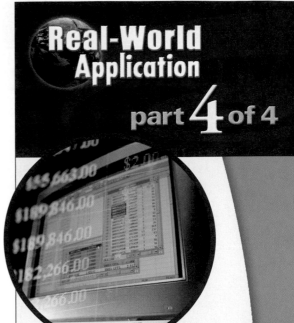

✓ Fast Review

1. What is the difference between a canceled check and an outstanding check?
2. What charges do you need to add and subtract from your check register to reconcile it with your bank statement?

Summary

1. Banks offer regular checking accounts, interest-bearing accounts, and joint accounts.

2. Checking account services include overdraft protection, stop payment orders, debit cards, and online checking.

3. Canceled checks, check registers, and bank statements are used to keep track of account transactions.

4. You reconcile an account by matching your check register with your bank statement.

Using Business Key Words

One of the most important services banks provide is the checking account. If you don't have one already, you probably will very soon. Understanding key terms about checking accounts will help you be a more informed user of your account. Write the term that best completes the sentence.

- **demand deposits**
- **bank reconciliation**
- **overdraft protection**
- **outstanding checks**
- **signature card**
- **endorsement**
- **check register**
- **interest-bearing account**
- **overdrawing**
- **stop payment**
- **debit card**
- **bank statement**
- **canceled checks**

1. A(n) _____ is used by the bank to verify your identity.

2. The process of seeing whether your records agree with the bank's records for your account is called _____.

3. Checks that have been written but haven't yet reached the bank are _____.

4. Checking accounts are often called _____ because each check a customer writes and signs is an order to the bank to release the specified amount.

5. The _____ is necessary for cashing a check.

6. The _____ is the section of your checkbook where you keep track of all your transactions.

7. A prearranged line of credit for overdrawn checks is called _____.

8. A(n) _____ earns interest on the balance left in the account.

9. _____ is when you write a check for more money than there is in your checking account.

10. A(n) _____ orders the bank not to cash a particular check.

11. A(n) _____ is like using a credit card but money is deducted directly from a checking account rather than a credit account.

12. A bank's record of all the transactions in a checking account is called a(n) _____.

13. _____ are checks that are written that have been cashed.

Review What You Learned

14. What major services do banks provide?
15. Why do most businesses and most people have checking accounts?
16. What percentage of U.S. households have checking accounts?
17. When would you want to use a stop payment order?
18. What is the most important part of the signature card? Why?
19. Why is it important to review your monthly bank statement?
20. When you reconcile your bank statement, you might not be able to balance it. List the steps you can follow to find the problem.
21. What should you do if you absolutely cannot reconcile your balance with the bank statement balance?
22. Define the payee, the drawer, and the drawee.

Understanding Business Concepts

23. Why should you shop around before opening a checking account?
24. Why is overdrawing your checking account poor financial management?
25. How does a debit card differ from a credit card?
26. Do you think the bank could make a mistake on your bank statement? Explain.
27. Why is recording your check in the check register before you actually write the check a good idea?
28. Where should the endorsement be written on a check?

Critical Thinking

29. Banks will not accept a check that has been postdated, that is, dated for a future date. Why do you think banks have this policy?
30. Some people are concerned that banking online is risky. They're worried about security, hackers, and not being able to access their money when needed. How would you answer someone who asks you whether or not he or she should consider banking online?
31. What information might the bank or financial institution need from you when you open a checking account?
32. Would you consider taking overdraft protection? Why or why not?

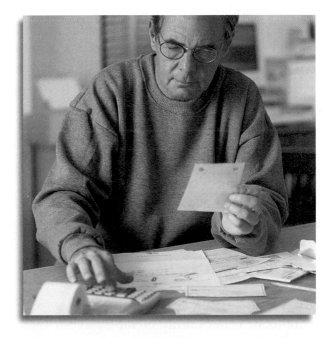

Viewing and Representing

Examining the Image. Look at the photograph and list details that you see. What bills do you or your family pay by check? What needs or wants of your family are met by paying these bills?

Building Academic Skills

Researching Services

In a team, choose a local bank to research. Each team member should concentrate on a different service offered by the bank. Visit or telephone the bank for information. The Internet may also be a resource that could be used. Create a chart of the bank's services and share this information with the class.

COMPUTER TECHNOLOGY **Comparing and Contrasting**

Some banks don't return canceled checks to their customers. Use online research to collect information about the pros and cons of this practice. Write a two-page report about the advantages and disadvantages of this practice for both the banks and their customers.

Social Science **Create a Teaching Tool**

In a group, create a board game that could be used to teach middle-school students about checking accounts. Emphasize the reasons why someone should have a checking account, how to reconcile a check register with a bank statement, and the trend towards online banking. Test the game by playing it in class; then offer to take the game to a middle-school class and use it as a teaching tool.

Reconciling an Account

Review the check register, bank statement, and steps for reconciling a checking account presented in this chapter. Then, reconcile the balance on the check register shown below with a bank statement balance of $844.71. The bank has charged a $4 service fee. The statement doesn't include check numbers 578 and 581. Also missing is a deposit in the amount of $47.86. Write an explanation of what you did.

No.	Date	Description	Payment	Deposit	Balance
					624.83
575	6/27	Sam's Good Gifts	22.95		601.88
-	7/1	Paycheck		650.77	1252.65
576	7/1	Finer, Fresher Foods	42.13		1210.52
577	7/10	Cash	100.00		1110.52
578	7/15	Rent	435.00		675.52
579	7/21	Phone Bill	34.67		640.85
580	7/25	World Wide Airlines	227.14		413.71
581	7/29	Electric Bill	32.90		380.81
-	7/31	Al's Check		47.86	428.67

Linking School to Home

Surveying Bank Services. Interview your parents or other family members about their checking accounts. Find out which bank they use, why they chose that particular bank, what type of checking account they have, the service charges they pay, and anything else you think is important.

Linking School to Work

Reporting About Financial Institutions. Call several financial institutions in your area and find out what you would have to do to open a checking account. Ask about the age requirements, initial deposit, service charge, and whether or not they offer interest-bearing accounts. Share your findings with the class.

E-Homework

Applying Technology

Online Banking. Use the Internet to research online banking. Find two different banks that offer the service online and evaluate them based on the following information:

- How is online banking different from doing business at your local bricks-and-mortar bank branch?
- Is online banking suitable for businesses as well as individuals?
- Are there cost savings with online banking? Or is it more expensive?
- What type of security is in place to protect consumers who choose to bank online? Share your findings with the class.

Upcoming Checking Accounts. Checking accounts might look very different in just a few years. Use the Internet to research one of the following topics: digital checks, digital coupons, digital cashier's checks, and divisible cash, e-money, or smart cards. Write a two-page paper with your findings.

Connecting Academics

Math. You and your friend Sal spend Saturday shopping. Sal uses checks to make the purchases, but needs help writing out the dollar amount. Practice writing out the following amounts as you'd write them on a check: $36.45, $152.79, $16.14, and $1,311.35.

Language Arts. Pair up with a partner and create a system to review topics in this chapter. For example, the system could be using questions and answers on 3" by 5" cards. Join with another pair and share ideas to improve both study systems.

BusinessWeek Analyzing the Feature Story

You read the first part of "The Dynamo of E-Banking" at the beginning of this chapter. Below are a few questions for you to answer about Nordea. You'll find the answers to these questions when you're reading the entire article. First, here are the questions:

33. How has online banking helped Nordea's bottom line?
34. What advantage do banks like Nordea have over banks that offer their services exclusively online?

CREATIVE JOURNAL ACTIVITY

Interview three adults to find out if and why they use online banking. Write a short report summarizing the similarities and differences between the three responses.

BUSINESS *Online*
The Full Story
To learn more about e-banking, visit the *Introduction to Business* Web site at **www.introbus.glencoe.com**, and click on *BusinessWeek* Feature Story, Chapter 29.

Chapter 30

Savings Accounts

Learning Objectives

After completing this chapter, you'll be able to:

1. **Name** reasons for saving money.
2. **Explain** how interest is earned.
3. **Identify** types of savings accounts.
4. **Describe** savings accounts.

Why It's Important

Savings accounts allow you to put money aside and help make your money grow.

Key Words

savings
opportunity cost
simple interest
compound interest
passbook savings account
statement savings account
certificate of deposit (CD)
maturity date
money market fund
money market deposit account
Federal Deposit Insurance
  Corporation (FDIC)
liquidity
inflation risk

BusinessWeek Feature Story

How to Cash Out Your College Fund

The Tricky Part Is Curbing Taxes and Boosting Aid. Congratulations! Your parents have been saving ever since you were a toddler, and now that you're a strapping high schooler, you have a hefty sum stashed away in growth stocks for college. You're among a tiny elite: By some estimates, only 2 percent of families with children have $5,000 or more saved for college expenses.

Now, how are you going to get those funds out of your account and into Wattasmatta U's? College planning focuses so much on the first phase—savings—that few are aware of the hurdles that await during the endgame.

Source: Excerpted with permission from "How to Cash Out Junior's College Fund," *BusinessWeek Online*, March 12, 2001.

An Extension Activity

Find a college, university, or institution that you're interested in attending after high-school graduation. How much money will you need to afford the tuition plus expenses? What steps do you need to take in order to pay for your future?

BUSINESS Online
The Full Story

To learn more about savings plans, visit the *Introduction to Business* Web site at **www.introbus.glencoe.com**, and click on *BusinessWeek* Feature Story, Chapter 30.

A Guide to Saving

You work part-time as a sales associate at the local department store. Every other week you receive a paycheck. You decide to start setting some financial goals since your checking account is almost empty by the time your next pay period comes around. You also decide to analyze your lifestyle costs. How can you manage your cash to save for your future?

Why You Should Save

A personal budget isn't complete without a plan for regular savings. **Savings** is money put aside for future use. The amount of money you save depends on how much of your income you're willing not to spend. Figure 30.1 illustrates the average account balance. What do you think this says about people's attitude toward lifestyle choices, money, and the future? All savings involve some sacrifice. When you save money, you're putting off spending money now to get something later. This is called the **opportunity cost**, or trade-off; this is what you give up when you make one choice instead of another. The opportunity cost of going to college is working at a full-time job. Choosing between alternatives involves knowing what you gain.

Figure 30.1

THE AVERAGE NEST EGG

➡️The average retirement account balance is about $41,000.
How much are you willing to save today in order to support your future?

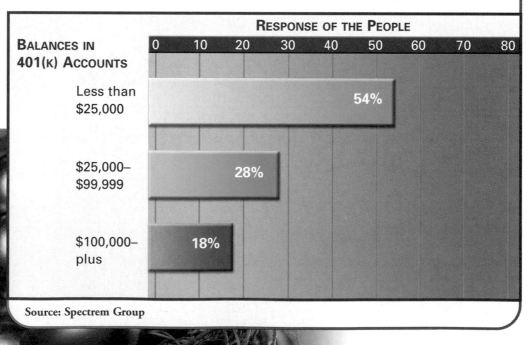

BALANCES IN 401(K) ACCOUNTS	RESPONSE OF THE PEOPLE
Less than $25,000	54%
$25,000–$99,999	28%
$100,000–plus	18%

Source: Spectrem Group

Why do people save money? People set up and maintain a savings plan for three major reasons: to make major purchases, to provide for emergencies, and to have income for retirement.

Major Purchases

Suppose you would like to have a really nice sound system, a top-of-the-line guitar, a car, or a two-year degree from a technical college. You'll probably need to save money before you can buy these. You might even need to save for an entire year or two before you have enough.

Remember, if you purchase items on credit or borrow money to make purchases, you have to pay finance charges. If you use cash for the purchase, you don't have to pay those charges. Finance charges can average 15 to 18 percent, which adds a lot to the cost of the item.

Emergencies

You might face financial emergencies in your life—your car breaks down, you lose your job, or you develop a health problem. Experts in personal finance strongly recommend that each person have money saved for emergencies. In fact, they recommend that you have at least six months of income set aside in case of an emergency.

Retirement

It might seem too early to think about saving for retirement, but it's best to begin early. Most workers in the United States receive some income from the federal social security program when they retire. Many, but not all, people have some type of retirement plan where they work, which will provide additional income. Individuals with their own businesses can also set up retirement plans.

For most people, though, social security and retirement plans still don't provide enough money to retire comfortably. A third source of income is savings made through the years. If you start early in your life, you can easily accumulate quite a nest egg from which to draw retirement income. For example, if you put away just $20 per week starting now, by the time you retire you would have $50,000. With interest earned on a savings account, it could come to several times more than that.

Real-World Application

part 1 of 4

HOW LONG IS A CD'S LIFE?
You've invested loads of money in audio CDs, CD-ROM multimedia games, and photo CDs. A CD's spiral track of pits stores your favorite data for at least 100 years if you treat them like investments. **The opportunity cost of carefully handling your CD collection is what?**

continued on p. 489

✓ **Fast Review** _____

1. What is a major advantage of saving to buy an item instead of buying it on credit?
2. What are the three main sources of retirement income?

A Specialized Plan

This activity gives you the chance to add to your portfolio. Communicate, interview, research, and write your way into a story. Choose one imaginary path, The Way to Catering or A Bookish Party. Follow your path's steps to complete your own story.

pick a path

The Way to Catering

The Setting. You're a great cook and plan to start a catering business, specializing in Kosher meats.

Rising Action. You continue working at your current job to save enough for a down payment on Kosher cooking equipment. You decide to save $25 per week from your paycheck.

Step 1. Call a bank and ask for interest rates for savings accounts, money market accounts, and certificates of deposit. Also find out the qualifications to open an account. Can you qualify for any? If not, calculate how long you would have to save in order to qualify.

Step 2. Assuming you do qualify, make a chart comparing the different benefits and risks of each savings plan. Decide which you would invest in and write a paragraph explaining why.

A Bookish Party

The Setting. Your book club just finished Myla Goldberg's *Bee Season*, and you're to host the next book party.

Rising Action. You've always wanted to throw a party, with lots of interesting foods. Use your savings to invest in creating a party worth remembering.

Step 1. Find a cookbook of recipes for Kosher food. Select three recipes that seem to call for inexpensive ingredients. Make a list of all the ingredients. Go to a Kosher food store or the Kosher section of your grocery store and write down the price of all the ingredients.

Step 2. Calculate how much it would cost to make enough of each recipe to feed 15 people.

Conclusion

Now it's time to write your own story and write a personal narrative about your path. Be sure to include your insights into the experiences that have shaped your decisions. What details will you keep or discard? Use vivid descriptions to reveal your own character. Specific details draw the reader into your narrative. Be creative.

Earning Interest on Savings

All savings don't necessarily earn income. For those who put their savings into a jar or under the mattress, no income is earned. Remember what you learned about credit in previous chapters. If you get a loan you must pay interest, which is like a rental fee for using someone else's money.

In this case, *your* money is being used to lend money to someone else, so *you* receive the rental fee or interest. Many different financial institutions, such as banks and credit unions, want to use your savings to make loans. If you put money into one of their savings accounts, you're actually lending them your money. They then use your money to make loans to other people. In return for letting them use your money, part of the interest they receive is used to pay interest to you.

Simple Interest

Simple interest is interest earned only on the money you deposited into your savings account, or the principal. The amount of interest you receive depends on three major factors—the amount of savings, the interest rate, and the length of time of the account. Does this sound familiar? A person who starts a savings account is actually a creditor with the same conditions for lending money.

For example, if you have a savings account that pays you 5 percent annual interest and $1,000 is in the account for the entire year, you'll receive $50 in interest. If you had $2,000 in that account during the year with the same interest rate, you would earn $100 in interest. In this case, the interest doubled because of doubling the amount of savings. If the account pays 10 percent interest and you have $1,000 for one year, you would also earn $100. When moving from 5 to 10 percent interest for the same amount of principal and the same time span, the interest doubles from $50 to $100.

Compound Interest

Compound interest is interest earned on both the principal—the money you deposited in your savings account—and any interest you earned on it. In other words, compound interest is interest on interest. For example, suppose you had $50,000 in a savings account at 6 percent annual interest. After one year, you would earn $3,000 in interest. With simple interest, you would continue to earn interest on the $50,000 principal. With compound interest, the $3,000 would be added to the $50,000 and you would start earning interest on $53,000. With simple interest, after 15 years you would earn $45,000. With compound interest, you would earn almost $70,000, or about $25,000 more.

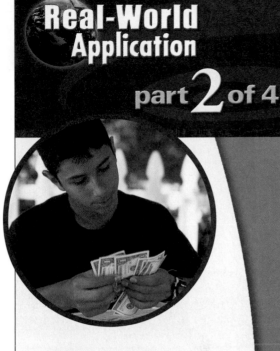

HOW LONG IS A CD'S LIFE?
You wouldn't leave your digitally remastered import CDs in plastic sleeves under the summer's sun; this isn't proper care. Assume you start lending out your CDs to friends at school because they love your eclectic taste in music. Often it's weeks before you get them back, which is just too long. You decide to start charging interest when they return the CDs late.
What can you do with the interest you earn?

continued on p. 491

Compound interest is usually earned daily, monthly, quarterly, or annually. The more often interest is compounded, the more you make in extra interest.

✓ Fast Review

1. Why do financial institutions pay interest on savings accounts?
2. What is the difference between simple interest and compound interest?

Types of Savings Accounts

Banks, savings and loans, savings banks, credit unions, and brokerage firms all offer different types of savings accounts. There are three

Figure 30.2 THE POWER OF COMPOUNDED INTEREST

➡Compounded interest makes your money grow faster when interest is left to accrue.
Which account earned more interest? What is the difference in the account totals after 15 years?

	SIMPLE INTEREST			COMPOUNDED INTEREST		
Year	Principal	6% Interest Earned	Account Total	Principal	6% Interest Earned	Account Total
1	$50,000	$3,000	$53,000	$50,000	$3,000	$53,000
2	$50,000	3,000	53,000	53,000	3,180	56,180
3	$50,000	3,000	53,000	56,180	3,371	59,551
4	$50,000	3,000	53,000	59,551	3,573	63,124
5	$50,000	3,000	53,000	63,124	3,787	66,911
6	$50,000	3,000	53,000	66,911	4,015	70,926
7	$50,000	3,000	53,000	70,926	4,256	75,182
8	$50,000	3,000	53,000	75,182	4,511	79,692
9	$50,000	3,000	53,000	79,692	4,782	84,474
10	$50,000	3,000	53,000	84,474	5,068	89,542
11	$50,000	3,000	53,000	89,542	5,373	94,915
12	$50,000	3,000	53,000	94,915	5,695	100,610
13	$50,000	3,000	53,000	100,610	6,037	106,646
14	$50,000	3,000	53,000	106,646	6,399	113,045
15	$50,000	3,000	53,000	113,045	6,783	119,828
TOTAL INTEREST EARNED	$45,000			$69,828		

Amounts are rounded to the nearest dollar.

basic types of savings accounts: traditional, certificates of deposit, and money market accounts.

Traditional Savings Account

This account is offered by all of the institutions named previously except brokerage firms. Generally, a low minimum deposit, such as $100, is required to open a traditional savings account. The interest rate varies from one financial institution to another. The rate can also change over time.

There are two types of traditional savings accounts. One is a **passbook savings account** in which all of the deposits and withdrawals are recorded in a book that the depositor keeps. With the **statement savings account**, all of the activity in the account is recorded on a statement that is sent to the person who has the account. With either account, you can withdraw money from your account at any time without any penalty. The interest rate on the traditional savings accounts is usually quite low. Many banks also charge a service fee if the savings account falls below a certain minimum balance.

The traditional savings account is a place for a small amount of money that you might need in the near future. You won't earn much interest on your savings, but the money is easy to get when you need it.

Certificate of Deposit

Another type of savings account, called a **certificate of deposit (CD)**, requires you to deposit a minimum amount of money in an account for a minimum period of time. The amount is usually at least $500. The length of time might be 6 months, 1 year, or 5 years. A CD has a **maturity date**, which is when the money becomes available to you. The interest rate on a CD is higher than a regular savings account. If you cash in the CD before the maturity date, however, you lose interest and might have to pay a penalty fee.

Money Market Fund

Brokerage firms, financial institutions that buy and sell stocks and bonds, offer a special type of savings account called a money market fund. A **money market fund** is a kind of mutual fund, or pool of money, put into a variety of short-term debt (less than one year) by business and government. In a way, you're lending your money to a business or the government to invest.

The interest rate on a money market fund varies from month-to-month. An advantage is that you can withdraw your money at any time. There are,

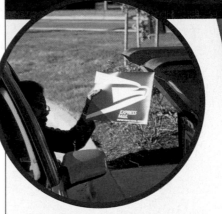

HOW LONG IS A CD'S LIFE?

A friend suggests you save some money on CD purchases by joining a music club, where you get 12 CDs free. In the club's brochure the fine print requires that each member order five full-priced CDs *before* choosing the free CDs. **What is the maturity date of those free CDs?**

continued on p. 493

however, two disadvantages. You usually need to put at least $1,000 into a money market fund, and you can only write a limited number of checks. Each check might have to be above a certain minimum, such as $500.

Money Market Deposit Account

Banks, savings and loans, and credit unions have their own form of money market fund called a **money market deposit account**. It has the same basic requirements and characteristics of a money market fund. One difference between them is that the federal government insures the money in a market deposit account.

✔ Fast Review

1. What happens if you cash in a CD before the maturity date?
2. What is the difference between a money market fund and a money market deposit account?

Advantages and Disadvantages of Savings Accounts

As with any choice, there are trade-offs to having a savings account. The opportunity cost, in which you give up something in order to get something later, has a trade-off. The main advantage of a savings account, of course, is that you earn interest on it. There are other advantages and disadvantages as well.

You Make the Call

Risking Someone Else's Future

As a financial planner, you work hard for your clients. This morning one of your best clients talked with you about his investments. He is 67, retired, and has a moderately strong portfolio. He wants to shift all his money from conservative investments such as savings accounts, CDs, and municipal bonds to high-risk stocks. You know that if he uses your services to buy stocks, you stand to gain more in service charges than if he keeps his investments in bank accounts. On the other hand, you believe at his age, he is better off not risking so much of his secure investments.

Making an Ethical Decision

1. What should you do?
2. What if he insists on transferring his money to high-risk stocks?
3. What if he were 87 years old?

Insurance Against Loss

Banks, savings and loans, and credit unions all have insurance. For example, the **Federal Deposit Insurance Corporation (FDIC)**, a government agency, insures bank accounts. Even if a bank fails, the FDIC will replace depositors' accounts for up to $100,000. Money market funds offered by brokerage firms aren't federally insured, but most brokerage firms have insurance on their accounts.

Liquidity

Liquidity means the ability to quickly turn an investment into cash. An investment such as a car or a business isn't very liquid because you have to sell it in order to get cash. Savings accounts, on the other hand, are highly liquid because you can easily withdraw cash from them. You can even cash in a CD before it matures. You won't get its full value, though, and you'll have to pay a penalty fee for cashing it in before the maturity date.

Inflation Risk

Inflation is a general increase in the cost of goods and services. **Inflation risk** is the risk that the rate of inflation will increase more than the rate of interest on savings. Suppose you have $1,000 in a savings account that earns 4 percent interest. During the next year, inflation increases by 6 percent. That means it cost $1,060 at the end of the year to buy what you could for $1,000 at the beginning of the year. With interest, your savings only increased to $1,040, so you actually lost money. The interest rates on most savings accounts, however, increase with inflation. The main risk is with CDs, where you're locked into an interest rate over a long period of time.

HOW LONG IS A CD'S LIFE?

Four years or so later, your music tastes have greatly changed. As a matter of fact, you can't believe you bought and listened to some of the things you did. A used audio CD store just opened in your town. You decide to sell your CDs to the store and it gives you cash in return. **Is this an example of liquidity or inflation?**

Costs of Savings Accounts

Savings accounts earn interest but they can also cost money. Some accounts charge a penalty fee for early withdrawal or if the account balance falls below a certain minimum. Other accounts charge a fee for each deposit and withdrawal. The money you earn in interest on a savings account is also considered income. As a result, you have to pay income tax on it.

 Fast Review _____

1. What kinds of savings accounts doesn't the FDIC insure?
2. In what ways can a savings account cost you money?

Summary

1. The three main reasons for saving money are for major purchases, for emergencies, and for retirement.

2. Financial institutions pay interest on savings accounts in return for using (or borrowing) the money. As with a credit account, the amount of interest earned depends on the interest rate, the size of the account, and the length of time you keep the account.

3. Passbook savings, statement savings, certificates of deposit, money market funds, and money market deposit accounts are different types of savings accounts.

4. Savings accounts earn interest, are usually insured, and have high liquidity. They can also cost money in fees, in taxes, and by not keeping up with inflation.

Using Business Key Words

Saving money is important. More important, however, is making that money you save work for you. See how many of the following terms you know by matching each one with its definition.

- **savings**
- **certificate of deposit (CD)**
- **compound interest**
- **money market fund**
- **money market deposit account**
- **passbook savings account**
- **liquidity**
- **opportunity cost**
- **statement savings account**
- **inflation risk**
- **simple interest**
- **maturity date**
- **Federal Deposit Insurance Corporation (FDIC)**

1. The depositor keeps money in an account for a higher rate of interest.
2. Interest that is calculated on the principal and previously accumulated interest.
3. The ability to turn your savings into cash.
4. The loss of your savings dollar.
5. A safe mutual fund offered by brokerage houses.
6. An account where all the deposits and withdrawals are recorded in a book the depositor keeps.
7. An account where all of the activity in the account is recorded on a statement that is sent to the person who has the account.
8. A safe mutual fund offered by banks, savings and loan associations, mutual savings banks, and credit unions.
9. Money you put aside for the future.
10. Giving up the opportunity to buy something in order to buy something else.
11. Interest earned only on the principal, or the money deposited into a savings account.
12. The date when money in a certificate of deposit becomes available to the depositor.
13. A government agency that insures commercial bank accounts for up to $100,000.

Review What You Learned

14. Why is it best to begin saving for retirement early?
15. The amount of interest you receive from your savings depends on three factors. What are they?
16. How do savers benefit from compound interest?
17. Explain what the FDIC is and what it does.
18. What type of savings account would be appropriate for a small amount of money you may need in the near future?
19. Why are banks or other financial institutions willing to pay a higher rate of interest for a CD than for a traditional savings account?
20. Can you withdraw money from a money market fund at any time without penalty?
21. What type of savings account would be appropriate for a large amount of money that you might want to use for something in the near future?
22. Explain why all savings involve some trade-off.

Understanding Business Concepts

23. What three sources of income are people able to rely on when they retire?
24. Explain how your savings account is like a loan to the bank or financial institution.
25. Which earns you more money—interest compounded daily or interest compounded yearly? Explain your answer.
26. If you're planning to go to college next year, what type of savings account should you have? Why?
27. What is the tradeoff for savings accounts that are liquid and safe?

Critical Thinking

28. Are you currently saving money? If so, what are you saving for? If not, why not?
29. Describe a person who would be a good candidate to use CDs as a method of saving money.
30. What do you think would happen if the FDIC didn't exist?
31. How does inflation affect your savings decisions?

Viewing and Representing

Examining the Image. Look closely at the photograph. What's important in this picture? Name something you want to buy that's expensive. What type of account would you choose to hold your money?

Building Academic Skills

 Research the Federal Deposit Insurance Corporation (FDIC)

Write a paragraph about how and why the FDIC impacted U.S. history and continues to do so today.

 Calculating Interest

If you have a savings account that pays you 6 percent annual interest and $1,000 is in the account for the entire year, how much interest will you earn? If your savings plan pays 6 percent interest compounded daily, how much will you earn?

 Creating a Visual Aid

As a group, choose one type of savings account. Conduct research and prepare a visual display describing the advantages and disadvantages of the selected savings account. Use local banks and the Internet as resources for your research. Share your visual display with the class.

COMPUTER TECHNOLOGY **A Comparative Spreadsheet**

Survey banks, savings and loan associations, and credit unions about the interest rates they pay on their savings accounts, certificates of deposit, and money market accounts. Also, compile information on their minimum deposits and balances, allowable number of transactions, minimum balances to earn interest, and limits on withdrawals. Create a spreadsheet with the information you gather that will calculate the return for each kind of savings account you discover. Input varying amounts of money from small to very large and print out the results. Then decide which institutions are best for growth when small amounts are saved and which are best for larger amounts. Write a paragraph with your decision.

Linking School to Home

Money Left Over. Savings is money put aside for future use. The amount of money you save depends on how much of your income you're willing not to spend. Obtain a large jar or other container and ask everyone in your family to "deposit" their change there each night when they come home from work or school. After one month, count the money. How much have you saved? As a family, decide what you would like to do with the money—for example, you could go out to dinner, see a movie, or donate it to a local charity.

Linking School to Work

Rephrasing Documentation. A brokerage firm might insure the money market fund. This is one of the many opportunities made available to you by a financial institution. Financial institutions generally have brochures or other written documentation about their various savings accounts. Obtain one of them and rewrite it in terms that a preteen might understand.

● E-Homework

Applying Technology

Calculating Compound Interest. Compound interest is interest earned on both the principal—the money you deposited in your savings account—and any interest you earned on it. Create a spreadsheet and the formulas necessary to calculate interest compounded daily, monthly, and yearly. The spreadsheet should contain at least five different interest rates.

Online Research. Use the Internet to find out if there are any local banks or online banks that offer special savings accounts for students.

● Connecting Academics

Math. Use the data below to compute the total savings on a $1,000 deposit at the end of one year. This might be a good opportunity to use spreadsheet software.

a. passbook savings account — 3.5 percent simple interest

b. certificate of deposit (CD) — 7 percent compounded quarterly

c. certificate of deposit (CD) — 3.5 percent compounded monthly

Social Science. Social skills on the job are important for success. You're a member of a news team for a public television program. Together, with several of your coworkers (classmates), develop and present a two-minute segment for the afternoon news called, "Savings Today." Assign one team member to observe the development process and report on how each team member relates to the others.

BusinessWeek Analyzing the Feature Story

You read the first part of "How to Cash Out Your College Fund" at the beginning of this chapter. Below are a few questions for you to answer about savings plans. You'll find the answers to these questions when you're reading the entire article. First, here are the questions:

32. What is the first step for parents who wish to begin a savings plan for their child's college tuition?

33. Why shouldn't parents keep college savings in their child's name?

CREATIVE JOURNAL ACTIVITY

Consider a family's expenditures. How much needs to be saved to afford them? What is a reasonable savings goal for each item? Estimate how much time the family will need to save for each expenditure.

BUSINESS Online
The Full Story

To learn more about savings plans, visit the *Introduction to Business* Web site at **www.introbus.glencoe.com**, and click on *BusinessWeek* Feature Story, Chapter 30.

Chapter 31

Investing in Stocks

● Learning Objectives

After completing this chapter, you'll be able to:

1. **Define** stock.
2. **Explain** how stock is bought and sold.
3. **Identify** the indexes that track stock prices over the long run.

● Why It's Important

Making good investment decisions helps you reach your financial goals.

● Key Words

investing
stock
yield
dividends
capital gain
capital loss
common stock
preferred stock
broker
stock exchange
mutual fund
blue-chip stocks
speculative stocks

BusinessWeek Feature Story

Where Kids Can Log On to Learn Their Investing ABCs

Intelligent and Fun Personal Finance Sites for Kids. Kids today seem to spend half their lives surfing the Web and the other half spending money. This year teens will spend $153 billion, including $105 billion of their own, according to Teenage Research Unlimited of Northbrook, Ill. So parents and teachers should be able to use the Internet to find communities that teach youths how to manage finances. But it turns out that learning about dollars and cents online is tougher than spending money there.

Source: Excerpted with permission from "Where Kids Can Log On to Learn Their Investing ABCs," *BusinessWeek Online*, November 12, 1999.

An Extension Activity

How much should your parents pay you? Be reasonable. Who can live on the least amount of money? Who has the greatest wants or needs? How do your wants and needs fit into your family's budget? Create an interactive debate to challenge each other to find a solution.

BUSINESS *Online*
The Full Story

To learn more about investing, visit the *Introduction to Business* Web site **www.introbus.glencoe.com**, and click on *BusinessWeek* Feature Story, Chapter 31.

Fundamentals of Investing

You won a youth national writing contest, with a cash reward of $3,000. Instead of placing all of the money in your savings account, you decide to invest some of the money so that it can earn a potentially higher return. With money you set aside for long-term goals like college, a house, or retirement, you'll need more than the rates usually paid on a savings account to stay ahead of inflation and taxes.

Investing in Stocks

Investing is putting your money to use in order to make money on it. Putting money in a savings account is a form of investing. Savings are loans made to banks or other financial institutions in return for earning interest. Investing in stocks, however, is quite different. Figure 31.1 illustrates the types of investments with the severity of their risk.

You might remember from Chapter 6 that there are three primary forms of business ownership: sole proprietorships, partnerships, and

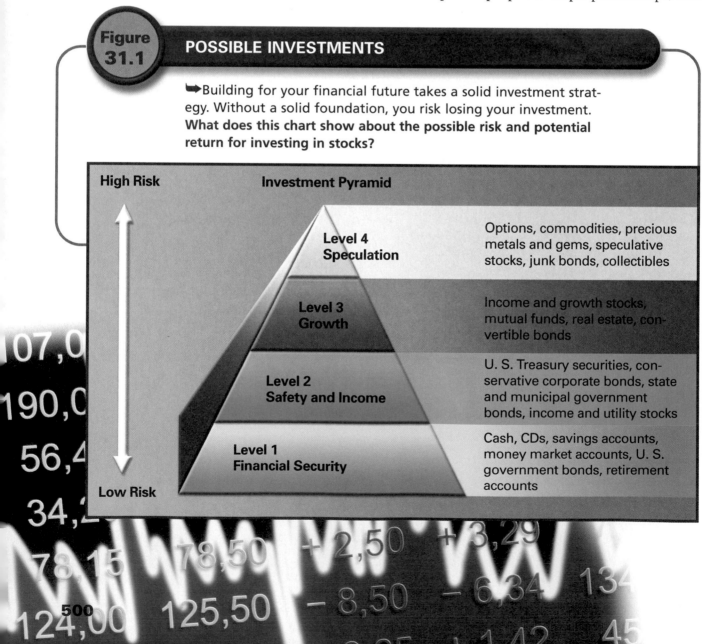

Figure 31.1

POSSIBLE INVESTMENTS

➡Building for your financial future takes a solid investment strategy. Without a solid foundation, you risk losing your investment. **What does this chart show about the possible risk and potential return for investing in stocks?**

High Risk

Low Risk

Investment Pyramid

Level 4 Speculation — Options, commodities, precious metals and gems, speculative stocks, junk bonds, collectibles

Level 3 Growth — Income and growth stocks, mutual funds, real estate, convertible bonds

Level 2 Safety and Income — U. S. Treasury securities, conservative corporate bonds, state and municipal government bonds, income and utility stocks

Level 1 Financial Security — Cash, CDs, savings accounts, money market accounts, U. S. government bonds, retirement accounts corporations. One way a corporation raises money to start or to enlarge its business is by selling stock. **Stock** is a share of ownership in a business. When you buy stock in a company, you aren't lending it money. When you buy stock, you receive a stock certificate indicating that you are now part owner of the company. Sole proprietorships and partnerships, on the other hand, don't sell stock.

Return on Stocks

The return on an investment, or **yield**, is the amount of money the investment earns. The return on a stock investment depends on the type of return and the rate of return.

Types of Return. There are two ways that you can make a return on stocks. One is through the payment of **dividends**, which is a share of profits. If a corporation makes a lot of money over a certain period of time, it distributes the profits among its shareholders in the form of dividends. Dividends are usually paid quarterly.

Stockholders can also earn income on their stocks by selling their stock shares for more than they paid for them. For example, if Juanita buys 100 shares of stock at $25 (total cost = $2,500) and sells it for $35 (total return = $3,500), she will earn additional income of $1,000 ($3,500 − $2,500).

Selling stock for *more than* you paid for it is called a **capital gain**. Juanita might also sell her stock for *less than* she paid for it because she needs the cash or the company is doing badly. In that case, she would be taking a **capital loss**. As with any form of income, the government taxes the amount you make in dividends or in capital gains.

Rate of Return. The rate of return on stocks is always expressed as a percent of the original investment and figured on an annual basis. For example, suppose $1,000 in a savings account earns a $50 interest payment for one year. The rate of return on the investment is 5 percent ($50/$1,000 = 0.05). A single share of stock whose value increases from $50 to $55 in a year and pays a $5 dividend during the year has a 20 percent rate of return ($10 return/$50 original investment = 0.20).

Types of Stocks

When a company sells stock, it usually offers two different types: common stock and preferred stock. **Common stock** is the primary form of ownership in a corporation. All corporations must issue common stock and many issue common stock only. For each share of common

Real-World Application
part 1 of 4

TYPICAL DAY ON THE FLOOR
You made a decision to sell some of your stock. The next morning your account executive receives your order to sell stock and relays the order electronically to the brokerage firm's representative on the stock exchange.
What are some reasons why you might sell your stock?

continued on p. 503

stock that you own, you get a vote in how to run the corporation. Every year the stockholders have a meeting where they vote on various issues and elect members to the Board of Directors. The Board of Directors is responsible for representing the interests of the stockholders in the running of the corporation.

A company might also issue **preferred stock**. Preferred stock gives its holders certain privileges that common stockholders don't have. If the company pays dividends, dividends on preferred stocks are paid before dividends on common stocks. If a company fails, preferred stockholders get a share of whatever assets are left after the company's debts are paid before the common stockholders do.

Business Building Blocks

Reading Stock Market Quotations

Math

If you're involved in the world of business, or have invested part of your savings in shares of corporate stock, you must be able to understand stock market quotations in newspaper financial pages. During a single day, the price of a stock may go up and down several times.

Practice

Study the examples of the stock quotation in the box and answer these questions:

1. What was the closing price for MCD?
2. What was the lowest price paid for MCD during a 52-week period?
3. How many shares of MCD were traded?
4. If you had bought 100 shares of MCD at the year's lowest price, how much more would they be worth today?

Example of a Stock Quotation Table

COLUMN										
1	2	3	4	5	6	7	8	9	10	11
52-Week Hi Lo	Stock	Sym	Div	Yld %	PE	Vol 100s	Hi	Lo	Close	Net Chg
66½ 45¼	McDonald's	MCD	.33	.5	28	30,124	66	63½	65⅞	+3¹/₁₆

Column 1 Highest and lowest selling price of the stock during the preceding 52 weeks.
Column 2 Company's name
Column 3 Ticker symbol
Column 4 Last year's dividend
Column 5 Yield. Last year's dividend divided by current price
Column 6 Price to earnings ratio. Current price divided by earnings per share

Column 7 Number of shares traded this day X 100
Column 8 Highest price the stock traded during this day
Column 9 Lowest price the stock traded during the day
Column 10 Last price the stock traded during this day
Column 11 Change between the closing price yesterday and this day

Stockbrokers

A **broker** is a person who acts as a go-between for buyers and sellers. Brokers process the purchase and sale of stocks. They charge either a percent of the value of the stock or a set amount for each transaction as a fee for their services, which could be up to $500.

Stock Exchanges

Most stocks are bought and sold through a trading market known as a **stock exchange**. These exchanges provide a central place where traders meet to buy and sell stock. When people sell stocks through their stockbrokers, their wishes are sent to the broker's representative on the stock exchange floor. A process like an auction takes place at a booth where the stock is bought and sold.

Some of the best-known exchanges are the New York Stock Exchange (NYSE) in New York City, regional exchanges—such as the Midwest Stock Exchange in Chicago—as well as the London Stock Exchange and the Tokyo Exchange. Only the stocks listed on an exchange can be traded. For example, if the ABC Corporation isn't listed on the New York Stock Exchange, then its stock isn't traded there. Exchanges have rules about what types of companies they'll list. To be listed on an exchange, a corporation must prove to the exchange that it's in good financial condition.

Over-the-Counter Markets

Many stocks not listed on a major exchange can be bought and sold through the National Association of Securities Dealers Automated Quotations (NASDAQ) market. The NASDAQ is a system that quotes over-the-counter securities—all investments bought and sold. In this case, a brokerage house makes a market in a particular stock, or provides a place where that stock can be bought and sold. For example, if you want to sell a stock that isn't listed on any of the exchanges in the United States, your broker will find out if any brokerage house is making a market in that stock.

Mutual Funds

An investor can participate in the stock market without buying stocks in a specific corporation by buying shares in a stock mutual fund. To determine your financial risk-taking personality, take the quiz in Figure 31.2 (on page 504). A **mutual fund** is a fund created by an investment company that raises money from many shareholders and invests it in a variety of stocks. A mutual fund has much greater buying power because

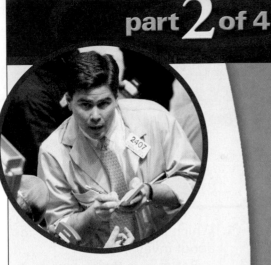

Real-World Application

part **2** of 4

TYPICAL DAY ON THE FLOOR
On the stock exchange floor a clerk for the firm signals the transaction to a floor broker on the stock exchange floor.
Name one of the best-known exchanges.

continued on p. 505

it has a greater amount of money available to invest. If the stocks owned by the mutual fund make a profit, then the mutual fund shareholders earn a dividend. Mutual fund shareholders, like stock shareholders, also have capital gains or losses when they sell their shares.

Mutual funds are a way to limit your risk of investing in the stock market. The risk is spread out because a mutual fund consists of stocks in many companies. If one stock performs poorly, the loss is limited and can be made up by other, better-performing stocks. Many people also prefer mutual funds because the professional managers of the mutual funds have more experience in selecting stocks than they do.

Stock Indexes. There are many ways to determine the value of your stock at any given time. The various stock exchanges' figures can be found in major newspapers, such as the *Wall Street Journal* or the *New York Times*, as well as on their Web sites.

There are some general indexes, or indicators, which are commonly reported on television and radio. An index is a measuring system that tracks stock prices over the long run. The Dow Jones Industrial Average (DJIA) and Standard & Poor's (S&P) are the two most common indexes.

The DJIA represents the 30 largest U.S. companies to measure the well-being of the stock market as a whole. Have you ever heard a report on a TV broadcast say that "the Dow went down 20 points today?" This doesn't mean that all stocks went down 20 points. A change of 20 points in the Dow means that the average for 30 selected stocks listed on the NYSE that the Dow represents went down 20 points.

The S&P 500 index tracks how the top 500 companies are doing. It's a gauge against which they compare their returns on stocks. Investing in an index fund over the long run is better than investing in individual stocks.

✔ **Fast Review** _____

1. What kinds of businesses can sell stock?
2. What privileges do preferred stockholders get?
3. What kinds of fees do brokers charge for their services?
4. Name the advantages of a mutual fund.

Real-World Application

part **3** of 4

TYPICAL DAY ON THE FLOOR
The floor broker goes to the trading post at which your specific stock is traded and trades with a floor broker (employed by another firm) who has an order to buy.
True or false: An exchange trades companies it wants.

continued on p. 507

Advantages and Disadvantages of Stocks

There is a general principle at work in the world of investing—the greater the risk, the greater the possibility of a larger return. You have much more risk of losing your investment when putting your money into stocks rather than savings accounts, certificates of deposit, or money market funds. Stocks generally carry more risk but they also carry the possibility of a better return. Long-term comparisons of returns on stocks compared to savings show that stocks do better over time.

Levels of Risk

The risk of losing your investment varies from stock to stock. There are, however, two basic categories of stocks that offer different levels of risk.

Blue-Chip Stocks. The safest investment is in blue-chip stocks. **Blue-chip stocks** are stocks in large, well-established companies that have a good track record of profitability and success. International Business Machines (IBM) and General Motors (GM) are examples of blue-chip stocks. There is little likelihood that you'll lose your money when you invest in those stocks. However, even the value of blue-chip stocks goes up and down. You could still lose money if you sell them when the value is lower than what you paid for them.

Working Lifestyle

What are you doing at 10 A.M.?

In Stock

When he was a high school student, Thomas Zuttermeister's reading and television viewing habits were very focused. He and his mother watched the Financial News Network together. As he began advising his mother and investing some of his own resources, the financially precocious teenager managed to do very well—and not very well.

Most of Zuttermeister's clients are retired. It's important for him to help them invest their money safely. "I deal mostly in mutual funds, which helps distribute the risk. And when the market experiences fluctuations, I tell my clients, 'Don't *you* worry—that's part of my job.'"

As the Claremont, N.H., financial advisor reads the 10:00 A.M. stock market report, he says the rewards of his job are more than financial. He says, "It's a good feeling when you know you've helped someone. And those clients are very appreciative—they come back."

Salary

A typical stockbroker earns a median base salary of $46,210. Half of the people in this job earn between $40,136 and $50,025.

Outlook for This Career

The need for stockbrokers is strong. People often seek better returns on their investments.

Connecting Careers Activity

Zuttermeister turned his teenage interest into a career. What's more important to you: doing something you're passionate about or making a lot of money?

CAREER PATH *finance*

Speculative Stocks. The story is different with speculative stocks. **Speculative stocks** are stocks in relatively new firms that don't have an established track record of success. They're often small firms that are developing new types of goods and services. Many technology stocks offered in the late 1990s and early 2000s were examples of speculative stocks. A few succeeded and made big money for their owners.

Day Trading

Some people have attempted to make quick money in the stock market by *day trading*. This means they're buying and selling stock, usually on the Internet, based on minute-by-minute changes in the price of the stock. This is extremely risky. You not only risk losing your original investment but also risk sustaining great financial losses.

Liquidity

Liquidity refers to how easily an investment can be turned into cash. In general, stocks are very liquid because they can be turned into cash quickly by selling them. You're not guaranteed to get all the money out of your investment, however, because the value of the stock might have gone down since you bought it. If the stock isn't listed on one of the exchanges or on the NASDAQ market, liquidity can be a problem. If it's not listed anywhere, there's no market for it and you won't be able to sell it.

Inflation Risk

Inflation risk is whether a rate of return or an investment keeps up with the rate of inflation. For example, if there is 4 percent inflation over the year, you must have 4 percent more money at the end of the year than at the beginning of the year to buy the same amount of goods and services. That means your stock needs to go up in value more than 4 percent to earn a return on your investment. Stocks have generally done very well in this category.

Real-World Application

part 4 of 4

TYPICAL DAY ON THE FLOOR
The floor broker signals the transaction back to the clerk. Then a floor reporter—an employee of the exchange—collects the information about the transaction and inputs it into the ticker system. The sale appears on the price board, and a confirmation is relayed back to your account executive, who then notifies you of the completed transaction. **Are stocks considered to have great liquidity?**

✓ **Fast Review** _____

1. What is the difference between blue-chip stocks and speculative stocks?
2. Why is online trading very risky?

Summary

1. Stocks are shares in ownership of a business. Only corporations sell stock.

2. Brokers buy and sell stock at stock exchanges. Brokers may research, advise, buy, and sell various stocks for you. When you tell a broker to buy or sell a stock, the broker contacts his or her representative on a stock exchange floor. The process is like an auction. Unlike organized exchanges, over-the-counter stocks are not traded in a specific place. Instead, brokerage firms hold these stocks for investors. The NASDAQ lists these over-the-counter stocks.

3. The DJIA and S&P 500 are two indexes that track stock prices over the long run.

Using Business Key Words

Investors have the ability to choose among many different options. Understanding the terminology is the first step to successful investing. Rewrite the sentences by filling in the blank with the term that best completes the sentence.

- **investing**
- **preferred stock**
- **stock**
- **yield**
- **broker**
- **stock exchange**
- **mutual fund**
- **dividends**
- **blue-chip stocks**
- **capital gain**
- **speculative stocks**
- **capital loss**
- **common stock**

1. A(n) _____ is created by an investment company, which purchases the securities of many corporations by selling shares in the fund.

2. _____ are generally stocks in relatively new firms, and which don't have a track record for success.

3. A positive return on stock when you sell stock for more than the purchase price is called a(n) _____.

4. Stock that gives its holders certain privileges is called _____.

5. A(n) _____ is a share of ownership in a business.

6. _____ is using money to gain a return.

7. The rate of return on an investment or amount of money an investment earns is the _____.

8. IBM and General Motors are examples of _____.

9. A negative return on stock when you sell the stock for less than the purchase price is called a(n) _____.

10. A dealer who specializes in buying and selling stock is called a(n) _____.

11. _____ is the stock that all corporations must issue.

12. A market where stocks are bought and sold is the _____.

13. A share of the profits of a corporation paid to stockholders is called _____.

Review What You Learned

14. What is the difference between saving and investing?

15. What is one way that a corporation raises money to start or grow its business?

16. What privileges do preferred stockholders have?

17. What is the function of a stockbroker?

18. Why is the investment risk generally lower for mutual funds?

19. What is the Dow Jones Industrial Average?

20. Do you have more or less risk of losing your investment when you put your money into stocks rather than a savings account? Explain.

21. Describe day trading.

22. What are the differences between growth stocks and income stocks?

23. Are stocks considered liquid investments? Explain.

Understanding Business Concepts

24. How do stockholders earn income?

25. Is it possible for a company to issue only preferred stock?

26. Is it possible to buy stock without going through a stock exchange? If so, give an example.

27. What is the difference between the DJIA and the S&P 500?

28. Do you believe the following general principle? The higher the risk, the higher the possibility of a greater return. Explain your answer.

29. If you had $1,000 to invest, how much investment risk would you feel comfortable with?

Critical Thinking

30. Imagine you own 100 shares of a particular stock. What do you think will happen to your investment if the company goes out of business?

31. If you have only a small amount of money, would you invest it in a high-risk stock or a low-risk stock? Explain why.

32. Given the current business climate, would you invest $5,000 in tech-sector stocks? Explain why or why not.

33. Investing is a very personal decision. Do you agree or disagree with her? Explain your answer.

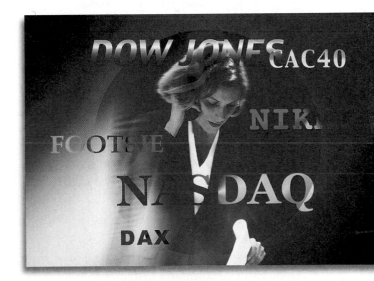

Viewing and Representing

Examining the Image. Focus on the background of this photograph and list details you see. Pair up with a classmate and discuss the following question: Before investing in stock, what resources would you use to make informed decisions?

Building Academic Skills

 Reading the Financial Section

Locate the financial section of the newspaper. Choose three different stocks and study the stock listings for the following information:

- Which stock traded the most shares on this day? How many shares were traded?
- Which stock lost the most from the day before? How much did it lose?
- If you buy $100 shares of each stock you selected, how much would it cost you?

 Industry's Stock Research

In a group, select an industry in the business world. Each member of the group should collect current information on the stock prices for one company in that industry. Then, use the Internet to check on the stock information from six months ago and one year ago. Use the information to answer the following questions:

- What was the selling price of the stock six months ago? One year ago?
- What rate of return or yield does the company report?
- What was the amount of the most recent dividend the company distributed?

- What were the high and low prices during the year?
- Compare the performance of the companies your group researched. Was one much better than another? Much worse?

Use the information you collect about the companies to make an industry profile. Explain whether you think companies in this industry might be a good investment and why.

 Online Trading

Research e-trading or online trading. Use the Internet to gather information about at least two different companies that offer trading online. Find out what services are offered online and how much it costs per transaction.

Writing About Stock Exchanges

Research one of the leading stock exchanges in the world. (Examples include the NYSE, the London Stock Exchange, or the Nikkei Exchange in Tokyo.) Write a two-page paper with your findings. Be sure to include how the exchange began, the average amount of trading that occurs each day, and the process used to buy and sell stocks.

Linking School to Home

Financial News. With family members and friends, listen to or watch a radio or television broadcast that focuses on the stock market. (Examples include *MG and the Stock Doctor*, CNBC's *Bloomberg's Market Watch*, and CNN's *Moneyline News Hour*.) Evaluate the experts and the stock advice they offer. Ask your family members and friends for their opinions as well.

Linking School to Work

Local Brokerage Firm. Investigate one of the brokerage firms in your community. Ask about the services they provide, the educational outreach they offer, and the fees they charge. If possible, invite a stockbroker to your classroom to discuss his or her job.

E-Homework

Applying Technology

E-Trading Behavior. The values of stocks or mutual funds go up and down in value over time. There are many Internet sites that provide information about prices and sales as they occur. Many magazines and publications are devoted to studying stocks and mutual funds and are another source of information about investments. Use the Internet to research how the Internet has changed our investment behavior. What resources are available online? How have chat rooms and discussion groups impacted investment decisions?

NASDAQ Research. Stocks represent ownership in a business. There's no promise that the business will succeed. It could fail and you could lose all of your investment. There is no federal agency insuring your investment in stocks as there is with banks, so you won't get your money back if the company goes out of business. Therefore, it's important to make tactical, wise decisions despite all the hype you hear in the media. Most of the technology stocks are traded on the NASDAQ. Find out what the NASDAQ stands for, where it's located, its history, and how many different stocks are traded there.

Connecting Academics

Math. Sarah buys 500 shares of stock at $18 and sells the holding for a capital gain of $3,000. What was the share price at the time of sale?

Language Arts. When faced with making hard decisions, your integrity or honesty might be tested. A debate sharpens your skills of discernment and decision making. As a class, debate the following: Buying stock is a good way to invest money and to promote the entrepreneurial spirit.

BusinessWeek Analyzing the Feature Story

You read the first part of "Where Kids Can Log On to Learn Their Investing ABC's" at the beginning of this chapter. Below are a few questions for you to answer about managing finances. You'll find the answers to these questions when you're reading the entire article. First, here are the questions:

34. Why is it important for kids to learn how to manage finances?
35. What are some of the strong points of Younginvestor.com?

CREATIVE JOURNAL ACTIVITY

Visit Kiplinger.com's Kids & Money page, **www.kiplinger.com/managing/kids**, KidsBank.org, **www.kidsbank.org**, or another financial educational Web site for kids. Surf the site. What do you like about it? What would make it more useful? Write a one-page review of the site.

The Full Story

To learn more about investing, visit the *Introduction to Business* Web site at www.introbus.glencoe.com, and click on *BusinessWeek* Feature Story, Chapter 31.

Bonds and Real Estate

BusinessWeek Feature Story

Will Refis Help Refloat the Economy?

Equity Into Cash: So Far, Owners Are Spending, Not Paying Down Debt. When Anton and Audrey Scholl bought their $249,000 townhouse in Itasca, Ill., a year ago, they had no idea they'd refinance their mortgage within a year. But when their broker called in January advising they convert their 30-year adjustable rate mortgage to a 30-year fixed mortgage with a lower interest rate and no closing costs, the Scholls bit. The new 7.25 percent rate, a reduction of 1.25 percentage points, cuts their monthly payments by $225.

Source: Excerpted with permission from "Will Refis Help Refloat the Economy?" *BusinessWeek Online*, April 2, 2001.

An Extension Activity

Imagine you receive a cash payment of $20,000 or more. Would you seek professional advice on how to invest your newfound wealth? Explain the details of your decision-making process.

The Full Story

To learn more about mortgage rates, visit the *Introduction to Business* Web site at **www.introbus.glencoe.com**, and click on *BusinessWeek* Feature Story, Chapter 32.

Common Investment Choices

There are many ways you can invest your money. The type of investment you choose depends on your goals. Do you want a return in the quickest time possible? Or do you want a steady, reasonable, and predictable flow of cash? Selecting a bond or purchasing real estate is an investment option. You can tailor an investment program to meet your individual needs. Choosing an investment program means making and completing your financial plan to make your money grow.

Bonds

Corporations can raise money by selling stock, but they can also raise money by borrowing. When a corporation or the government needs to borrow a large amount of money for a long time, they often issue bonds. **Bonds** are written promises to repay a loan with interest on a specific date (the *maturity date*). (See Figure 32.1 to examine a bond.) The buyer

Figure 32.1 — A TYPICAL CORPORATE BOND

➡ Important Papers. This bond issued by the Mobil Corporation is a typical corporate bond with a face value of $1,000.
What is this bond's maturity date?

of a bond becomes a creditor (or lender) to the corporation or government that issued the bond.

Characteristics of Bonds

Like savings accounts and other types of investments, bonds earn interest. The rate of interest on a bond is referred to as the **coupon rate**. Interest is usually paid once or twice a year. For example, a $1,000 bond with a 6 percent coupon rate will pay $60 once a year or $30 twice a year. Many bonds are sold at a discount, or below their face value, and gather interest until they reach their full value. The difference between the amount you pay for the bond and its face value is the **bond discount**.

The prices of bonds are listed in the financial section of newspapers and are also found on the Internet. Bonds are rated according to their risks by several agencies, such as Standard & Poor's and Moody's. Bonds are usually rated from *secure* (the highest rating) to *speculative* (the lowest rating). Bonds with more risk carry a higher interest rate than those that are more secure.

Bonds are generally considered a safe place to invest your money. If the corporation or government doesn't pay back the loan or the interest, you can take legal action to collect the amount owed. Even if the corporation that issued you a bond goes bankrupt, you would be repaid before the stockholders. Although the prices of bonds don't go up and down as much as stocks, they do fluctuate. There are three types of bonds you can buy: federal, municipal, and corporate.

Federal Bonds

Bonds that are sold by the federal government are called **savings bonds**. U.S. savings bonds are considered one of the safest kinds of investments and are bought through a bank or a payroll plan at work. There are several types of government-issued bonds.

EE Bonds. A series EE savings bond costs half the amount of its face value to buy. For example, a $100 bond costs $50 and a $1,000 bond costs $500. After a certain number of years the bond becomes worth its full face value. The time it takes to reach its maturity rate depends on the rate of interest. If you cash in an EE bond before its maturity date, you have to pay a penalty. On the other hand, if you keep an EE bond past its maturity, it continues to earn interest for up to 30 years and can become worth more than its face value.

Real-World Application

part **1** of 4

HUNTING FOR A HOME

Just look in the real estate section of a newspaper and the options might make you dizzy. House. Townhouse. Cooperative. Mobile home. Let's break down the differences. For a homeowner, he or she takes on all aspects of ownership. That means the owner is responsible for maintaining the lawn, painting, repairs, and taxes.
What are some other costs that come along with owning a home?

continued on p. 517

I Bonds. Another type of U. S. savings bond is the I bond. This is a bond for which you pay the face value. If you buy a $500 I bond, you would pay $500. The interest rate on this bond fluctuates over time with the rate of inflation. The higher the rate of inflation, the higher the interest rate on the bond. The interest doesn't fall if there is deflation during a period of time. You can lose interest if you cash it in early (much like the EE bond). Like the EE bond, there are certain restrictions on how much you'll receive if you cash it in before its maturity date. For example, if you earn an I bond during the first five years of your investment, you'll forfeit, or lose, three months of interest.

EE bonds and I bonds are attractive to people who want safe, guaranteed long-term investments. There are also tax advantages for the income earned on these bonds. Interest from savings bonds isn't subject to state and local income taxes. You pay reduced taxes or no taxes at all if you're paying for college and your household income is below a certain level.

Other Federal Bonds. The U.S. Treasury issues three kinds of bonds. The main difference between them is the length of time it takes to mature. *Treasury bills* (or *T-bills*) are issued for three months to one year, *Treasury notes* are issued for two to ten years, and *Treasury bonds* are issued for ten or more years. The longer the maturity, the higher the interest rate. The smallest amount of any of these bonds is $1,000 (treasury bonds). T-bills are only available as $10,000 bonds, and T-notes range from $1,000 to $5,000. You can buy (and sell) these bonds through brokerage firms, banks, and other financial institutions, at a Federal Reserve Bank, or over the Internet.

They can be sold just like stocks at any given time before their maturity date. The U. S. government, based on its ability to tax and collect money from its citizens, guarantees treasury bonds. T-bills are sold at a discount like EE bonds.

Municipal Bonds

Local and state governments issue **municipal bonds**. They're sold to finance projects such as schools, highways, and airports. You can buy them from a broker or directly from the government. The main advantage of municipal bonds is that the government doesn't generally tax the interest you earn on them. Like treasury bonds, you don't have to hold on to a municipal bond until it reaches its maturity date. If you sell it before it matures, however, you might receive less than the face value of the bond.

Corporate Bonds

Bonds issued by corporations are called **corporate bonds**. Corporate bonds can be bought and sold through brokerage firms. They're usually used to finance building and equipment. The value of a corporate

Consider This...

Spending Your Windfall Wisely

Smart people who inherit large sums of money don't spend their windfall quickly. Instead, more than half seek financial advice and invest it. If you're newly rich, you might need to pay off high-interest credit cards or other debts. Windfalls starting at $50,000 require a financial plan. This would include your home and retirement account, mutual funds, tax-free bonds, and real estate.

ANALYZE

What is your monetary attitude toward investing versus spending?

bond fluctuates according to the overall interest rates in the economy. If you buy a corporate bond with a high interest rate and interest rates fall, the corporation may be able to *call* your bond, or buy it back before the maturity date. This way the corporation doesn't have to pay off the bonds at the higher interest rate. It then issues new bonds at lower rates.

Junk Bonds. Junk bonds belong to a special category of corporate bonds. **Junk bonds** are bonds that have a low or speculative rating and are issued by companies that don't have successful track records. They offer a high rate of interest and a high rate of risk. Remember risk and return trade off. They are not considered a very safe investment. If a company defaults on its junk bonds, there's little chance you'll be able to get any of your money back. In fact, many junk-bond holders lose their entire investment.

✔ Fast Review

1. How much does an EE bond cost to buy?
2. What is the main difference between a Treasury bill, a Treasury note, and a Treasury bond?
3. What is the main advantage of municipal bonds?

Real Estate

You would think that there couldn't be a safer, surer investment than real estate. **Real estate** is land and anything attached to it, such as buildings or natural resources. Real estate is considered the safest form of investment for one simple reason: As the population continues to increase and the demand for land increases, the supply of desirable land remains the same. According to the law of supply and demand, the more demand exceeds supply, the more the item in demand increases in value. In fact, the value of real estate only seems to increase over time.

People buy real estate for a number of reasons. Most people buy property for the safety and security of owning their own home. Some people buy property to make an income from it, like raising crops or renting office space. Others buy unused property hoping its value will increase. Buying real estate is a major investment.

How then can anyone make a poor real estate investment? There are a number of mistakes that people can make. When demand decreases, the value of real estate goes down. For instance, people can buy in the wrong location—one that is or becomes unpopular or unattractive to others. When the owner wants to sell such property, its value may be less

HUNTING FOR A HOME
From San Francisco to Brooklyn, people also invest in townhouses. The owner owns both the structure and the land, except it isn't free standing. There may be a front yard or back yard, but each townhouse connects to the next. **How does a townhouse differ from a house?**

continued on p. 519

than what the owner has invested in it. People can choose (or need to buy or sell) at a poor time. They can pay too much—either initially or through unexpected hidden costs. Perhaps they might make a poor choice regarding the type of real estate in which they invest.

Home Ownership

Buying a home is the most expensive purchase most people make in their lives. Before buying a home, there are a number of factors to consider.

Types of Homes. There are different types of homes you can buy depending on your income and needs. The most popular is the single-family house. It usually sits on its own lot, with its own yard. It's separate from other buildings and provides privacy. Single-family houses range from modest two-bedroom homes to huge mansions.

Figure 32.2

AFFORDABLE HOUSING

➡People buy a home to live in for a variety of reasons. Some people see the purchase of a home as a safe investment. Others buy a home because of the feeling of security that they receive from home ownership. Others invest with the hope of making money on their home. Still others want to own a home in order to build equity—the amount of value in the home. Read the table below.
According to your geographic location, what do you think your city's homes are worth?

MOST AFFORDABLE COSTS FOR SINGLE-FAMILY HOMES		
Location	Percent of income	Median
1 Oklahoma City, Okla.	17.4	$41,300
2 Richmond, Va.	17.8	$52,600
3 Kansas City, Kans.	18.4	$52,600
4 Knoxville, Tenn.	18.6	$42,300
5 Raleigh-Durham, N.C.	18.9	$54,700
6 Indianapolis, Ind.	19.0	$51,100
7 Tulsa, Okla.	19.1	$41,400
8 Houston, Tex.	19.6	$50,400
9 Charlotte, N.C.	19.7	$49,600
10 Dallas-Ft. Worth, Tex.	19.7	$53,600

Multi-unit housing includes duplexes, townhouses, and condominiums. Multi-unit houses are usually single buildings divided into various units, with a separate person or family living in each unit. They are like apartment buildings only the people who live in them own rather than rent the space.

Mobile homes are usually produced in parts by a factory and assembled on a building site. They're sometimes referred to as prefabricated houses. The owner often doesn't own any land but rents space for the house in a mobile-home park. Because the parts of these homes can be mass-produced cheaply, they usually cost much less than other types of houses.

Buying a Home. Few people have enough money to pay for a house in full and have to finance it with a *home mortgage loan*, or a long-term property loan. To buy a house also requires a down payment, usually about 20 percent. The down payment is money you have to come up with yourself. That means if you want to buy a house for $100,000, you need $20,000 for the down payment.

Homebuyers often use the services of a real estate agent to help them find a home. A **real estate agent** is a person licensed to arrange the buying and selling of homes as well as other types of real estate. Real estate agents charge a fee for their services, but it is usually charged to the seller and not the buyer.

Once you find a house you're interested in buying, it's a good idea to hire a qualified building inspector. A house that looks good on the surface might have serious plumbing or electrical problems. The cost of a building inspection can be high, but it can save a lot of money in repairs.

Home Values. There are a number of factors that affect the value of a house, such as the size, condition, and location. Location is especially important. A house that seems like a bargain might turn out to be in a bad neighborhood or in the path of a noisy airport. If you buy a house in an area where many businesses are closing, the value of your house will go down as more people move out to find other jobs and the demand for housing decreases.

Home Equity. The amount of equity you have in a home is very important. Your home equity is the amount on the house you actually own as opposed to how much you owe. As you pay off the mortgage on the house, your equity increases. For example, if you make a $20,000 down payment on a $100,000 house and pay off $3,000 over four years, your equity increases from $20,000 to $23,000. Your equity also increases as the value of your home increases. Suppose over those four years, the value of your house increased by $20,000. Your equity would then be $43,000 instead of $23,000.

Real-World Application

part 3 of 4

HUNTING FOR A HOME

Depending on the context, cooperative means either helpful or a company. In the context of real estate, a cooperative (or co-op) is just that—you share ownership in a cooperative corporation. You can live in the co-op, but you don't get complete ownership. As a co-op member you help pay for building maintenance, shared spaces, and management issues.

Do you foresee any problems with being part owner of a co-op?

continued on p. 521

Advantages of Home Ownership. Some of the advantages of owning a home have already been stated. First of all, the value of a home usually increases over time, so it's a good investment. Owning your own home rather than renting provides a sense of security and stability. Homeowners also get tax breaks. You can deduct the interest you pay on your mortgage loans and the taxes you pay on your property from your federal income taxes.

As a homeowner, you will also reap financial benefits. You can deduct the interest charges on your loan payments from your federal income taxes each year. Your property taxes are also deductible. Moreover, the value of many homes rises steadily, so homeowners often can sell their homes for a profit depending on their *equity*—the value of the home less the amount still owed on the money borrowed to purchase it. Finally, once the money they borrowed is paid off, homeowners have no further financial obligation other than property taxes, homeowner's insurance, and maintenance costs.

Disadvantages of Home Ownership. Of course, buying a house doesn't guarantee happiness. Home ownership involves financial risk. Saving money for a down payment is very difficult for many people. Property value doesn't always go up, either; in some cases, they may even decline.

As with any investment, owning a home also has some disadvantages. While owning a home gives you more stability, it also gives you less mobility. If you want to move, you have to sell your house first. Because it can take a long time to sell a house and turn it into cash, it's the least liquid of all investments. In both cases, the process can be slow and may result in a financial loss.

There are also several costs to owning a house besides mortgage payments. You have to buy homeowner's insurance and pay property taxes. You also

You Make the Call

One Person's Junk Is Another Person's...

The second-hand shop you own is a popular spot for antique shoppers in search of reasonably priced furniture and collectibles. You build your inventory from attending auctions and buying objects brought in by individuals. One day, a man brings a box full of odds and ends from his great aunt's attic. He says it's all just junk and asks for $10. You glance through it and agree. After he leaves, you notice a pocket watch that is lodged in the corner. As you lift it out and look at it, you realize it is worth hundreds of dollars.

Making an Ethical Decision

1. What should you do?
2. What if the watch was worth thousands of dollars? Would that change your answer?
3. Let's say you're a pocket-watch collector? Would that change your view of what is ethical behavior?

need to pay for repairs and maintenance, such as fixing the plumbing, putting on a new roof, or repainting the house. Repairs can be very costly, and if neglected, lower the value of your home. The cost of taking care of a home can be quite high, even if the homeowners do most of the work themselves.

Income Property

Another reason for buying real estate is to obtain **income property**, or property used to generate an income. A common type of income property is farmland for producing and selling crops. Land can also be used for raising sheep or cattle. Natural resources found on land, such as oil, timber, or gas, can be produced and sold.

Stores, factories, and office buildings are other kinds of income property. You could buy an apartment building and rent out the units to earn an income. Some people buy a multi-unit home, move into one unit, and rent out the others. The rental income can then be used to pay the mortgage and taxes on the property. With income property, the owner can produce income in two ways. First, the owner can make money from the rent, crops, or natural resources on the property. Second, the owner can make investment income by selling the property for a profit after its value increases.

Undeveloped Property

Undeveloped property is unused land intended only for investment purposes. Usually the land isn't cleared and has no utility services such as drinking water, sewage, or electricity. Within large tracts of undeveloped land there are usually no public roads. This type of land is often inexpensive to buy.

Investors in undeveloped property hope that its value will increase sharply over the years. The land might be chosen as the site of a shopping center, housing development, or industrial park. In other cases, however, the land's value might stay the same or even decrease. For example, a planned highway might never be built, leaving the land along its proposed route undeveloped. With undeveloped land, there is no return, like rent or the sale of crops. The income earned on undeveloped property comes through the sale of the property after it has gone up in value.

HUNTING FOR A HOME

A mobile home is also one of the most common types of real estate investments. When you buy this home you're the owner, but its value depreciates unlike other real estate investments. Depending if you hit the open road with your mobile home or decide to settle in a mobile home park, each situation has different taxes and fees involved.

Why isn't buying a mobile home considered a safe investment?

✔ **Fast Review** _____

1. Why does the value of real estate generally increase over time?
2. What are the two ways the equity in your home can increase?
3. What are the two ways an owner can produce income with income property?

Summary

1. Bonds are written promises to repay a loan on a specific date. They earn interest like savings accounts and are considered a safe place to invest your money.

2. The federal government sells U.S. savings bonds, state and local governments sell municipal bonds, and corporations sell corporation bonds and junk bonds.

3. The main reasons people buy real estate are to own a home, to generate an income, and to make an investment.

4.
Home Ownership

Advantages	Disadvantages
• A good investment	• Less mobility
• Provides security and stability	• Have to buy insurance and pay property taxes
• Homeowners earn tax breaks	• Have to pay for maintenance and repairs

Using Business Key Words

Understanding these investment terms will help you when you decide to invest in bonds and real estate. Match each term with its definition.

- **bonds**
- **real estate**
- **coupon rate**
- **bond discount**
- **municipal bonds**
- **savings bonds**
- **corporate bonds**
- **undeveloped property**
- **real estate agent**
- **income property**
- **junk bonds**

1. Bonds that can be bought or sold through brokerage firms.

2. Debt obligations that are written promises to repay not only the loan but also the interest on the loan.

3. A person licensed to arrange the buying and selling of homes.

4. The rate of interest on a bond.

5. Land in its natural state.

6. The difference between the amount paid for a bond and its face value.

7. Bonds sold by the federal government.

8. Bonds that carry a high rate of interest but also carry a high rate of risk.

9. Bonds sold to finance projects by local or state governments and by certain government agencies.

10. Land and anything attached to it, such as buildings or natural resources.

11. Property used to generate an income, such as a farm or apartment building.

Review What You Learned

12. The corporation or government issuing the bond makes two promises. What are they?
13. Why are bonds considered a safe place to invest your money?
14. What is the difference between the EE and the I bonds?
15. What is the tax advantage for the income earned on savings bonds?
16. What do municipal bonds finance?
17. How are bonds rated?
18. How are poor real estate investments made?
19. Which possess less risk—bonds or real estate? Explain.
20. Which of the following is the least liquid—CDs, stocks, bonds, or real estate? Explain.

Understanding Business Concepts

21. Why do you think the U.S. government issues bonds?
22. Describe the differences between T-bills, Treasury notes, and Treasury bonds.
23. The costs of home ownership include more than the purchase price, which is most often financed through a long-term mortgage. Property taxes, the cost of utilities, gas, water, and sewage add to the monthly costs. With all these expenses, why do you think people buy a home?
24. Why is the timing of a sale of a home important?
25. How do people earn income by investing in undeveloped property?
26. What criteria should you use to evaluate various types of investments?

Critical Thinking

27. Do you believe bonds are less risky than stocks? Explain your answer.
28. Do you think home ownership is a good investment? Explain why or why not.
29. What proportion of your savings would you consider putting in bonds? In stocks? Explain your answer.
30. What would your advice be to a friend who is considering buying a home?

Viewing and Representing

Examining the Image. Give a written description of this picture. What's the message? To prevent this happening to you, how do you plan to invest in the future? Together with a partner share and discuss your investment plans.

Chapter 32 Review

Building Academic Skills

 Planning a Dream House

Create a poster of your dream house. Use magazines, the Internet, or your own drawings to depict what features it will have, where it will be located, and what it will look like. Then, use the newspaper or the Internet to locate a real home that might look like what you designed. Use the real home's price to create a reasonable purchase price for your home.

 Researching Social Responsibility

Habitat for Humanity builds houses for families in need. Its mission is to eliminate homelessness from the world and to make decent shelter a matter of conscience and action. Research the history of Habitat for Humanity and its plans for the future. Write a two-page paper with your findings.

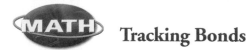 **Tracking Bonds**

Imagine you have $5,000 to invest and you decide to buy bonds. Using the newspaper or the Internet, choose two bonds in which to invest your imaginary money. Note today's actual market price for your bonds. In two weeks, check the price again. Do the same in one month. How do they compare?

Comparative Research

In groups of three or four, research the average price for a home in your area. Include single- and multiple-family housing. Create a spreadsheet with your findings.

Linking School to Home

Conducting a Mini-Survey. Do you own any savings bonds? Many people give savings bonds as gifts for birthdays or to be used for college tuition. You can buy and sell U.S. savings bonds at banks and other financial institutions. The minimum face value of such a bond is $50; the maximum is $10,000. Conduct a mini-survey among your family and friends and find out if they have any bonds, what they plan to do with them, and whether or not they have given any as gifts. Also, ask them what they think of savings bonds as an investment.

Linking School to Work

Profiling a Career. Research the careers associated with the real-estate profession. Choose one of the following: sales agents, brokers, real-estate lawyers, commercial real estate investment counselors, appraisers, urban planners, and real-estate researchers. Interview someone in the profession. What skills does it take to have that job? How do you prepare for that job? Remember to use the journalist questions: who, what, where, when, why, and how. Write a two-page paper with your findings. Be sure to include a description of the career, the education and training necessary to succeed, average earnings, and the opportunities in the field.

● E-Homework

Applying Technology

Comparing Municipal Bonds. Municipal bonds are sold to finance projects by local or state governments and by certain government agencies. Municipal bonds finance highway construction, schools, and other government projects. They can be bought and sold like stocks. In other words, like treasury bonds, you don't have to hold on to a municipal bond until it matures. Using the Internet, research the relationship between the current interest rate and the interest earned from the purchase of municipal bonds. Write a paragraph describing the relationship.

Researching the Process. Research the steps necessary to purchase U.S. savings bonds online. Then, find out if there are other types of bonds you can purchase online. Create a flowchart with the steps.

● Connecting Academics

Math. Maria is considering a $10,000 corporate bond offering 7 percent or a $10,000 municipal bond paying 5 percent. Maria pays a tax of 31 percent on her income. Which of the investments will result in the greatest gain?

Computer/Technology. You're an employee in a real-estate office that has just acquired new computer equipment. Your coworkers are useless with new technology and look to you as the technology expert. What technical problems might arise, and what steps do you take to solve them?

BusinessWeek Analyzing the Feature Story

You read the first part of "Will Refis Help Refloat the Economy?" at the beginning of this chapter. Below are a few questions for you to answer about mortgage rates. You'll find the answers to these questions when you're reading the entire article. First, here are the questions:

31. What are some of the reasons for lower mortgage rates?
32. Why are homeowners like Anton and Audrey Scholl choosing to refinance their mortgages?

CREATIVE JOURNAL ACTIVITY

You just inherited $300,000 after taxes. Create a financial plan for this windfall. How much of your new wealth would you like to invest in real estate? Stocks? Bonds? Collectibles? Do you plan to borrow money for your real-estate investment? Why or why not? Break into teams and share your financial plan with a partner. How would you improve your partner's plan?

The Full Story

To learn more about mortgage rates, visit the *Introduction to Business* Web site at **www.introbus.glencoe.com**, and click on *BusinessWeek* Feature Story, Chapter 32.

Tracking Investments on the Internet

Buy in and sell at the right time to make your money grow. Sometimes the stock market is the quickest game of chance. In Chapter 31, you read about investing in stock. The Internet has made information about stocks and investing much more accessible than ever before. Never before has it been easier for you to become your own financial manager. All it takes is lots of research, reading, and analysis. This seminar gives you a chance to discover the information only stockbrokers had in the past. Today this information is available to anyone with Internet access.

Factoids

Paying a Financial Planner. If you need a money makeover, consider consulting a financial planner. Call around for different planners to find out what they charge for their services. Determine whether you can afford a commission-only planner, fee-based planner, or fee-only planner.

Match Your Employer. Assume you sock away $100 a month to your 401(k) and your company matches that amount by 50 percent. In 20 years you'll be sitting on about $184,000.

Fund Tracker. The past performance of a stock is no indicator of its future results.

Risk Taker. Fund managers often fall into two categories of risk takers: popular high-earnings growth and undiscovered bargain stocks.

Choose One. There are about 8,000 mutual funds available. Most people have only heard of 250 of them.

Investigate the Images

Look at the photographic collage on the left page. What grabs your attention first? Is it the color or the words? The power in reading visuals is in analyzing and dissecting your observations. On a separate piece of paper, respond to the questions listed below. These questions might help sharpen the focus of your visual mind.

Your Observations

1. How many photographs do you see?

2. Examine each photograph. How are they assembled in relation to one another?

3. What is the subject of each photograph? Is place or location the subject?

4. Does color signify a message?

5. What issues do you take from these images?

Information

6. Summarize what you know about the photographs from your observations.

Exploring Culture

7. Why do you think investing in stocks or mutual bonds can be a stressful, anxiety-ridden activity?

8. Corporate profits represent an average of 9.2 percent of the GDP. Over long periods of time corporate profits reflect the state of the nation's economy. In today's economy, what can you glean from this?

Taking Aim at Technology

Preparation

Research, discover, and track a stock as if it were your own investment.

Objective

In this *BusinessWeek* seminar, you'll:

- **Research** companies on the Internet. Discover the stocks you're hypothetically interested in buying.
- **Select** a particular stock and track its progress for one week. Calculate earnings and losses for one year.
- **Create** a chart to display your chosen stock's performance that year.

Materials Needed

- ✓ Internet access (Note: Internet access is preferable but not necessary. The Internet just makes the information easier to find.)
- ✓ Copies of recent business news publications such as *BusinessWeek* and the *Wall Street Journal*
- ✓ Paper, pens, and pencils
- ✓ Posterboard and markers

Procedures

1. Find and read articles about investing. To use the Internet, access the Web site of a business magazine, such as *BusinessWeek* at **www.businessweek.com**. Click on the tab labeled "Investing" and scan the various articles, columns, and reports available. Read those that interest you until you find a specific company that you would like to research.

2. Research how a company's stock performed over time. To use the Internet, again access *BusinessWeek Online* and find a blank field labeled "Stock Lookup." Enter the name of the company. Write a brief summary of your findings by completing your own stock quotation table. (See a sample of this in Chapter 31 on page 502.)

3. Check these same figures in one week. How do they compare? Write another brief summary like the one in No. 2.

4. Imagine that a year ago you purchased 40 shares of the stock you've been researching. Using the "Historical Quotes" link, calculate whether your stock has increased or decreased in value. If you sold your stock today, how much would you earn or lose?

Chart It

On posterboard, draw a graph that shows the changes in price per share of your stock over the past year. Use the price per share for the first day of each month to create the graph. Display your graph in class.

EXAMPLE:

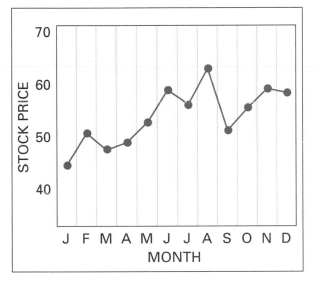

Analyze and Conclude

After considering your research and your chart, answer the questions below.

1. **Interpreting and Communicating Information.** When was the price per share at its highest this past year? When was the price per share at its lowest this past year?

2. **Knowing How to Learn.** Overall, is the price per share of your stock increasing or decreasing in value? Would you recommend buying this stock? Why or why not?

3. **Decision Making.** Why did you choose to research the stock of this company?

Becoming an Informed Citizen

Congratulations, you finished the seminar. Now it's time to reflect on the decisions you made.

Allocating Money. How do you know how much money you'll allocate to stocks in the future? What factors will influence your decisions?

Analyzing Your Future. Why is it important to start investing for your future today?

Further Exploration
To find out more about investing, visit the *Introduction to Business* Web site at **www.introbus.glencoe.com**.

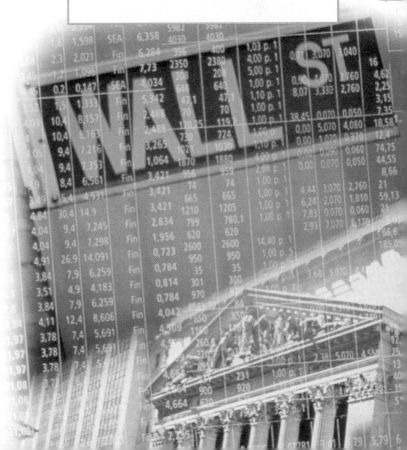

Unit 11

Risk Management

Insurance of the Weird

For every type of risk there is some form of insurance coverage. You can buy insurance for pets, insurance against crocodile attacks, and insurance against employees who quit if they win the lottery. What can you do if aliens abduct you? In fact there are a few companies that provide alien abduction insurance. One company offers coverage not only for alien abductions, but also for injury caused by an asteroid or a piece of falling satellite.

● **Fancy Feet**
Fred Astaire, the famous dancer, had his legs insured for $650,000.

● **Famous Face**
When the *Mona Lisa*, valued at $100 million, was transported from Paris to the United States for an exhibition, the painting wasn't insured because the premiums were too high.

● **For Ransom**
Many U.S. corporations buy kidnap and ransom insurance for their overseas executives, since over 1,000 are kidnapped each year and the average ransom is $10 million.

● **Fore!**
In Japan, many golfers buy "hole-in-one" insurance, since the lucky occasion calls for buying expensive dinners and gifts that can cost as much as $15,000.

Chapter 33

Vehicle Insurance

Learning Objectives

After completing this chapter, you'll be able to:

1. **Name** the different types of vehicle insurance coverage.
2. **Explain** the laws on vehicle insurance.
3. **Describe** the factors that affect the costs of vehicle insurance.

Why It's Important

Most states require you to have some form of vehicle insurance. To get the best value, you need to know the choices in coverage and the costs of insurance.

Key Words

insurance
policy
liability insurance
actual cash value
depreciation
financial responsibility law
compulsory insurance law
no-fault insurance
claim
premium
deductible

BusinessWeek Feature Story

An Insurance Hunter's System of Choice: The Web

The Do's and Don'ts of Finding an Affordable Policy Online. Buying insurance has never been a very consumer-friendly experience. Until recently, scouting out the best deal meant spending hours on the phone with various salespeople to compare policies. Even then, you could never hope to sample more than a fraction of the insurers licensed by your state.

Source: Excerpted with permission from "An Insurance Hunter's System of Choice: The Web," *BusinessWeek Online*, June 11, 2001.

An Extension Activity

Take an industry that you know a little about. What industry is it? How would you change things to make it more consumer oriented, friendly, and efficient?

BUSINESS *Online*
The Full Story

To learn more about vehicle insurance, visit the *Introduction to Business* Web site at **www.introbus.glencoe.com**, and click on *BusinessWeek* Feature Story, Chapter 33.

Preparing to Drive Safely

No one wants to pay for an accident for the rest of his or her life. Not only is being a smart, careful driver good for everyone on the road, but becoming a vehicle insurance holder will protect you against any number of situations. Even before you start looking at cars in the used or new sales lot at the local auto dealer, remember to carefully consider the expenses of any vehicle's insurance before making a decision to buy a car.

Types of Vehicle Insurance

Headlines like "Icy Roads Cause Fender-Benders" and "Wet Freeways Lead to Accidents" show how accidents might happen. How can drivers reduce the risk of financial losses resulting from accidents? One way is to buy insurance. **Insurance** is paid protection against losses due to injury or property damage. To get insurance, you have to purchase a contract called a **policy** from an insurance company. The policy explains how much and what kinds of protection you have. The company that issues the policy is called the *insurer* and the buyer of the policy is called the *policyholder*. Figure 33.1 covers the types of vehicle insurance.

Figure 33.1

TYPES OF VEHICLE INSURANCE COVERAGE

➡ The kinds of vehicle insurance coverage listed here are often included in a single policy or package policy.
Which types cover injuries, and which types cover only property damage?

VEHICLE INSURANCE COVERAGE	
Type of Coverage	**Covers Financial Risk Due To**
Bodily Injury Liability	Injury or death to person(s) not in policyholder's car
Property Damage Liability	Damage to another person's property during an accident
Medical Payments	Medical expenses resulting from injury to the driver or others in policyholder's car
Collision	Damage during an accident to policyholder's car
Comprehensive Damage	Storms, floods, falling objects, fire, vandalism, and theft of policyholder's car
Uninsured Motorists Protection	Accidents caused by people who have no liability insurance and no money to pay for damage (bodily injury and property damage) they cause

The type and amount of protection you have with an insurance policy depends on how much you're willing to pay. Vehicle insurance offers seven types of protection:

- bodily injury liability
- property damage liability
- collision
- medical payments
- comprehensive coverage
- uninsured motorist protection
- miscellaneous coverage

The most basic type of coverage (required by most states) is liability insurance. **Liability insurance** protects you from claims of injury or property damage to others in case you're held responsible for an accident. A policyholder should at least have liability insurance and then add other types of coverage.

Bodily Injury Liability

Bodily injury liability insurance covers injuries to someone else. It is a must for all drivers. The policy states the amount of protection in thousands of dollars. One figure applies to injuries to one person, and the second is a total for one accident. For 100/300 bodily injury coverage, the insurance pays up to $100,000 for injuries to one person. For one accident, it pays up to $300,000 for all claims. How much coverage do you need? A good rule is to buy as much as you can afford. Once you have basic insurance, it doesn't cost that much to increase protection.

Property Damage Liability

Property damage liability insurance covers damage to another person's vehicle or other property. It also covers damage to property, such as telephone poles or street signs. All drivers should have both bodily injury and property damage liability insurance. A policy might quote all liability limits together. The figure 100/300/50 means $100,000 and $300,000 for bodily injury and $50,000 for property damage. Drivers should carry as much coverage as they can afford.

Collision Insurance

Property damage liability insurance covers damages to *someone else's* vehicle. Collision insurance covers damages to your *own vehicle*. The maximum amount covered is based on the **actual cash value** of your vehicle, which is the value of the car when it's new minus depreciation. **Depreciation** is the decline in value of a vehicle because of use. In other words, its actual cash value is how much the car is worth used.

Suppose you get into an accident and the estimate for repairs on your car is $3,000. If the current value of your car, the actual cash value, is only $2,000,

BEWARE OF THE COMBINATIONS
Before getting into a motor vehicle with your driving-age friends, carefully consider this fact: The more teens you have in a car, the higher the crash risk. **Why do you think teenagers' vehicle insurance is expensive?**

continued on p. 537

the insurance won't pay more than $2,000. If you have an old car that's cheaper to replace than to repair, you might not need collision coverage.

Medical Payments Coverage

Medical payments coverage is also called personal injury protection. It covers injuries to you and anyone else in your car. If you're injured in an accident and have to go to the hospital, this coverage pays your medical bills. Since medical costs are rising, you should have as much medical coverage as you can afford. Drivers often carry coverage of $5,000 or $10,000.

Comprehensive Coverage

Comprehensive insurance covers damage to a policyholder's vehicle caused by things other than a car accident. It covers losses from falling

Business Building Blocks

Analysis

Predicting Consequences

You attend a rock concert. As a result, you enjoy yourself, but have less money to spend on a movie next week. These consequences—good and bad—are easy to predict. However, not all decisions and actions give you clear-cut consequences.

Businesspeople often find their success depends on their ability to predict the consequences of business decisions and actions. Predictions are so important that successful businesspeople try to follow a logical process of predicting outcomes. They first try to learn as much as possible about the decision or action.

Practice

Using what you've learned about financing a business, follow the "steps for predicting consequences" to clarify the possible results of each action. Write an explanation of this problem: You want to start a business producing all-natural jams. Your savings are small and your start-up costs will be large. You could: (1) ask a local bank for a loan, (2) accept the offer of money from your Uncle José, or (3) talk to an investment firm in your city.

Steps for Predicting Consequences

1. Gather information about the decision or action.
2. Identify as many consequences as possible.
3. Analyze each consequence by asking how likely it is to occur.
4. Figure out ways to ensure favorable consequences and prevent unfavorable ones.

objects, theft, flood damage, vandalism, and other causes. With this type of insurance, you're covered if someone smashes your window and steals your car stereo. Like collision coverage, comprehensive coverage will not cover more than the actual cash value of your car.

Uninsured Motorist Protection

What if you're in an accident caused by someone without insurance? Uninsured motorist coverage protects you from people who can't pay insurance claims. If you have this kind of coverage, anyone riding with you is also protected. It also protects you if you're hit by a vehicle while walking or if you get into an accident caused by a hit-and-run driver. Most states require this coverage.

Miscellaneous Coverage

Besides these basic types of coverage, you can add other types of protection. For example, you can add coverage for a rental car. Insurance might pay the cost of towing. You need to add insurance to cover someone else who uses your car. If you're required to drive a vehicle for your job, you can add that vehicle to your policy. Your insurance agent can help you add the protection you need.

People who ride motorcycles, motor scooters, or snowmobiles need insurance, too. Most policies won't cover any damages caused as a result of racing. They might not cover passengers or anyone who borrows your motorcycle or snowmobile. Some policies don't include medical payments coverage for the owner.

BEWARE OF THE COMBINATIONS
The Fatality Analysis Reporting System (FARS), a census of fatal motor vehicle crashes on the U.S. public roads, found that 64 percent of the deaths of 13- to 19-year-old passengers occurred when other teenagers were driving.
In case of an accident, how much medical coverage should your vehicle insurance cover?

continued on p. 539

✓ **Fast Review** _____

1. What does liability insurance cover?
2. What do the figures 100/300 mean?
3. What is the maximum amount an insurance company will cover in damages to a vehicle?
4. What types of losses will comprehensive insurance cover?

Laws on Vehicle Insurance

If you drive an old car that's not worth much, consider yourself a safe driver, or just don't have the money, you might think you don't need insurance. States have laws requiring drivers to show proof that they can pay for any injuries or damages they may cause. This not only makes you responsible for any accidents you cause, but protects you from others drivers. Vehicle insurance laws vary from state to state.

News Reporting and Writing

This activity gives you a chance to add to your portfolio. Communicate, interview, research, and write your way into a story. Choose one imaginary path, Civic Journalism or Investigative Reporter. Follow your path's steps to complete your own story.

pick a path

Civic Journalism

The Setting. You're a journalist for the local newspaper. Your editor has assigned you to write a story about car accidents involving young drivers.

Rising Action. Take careful notes during your interviews in order to create a final feature article. Arrange a series of quotes from your sources that you would like to include.

Step 1. Interview the crew of a local automobile towing and wrecking company. Prepare questions ahead of time.

Step 2. Interview one of the wrecker drivers and, if possible, the company owner. Try to find out their perspectives on car accidents. Ask if they have any particularly interesting stories about their work. Did their own driving habits change after they began working as wrecker drivers?

Investigative Reporter

The Setting. From what you've heard young drivers' vehicle insurance is expensive.

Rising Action. Investigate and develop an article on why young people pay high insurance rates. Summarize your interview in an outline that you can expand into a feature article.

Step 1. Talk with a local insurance agent about insurance for young drivers. Why are insurance rates for young drivers higher than those for more mature individuals? Why are young men charged more for insurance?

Step 2. Gather compelling statistics about how certain behaviors—underage drinking, loud music, and too many passengers—increase the risk of accidents.

Conclusion

Journalists determine the importance of a news story based upon timeliness, impact (on the reader), conflict, unusual events, and interest in ongoing issues. How newsworthy is your story? Write a one-page query letter, persuading a newspaper editor to publish your story.

Financial Responsibility Law

All states have some form of financial responsibility law. A **financial responsibility law** says you must pay for any damage or injury you cause in an accident either with insurance, with savings, or by selling property. If you can't pay, you can be sued, lose your license, or even lose your car. The best way to demonstrate financial responsibility is to have car insurance.

Compulsory Insurance Law

Most states also have some form of compulsory insurance law. A **compulsory insurance law** legally requires drivers to have a minimum amount of car insurance. This ensures that drivers will be held responsible for any accidents or injuries they cause as a result of bad driving. According to the law, you have to show proof of insurance before you can get a license or register your car. You might also have to show proof of insurance if the police stop you for a moving violation.

No-Fault Insurance

Suppose you get into an accident with another driver where both of you are injured and there's some dispute about whose fault it is. It can lead to costly lawsuits and take a long time to settle the insurance claims. In order to reduce the amount of time and money it takes to settle injury cases, many states have no-fault insurance laws. Under **no-fault insurance**, it doesn't matter who caused the accident. It requires drivers involved in accidents to collect damages from their own insurance companies no matter who is at fault.

✓ Fast Review

1. What is the difference between a financial responsibility law and a compulsory insurance law?
2. What can happen if you can't show proof of financial responsibility or insurance?

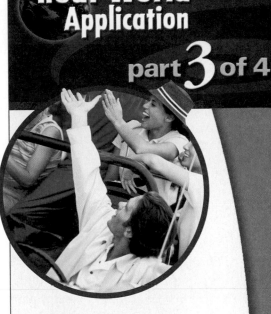

Real-World Application

part **3** of 4

BEWARE OF THE COMBINATIONS
When you've got two or more passengers with a teenage driver the fatal crash risk jumps five times as high as driving alone. Distractions such as music playing, turning to talk with someone in the rear seat, and passengers fooling around are largely the result of the risk-taking factors. **Should there be a law to improve the safety of teenage drivers?**

continued on p. 541

The Costs of Insurance

Paying for car insurance can take a lot out of your budget. The average person pays about $1,200 in car insurance per year. The costs of insurance are directly affected by the amount of money insurers pay each year in insurance claims. A **claim** is a request for payment from an insurer for any damages covered by a policy. The more money insurance companies have to pay in claims, the more they have to charge for insurance to make up for it.

Insurance Premiums

The amount an insurance company charges a policyholder for an insurance policy is called the **premium**. The premium covers the policyholder for a limited period of time, usually for a month, six months, or a year. At the end of the period, the policy is renewed. The insurance company can also cancel a policy or refuse coverage for someone with a record of accidents. (See Figure 33.2 for more specifics on an insurance policy.)

Deductible

Most collision insurance has a deductible. A **deductible** is an amount in damages a policyholder must pay before the insurance company pays anything. For example, you get into an accident and it costs $700 to repair the damage to your car. If your deductible is $200, you pay for $200 of the damages and the insurance company pays the other $500. A deductible makes you responsible for small losses and the insurance helps pay for the larger losses.

Figure 33.2

SPECIFICS OF AN INSURANCE POLICY

➡The amount of coverage you want and the amount of your deductible determines the basic cost of your premium.
If the policyholder has a claim under comprehensive coverage, how much must he or she pay before the insurance company pays? How much must the policyholder pay first in case of a collision?

COVERAGES**	LIMITS
Personal Liability (per accident)	$300,000
Medical Payments	$5,000
Uninsured/Underinsured Motorists (including property damage)	$300,000
Comprehensive	$50 deductible
Collision	$500 deductible
Towing	$50
Rental Reimbursement	$30 a day/maximum of $900

**Discounts for no accidents or moving violations in three years, seat belt/air bags

Factors Affecting the Costs of Insurance

The costs of paying claims affect the costs of insurance in general. The amount of coverage you want and the amount of your deductible determines the basic cost of your premium. In addition, there are a variety of specific factors that affect the cost of your premium: type of vehicle, vehicle usage, geographic location, and your age.

Type of Vehicle. The amount of your premium will vary according to the make, model, and year of the vehicle you drive. A brand new $30,000 car will cost more to insure than an old car worth about $2,000. That's because if the new car is wrecked, it can cost the insurance company a lot more to replace. Similarly, cars with parts that are expensive to repair will cost more to insure.

Location. The area where you live has an affect on your insurance premium. If you live in an area with a high crime rate where vehicles are vandalized or stolen more often, your premium will be higher than in areas with a lower crime rate. City drivers usually pay more than drivers in rural areas because there is a greater likelihood of accidents in the city.

Driver Classification. Driver classification includes factors like your age, gender, and marital status. Drivers under the age of 25 or over the age of 70 have accidents more often so they pay more in insurance premiums. Young men often have more accidents than young women, so they have to pay more. On the other hand, middle-aged drivers are generally considered less of a risk because they have more driving experience.

Driving Record. Your driving record is a major factor in the cost of your premium. Drivers with a record of accidents or traffic violations pay the most in premiums, because they pose the greatest risk. You can qualify for a lower premium if you complete a driver education course or have good grades. Some companies find that good students have a better safety record, so their rates are lower.

BEWARE OF THE COMBINATIONS
An Auto Club of Southern California study found that the Graduated Drivers License Law has improved the safety of teen motorists. Under this law, new drivers under the age of 18 must hold their learner's permit for at least six months before getting a license. During this time, the teen motorist must spend at least 50 hours behind the wheel, with a parent or guardian aboard. The number of passengers killed or injured in crashes involving 16-year-old motorists dropped 40 percent.
Has your state adopted a version of this law?

✓ Fast Review

1. How does a deductible affect the cost of a premium?
2. Why do drivers under the age of 25 and over the age of 70 pay more in premiums?
3. How can younger drivers qualify for a lower premium?

What Happens During a Crash Test?

1

2

2. The dummies are placed in the car, which is outfitted with 15 different high-speed cameras to record the crash.

1. The crash-test dummies are prepared with sensors to monitor the crash and paint on the body parts most likely to hit something during the crash.

3

3. The fuel tank is drained and replaced with water.

4. The car, mounted on a track, crashes into a barrier at anywhere from 5 to 100 mph.

5. The crash-test dummies are removed from the car.

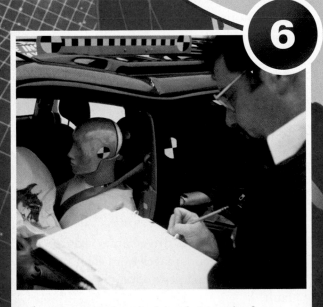

6. Researchers study paint marks from the dummies, sensor monitors, and film of the crash to assess the damage to the vehicle and occupants.

Now *You* Take a Shot...

How Safe Is Your Family's Car?
The main organization that tests car safety is the National Highway Traffic Safety Administration (NHTSA). Go online to find out how safe your family's car is. You can reach the NHTSA at <u>www.crashtest.com</u>. What are the categories that the NHTSA rates and how does it rate them? How did your family's vehicle rate overall?

Summary

1. Types of vehicle insurance include bodily injury liability, property damage liability, medical payments, collision, comprehensive coverage, uninsured motorist protection and miscellaneous coverage. Liability insurance protects you from claims of bodily injury or property damage to others.

2. State law requires drivers to prove financial responsibility in case of an accident. Most states also require you to carry a minimum amount of insurance. No-fault insurance requires drivers involved in accidents to collect damages from their own insurance companies no matter who is at fault. These laws vary from state to state.

3. The costs of insurance premiums are affected by:
   - The costs insurance companies pay in claims.
   - The amount of coverage and the deductible on a policy.
   - The type of vehicle, the area where the vehicle is used, the driver's age, gender, and marital status, and the driver's driving record.

Using Business Key Words

Vehicle insurance is something you'll probably purchase during most of your adult lifetime. Knowing the terms surrounding the insurance industry will help you become a better consumer. Match the terms with their definitions.

- insurance
- policy
- deductible
- liability insurance
- compulsory insurance law
- depreciation
- financial responsibility law
- premium
- no-fault insurance
- claim
- actual cash value

1. Paid protection against losses due to injury or property damage.
2. A contract between an insurance company and policyholder.
3. A law that requires drivers to have a minimum amount of car insurance.
4. The amount of damages that an insurance policyholder must pay before the insurance company pays.
5. Amount of money charged by an insurance company for protection for a given time period.
6. Requires proof that drivers can pay for damages in an accident.
7. Protection against claims of injury or property damage.
8. Decline in value of a vehicle because of age, and wear and tear.
9. A law that requires drivers involved in accidents to collect damages from their own insurance companies no matter who is at fault.
10. A request for payment from an insurer for any damages covered by an insurance policy.
11. How much the used item is worth.

Review What You Learned

12. How does insurance reduce the risk of financial loss?

13. Which type of insurance is the most important protection? Why?

14. How much insurance should a driver purchase?

15. Which type of insurance covers damage to a telephone pole or street sign?

16. What does comprehensive insurance cover?

17. When would it be possible to drop your collision and comprehensive insurance coverage?

Understanding Business Concepts

18. Why do you think the laws in most states require proof that drivers can pay for damages in an accident?

19. What does 100/300/50 mean?

20. How does a deductible cut the cost of insurance?

21. What does uninsured motorist coverage protect?

22. Why do you think an insurance policy would not cover a driver in a motorcycle-racing contest?

23. Why do you think insurance for a sports utility vehicle would cost more than a mid-size sedan?

Critical Thinking

24. Teenage boys usually pay more for vehicle insurance than teenage girls. Why do you think this is the case? Is it fair?

25. Create a list of ways you can reduce your vehicle insurance premiums.

26. Do you agree that no-fault insurance is a good thing? Explain your answer.

27. How might knowledge of the different types of vehicle insurance coverage help you?

Viewing and Representing

Examining the Image. Draw a sketch of things that stand out in this picture. Do you think the photographer took this picture with a point of view in mind? What does the photographer want you to think or do? Group with three other students. Share your knowledge and experience of vehicle accidents and vehicle insurance.

Building Academic Skills

 Role-playing

With a partner, role-play an imaginary meeting with an insurance agent. Use at least eight new terms you learned from this chapter in your role-play and present it to your class.

Social Science **Researching State Insurance**

Research the laws in your state regarding motor vehicle insurance. Find out if drivers are required to carry insurance, the type of coverage required, and what penalties exist if a driver does not carry vehicle insurance. Then choose another state and compare the same information with what you found out about your own state.

COMPUTER TECHNOLOGY **Brainstorming About Risks**

Work in teams of four to create a spreadsheet. The first column of the spreadsheet should be "Driving Risks." The second column should be titled, "Ways to Reduce Risks." The third column should be titled, "Ways to Avoid Risks." As a group, brainstorm risks you might face while driving. Enter those into the spreadsheet and then complete the other two columns. Print your spreadsheet.

 Reading a Chart

Using the chart below, answer the following questions:

- Which age group has the highest number of fatal crashes caused by speeding?
- Which age group has the second-highest number of fatal crashes caused by driver error?
- Which age group has the highest number of fatal crashes caused by drinking and driving?

Percentage of Fatal Crashes by Characteristic			
Driver Age:	16	17–19	20–49
Driver error	80	75	62
Speeding	36	31	22
3+ occupants	33	26	19
Single vehicle	41	37	30
Drivers killed with 0.01+ BAC (blood alcohol content)	8	25	47

Source: Insurance Institute for Highway Safety.

Linking School to Home

Family Vehicle Insurance. Ask your parents about the vehicle insurance coverage they carry. Find out what types of protection they carry, how much coverage they carry, and the cost of the insurance premium. If you're insured under their policy, find out what your coverage costs. Share your findings with the class.

Linking School to Work

Comparing Reasons. Millions of Americans carry vehicle insurance. However, millions of others don't. Write a paragraph explaining the advantages and disadvantages of having car insurance. Address this complaint: "I sure am wasting a lot of money. I'm a careful driver, and I probably will never have an accident."

E-Homework

Applying Technology

Examine Crime. Premiums are also higher for vehicles that are known to break down or get stolen often. You'll pay more for insurance if you live in an area where there is a higher rate of car accidents. Use the Internet to research the type of car that has the highest theft rate in the United States. Write a paragraph explaining why you think this is the case.

Researching Insurance Premiums. Many new vehicles come equipped with safety features like air bags and security systems. How a vehicle is used affects the cost, too. If you drive your vehicle to work every day, your insurance might cost more than if you only use it on weekends. Use the Internet to create a list of those features that are currently available and those that will be in the near future. Then, contact an insurance company and find out how these features can help reduce insurance premiums.

Connecting Academics

Math. Insurance companies rely on the laws of probability. These laws enable an insurance mathematician, called an actuary, to determine the likelihood that an event will actually take place. Find out about actuarial figures and create a poster display of your findings.

Social Science. Imagine you'll get delivery of the car of your dreams in two weeks. You need to research the different types and costs of insurance, but with your busy schedule when will you have the time? If you don't already have a weekly planner or schedule, make one for next week. Estimate how much time you'll need to research insurance, and which times of day are best to be online or to make telephone calls. Mark the time slots on your schedule.

BusinessWeek Analyzing the Feature Story

You read the first part of "An Insurance Hunter's System of Choice" at the beginning of this chapter. Below are a few questions for you to answer about insurance hunter's choices. You'll find the answers to these questions when you're reading the entire article. First, here are the questions:

28. What percentage of insurance policies is sold online?

29. What kind of insurance is purchased the most online?

CREATIVE JOURNAL ACTIVITY

People who have been driving for years without any accidents or traffic tickets enjoy the lowest premiums. Investigate some other conditions that will lower your car insurance premiums. Interview an auto insurance agent or research rates on the Internet. What did you learn?

BUSINESS Online
The Full Story

To learn more about buying insurance, visit the *Introduction to Business* Web site at **www.introbus.glencoe.com**, and click on *BusinessWeek* Feature Story, Chapter 33.

Chapter 34

Property Insurance

Learning Objectives

After completing this chapter, you'll be able to:

1. **Describe** what kinds of property you can insure.
2. **Explain** the different types of property insurance.
3. **Name** the six kinds of homeowner's policies.
4. **Identify** the factors that affect the cost of property insurance premiums.

Why It's Important

Property insurance can protect you financially if your home is destroyed or your possessions are stolen.

Key Words

property insurance
real property
personal property
renter's insurance
standard fire policy
extended coverage
homeowner's policy
eleven perils
rider
replacement value

BusinessWeek Feature Story

Containing Your Risk

And You Thought Insurance Was Dull? Flood, fire, death, even clerical errors. Until now, Stefan E. Szyszko, president of United Planet in Novi, Mich., has had the right insurance to cover just about any disaster that could befall his nine-person direct-marketing firm. He's not an insurance junkie. Mostly, Szyszko was motivated by the experience of a friend whose business burned to the ground, but got back up and running again in just three weeks' time using proceeds from his coverage.

Source: Excerpted with permission from "Containing Your Risk," *Business-Week Online*, April 27, 2000.

An Extension Activity

Are you aware of any work-related lawsuits? How do businesses protect themselves against work-related injuries and illnesses? Research workers' compensation laws to find out about your rights as an employee. The law requires businesses to have workers' compensation.

BUSINESS Online
The Full Story

To learn more about risks and insurance, visit the *Introduction to Business* Web site at **www.introbus.glencoe.com**, and click on *BusinessWeek* Feature Story, Chapter 34.

Insuring Your Valuable Property

Hurricane Floyd swept through 16 different states on the East Coast, from Maine to Florida, destroying homes and businesses, and causing billions of dollars in property damage. Each year property is destroyed due to earthquakes, fires, floods, and various other disasters. More property is lost or damaged due to lesser causes such as accidents, theft, and vandalism. Almost everyone at some point has his or her property damaged or stolen. You can protect yourself from financial loss on your property with **property insurance**.

Types of Property Insurance

The two kinds of property you can insure are real property and personal property. **Real property** is property attached to land, like a house, business, garage, or other building. **Personal property** consists of possessions that can be moved, like furniture, jewelry, and electronic equipment. Insurance companies offer different kinds of protection for real and personal property. The cost of insurance might seem high, but it's nothing compared to losing everything with no financial backing.

Renter's Insurance

When people first start out on their own, they usually rent an apartment rather than buy a house. Suppose you're living in an apartment and someone breaks in and steals your computer. Is there anything you can do about it? The owner of the building will probably have property

You Make the Call

Risky Business?

A man comes to your insurance agency asking for renter's insurance. After talking to him, you find out that he lives in a high-crime part of town where the number of burglaries is particularly high.

Making an Ethical Decision

1. Do insurance companies have an obligation to insure any potential client? If so, how might insuring high-risk clients affect their business? If not, how might the refusal to sell insurance affect individuals and neighborhoods?
2. Insurance companies can't "redline" clients in certain neighborhoods (i.e., refuse residents insurance simply because of their economic or ethnic backgrounds). On the other hand, they raise rates in high-risk areas. How would you balance these conflicting issues?

insurance, but it won't pay for loss or damage to a renter's personal property.

You might not realize that you can buy **renter's insurance** to cover any loss or damage to your personal possessions. Renter's insurance covers such items as televisions, large appliances, and furniture. It can also include liability protection in case someone is injured in your apartment. The cost of renter's insurance depends on the amount of coverage, the type of building, and the location. It's fairly inexpensive and offers you the same kinds of protection homeowners get.

Standard Fire Policy

Property owners can buy individual insurance policies to protect themselves against specific types of threats, such as floods or earthquakes. The greatest threat to property is fire. Fires account for 85 percent of all property damage in the United States. Whereas earthquakes and floods are rare natural disasters, a fire can start any time because of an electrical short, an overturned candle, or a towel left too close to a heater. For that reason, many people buy a **standard fire policy** to insure against damage due to fire or lightning.

A policyholder can add other types of protection to this basic policy. **Extended coverage** also protects against damage from riots, car or airplane crashes, windstorms, hail, and even explosions. Extended coverage also pays for damages if someone breaks into your house or vandalizes your property.

Liability Protection

What if someone slips on your kitchen floor and breaks an arm? Even if it wasn't your fault, you might be sued. Just as vehicle owners can buy liability insurance to cover injury to others, so can property owners. Liability insurance protects you from the costs of injuries to others on your property. It pays for two things. First, it pays for the actual damages for which you are held liable, such as medical expenses. Second, it pays legal expenses for the accident in case you're sued.

Additional Living Expenses

What if your house or apartment building burns down and you have to live somewhere else while it's being rebuilt? Vehicle insurance often pays for a rental car if you can't use your car while it's being repaired. Additional living expenses insurance provides similar coverage. It pays

Real-World Application

part 1 of 4

TIDAL WAVE IN AN APARTMENT
Tricia Musel heard one of her roommates scream her name followed by a "get down here, now." This stopped Musel writing mid sentence as she neared the end of her screenplay's first draft. Musel raced downstairs where she was stopped by an unusual sound. She put her ear to the wall: Water was rushing behind the wall, like a dishwasher.
An apartment is an example of real or personal property?

continued on p. 553

for the cost of renting another place to live if your home is damaged. The amount of coverage might be limited to 10 or 20 percent of the coverage on your home. For example, if the coverage on your home is $150,000, additional living expenses insurance will cover only up to $15,000 or $30,000 of your costs while you live somewhere else. The

Figure 34.1 — PERILS COVERED BY A HOMEOWNER'S POLICY

➡This chart shows coverages provided by different forms of home-owner's insurance. HO-5, the comprehensive or all-risks policy, covers all but a few perils.
What perils are not covered?

COMPREHENSIVE

BROAD

BASIC

Perils
1. Fire or lightning
2. Loss of property removed from premises endangered by fire or other perils
3. Windstorm or hail
4. Explosion
5. Riot or civil commotion
6. Aircraft
7. Vehicles
8. Smoke
9. Vandalism and malicious mischief
10. Theft
11. Breakage of glass constituting part of a building

12. Falling objects
13. Weight of ice, snow, sleet
14. Collapse of building(s) or any part thereof
15. Sudden and accidental tearing asunder, cracking, burning, or bulging of a steam or hot water heating system or of appliances for heating water
16. Accidental discharge, leakage, or overflow of water or steam from within a plumbing, heating, or air-conditioning system or domestic appliance
17. Freezing of plumbing, heating, and air-conditioning systems and domestic appliances
18. Sudden and accidental injury from artificially generated currents to electrical appliances, devices, fixtures, and wiring (TV and radio tubes not included)

All perils EXCEPT: flood, earthquake, war, nuclear accidents, and others specified in your policy. Check your policy for a complete listing of perils excluded.

length of time you're covered might also be limited to six months or a year.

Business Insurance

Business owners need property insurance just like renters and homeowners. Suppose you own a café and a falling tree or vandals destroy your plate-glass window. A large store window can cost thousands of dollars to replace. If your business property isn't insured and you don't have the money to replace it, you could go out of business.

Business owners can get insurance to cover the costs of property. They can also get liability insurance to protect themselves from claims by anyone injured on the premises. It's especially important for business owners to carry insurance because of the potential loss of income if they have to close down for a while.

✓ Fast Review

1. What is the difference between real property and personal property?
2. What is the main cause of property damage?
3. What does additional living expenses insurance cover?

The Homeowner's Policy

Many insurance companies offer a combination policy with different kinds of home protection called a **homeowner's policy**. Homeowner's policies provide protection against loss from the eleven perils. The **eleven perils** are the most common causes of property damage or loss. They include fire, smoke, windstorms, vehicles, riots, theft, vandalism, and breaking glass. All homeowner's policies cover the eleven perils. Figure 34.1 illustrates the perils covered by a homeowner's policy.

There are six standard homeowner (HO) policies, or forms, for different kinds of risks:

- HO-1 Basic Form
- HO-2 Broad Form
- HO-3 Special Form
- HO-4 Renter's Form
- HO-5 Comprehensive Form, or All-Risks Policy
- HO-6 Condominium Owner's Form

Basic Coverage

HO-1, the basic form, is the least expensive policy, but provides less coverage than some of the other forms. This policy protects a home and

TIDAL WAVE IN AN APARTMENT
Musel walked into her college roommate Jamie Caslavaka's bedroom. Caslavaka stood underneath the room's ceiling light with the kitchen trashcan catching the steady stream of water coming from the light. Suddenly, the water started gushing and pouring into the trashcan as it nearly topped off. Musel ran out of the room to the kitchen to get pots and pans.
What basic insurance provides coverage against the eleven perils?

continued on p. 555

personal property against the eleven perils. It provides liability protection for the homeowner if someone is injured on the insured property. If you break a valuable item while visiting someone else's home, the policy might cover the cost. It also covers additional living expenses if you are temporarily displaced because of damage to your home.

Additional Coverage

HO-2, the broad form, adds more coverage to the HO-1. This policy also covers damage from falling objects, collapse of a building, ice and snow, steam, water, and electrical systems. It's the most popular homeowner's policy. (See Figure 34.2 as a snapshot of a homeowner's policy.)

The second most popular policy is HO-3. It provides maximum protection for the house itself, with less coverage for contents or personal property. The extra protection on the building is worth the extra cost to policyholders.

HO-4 is the policy for renters. It covers the personal property of the renter and includes additional living expenses coverage. The policyholder doesn't own the building, so it's not covered.

HO-5, the all-risks policy, provides the most comprehensive coverage. It insures a building and its contents with maximum coverage. Because it offers the most protection, it's also the most expensive.

HO-6 is a policy for condominium owners. It covers personal property and anything else inside the unit. The building itself is covered under a separate policy.

Figure 34.2

SNAPSHOT OF A HOMEOWNER'S POLICY

➡ This chart shows the coverage and premiums charged for home protection for one homeowner.

a. What is the value of the home that is insured? How much coverage does the homeowner have for the home, contents, and other items covered?
b. How much liability coverage does the homeowner have?
c. What is the cost per year for this coverage?

DESCRIPTION	COVERAGE	ANNUAL PREMIUM
Property Location Limit (200% of residence value of $117,000)	$234,000	$421.00
Personal Liability	$300,000	
Medical Expense	$5,000	

Discounts applied: Fire Alarm and Smoke Detectors Discount

Special Coverage

Most standard homeowner's policies cover special items for limited amounts. For example, a homeowner's policy might cover jewelry for up to $500. A homeowner can buy this extra coverage with a rider. A **rider** is an addition to a policy that covers specific property or damages. The extra cost is usually low. Riders are often used for antiques, art, or silver. Homeowners can also buy extra burglary and robbery protection. The premium depends on the crime rate in the area.

None of the homeowner's policies cover loss from floods, earthquakes, landslides, acts of war, or nuclear hazards. Homeowners, however, can also get riders to cover these conditions. Earthquake insurance is available, but it's more expensive where earthquakes occur often, such as California. The federal government offers low-cost flood insurance through the National Flood Insurance Program. If you live where floods are a problem, such as the Midwest, you might be able to buy flood insurance.

✔ **Fast Review** _____

1. What type of protection is covered by all homeowner's policies?
2. Which homeowner's policy provides the most coverage?

Buying a Policy

The type of policy you buy depends on your particular needs. Most homeowners get either the HO-2 or HO-3 form, but the HO-5 form is better if you can afford the extra cost. If you rent an apartment rather than own a house, the HO-4 renter's form is obviously better suited to your needs. Many people buy only the standard fire policy and add extended coverage. Before you buy insurance, it's important to know how much insurance you'll need and the costs of insurance.

Real-World Application

part **3** of 4

TIDAL WAVE IN AN APARTMENT
By the time Musel returned with pots and pans, Caslavaka stood by the bedroom door just staring at the ceiling's plaster starting to flake onto her bed. After a loud creaking sound, the entire ceiling fell in one large piece followed by a tidal wave bursting through. **What kind of insurance might cover any loss or damage of personal possessions?**

continued on p. 557

Amount of Insurance

Insurance companies recommend that you insure your home for 80 percent of its market value. That's because even a large fire or flood doesn't destroy a building completely. The land and the building's foundation won't be destroyed and will hold their value. Real estate increases in value, so increase your coverage every few years. If the value of your home increases from $200,000 to $300,000 and you didn't increase your coverage, the insurance company will still only pay $160,000 if it's destroyed.

You can also insure property for either its actual cash value or its replacement value. The actual cash value is the value of the property new minus devaluation from use. For example, suppose you bought a new bike for $300 but it's depreciated in value by $100. If the bike is stolen, the insurance company will only pay you $200. The **replacement value**, on the other hand, is the full cost of repairing or replacing the property, regardless of the depreciation value. If your bike is stolen, the insurance company will pay you the full $300 you paid for it.

Working Lifestyle

What are you doing at 10 A.M.?

Creative Construction

Standing in what will eventually be the kitchen of a new home, Don Otto is surrounded by piles of lumber, an uninstalled dishwasher, half-a-dozen plumbing pipes, two carpenters, an electrician, and a lot of sawdust. It's only 10 A.M. and this general contractor discusses the next step with the skilled builders.

Otto's business, DPO Construction in Iowa City, Iowa, has one employee—him. He doesn't work solo, however, but directs the efforts of dozens of skilled builders, sometimes at several different job sites at once. He's involved in organizing and directing every aspect of building a house, from the design through construction.

"My job," he says, checking his watch, "is to keep things on schedule and know every detail about the house. I always try to make sure this is a team effort—and the customers are a vital part of that team."

He negotiates contracts, schedules production, maintains a dialogue with the owners and crewmembers, inspects the work, and monitors the project's progress. Sometimes he can be found standing on a ladder sealing duct joints or disappearing into an attic to check out the insulation.

A DPO-built house won the first five-star rating from the Energy Rated Homes of Iowa Program. Don's commitment to energy-efficient design and construction spurs him to attend conferences around the country where he learns about the latest products and developments in his field.

Salary

A typical construction manager earns $47,610. Half of the people in this occupation will earn between $36,360 and $70,910.

Outlook for This Career

Employment of construction managers will increase faster than the average occupation. The increasing complexity of construction projects will increase demand for positions at the managerial level.

Connecting Careers Activity

Construction managers must be "on call" 24 hours a day to deal with delays, bad weather, or emergencies at the site. What other careers might require someone to be "on call"?

CAREER PATH — *Architecture & Construction*

Costs of Insurance

Property insurance has many of the same costs vehicle insurance does. The number of claims insurance companies have to pay each year affects the overall cost of insurance. Your premium, or the amount you pay for your policy, depends on the amount of coverage and the type of policy you want. It'll cost you less for a standard fire policy than it'll for comprehensive homeowner's insurance. Replacement value coverage costs more than actual cash value coverage. The amount of your premium is also determined by specific factors.

Deductible. The deductible, as you'll recall from the last chapter, is the amount of money you pay out of your own pocket before the insurance company pays for any losses. If your deductible is $250 and damage to your property is $600, you pay $250 and the insurance company pays the other $350. The higher your deductible is, the lower your premium is since it costs the insurance company less to pay your claims.

Location. The location of a home affects the cost of your insurance. If you live in high-crime area or an area with no fire department, your premium will be higher. Insurance will cost you more if you live in an area with frequent brushfires or tornadoes. A fire hydrant near your property, on the other hand, can reduce the cost.

Type of Building. The type of home and building materials used also affect the cost of your insurance. A house made of brick will cost less to insure than a house made of wood. A house that's worth $500,000 will cost more to insure, of course, than a house that's worth $150,000. It might also cost more to insure a house that's 100 years old than a new house.

Preventive Measures. You can get discounts on your insurance rates by taking preventive measures to protect your property. For example, if you install deadbolts and burglar alarms to prevent theft, your insurance will be lower. Similarly, your rates will be lower if you have smoke detectors, fire extinguishers, or sprinklers in your home.

TIDAL WAVE IN AN APARTMENT
Firefighters came and turned off the building's sprinkling system, which was the culprit of the disaster. Then their landlord walked in and said, "I hope someone has renter's insurance." They didn't have renter's insurance. Instead they were left with sodden insulation and drywall covering furniture, clothes, computers, notebooks, and photo albums.
Why is it important to have renter's insurance?

✓ Fast Review

1. Why does replacement value coverage cost more than actual cash value coverage?
2. What preventive measures might lower your insurance rates?

Summary

1. You can insure both real property (for example, a house, business, or other type of building) and personal property (for example, furniture, jewelry, and electronic equipment).

2. There are many different kinds of property insurance, including renter's insurance, standard fire policy, liability, additional living expenses, and business insurance.

3. There are six kinds of homeowner's policies for different needs: basic, broad, special, renter's, comprehensive, and condominium owner's. All of them include protection against the eleven perils, which are the most common causes of property damage or loss.

4. The cost of property insurance premiums is affected by the type of policy, amount of coverage, deductible, location, type of building, and preventive measures you might take.

Using Business Key Words

Insuring your property, both real and personal, is necessary to protect your investments. Complete the following sentences with these terms to see how well you understand these property insurance concepts.

- **real property**
- **personal property**
- **rider**
- **standard fire policy**
- **property insurance**
- **renter's insurance**
- **extended coverage**
- **homeowner's policy**
- **eleven perils**
- **replacement value**

1. Some examples of _____ are furniture, jewelry, and electronic equipment.
2. Some examples of _____ are houses, barns, garages, and other buildings.

3. A(n) _____ is an addition to a policy that covers specific property.
4. Protection from financial loss on property due to damage or theft is called _____.
5. If smoke and heat from an explosion damages your property, a(n) _____ covers the loss.
6. It's important to obtain _____ when you first move into an apartment.
7. If your insurance company fully pays for the cost of your stolen bike, it's paid you the _____ of the bike.
8. A homeowner's policy provides protection against such things as fire, smoke, windstorms, and riots, or otherwise known as the _____.
9. Insurance coverage added to a standard fire policy that protects against other types of property damage is _____ coverage.
10. A(n) _____ is a combination policy offering different kinds of home protection designed for homeowners.

Review What You Learned

11. What does renter's insurance cover?
12. What does extended coverage insurance cover?
13. Name the least expensive form of homeowner's insurance.
14. Which homeowner's policy provides the most comprehensive coverage?
15. Why is insurance for 80 percent of the market value of a home usually enough?

Understanding Business Concepts

16. When you buy a home, why do you think the bank or mortgage company will insist you buy insurance on it?
17. Renter's insurance covers any loss or damage to your personal possessions. Explain how renter's insurance is different from homeowner's insurance.
18. Give an example of an accident that could happen around your house.
19. There are numerous types of coverages in a homeowner's policy: basic, broad, and comprehensive. Each coverage provides more and different coverage than the next step. What type of homeowner's policy would cover damage caused by ice and snow?
20. Why do you think you have to buy a special insurance policy for flood, earthquake, and landslide protection?
21. What is wrong with carrying too much insurance on your home?
22. In Chapter 33 you learned about vehicle insurance. Remember that insurance is paid protection against losses due to injury or property damage. To get insurance, you have to purchase a policy from an insurance company. What is the main point of insurance?

Critical Thinking

23. Property insurance rates are sometimes lower for people who live near fire stations or who have homes built out of brick or stone rather than wood. Is this fair? Explain your answer.
24. Why do you think an insurance company would not want to insure every home in the same neighborhood?
25. Do you think it's a good idea for renters and homeowners to review their insurance coverage every two years? Why or why not?
26. Describe the steps you would take to research property insurance before you purchase a policy.

Viewing and Representing

Examining the Image. Write down your impressions of this picture in your journal. How would you feel if you lived there? What are the eleven perils covered by property insurance? Do you know of someone who suffered property loss? Was the property covered by insurance? Write about the experience.

Building Academic Skills

 Estimating Replacement Cost

Imagine you were going to buy insurance on the contents in your room. Take an inventory of the items in your room and estimate the total cost to replace each item. Then figure a total replacement cost.

 Promoting Fire Safety

In groups of three or four, create a poster to promote fire safety. The poster should include information about how to protect your home from fire and smoke damage. Display the posters in your school or take them to a local elementary or middle school and display them there.

 Delving Into the Past

Research the historical development of the insurance industry. Find out about bottomry contracts, early commercial and maritime insurance, and fire insurance. Present your findings orally to the class.

 Compiling Information

Before making a decision about insurance policies, it's important to research and compile data. This will help you make an informed decision. Compile and print out a spreadsheet related to the various kinds of property insurance, coverages, and premiums.

Linking School to Home

Inquiring About Insurance. You may take shelter for granted if it's something you've always had. Imagine that your home is damaged and uninhabitable. What will happen to you and your family's belongings? How are you protected against loss or damage? Interview your parents or other family members about the various types of property insurance coverage they carry. Ask them what factors affected their purchasing decisions.

Linking School to Work

Contacting an Agent. The time has come and you've officially entered into adulthood: You're renting an apartment and you're financially independent. It's your responsibility to call around on insurance rates for your new apartment. Using the amount you figured your personal property was worth in the math activity above, contact an insurance agent and find out the cost of renter's insurance.

E-Homework

Applying Technology

Focusing Your Search. Use the Internet to research one insurance trade association. Write a one-page paper explaining the association's mission, how and when it was founded, and the key issues upon which it focuses.

Obtaining a Quote. Imagine that you have approximately $10,000 in property you wish to insure. Using the Internet, obtain a quote for renter's insurance. In addition, evaluate the Web site for ease of use. Share your findings with other classmates.

Connecting Academics

Math. As you learned earlier, there are numerous factors that influence the cost of insurance. Location and type of building are two examples that influence costs. Find out the cost of renter's insurance offered by insurance companies in your area. Get at least five estimates. Draw a bar graph of your findings. Include an analysis of why some insurance companies might vary in prices when your personal property value remains constant.

Social Science. Keeping current, easily-accessible records of your possessions' values and our insurance coverage is essential. Ask family members what record-keeping methods they use. Write two paragraphs outlining your findings and your plan for keeping insurance information.

BusinessWeek Analyzing the Feature Story

You read the first part of "Containing Your Risk" at the beginning of this chapter. Below are a few questions for you to answer about risks and insurance. You'll find the answers to these questions when you're reading the entire article. First, here are the questions:

27. What is the range of costs for an insurance policy to protect a business online?
28. What are some of the new risks in the global New Economy?

CREATIVE JOURNAL ACTIVITY

It's summertime and you'd like to barbeque with your friends. Your parents' old grill doesn't work anymore so you go shopping for a new one. The local store has a gas grill that bears the mark of an independent testing laboratory. This is reputable, so you buy it and take it home. What are the risks of having a gas grill near your home? Can you think of any preventative measures you should take to insure a safe grilling experience?

BUSINESS
Online
The Full Story

To learn more about risks and insurance, visit the *Introduction to Business* Web site at **www.introbus.glencoe.com**, and click on *BusinessWeek* Feature Story, Chapter 34.

Chapter 35

Life and Health Insurance

Learning Objectives

After completing this chapter, you'll be able to:

1. **Define** cash-value and term insurance.
2. **Identify** the factors that affect the cost of life insurance.
3. **Describe** the types of health insurance.
4. **Name** the types of health insurance plans.

Why It's Important

Life insurance and health insurance protect you and your loved ones financially.

Key Words

proceeds
beneficiary
cash-value insurance
term insurance
coinsurance
health maintenance
    organization (HMO)
Medicare
Medicaid
copayment
pre-existing condition

BusinessWeek Feature Story

Staying Insured When You're on Your Own

How to Sort Out Health-Care Options for the Self-Employed. Obtaining health insurance if you're leaving the corporate fold or already on your own can be a grueling endeavor. Ask Ruth Sheridan, a freelance business writer from New York. When she wanted a change from her health maintenance organization recently, Sheridan turned herself into a one-woman search engine. She scoured the yellow pages, read articles, and grilled friends to find insurance companies with plans for the self-employed.

Source: Excerpted with permission from "Staying Insured When You're on Your Own," *BusinessWeek Online*, September 6, 1999.

An Extension Activity

Think of a situation when you had to shop wisely for a service or product. What was your process? How did you find out where to shop? Share your process with the class.

BUSINESS Online
The Full Story

To learn more about health and life insurance, visit the *Introduction to Business* Web site at **www.introbus.glencoe.com**, and click on *BusinessWeek* Feature Story, Chapter 35.

Ensuring Safety for Your Family

What would happen to a family if one of the wage earners dies? How will the survivors support themselves? What would happen if the wage earner was seriously injured and couldn't work for months? You might not think you need life or health insurance, but you might if there are people financially dependent on you or you have a dangerous job.

Life Insurance

Life insurance protects the standard of living of the survivors. Figure 35.1 is a chart on life expectancy to illustrate how life insurance premiums are affected by life spans. At the policyholder's death, the insurance company pays survivors the face value of a life insurance policy. The money paid to the survivors is called the **proceeds**. Each person who receives part of the proceeds is a called a **beneficiary**. The person who buys the policy names the beneficiaries. There are several types of life insurance to fit different needs.

Figure 35.1

THE LENGTH OF A LIFE

➡️This chart shows the life expectancy of males and females. Answer the questions below based upon the chart's information.

1. How many more years would a 15-year-old girl expect to live compared to a 15-year-old boy?
2. A baby girl born today can expect to live to what age?
3. What effect do you think these figures have on the premiums for whole life insurance?

YEARS | 0 | 10 | 20 | 30 | 40 | 50 | 60 | 70 | 80 | 90 | 100

Life expectancies for persons born today
- 73.8
- 79.5
- 76.7

Life expectancies for 15-year-olds
- 59.7
- 65.2
- 62.5

- Males
- Females
- All persons combined

564

Cash-Value Insurance

Cash-value insurance provides both savings and death benefits. Part of the premium pays for death benefits. The rest builds up cash value like a savings account. The cash value increases throughout the life of the policy. If you cancel the policy, you can collect the amount of the cash value. In an emergency, you can borrow part or all of the cash value, but you have to pay interest on it just as you would on any loan. Policyholders can buy different forms of cash-value insurance.

Whole Life Insurance. With whole life insurance, a policyholder pays a premium that stays the same throughout his or her lifetime. The policy stays the same until the insured dies as long as the premiums are paid. Whole life insurance provides savings during the policyholder's life and pays benefits at death.

Limited-Payment Life Insurance. The policyholder pays premiums for a certain number of years for limited-payment life insurance. For example, if you have a 20-payment life policy, you pay premiums for 20 years. Then your policy is considered paid up and you don't have to pay any more premiums. One popular type of limited-payment life insurance is "paid up at age 65." Since many people retire at age 65, they won't have to pay premiums after their paychecks stop.

Variable Life Insurance. With variable life insurance, the cash value part of the premium is invested in things like stocks, bonds, and mutual funds rather than in savings. Like other types of cash-value insurance, the rest of the premium is used for guaranteed death benefits. The cash value is variable because it can increase or decrease in value depending on how the investments do. For example, if part of the premium is used to invest in stocks and the stocks double in value, the cash value will be worth double.

Endowment Insurance. Endowment insurance is a special type of cash-value insurance. An endowment policy is based more on savings than on death benefits. It provides coverage for a specific period of time, usually 20 to 30 years. The proceeds go to the policyholder if he or she is still alive at the end of that period. If the policyholder dies during the endowment period, the beneficiary receives the proceeds. Policyholders often use endowment insurance to provide retirement income or an education fund. To provide funds for college, parents might buy an 18-year, $15,000 endowment policy when a child is born.

Real-World Application

part 1 of 4

INSIDE THE ER

On TV, the emergency room (ER) appears like mass chaos. Doctors and nurses zigzag in and out of the frame, while patients with life-threatening conditions lie on gurneys. Patients' families wait in tense silence. The emergency physician wipes her brow before the scalpel makes an incision. In the real world, the ER is a highly orchestrated place, with a slew of trained professionals.
What should you have before being admitted to a hospital?

continued on p. 567

Term Insurance

Term insurance covers a person for a specific period of time. The length of the term might be 5, 10, or 20 years. It pays benefits only if the insured dies during the term of the policy. If the insured person lives beyond the term of the policy, the policy has no value. It can be renewed, but usually with a higher premium. Term insurance is sometimes called "pure protection," since it's used only to pay death benefits and doesn't build cash value. The major advantage of term insurance is its low cost.

How does term insurance work? If Gabriel buys a five-year, $10,000 policy, it covers him for five years. If he dies during that five years, his beneficiary will receive $10,000. After five years, his coverage ends. Gabriel can then renew the policy. As he gets older, however, his premium will increase.

Policyholders often have term insurance as a part of group life insurance. An employer or organization might provide term insurance to

Working Lifestyle

What are you doing at 10 A.M.?

Settling Medical Disputes

Helen Walthier is sitting in the Pima County Courthouse, reading papers she has prepared for a medical malpractice case. Roberts and one of the senior attorneys in her law firm will try to convince a judge to dismiss the case against one of their clients, a local pediatrician.

This Tucson, Ariz., attorney enjoys handling very complex cases.

"In Arizona, a medical malpractice plaintiff must prove two things," Walthier says. "First, a plaintiff must prove that the health care professional did not meet Arizona's standard of reasonable medical care. Next, they must prove that this failure caused damage to the plaintiff." Walthier's clients can be doctors, nurses, physician's assistants, physical therapists, or hospitals.

"Good legal practice involves adopting the best strategy to help your client," Walthier says. She gathers up her papers, puts them in her leather briefcase, and walks into the courtroom for the 10:00 A.M. hearing.

Salary

A typical lawyer of earns $78,170. Half of the people in this job earn between $51,450 and $114,520.

Outlook for This Career

Employment will grow at roughly the same rate as the average for all occupations. Opportunities in health care law, intellectual property, elder law, sexual harassment issues, and environmental law look promising.

Connecting Careers Activity

Most careers require formal training. Discover the formal training requirements you'll need as you pursue your career. Share your findings with your family.

CAREER PATH Law & Public Safety

employees or members. One master insurance policy covers everyone in the group. When a member of the group leaves, the coverage ends for that person. For example, if you work for a company that provides term insurance as a benefit, you lose that coverage if you leave the company.

Workers or their companies usually pay less for a group policy than for individual policies. If the company provides coverage as a benefit, the employee often pays nothing for the coverage. The employer pays the entire cost of the insurance.

Costs of Life Insurance

As with any type of insurance, the amount of the premium on a life insurance policy depends on the type of policy and the amount of coverage. Term insurance costs less than cash-value insurance. A policy for $100,000 costs more than a policy for $50,000.

Like other forms of insurance, there are specific factors that also affect the cost of the premium on life insurance, such as age, health, and occupation. Many people have to take a physical before they're sold an insurance policy to ensure they're in good health. The older a person is, the higher the premium will be because of the likelihood the company will have to pay benefits sooner. Life insurance also costs more for people in dangerous occupations, such as a high-rise construction worker or a stunt pilot.

✔ Fast Review

1. How is variable life insurance different from other types of cash-value insurance?
2. Why is term insurance sometimes called "pure protection?"
3. What are three of the specific factors that affect the cost of a life insurance premium?

Health Insurance

Many people are concerned about their families if they should die, and they also worry about what happens if they become sick or disabled. Health care for a serious illness or accident is very expensive. Few people have enough savings to pay for medical costs on their own. In fact, medical expenses can be financially disastrous. The average cost of a stay in the hospital is $5,000 *per day*. Health insurance provides protection against the costs of illness and accidents. Figure 35.2 on page 568 shows the percentage of the U.S. population that isn't covered by any health insurance.

Real-World Application

part **2** of 4

INSIDE THE ER
How many of you can afford to spend $5,000 per day? Probably not many of you, but that's how much it costs on average to stay in the hospital. Depending on the severity of your health problem when you check into the ER, a nurse will categorize your condition: life threatening, urgent but not life threatening, or less urgent. The nurse monitoring your vital signs determines your category.
Why is it important to know about your medical history?

continued on p. 569

Major Medical Insurance

Major medical insurance, sometimes called catastrophe insurance, is the most important coverage for a serious illness or accident. Major medical pays for most kinds of care in and out of the hospital. It covers hospital care, doctors' bills, tests and x-rays, and nursing care. Most policies have a deductible, or an amount the policyholder must pay, of several hundred dollars.

With some plans, you also have to pay coinsurance. **Coinsurance** is a percentage of medical expenses a policyholder must pay beyond the deductible. Major medical insurance is intended to cover the health costs not covered by other types of insurance. The insurance company usually pays 75 or 80 percent of the costs and the policyholder pays the other 20 or 25 percent. For example, suppose your insurance has a $1,000 deductible and a coinsurance payment of 20 percent. If you're hospitalized and your medical bills come to $6,000, you have to pay $2,000 ($1,000 deductible plus 20 percent of $5,000).

Figure 35.2

WHO'S COVERED?

➡This chart shows the percentage of the U.S. population (by gender and by age) that isn't covered by any health insurance. Answer the questions below based upon the chart's information.

1. Are there more males or females who have no insurance?
2. What age group has the largest percentage without health insurance coverage?
3. Why do you think the age group 65 and over has such a small percentage of population not covered by health insurance?

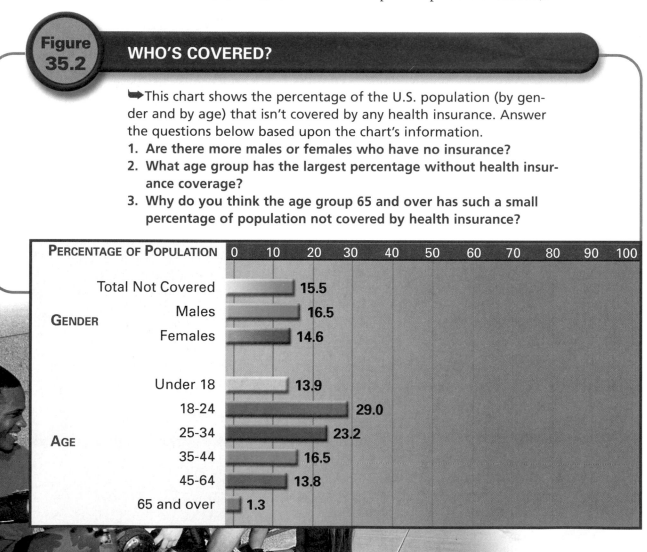

PERCENTAGE OF POPULATION	0	10	20	30	40	50	60	70	80	90	100

GENDER
- Total Not Covered: 15.5
- Males: 16.5
- Females: 14.6

AGE
- Under 18: 13.9
- 18-24: 29.0
- 25-34: 23.2
- 35-44: 16.5
- 45-64: 13.8
- 65 and over: 1.3

Hospital Expense Insurance

Hospital expense insurance pays for hospital care for a given period of time. It covers room and board, tests and x-rays, operating room costs, nursing care, and fees for drugs and treatments. Like major medical insurance, it might have a deductible. Some policies set a limit for each specific expense. Others set a maximum amount per day for up to a maximum number of days. Hospital expense is the most popular type of health insurance because hospitalization is so expensive.

Surgical Expense Insurance

Surgical expense insurance pays part of a surgeon's entire fee for an operation. Most policies set a maximum payment for a particular surgical expense. A policy lists the surgical procedures and the costs allowed. In many cases, major medical picks up where this coverage ends. Surgical expense insurance is usually bought with hospital expense insurance. The higher the maximums for each operation, the higher the premium for surgical expense insurance.

Medical Expense Insurance

Medical expense insurance covers the costs of a doctor's care *not* involving surgery. It might cover visits to a doctor's office or a doctor's calls at the hospital. This insurance is usually bought with hospital and surgical expense insurance. An insurance company might combine all three types of insurance into a basic health coverage plan.

Group Health Insurance

A group health insurance plan is the least expensive form of health insurance for most people. A company or organization usually provides group insurance for its employees or members. The company pays for part or all of the cost of the plan and employees can add extra coverage at their own expense.

Most private insurance companies offer group health insurance plans. Under these plans, you choose where and to whom you want to go for health care. A **health maintenance organization (HMO)** provides health care at its own health center for a fixed fee per month.

What's the difference between regular group insurance and an HMO plan? With an HMO, you must go to its own clinic. You must choose a doctor from its network. HMO plans stress preventive health care to keep medical costs down.

INSIDE THE ER
The nurse asks to see your insurance information once you're categorized. This might be your Medicare, Medicaid, or your HMO card. This lets you and the hospital know how much you pay versus how much the insurance company pays for tests or procedures. Most health insurance plans have a deductible.
What is a deductible?

continued on p. 571

Constructing Your Opinion on HMOs

This activity gives you the chance to add to your portfolio. Communicate, interview, research, and write your way into a story. Choose one imaginary path, Evaluating Evidence or Stating Your Case. Follow your path's steps to complete your own story.

pick a path

Evaluating Evidence

The Setting. Health maintenance organizations (HMOs) generally cost less than private practitioners, but patients can't always choose which of the clinic doctors they will see.

Rising Action. You're interested in surveying community members on their experiences and opinions of health care.

Step 1. Survey at least 20 individuals in your community about their health care. Ask at least five questions to find out what kind of health care service they receive, whether they are satisfied with it, and how they think it might be improved.

Step 2. Make a chart to organize the responses.

Stating Your Case

The Setting. A local hospital that operates like an HMO is associated with the state university. The hospital and its clinics, which serve patients from a three-state area, are renowned for its cardiovascular (heart) research.

Rising Action. Hospital administrators have asked your advertising company to draw up a marketing campaign to get the word out about the quality of the hospital and its specialization.

Step 1. Research other hospital marketing campaigns (either nationally or locally). Observe their techniques, messages, and layout.

Step 2. Using a design program on a computer or traditional art materials, design a poster that will help market the hospital.

Conclusion

To make a message persuasive, it needs to be clear, concise, and direct. This focus captures your reader's attention and helps hold his or her interest. Describe the strategy you used to organize your position. How did the evidence you gathered help you conclude your position? How did you know in what order of importance to list them? A strong opinion is also more persuasive when backed with facts, reasons, and examples.

Government Health Insurance

Most people who have health insurance receive it through their jobs or buy it from private companies. Many people also receive health insurance through state and federal government programs.

Medicare. **Medicare** is a major health insurance program set up by the federal government. Medicare coverage has two parts. Part A is hospital insurance that covers hospital care. Part B is medical insurance that covers doctors' fees and tests.

People covered by Medicare pay a deductible, coinsurance, and a monthly premium for their medical insurance. For their hospital insurance, they also have to pay a deductible. Many medical services aren't covered by Medicare.

Medicaid. **Medicaid** is another government health care plan for certain groups of citizens. It provides care for those who are unable to pay for insurance or health care. The coverage it provides is much more comprehensive than Medicare.

Costs of Health Insurance

Many policies have a *coinsurance clause* that requires you to pay a certain percentage of medical expenses beyond the deductible. Many policies also require a **copayment**, or a fee paid each time a service is used. For example, you might have to pay between $5 and $15 every time you visit the doctor or fill a prescription. Another factor is the number of people covered by a policy, such as dependent children. The more people covered by the policy, the higher the premium.

Some services, such as dental, vision, or mental health care, might not be covered by a policy. In those cases, you have to pay out of your own pocket and pay for additional insurance. Many policies won't cover a **pre-existing condition**, which is a serious health condition diagnosed before a person obtained health insurance. For example, if someone suffers from a heart condition, an insurance company might refuse to cover it.

Real-World Application

part **4** of 4

INSIDE THE ER
At any point in the ER, you may encounter an emergency physician, emergency nurse, physician assistant, emergency department technician, unit secretary, or a physician in training. Every one has a specific, important job to do and looks out for you. A physician assistant gives your ailment an educated diagnosis. You don't need surgery.
According to these facts, what kind of health insurance probably covers this visit?

✓ Fast Review

1. What is the least expensive form of health insurance for most people?
2. What is the difference between an HMO plan and regular group insurance?

Summary

1. Cash-value life insurance provides both protection and builds up savings. Term life insurance, or pure protection, provides death benefits only.

2. The cost of life insurance depends on the type of policy, the amount of coverage, and the age, health, and occupation of the insured.

3. Types of health insurance include major medical, hospital expense, surgical expense, medical expense, group health, and government health.

4. Companies and organizations provide group medical insurance to their employees and members. An HMO is a type of group insurance plan that has its own facilities and doctors, costs less than other plans, and stresses preventive health care. Medicare and Medicaid are government health insurance programs for retired persons, low-income families, people with medical needs, dependent children, and people receiving government assistance.

Using Business Key Words

Life and health insurance protect people from the financial risks associated with injury, illness, or death. See how many of the insurance-related terms you can match with the sentences below.

- **proceeds**
- **health maintenance organization (HMO)**
- **cash-value insurance**
- **term insurance**
- **Medicare**
- **beneficiary**
- **copayment**
- **pre-existing condition**
- **coinsurance**
- **Medicaid**

1. Covers a person for a specified period of time.
2. Provides health care at its health-care center for a fixed fee per patient.
3. A major health insurance program set up by the federal government.
4. Money paid from the policy.
5. Provides both savings and protection.
6. Specifies the percentage of costs, after the deductible, which the insurance company will pay.
7. Provides care for those who are unable to pay for other insurance or for health care.
8. Person who receives part or all of the proceeds from a life insurance policy.
9. A fee paid each time a service covered by a health insurance plan is used, such as a doctor's visit or a prescription.
10. A serious health condition diagnosed before a person obtained health insurance and which might not be covered by a policy.

Review What You Learned

11. What does life insurance protect?
12. Who names the beneficiary of a life insurance policy?
13. What is the difference between whole life insurance and term insurance?
14. Major medical insurance usually covers what kinds of care?
15. What does medical expense insurance cover?
16. Name two differences between a regular group insurance plan and an HMO.
17. Describe the two parts of Medicare.

Understanding Business Concepts

18. A person who receives part of a life insurance policy's proceeds is called a beneficiary. Why do you think the person who buys the life insurance policy names the beneficiary?
19. Cash-value insurance provides both savings and death benefits. Part of the premium pays for death benefits and the other builds up cash value like a savings account. Limited-payment insurance and endowment insurance are two types of cash-value insurance. What is the difference between limited-payment life insurance and endowment insurance?
20. If you work for a company that provides term insurance as a benefit, why do you think you would lose that insurance coverage if you leave the company?
21. Why do you think companies offer health insurance benefits for their employees?
22. Why do you think the federal government provides health care coverage for retired persons who are 65 and older?

Critical Thinking

23. Do you think a young, single person needs life insurance? Explain your answer.
24. Why do you think HMO plans are generally less expensive than other health care plans?
25. Would you work for a company because it offers good health benefits? Explain your answer.
26. Do you think that providing health care for retired persons should be the role of government? Explain why or why not.

Viewing and Representing

Examining the Image. Examine the picture. If you buy health and life insurance, what coverage would you probably purchase now, in five years, or in ten years? What assumptions are you making? Create a chart summarizing your decisions.

Building Academic Skills

 A Debatable Issue

Health care is nearly unaffordable without health insurance. Eighteen percent of the population in the United States lack insurance. Why do you think so many don't have insurance? With a partner, debate the ethics issues surrounding a doctor who charges a lower fee when the patient doesn't have health insurance.

COMPUTER TECHNOLOGY **Prefiguring Your Premiums**

Use a spreadsheet program to figure your health insurance premiums for the next ten years. Assume they are currently $800 per year and will increase at a rate of 5 percent per year. Calculate the increase at 4 percent and 6 percent as well. Print out your spreadsheet.

MATH **Calculating Percentage**

Suppose a policyholder's medical bills come to $11,000. The policyholder has a $100 deductible. The coinsurance clause states that the insurance company will pay 75 percent of the remaining balance and the policyholder will pay the other 25 percent. How much will the policyholder actually pay?

Social Science **Covering Controversy**

In groups of three or four, research the controversy surrounding national health care coverage in the United States. Include information about the political, social, and economic issues involved. Create an oral presentation with visuals to share your findings with the class.

Linking School to Home

Sharing a Scenario. Consider these facts about the uninsured:

- Sixty-five percent earn less than $26,580 for a family of three.
- Forty percent have no family physician.
- Forty percent go without recommended medical tests or treatments.

Discuss with your parents or other family members the importance of having health insurance. Together, describe a scenario where a high school student would need health insurance. Share your scenario with the class.

Linking School to Work

Inquiring About Local Charges. The uninsured are more likely to be hospitalized than those insured, because of avoiding medical tests or treatments. Do you have any idea how this might financially cripple an uninsured family? In groups of three or four, contact a local hospital and find out how much it costs for room and board during a hospital stay. Find out if there are additional charges for intensive-care rooms. Then research the cost of an average hospital stay today and ten years ago.

E-Homework

Applying Technology

Explore a Career. Use the Internet to research the variety of careers in the insurance industry. One good resource is the *Occupational Outlook Handbook* by the U. S. Department of Labor. This handbook describes jobs, working conditions, training and education needed, earnings potential, and expected job growth. Choose one and find out the:

- educational requirements
- salary range
- duties and responsibilities

Lifestyle Choices. Use the Internet to obtain a quote for term life insurance for yourself. What are the lifestyle choices that might impact the cost of term life insurance?

Connecting Academics

Math. Nin lost her job. She could continue the group health coverage of her former employer through the COBRA plan, but the monthly payment is 18 percent higher than an ample coverage she can purchase herself. Nin decides to buy independent health coverage, with monthly payments of $143. How much would have the COBRA plan cost Nin?

Language Arts. Working in a team of four, choose one of the following insurance topics: cash-value life, term life, government health, group health, or other health insurance. Together, assess the knowledge and skills of the members of your team then decide on the best person for each task of the team project. Research the team's chosen topic and prepare a visual presentation.

BusinessWeek Analyzing the Feature Story

You read the first part of "Staying Insured When You're on Your Own" at the beginning of this chapter. Below are a few questions for you to answer about health insurance. You'll find the answers to these questions when you're reading the entire article. First, here are the questions:

27. How long can someone continue the health insurance offered by their former employer under COBRA?
28. What is one of the least expensive ways for a self-employed person to buy coverage?

CREATIVE JOURNAL ACTIVITY

Go to the library or online and research federal laws such as COBRA or HIPAA. What information or programs does your state offer related to one of these acts? Summarize your findings in a short report.

BUSINESS Online

The Full Story

To learn more about health or life insurance, visit the *Introduction to Business* Web site at **www.introbus.glencoe.com**, and click on *BusinessWeek* Feature Story, Chapter 35.

Investigating Business Schools

Throughout this book, you've read about the different ways businesses are managed—from finances and technical resources to risk. To make informed decisions, it's important to obtain as much information as possible. Education is the best training for this. Therefore, examine both undergraduate and graduate college degrees in business. In this seminar, you'll research a business school and find out about the different programs available.

Factoids

Not Just Another Degree.
With an MBA (Masters of Business Administration) on your résumé you're guaranteed more money in an industry. Starting salaries of the top graduates start at about $75,000 including stock options and signing bonuses.

Higher Education Near You.
Nearly 700 universities and colleges offer MBA programs.

In Your Future. The typical new business-school grad is 28 years old.

Reap the Benefits. Investing in business school usually pays off in five to eight years, including the two full years you spent in graduate school.

Expanding Your Horizons.
About 75 percent of full-time MBA graduates change the direction of their career after completing the degree. It's an excellent opportunity to broaden your career opportunities.

Investigate the Images

Look at the photographic collage on the left page. What grabs your attention first? Is it the color or the words? The power in reading visuals is in analyzing and dissecting your observations. On a separate piece of paper, respond to the questions listed below. These questions might help sharpen the focus of your visual mind.

Your Observations

1. How many photographs do you see?

2. Examine each photograph. How are they assembled in relation to one another?

3. What is the subject of each photograph? Is place or location the subject?

4. Does color signify a message?

5. What issues do you take from these images?

Information

6. Summarize what you know about the photographs from your observations.

Exploring Culture

7. Reprimand in private, and praise in public is a manager's old adage. As a future employee or employer, why is feedback important to success? How do you gain the respect of an employer?

8. Does an increase in salary indicate your worth to a company? Why or why not?

Taking Aim at Careers

Preparation

Learning to manage the different aspects of a business requires training and education.

Objective

In this *BusinessWeek* Seminar, you'll:
- **Research** a business school.
- **Investigate** the school's admissions procedures.
- **Create** a brochure that describes the business school you'd like to attend.

Materials Needed

✓ Copies of recent news publications such as *BusinessWeek*, the *Wall Street Journal*, or *US News and World Report*

✓ Access to the Internet or your local or school library

✓ Paper, pens, pencils, and markers

✓ Copies of magazines you can cut up

Procedures

1. Find and read articles about business schools—colleges and universities that offer degrees in business administration. Business magazines and newspapers publish articles about business schools. At **www.businessweek.com** there is a link to "B-Schools" where you can access information about business schools.

2. Choose a specific school to investigate. Select one that is nearby, one that is highly ranked, or one that interests you.

3. Research your chosen school and a particular business program, such as marketing or business administration. Find information on admissions, tuition and fees, and requirements for graduation. Find out about campus life and extracurricular activities. If you'd like, research scholarships, loans, and other financing arrangements.

4. Create a brochure that describes your chosen business school. Explain why you've chosen this school and include information on the business program that interests you. Cut up old magazines for visuals and be sure to include contact information.

5. As a class, create a display of the brochures. Be sure to review other students' brochures and ask questions about their research to compare your business school to theirs.

Chart It

As a class, make a chart on the board that lists the business schools researched, the programs students are interested in, and why they were chosen.

Business Schools	Business Programs	Why Did You Choose These?

Analyze and Conclude

After reviewing the chart, answer the questions below.

1. **Acquiring and Evaluating Information.** Did more than one student research the same school and/or program? Name the school(s) and program(s).

2. **Building Self-Esteem.** What are the benefits of selecting a business school appropriate for your wants and needs?

3. **Decision Making.** What reason was given most often for the student's choice of school and/or program?

Becoming an Informed Citizen

Congratulations, you finished the seminar. Now it's time to reflect on the decisions you made.

Creative Thinking. Business schools like applicants with a variety of backgrounds and different objectives. How would you sell yourself in a personal statement to a business school? Examine how your different experiences would compliment your classmates.

Analyzing Your Future. What actions can you take today in order to prepare yourself for a future you really want? What is your purpose in life?

Further Exploration
To find out more about business schools, visit the *Introduction to Business* Web site at **www.introbus.glencoe.com**.

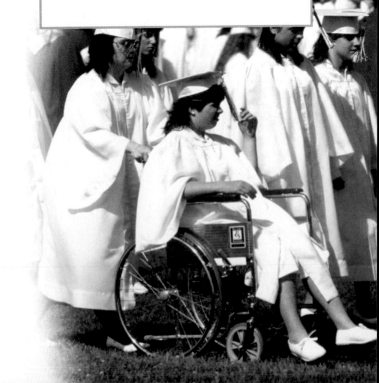

Math Skills Builder

WRITING NUMBERS AS WORDS AND ROUNDING NUMBERS

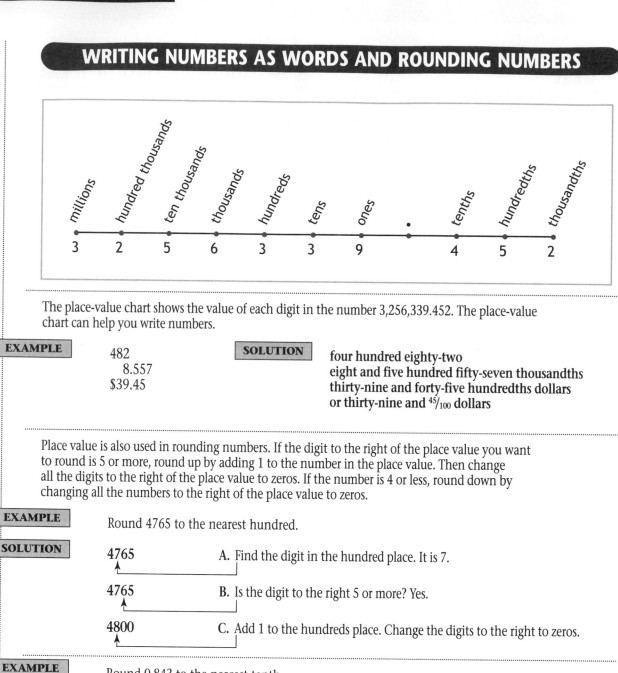

The place-value chart shows the value of each digit in the number 3,256,339.452. The place-value chart can help you write numbers.

EXAMPLE

482
8.557
$39.45

SOLUTION

four hundred eighty-two
eight and five hundred fifty-seven thousandths
thirty-nine and forty-five hundredths dollars
or thirty-nine and $^{45}/_{100}$ dollars

Place value is also used in rounding numbers. If the digit to the right of the place value you want to round is 5 or more, round up by adding 1 to the number in the place value. Then change all the digits to the right of the place value to zeros. If the number is 4 or less, round down by changing all the numbers to the right of the place value to zeros.

EXAMPLE

Round 4765 to the nearest hundred.

SOLUTION

4765   A. Find the digit in the hundred place. It is 7.

4765   B. Is the digit to the right 5 or more? Yes.

4800   C. Add 1 to the hundreds place. Change the digits to the right to zeros.

EXAMPLE

Round 0.843 to the nearest tenth.

SOLUTION

0.843   A. Find the digit in the tenth place. It is 8.

0.843   B. Is the digit to the right 5 or more? No.

0.8   C. Do not change the tenths digit. Drop the digits to the right.

WRITING NUMBERS AS WORDS AND ROUNDING NUMBERS

Dollar and cents amounts are often rounded to the nearest cent, or the hundredths place.

EXAMPLE $26.7443
$683.1582

SOLUTION $26.74
$683.16

PROBLEMS

Write as numbers.
1. three thousand four hundred ninety-nine
2. one hundred eleven and ³²/₁₀₀ dollars
3. two hundred six and eighty-eight thousandths

Write in word form.
4. 572
5. 2.897
6. $325.10

Round to the nearest place value shown.

7.	ten thousand	327,975	11.	one	28.91
8.	thousand	816,777	12.	tenth	86.379
9.	hundred	26,312	13.	hundredth	5.5787
10.	ten	6336			

Round 23,793,611 to the place value shown.
14. millions
15. ten millions
16. thousands
17. hundreds
18. ten thousands
19. hundred thousands

Round to the nearest place value shown.

20.	cent	$87.2671	23.	ten dollars	$5,982
21.	ten cents	$213.432	24.	hundred dollars	$12,785
22.	one dollar	$671.98			

APPLICATIONS

25. As an accountant for the advertising agency of Phillips & Phillips, Marcia Strasser writes many checks. Write each check amount in words.
    a. $27.83
    b. $121. 77
    c. $569.14
    d. $8,721. 65

26. Juan Sanchez, an inventory clerk for a lumber yard, often rounds inventory figures for easier handling. Round the number from the inventory list to the nearest ten.
    a. grade 1 oak   519 ft.
    b. grade 2 oak   795 ft.
    c. grade 1 pine   323 ft.
    d. grade 2 pine   477 ft.

ADDING AND SUBTRACTING DECIMALS

When adding decimals, write the addition problem in vertical form. Be sure to line up the decimal points. When adding amounts with different numbers of decimal places, write zeros in the empty decimal places.

EXAMPLE $15.27 + 16.39 + 36.19$

SOLUTION

```
  15.27
  16.39
+ 36.19
───────
  67.85
```

EXAMPLE $58.2 + 3.97 + 8 + 123.796$

SOLUTION

```
   58.2          58.200
   3.97           3.970
   8.             8.000
+123.796       +123.796
             ──────────
               193.966
```

When subtracting decimals, write the subtraction problem in vertical form. Be sure to line up the decimal points. When subtracting amounts with different numbers of decimal places, write zeros in the empty decimal places.

EXAMPLE $78.63 - 42.41$

SOLUTION

```
  78.63
- 42.41
───────
  36.22
```

EXAMPLE $149.9 - 28.37$

SOLUTION

```
  149.9         149.90
- 28.37        - 28.37
              ────────
                121.53
```

Adding and subtracting amounts of money is just like adding and subtracting decimals. The decimal point separates the dollars and cents. Remember to put a dollar sign in the total.

EXAMPLE $74.99 + $8.76

SOLUTION

```
 $74.99
 + 8.76
───────
 $ 83.75
```

EXAMPLE $750 - $43.29

SOLUTION

```
 $750.00
 - 43.29
────────
 $706.71
```

PROBLEMS

```
1.   19.87        2.   4.377        3.    8.3          4.   46.65        5.  $  2.77
     32.24             6.829            12.78                 3.5            35.96
   + 27.55           + 2.707        + 322.437           + 125.397        + 10.37
```

6. $22.19 + 47.75 + 13.88 + 19.85$
7. $0.78 + 9.82 + 36.242 + 37.4$
8. $6.7 + 27.81 + 653.47 + 5.5$
9. $54.32 + 0.37 + 2.5 + 0.797$
10. $6.22 + $53.19 + $ .33 + $7.85
11. $4.78 + $12.50 + $22 + $17.10

```
12.   3.75       13.  376.55       14.  468.47       15.  367.05       16.  $363.27
    - 2.18           - 27.42          - 233.55          - 219.87          - 79.14
```

ADDING AND SUBTRACTING DECIMALS

17. $547.7 - 127.6$	18. $76.99 - 3.87$
19. $695.13 - 428.1$	20. $3076 - 2205.50$
21. $\$300 - \$5.75$	22. $\$445.19 - \$175.76$

APPLICATIONS Complete the sales receipts by finding the subtotals and the totals.

23.

Date 6/1/--	Auth. No. 86430	Identification	Clerk DL	Reg./Dept.	☑ Take ☐ Send
Qty	Class	Description	Price	Amount	
1		dress		77	98
1		jacket		85	99
2		hosiery	12.99 ea	25	98

a. Freight charges will be included with your invoice at the time of shipping. You will be billed the published rates from UPS, US Postal Service.

Subtotal	?	
CUSTOMER SIGNATURE X _Shelley Turner_	Tax	13	30
b. Sales Slip	Total	?	

24.

Date 3/14/--	Auth. No. 42	Identification	Clerk JR	Reg./Dept.	☑ Take ☐ Send
Qty	Class	Description	Price	Amount	
1		couch		599	95
1 pr		draperies		279	88

a. Freight charges will be included with your invoice at the time of shipping. You will be billed the published rates from UPS, US Postal Service.

Subtotal	?	
CUSTOMER SIGNATURE X _Betty Clark_	Tax	57	19
b. Sales Slip	Total	?	

Complete the bank deposit slips by finding the subtotals and the total deposits.

25.

		DOLLARS	CENTS
CASH	CURRENCY	72	00
	COINS		
CHECKS	LIST SEPARATELY 95-76	413	12
	98-11	25	00
	95-13	211	10
a.	SUBTOTAL	?	
↩	LESS CASH RECEIVED	50	00
b.	TOTAL DEPOSIT	?	

a.
b.

26.

		DOLLARS	CENTS
CASH	CURRENCY	23	00
	COINS	7	44
CHECKS	LIST SEPARATELY 85-76	175	66
	88-11	23	33
		12	87
a.	SUBTOTAL	?	
↩	LESS CASH RECEIVED	75	00
b.	TOTAL DEPOSIT	?	

a.
b.

27.

		DOLLARS	CENTS
CASH	CURRENCY		
	COINS	4	75
CHECKS	LIST SEPARATELY 57-12	25	95
	57-10	38	11
a.	SUBTOTAL	?	
↩	LESS CASH RECEIVED	25	00
b.	TOTAL DEPOSIT	?	

a.
b.

28. You are a cashier at a coffee shop. Compute the correct change for each of the following orders.

	Customer's Order	Customer Gives You	Change
a.	$8.76	$10.00	
b.	$12.94	$15.00	
c.	$9.30	$10.50	
d.	$16.11	$20.00	
e.	$5.57	$5.75	
f.	$22.02	$25.00	
g.	$7.12	$7.15	
h.	$3.33	$5.00	
i.	$28.04	$30.04	
j.	$6.12	$10.25	

MULTIPLYING AND DIVIDING DECIMALS

When multiplying decimals, multiply as if the decimal numbers were whole numbers. Then count the total number of decimal places in the factors. This number will be the number of decimal places in the product.

EXAMPLE

```
   18.7  ◄  factor
 × 0.34  ◄  factor
   748
   561
  6358   ◄  product
```

SOLUTION

```
   18.7   ◄   1 decimal place
 × 0.34   ◄ + 2 decimal places
   748
   561
  6.358   ◄   3 decimal places
```

If the product does not have enough digits to place the decimal in the correct position, you will need to write zeros. Start at the right of the product in counting the decimal places and write zeros at the left.

EXAMPLE

```
   0.63
 × 0.05
   315
```

SOLUTION

```
   0.63   ◄   2 decimal places
 × 0.05   ◄ + 2 decimal places
 0.0315   ◄   4 decimal places
```

When multiplying amounts of money, round the answer to the nearest cent. Remember to put a dollar sign in the answer.

EXAMPLE

```
  $2.25
 × 1.5
  3.375
```

SOLUTION

```
 $ 2.25  ◄   2 places       $2.25 × 1.5 = $3.375
 × 1.5   ◄ + 1 place                     = $3.38
 $3.375  ◄   3 places       rounded to the nearest cent
```

When multiplying by 10, 100, or 1000, count the number of zeros. Then move the decimal point to the right the same number of spaces.

EXAMPLE

8.32 × 100

SOLUTION

8.32 × 100 = 8.32 = 832   100 has 2 zeros; move
                           decimal 2 places.

PROBLEMS

1.
```
   18.3
 × 2.5
```

2.
```
   27.5
 × 8.2
```

3.
```
   56.8
 × 0.33
```

4.
```
   88.1
 × 0.23
```

5.
```
   0.57
 × 0.14
```

6.
```
   0.88
 × 0.07
```

7.
```
   0.93
 × 0.04
```

8.
```
   0.323
 × 0.005
```

9. $17.85 × 15.5 = $276.675 =

10. $25.24 × 6.3 = $159.012 =

11. $18.15 × 6.5 = $117.975 =

12. $14.98 × 8.7 = $130.326 =

13. 33.8 × 10 =

14. 55.399 × 100 =

15. 0.518 × 1000 =

16. 532.788 × 10,000 =

MULTIPLYING AND DIVIDING DECIMALS

APPLICATION

17. Below are partial payroll records for Fanciful Flowers. Complete the records by calculating gross earnings (hourly rate x hours worked), Social Security tax (gross earnings $\times$ 0.062), Medicare tax (gross earnings $\times$ 0.0145), federal income tax (gross earnings $\times$ 0.15), and state income tax (gross earnings $\times$ 0.045). Round each deduction to the nearest cent. Find the total deductions and subtract from gross earnings to find the net pay.

	Employee	Hourly Rate	Number of Hours	Gross Earnings	Social Security Tax	Medicare Tax	Federal Inc. Tax	State Inc. Tax	Total Deductions	Net Pay
a.	M. Smith	$8.25	24	198.00	12.28	2.87	29.70	8.91	53.76	144.24
b.	R. Nash	$9.15	33	301.95	18.72	4.38	45.29	13.59	81.98	219.97
c.	C. Young	$7.75	15	116.25	7.21	1.69	17.44	5.23	31.57	84.68
d.	D. Cha	$9.15	30	274.50	17.02	3.98	41.18	12.35	74.53	199.97

When dividing decimals, if there is a decimal point in the divisor, you must move it to the right to make the divisor a whole number. Move the decimal point in the dividend to the right the same number of places you moved the decimal point in the divisor. Then divide as with whole numbers.

$$\begin{array}{r} 140 \leftarrow \text{quotient} \\ \text{divisor} \rightarrow 6\overline{)840} \leftarrow \text{dividend} \end{array}$$

EXAMPLE

$3.44\overline{)15.5488}$

SOLUTION

$3.44\overline{)15.5488}$

$$\begin{array}{r} 4.52 \\ 344\overline{)1554.88} \\ -1376 \\ \hline 1788 \\ -1720 \\ \hline 688 \\ -688 \end{array}$$

Add zeros to the right of the decimal point in the dividend if needed.

EXAMPLE

$0.42\overline{)0.147}$

SOLUTION

$0.42\overline{)0.147}$

$$\begin{array}{r} 0.35 \\ 42\overline{)14.70} \\ -126 \\ \hline 210 \\ -210 \end{array}$$ zero added

When the dividend is an amount of money, remember to place the dollar sign in the quotient and round the answer to the nearest cent.

EXAMPLE

$48\overline{)\$95.12}$

SOLUTION

$$\begin{array}{r} \$1.981 \\ 48\overline{)\$95.120} \end{array}$$

$\$95.12 \div 48 = \$1.98$ rounded to the nearest cent.

Appendix

MULTIPLYING AND DIVIDING DECIMALS

When dividing by 10, 100, or 1000, count the number of zeros in 10, 100, or 1000 and move the decimal point to the left the same number of places.

EXAMPLE

$15{,}213.7 \div 1000$

SOLUTION

$15{,}213.7 \div 1000 = 15213.7$

$= 15.2137$

1000 has 3 zeros; move decimal 3 places

PROBLEMS

Round to the nearest hundredth or the nearest cent.

18. $2.7 \overline{)11.61}$

19. $1.3 \overline{)7.67}$

20. $6.2 \overline{)44.02}$

21. $0.3 \overline{)1.62}$

22. $.05 \overline{)1.47}$

23. $.04 \overline{)28.4}$

24. $8.3 \overline{)46.99}$

25. $3.4 \overline{)178.3}$

26. $88 \overline{)\$356.68}$

27. $45 \overline{)\$42.79}$

28. $15 \overline{)\$87.32}$

29. $14.1 \overline{)7.823}$

APPLICATIONS

30. Your family is looking into buying a late model, used car. Calculate (to the nearest tenth) the gas mileage for the following types of cars.

	Type of Vehicle	Miles	Gallons of Fuel	Miles per Gallon
a.	Subcompact	631	17.8	
b.	4-door sedan	471.4	16.6	
c.	Minivan	405.1	18.2	
d.	Compact	512.2	15.7	
e.	SUV	298.1	23.2	

FRACTION TO DECIMAL, DECIMAL TO FRACTION

Any fraction can be renamed as a decimal and any decimal can be renamed as a fraction. To rename a fraction as a decimal, use division. Think of the fraction bar in the fraction as meaning "divide by." For example, $5/8$ means "5 divided by 8." After the 5, write a decimal point and as many zeros as are needed. Then divide by 8.

EXAMPLE   Change $3/8$ to a decimal.

SOLUTION

$$3/8 \rightarrow \begin{array}{r} 0.375 \\ 8\overline{)3.000} \\ -24 \\ \hline 60 \\ -56 \\ \hline 40 \\ -40 \end{array}$$

EXAMPLE   Change $1/5$ to a decimal.

SOLUTION

$$1/5 \rightarrow \begin{array}{r} 0.2 \\ 5\overline{)1.0} \\ -10 \end{array}$$

If a fraction does not divide evenly, divide to one more decimal place than you are rounding to.

EXAMPLE   Change $5/7$ to a decimal rounded to the nearest hundredth. (Divide to the thousandths place.)

SOLUTION

$$5/7 \rightarrow \begin{array}{r} 0.714 = 0.71 \\ 7\overline{)5.000} \\ -49 \\ \hline 10 \\ -7 \\ \hline 30 \\ -28 \\ \hline 2 \end{array}$$

EXAMPLE   Change $2/7$ to a decimal rounded to the nearest thousandth. (Divide to the ten thousandths place.)

SOLUTION

$$2/7 \rightarrow \begin{array}{r} 0.2857 = 0.286 \\ 7\overline{)2.0000} \\ -14 \\ \hline 60 \\ -56 \\ \hline 40 \\ -35 \\ \hline 50 \\ -49 \\ \hline 1 \end{array}$$

To rename a decimal as a fraction, name the place value of the digit at the far right. This is the denominator of the fraction.

$$0.83 = 83/100$$

3 is in the hundredths place, so the denominator is 100.

$$0.007 = 7/1000$$

7 is in the thousandths place, so the denominator is 1000.

Note that the number of zeros in the denominator is the same as the number of places to the right of the decimal point. The fraction should always be written in lowest terms.

$$0.25 = 25/100 = 1/4$$

$$3.375 = 3\ 375/1000 = 3\ 3/8$$

Appendix

FRACTION TO DECIMAL, DECIMAL TO FRACTION

Change the fractions to decimals. Round to the nearest thousandth.

1. $2/5$
2. $5/6$
3. $4/9$
4. $7/10$
5. $9/25$
6. $115/200$
7. $1/7$
8. $13/40$
9. $4/15$
10. $5/12$
11. $11/16$
12. $1/4$

Change the fractions to decimals. Round to the nearest hundredth.

13. $1/8$
14. $5/9$
15. $33/35$
16. $12/25$
17. $7/20$
18. $2/25$
19. $15/16$
20. $2/9$
21. $3/7$
22. $3/4$
23. $1/6$
24. $31/32$

Change the decimals to fractions reduced to lowest terms.

25. 0.275   o
26. 0.3
27. 0.15
28. 0.8
29. 1.125
30. 0.117
31. 0.32
32. 2.5
33. 44.755
34. 0.005
35. 5.545
36. 0.2

37. Stock prices have traditionally been quoted as dollars and fractions of a dollar. Change the stock prices to dollars and cents. Round to the nearest cent.

Stock	Price
a. AdobeSy	$61\,5/16$
b. AirTran	$4\,15/32$
c. CNET	$50\,3/4$
d. ETrade	$20\,1/4$
e. Omnipoint	$112\,5/8$
f. Qualcomm	$142\,1/16$
g. WebLink	$17\,13/16$
h. Winstar	$70\,23/32$

38. Individual bowling averages in the Southern Community League are carried to the nearest hundredth. Convert the decimals to fractions reduced to the lowest terms.

Name	Average
a. B. Taylor	220.13
b. J. Scott	217.02
c. T. Anfinson	216.97
d. G. Ingram	212.08
e. D. Ingram	210.50
f. B. Jordan	209.25
g. G. Maddux	207.88
h. A. Jones	205.15

PERCENT TO DECIMAL, DECIMAL TO PERCENT

Percent is an abbreviation of the Latin words *per centum*, meaning "by the hundred." So percent means "divide by 100." A percent can be written as a decimal. To change a percent to a decimal, first write the percent as a fraction with a denominator of 100, then divide by 100.

EXAMPLE   Change 31% to a decimal.

SOLUTION $31\% = {}^{31}/_{100} = 0.31$

EXAMPLE   Change 17.3% to a decimal.

SOLUTION $17.3\% = {}^{17.3}/_{100} = 0.173$

When dividing by 100, you can just move the decimal point two places to the left. When you write a percent as a decimal, you are moving the decimal point two places to the left and dropping the percent sign (%). If necessary, use zero as a placeholder.

EXAMPLE

A.   31%

B.   7%

SOLUTION

$31\% = 31. = 0.31$ ←——— Drop % sign.
————— Move decimal 2 places.

$7\% = 07. = 0.07$ ——— Insert a zero as a placeholder.

To write a decimal as a percent, move the decimal point two places to the right and add a percent sign (%).

EXAMPLE

A.   0.31

B.   0.07

C.   2.5

D.   0.008

SOLUTION

$0.31 = 0.31 = 31\%$ ← Add % sign.
————— Move decimal 2 places.

$0.07 = 0.07 = 7\%$

$2.5 = 2.50 = 250\%$

$0.008 = 0.008 = 0.8\%$

PROBLEMS

Write as decimals.

1. 35%   2. 22%   3. 68%   4. 30%

5. 49.2%   6. 88.7%   7. 11.5%   8. 92.9%

9. 322%   10. 526%   11. 663%   12. 275%

13. 9%   14. 5%   15. 4%   16. 12%

17. 7.03%   18. 9.02%   19. 2.0725%   20. 3.0843%

Write as percents.

21. 0.75   22. 0.17   23. 0.44   24. 0.26

Appendix

25. 0.06   26. 0.07   27. 0.01   28. 0.02

29. 0.003   30. 0.009   31. 0.0045   32. 0.0029

33. 3.12   34. 4.14   35. 6.007   36. 5.000

37. 0.1   38. 0.5   39. 325.5   40. 0.2015

APPLICATIONS

41. The percent changes in retail sales were reported as a decimal in the October issue of *Retail Monthly* magazine. Change the decimals to percents.

	Retail Sales	
	Month	Change
a.	February	0.012
b.	March	0.006
c.	April	0.013
d.	May	0.038
e.	June	0.043
f.	July	0.011
g.	August	0.022

42. The commission rate schedule for a stockbroker is shown. Change the percents to decimals.

	Commission Rate Schedule	
	Dollar Amount	% of Dollar Amount
a.	$0 – $2,499	2.3%, minimum $30
b.	$2,500 – $4,999	2.0%, minimum $42
c.	$5,000 – $9,999	1.5%, minimum $65
d.	$10,000 – $14,999	1.1%, minimum $110
e.	$15,000 – $24,999	0.9%, minimum $135
f.	$25,000 – $49,999	0.6%, minimum $175
	$50,000 and above	negotiated

PERCENT TO DECIMAL, DECIMAL TO PERCENT

43. During the National Basketball Association season, the teams had these won–lost records. The Pct. column shows the percent of games won, expressed as a decimal. Change the decimals to percents.

EASTERN CONFERENCE
Atlantic Division

	W	L	Pct.	GB
a. Miami	28	16	.636	-
b. New York	27	17	.614	1
c. Philadelphia	25	21	.543	4
d. Boston	21	25	.457	8
e. Orlando	21	26	.447	8 1/2
f. New Jersey	17	29	.370	12
g. Washington	15	31	.326	14

WESTERN CONFERENCE
Midwest Division

	W	L	Pct.	GB
p. San Antonio	30	16	.652	-
q. Utah	27	17	.614	2
r. Minnesota	25	18	.581	3 1/2
s. Denver	21	22	.488	7 1/2
t. Houston	19	27	.413	11
u. Dallas	18	27	.400	11 1/2
v. Vancouver	12	32	.273	17

Central Division

	W	L	Pct.	GB
h. Indiana	29	15	.659	-
i. Milwaukee	26	21	.553	4 1/2
j. Charlotte	24	20	.545	5
k. Toronto	24	20	.545	5
l. Detroit	22	23	.489	7 1/2
m. Cleveland	19	26	.422	10 1/2
n. Atlanta	17	26	.395	11 1/2
o. Chicago	9	34	.209	19 1/2

Pacific Division

	W	L	Pct.	GB
w. L.A. Lakers	34	11	.756	-
x. Portland	34	11	.756	-
y. Sacramento	28	16	.636	5 1/2
z. Seattle	29	18	.617	6
aa. Phoenix	26	18	.591	7 1/2
ab. Golden State	11	32	.256	22
ac. L.A. Clippers	11	34	.244	23

44. How many teams have won more than 75% of their games? _____
Who are they? _____

45. How many teams have won more than 50% of their games? _____

46. How many have won less than 30% of their games? _____

Appendix

FINDING A PERCENTAGE

Finding a percentage means finding a percent of a number. To find a percent of a number, you change the percent to a decimal, then multiply it by the number.

EXAMPLE 30% of 90 is what number?

SOLUTION

$30\% \times 90 = n$ — In mathematics, *of* means "times" and *is* means "equals."
Let n stand for the unknown number.

$0.30 \times 90 = n$ Change the percent to a decimal.

$27 = n$ Multiply.

30% of $90 = 27$ Write the answer.

EXAMPLE The delivery charge is 8% of the selling price of $145.00. Find the delivery charge.

EXAMPLE The student had 95% correct out of 80 questions. How many answers were correct?

SOLUTION

$8\% \times \$145.00 = n$
$0.08 \times \$145.00 = n$
$\$11.60 = n$
$8\% \times \$145.00 = \$11.60$ delivery charge

SOLUTION

$95\% \times 80 = n$
$0.95 \times 80 = n$
$76 = n$
$95\% \times 80 = 76$ correct

PROBLEMS

Find the percentage.

1. 25% of 60
2. 45% of 80
3. 40% of 30
4. 33% of 112

5. 58% of 420
6. 50% of 422
7. 3% of 100
8. 2% of 247

9. 110% of 65
10. 7% of 785
11. 1% of 819
12. 4% of 19.5

13. 185% of 95
14. 200% of 720
15. 135% of 860
16. 120% of 3.35

17. 4.5% of 50
18. 1.25% of 300
19. 33.3% of 80
20. 67.2% of 365

Round the answer to the nearest cent.

21. 7% of $35.78
22. 6.5% of $80
23. 10% of $93.20
24. 5.5% of $135

25. 4.25% of $65.00
26. 2.75% of $115
27. 125% of $98
28. 7.5% of $150

29. 0.3% of $450
30. 0.15% of $125
31. 8.2% of $19.89
32. 5.25% of $110.15

FINDING A PERCENTAGE

33. The following items appeared in a sales flyer for a major department store. Calculate the amount saved from the regular price as well as the sale price for each item. Round to the nearest cent.

		Amount Saved	Sale Price
a.	Save 25% on juniors knit shirts. Reg. $18.		
b.	Save 30% on women's dresses. Reg. $69.99		
c.	Save 20% on men's shoes. Reg. $135.		
d.	Save 25% on all nursery cribs. Reg. $119.99		
e.	Save 25% on all boxed jewelry sets. Reg. $19.99		
f.	Save 30% on family athletic shoes. Reg. $59.99		

34. Student Sean Hu received these test scores. How many answers were correct on each test?

	Subject	Test Score	Number of Items	Correct Answers
a.	Math	90%	80	
b.	English	70%	90	
c.	Science	80%	110	
d.	Spanish	90%	50	
e.	Government	85%	100	

35. Sales taxes are found by multiplying the tax rate times the selling price of the item. The total purchase price is the selling price plus the sales tax. Find the sales tax and total purchase price for each selling price. Round to the nearest cent.

	Selling Price	Tax Rate	Sales Tax	Total Purchase Price
a.	$14.78	4%		
b.	$22.50	5%		
c.	$3.88	6%		
d.	$95.85	6.5%		
e.	$212.00	7.25%		
f.	$85.06	8.25%		
g.	$199.99	7.455%		

AVERAGE (MEAN)

The average, or mean, is a single number used to represent a group of numbers. The average, or mean, of two or more numbers is the sum of the numbers divided by the number of items added.

EXAMPLE Find the average of 8, 5, 3, 7, and 2.   Add to find the total.

SOLUTION
$$\frac{8 + 5 + 3 + 7 + 2}{5} = \frac{25}{5} = 5$$ Divide by the number of items.

EXAMPLE Find the average of 278, 340, 205, and 235.

SOLUTION
$$\frac{278 + 340 + 205 + 235}{4} = \frac{1058}{4} = 264.5$$

EXAMPLE Find the average of 4.3, 7.1, 1.5, 3.2, and 6.4. Round to the nearest tenth.

SOLUTION
$$\frac{4.3 + 7.1 + 1.5 + 3.2 + 6.4}{5} = \frac{22.5}{5} = 4.5$$

EXAMPLE Find the average of $12, $35, $19, $23, $11, and $21. Round to the nearest dollar.

SOLUTION
$$\frac{\$12 + \$35 + \$19 + \$23 + \$11 + \$21}{6} = \frac{\$121}{6} = \$20.17 = \$20$$

PROBLEMS

Find the average for each group.

1.   3, 5, 7, 9, 11
2.   25, 40, 35, 50
3.   211, 197, 132
4.   416, 310, 344, 430
5.   4.4, 2.9, 3.7, 1.8, 6.5
6.   3.6, 7.1, 4.8, 4.7, 6.3, 5.3
7. $23, $21, $25, $24, $26
8. $98, $87, $79, $85, $88, $91

Find the average for each group. Round to the nearest hundredth or cent.

9.   8.1, 8.6, 7.7, 9.2, 5.5, 6.9, 7.3
10. 3.3, 5.8, 4.6, 2.8, 3.4, 5.2
11. $31.70, $33.91, $36.17, $33.85
12. $4.37, $3.74, $4.90, $5.74, $6.11
13. $55.78, $44.20, $43.95, $34.36

AVERAGE (MEAN)

14. $121.19, $115.08, $135, $129.05, $111.88

15. Ben Agars had bowling scores of 187, 154, and 130. What was his average?

16. Kelley O'Reilly's tips from being a waitress were $5.00, $5.50, $4.75, $3.00, $4.50, $2.00, $5.75, and $4.50. What was her average tip?

17. Last year, Michael Legato's telephone bills averaged $66.12 a month. What was his total bill for the year?

18. Mark Purdue recorded his math test scores this quarter. What is his average?

Test Number	1	2	3	4	5	6	7	8
Score	65	77	81	79	90	86	92	98

19. What does he need on the next test to have an average of 85?

20. If Mark got a 97 on test 9 and 100 on test 10, what would be his average?

APPLICATIONS

21. As captain of the school golf team, Erica Samuelson has to complete this form after each game. Help her by computing the total and the average for each golfer. She also computes the total and the team average for each game. Round to the nearest whole number.

	Golfer	Game 1	Game 2	Game 3	Total	Average
a.	Samuelson	86	78	75		
b.	Haas	80	81	70		
c.	Sutherland	82	77	71		
d.	Beck	80	66	73		
e.	McCarron	78	81	82		
f.	Total					
g.	Team average					

ELAPSED TIME

To find elapsed time, subtract the earlier time from the later time.

EXAMPLE Find the elapsed time for Kaitlin Harper who worked from:
  A. 4:30 P.M. to 11:45 P.M.   B. 5:15 A.M. to 10:33 A.M.

SOLUTIONS

$$
\begin{array}{r}
11:45 \\
-\ 4:30 \\
\hline
7:15
\end{array}
$$
= 7 hours 15 minutes
written as 7 h: 15 min

$$
\begin{array}{r}
10:33 \\
-\ 5:15 \\
\hline
5:18
\end{array}
$$
= 5 hours 18 minutes
written as 5 h: 18 min

You cannot subtract 45 minutes from 30 minutes unless you borrow an hour and add it to the 30 minutes. Remember that 1 hour = 60 minutes.

EXAMPLE Find the elapsed time from 2:50 P.M. to 9:15 P.M.

SOLUTION

$$
\begin{array}{rcl}
9:15 & = & 8:15\ +\ :60\ = & 8:75 \quad \text{borrowed 1 hour} \\
-\ 2:50 & = & -\ 2:50 & -\ 2:50 \\
\hline
& & & 6:25 \quad = 6\text{ h}: 25\text{ min}
\end{array}
$$

To find elapsed time when the time period goes past noon, add 12 hours to the later time before subtracting.

EXAMPLE Find the elapsed time from 6:00 A.M. to 3:15 P.M.

SOLUTION

$$
\begin{array}{rcl}
3:15 & = & 3:15\ +\ 12:00\ = & 15:15 \\
-\ 6:00 & = & -\ 6:00 & -\ 6:00 \\
\hline
& & & 9:15 \quad = 9\text{ h}: 15\text{ min}
\end{array}
$$

EXAMPLE Find the elapsed time from 10:35 P.M. to 3:12 A.M.

SOLUTION

$$
\begin{array}{rcl}
3:12 & = & 15:12\ = & 14:12\ +\ :60\ = & 14:72 \\
-\ 10:35 & = & -\ 10:35\ = & -\ 10:35 & -\ 10:35 \\
\hline
& & & & 4:37 \quad = 4\text{ h}: 37\text{ min}
\end{array}
$$

PROBLEMS

Find the elapsed time.

1. From 2:30 P.M. to 6:35 P.M.
2. From 1:18 P.M. to 7:25 P.M.
3. From 4:40 A.M. to 8:57 A.M.
4. From 3:33 a.m. to 10:47 A.M.
5. From 3:15 A.M. to 5:20 A.M.
6. From 1:25 P.M. to 9:05 P.M.
7. From 7:35 P.M. to 11:12 P.M.
8. From 8:43 A.M. to 11:30 A.M.
9. From 6:00 A.M. to 3:30 P.M.
10. From 10:30 A.M. to 6:45 P.M.
11. From 5:45 A.M. to 9:16 A.M.
12. From 1:45 A.M. to 7:05 A.M.
13. From 6:10 P.M. to 8:08 P.M.
14. From 3:28 A.M. to 11:16 A.M.
15. From 2:27 P.M. to 9:11 P.M.
16. From 3:56 P.M. to 10:22 P.M.

ELAPSED TIME

17. From 12:07 A.M. to 7:25 A.M.
18. From 12:35 P.M. to 6:45 P.M.
19. From 8:10 A.M. to 4:45 P.M.
20. From 7:45 A.M. to 5:30 P.M.
21. From 7:00 A.M. to 3:00 P.M.
22. From 8:30 A.M. to 5:00 P.M.
23. From 7:30 A.M. to 4:10 P.M.
24. From 8:23 A.M. to 5:04 P.M.
25. From 5:45 A.M. to 2:15 P.M.
26. From 7:43 A.M. to 4:21 P.M.
27. From 8:45 P.M. to 1:18 A.M.
28. From 9:47 A.M. to 7:08 P.M.
29. From 11:27 P.M. to 4:11 A.M.
30. From 5:55 P.M. to 1:55 A.M.

APPLICATIONS

31. Jack Keegan worked from 7:15 A.M. to 5:00 P.M. How long did he work?

32. Elena Diaz took a bus that left Cincinnati at 5:45 P.M. and arrived in Cleveland at 1:10 A.M. How long was the trip?

33. National Delivery Service (N.D.S.) ships hundreds of packages across the United States every day by air freight. Below is an N.D.S. air freight schedule. Calculate the total transit time for each shipment. (Note that all times given are Eastern Standard Time; therefore, time zones do not need to be taken into account.)

	Shipped From	Shipped To	Departure Time	Arrival Time	Total Transit Time
a.	Chattanooga, TN	Atlanta, GA	7:35 A.M.	8:20 A.M.	
b.	Chicago, IL	Houston, TX	8:10 A.M.	12:57 P.M.	
c.	Los Angeles, CA	New Orleans, LA	8:35 A.M.	2:17 P.M.	
d.	New York, NY	Cleveland, OH	5:25 P.M.	7:25 P.M.	
e.	Boston, MA	Phoenix, AZ	11:45 A.M.	7:28 P.M.	
f.	Atlanta, GA	Miami, FL	7:07 A.M.	9:00 A.M.	

READING TABLES AND CHARTS

To read a table or chart, find the *column* containing one of the pieces of information you have. Look across the *row* containing the other piece of information. Read down the column and across the row. Read the information you need where the column and row intersect.

Shipping Costs

Not Over (lbs)	Zone 2 & 3	Zone 4	Zone 5	Zone 6	Zone 7
1	$4.00	$4.00	$4.00	$4.00	$4.00
2	$4.00	$4.00	$4.00	$4.00	$4.00
3	$5.10	$5.10	$5.10	$5.10	$5.10
4	$6.20	$6.20	$6.20	$6.20	$6.20
5	$7.30	$7.30	$7.30	$7.30	$7.30
6	$8.60	$8.90	$9.10	$9.45	$9.70
7	$8.70	$9.30	$9.70	$10.40	$10.90
8	$8.80	$9.70	$10.30	$11.35	$12.10
9	$8.90	$10.10	$10.90	$12.30	$13.30
10	$9.00	$10.50	$11.50	$13.25	$14.50

EXAMPLE What is the cost to ship a 6-lb package to Zone 5?

SOLUTION
a. Find the Zone 5 column.   b. Find the 6-lb row.
c. Read across the 6-lb row to the Zone 5 column. The cost is $9.10.

To classify an item, find the row that contains the known data. Then read the classification from the head of the column.

Men's Body Measurement

Size	S	M	L	XL	XXL
Neck	14–14 $1/2$	15–15 $1/2$	16–16 $1/2$	17–17 $1/2$	18–18 $1/2$
Chest	34–36	38–40	42–44	46–48	50–52
Waist	28–30	32–34	36–38	40–42	44–46
Reg. Sleeve	32–33	33–34	34–35	35–36	36–37
Tall Sleeve	33–34	34–35	35–36	36–37	37–38
Height	Reg. 5'8"–6'	Tall 6'1"–6'4"			

Talls: Measure 2" longer overall, 1" at sleeves

EXAMPLE What size shirt should a man with a 42-inch chest order?

SOLUTION
a. Find the row for the Chest measurements.   b. Read across the row to 42–44.
c. Read the size at the head of the column (L). A man with a 42-inch chest should order a size L, which stands for large.

PROBLEMS

Use the shipping chart above to find the cost to ship each package to the indicated zone.

1. 3 lb, Zone 3
2. 4 lb, Zone 7
3. 9 lb, Zone 4
4. 2 lb, Zone 6
5. 6 lb, Zone 2
6. 5 lb, Zone 5
7. 1.5 lb, Zone 5
8. 6.4 lb, Zone 7
9. 8.2 lb, Zone 3
10. 7.1 lb, Zone 6
11. 5.8 lb, Zone 4
12. 9.3 lb, Zone 3

READING TABLES AND CHARTS

Use the size chart on the previous page to determine what size to order. In-between sizes should order the next size up.

13. Shorts—waist 33
15. Jacket—chest 47
17. Sweater—chest 43

14. Shirt—chest 37
16. Pants—waist 43
18. Shirt—height 6'2", sleeves 36

APPLICATIONS

19. Use the shipping chart on the previous page to determine the maximum amount a package can weigh.

	a.	b.	c.	d.	e.	f.
Shipping Zone	2	5	7	3	6	4
Shipping Cost	$7.30	$4.00	$13.30	$8.90	$7.30	$5.10
Maximum Weight						

Use the Federal Income Tax Table to find the amount of tax withheld in questions 20–25 and the amount of wages earned in questions 26–31:

Federal Income Tax Table
MARRIED Persons—WEEKLY Payroll Period

If the wages are—		And the number of withholding allowances claimed is—							
At least	But less than	0	1	2	3	4	5	6	7
		The amount of income tax to be withheld is—							
$480	$490	$63	$56	$50	$44	$38	$32	$25	$19
490	500	64	58	52	45	39	33	27	21
500	510	66	59	53	47	41	35	28	22
510	520	67	61	55	48	42	36	30	24
520	530	69	62	56	50	44	38	31	25
530	540	70	64	58	51	45	39	33	27
540	550	72	65	59	53	47	41	34	28
550	560	73	67	61	54	48	42	36	30
560	570	75	68	62	56	50	44	37	31
570	580	76	70	64	57	51	45	39	33
580	590	78	71	65	59	53	47	40	34
590	600	79	73	67	60	54	48	42	36
600	610	81	74	68	62	56	50	43	37
610	620	82	76	70	63	57	51	45	39
620	630	84	77	71	65	59	53	46	40

	20.	21.	22.	23.	24.	25.
Income	$491.77	$501.07	$617.30	$525.00	$600.00	$531.13
Allowances	2	1	3	0	4	6
Amount Withheld						

	Number of Allowances	Tax Withheld	Wages At least	But less than
26.	5	$47		
27.	2	$71		
28.	3	$53		
29.	1	$62		
30.	4	$38		
31.	0	$76		

Appendix

CONSTRUCTING GRAPHS

A **bar graph** is a picture that displays and compares numerical facts in the form of vertical or horizontal bars. To construct a vertical bar graph, follow these steps:

a. Draw the vertical and horizontal axes.
b. Scale the vertical axis to correspond to the given data.
c. Draw one bar to represent each quantity.
d. Label each bar and the vertical and horizontal axes.
e. Title the graph.

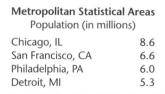

Metropolitan Statistical Areas
Population (in millions)

Chicago, IL	8.6
San Francisco, CA	6.6
Philadelphia, PA	6.0
Detroit, MI	5.3

EXAMPLE Construct a vertical bar graph of the given data.

SOLUTION
a. Draw vertical and horizontal axes.
b. Scale the vertical axis.
c. Draw one bar to represent each quantity.
d. Label each bar and the vertical and horizontal axes.
e. Title the graph.

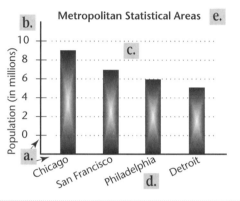

A **line graph** is a picture used to compare data over a period of time. It is an excellent way to show trends (increases or decreases). To construct a line graph, follow these steps:

a. Draw the vertical and horizontal axes.
b. Scale the vertical axis to correspond to the given data.
c. Label the axes.
d. Place a point on the graph to correspond to each item of data.
e. Connect the points from left to right.
f. Title the graph.

Percentage of Women in the Total Workforce

1950	29.6%
1960	33.4%
1970	38.1%
1980	42.5%
1990	45.8%
2000	47.5%

EXAMPLE Construct a line graph of the given data.

SOLUTION
a. Draw the vertical and horizontal axes.
b. Scale the vertical axis.
c. Label the axes.

d. Place a point to correspond to each item of data.

e. Connect the points from left to right.

f. Title the graph.

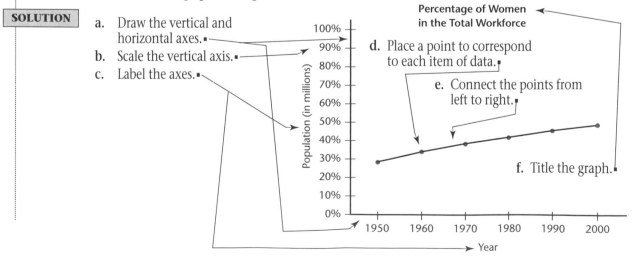

CONSTRUCTING GRAPHS

1. Construct a vertical bar graph of the given data.

Wrenn's Department Store
Total Sales by Department (in thousands)

Housewares	122
Men's Clothing	145
Women's Clothing	160
Appliances	183
Electronics	214

2. Read the vertical bar graph.

   a. Of the metropolitan areas listed, which is projected to have the largest population in 2033?

   b. Which of the metropolitan areas listed is projected to have the smallest population in 2033?

   c. What is Chicago's projected population for 2033?

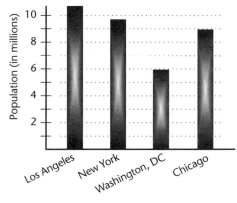

3. Construct a line graph of the given data.

Tollhouse Industries Stock

Month	Average
Jan.	16.50
Feb.	17
Mar.	16.25
Apr.	15
May	17.50
June	18

Appendix

UNITS OF MEASURE

Here are abbreviations and conversions for units of measure in the customary measurement system.

Length	Volume	Weight
12 inches (in) = 1 foot (ft)	2 cups (c) = 1 pint (pt)	16 ounces (oz) = 1 pound (lb)
3 ft = 1 yard (yd)	2 pt = 1 quart (qt)	2000 lb = 1 ton (t)
5280 ft = 1 mile (mi)	4 qt = 1 gallon (gal)	

Here are symbols and conversions for units of measure in the metric system.

Length

1000 millimeters (mm) = 1 meter (m)
100 centimeters (cm) = 1 m
1000 m = 1 kilometer (km)

Volume

1000 milliliters (mL) = 1 liter (L)

Mass

1000 grams (g) = 1 kilogram (kg)

To convert from one unit of measure to another, use the conversions lists above.

When converting to a smaller unit, multiply.

EXAMPLE

SOLUTION

Convert 5 feet to inches.

Use 12 in = 1 ft
5 ft: $5 \times 12 = 60$
5 ft = 60 in

Convert 4 meters to centimeters.

Use 100 cm = 1 m
4 m: $4 \times 100 = 400$
4 m = 400 cm

When converting to a larger unit, divide.

EXAMPLE

SOLUTION

Convert 6 pints to quarts.

Use 2 pt = 1 qt
6 pt: $6 \div 2 = 3$
6 pt = 3 qt

Convert 6500 grams to kilograms.

Use 1000 g = 1 kg
6500 g: $6500 \div 1000 = 6.5$
6500 g = 6.5 kg

PROBLEMS

Make the following conversions.

1. 12 yd to feet
2. 8 gal to quarts
3. 9 lb to ounces
4. 2 ft to inches
5. 3 lb to ounces
6. 5 L to milliliters
7. 2.4 km to meters
8. 24 pt to cups
9. 3.6 kg to grams
10. 99 in to yards
11. 15 qt to gallons
12. 66 oz to pounds
13. 18 qt to gallons
14. 24 oz to pounds
15. 7000 g to kilograms
16. 60 cm to meters
17. 2200 mL to liters
18. 350 cm to meters
19. 29 kg to grams
20. 17.3 L to milliliters
21. 522 g to kilograms
22. 10.122 mL to liters
23. 72 cm to millimeters
24. 432.2 cm to meters
25. 1 yd 7 in to inches
26. 5 ft 7 in to inches
27. 3 qt 1 pt to pints
28. 6 lb 9 oz to ounces
29. 4 gal 1 qt to quarts
30. 3 yd 1 ft 5 in to inches
31. 5 gal 3 qt 1 pt to pints
32. 3 m 57 cm 29 mm to millimeters

UNITS OF MEASURE

33. How many quarts will a 6-gallon bucket hold?

34. How many milliliters will a 2-liter bottle hold?

35. How many cups of coffee does a 4-quart coffeepot hold?

36. How many cups of hot chocolate will a 1.5-gallon thermos jug hold?

37. How many inches long is an 8-yard roll of aluminum foil?

38. Strawberries are sold in 1-pint containers. How many pints must be purchased to have enough for a recipe that calls for 3 cups?

39. James Jones knows that his jogging stride is about 1 meter long. The jogging trail he uses is 4.2 kilometers long. How many strides does it take him to go around the trail once?

40. The cafeteria receives 49 cases of milk each day. Each case contains 24 half-pint cartons. How many gallons of milk are received each day?

41. A soft drink is sold in 355 mL cans. How many liters are in a six-pack?

42. Katie Karanikos baked a chocolate layer cake weighing 1.5 kilograms. How many 75-gram servings can be cut from the cake?

43. Joan Baird ordered baseboard molding for the rooms of a new house. Joan needs to complete this chart to determine the total number of feet of molding needed. How much molding is needed?

Length	Width	2 lengths	+ 2 widths	= Perimeter
12 ft	10 ft	24 ft	+ 20 ft	= 44 ft
11 ft	8 ft	22 ft	+ 16 ft	=
a. 11 ft	19 ft			
b. 12 ft	12 ft 2 in			
c. 15 ft	16 ft 8 in			
d. 11 ft 8 in	12 ft 2 in			
e. 12 ft 10 in	16 ft 10 in			
f. 16 ft 9 in	24 ft 3 in			
g. 9 ft 4 in	10 ft			
h.		Total		

PROBLEM SOLVING: USING THE FOUR-STEP METHOD

The problem-solving process consists of several interrelated actions. The solutions to some problems are obvious and require very little effort. Others require a step-by-step procedure. Using a procedure such as the four-step method will help you to solve word problems.

The Four-Step Method

Step 1: Understand   What is the problem? What is given? What are you asked to do?

Step 2: Plan   What do you need to do to solve the problem? Choose a problem-solving strategy.

Step 3: Work   Carry out the plan. Do any necessary calculations.

Step 4: Answer   Is your answer reasonable? Did you answer the question?

EXAMPLE   The Gordons own several rental homes that need replumbing. It will take 2 plumbers 5 days to do the work. Each plumber works 8 hours a day at $33 per hour. How much will the project cost?

SOLUTION

Step 1: Given   2 plumbers, 5 days, 8 hours, $33 per hour

        Find   The cost per day for 1 plumber.
                 The cost per day for 2 plumbers.
                 The cost of 2 plumbers for 5 days.

Step 2: Plan   Find the cost per day for 1 plumber, then multiply by the number of plumbers, and then multiply by the number of days.

Step 3: Work   8 hours per day $\times$ $33 per hour = $264 per day for 1 plumber
                 2 plumbers $\times$ $264 per day for 1 plumber = $528 per day for 2 plumbers
                 5 days $\times$ $528 per day for 2 plumbers = $2640 for 2 plumbers for 5 days

Step 4: Answer   It will cost $2640 for 2 plumbers for 5 days.

PROBLEMS

Identify the plan, work, and answer for each problem.

1. It takes 3 electricians 10 days to rewire some apartment buildings. Each electrician earns $37.50 per hour and works $7\frac{1}{2}$ hours per day. How much will the rewiring cost?

2. Eric Cortez makes a car payment of $227.15 every month. His car loan is for 5 years. How much will he pay in 5 years?

3. Jessica Henderson and Kyle Casey spent a total of $213.58 on their prom date. Dinner cost $60.12. How much did everything else cost Jessica and Kyle?

4. Marcus Johnson purchased 2 shirts at $38 each, a belt for $19.50, jeans for $29.50, shoes for $89.99, and 3 pairs of socks at $6.99 a pair. How much did Marcus spend?

5. A contractor is building 5 new homes. It will take 4 carpet layers 3 days to install the carpet for all 5 homes. The carpet layers work 8 hours per day and earn $18.00 per hour. How much will it cost for the carpet installation?

6. The same 5 new homes will each have a foyer measuring 12 feet by 12 feet. Wood parquet floors for each foyer cost $55.30 per square yard. What is the cost of the wood parquet floors for the foyers in all 5 homes?

PROBLEM SOLVING: USING THE FOUR-STEP METHOD

7. Beth Anderson charges $2.50 per page for typing rough drafts and an additional 75¢ per page for changes and deletions. A manuscript had 318 pages, of which 165 pages had changes and deletions. What was the total cost of typing the manuscript?

8. Fred Woo is paying $53.50 per month for a computer. The total cost of the computer was $855.99. How long will it take Fred to pay for the computer?

9. Mitch Elliot rode his bicycle on a 3-mile path. Approximately how many rotations did Mitch's 26" bicycle wheels make on this path? (Hint: The circumference of a circle is approximately 3.14 times the diameter and a mile = 5280 feet.)

10. Nicole and Joseph Conti drove to St. Louis, a distance of 781 miles. Their car gets 22 miles per gallon of gasoline. Gasoline costs them $1.36 per gallon. How much did Nicole and Joseph spend for gasoline on their trip?

11. Joy and Ernie both live in Columbus, Ohio. Joy drove due north for 3 hours at 60 miles per hour. Ernie drove due south for 2 hours at 65 per hour. How far apart were they after their trip?

12. Cindee Adams bought 3 boxes of cereal at $2.79 each, a roll of paper towels for 88¢, and 10 pounds of chicken at 65¢ a pound. How much change would Cindee get back from $20?

13. Thelma Wicker's pound cake is 30 cm long. She slices each cake into 2 cm slices. Thelma is serving 115 people for lunch. How many pound cakes will she need to bake?

PROBLEM SOLVING: IDENTIFYING INFORMATION

Before you begin to solve a word problem, first read the problem carefully and answer these questions:

- What are you asked to find?
- What facts are given?
- Are enough facts given? Do you need more information than the problem provides?

Some word problems provide more information than is needed to solve the problem. Others cannot be solved without additional information. Identifying what is wanted, what is given, and what is needed allows you to organize the information and plan your solution.

EXAMPLE Jonathan Klein is a lab technician at Laminates, Ltd. He earns $25.20 per hour. He is single and claims 1 withholding allowance. Last week he worked 40 hours at the regular rate and 4 hours at the weekend rate. He is 28 years old. Find his gross pay for last week.

SOLUTION

A. Wanted: Jonathan Klein's gross pay for last week
B. Facts given: $25.20 hourly rate
                              40 hours worked at regular rate
                              4 hours worked at weekend rate
C. Additional facts needed: Weekend rate

This problem cannot be solved.

EXAMPLE Martha Henderson, age 43, runs 3 miles every day. How many miles does Martha run in a week?

SOLUTION

A. Wanted: Number of miles run in 1 week
B. Facts given: Runs 3 miles every day
C. Additional facts needed: None

This problem can be solved. Multiply the number of miles run per day (3) by the number of days in 1 week (7). The answer is 21 miles.

PROBLEMS

Identify the wanted, given, and needed information. If enough information is given, solve the problem.

1. Kelly Jenkins bought a new car with a $4500 down payment and monthly payments of $375. How much did Kelly pay, in total, for her new car?

2. The Great Outdoors is having a sale on sports equipment. The Yosemite dome tent is priced at $99, the GlacierPoint mountain bike is $69, and Shenandoah in-line skates are $49. What is the total cost of the Yosemite dome tent and Yellowstone backpack?

3. Lisa Smith paid $175 each way to fly round-trip from Atlanta to Denver. Brittany Cruz paid $335 for the round-trip fare. Who paid more? How much more?

PROBLEM SOLVING: IDENTIFYING INFORMATION

4. The Northside Fruit Farm pays pickers $1.50 per pound to pick blueberries, which are packed in one-pint baskets and sold at market for $2.25 per pint. How many pint baskets need to be sold to pay one worker one day's wage?

5. Tyler Fulgum paid $95 each for two tickets to a concert. He paid for the tickets with four $50 bills. How much change did he receive?

6. How much would four sets of towels cost if they were 25 x 20 inches and priced at three for $9.99?

7. Bill Hale bought a boneless shoulder roast with a $20 bill. He received $3.17 in change. How much did Bill pay per pound for the roast?

8. The party platter cost $65, beverages cost $35.77, and party supplies cost $18.13. Brandon and his friends agreed to share the total cost of food, beverages, and supplies for the party equally. How much did each pay?

9. Dana Edwards is 5 feet 2 inches tall and weighs 108 pounds. She grew 3 inches in the past year. How tall was she last year?

10. Greg Jones has finished 55 of the 60 math problems on his test. It is now 11:20 A.M. The 1-hour test started at 10:30 A.M. What is the average number of minutes he can spend on each of the remaining problems?

11. A two-drawer file cabinet and a box of files cost $110. What is the cost of the file cabinet?

12. A designer fragrance gift set is on sale for 40% off its original retail price of $65. If the retailer discounted it an additional 10% of the sale price, what would the final sale price be?

13. Matthew Travino sells stereo equipment and receives a weekly salary of $300 plus a 5% commission on sales. Last week his gross pay was $660. What is the dollar amount of stereo equipment sold by Matthew last week?

14. Darien Dromboski was shopping for coffee makers. The Javamaker model was $11.43 more than the BestBrew model and the Coffee Time model was $4.95 less than the BestBrew. How much more than the cost of the Coffee Time was the Javamaker?

Appendix

PROBLEM SOLVING: USING MORE THAN ONE OPERATION

Some problems require several operations to solve. After deciding which operations to use, you must decide the correct order in which to perform them.

EXAMPLE

The cash price of a new car is $22,885. Marcie Cunningham cannot pay cash, so she is making a down payment of $3300 and 60 monthly payments of $385 each. How much more does it cost to buy the car this way?

SOLUTION

A. Given: Cash price of $22,885
                    $3300 down + 60 payments of $385 each

B. Multiply: To get total of payments
                    60 × $385 = $23,100

   Add: $3300 to total payments
                    $3300 + $23,100 = $26,400

   Subtract: Cash price from total payments
                    $26,400 − $22,885 = $3515

It cost $3515 more to buy the car this way. In this example, the order of operations is very important; that is, multiply, then add, then subtract.

EXAMPLE

Juan Perez bought 2 gallons of milk costing $2.69 per gallon. He gave the cashier a $20 bill. How much change did he receive if there was no sales tax?

SOLUTION

A. Given: Bought 2 gallons of milk at $2.69 per gallon, no sales tax
                    Gave cashier $20.00

B. Multiply: To get total cost
                    2 × $2.69 = $5.38

   Subtract: To find change
                    $20.00 − $5.38 = $14.62

Juan received $14.62 in change. In this example, the order of operations is multiply, then subtract.

PROBLEMS

Give the sequence of operations needed to solve the problems, then solve.

1. Your entertainment budget for the month is $50. If you spent $18.50 at the movies, $12 for tickets to a college basketball game, and $11.75 at a concert, how much is left in your entertainment budget?

2. Steve Sorrells works 9 hours a day 5 days a week. So far this year, he has worked 540 hours. How many weeks has he worked?

3. The Parent/Teacher Organization (PTO) sells soft drinks and popcorn at home basketball games. Last week they sold 225 cups of soft drinks at $1.00 per cup and 185 bags of popcorn at 75¢ per bag. What were the total sales?

PROBLEM SOLVING: USING MORE THAN ONE OPERATION

4. Gerry Hanson pays his electric bills through a payment plan of $65 per month regardless of usage. At the end of one year, he is billed for the difference if his usage is more, or sent a refund if his usage is less. His usage for the last three months was $62, $64.35, and $68.20. Is he over or under his payment plan schedule so far this year? By how much?

5. Daniel Dalton sold 16 watermelons for $5 each, 20 for $4 each, and 30 for $3 each. He makes 50% commission for each watermelon he sells. How much money did Daniel make?

6. Henry Mack has a new job as an insurance adjuster and has read 272 pages of a 512-page training manual. It took him two days to read through the remaining pages. If he read the same number of pages each day, how many pages did he read each day?

7. Leah Mattison worked 40 hours for $7.25 per hour. She worked 5 hours for $18.13 an hour. How much money did Leah earn?

8. In one month, the Bowens spent $95.78, $112.13, $98.66, and $124.33 for groceries. Their monthly food budget is $450. How much money do they have left to spend for food?

9. The temperature in the greenhouse is 25 degrees Celsius at 9:00 A.M. If the temperature increases 1.5 degrees every hour, what will the temperature be at 3:00 P.M.?

10. Daryl Harden walks 3 miles round-trip to work 5 times a week. How far will he walk in one year?

11. Zach McCain assembled a total of 788 circuit boards in 4 days of work. During the first three days, he assembled 201, 196, and 198, respectively. How many did he assemble the last day?

12. In a one-month reading contest at school, Rick Gonzalez earned 3 half-point certificates, 5 one-point certificates, and 4 two-point certificates. How many points did he earn for the month?

13. The Athens Historical Society sold 1245 $5 tickets as a fund-raiser. Prizes were a $2,000 handmade quilt, 4 framed prints that cost $500 each, and 10 books that cost $25 each. How much money did the Historical Society make?

14. Drew Young sold candy bars at school to raise money for a band trip. He sold 47 $1-candy bars. If his sales totaled $68 dollars, how many $3-candy bars did he sell?

15. Spencer Baird bought 2 sweatshirts for $15.75 each and 2 T-shirts for $8.50 each. How much change did he receive from a $50 bill?

16. Josey Chandler saved $550. After she earned an additional $125, she spent $320 for a chair, $50 for a rug, and $30 for a lamp. How much money did Josey have left?

PROBLEM SOLVING: WRITING AN EQUATION

A word problem can be translated into an equation that is solved by performing the same mathematical operation (adding, subtracting, multiplying, or dividing) to both sides. Solving the equation then leads to the solution of the problem.

To set up the equation, look for words in the problem that suggest which of the four mathematical operations to use.

Words	Symbol	Operation
The total, how many in all, the sum, plus	$+$	Addition
The difference, how much more, how much smaller, minus	$-$	Subtraction
The total for a number of equal items, the product	$\times$	Multiplication
The number left over, the quotient	$\div$	Division

EXAMPLE

In 40 hours at your regular rate of pay plus 10 hours of double time (twice your regular rate of pay), you earn $855. What is your regular rate of pay?

SOLUTION

Use the letter x to stand for your regular rate of pay.

$40x + 10(2x) = \$855.00$

$40x + 20x = \$855.00$

$60x = \$855.00$ (Divide each side by 60.)

$x = \$14.25$

EXAMPLE

A rectangle with a perimeter of 64 mm is 25 mm long. What is the width of the rectangle?

SOLUTION

Let w equal the width of the rectangle.

$w + 25 + w + 25 = 64$

$2w + 50 = 64$ (Subtract 50 from both sides.)

$2w = 14$ (Divide both sides by 2.)

$w = 7$ mm wide

PROBLEMS

1. The sum of 2 consecutive numbers is 47. What is the smaller number?

2. One brand of computer scanner can read 83 documents per hour while a second scanner can read 97 documents per hour. How many hours will it take to read 900 documents?

3. A jar of mayonnaise costs 97¢. The mayonnaise costs 55¢ more than the jar. How much does each cost?

4. A robot travels 36 meters around the edge of a rectangular assembly room. If the rectangle is twice as long as it is wide, how long is each side?

PROBLEM SOLVING: WRITING AN EQUATION

5. A football field is 100 yards long and has a distance around of 308 yards. How wide is it?

6. Ed and Maria Zavala-Waterman make monthly payments of $845 on their $120,000 mortgage. They will have paid $184,200 in interest when their mortgage is paid off. For how many years is their mortgage?

7. Carol Austin had gross earnings of $804.86 last week. She earns $10.25 per hour plus a 4.5% commission on all sales. She knows she worked 40 hours last week but can't remember her total sales. What were her total sales?

8. Luis Rivera earns $8.10 per hour plus double time for all hours over 40 per week. How much did Luis earn for working 48 hours last week?

9. Sandy Brubaker has 4 Guernsey cows and 3 Holstein cows that give as much milk in 5 days as 3 Guernsey and 5 Holstein cows give in 4 days. Which kind of cow is the better milk producer, the Guernsey or the Holstein?

10. The Maren Manufacturing Company building is 6 times as old as the equipment. The building was 40 years old when the equipment was purchased. How old is the equipment?

11. The sum of 3 consecutive odd numbers is 33. What are the 3 numbers?

12. Ingram, Inc. stock sells for $23 3/4 a share. The Morrison Brokerage Company charges a flat fee of $45 for every transaction. How many shares could you buy for $900?

13. Keesha is working with fabric that is twice as long as it is wide. It is 6 1/2 yards long. How wide is it?

14. If the fabric were 4 yards, 6 inches wide, how long would it be?

15. Tom, Darren, and Kerry have a combined weight of 600 pounds. Kerry weighs 15 pounds more than Darren, while Darren weighs 15 pounds more than Tom. How much does each man weigh?

Glossary

A

accounting The systematic process of recording and reporting the financial position of a business.

actual cash value The value of an item new minus depreciation as a result of wear and tear, or how much the item is worth used.

advertising A paid, non-personal form of communication that businesses use to promote their products.

ageism Discrimination on the basis of age.

Americans with Disabilities Act (ADA) A federal law that requires businesses to provide facilities for people with special needs.

annual percentage rate (APR) The rate at which interest is charged for credit on a yearly basis.

antitrust laws Laws that allow the federal government to break up, regulate, or take over monopolies and trusts.

apprenticeship Learning a trade by working under the guidance of a skilled worker.

aptitudes Talents or abilities that come naturally.

asset Anything of value that a business or individual owns.

autocratic leadership A leadership style in which one person runs everything and makes all decisions without consulting others.

B

baby boom generation People born between 1946 and 1964.

bait and switch Advertising an item at a low price to lure customers into the store and then trying to get them to switch to a more expensive item.

balance of trade The difference in value between how much a country imports and how much it exports.

balance sheet A report of the financial state of a business on a certain date.

bank account A record of how much money a person has put into and taken out of a bank.

bank reconciliation The process of seeing whether one's own checking account records agree with the bank's records.

bank statement A bank's record of all the transactions in a checking account.

bankruptcy A legal process in which a person is relieved of debts but creditors can take some or all of the person's assets.

banner ads Internet ads that are displayed across the top or bottom of the screen.

beneficiary Person who receives part or all of the proceeds from a life insurance policy.

Better Business Bureau (BBB) A nonprofit organization that provides information and handles complaints about local businesses.

blue-chip stocks Stocks in large, well-established companies that have a good track record of success.

body language Non-verbal communication, such as posture, eye contact, facial expressions, and gestures.

bond discount The difference between the amount paid for a bond and its face value.

bonds Written promises, issued by a corporation or the government, to repay a loan with interest on a specific date.

boycott Refuse to buy a company's products or services.

brand name A word or name on a product that helps consumers distinguish it from other products.

breach of contract The failure of a party to live up to the terms of a contract.

break-even point The amount of money a company has to make on a product to pay for the cost of producing it.

bricks-and-mortar Stores, warehouses, and other buildings businesses use.

broker A dealer who specializes in buying and selling stock.

budget A plan of expected income and expenses over a certain period of time.

budget deficit When the government spends more on programs than it collects in taxes, or expenses exceed income.

budget surplus When the government collects more in taxes than it spends on programs, or income exceeds expenses.

budget variance The difference between planned spending and actual spending.

bureaucracy A formal organization consisting of many levels of management.

business Any activity that seeks profit by providing goods or services to others.

business cycle The rise and fall of economic activity over time.

business ethics The rules that govern how businesses should conduct themselves.

business etiquette Acceptable social behavior and manners in business.

byte Amount of memory it takes to store a single computer character.

C

canceled checks Checks written that have been cashed.

capital gain Selling stock for more than it cost to buy it.

capital loss Selling stock for less than it cost to buy it.

capital resources Things such as buildings, materials, and equipment used to produce goods and services.

career An occupation or field in which a person works over a long period of time.

career counselor A person trained to provide information and guidance on choosing and preparing for a career.

career ladder Job levels within an occupation.

career planning The steps necessary to choose and prepare for a career.

cash advance Using a credit card to borrow money rather than to charge a purchase.

cash-value insurance Life insurance that provides both a savings plan and death benefits.

centralized organization An organization that puts authority in one place, with top management.

certificate of deposit (CD) A type of savings account that requires a minimum amount of money deposited in the account for a minimum period of time.

channel of distribution A particular means of directing products from producers to consumers, such as a wholesaler or retailer.

charge account Credit provided by a store or company for customers to buy its products.

check register A checkbook or log used to record checking transactions.

claim A request for payment from an insurer for any damages covered by an insurance policy.

clearance sale A sale to clear out goods that are going out of season or are no longer profitable to make room for new merchandise.

clicks-and-mortar The use of both the Internet and buildings, such as stores and warehouses, to do business.

code of ethics A strict set of guidelines in a profession or company for upholding ethical behavior in the workplace.

coinsurance A percentage of medical expenses an insurance policyholder must pay beyond the deductible.

collateral Something valuable, such as a house or car, used as guarantee for a loan that the lender can take if the borrower doesn't repay the loan.

collection agent A person or business that collects overdue bills.

command economy A system in which a central authority such as the state makes the key economic decisions.

commercial credit Credit used by business.

common stock The primary, or common, form of ownership of a corporation.

comparison shopping Checking the price and quality of a product in more than one store.

compensation The pay and benefits a company offers for a job.

competition The contest between businesses to win customers.

compound interest Interest earned on both the principal amount in an account and the interest already earned on the account, or interest on interest.

compulsory insurance law A law that requires drivers to have a minimum amount of car insurance.

computer-aided design (CAD) Software for designing products with a computer.

conflict of interest When a business puts its interests before the interests of society.

conservation The process of preserving, protecting, and managing resources.

consolidation loan A loan that combines several debts into one loan with lower payments.

consumer A person who selects, purchases, uses, or disposes of goods or services.

consumer advocates Groups and individuals that work to protect, inform, and defend consumers.

consumer credit Credit used by individuals for personal reasons.

Glossary

Consumer Credit Protection Act A federal law, also known as the Truth in Lending Law, that requires creditors to inform consumers of the costs and terms of credit and protects consumers from lost or stolen credit cards.

consumer movement A movement to pass laws protecting consumers from unfair and unsafe business practices.

consumer reporter A radio or TV reporter who reports on issues important to consumers, such as product safety.

consumer rights Consumers' rights to safety, to be heard, to choose, to be informed, to have problems corrected, to consumer education, and to service.

contract A legal agreement between two or more parties to conduct business.

cookies Pieces of information about a computer user, stored on the user's hard drive, that can be accessed by a Web server whenever the user goes on the Internet.

cooperative An organization of businesses owned and operated by the members, who pool their resources and share the benefits.

copayment A fee paid each time a service covered by a health insurance plan, such as a doctor's visit or a prescription, is used.

copyright A legal grant for the sole right to own a creative property, such as a book or video game.

corporate bonds Bond sold by corporations to finance building and equipment.

corporate culture A company's shared values, beliefs, and goals.

corporation A business treated by law as separate from its owners.

cosigner A person who signs a loan for someone else and is responsible for repaying the loan if the borrower doesn't repay it.

coupon rate The rate of interest on a bond.

cover letter A one-page letter accompanying a résumé that tells an employer about an applicant and why the applicant is interested in a job.

credit An agreement to get money, goods, or services now in exchange for a promise to pay in the future.

credit bureau An agency that collects information about consumers of credit.

credit counselor A person who helps consumers with their credit problems.

credit limit The maximum amount a person can spend or charge on a credit account.

credit rating A measure of a person's ability and willingness to pay debts on time.

creditor One who lends money or provides credit.

culture Beliefs, customs, and attitudes of a distinct group of people.

cyber ads Advertisements on the Internet.

D

database A computerized collection of information, usually kept in a list.

debit card A bank card used like a credit card but which takes money directly from a checking account.

debtor One who borrows money or uses credit.

decentralized organization An organization that gives authority to a number of different managers to run their own departments.

deductible The amount of damages that the holder of an insurance policy must pay before the insurance company pays.

deductions Amounts of money taken out of a paycheck for expenses such as taxes, health insurance, retirement, and union dues.

deflation A general decrease in the cost of goods and services.

delegate Give employees the power to run things and make decisions.

demand The amount of goods and services that consumers are willing to buy at various prices.

demand deposits Checks, or orders to a bank to release money from a checking account on demand.

democratic leadership A style of leadership in which managers work with employees to make decisions.

demographics Facts about the population in terms of age, gender, income, and education.

departmentalization Dividing responsibilities in an organization among specific units, or departments.

deposit Money put into a bank account.

depreciation Decline in the value of an item, such as a house or car, because of use.

depression A deep, long-term decline in economic activity.

desktop publishing Writing, designing, and laying out documents on a computer like a professional publisher.

digital workflow Linking all the steps in a process, such as printing, electronically.

direct distribution Selling goods and services directly from producers to consumers without using intermediaries.

direct-mail advertising Advertising sent to people's homes by mail.

discrimination Excluding someone on the basis of age, gender, ethnicity, or other difference.

diversity Variety of people with different backgrounds and identities.

dividends A share of the profits of a corporation paid to stockholders.

dot-com A company that does business on the Internet.

down payment A portion of the total cost of an item that is paid at the time the item is purchased.

E

e-commerce Electronic commerce, or business conducted on the Internet.

economics The study of how society chooses to use resources to produce and distribute goods and services for people's consumption.

electronic funds transfer (EFT) The transfer of money from one account to another using computers.

eleven perils The most common causes of property damage or loss, covered by all homeowner's insurance policies.

embargo A ban on the import or export of a product.

employability skills Qualities that employers look for in a person, including education, experience, character, and ability to work with others.

employment agencies Professional services that help people find jobs.

employment objective A statement in a résumé of one's career goals or interest in a business.

endorsement The signature of the payee on the back of a check, necessary for cashing a check.

entrepreneur A person who recognizes a business opportunity and assumes the risks of starting a business.

entrepreneurial resources The initiative to improve goods and services or create new ones.

entrepreneurship Accepting the risk of starting a business, or a business started by a risk taker.

entry-level job A beginning career job.

Environmental Protection Agency (EPA) A federal agency that enforces rules to protect the environment and control pollution.

Equal Credit Opportunity Act A federal law against denying credit on the basis of gender, age, ethnicity, or other difference.

Equal Employment Opportunity Act A federal law that prevents discriminating against workers on the basis of gender, ethnicity, or other difference.

Equal Pay Act A federal law requiring that men and women be paid the same wages for doing equal work.

equilibrium price The price at which the amount of goods producers supply meets the amount of goods consumers demand.

e-tail Electronic retailing, or selling products on the Internet.

ethics A set of moral principles by which people conduct themselves personally, socially, or professionally.

e-tickets Electronic tickets, or tickets sold using computers.

e-workforce People who work with computers while doing business.

exchange rate The price at which the currency of one country can buy the currency of another country.

expenditures Items you have to spend money on such as food, rent, and clothing, or expenses.

expert system Computer software that stores and uses knowledge that a human expert would have on the same subject.

exports Goods and services one country sells to another country.

extended coverage Coverage added to a basic insurance policy that protects against other types of property damage.

extranet A semiprivate computer network that allows more than one company to access the same information.

F

factors of production The economic resources used to produce goods and services.

Glossary

Fair Credit Billing Act A federal law requiring creditors to correct billing mistakes brought to their attention.

Fair Credit Reporting Act A federal law giving people the right to know what is in their credit files at credit bureaus.

Fair Debt Collection Practices Act (FDCPA) A federal law that protects debtors from unfair methods and practices by collection agents.

Federal Deposit Insurance Corporation (FDIC) A federal government agency that insures commercial bank accounts for up to $100,000.

Federal Reserve System The central banking system of the United States, also called the Fed.

finance charge The total amount it costs to finance a loan, including interest and fees, stated in dollars and cents.

financial forecast An estimate of what business conditions will be like in the future.

financial institution An organization for managing money, such as a bank, credit union, or brokerage firm.

financial manager The person in charge of a business's financial planning, funding, and accounting.

financial plan An outline of a business's expenses, needs, and goals, and how it expects to meet them.

financial responsibility law A law requiring drivers to pay for any damages or injuries they cause in an accident.

fiscal year An accounting period in business of one year.

fixed expenses Expenses that occur regularly and must be paid regularly, such as rent and car insurance.

Food and Drug Administration (FDA) A government agency that protects consumers from dangerous or falsely advertised products.

franchise A contractual agreement to use the name and sell the goods or services of an existing company.

fraud Deliberately misleading business practices.

free-rein leadership A style of leadership in which managers and employees are given goals and then left alone to get their jobs done.

free trade Few or no limits on trade between countries.

G

garnishment of wages A creditor's legal right to take all or part of a debtor's paycheck for an unpaid dept.

generic products Products that are plainly labeled, unadvertised, and sold at lower prices.

goods Material things that can be physically weighed or measured.

grace period An amount of time to pay off a debt without having to pay interest on it.

grade labels Labels that indicate foods have been inspected by the federal government and the quality of the foods.

gross domestic product (GDP) The total value of the goods and services produced in a country in one year.

gross pay The total amount of money earned in a specific period of time before deductions.

group training Learning a new job from an instructor or manager with a group of other employees, like a class.

groupware Computer software that enables members of a team to share information on the same project, also called project management software.

H

hacker A person who breaks into computer systems for illegal purposes.

hardware The physical components of a computer.

health maintenance organization (HMO) A group health program that provides health care at its own center for a fixed fee per month.

hierarchy A formal chain of command with one person at the top.

homeowner's policy An insurance policy designed for homeowners that combines different kinds of home protection.

human relations The ability to communicate with people.

human resources The knowledge, efforts, and skills people bring to their work, also called labor.

human resources management The process of finding, selecting, training, and evaluating employees.

I

imports Goods and services one country buys from another country.

impulse buying Purchasing things on the spur of the moment.

income The amount of money a person earns or receives during a given period of time.

income property Property used to generate an income, such as a farm or apartment building.

income statement A report of a business's net income or net loss over a specific period.

indirect distribution Moving goods from producers to consumers using one or more intermediaries.

inflation A general increase in the cost of goods and services.

inflation risk The risk that the rate of inflation will increase more than the rate of return on an investment.

infomercial A television program, usually 30 minutes long, made to advertise a product.

information technology Hardware and software for creating, processing, storing, and communicating information.

initiative Taking action to get things done.

installment loans Loans repaid in regular payments over a period of time.

insurance Paid protection against losses due to injury or property damage.

integrity Holding to principles like honesty, loyalty, and fairness.

interest A fee charged for the use of money.

interest-bearing account A checking account that earns interest on the balance left in the account.

intermediaries Businesses that act as go-betweens in moving goods from producers to consumers, such as wholesalers, retailers, and distributors.

Internet A collection of tens of thousands of connected computer networks.

internship A program that provides hands-on experience for a beginner in an occupation, usually as a temporary, unpaid trainee.

interstate commerce Business that take place across states, overseen by the federal government.

intranet A private computer network that connects employees from the same company together.

intrastate commerce Business that takes place within a state, overseen by state governments.

investing Putting money to use in order to make money on it.

J

job description A detailed description of the duties, qualifications, and conditions required to do a specific job.

job interview A formal face-to-face discussion between an employer and a potential employee.

job lead Information about a job opening.

journeyworker A skilled craftsperson who has completed an apprenticeship.

junk bonds Corporate bonds that have a low rating and are issued by companies that don't have successful track records.

L

leadership Providing direction and vision.

legal monopolies Companies, such as public utilities, that are allowed to operate without competition.

liability insurance Protection against claims of injury or property damage to others.

licenses Legal permits to conduct business, usually issued by states.

limited liability Financial responsibility of business owners only for what they invested in a business.

line authority An organizational structure in which managers at the top of the line are in charge of those beneath them.

liquidity The ability to quickly turn an investment into cash.

loss leaders Advertised products that sell for a loss to bring customers into a store so they'll buy other things.

M

management plan A business plan that divides a company into different departments run by different managers.

manufacturers Businesses that make finished products out of raw or processed goods.

market A group of customers who share common wants and needs.

Glossary

market economy A system in which economic decisions are made in the marketplace according to the laws of supply and demand.

market research Gathering and studying information about the buying habits of consumers to determine what goods and services to produce.

marketing The process of creating, promoting, and presenting a product to meet the wants and needs of consumers.

marketing concept A plan for how to market a product or service to consumers.

marketing mix The four main elements of marketing, also called the four Ps: product, place, price, and promotion.

mass media Means of mass communication such as TV, radio, and newspapers.

maturity date The date when money invested in a bond or certificate of deposit becomes available to the investor.

Medicaid A health care program provided by state governments for low-income families.

Medicare A health care program provided by the federal government primarily for retired persons.

middle managers Managers who carry out the decisions of top management and oversee specific departments.

mixed economy A combination of a command and a market economy.

monetary system A system in which goods and services are exchanged indirectly using money as a medium.

money Anything that people accept as a standard of payment.

money management The process of planning how to get the most from your money.

money market deposit account A type of savings account offered by banks, savings and loans, and credit unions similar to a money market fund or mutual fund.

money market fund A type of savings account offered by brokerage firms to finance business and government debts.

monopoly Control of an entire industry by one company or a trust.

mortgage Property put up for a loan that the lender can take if the loan is not paid back.

multi-channel retailer A company that uses several means to sell products, such as retail stores, mail-order catalogs, and the Internet.

multinational corporation A company that does business and has facilities in many countries around the world.

municipal bonds Bonds issued by local and state governments to finance government projects.

mutual fund A fund, or pool of money, created by an investment company that raises money from many shareholders and invests it in a variety of stocks and bonds.

N

national debt The total amount of money owed by the federal government.

natural resources Raw materials found in nature used to produce goods.

needs Necessary wants, such as food, shelter, and clothing.

net pay Gross pay minus deductions, also called take-home pay.

networking Meeting and talking to people in different occupations to find out what they do and make connections.

no-fault insurance A law that requires drivers involved in accidents to collect damages from their own insurance companies no matter who is at fault.

nonprofit organization A business whose main purpose is to provide a service rather than to make a profit.

O

Occupational Safety and Health Administration (OSHA) A division of the Department of Labor that sets and enforces work-related health and safety rules.

oligopoly Control of an industry by a small number of companies.

on-the-job training Learning a new job by actually doing it.

operational managers Managers who are responsible for the daily operations of a business, such as supervisors and office managers.

opportunity cost Giving up the opportunity to buy something now in order to buy something else later.

organizational chart A chart that shows how a business is structured and who is in charge of whom.

orientation The process of helping new employees adjust to a company.

outstanding checks Checks that have been written but haven't yet been cashed.

overdraft protection A line of credit offered by banks to cover an overdrawn checking account.

overdrawing Writing checks for more money than there is in a checking account.

owner's equity The difference in value between a business's assets and liabilities, or what a business owns and what it owes.

P

partnership A business owned by two or more persons who share the risks and rewards.

passbook savings account A traditional savings account in which all transactions are recorded in a book that the depositor keeps.

patent A legal grant for the sole right to own an invention.

performance appraisal An evaluation of how well an employee is doing his or her job.

personal digital assistant (PDA) A hand-held computer that can be used as an address book, appointment book, voice recorder, and to access the Internet.

personal property Possessions that can be moved, like furniture, jewelry, and electronic equipment.

policy A contract between an insurance company and policyholder that explains the amount and types of coverage.

pollution Contamination of air, water, and land.

pop-up ads Internet ads that appear briefly when a user logs onto the Internet or clicks on a site.

pre-existing condition A serious health condition diagnosed before a person obtained health insurance and which might not be covered by a policy.

preferred stock A form of ownership of a corporation that gives stockholders certain privileges.

premium The amount an insurance company charges a policyholder for an insurance policy.

principal The actual amount of money owed or deposited in an account, upon which interest is based.

proceeds Money paid from a life insurance policy to a beneficiary.

processors Businesses that change raw goods into more finished products.

producer A business that gathers raw products in their natural state.

product liability The legal responsibility manufacturers have to make a safe product.

profession A field that requires a high level of education, such as law, medicine, or architecture.

profit The amount of money left over after a business has paid for the cost of producing its goods and services.

promotion A move to a higher level job with more authority, responsibility, and pay.

promotional sale A sale that gives you a special buy on a new product or a product that's in season.

property insurance Protection from financial loss on property due to damage or theft.

prosperity The peak of economic activity.

protectionism Limiting trade with other countries to protect businesses at home.

Q

qualifications The education, skills, and experience required to do a particular job.

quota A limit placed on the quantities of a product that can be imported.

R

random access memory (RAM) Computer memory that stores information temporarily and loses it when the computer is turned off.

real estate Land and anything attached to it, such as buildings or natural resources.

real estate agent A person licensed to arrange the buying and selling of homes and other types of real estate.

real property Property attached to land, like a house, business, or garage.

recall An order to take back and repair or replace defective products.

recession A decline in economic activity.

recovery A rise in business activity after a recession or depression.

recruitment Actively looking for the most qualified people to fill a job position.

recycling Collecting products for processing so that they can be used again.

reference A person an employer can contact to find out about a job applicant.

Glossary

referral A personal recommendation to an employer for a job applicant.

refund Return the cost of a product.

relationship marketing Building customer loyalty through good customer relations.

renter's insurance Insurance available to renters, as opposed to homeowners, to cover any loss or damage to personal possessions.

replacement value The full cost of repairing or replacing property by an insurance company regardless of its depreciation value.

repossess To take back collateral put up for a loan, such as a car, if the loan is not paid back.

resource Anything that people can use, such as fuel, labor, or money, to make or obtain what they need or want.

résumé A written summary of one's skills, education, and work experience.

retailer A business that sells goods or services directly to the public.

revenue Government or business income.

revolving account A form of credit which allows one to borrow or charge up to a certain amount of money and pay back a part of the total each month.

rider An addition to an insurance policy that covers specific property or damages.

risk taker Someone willing to take chances in business, considered a key characteristic of an entrepreneur.

S

safety-deposit box A place at a bank for storing valuable items.

savings Money put aside for future use.

savings bonds Bonds sold by the federal government to pay for government projects.

scanner A computerized device that can read images and record or transfer them.

scarcity The shortage of economic resources.

screen ads Internet ads displayed on the right or left of a screen and that can be printed out.

secured loan A loan that is backed by collateral.

self-managed teams Work groups that supervise themselves.

separation Leaving a company because of retirement, resignation, layoff, or termination.

services Tasks that people or machines perform.

shadowing Following a person throughout a workday to see what a job involves.

signature card A record of an account holder's signature used by a bank to verify the person's identity.

simple interest Interest earned only on the money deposited into a savings account, or the principal.

skills Abilities developed through training and experience.

small business An independently owned business that employs fewer than 500 people.

small claims court A court that settles cases involving relatively small amounts of money.

social responsibility The obligation to do what is best for the welfare of society.

software A computer program containing a set of instructions that tells a computer what to do.

sole proprietorship A business owned by only one person.

speculative stocks Stocks in relatively new firms that don't have an established track record of success.

spreadsheet program A computerized worksheet.

standard fire policy Insurance against property damage due to fire or lightning.

standard of living The amount of goods and services the people of a country can buy.

start-ups Businesses just starting out.

statement savings account A traditional savings account in which all transactions are recorded in a statement sent by the bank to the account holder.

stereotype Identify someone by a single trait or as a member of a certain group rather than as an individual.

stock Shares of ownership in a corporation.

stock exchange A marketplace where stocks are bought and sold.

stop payment An order for a bank not to cash a particular check.

subsidies Payments the government gives to businesses to make up for their business losses.

supply The amount of goods and services that producers will provide at various prices.

sweatshops Factories that pay poorly, have unsafe working conditions, and treat workers badly.

T

target marketing Finding and analyzing potential consumers for a product.

tariff A tax placed on imported products to make them more expensive than domestic products.

tax incentives Reductions in taxes government gives to businesses to encourage socially responsible behavior.

telecommuting Using communications technology, such as computers, to keep in touch with the workplace while working away from it.

term insurance Life insurance that covers a person for a specific period of time.

top-level managers Managers responsible for setting goals and planning the future for a company.

trade A field that requires a high level of manual or technical skill, such as carpentry, mechanics, or computer programming.

trademark A legally-protected brand name, trade name, or trade characteristic that distinguishes one product from another.

transfer A move to another job within a company at the same level and pay.

transit advertising Advertising that uses public transportation to display ads.

trust A group of companies that band together to form a monopoly and eliminate competition.

truth-in-lending disclosure A statement creditors must give to consumers informing them of the costs and terms of credit.

U

undeveloped property Unused land intended only for investment purposes.

unit price The cost of an item for a standard unit of measurement, such as an ounce.

unlimited liability Full legal and financial responsibility for a business.

unsecured loan A loan that is not backed by collateral.

usury law A law that restricts the amount of interest that can be charged for credit.

V

variable expenses Expenses that fluctuate and over which you have some control, such as food and entertainment.

variable rate Interest rate on a loan that changes as interest rates in the banking system change.

virtual business A company that does business only on the Internet.

W

wants Things we wish we could have, as opposed to needs.

warranty A legal document that states the rights and responsibilities agreed to by the consumer and the store or manufacturer.

wearable computers Small, lightweight computers that workers can carry with them to assist them on the job.

Web browser A program that makes it easy to search and retrieve information on the Web.

webcast A broadcast, like a TV or a radio broadcast, sent and received over the Internet.

wholesaler A type of business that buys goods in large amounts and resells them to other businesses in smaller lots.

withdrawal Money taken out of a bank account.

withholding Money subtracted from a paycheck for taxes, social security, and other deductions.

Y

yield The rate of return on an investment, or the amount of money an investment earns.

Index

Index

Index

Index

Photo Credits